AF324913

DOMENICO BOLLANI

BIBLIOTHECA

HUMANISTICA & REFORMATORICA

VOLUME XV

Fig. 1 Domenico Bollani.

DOMENICO BOLLANI

Bishop of Brescia

DEVOTION TO CHURCH AND STATE
IN THE REPUBLIC OF VENICE
IN THE SIXTEENTH CENTURY

by

CHRISTOPHER CAIRNS

WITH 28 PLATES

NIEUWKOOP
B. DE GRAAF
1976

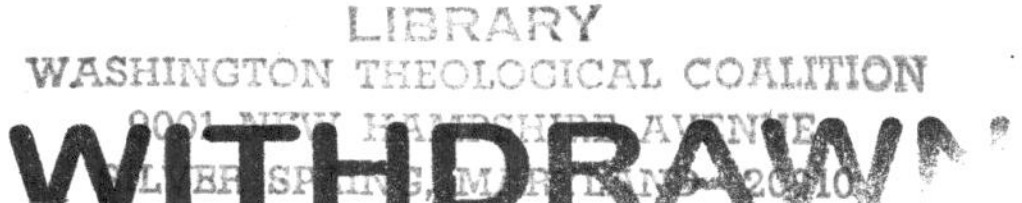

DOMENICO BOLLANI, BISHOP OF BRESCIA:
DEVOTION TO CHURCH AND STATE IN THE REPUBLIC OF VENICE
IN THE SIXTEENTH CENTURY

CONTENTS

Part I

1

2

ABBREVIATIONS USED FOR REFERENCE TO ARCHIVAL SOURCES

Brescia	A.C.S.B.	Archivio Civico Storico Bresciano (Biblioteca Queriniana, Brescia)
	A.S.B.	Archivio di Stato, Brescia
	A.V.B.	Archivio Vescovile, Brescia
	A.P.P.B.	Archivio dei Padri della Pace, Brescia
Cremona	Arch. Nav. Crem.	Archivio del Naviglio Cremonese (now in A.S.C.)
	A.S.C.	Archivio di Stato, Cremona
Milan	A.A.M.	Archivio Arcivescovile, Milan
	A.S.M.	Archivio di Stato, Milan
Rome	Nunz. Ven.	Archivio Segreto Vaticano, Segreteria di Stato, Nunziatura di Venezia. (microfilmed copies used in the Fondazione Cini, Isola di San Giorgio, Venice)
Udine	A.C.U.	Archivio Civico Utini, (Bibioteca V. Ioppi, Udine)
Venice	A.S.V.	Archivio di Stato, Venice

ACKNOWLEDGEMENTS

I am conscious of many debts in the preparation of this work: from the courtesy and interest of many libraries and archives in Italy, to the encouragement of historians in England. I cannot hope to recognise all these debts here, but remember with gratitude many friendships and contacts which contributed at all times to the enjoyment of research.

I owe much to many friends in Brescia, from the genial encouragement of Padre Felice Muracchelli, who first pointed out to me the need for a modern study of Domenico Bollani, to the courteous advice of the late Prof. Carlo Pasero, expert in the Cinquecento Bresciano, and the patient advice of Prof. Don. Alberto Nodari, promoter of Brescian ecclesiastical history. I am grateful, too for the friendship of Dott. Ornello Valletti, archivist of the Archivio Civico Storico Bresciano, and director of the Biblioteca Queriniana, for his courteous cooperation in four years, and for opening those doors which sometimes close inexorably on Italian historical sources during the hot summer months.

In Cremona, my friend Ing. Bruno Loffi followed with passion and professional skill my work on Chapter V, and patiently criticised an early draft. If I have been less than fair to Cremona in my account of the Oglio dispute, it is not his fault. My debt is considerable too, to Count Aleramo Custoza for his friendship and encouragement. A descendant of the Bollani and Da Ponte families, he spent much time in an attempt to trace the Bollani family archive which contained a considerable bulk of documents at the fall of the Republic.

Finally the help and encouragement constantly offered by historians has been invaluable. I have taken much from helpful discussions with Dr. Oliver Logan, Professor Brian Pullan and Dr. Peter Laven — who very kindly criticised an early draft of Chapter IV from the standpoint of his expert knowledge of Friuli. But perhaps above all I have benefited from discussions with Professor Gaetano Cozzi, who unstintingly offered me the benefit of his learning and experience of Venetian History. The interpretation of the life and relevance of Domenico Bollani is my own, but the community of scholars working on the history of the Venetian Republic has its own rich character, and is unfailingly charitable in sharing its knowledge.

I should like to acknowledge the assistance of the Ford (Dagenham) Trust, the Dante Alighieri Society, the Italian Government and the university of Southampton, for grants at various times facilitating extended periods of research in Italy. Professor Stuart Woolf introduced me to the study of history through stimulating and dynamic discussions, and he partakes of any value which the following chapters may have.

Acknowledgment is made to the following for permission to reproduce photographs, portraits and documents as illustrations: The Frick Collection, New York (4), The National Portrait Gallery, London (7, 8), The National Gallery of Canada, Ottawa (10), The Petworth Collection (5), Istituto Lombardo, Accademia di Scienze e lettere, Milan (18, 21, 23, 25), Museo Correr, Venice (9), Archivio di Stato, Milan (15), Archivio di Stato, Venice (12–14, 16), Museo Civico e Gallerie d'Arte Antica e Moderna, Udine (11), The British Museum (6).

INTRODUCTION

In the year 1579, two events important for this study occurred: Domenico Bollani, the great reforming Bishop of Brescia died in the arms of his mentor, Carlo Borromeo, and Paolo Paruta published his dialogue on the merits of the active and contemplative life: *Della Perfettione della Vita Politica*, using Bollani as a voice in support of the claims of the Church. In many ways an era was ending. Venice had adopted an uneasy neutrality in European politics, permanently weakened by the after effects of Cambrai. At home, the seeds were already sown of that consitutional and political dissatisfaction that was about to break the peace of oligarchical rule by a closed aristocracy in the suspension of the *Zonta* in 1582. The impact of the reformation of the Catholic Church had brought jurisdictional conflicts between the zealous reformer Pope Pius IV and his successors and the Venetian consciousness of her own traditional powers of ecclesiastical preferment. And now, sixteen years after the publication of the Tridentine Decrees, the first difficult phase in their implementation was complete.

In some ways, Paruta's dialogue symbolises the dualism inherent in the career of Domenico Bollani. Its author, of his own volition or through political necessity, had chosen the path of literary fame to political success, and had summarised much of the spirit of his time. The discussions of the legates, ambassadors and observers at Trent in 1563 — whether fictional fancy or reported fact — had introduced the ideas of an active participatory career in government magistracies and embassies, and a contemplative, spiritual and pastoral life in renunciation of the world. Paruta had introduced a note of disquiet in his figure of Francesco da Molin, standing for an emergent faction of the disgruntled which was to challenge the oligarchical rule of the Council of X.

The co-existence of the two principles — of contemplative and active, directive and pastoral, in short, of Church and State — is a peculiar feature of Venetian society in the sixteenth century. Their union, or the possibility of their conflict provided the core of Domenico Bollani's life. The demands of citizenship in the Republic of Venice were severe: service to the state was the highest form of service to which life, work and wealth might be sacrificed. The *Ragion di Stato* had achieved a supremacy in the Venetian mind which attracted a continuous flow of contemporary commentary, and is perhaps unequalled down to modern times. But the impetus of the Catholic Reformation, pioneered by men like Giberti in Verona, and spearheaded by Borromeo in Milan, made new demands on its officers. The function of the bishop in the organisation of this movement — itself an innovation exciting much comment throughout the century — motivated by the example of Borromeo, was crucially important. The Reformation bishop needed a new spirituality, a sanctity of life for inspiration through example, and a dynamic organisational skill. Only with these attributes could Borromeo's example be followed and his vision realised.

In Venice, the possibility of conflict between these two principles had long been inherent. Both government recommendation and dynastic intrigue had been the traditional means to ecclesiastical preferment in Venetian dominions, ensuring a political control both through traditional means, and through Venetian clerics.

6

Every Venetian bishop on the *Terraferma* exercised this quasi ambassadorial function. At its centre, the problem of conflicting interests was not to reach its crisis until the Papal Interdict of 1606. But locally, there was always the possibility that the Pope, Borromeo or the Inquisition would make demands unacceptable to the Venetian patriotic conscience. The more so in a Diocese where the organisational dynamism of civil experience was being applied to the application of the Tridentine Decrees.

Domenico Bollani as bishop of Brescia was in precisely this position. This study is an attempt to show how the experience of the government of men was used in the cure and organisation of souls with outstanding success. For Bollani was unique in one sense. There were several Venetian reformation bishops whose previous experience had been in civil and government posts — and perhaps the examples of Vincenzo Diedo and Lorenzo Priuli, Patriarchs of Venice, and Leonardo Mocenigo, Bishop of Ceneda, provide the most direct analogies — but none had passed from the government of a city to the Bishopric of that same city. Possibly, too, none had been elected for so transparently political reasons — such as to cause the new incumbent a very genuine embarassment. The principle of success in many spheres was not new in Bollani's day, and is immortalised in Castiglione's treatise *Il Cortegiano*, but the abruptness of the change is important, and the degree of success significant. Not only did the experience of civil government help Bollani to avoid the rocks of intrigue and the objections to the Reformation of self-interest, but they brought him an understanding of men and a common bond with his Diocese that helped to bring him closer to the Borromeo ideal.

Paruta's dialogue does not paint Bollani in these colours. For his author, the character typified the spirit of the Reformation, but it was a spirit in which civil experience does not play a part, and into which practical skill and diplomacy hardly enter. The Bollani of history does not emerge personally from the work. Far from representing the bishop of Brescia as a dynamic organiser and accomplished diplomat, Paruta was content to use him simply as a member of the Church enclave. This study will attempt to elaborate this picture: to depict the career of a typical but gifted member of a modest Venetian noble family, to take him through his apprenticeship in government, as ambassador, rector of a province, to posts of weight and importance in the Venetian Republic. It will describe his arbitration of the river Oglio dispute — perhaps his most accomplished feat of diplomacy — and will watch him swept into the Bishop's palace in Brescia on a tide of local popularity and international political expediency. It will then examine his ecclesiastical career from the standpoint of his civil training, and attempt to show how diplomatic skills were harnessed willingly and successfully to the Reformation movement.

It will also look at him in a wider context. As a Venetian, he trod the difficult path between governmental anxiety for his province as an outpost of the Venetian Empire on the frontiers of Milan and the Empire, and suspicion of Papal initiatives that might be motivated by territorial considerations. Through this his dual allegiance never wavered. Faithful to the interests of his home government, he yet remained a devoted servant of the Church, the Pope and Borromeo. Such a path was not without its pitfalls, but tenacity and resoluteness were also virtues which had served the State. The measure of his achievement must surely lie in the effective reconciliation on a local plane of those two principles which were exercising the minds of thinkers such as Paolo Paruta and of rulers like the Venetian Senate.

We shall attempt, then, to pose the question of how far it was possible to be a Venetian and a faithful servant of the Catholic Reformation: how far one could serve two masters who were capable of rival demands. Perhaps it was only the combination of civil training and episcopal experience that could bring success in the re-organisation and codification of Roman Catholicism after the Council of Trent. Perhaps the old dualism, taken up by Paruta from his classical forbears, was being resolved by his own characters in the new ecclesiastical administration that the Council of Trent and local councils were creating.

PART ONE

CHAPTER I

Origins and Family

The origins of the Bollani family are obscure before the beginning of the fourteenth century. The family trees of the genealogist Marco Barbaro[1] give the clearest idea of the history of many Venetian patrician families, with details of births, marriages and deaths of their members, as well as allusions to contemporary chronicles and diaries.[2] The minority view was that the Bollani family came to Venice from Aquileia in 961, but Barbaro states that *'la maggior parte convengono'* that the family arrived in Venice about 1125 from Constantinople. The earliest records state that members of the family were assuming political office by the middle of the thirteenth century, and that a Piero Bollani was elected to the *Gran Consiglio* from 1264 to 1268, and a G. Pantalon Bollani was elected in 1278, 1280 and 1281. On the other hand, there is a reference to the transfer of the Bollani family from Friuli to Venice in 962 in the History of Friuli of Gio. Francesco Palladio degli Olivi.[3] Here the Bollani family is stated to be a noble family from Aquileia:

'L'anno a questa incoronattione antecedente si portarono due altre nobili Famiglie ad habitare in Venetia, la Bolani d'Aquileia, e la Donzorzi da Trieste.'

Whatever their origins, it is clear that the Bollani family was established in Venice by the beginning of the sixteenth century, that two main branches had had a tradition of office in the Venetian government for several generations as nobles, and that the branch that produced Domenico (1513–1579) had held office in various capacities since the fifteenth century and acquired some prestige thereby.[4] Domenico's grandfather, Domenico Bollani (1450–1504) had been a member of the Gran Consiglio and Podestà of Cremona, and his father, Franceso Bollani (? –1566) had been a judge[5] and member of the *Pregadi*.[6] So on the face of it, it would seem that Domenico was destined for a political career. Essentially, there were two career opportunities open to the young Venetian nobleman at the beginning of the sixteenth century. If he were studiously inclined he might be sent to the University of Padua, returning home later to begin the arduous climb up the ladder of government posts to important office. Alternatively, he might be educated at home, beginning practical training for the family business (in commerce and trading) at an early age.[7] But in sixteenth century Venice political fortunes and economic stability were so inextricably linked that some comment on the financial position of the Bollani family will be necessary. As we shall see, the family was relatively poverty-stricken when Domenico was born in 1513, and his rise to positions of political and ecclesiastical distinction happened in spite of economic disadvantages at first, but was later aided by family inheritance.

First it must be said that the society into which Domenico was born had certain specific characteristics. Wealth had become an important prerequisite for office in the government both from the point of view of the specialised education required for such office and because ambassdorships and governorships — which alone provided the experience and prestige for the highest offices — were expensive demands on the wealth of the family. For traditions of service and patriotic devotion to the state demanded that a Venetian envoy should finance himself to a very considerable extent.[8] When this is borne in mind, and it is also realised that a general decline in the wealth of the Venetian nobility accompanied the decline in trading and mercantile interests and a transfer of the activities of many nobles from the sea to the land, we shall find that many noble families at the time Domenico lived were able only with great difficulty to supply qualified manpower for administrative posts in the Venetian government.[9]

The evidence for the poverty of the Bollani family during Domenico's childhood is now conclusive, and it is clear that his later career was facilitated by two inheritances from his mother's side of the family. Domnico's father, Francesco, seemed to have been a member of two family *fraterne* in 1534 and 1537,[10] and the income from houses and lands in those years seems to have been small.[11] Further, both Domenico's father and his uncle had been obliged to petition the Senate to defer payments of debts incurred in the collection of taxes.[12] But 1538, the year of Domenico's majority, was the important year, for it will be seen that the family's hopes for a distinguished government career rested with Domenico. If his father had declared his 'povertà et impotentia' in 1536, his mother, Benedetta Bollani, had an income of her own, received from her mother on her death in 1530. It is perhaps ironical that this property, a series of houses in the *Contrada dei SS. Apostoli*, probably contributed to the fact that Domenico was able to accept the expensive embassy to England in 1547 — and provided the family with endless trouble from their tenant, Pietro Aretino, which may have ended in a lawsuit.[13]

When Domenico began his career in government service, therefore, the family income was modest. After 1538, however, they had some small reserves in the shape of property inherited from the Dolfin family. Traditionally, the preservation of the patrimony of a Venetian noble family was aided by its transmission through inheritance to the male heirs, once dowries or fees to monasteries for unmarried daughters who became nuns had been provided for.[14] The two principal causes of impoverishment of the Venetian nobility in the sixteenth century were service to the state in expensive positions and the provision of dowries. We shall see that Domenico's early career reflects the modest financial standing of his family between 1538 and 1562, but that sacrifices were clearly made after 1547 to allow him to accept the embassy to England (1547–1549), the *Luogotenenza* in Udine (1555–1556) and the post of *Podestà* in Brescia (1558–1559) – all posts whose prestige required some degree of expenditure.[15] The financial standing of the family in 1559 – with the demands that Domenico had made on it during the previous ten years – and the provision of dowries for his sister and seven nieces, may well have influenced his decision to accept the Bishopric of Brescia when it was offered in that year.[16]

After the election of Domenico Bollani to the Bishopric of Brescia in 1559, there are indications that the economic situation of the family took a turn for the better. In 1562, they received an important legacy from Lugrecia Memmo, who left her fortune to Benetta Bollani, Domenico's mother.[17] This rise in the family fortunes is reflected in the will of Giacomo Bollani, in which the situation of the family is described in 1568, and in Giacomo's *Condizione* of 1566, in which some 85 shops and houses in Venice and extensive lands on the Terraferma are described.[18] The seriousness of the family position during Domenico's childhood (before 1530) was described by Giacomo in his will: 'Assai povera l'abbiamo trovata', his legacies are acknowledged, and now, after the acquisition of the Memmo fortune, 'Si è fatta convenientemente comoda.'[19]

Further indications of the family's financial status are provided by an examination of the dowries in the wills of Giacomo and Domenico.[20] In 1568, Giacomo left 600 ducats to any of his daughters who might enter monasteries after his death,[21] and a dowry of 5,000 ducats to any who might marry.[22] Domenico left sums to any who entered monasteries so that they might have an income of 30 ducats a year, and increased the dowries for those marrying from 5,000 to 6,000 ducats.[23] It has been shown that dowries provided by members of the upper half of the Venetian patriciate were often around 20,000 ducats,[24] so that the figures given by Giacomo – in a period, as we have seen, of no legal restriction – are highly significant. Even after Domenico had begun to help in the financial support of the family with the revenues from his bishopric, the family must still have been among the poorer half of the Venetian patriciate. If Giacomo was able to offer only 5,000 ducats to his daughters on their marriage, and was still able to congratulate himself in 1568 on the state of the patrimony being 'convenientemente comoda', then it becomes clear that the situation in which the young Domenico Bollani grew to maturity was one of financial difficulty and restraint. Further, there is every reason to suppose that the family was not less subject to bad luck, circumstantial hardship and factors associated with rising prices and economic decline than others.[25]

We have seen that service to the state was both the duty and the summit of ambition of a young Venetian nobleman.[26] It is also true that promotion in government offices was often hindered by financial embarrassment.[27] In a survey of the minor government posts occupied by Domenico and his brother, it will

Fig. 2 Palazzo Bollani on the Grand Canal, Venice, at the corner of the *rio di*
S. Giovanni Grisostomo.

Fig. 3a   The Grand Canal: Pallazo Bollani in the eighteenth century as seen by Marieschi.

Fig. 3b   The Grand Canal: Palazzo Bollani as it is today.

Fig. 4 Pietro Aretino by Titian.

Fig. 5   King Edward VI. From a portrait at Petworth.

Fig. 6   Bollani's knighthood from Edward VI.

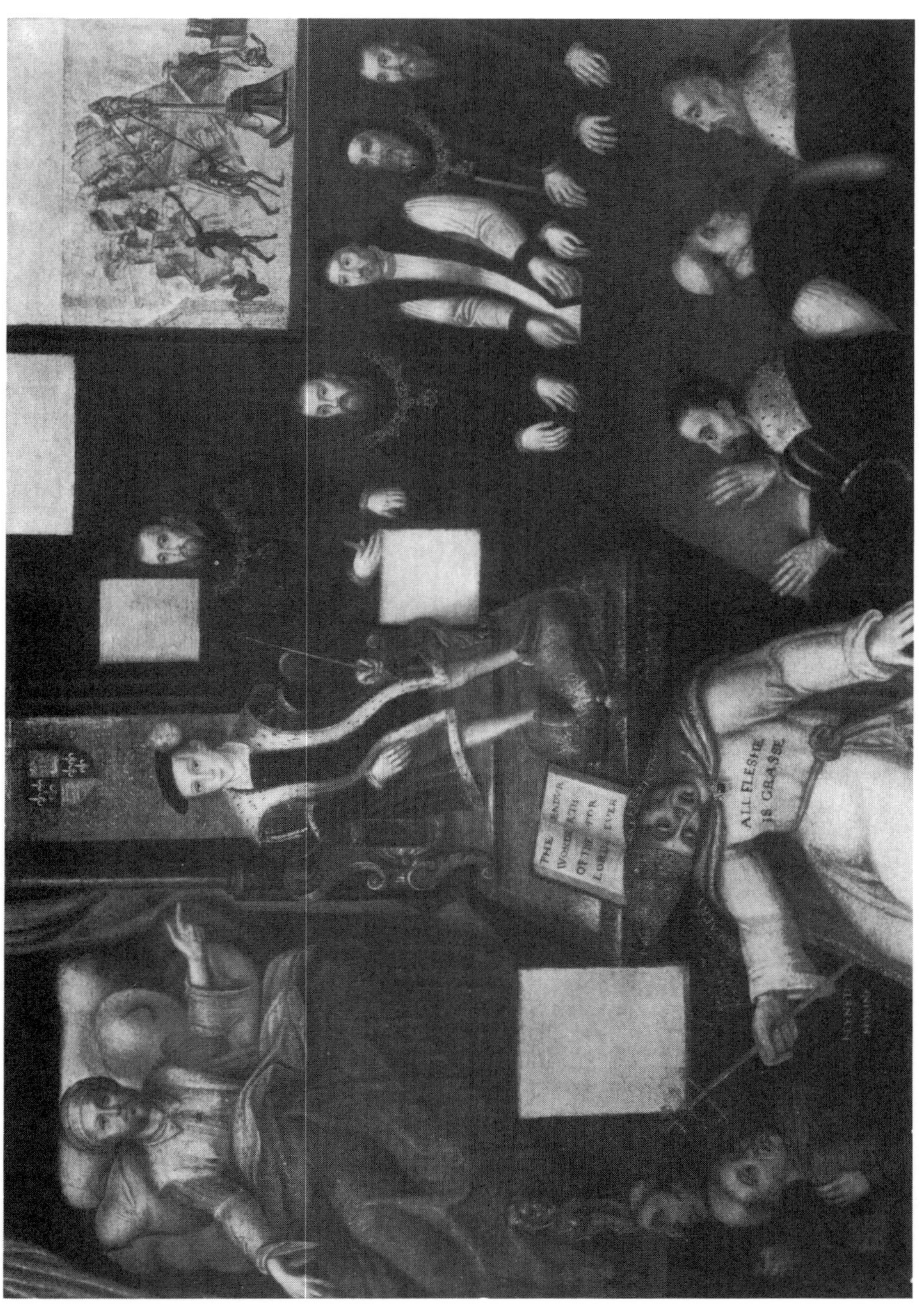

Fig. 7   Edward VI and the Roman Church: Anti-papal allegory.

Fig. 8   Cardinal Pole.

Fig. 9   The official robes of a *Savio* in the Venetian Government.

Fig. 10 Daniele Barbaro by Titian.

Fig. 11   The Bollani Arch, Udine, built in recognition of Bollani's efforts during the plague of 1556.

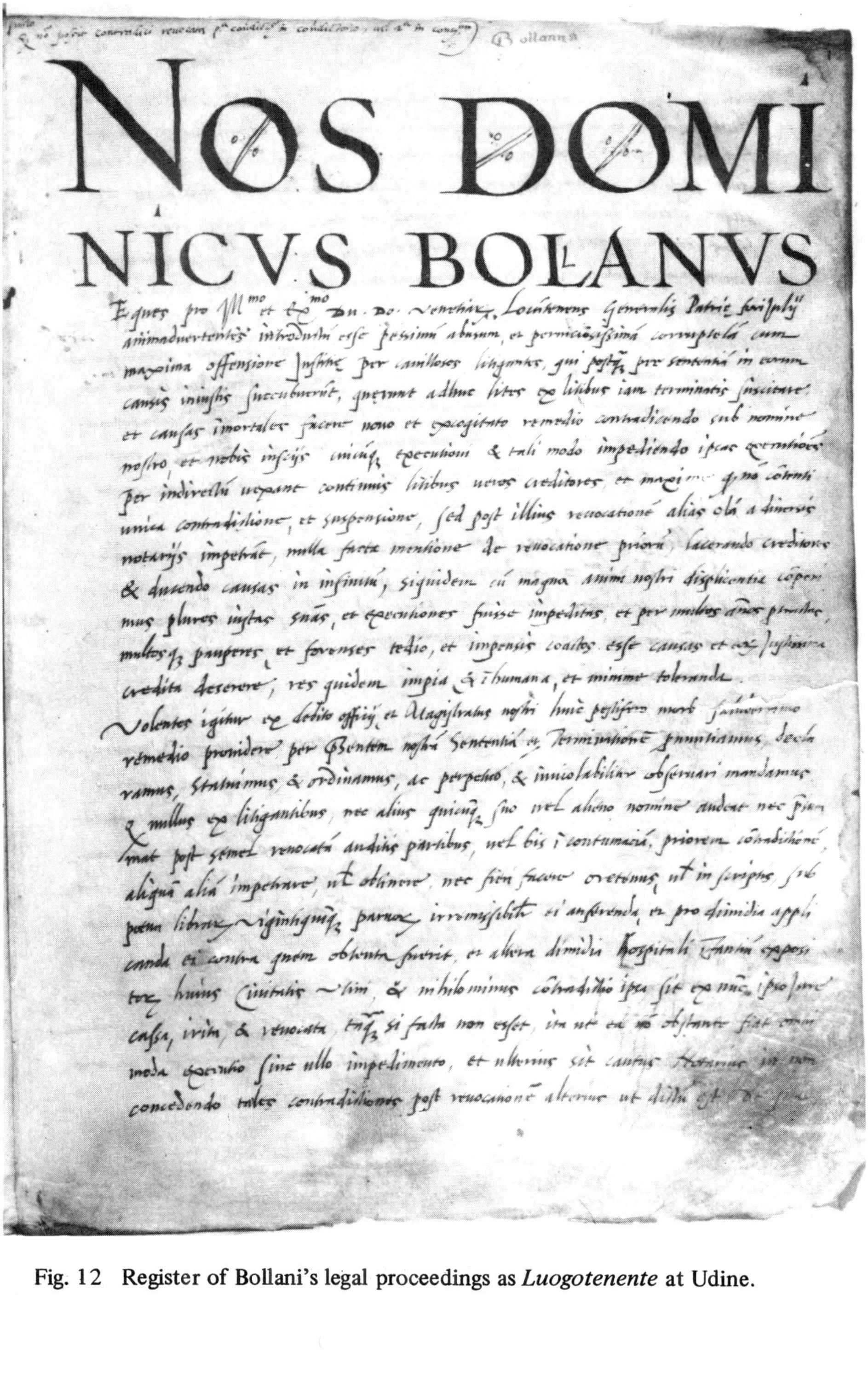

NOS DOMI NICVS BOLANVS

Fig. 12   Register of Bollani's legal proceedings as *Luogotenente* at Udine.

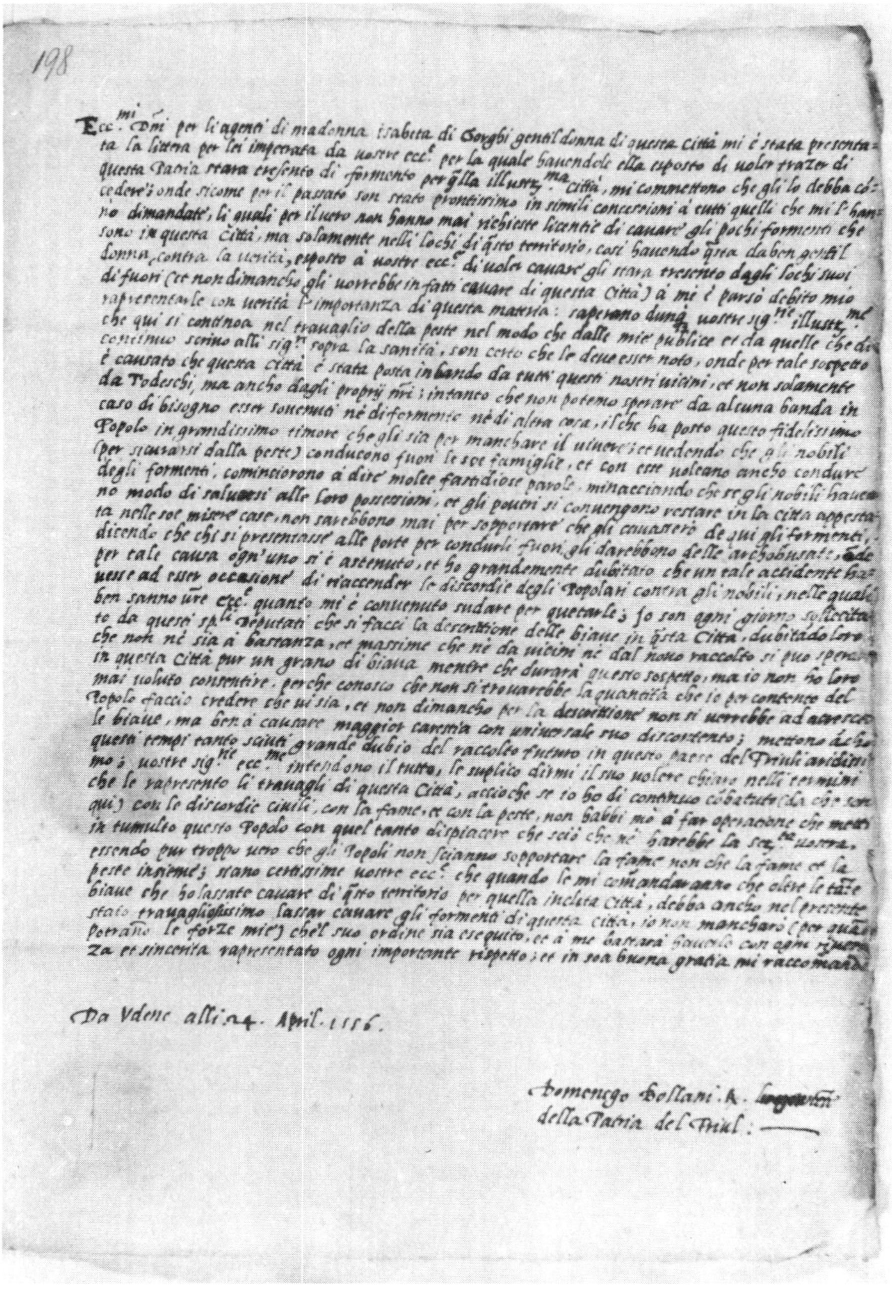

198

Da Vdene alli 24. April. 1556.

Domenego Bollani K. Luogotenente
della Patria del Friul: ———

Fig. 13   A letter from Bollani to Venice while *Luogotenente* at Udine.

VOLENDO IL CLARISSIMO M. DOMENEGO BOLLANI
Caualier dignissimo Podesta di Bressa, & suo distretto, prouedere che non solamente la
Città di Bressa, ma anco il territorio Bresciano sia abondante de biaue, & hauendo inteso che
si ritrouano in questo territorio, alcuni liquali contra il debito della Carità, & contra la men
te della Sereniss. Signoria, & non senza graue danno de poueri comprano biaue per incane/
uar, però per prouedere a simili male operationi, & à molte fraudi, che si cometteno, si fa à sa/
pere per parte, & comandamento di sua Magnificentia Clarissima che non sia persona alcuna
di qual grado & conditione essere si voglia, che senza espressa licentia di sua Magnificentia in
scrittura, laquale senza alcuna spesa sara concessa à chi conuenientemente la douera hauere, ar
disca ne presuma di comprar far mercato ouero incaparar biaue paesane di qual si voglia sor
te lequal siano raccolte sopra questo territorio per incauenarle ouero per riuederle, sotto pe/
na di perder dette biaue, & etiam vno ducato per soma, la mita dellequal biaue & pena pecu/
niaria sia dell'accusator che sara tenuto secreto, & l'altra mita sia applicata ad arbitrio di sua
Magnificentia Clarissima, & in oltre incorrino tal contrafacenti in quelle pene piu rigorose
di pregione galea, & bando che pareranno al arbitrio di esso Clarissimo Signor Podesta.

Quanto veramente al comprar biaue forestiere si dechiara espressamente che cadauno possa li/
beramente comprar biaue forestiere per incaneuar, domente però che le non comprino so/
pra li publici mercati che ordinariamente si fanno nelle terre dil territorio Bresciano, & cum
conditione che tutti quelli che compraranno biaue forestiere per incaneuar vt supra siano te
nuti, & obligati venirsi à dar in nota nella cancellaria di sua Magnificentia, ouero se senza incaneuare volessero condurle per il paese
si come fanno li conduttori ordinarii, venghino à tuor le sue licentie in scrittura che li saran/
no date senza alcuna spesa, & contrafacendo caschino nelle pene predette; & accioche non si
cometta fraude circa cio, & che sotto il nome de biaue forestiere non si comprino delle paesa
ne, tutti quelli che fino hora si ritrouano hauer comprato, & incaneuato biaue ò forestiere ò
paesane siano similmente tenuti denuntiarle, & darle in nota nella Cancellaria vt supra in ter
mine de giorni quattro dappoi bublicato il presente proclama; altramente passato ditto ter/
mine, & non hauendo datta la nota ouero tolto le licentie predette, caschino nelle pene sopra
dette da esser diuise vt supra: lequal irremissibilmente saranno mandate ad essecutione con/
tra li inobedienti.

Et alla istessa conditione s'intendano esser tutti quelli mercadanti che scoderanno biaue, dalli
suoi debitori, & le incaneuaranno senza licentia vt supra.

Preterea li Consuli de le terre, & ville del territorio siano tenuti hauer circa questo diligentiss
ma custodia per venir à manifestar à sua Magnificentia tutti quelli che saranno inobedienti
à cadauna delle cose comandate nel presente proclama in termine de giorni tre doppo che
per alcuno fusse stata comessa alcuna contrafattione, altramente li consuli di quel loco doue sa
ra ritrouato essere comessa la inobedientia & contrafaccion, siano, & se intendino imediate in
corsi in le predette pene statuite contra li istessi disobedienti & contrafacienti.

Fig. 14 An edict by Bollani when *Podestà* of Brescia.

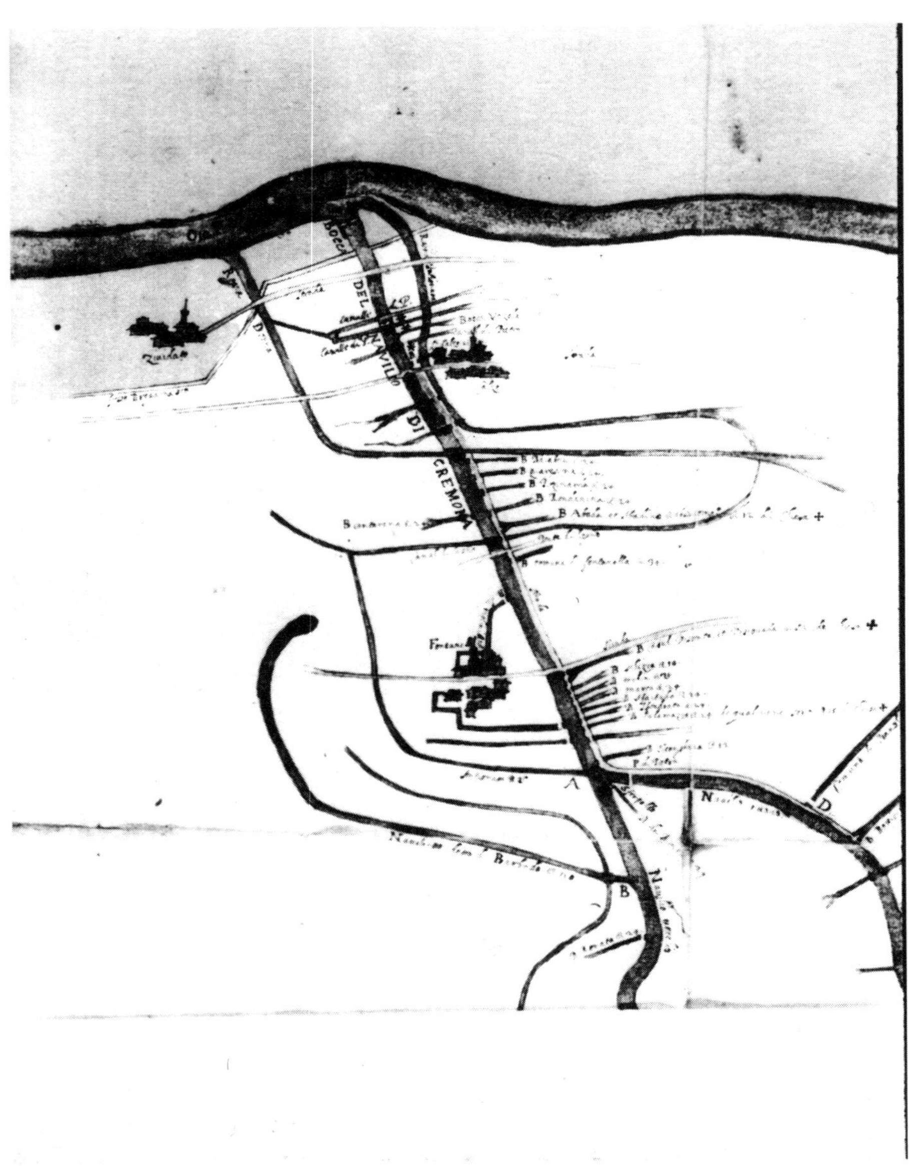

Fig. 15 Milanese sketch-map of the *Naviglio Cremonese*, pen and watercolour, showing Cremonese installations on the canal.

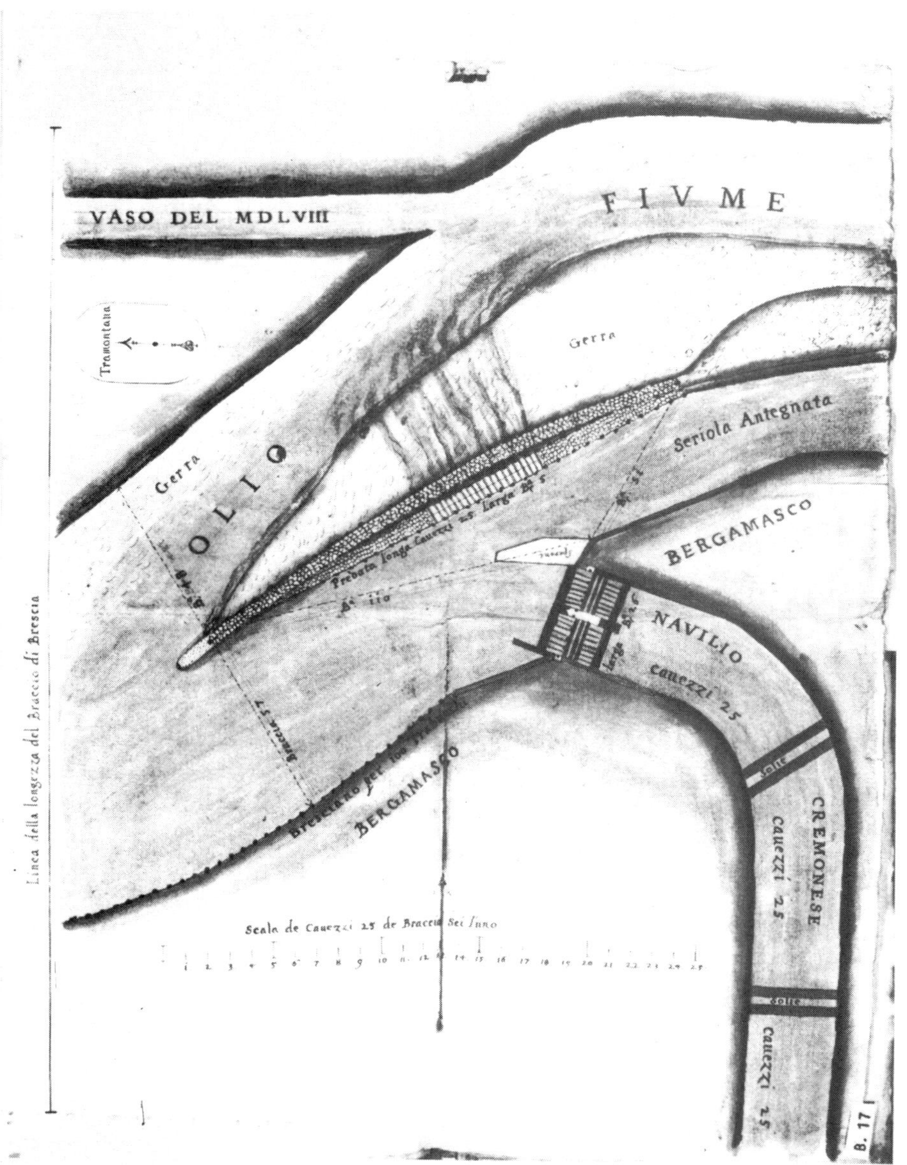

Fig. 16 Venetian sketch of the mouth of the *Naviglio*, pen and watercolour, showing the canal gate, the Brescian diversionary canal of 1558, *soglie* (floor levels) and measurements.

Fig. 17   The site of the Oglio dispute in 1932, when much of the original structure of the spur (*Predata*) survived and (below) as it is today.

Fig.18 Count Giovanni Anguissola, Bollani's adversary in the Oglio dispute

Fig. 19   Count Giulio Martinengo, Bollani's host at Urago d'Oglio.

Fig. 20 The Palace at Urago d'Oglio where Bollani stayed during the Oglio dispute.

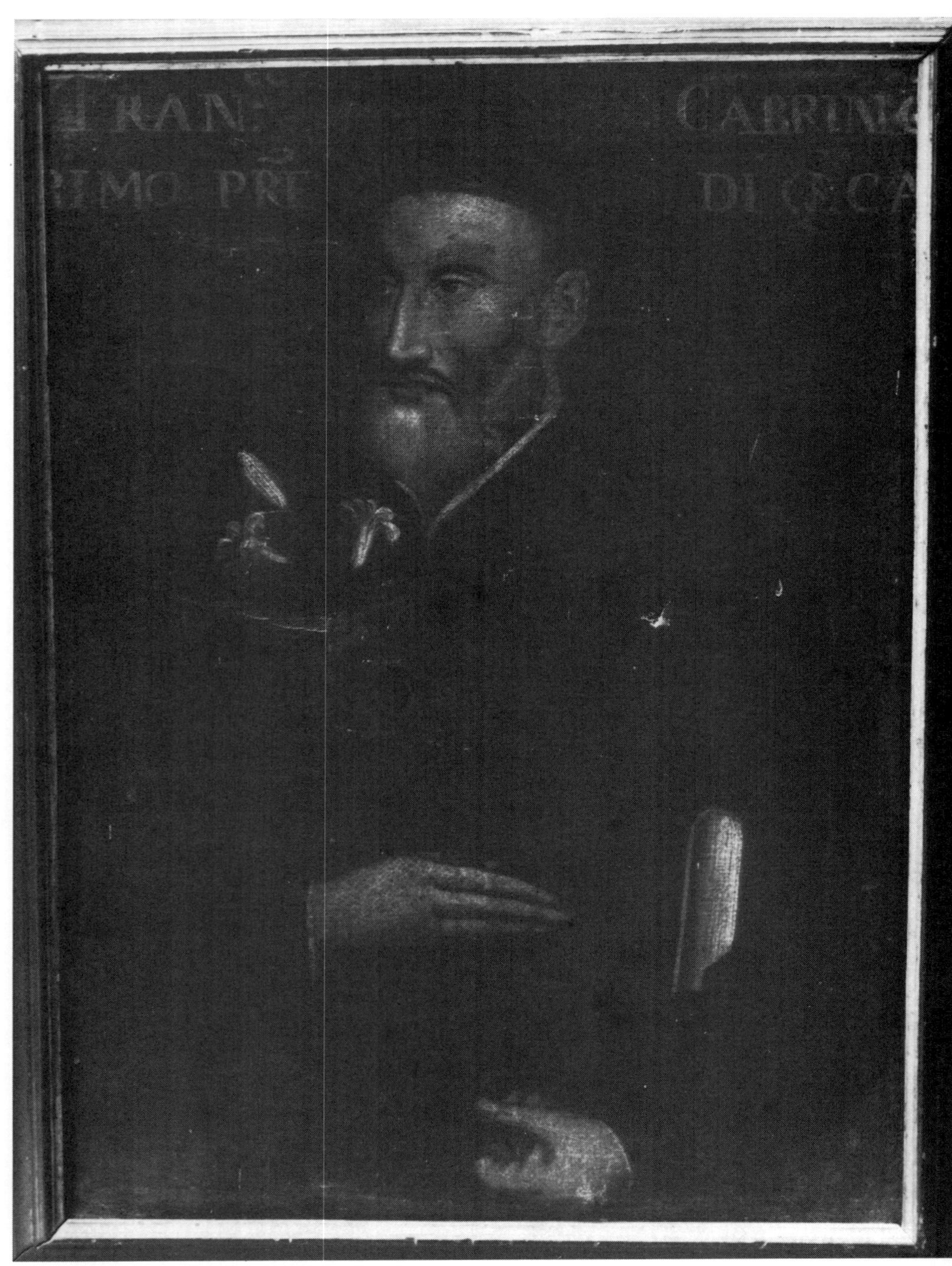

Fig. 21   Francesco Cabrino, Bollani's confessor and advisor.

Fig. 22   Portrait of Bollani from the *Acta Ecclesiae Brixiensis* ... (Venice, 1608) possibly made from a lost original portrait by Titian.

Fig. 23   Cardinal Francesco Gambara, Bollani's opponent in reform.

Fig. 24 The entrance to the bishop's palace, Brescia, with Bollani's inscription.

Fig. 25 Giacomo Roveglio, Bollani's confidant.

Fig. 26 Recent recognition of Bollani's efforts in connection with the first Brescian seminary: the approach road to the new seminary in Brescia.

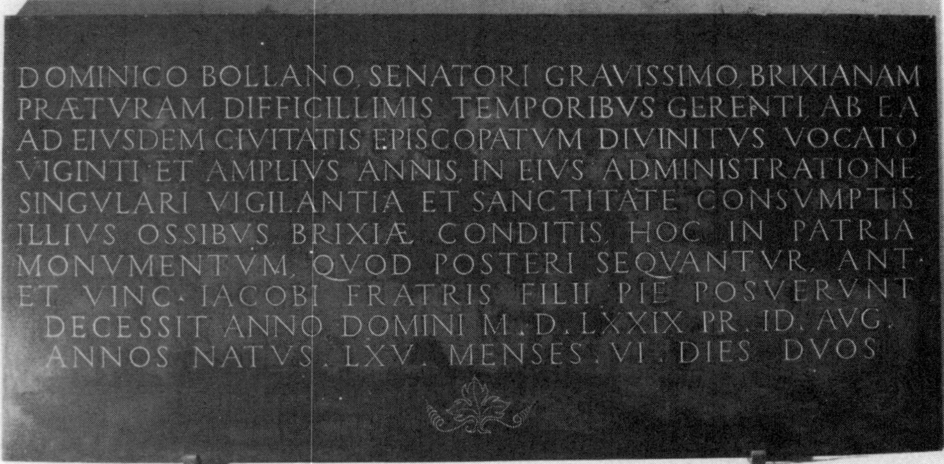

Fig. 27 All that remains of Bollani's tomb monument. The inscription is now in the Duomo Vecchio; the sculptures by Alessandro Vittoria for the tomb in the Duomo (destroyed when the tower fell in 1708) of the Redeemer, Faith and Charity, are now in the Museo di Età Christiana, Brescia.

Fig. 28 The only near contemporary painted portrait of Bollani in the bishop's palace, Brescia.

appear that Domenico's initiatives were directed towards positions of calculated financial benefit.[28]

But at this point it is worth pausing to consider the kind of society in which Domenico Bollani grew up. The period was one of social change and critical self-examination in politics. The events following the League of Cambrai — and particularly the Venetian defeat at Agnadello — had administered a severe shock to the myth of Venetian invulnerability.[29] It invited caution in international relations and a more outward-looking attitude. 'The devastation for the first time of territories on which she was heavily dependent for food, for men, and for access to her customers, taught her that she could no longer expect to make war in Italy at a comfortable distance and minimum expense.'[30] And a wider political horizon was accompanied by agricultural development of the *Terraferma* and by a shift of emphasis in economic priorities from the sea to the land.[31] For the poorer nobility in Venice, there seems to have been a gradually more rigid definition of claims to the advantages of the patriciate. Registration of marriages and births, the requirement of strong evidence of status for admission to the Great Council, centralisation of power within the government in the Council of Ten, all tended to concentrate the real power in the hands of a few powerful families.[32] Thus, with a small measure of trafficking in office, and the system of clientage developing in the upper echelons of the nobility, there was some breakdown in the kind of 'absolute democracy' on which Venice prided herself, and families like the Bollani must have felt excluded from power and influence if their members were not endowed with quite exceptional talent.[33]

Domenico Bollani was born in 1513 on 10th February, four years after the defeat at Agnadello, in the year in which the Council of Ten accepted Titian's offer to fresco the Palazzo Ducale, and Marco Bollani, Domenico's second cousin, was elected to the Procuratorship of St. Mark.[34] He was born into a world of colourful cultural exploration, a world painted by Titian, Giorgione and later, Tintoretto, a world which saw the domination of literate Europe by the Venetian printing presses, and the literary primacy of Pietro Bembo. It was a world of self-examination not only in the field of historiography, but also by grammarians, editors, commentators, translators and those writers like Baldassare Castiglione who examined through the printed word every conceivable aspect of Venetian public, cultural and private life.[35] It was also the world of Pietro Aretino, and that brand of literary blackmail through the recent invention of printing which the tolerant constitution of the Venetian Republic was alone broad enough to tolerate. There are few references to Domenico's activities in his younger years, but we know from Barbaro[36] that he was *provato* in 1533, when he was 20, so that by this point his education would have been finished and he would have been ready to embark on public life. The earliest record of Domenico occurs in the correspondence of Pietro Aretino with the Bollani family over the tenancy of the palace owned by the family and occupied by Aretino from 1529 to 1552.[37] It is clear by 1537, the year before Domenico would have entered the Grand Council by right on his twenty-fifth birthday, that he had already received a good education and was preparing to undertake tasks imposed on him by the government, for Aretino alludes to him in flattering terms in a letter to the family that year.[38]

Even if this letter were part of that groundless flattery for which Aretino is famous, or were an early attempt to 'pagar con la lode'[39] part of the rent which he owed to the Bollani, it would have been inappropriate had not Domenico achieved some distinction in learning by this time. Further it is from about this time that a letter from Francesco Coccio, inserted into an edition of Aretino's *Ragionamenti*,[40] can be dated.[41] Apparently Aretino had promised to write a *Trattato de la Libertà e de la Servitù* 'al Magnifico e dottissimo giovane M. Domenico Bollani'.[42] So we now have two testimonies to Domenico's education up to the age of 24 (1537) and his preparedness for election to an active part in the government of the Republic.

Of Domenico Bollani's formal education little concrete evidence remains. A tradition persists that he attended the *Studio* at Padua[43] but no contemporary evidence has survived.[44] It seems highly likely that he attended the University, however, for two main reasons. We have seen contemporary judgements of him in his youth as *dotto* and as having experience of *lettere*. For a Venetian patrician coming to maturity in 1538, Padua would have been the only institution where further education could have been obtained. Secondly, he was appointed later to the office of *Riformatore dello Studio di Padova*.[45] The election to a magistracy with such complete control over all matters pertaining to the university adds some weight to the hypothesis that he studied there, though is hardly conclusive.

While at Padua, Domenico would have gained useful experience besides his formal training in law. The *Studio*, recovering fast after the suspension of its activities at the time of Cambrai up to 1517, was an international community of world renown. Scholars from the farthest corners of Europe were attracted by its freedom and the excellence of its teachers.[46] Schools of Law, Medicine, Theology and Philosophy thrived during the period of his attendance, Professors were still elected by the students at this time, and the teaching of men like Pomponazzi had already given the university the reputation of the cradle of Humanist thinking. Importantly, Domenico Bollani had ample opportunity of direct experience of Protestantism in these early years through contacts with German Lutherans and other northerners.[47]

Possibly Giacomo, Domenico's brother, had not had the benefit of the Paduan experience, but had elected to safeguard the family commercial enterprises.[48] For it was often the case for a Venetian noble family of modest means that an economic division of effort among the active members was agreed.[49] If Domenico had shown early promise in learning and administrative capacity, then he would have been elected to serve the state in a bid to secure for the family the prestige that would derive from high office. There is no way of telling whether Domenico was selected early to represent the family in politics, or even whether a 'policy' was ever decided. What is certain, however, is that the fortunes of the family had turned dramatically in 1530 and 1562 as a result of inheritances from the Dolfin and Memmo families respectively, and that on Domenico's election to the English embassy through his evident talent (combined with some good fortune in financial matters) the family decided, so to speak, to put its eggs in one basket.

Before this stage had been reached, it is quite clear that the family had offered itself for election to offices that held out some hope of financial security or

12

benefited the family trading enterprises, as a survey of these posts will show.[50] Domenico's father, Francesco, seems to have been concerned exclusively in tax-collection from 1536, when he was conspicuously unsuccessful,[51] until 1538. He had been a member of the Council of 30 when he was proposed *Sopra le rendite de Beni* in that year, but came last in a poll of 24. He succeeded in being elected to collect taxes levied on wine (*Dacio del Vin*) a month later, but was again last in the poll for election of members to the Council of 30 a week later.[52] Possibly the experience of 1536 induced him to abandon the world of finance in 1538, as we know from Barbaro and Sanuto[53] that he held legal office as a member of the *Quarantie*. Possibly, too, a move of this kind had been prompted by his misfortune in 1536, as the *Quarantie* was becoming the preserve of the poorer nobility.[54] Whatever the reason — financial caution in the 1530s or the wish to leave a clear field for his sons — Francesco Bollani does not again appear in the lists of candidates for fiscal offices.[55]

There is less evidence of the participation in government of Giacomo Bollani for we have suggested that he may have been occupied in family trading enterprises. He was elected *Camerlengo a Verona* in 1544, and tried unsuccessfully three times for election to the *40 Civil Novi* (a minor fiscal office) in 1547.[56] He was also unsuccessful in an attempt at a post in Dalmatia in 1549. Possibly his entry into the lists at this point (1547) reflects an attempt to take advantage of the prestige which followed Domenico's election to the important and expensive English Embassy in the spring. Possibly, too, it reflects the rise in the family fortunes after 1530. Whatever the reason for Giacomo's brief excursion into public life, it is certainly true that his choice of office was typical of a nobleman of relatively modest means.[57]

Domenico Bollani's apprenticeship in minor government office follows the pattern we have seen gradually emerging of offices appropriate to the poorer nobility, but he was a much more persistent candidate. Compared with the career of his brother above, who was ballotted 4 times between 1538 and 1547, Domenico stood for office no less than 14 times before his 'breakthrough' in 1547. It is clear that in him resided the family hopes for a distinguished public career. But the ballots in which he participated yield another important fact. When Domenico began his apprenticeship in the mid-1530s, he was without influential support among the electors as he was frequently unsuccessful in the poll. Clearly a young nobleman without this support who had to depend on his own individual talent for election was bound to experience difficulty in the early stages and could hardly aim at the highest offices.[58] Domenico's first office seems to have been *Provveditore Sopra le Acque*,[59] a position of some importance in the organisation of the lagoon-city. It implied membership of the committee responsible for the upkeep of the lagoon, canals, river banks and waterways, and carried criminal jurisdiction in these matters and the levying of a tax on unearned income of 5%.[60] Between 1540 and 1543, he was proposed for office eight times without being elected, almost always for fiscal offices.[61]

When Domenico Bollani was elected to office on September 14th 1543 as *Provveditore al Cottimo di Damasco*, he had been contesting elections for five years or thereabouts.[62] He had offered himself for six different fiscal posts without success in an attempt, perhaps, to make a modest living while gaining access to the Senate.[63] When we compare the careers of Domenico's contemporaries, Daniele Barbaro and Nicolò da Ponte, it becomes clear that his early career was hindered by a lack of the right political support and probably the relative poverty of his family.[64] The choice of this post hardly departs from the pattern of offices for which men in Domenico's position were eligible.[65]

The post itself had important commercial connections.[66] In each of the Venetian outposts in the Levant the Republic had established *Consuls* and two *Provveditori* whose responsibility it was to protect Venetian trading interests in Alexandria, Damascus and London. F.C. Lane has shown that the Venetian Spice trade recovered fast from its initial setback at the beginning of the century from competition with the Portuguese, and until the 1560s at least, Damascus was the important centre for all eastern spices reaching Europe through Venice.[67]

From 1544–5 until 1547, Domenico was in Venice awaiting election to further office. He was proposed five times in this period without election — nearly always for fiscal offices. It seems that he continued to favour posts with some small financial benefit that would provide access to the Senate. Further it may be significant that he was proposed twice for the post of *Provveditore di Comun.* Besides offering voting rights in the Senate, this post was of great importance as the three *Provveditori* exercised control over all merchandise, including wool, silk, gold and glass industries. They were also responsible for doctors, surgeons, minor schools, and dealt with matters relating to the upkeep of roads, bridges, riverbanks and small canals. Perhaps important for Domenico Bollani was the fact that they exercised criminal jurisdiction over dealings in merchandise. It seems a logical progression from a period concerned with trade.[68]

So it can be seen that Domenico Bollani's debut in public life was anything but smooth. Hindered by a lack of strong support from influential members of the Senate and Great Council, his progress had been slow. Prevented by the economic situation of his family from choosing the path of expensive appointments that Daniele Barbaro and Nicolò da Ponte had been able to choose, he had had to gain access to the Senate — and the influence that this would have provided — by means of fiscal posts with a secure small income.

The turning point had come in 1547 with the election to the English Embassy. There had been a rise in the family fortunes shortly before this to allow him to accept one of the most expensive posts in the Venetian government. At this point, too, his brother, Giacomo, retired from full participation in the life of the government to devote himself to the family business. Also to the business of a family, as he married Marietta Longo in 1550. The embassy to England had given a clear indication of the roles of the brothers in the Bollani *fraterna*: Domenico became a full-time government servant from this point, and Giacomo provided heirs to continue the tradition.

The epilogue is a sad one in many ways. The pattern of division of labour was continued by the next generation, as Domenico, the eldest son, entered the church to become a Bishop later.[69] Vincenzo seems to have been elected to undertake government service, but little remains to indicate distinguished service.

14

Antonio, the youngest of Giacomo's sons, married late in 1586, became *Savio agli Ordini*, and had one son before his early death in 1587.[70]

On Giacomo's death in 1571, the patrimony passed to the three sons, with Domenico, now Bishop of Brescia named as chief executor. The family business was carried on in Venice by their mother Marietta (Longo) Bollani, and Domenico's brothers-in-law, Francesco and Marcantonio Longo, while Domenico supervised the education of his nephews Domenico, first a friar in the monastery of San Domenico in Brescia, and later a Bishop, and Antonio and Vincenzo Bollani, who were brought up at Salò, Antonio returning to Venice to learn the business of the family affairs, and Vincenzo completing his education at a boarding school in Verona.[71] On Domenico's death in 1579, the family fortune was added to by his bequests, as he mentioned the facility granted to him by the Pope to bequeath revenues from his bishopric. The family property then passed to Vincenzo Bollani, who died without issue in February, 1609, leaving the property to his only remaining unmarried sister, Cecilia, as his nephew, Giacomo, would not have reached maturity until 1611.[72] There is no mention of Giacomo in Vincenzo's will, however, as he had been recently banished for theft. Four months after the death of Vincenzo, Giacomo returned to Venice in contravention of his banishment, and was beheaded between the columns of St. Mark's Square on June 1, 1609.[73]

This macabre event marked the extinction of this branch of the Bollani family, as Cecilia was now the only surviving niece of the bishop of Brescia outside monasteries.[74] Its extinction at this point occasioned a complete inventory of the property in 1624, as Cecilia was forced to leave it equally divided between the Molin and Loredan families, the descendents of her two married sisters, Elena and Laura Bollani.[75] It is not difficult to imagine the situation of Cecilia. She had begun life in the shadow of the universally respected church reformer and Bishop of Brescia, her uncle, had lived through the unprisings in the government of 1582, and the Interdict of 1606, finally to witness the public execution of her nephew in 1609, and with him the hopes for the continuation of the family tradition. Something of the pathos of her position comes through her division of the family property — a patrimony that had been jealously and carefully put together by previous generations — between the families of the Molin and the Loredan in 1624: 'De questa mia facultà ne farò due parte, una all'SS. Loredani, et una all'SS. Molini, et questo, che siano hubbligati a metter nell'loro arme l'arma mia da Ca Bollani come gla sce retrova al presente, et mantenerla perpetuamente, et perchè non pari questa mia hordinattione ad alcuno superflua, et protestando li dico che non hordino questo ad altro fine sce non che godendo gli miei beni, et beni da Ca Bollani sci ricordino di pregar, et far pregar el S.D. pel'anima mia, et per li miei antenati . . .'

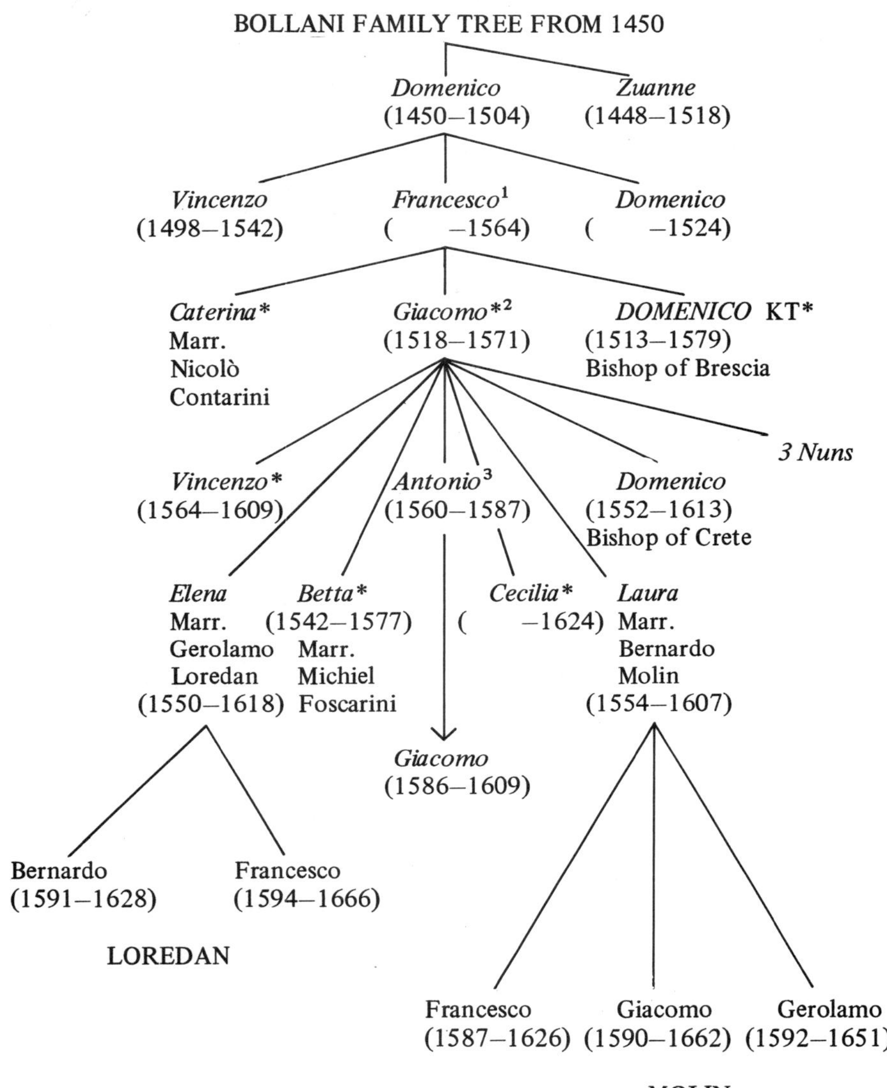

*   Indicates that a will exists in the *A.S.V.*
1 Married daughter of Giacomo Capello di Michiel.   (1511)
2 Married daughter of Antonio Longo di Francesco.   (1550)
3 Married daughter of Nicolò Bragadin di Zuanne.   (1586)

For these marriages see the *Libro di Nobili* in the Biblioteca di San Marco, Venice, MS. It. VII. 154 (8866) p. 32.

16

NOTES TO CHAPTER I

1   See Marco Barabaro, *Arbori dei Patrizi Veneti*, Ms book, (in the Archivio di Stato, Venice, henceforward A.S.V.) pp. 31—47. Barbaro began to record genealogies of the Venetian patriciate in the sixteenth century, continued after his death by other compilers. Their chief deficiency is the lack of female descendents, but by cross-reference with Cappellari, *Genealogie* I, p. 168, and with family wills preserved in the *Cancelleria Inferiore* and *Archivio Notarile* (A.S.V.) a fairly accurate idea of the family history — particularly for what concerns the transfer of property — may be obtained. Copy dated 1679 in BM.MS. Egerton 1155. Plut. K. 541 has no dates in family trees and is therefore of very limited use. Cf. Yriarte, *La vie d'un patricien de Venise* (Paris, 1874) p. 21. J.C. Davis in his *The Decline of the Venetian Nobility as a Ruling Class* (Baltimore, Johns Hopkins, 1962) pp. 130—132, found the genealogies of Barbaro 'a comparatively dependable and solid work'.
2   Barbaro, *op. cit.*, pp. 31—33. The unspecific reference is to *alcune Croniche*, probably to sources now lost.
3   *Historie della Provincia del Friuli*, (Udine, 1660 {1966}), I, p. 138.
4   See Barbaro, *loc. cit.* The earliest recorded names in the family tree are the brothers Andrea and Tommaso in the mid-thirteenth century. Andrea's son Tomà was a member of the *Gran Consiglio* in 1293, and Tommaso's son, Marco, was a member in 1317.
5   'Fu Zudece del Proc. e di 40 . . .' Barbaro, *op. cit.* p. 41. He is also mentioned in this capacity in the *Diarii di Marin Sanuto* (1496—1533) 58 vols. (Venice, 1879—1902), LV, pp. 107, 666, LVI, p. 71. This was the *Quarantia Criminale*, the highest judicial body in the government. For this office see G. Orlandini, *loc. cit.*, and for important comments on its relative financial standing, B. Pullan, 'Poverty, Charity and the Reason of State' in *Bollettino dell'Instituto di Storia della Società e dello Stato*, II, (1960) pp. 48—49, and *idem*, 'Service to the Venetian State: Aspects of Myth and Reality in the early Seventeenth Century,' in *Studi Secenteschi* V (1964), pp. 121—122.
6   The Senate. For a concise modern summary of the function of the Venetian Senate or *Pregadi* see W.J. Bouwsma, *Venice and the Defence of Republican Liberty: Renaissance Values in the age of the Counter Reformation*, (California, 1968), p. 61, and bilbliography in n. 31. For the structure of positions in the Venetian government, see *idem*, pp. 53—70, E. Besta, *Il Senato Veneziano*, (Venice, 1899) *passim*, H. Brown, *Studies in the History of Venice*, (London, 1907) I, pp. 288—303, G. Orlandini, 'Lineamenti di Storia dell'Amministrazione della Republica Veneta' in *Ad Alessandro Luzio gli Archivi di Stato Italiani — Miscellanea di Studi Storici*, (Florence, undated offprint), pp. 241—249.
7   For the education and career prospects of a typical Venetian nobleman, see J.C. Davis, *op. cit.*, pp. 26—33.
8   See below pp. 13—14.
9   On the complex economic phenomenon of the changing fortunes of the Venetian patriciate, see J.C. Davis *op. cit.*, pp. 34—53 for some causes of the decline in wealth; for the contribution of Turkish pressure and European trade competition, see G. Luzzatto, *Storia dell'Età Moderna e Contemporanea* (Padua, 1955) I, pp. 78—87; For the transfer of the activities of the nobility from trade and mercantile enterprises to investment in land on the *Terraferma*, see, for example, G. Cozzi, Il Doge Nicolò Contarini: *Ricerche sul Patriziato Veneziano agli inizi del Seicento* (Venice/Rome, 1958) pp. 14—15, and for the economic implications of this transfer, S.J. Woolf, 'Venice and the Terraferma, Problems of the change from Commercial to landed activities' in *Bollettino dell'Istituto di Storia della Società e dello Stato Veneziano*, IV (1962) pp. 415—441. In addition, B. Pullan has shown how the necessity for qualified manpower for office, among other factors ('reasons of state') were probably responsible for the growth of beneficent institutions more than charitable considerations. ('Poverty, Charity . . .' *cit.*)
10   First with Nicolò and then with Vincenzo Bollani respectively, as Francesco's *Condizione*, or tax-return, is a joint declaration with Nicolò in 1534 (*A.S.V., Dieci Savi sopra le Decime*, (Nuovissima, 1534, *busta* 89, n. 157) and with Vincenzo in 1537 (*Ibid, Castello, busta* 80, {1537} n. 145). (It should be noted that Barbaro's genealogies do not confirm the existence of Nicolò Bollani, but the internal evidence of the *Condizione* points to an uncle or

more distant relative of Domenico Bollani, joined in a *fraterna* with Francesco in 1534, and who probably died between 1534 and 1547.)

11 In his *Condizione* of 1514, Francesco declared the family house in Santa Maria Formosa and some low yield properties in the Este region (Santa Maria Formosa, {1514} *busta* 47, n. 80). In conjunction with Nicolò Bollani, Francesco declared *accrescimenti*, or additional acquisitions in 1534 to a total of less than 15 ducats. In 1538, the year of the *redecima*, (and Domenico's entry into the Grand Council), Francesco and Vinzenzo Bollani, his father and uncle respectively, declared their holdings as the family house in Sta. Maria Formosa (annual income value 27 ducats) a vineyard with an annual yield of 22 ducats and 30 fields in the Este region (annual income 34 ducats) giving them a total annual income from immovable goods of 83 ducats. It should be added, however, that these figures represent income from *stabili* (taxable income from house and land property), and that there is evidence that the Bollani family had a tradition of commercial and trading interests, so that wealth may well have been tied alsewhere.

12 On July 26, 1519, 'Fu posto per li consieri e Capi di XL e Savi una gratia, suspender li debiti per do anni di Ser Vincenzo Bollani {Domenico's uncle} fo di ser Domenego e fu presa . . .' (M. Sanudo, *Diarii, cit.* XXVII, col. 526). In 1536 (when Domenico was 23) the other member of the fraterna, Francesco, was granted the same facility to defer payment of a government debt: '. . . la povertà et impotentia nella quale si attrova il Nobil homo Franc.o Bolani fu de Domenego, li debiti sui quali si attrova haver all'officio nostro dell Rason Nove per perdeda delli Datii della Insida et delle Legne siano suspesi per anni due pro X futuri siccome ad altri in simili casi e stato concesso.' (*A.S.V., Senato Terra*, Ro. 1536–1537, f. 36, for July 8, 1536). Although these two petitions cannot be taken as a direct index of poverty in the family, they show at least that at two moments in Domenico's childhood, the family had been unable to meet its financial commitments, being obliged to make them public in this way. The reference to 'altri in simili casi' shows that this was far from an isolated case, however. Later, papers relating to such cases were collected in *Filze*, where more information relating to the family in question may be found. For another example, see *Ibid. Senato Terra*, Ro. 1534–1535, f. 175. (I am grateful to Dr. Pullan for drawing my attention to the 1536 petition.) By a stroke of irony, Domenico Bollani himself wrote about a similar request by the Duodo family from Udine twenty years later (*Ibid., Filza* 23, April 23, 1556). The phenomenon of tax-farming, its motivations and results, with various examples of losses incurred by noblemen, is now discussed fully in B. Pullan, 'The Occupations and Investments of the Venetian Nobility . . .' in *Renaissance Venice* (Ed. J.R. Hale) (London, 1973) pp. 392–3.

13 For Pietro Aretino's relations with the family, see below, pp. 11–12. Benedetta Bollani inherited houses in this district from her mother, Isabetta Dolfin (widow of Giacomo Capello) on her death in 1530, which totalled 62 ducats of annual income in her *Condizione* of 1534 (*Decima 'Nuovissima'* {1534} *busta* 89, n. 157), and by 1538, (the year of Domenico's majority) his mother owned properties with an annual yield of 162 ducats – twice the income from *stabili* declared by Domenico's father and uncle together – divided as property at Mirano {56 ducats}, houses there {12 ducats} and further property {12 ducats}. Importantly this property was now jointly owned by 'Nui benetta Bollani consorte del M. Francesco et fioli Domenico e Giacomo' (*Condizione* 1538, *Castello*, n. 335).

14 This has been studied in detail by J.C. Davis, *op. cit., passim*, and see particularly, B. Pullan, 'Service to the Venetian State . . .' *cit.* pp. 135–143.

15 See below, pp. 13–14, for his early career and attempts to gain election to posts with some secure financial yield.

16 See below, Chap. VI. Domenico's sister Catterina Bollani married Nicolò Contarini in 1535, and the family was obliged to pay her dowry over a considerable period (*A.S.V., Avogaria di Comun*, Ro. 106/1 (*Matrimoni di Nobili Veneti {1400–1560}*, and for the marriage contract, its terms and provisions, *Libro Contratti*, Ro. 143/4.) The strain on the family's resources exercised by the provision of dowries is amply illustrated by the case of Domenico's niece Betta Bollani (1542–1577), who married Michele Foscarini in 1572. (See family tree, p. 16). On her death in 1577, Betta left her dowry intact to her husband (see her will in *A.S.V., Atti Ziliol, busta* 1257, n. 303, dated November 29, 1572). It is clear from Domenico's correspondence at this time that the family regarded this will as an act of

treacherous coercion on the part of the husband, and that, further, a sizeable proportion of it remained to be paid: 'Mi e succeduto anco in questi giorno un'altra tribulatione della morte di mia sorella de questi poveri figlioli { Antonio and Vincenzo Bollani. Domenico is therefore describing his niece } con haver lasciata tutta la sua dote di ducate 12 M. a suo marito et cosi privare il suo sangue et massime le sue sorelle che si trovano senza alcuna provisione de esser maritate; { Giacomo had seven daughters } et de peggio ci resta ancora da pagare una buona parte di detta dote; in fatti questo mondo et comune viver de gli huomini e pur iniquo et perfido; guardate di gratia che fraudulente deduttione e stata di quel assassino marito . . .' (Bollani to Roveglio, June 8, 1577 in *Lettere Bollani* MSS, *Biblioteca Queriniana*, Brescia, B.V. 31–32). It is clear that the family intended to contest the will, as Domenico wrote of the assistance lent by his brother-in-law, Francesco Longo, 'per farci questo ritornare a casa con ogni honore, si come ne sono sicurissimo' (*Ibid.*). We do not know the outcome of the affair, except that Bollani was sending money to Venice to settle 'quel debito Foscarini' on September 22, 1577 (*Ibid.* Bollani to Roveglio on that date), and so a sizeable debt remained. For further discussion of the family dowries, see below, n. 25.

17 See the will of Lugrecia Memmo q. Bernardo in *A.S.V., Atti Marsilio, Busta* 1209, p. 527 (dated December 24, 1554) and the far more ligible *protocollo* (notary's copy) in *busta* 1218, XI, pp. 94–98. Lugrecia Memmo was the aunt of Benetta Bollani, Domenico's mother, who inherited most of the fortune of an entire generation, surviving her three sons. (See Barbaro, *ad vocem*, and for the size and nature of the fortune, see the *Condizione* of Lugrecia's uncle, Bernardo Memmo q. Piero in 1514 (San Trovaso). A comparison of the Bollani *Condizioni* before and after receipt of this legacy makes it clear that the vast majority of the family property by 1566 came from this source, including the house on the Rio di San Trovaso, to which the Bollani family moved in 1562 from their previous lodging in Sta. Maria Formosa.

18 Giacomo's will is in *A.S.V., Atti Ziliol, busta* 1258, f. 451. His *Condizione* for 1566 (*Ibid. Dieci Savi . . ., Dorsoduro, busta* 139, n. 125) lists the combined assets of the Dolfin and Memmo fortunes. It is also clear from this document that the family had invested in land on the *Terraferma* to a considerable extent, some of which was held in *consortia* with the Dolfin, Trevisan and Coccho families.

19 Giacomo's will (*cit.*).

20 See B. Pullan, 'Service to the Venetian State . . .' *cit.* pp. 135–143, and 'The Occupations and investments of the Venetian Nobility in the Middle and Late Sixteenth Century' (*cit.*) for discussion of the economics of dowries in Venice, and S.J. Woolf, *Studi sulla Nobiltà Piemontese nell'Epoca dell'Assolutismo*, (Turin, 1963) pp. 34–35, 153–158, for comparable structures in Piedmont. (I am grateful to Professor Pullan for allowing me to consult his work before its publication).

21 They had already been left an income of 12 ducats a year by their grandmother's will. In fact three of Domenico's nieces entered the Convent of Sant'Anna in Padua in February 1576, when Domenico described his visit to Padua to hear their profession to Roveglio (*Carteggio Bollani-Roveglio, cit.*, Bollani To Roveglio, 24 February, 1576 from Padua).

22 Giacomo's will, *cit.* p. 2. Interestingly however, Betta Bollani, who married the year after her father's death, was to receive 12,000 ducats – possibly helped by the revenues from Domenico's bishopric.

23 See App. 1, pp. 244–247, and notes. Both brothers provide a comment on the inflation of sixteenth century Venetian dowries. Between 1564 and 1575 the legal limits on dowries had been removed, so that Giacomo lamented not being able to offer more to his daughters in 1568, adding that 'al presente corrono le doti tanto eccessive desiderarei il modo di poter loro proveder di qualche maggior suma ma convenendo io haver riguardo al tanto numero di figlioli che mi trovo . . .' By 1579, when Domenico made his will, the limit imposed was 6,000 ducats 'tanto per le leggi della Patria notra è ultimamente statuito potersi dare in dote' (App. I, p. 244).

24 Pullan, 'Service to the Venetian State . . .' *loc. cit.*

25 First among these must have been the arrival of seven daughters, but Giacomo described various pernicious influences on the family fortune in 1568. When restoring his wife's dowry to its source, he hopes that she will help in the provision of dowries, should their extraction from the patrimony make this necessary, since 'il mio ressiduo verrà a restare molto gravato.'

He complained of the many 'riparationi notabilissimi delli nostri stabeli dentro et fuori,' (echoing similar comments in his *Condizione* of 1566) which call to mind the cases of the Zen and Barbarigo families, and of 'that class of poor noblemen who lived off the rent of old and ruinous houses with heavy expenses for repairs.' (cited by B. Pullan, 'Service . . .' p. 137) We have also suggested (p. 8, n. 18) that he had attempted to offset these disadvantages in investment in the *Terraferma* in conjunction with other families. He lamented losses caused by misfortunes in business ('la pocha sorte che ho avuto di guadagno nella compera d'ogli . . . et medesimamente nella bottega de panni . . . per ragione di compera in portione della mietta . . .'), and losses resulting from the Turkish war: 'Onde io vengo a perdere un cavedale di forse ducati diecimille mandati l'anno passato in tanti panni et danari contanti al viaggio d'Alessandria . . . et in oltre è da dubitare grandemente che le nostre entrate de fitti di case in Vinetia habbiano per causa di detta guerra a deteriorare non pocho . . .' Thus it seems that the family had been unlucky in the various trading enterprises in which their money had been invested. It is tempting to assume from a comparison of Giacomo's *Condizione* of 1566 (where extensive land holdings on the *Terraferma* appear) with the will of Cecilia Bollani in 1624, that the investment in land of the family's capital had been reversed. Cecilia was the last surviving niece of the Bishop of Brescia, and in her will (in *A.S.V., Atti Fabrizio Bencian, buste* 56–58, pp. 100. 352–353) a complete inventory of the family property was occasioned bv its division between the Molin and Loredan families at this moment of the extinction of Domenico's branch of the Bollani family. (See below, and family tree p. 16) The houses and shops in Venice that had passed into the family from the Dolphin and Memmo inheritances are still there, but the land holdings are noticeably absent.

26 See the full discussion of the 'Venetian Political Tradition: The Republic's Consciousness of itself' in contemporary treatise literature in W.J. Bouwsma, *op. cit.*, pp. 52–162.

27 See the comparison with the Barbaro and da Ponte families below.

28 See below, pp. 13–14.

29 On the myth of Venice, see particularly F. Gaeta, 'Alcune considerazioni sul mito di Venezia' in *Biblioteque d'Humanisme . . .* XXIII (1961).

30 W.J. Bouwsma, *op. cit.*, p. 107.

31 For the political events, for example W. Carew Hazlitt, *The Venetian Republic* etc. (London, 1900) II, pp. 174–223, P. Daru, *Storia della Repubblica di Venezia*, (Capolago, 1837) V passim., S. Romanin, *Storia Documentata di Venezia*, (Venice, 1925) V, pp. 425–477, VI, passim.

32 G. Cozzi, *Il Doge Nicolò Contarini cit.* pp. 7–9, W.J. Bouwsma, *op. cit.* pp. 111–1¨2.

33 *Ibidem.* And for the Democratic/Oligarchic nature of the government at this time, see the conflicting contemporary *Relazioni* quoted by B. Pullan in *Service to the Venetian State cit.* pp. 95–108.

34 Barbaro, *op. cit.*, pp. 40–41, R.M. della Rocca and M.F. Tiepolo, 'Cronologia Veneziana del Cinquecento' in *La Civiltà Veneziana del Rinascimento*, (Venice, 1958) p. 209.

35 Besides the many sources already cited, see particularly W.T. Elwert, 'Pietro Bembo e la Vita Letteraria del Suo Tempo' in *La Civiltà Veneziana cit.* pp. 127–176.

36 *Op. cit.* p. 40.

37 The house stands to this day on the Grand Canal at the corner of the Rio di San Giovanni Grisostomo, just below the Rialto. It has been the subject of much speculation, and the documents relating to the history of the Bollani family shed some new light on this. See my 'Ancora sulla casa dell'Aretino sul Canal Grande' in *Studi Veneziani*, XIV, (1972) pp. 211–217. (Figs. 2, 3a, 3b)

38 Aretino compares the beauty of the position of the house with the qualities of its owner, Domenico Bollani, who, had inherited it with his mother and brother from Isabetta Dolfin in 1530. As Aretino had moved into the house in 1529, Domenico has also inherited his troublesome tenant, unless Aretino's memory is at fault (See Aretino, *Lettere, cit.* VI, 23: 'io vi restituisco le chiavi di quella casa da me XXII anni habitata . . . {1551}). 'Ma dove si rimangono i lumi, che dopo la sera paiono stelle sparse, u' si vende la robba necessaria ai nostri desinari e a le nostre cene? Dove le musiche, che la notte poi mi grattano l'orecchie con la concordia de le lor consonanze? Prima si esprimerebbe il giudizio profondo che voi avete ne le

lett{e}re e nel governo pubblico, ch'io potessi venire al fine dei diletti ch'io provo ne le comodità del vedere.' (Pietro Aretino, *Lettere* (Paris, 1609) I, p. 212).

39 The subject of Aretino's correspondence with the Bollani family was the former's non-payment of rent due for the *palazzo*, and the attempt to pay part of what was owing by praising the family in his published collections of letters. For this, see my 'Distinguished Correspondent' *cit.* and Alessandro Luzio, *Pietro Aretino nei suoi primi anni a Venezia e la Corte dei Gonzaga*, (Turin, 1888) pp. 41–44. The letters are in *Lettere*, ed. *cit.* I, 212, (October 27, 1537) IV, 424 (1548) VI, 53.

40 Pietro Aretino, *Ragionamenti dell'Aretino*, (Cosmopoli, 1660) p. 417, quoted by G. Mazzuchelli in his *Vita dell'Aretino*, (Brescia, 1763^2) p. 298.

41 According to G. Innamorati, *Tradizione e Invenzione in Pietro Aretino*, (Messina/Florence, 1957) pp. 224–225, this letter must predate Aretino's *Dialogo delle Corti* which was published in 1538. It would therefore be contemporary with the above letter, or earlier.

42 As far as is known, this treatise was never written. See Innamorati, *loc. cit.*, where it is suggested it might have been 'illustrazione, o commento . . . della società contemporanea nei due 'stati' essenziali del vivere sociale'. (p. 224) Further testimony of Domenico's scholarly interests is provided by the letter to him of January 23, 1551, by Alvise Cornaro (in Museo Correr, Venice, Mss *Prov. Div.*, 399. p. 9) which refers to their discussions of a moral and academic nature and contains the writer's views on vices and virtues and an invitation to Bollani to visit him soon. (For Alvise Cornaro and land reclamation projects, see R. Cessi, *Storia della Repubblica di Venezia*, (Milan/Messina, 1968) II, pp. 116–117.

43 Initiated by Luigi Francesco Fè d'Ostiani, *Il Vescovo Domenico Bollani, Memorie Storiche della Diocesi di Brescia*, (Brescia, 1875) p. 3, and perpetuated by the writers of two theses on Bollani (see below). Fè d'Ostiani states that Domenico Bollani studied law at Padua, making contact with prominent jurists of the day. He gives no source, but states that details of early biography are from E.A. Cicogna, *Delle Iscrizioni Veneziane*, 6 vols (Venice, 1824). This writer, however, does not mention Bollani's legal studies. There is no complete biography of Domenico Bollani. Apart from the sketch in Barbaro (*loc. cit.*) the first attempt at collect-ing data connected with his life seems to have been E.A. Cicogna, *op. cit.*, I, pp. 133–134, IV, pp. 351, 451–457, 651, which draws on Morosini, *Degli Istorici delle Cose Veneziane*, (Venice, 1719), and Foscarini, *Della Letteratura Veneziana, ad vocem*. The only, biography is Fè d'Ostiani, *cit.* which deals in detail only with Bollani's activity as bishop, and is entirely derivative up to the Oglio dispute. Similarly derivative on the early life, are the two doctoral theses on Bollani's ecclesiastical reforms: Carmela Petroboni, 'Domenico Bollani e la sua Opera nella Controriforma Bresciana', (1937–1938), Facoltà di Magistero, Università Cattolica del Sacro Cuore, Milan, Tesi di Laurea n. 7889, and the most recent: Celestina Zanotti, 'Aspetti della figura e dell'opera di Domenico Bollani nella riforma Cattolica Bresciana' (1559–1579) Un. Catt. del S.C. tèsi 35101 (1963–1964). There are two pages towards a life of Bollani by the 19th century scholar Baldassare Zamboni: 'Notizie spettanti al Vescovo Domenico Bollani tratti dai libri delle Provvisioni', (Brescia, Biblioteca Queriniana, Ms F.IV.9), but these are merely summaries from the *Provvisioni* (see p.106 n. 12) from 1559. There is a brief biographical summary in Gradonigo, *Pontificum Brixianorum series commentario historico illustrata opera et studio Iohannis Gradonici*, (Brescia, 1755) pp. 366–372, and there were plans for a biography by Zamboni and Guadagnini in the nineteenth century, and a manuscript by the latter was due to be published about 1808, but of these, no trace remains. For discussion of these sources see Petroboni, thesis *cit.* pp. 5–14.

44 I am grateful to Dott. Rosetti of the Archivio Antico, Università di Padova for this information. There are no contemporary records of the university of Padua which indicate Domenico's presence there.

45 From May to November, 1552 (*A.S.V. Senato Terra*, Ro. 38 1551–1552) For discussion of the functions of this office, and Bollani's tenure see below, p. 54.

46 For the *Studio* in general see the very full 'Bibliografia dell'Università di Padova' by Lucia Rossetti in *Quaderni per la Storia dell'Università di Padova*, (Padua, 1968) pp. 179–311. For the structure, syllabus and courses, see B. Brugi, 'L'Università dei Giuristi in Padova nel Cinquecento: Saggio di Storia della Giurisprudenza e delle Università italiane' in *Archivio Veneto-Tridentino* I (1922) pp. 1–92.

47 For foreigners in Padua and their influence, besides the 'bibliografia' above, see *Idem*, 'La Nazione Tedesca dei Giuristi dello Studio di Padova nel Secolo XVII' in *Monografie Storiche sullo Studio di Padova* (Venice, 1922) passim, and for activities of scholars etc., *Idem*, 'Gli Scolari dello Studio di Padova nel Cinquecento' in *Per la Storia della Giurisprudenza e delle Università Italiane* (Turin, 1921) pp. 122–154. Apparently, Lutheranism was a favourite accusation levelled at Germans at the time of university elections. See also P. McNair, *Peter Martyr in Italy: An Anatomy of Apostasy*, (Oxford, 1967).

48 We have seen from Giacomo's will that he had been trading in oil, woollen cloth and grain, and that he had speculated in a voyage to Alexandria in 1567 (see above, p. 9, n. 25).

49 J.C. Davis has described a typical *Fraterna* in his *Decline of the Venetian Nobility cit*, pp. 26–27, and noted the 'high degree of coordination within the family and agreement as to family aims.' As we have seen, Domenico's father, Francesco, and his uncle, Vincenzo, were linked in a *fraterna* (see their combined tax return in 1537 in *A.S.V. Decime, Castello, busta 94/80*, n. 145) and Giacomo Bollani's brothers-in-law, Francesco and Marcantonio Longo were similarly united (see their combined tax return in 1582 in *Museo Correr*, Mss. P.D. 2065, cc. 45–48).

50 The only way to carry out such a survey for one family is through a systematic survey of the *Segretario alle Voci* in the *A.S.V.* There is, however, an Ms in the Marciana library which records all those noblemen elected to office between 1520 and 1580 (Ms. It. VII 813 *et seq.*) I used 813–871 for the years 1538–1558. (See J.C. Davis, *op. cit.*, pp. 130–138 for discussion of this and similar sources). This Ms. (the *Raccolta dei Consegi*) has the advantage in the present context of including all those *proposed* for office with votes cast for and against, so that it provides some evidence for the growth of influence of the noblemen by showing also those offices to which he was *not* elected and by what margin. (I am not aware that this system of assessment of progress through *minor* offices has been attempted before, as Gaetano Cozzi, *Niccolò Contarini, cit.*, Federico Seneca, *Leonardo Donà, cit.*, Charles Yriarte, *La Vie d'un Patricien de Venise* (Paris, 1874) etc. merely list minor offices and omit proposals for office that were unsuccessful.) It is almost impossible accurately to forecast the financial yield of offices. I have been guided in general by the conclusions of B. Pullan in 'Service to the Venetian State' *cit.* pp. 120–121 and n. 99, on the possibilities in government office for poor noblemen and their yield. In general 'it seems that legal offices and fiscal or administrative posts within Venice itself or occasionally in the provinces (as Chamberlains, *Camerlenghi* in the big towns) were the most popular receptacles for the poorer nobility. Naval commands and small civil or military governorships, either on the mainland of Italy, on the Dalmatian and Albanian coastline, in the Ionian Islands or in Crete, also absorbed much of the lesser nobleman's labour and energy.' (pp. 120–1) See also *Idem*, 'Occupations and investments . . .' *cit.*

51 See above p. 18, n. 12.

52 *Raccolta dei Consegi, cit.* IX, pp. 171, 174, 175, for, respectively, September 24, October 1 and October 6, 1538.

53 See above p. 17, n. 1.

54 Cozzi, *Nicolò Contarini, cit.*, p. 8, Pullan, *Service to the Venetian State, cit.*, pp. 121–123, *Idem* 'The Occupations and Investments . . .' *cit.*, pp. 394–5.

55 Except as proposer in 1547, when he proposes a Contarini as *Consolo* (6th February) and *40 Civil Novi* (5th June). (*Raccolta dei Consegi, cit.*, XI, pp. 64, 83). It is very likely that this was either his brother-in-law or son-in-law, as his daughter, Domenico's sister, married a Contarini. See family tree p. 16.

56 *Raccolta dei Consegi, cit.*, X, p. 199, XI, pp. 89, 90, 93, 268. It was often the case that candidates were proposed by their relatives (presumably if they lacked influential support from the upper ranks of the government). Giacomo was first proposed by his father on 10th July, 1547, Francesco proposed his in-laws in 1547, and Domenico was proposed *Dieci Savi sopra le Decime del Rialto* by his uncle, Antonio Longo on 7th June, 1545. (IX, p. 287).

57 See the summary cited by B. Pullan, *loc. cit.* Giacomo's withdrawal from public life about 1547 also receives support from the fact that he had taken over the business of letting the properties owned by the family, as we know from Aretino's letter of 1551 (*Lettere, cit.*, VI, p. 53, and see my 'Bollani correspondent of Aretino' *cit.*, pp. 200–201). For the financial

22

status of *Camerlenghi*, see the comment of Sieur de la Haye, who suggests that the post was often an opportunity for feathering the nest of the incumbent, quoted by B. Pullan *loc. cit.*
58 Before 1547, Domenico had not been proposed for office by any nobleman of real influence or political significance. This difficulty may be seen not only in choice of office and repeated unsuccessful candidature but also by comparison with two of Domenico's contemporaries, Daniele Barbaro and Nicolò da Ponte. The former parallels Domenico's later career exactly, following him in the English Embassy in 1549, and meeting him again at the Council of Trent as Patriarch-elect of Aquileia. Da Ponte was the future Doge, representing the continued devotion to State rather than Church. Both were powerful and wealthy families in contrast to the Bollani, and, importantly, all three were considered representative of their age by their contemporary Paolo Paruta, who included them as characters in his discussion *Della Perfettione della Vita Politica*, (Venice, 1579).
59 Information from a subsequent election: 'Domenico Bollani fu acque . . .' as I have been unable to find the date of this election in the *Raccolta dei Consegi*. It was almost certainly in 1538, however, the year of Domenico's entry to the Grand Council, as he reached the age of 25 in that year.
60 Created in 1505, the membership was increased from 15 to 25 in 1531, and its functions were radically altered later in 1543. See A. da Mosto, *L'Archivio di Stato di Venezia*, I, pp. 155–157, and G. Orlandini, 'Il Veneto Magistrato alle Acque' in *Ateneo Veneto* (1906) Fasc. 1, pp. 200–241, Fasc. 2, pp. 250–309. Undoubtedly Domenico's early experience of water control and legal aspects of water rights would have stood him in good stead when he later came to solve the question of water rights in the dispute over the river Oglio (Chap. V), just as Nicolò Contarini had found his experience of a similar magistracy useful in his later position in the Friuli. (Cozzi, *Nicolò Contarini, cit.*, pp. 58–62).
61 1. 10th October 1540: *Dieci Savi sopra le Decime in Rialto*, Bollani last in a poll of 4. This magistracy, whose membership was increased to 10 in 1477, was responsible for the census and assessment of incomes for tax purposes. (*Raccolta dei Consegi, cit.*, IX, p. 308, Da Mosto, *op. cit.*, I, 127–128, B. Canal, 'Il Collegio, l'Ufficio e l'Archivio dei Dieci Savi alle Decime in Rialto' in *Nuovo Archivio Veneto*, N. Serie, XVI, pp. 115–150, 279–310.
2. 21st September 1541: *Provveditore al Cottimo d'Alessandria.*
Bollani third in a poll of 4. (see below p. 24, n. 66)
3. 21st September 1541: *Provveditore sopra li Ufficii.*
Bollani second in a poll of 4. An important office, with responsibilities for auditing accounts involving expenditure of public monies, and voting rights in the Senate. (Da Mosto, *op. cit.*, I, p. 138)
4. 25th September 1541: *Provveditore sopra i Dazi.*
Bollani third in a poll of 4. An office slightly lower in the hierarchy than above, as the three members of this committee had access to the Senate, but without voting rights. The office was created in 1500 to prevent smuggling, police waterways and issue licences for the loading, export and import of goods. (Da Mosto, *op. cit.*, p. 124)
5. 10th April 1542: *Camerlengo de Comun.*
Bollani third in a poll of 4. The three members of this committee had offices at the Rialto and were, in effect, the cashiers of the Republic. They controlled transactions with public money and had the additional function of proposing economies in the expenditure of the State. They also had criminal jurisdiction over the Republic's debtors. (Da Mosto, *op. cit.*, p. 116)
6. 30th May 1542: *Provveditore al Cottimo d'Alessandria.*
Bollani third in a poll of 4. (See below p. 24, n. 66)
7. 17th September 1542: *Camera degli Imprestidi.*
Bollani second in a poll of 4. (An office connected with securities deposited against loans from the State.)
8. October 1542: *Provveditore sopra i Banchi.*
Bollani second in a poll of 4. An office which controlled Venetian Banks. (Da Mosto, *op. cit.*, p. 111.)
It seems that Domenico Bollani gained some ground in 1542, as in September of that year, Polo Querini, elected in (7) above had scored 738 votes for, and 425 against, while Bollani had had 557 for and 660 against. In October, Zuanne Donà had polled 656 for and

483 against in his election in (8) above, while Bollani scored 617 for and 517 against. For these elections see *Raccolta dei Consegi, cit.*, IX, p. 308, X, pp. 33, 34, 72, 79, 97, 141.

62 This was by no means unusual for a member of the poorer nobility. See examples in J.C. Davis, *op. cit.*, pp. 33–53.

63 See B. Pullan, 'Service to the Venetian State', cit., pp. 117–125. Prof. Pullan suggests that an average poor nobleman might earn 120–160 ducats a year from official sources, even if embezzlement was not common.

64 Daniele Barbaro had been proposed *40 Civil Novi* in 1540. Ambassador to the French King in 1541, Ambassador to the King of Rumania in 1542, all without success until he was elected *Provveditore sopra i Banchi* in 1544, and Ambassador to Edward VI of England in 1549. (*Raccolta dei Consegi*, cit., IX, p. 275, X, p. 63, 120, 276). Even if he had not had support from the Grand Council, his family had been – in theory at least – ready to support him in the most expensive ambassadorships for nine years. Nicolò da Ponte seems to have had both wealth and influence. By 1539 he had reached *Avogador* and was elected *Luogotenente a Udine* in 1540, and Ambassador to Charles V in 1542. (*Raccolta cit.*, IX, p. 329, X, p. 73.) Da Ponte's career up to his election as Doge in 1578 is too long to summarise here, but significantly (and unlike men of more modest means and power like Bollani and Barbaro) I have found no record of Da Ponte not succeeding in an election in which he was a candidate.

65 See p. 22, n. 50.

66 It will be remembered that Domenico had offered himself as *Provveditore al Cottimo d'Alessandria* in 1541 and again in 1542. The *Cottimo* was a tax levelled by the *Provveditore* on goods imported from Alexandria, London and Damascus. On the Venetian W ol Industry see Domenico Sella, 'The Rise and Fall of the Venetian Wool Industry'; on trade with the Levant, *Idem*, 'Crisis and Transformation in Venetian Trade' and F.C. Lane, 'The Mediterranean Spice Trade: Further Evidence of its revival in the Sixteenth Century: all in B. Pullan (Ed.) *Crisis and Change in the Venetian Economy in the Sixteenth and Seventeenth Centuries*, (London, 1968). For probable cargoes and details of trade, compare particularly examples given for 1511, 1525 and 1561 in Lane, *op. cit.*, p. 48 and notes. Giacomo Bollani was proposed for a minor post in Dalmatia in 1549, though was not successful. (*Raccolta de Consegi, cit.*, XI, p. 268, 22 September, 1549)

67 *Op. cit.*, pp. 51–52, and the *Relazioni* of Venetian Consults quoted n. 1. See also 'Cottimo' in Boerio, *Dizionario del Dialetto Veneziano*, (Venice, 1829) I, p. 161. It is interesting to find in the context of the post as a prerogative of poor noblemen that, on the suppression of the post in the seventeenth century, 'si volle non di meno indenizzare quella parte dei poveri patrizi che restava pregiudicata della detta soppressione, e quindi s'instituitiono tre specie di Magistrature annuali sotto il titolo . . . ch'erano come benefizi semplici nei quali si percepiva il salario mensuale di ducati 30 d'argento ma senza alcune attribuzione di affari.' Unfortunately, no source is given for this statement. The dispatches of the Venetian *Consoli* are collected in *A.S.V. 5 Savi alla Mercanzia*, (for which see M. Borgherini Scarabellini, 'Il Magistrato dei Cinque Savi alla Mercanzia dalla Instituzione alla Caduta della Repubblica' in *Miscellanea di Storia Ven. Tridentina* (1926, II.) but contains few significant documents before the eighteenth century.

68 For the polls after 1543, see the *Raccolta dei Consegi, cit.*, X, pp. 287, 314, XI, pp. 10, 39, 45.:

   1. 7th June 1545: *Dieci Savi Sopra le Decime del Rialto.* Fourth in poll of 4.

   2. 6th October, 1545: *Provveditore di Comun.* Second in a poll of 4. (Da Mosto, *op. cit.*, I, p. 178.)

   3. 2nd May, 1546: *Ditto.* Third in a very close poll of 4.

   4. 1st October, 1546: *Officiale alle Rason Vecchie:* Third in a poll of 4. These officers audited the accounts of the Venetian representatives in the *Terraferma*, and had considerable powers over debtors and other magistrates, particularly when the latter were lax in attending committees. They had rights of access and vote in the Senate. (Da Mosto, *vol. cit.*, pp. 139–140)

   5. 31st October, 1546: *Provveditore e Castellano a Cerigo:* (A minor governorship.)

69 'Vescovo della Canea' (1588–1613). Domenico's career was certainly facilitated by his uncle's reputation in Venice and Rome, and the possibility of recommending him for his

uncle's see of Brescia was discussed in *Collegio* in 1579 (for which see Stella, *Chiesa e Stato . . . cit.*, pp. 218–219, the *Relazione* of the Papal Nunzio Bolognetti) He seems to have had a career of misfortune, being under suspicion of friendship with the Spanish Ambassador (for which see Cicogna, *op. cit.*, IV, pp. 455–457) and, by a stroke of irony (when his uncle's firm stand at the Council of Trent is remembered) he was notoriously absent from his distant see. (On this see Logan, 'Studies in the Religious life of Venice . . .' *cit.*, pp. 291–293, and dispatches of the Papal Nuncio quoted there). See also Giovanni Botero, *Relatione della Republica Venetiana* (Venice, 1608) pp. 49–50, for further details of family history, *Idem, Discorso intorno allo Stato della Chiesa*, (Venice, 1608) dedicated to 'monsignor Domenico Bollani, Vescova di Canea', and Cicogna, *op. cit.*, IV, pp. 456–457.

70 See family tree, p. 16. Barbaro, *op. cit.*, p. 40. He had married Maria Bragadin q. Nicolò, q. Giovanni, in 1586, the year before his death. (*A.S.V., Avogaria di Comun, loc. cit.*)

71 Domenico's preoccupation with the education and upbringing of his two younger nephews – who had not reached maturity on their father's death in 1571 – is a frequent subject of his letters to Roveglio at Salò during the period 1576–1577 (see *Carteggio Bollani-Roveglio, cit., passim.*) Neither of the boys seems to have distinguished himself, which caused Domenico much heart-searching.

72 See Vincenzo's will in *A.S.V., Atti Fabrizio Bencian, busta* 58, p. 129.

73 It is perhaps curious to find that Giacomo Bollani was condemned for theft, when Domenico, bishop of Brescia, had described similar behaviour in Vincenzo Bollani, his nephew. He hopes Vincenzo will 'lasciar quel maledetto vitio di pigliar le cose dove egli capita, ch'altro non vuol dire che farsi tener per ladro.' (Bollani to Roveglio, October 1, 1577, *Carteggio, cit.*).

74 In fact, another niece, Lucrezia Bollani, was Abbess of the Monastery of Sant'Anna in Padua in 1636 (Capellari, *Famiglie Venete*, MSS. I p. 467).

75 Cecilia's will is in *A.S.V., Atti Fabrizio Bencian, buste* 56–58, pp. 100, 352–353.

CHAPTER II

AMBASSADOR TO EDWARD VI (1547–1549)

After conspicuous lack of success in his attempts to obtain election to the various fiscal offices in the Venetian government, Domenico Bollani was about to enter the theatre of European politics in 1547 with his election to the English embassy. Seen against the background of his small success in elections to date, this was a considerable advance. Moreover, the post was to involve him in the delicate relations between Venice and the Papacy, and was to send him into the heart of Protestant Europe. The details of this appointment and the fact that he was to be precipitated into a situation of constitutional and religious crises in England make it necessary briefly to sketch in the background of international relations between England and Venice.

The death of Henry VIII in England had precipitated crises which all Europe was concerned to watch closely. The problem of Henry's will and the assumption of the Tudor heritage by a Council under the protector Somerset was one thing, but it was difficult to see how Henry's headship of the Church could be vested in a Council. The balance of power in Europe could have been drastically altered by revolution or anarchy in England, poised as it was for England on the shifting sands of uneasy alliances with France and the Emperor Charles V. Importantly, too, emergent protestantism in England might favour alignment with German protestants, or a reversion to Catholicism might be engineered from the general confusion. A good contemporary description of England's position in August 1546, shortly before Henry's death was written by William Paget.[1]

Paget saw in England's relations with France and the Emperor no grounds for complacency, but rather every reason for vigilance. Henry VIII's annexation of Boulogne invited reprisal and revenge. Charles V could not be counted on in alliance since the schism, as he was much influenced by the policy of the Papacy to regain spiritual control of England. The German Protestant states were weak and in constant danger, and any alliance with them might produce a Catholic alliance of Charles and France against England. Paget saw one avenue to strength in the cultivation of relations with Venice (and we shall return to this) as she was constantly preoccupied with the threat to her northern frontiers from the Empire. Basically, then, the alliance between France and the Emperor was to be avoided at all costs, and any opportunity to sow seeds of discord should be grasped. One way to do this would be if Charles were to lend assistance against a French threat to Boulogne, another would be to favour a stronger German Protestant bloc as an insurance against duplicity on the part of Charles V, but above all, to build a strong and unified nation with singleness of purpose. It has been noted[2] that this summary of the English position in 1546 does represent Somerset's foreign policy at the beginning of his protectorate, but that this comes as no surprise, as Paget must have been instrumental in formulating it from his position of influence. It took no account of the problem of Scotland, however, and this was to be the cause of the failure of Somerset's foreign policy during the three years of Bollani's term of office as ambassador.

So on the death of Henry VIII, the position of English diplomacy in Europe was a complex of problems and potential dangers. Charles V was making some headway towards a better unity of German states — a potentially dangerous situation for England. Relations with France were momentarily settled by the Treaty of Campe by June, 1547, which confirmed English possession of Boulogne for the time being. The Pope was an obviously hostile force and would do everything to hinder English interests as she moved towards a definition of her Protestant position. The accession of the boy king Edward VI, who had been brought up as a Protestant, might bring England to her knees and might favour any of the varied European interests in English affairs.

For these reasons, the news of Henry's death was received with excitement and speculation in European capitals. The Venetian Ambassador to Charles V at the time was perhaps the least well informed. He wrote to the Doge and Senate to report on speculation at the Imperial Court about a possible revolution in England, and to predict that France would consider England's weakness an open invitation to re-take Boulogne,[3] but wrote again the next day to quote the English Ambassador to Charles[4] on the English need for an alliance with the Emperor. Francis I expressed formal condolences on the death of Henry on February 14.[5]

The Pope's attitude we must examine more closely. Internal confusion in England, with the possibility of revolution, and the dissipation of Tudor strength in Edward VI's Privy Council might lead to an English return to Papal obedience. The Pope's reaction to the death of Henry VIII was almost immediate, for on February 25th, 1547, the decision had already been reached in the Consistorium to send three Papal legates to the courts of France, Charles V and to Scotland in order to smooth the path towards the 'reduction' of England to Catholicism.[6] Cardinal Sfondrato was to go to Charles V, Cardinal Capodiferro to France, and the Pope elected Cardinal Pole to go to Scotland. As can be seen from the instructions issued to the two cardinals,[7] Paul III had conceived the idea of a combination of Catholic pressures to bring England to order. The plan was unrealistic as it turned out, but first reports reaching Europe after Henry's death had given rise to the speculation that anarchy was rife in England. That this judgement was premature will be seen from subsequent events, but the Venetian Secretary, Zambon, in London was able to write to his counterpart at the court of Charles V that 'per esser il figliolo di esso re in pueril età et il regno in governo de sui tutori, potria esser causa de molte revolutioni, si per li tanti di quel regno che sono stati offesi dal detto Re et per conto della religione et altre cause, come perchè Cesare potria forse pretendere che esso regno di ragione debbi pervenire alla figliola, che è germana di Sua Cesarea Maestà, oltra che è quasi commune oppinione ch'l Re di Franza vorrà hora almen tentare di ricuperar Bologna . . .'[8] This opinion of the English situation in February was transmitted to the Venetian Doge by the Venetian Ambassador to Charles, Alvise Mocenigo from Ulm on 10th February, but it might almost have reached the Pope, as it is a concise summary of his hopes for the re-conversion of England taking advantage of her several hypothetical weaknesses. If Zambon's report from London was precipitate and premature, the Pope can hardly have had better intelligence on which to base his plans. He acted with caution, however, instructing his Nuncios in France and Germany to try to discover what kind of a reception the legates would have. He also proposed to send Cardinal Pole first to the French court before proceeding to Scotland. The results of these enquiries were hardly encouraging from the outset. In France, the King forbade the arrival of Pole, fearing that the arrival of an English exile in France would hinder his negotiations with England over the return of Boulogne. The papal legate in Paris was not able to report a favourable reception for the idea of sending Cardinal Capodiferro either.[9]

At the Emperor's court, the atmosphere was even less propitious. The Papal Nuncio, Verallo, had tried to put the question to Charles, but had been told that the Emperor 'would not take up arms against the very worst of men' and that Charles 'would like to put the Nuncio and the Legate in the front line to see what effect their blessings would have.'[10] There is evidence that these soundings were not quite accurately transmitted to the Pope[11] — perhaps on the principle of reporting in a vein most likely to please the reader — but in any event, the Cardinals were dispatched with instructions to persuade Charles and Henry II to facilitate the re-conversion of England to Catholicism.

But even before the appointment of Papal legates there is some evidence that order was gradually emerging in England's relations with the Emperor. From the dispatches of the Venetian ambassador to Charles, it seems that Paget had begun early to sow the seeds of a foreign policy that would not leave England in isolation. A Venetian ambassador at the Emperor's court, although lamenting his lack of information and official commission, permitted himself the comment; 'Serà necessario che questo Re giovinetto si ritrovi un padre esterno, il qual bisogna che sia Cesare, et Dio volesse che la Illustrissima Signoria {Venice} fosse propinqua perchè la buona intelligentia fra lei et quel regno saria molto utile ad ambidoi,'[12] which seems to echo Paget's advice of 1546 to cultivate the Venetians and drive a wedge between the Emperor and France.

The commissions to the Papal legates on their dispatch to Henry II in France and Charles V in Germany leave no doubt about the Pope's intentions. Capodiferro in France was to press for unity between Catholic nations ('una vera pace et unione con la Maestà Cesarea') and to bring to the Pope 'allegrezza di vedere tra loro Maestà, avanti ch'ella muora, la pace tanto desiderata et procurata da Sua Beatitudine.'[13] But this 'pace tanto desiderata' was to mean war with England. For the 'reduction' of England, the Pope adds that 'si possa non manco procurare col mezzo della concordia che non quello dell'armi' and hopes that 'Sua Maestà Christianissima pigli questo assunto di procurare la reduttione di quel regno.'

To Sfondrato, the envoy to Charles V, the instructions are quite specifically to strike while the iron was hot. The death of Henry in England had 'opened the road' to the return to Catholicism, and 'una occasione tale' was not to be missed. Not only would Charles have the good of the Catholic Religion in mind, but would take up the cause 'per interesse proprio della cugina.'[14] The same wording is used for the exhortation to peace between Catholic monarchs, and the thought that 'concordia' was as good a weapon as arms to bring about the reduction of England. But he added that 'non è la mente di Sua Beatitudine di metter guerra tra lei et gl'Inglesi, ma solo della reduttione sopradetta,' knowing perfectly well that both the legate and Charles would infer the opposite.

28

Domenico Bollani's part in the Pope's plans begins on February 19th, when the Venetian Ambassador at the Papal Court referred to the Doge and Senate the Pope's request that the newly-appointed Venetian Ambassador to England should help to facilitate the re-conversion of England.[15] As we have seen, the Pope had been sounding reaction to his plans in European courts in February, so that Venice was also asked for help at this stage. They replied through their ambassador in Rome that they would do all they could, although they were concerned about the stability of the new government — a concern we have seen justified by Zambon's report from London — and it would not be appropriate to send a fully qualified envoy until a stable government had emerged from potential constitutional confusion.

In this situation lie the reasons for Bollani's election. He had only previously held one representative and one administrative post, and was therefore not 'fully qualified.'[16] But there is every reason to suppose that the election of a junior patrician was deliberate policy. The affair was linked with a number of diplomatic negotiations in European minds, even the possibility of a protestant alliance between Henry VIII, Francis I, Venice and German protestant princes in December, 1546. There was controversy when a letter presented in the Venetian Senate by the Secretary for England was heard in spite of attempts by the Papal Nuncio to block it. There were also rumours that the election was linked to the possibility that Pietro Strozzi was treating in Venice for a loan.[17]

A good summary of the reasons behind the election of an ambassador was given by Paolo Paruta in his history.[18] Henry VIII had been traditionally well-disposed towards Venetians, and had entrusted important affairs to the Venetian patrician Francesco Bernardo, who, resident in England for business reasons, had been instrumental in the conclusion of Peace between England and France (which was why the Pope had first suggested that a member of the Bernardo family might best further Papal aims in England.[19]) In December, 1546, before Henry's death, Bernardo Navagero, a well-known diplomat and the future cardinal had been elected ambassador to England, but on the death of the King, the job became uncertain and probably unpopular for experienced diplomats. Thus, bearing in mind the objections of the Nuncio to the recent Protestant initiative, and the efforts of the Pope to secure the 'reduction' of England to Catholicism, the election of Domenico Bollani in 1547, an untried man, may have been a concession to the Papal Nuncio. This is borne out by a dispatch from the Imperial Ambassador in Venice to Charles V: 'An ambassador has been demanded of this signory on behalf of the English even though it were one who has formerly served as secretary; therefore the present one was appointed . . .'[20]

But, the interests of the Pope aside, there were other reasons for the initial caution of the Republic over the appointment of a representative in England. For there had been a break in full diplomatic relations between the two countries of 12 years since the schism. The last Venetian ambassador with full powers had been Carlo Capello, resident from 1531—1535, who had returned home in the latter year leaving a secretary, Gerolamo Zuccato (later replaced by Giacomo Zambon) to hold the fort.[21] The death of the King now provided an opportunity for the resumption of diplomatic relations for three reasons. First a change in the government in England might lead to a reversal to Catholicism, and secondly, even if this did not happen, Venice had important commercial reasons for reinstituting a diplomatic life-line between London and Venice — to safeguard the interests of her merchants and bankers resident in England.[22] Lastly, the English Ambassador, Edmund Harvel, had been resident in Venice throughout the schism, and the accession of Edward VI to the English throne was an opportunity to remedy this diplomatic slight, although it must be added that the question of stationing an ambassador in London was not properly considered until March 2nd, when Harvel reminded the Venetian Senate of promises to send an ambassador — so far, unfulfilled.[23] Harvel's reminder must have jolted the Senate into action, for the decision to send an ambassador was final by March 5th, when the news of this was conveyed to the Pope via the Venetian representative at the Papal Court. Venice expressed her willingness to comply with the Pope's request, and stated that she would use her ambassador (Bollani) to facilitate the re-conversion of England to Roman Catholicism.[24] On the same day, dispatches left Venice for London, addressed to the King, the Protector, and the Venetian Secretary, Zambon, announcing the intention to send an ambassador.

So one of the functions of Domenico Bollani at the English Court was to test reaction to a possible re-conversion, a duty of observation and the transmission of intelligence. But there is a legitimate doubt about the complete sincerity of Venice's stated participation in the Pope's plans. For commercial reasons, she was anxious to resume normal diplomatic relations with England which the correspondence on the appointment of the ambassador clearly shows. It seems far more likely that the formula of 'doing what they could' was a vague expression implying little commitment.

England herself was not unaware of the Pope's machinations. Harvel in Venice had reported on March 7th that he had repeated the request for a Venetian Ambassador, and sent a warning about plans being hatched by the Pope and Cardinal Pole, repeated again in his dispatch to London of March 8th.[25]

We have seen that Charles V was little disposed to favour the Pope's plan and 'would not take up arms against the very worst of men'.[26] His conversations with the Papal Nuncio reached the ears of the Venetian Ambassador who reported on 21st March that 'oltra che lei teneva amicitia con esso Re novo d'Inghilterra, et che voleva mantenerla'[27] as the Pope was continually involving him in war and was deliberately delaying the meeting of the Council of Trent. Charles' own letter of 17th March to Diego de Mendoza is more explicit and stronger, adding that he 'understood his {the Pope's} manoeuvres too well now, for he had drawn us into this enterprise in Germany and left us in the lurch at the most critical point.'[28] So early in the spring of 1547, it cannot have seemed to anyone that the Pope's plan for an invasion of England had any chance of success. It is clear from subsequent events that he had dropped the plan by mid-summer. Fortunately for England, Charles V was in no position to take it seriously, being concerned with the complicated negotiations with his rebel German states, as well as with the question of the Council of Trent. France had been ill-inclined to support the plan either, being concerned with negotiations with England over Boulogne.[29]

Domenico Bollani was elected Ambassador to England on March 11. His commission from the Doge and Senate follows the pattern of such commissions, and only the formal function would have been recorded in the Senate minutes.[30] He was to present letters of authority to the young King, commiserating with him for the Republic on the death of Henry VIII, and congratulating him on his accession to the throne. He was also to do all in his power to promote the interests of Venetian merchants resident in England.

Good relations between England and Venice had been traditionally founded on commerce, and Bollani's success in this field is undoubted. Paruta expressed this special relationship as something which surpassed any specifically diplomatic considerations: 'della morte di Henrico {VIII}, come di prencipe per la lontananza del suo stato, men interessato nelle cose d'Italia, si tenne da gl'Italiani minor conto; ma più degli altri istimavano l'amicitia di quel Re, e di quel regno i Vinitiani, come quelli, che non pur per ragione di stato, ma per le loro private faccende mercantili venivano di tale buona intelligenza a riceverne molti comodi. Conciosiache ordinariamente da Vinetia si mandavano in Inghilterra varie sorti di mercantie, per il che ritornava il commercio con quella nattione utilissimo a'cittadini e mercanti Vinetiani.'[31] Clearly for this commercial ambassadorial role, Bollani would have been better suited, and it was this special relationship which gave rise to his success in England, where, in the words of Paruta, 'trovò nei signori principali, e di maggiore auttorità un'ottima corrispondenza di continuare l'amicitia, e il commercio con Vinetiani, promettendo di ben trattare tutti gli huomini della nattione, che fussero a quell'isola capitati.'[32]

Bollani's election had been recorded in mid-March, but the new ambassador did not leave Venice until June 6. The delay of three months between election and official commission and departure may have been occasioned by a complex of motives both personal and diplomatic. First on a personal level, there is evidence to show that Domenico Bollani was ill during the period March — June, 1547, unless this illness were of the diplomatic variety.[33] The illness is supported, if not confirmed, by a letter of Pietro Aretino to Domenico's brother Jacopo of 1548, in which he refers to Domenico's convalescence:

'In tanto mi rallegro del risanarsi del Clarissimo messer Domenico in Inghilterra imbasciadore, come cotal sua convalescenza risultasse in pro del mio corpo istesso . . .'[34]

But Venetian embassies abroad were often far from popular among the aristocrats elected to them[35] because of their inherent hardships and dangers, and also because they could often be ruinous from a financial point of view.[36] From this reluctance to accept office came a series of laws forbidding nobles to reject election to office.[37] But, illness apart, there was evidently an air of mystery surrounding Bollani's departure — at least in the mind of the Imperial ambassador in Venice. For he wrote to Charles on June 24, shortly after the ambassador's departure that 'the republic had settled upon an ambassador for England (March, 1547) and when the news of a league (between England and France) was confirmed by their ambassador in France, they commanded their new envoy to proceed to England at once. He has already departed, though the English Ambassador (Harvell) will not own up about this, but only because he objects to confession (a joke about English Protestantism). Your Majesty will be able to ascertain the facts of the matter.'[38]

So the League between England and France, concluded hastily by Somerset from his anxiety lest Francis I should strike at Boulogne while England was weak, was the reason for the urgency of Bollani's departure. This League had been concluded on April 1[39] only to be immediately invalidated by the death of Francis and the accession of Henry II. But Venice must have been keenly interested in this alliance, it being the first alignment to emerge since the death of Henry VIII which had given rise to so much speculation about England's future, especially as this alignment was with a Catholic power and not the German Protestants. Importantly, it would destroy the machinations of the Pope and Cardinal Pole, as Charles was hardly likely to consider an attack on England in these circumstances. With all these things in mind Venice was anxious for news of the situation, and Bollani was ordered to 'proceed at once'. This must have been before mid-April, when the news of Francis' death must have reached Venice. Possibly when it did, there was less urgency, but he had still not departed by May 31, when a motion was proposed in the Venetian Senate that he should depart on his legation at once on pain of a fine of 1,000 ducats.[40] Quite clearly, then, illness was the genuine reason for his delay, as the motion was defeated by 88 to 60 votes, but he undoubtedly left Venice in a hurry. When it is remembered that the new English government was an utterly unknown quantity in the Spring of 1547, that her religious position was to be vital test-case for European Protestantism, that Venice had given at least a vague undertaking that she would supply information on the situation to the Pope, and not least, that there had been no fully qualified Venetian ambassador in London for twelve years, the urgency and importance of Domenico Bollani's mission may be calculated. Even if the news of the League with France had diminished the possiblity of the intervention of Charles V in England, the Emperor's refusal was not known until July, and Venice's sources of information on the situation in England were almost exclusively limited to the gleanings of their ambassadors at the courts of Francis I and Charles V.

By the time of Bollani's departure for England on June 6th, he must have been well aware of the use that was to be made of his dispatches. Venice knew about the departure of Cardinal Sfondrato by April 20th, when the Council of X informed their ambassador in Germany of this.[41] While the ambassador was on his journey,[42] a second initiative towards the 'reduction' of England came from Rome, this time at the instigation of Cardinal Pole.[43] The plan was that the Pope would send a legate with his letters of authority to England in the hope that discussions with the English Privy Council might ensue, and that some ground could be gained towards the return of the kingdom to Catholicism.[44] As before, Pole hoped that the support of Henry, Charles and Venice might be enlisted to this end. France and Germany had already shown themselves unwilling to co-operate, and clearly did so again.[45] The rift between Charles V and Pope Paul was widening, as the Emperor replied to the Papal Legate that 'Quanto a fargli querra, disse che Sua Maestà al presente era occupata in altro et non poteva attendere a questa cosa et che non voleva più il Pontefice per compagno ad alcuna impresa'

In the face of this bleak prospect, Pole was forced to turn to Venice, in the hope that her ambassador might obtain an entry into the English Court for his representative in the absence of similar help from the ambassadors of France and Germany.[46] The proposal was, therefore, that Bollani should introduce the representative of Pole into the English Court, doing what he could to facilitate fruitful discussions. Venice had been justifiably cautious about this second initiative, replying to the Pope's request on 27th June that they were waiting for Bollani's report on conditions in England, and that he would 'inform them in detail of the mode in which to proceed.'[47]

It is now obvious that any moves that the Pope or Cardinal Pole might make in the direction of England would depend on the reports of Domenico Bollani — in the absence of co-operation from France and Germany — and these reports were transmitted to Rome from time to time during his period of residence in England.[48] The dispatches themselves do not appear to have survived, as Rawdon Brown noted in his compilations of the Venetian State Papers, but we can deduce their substance from various other sources.[49] The events in England on which he was to report down to the spring of 1549 left the Pope in no doubt about the inadvisability of direct initiatives towards England — until the accession of Mary brought about a *volte-face* in matters of religion.

Bollani had arrived at Hampton Court on August 6th, 1547, being warmly received by the Protector Somerset and the Privy Council as the first Venetian Ambassador since Henry VIII had severed English connections with the Papacy.[50] For Venice, his arrival signified the return to diplomatic support for Venetian commercial interests; for England, it meant importantly at least one European recognition of the legality of the Somerset administration. These attitudes are reflected to some extent in the elaborate welcome staged for Bollani at Hampton Court, and, on the Venetian side, in the warmth of his reception by resident Venetians.[51]

We have seen that his function was to be chiefly to transmit intelligence to Venice, and that these reports were certainly conveyed to the Pope. They would certainly have contained information on English progress in three fields; matters of religion, Scottish affairs, and internal constitutional matters. It may be convenient to deal with these topics separately, and to provide brief summaries of the events on which the ambassador reported.

In a general way, however, it can be noted that his task may not have been as difficult as at first appears. It will be remembered that Paget's summary of foreign policy of August, 1546 had advised overtures towards Venice.[52] It is also clear from his welcome that the ambassador had been subject to a 'staged' display of friendship. It further appears that all efforts were made to ingratiate the English government with Venice, as Bollani had reported a 'loving and confidential' *rapport* which had developed between him and Paulet by September 15th.[53] We shall look more closely at the relations between Bollani and the French Ambassador in London, Odet de Selve, but in the context of Bollani's access to information, Selve's reports show that the rulers of England were apparently more kindly disposed towards the ambassador of Venice than they were towards the ambassadors of Charles V or Henry II. Throughout his residence in England,

Bollani was often the first to receive information from Somerset or Paget, and would then be wooed for this information by the other two members of the Catholic ambassadorial community.[54] Leaving aside the passage of information between one ambassador and another, it is clear that Bollani (and with him, Venice) occupied a special place in English diplomatic circles.[55] Not only had she been the first to send a *resident* ambassador since the accession of Edward VI, but she was not directly involved in questions of border conflict (France, over Boulogne and in Scotland), nor was she involved in internal English affairs (Charles, in his relations with Protestants and his kinship with Mary). Finally, Venice was not in a position geographically or politically to play an active part in Roman schemes for interference in English religion.[56] She was, in a sense, an interested spectator to those vital issues affecting England's European destiny in the autumn of 1547.

Of Bollani's reports on the state of English religion in the period 1547—1549, no direct evidence has survived. His first report particularly, written probably in late August, 1547, eagerly awaited by the Pope and Cardinal Pole (not to say Venice) would be a fascinating document on the English Reformation if it came to light. However, the ambassador can have had little to report that was encouraging to Rome as English Protestant positions became more clearly defined after some legitimate doubt at Henry's death.[57]

Even before the arrival of the new Venetian ambassador, the last Henrician Catholic, Wriothesly, had been removed from the Council. By 12th March, 1547, effective control of English destiny was vested in the Protector Somerset, a Calvinist by 'persuasion' if not by any kind of dogmatic 'conviction'. If the protector was motivated primarily by the interests of the state in these early days of his administration, it is also true that ruling power in England was now in Protestant hands. Again, if measures taken by Somerset and Archbishop Cranmer to consolidate and codify England's protestant position were characterised by an exaggeratedly cautious liberalism, the appointment of Bishops by letters patent (for instance) would have seemed strange to a Catholic visitor. Similarly, the measures of Edward's first parliament, meeting a month after Bollani's arrival, might seem mild when seen against a background of sixteenth-century religious persecution, but must have been reported to Venice as the worst of ecclesiastical aberrations. Laws governing heresy, preaching and printing were repealed, the Chantries Act transferred control of institutions from Church to State, and the Prayer Book and new Liturgy had become law before Bollani left England. Similarly, the English language had taken the place of Latin in church services. These measures to open the eyes and minds of the uneducated to theological questions — even to invite debate — must have signified the abandonment of all restraint to the future Roman Catholic Bishop of Brescia.

It is hardly presumptuous, therefore, to assume a strong reaction to English Protestant Reforms in the Venetian ambassador,[58] and that this was clear in his reports to Venice for transmission to Rome and Turkey.[59] A good idea of the Venetian reaction to such measures is given by the *relazione* of Daniele Barbaro, written in 1551, which reports fully and in strong terms on the religious situation in England from the death of Henry VIII.[60] Barbaro saw the English Reformation

34

solely as a result of Henry's marital problems: 'In this confusion of wives, so many noblemen and great personages were beheaded, so much church plunder committed, and so many acts of disobedience perpetrated, that it may be said that all that ensued, and is still going on (which to say the truth is horrible and unheard of) — all, I say, is the penalty of that first sin.' And he went on to add that 'detestation of the Pope is now so confirmed that no one, either of the new or old religion, can bear to hear him mentioned.'[61] On the Dissolution of monasteries, Barbaro says 'they have made sheer plunder and one enormous act of sacrilege;' on liturgical reform, 'with regard to church ceremonies, it is true they have retained many of them; introducing many new ones, under pretence that the nature of the times requires this, as some had become idolatrous and superstitious;' and adds that 'the greater part of their lessons and sermons consists in abusing the Pope, in preaching the repudiation of wives, and maintaining whatever their masters choose.'[62] Barbaro's relation is an important document, for the Catholic reaction to English Protestantism.[63] It may be noted in this context that it contains a full description of events which took place during Bollani's period as ambassador in England, that Barbaro's introduction to the events he describes was through Bollani's reports in 1547—1549, and that Bollani introduced Barbaro to the English Court in the summer of 1549. It must therefore have been with the same kind of horror that Barbaro's *relazione* evidences that Bollani watched the gradual secularisation of the English Church in the first three years of Edward's reign.

Bollani undoubtedly reported the progress of the English Reformation to Venice and Rome in great detail, for we hear nothing of the Pope's plans to force a return to Catholicism until the end of Bollani's period of office, in the summer of 1549. By then, the climate seemed more propitious, the country being torn by rebellion and internal strife, for a new initiative. In fact the risings in Cornwall and Norfolk of 1549, and the general atmosphere of distrust and disunity throughout the country, were enough again to encourage the hope that England was weak enough for Catholic interference and intrigue.[64] This was obviously the tenor of Bollani's report of 3rd July, 1549, as Venice thought it worth sending to their Ambassador in Rome for passage to the Pope. We can easily imagine that Bollani attributed the causes of the revolts rather too exclusively to a reaction against religion, as he writes that 'the people have rebelled in several parts of the kingdom, not choosing to conform to the new religion. Commissioners were sent to quiet them, and some of the rioters boldly refused to submit unless the mass and all the other offices of the old religion were restored.'[65] Although England was weakened by the uprisings, there is no evidence to suggest that the people of England would have flocked back to the Pope's standard at this time,[66] but rather that Bollani's report contained a degree of wishful thinking. Possibly too, the reference to Mary[67] reminded the Pope that this link with the Emperor had been the cornerstone of his English policy in 1547. At all events, the Venetian Ambassador in Rome discussed Bollani's reports on the state of England very fully with the Pope, who 'was very much pleased with them'.[68] The report narrated 'much turmoil' — reference to the uprisings in the West and in Norfolk well under way — and prompted the Pope to send immediately for Cardinal Pole 'to consult with his Right Rev. Lordship how far that flock can be assisted to return to his bosom.'[69]

This initiative too was doomed to failure and the remaining events serve only to show the perseverance of Cardinal Pole in his hopes for an English return to Catholicism. By the end of July, it is clear from the State Papers that the Pope had had at least one first hand account of the English uprisings,[70] and that he had decided that Pole was to send two representatives to England to find out more about the situation there.[71] Finally a dispatch from Dandolo in Rome to the Venetian government dated September 14th, relates that 'with regard to English affairs, it seems that his Holiness is not much inclined towards them, awaiting ulterior advices; and he will rather employ Cardinal Pole in the congregations and consultations relating to the Council, instead of doing anything further about the matter of England.'[72] At this point the dispatches of the Venetian Ambassador in England cease to be important in the Pope's design's on England, and Domenico Bollani had by now returned to Venice.

The other sphere in which Domenico Bollani's dispatches from England had considerable importance was the Scottish war. As in the affairs of religion, his arrival in England coincided with a moment of national crisis, and renewed European interest. For the traffic of ambassadors from end to end of Europe in 1547 was occasioned by not one royal death, but two: Francis I of France had died on March 31.

The interference of France in Scottish affairs had been successfully avoided by Somerset by his treaty with Francis a matter of days before the French king's death. Henry II was a less predictable element, and far more inclined to favour the dynastic claims of Mary Queen of Scots if the plan included the recapture of Boulogne.[73] These attitudes being known, the effect was predictable on two fronts, and guerrilla activity began both in Scotland in the area round Boulogne, forcing English garrisons into a position of constant alertness. But the Emperor was also to be reckoned with. For, in the words of R.B. Wernham, 'however unwilling he might be to involve himself in war to replace Edward VI by Mary Tudor,[74] he would certainly not stand by while Henry II replaced both of them by Mary Stuart.'[75] Whereas he might have little cause to support the English in Scotland, it is also true that he had no reason to support growing French influence there. Nevertheless, French troops were in Scotland by June, 1547.

This was the situation which confronted Domenico Bollani when he arrived in London in August. No longer was the Scottish question the rising of a rebel prince. Now, since the death of Francis I, it was to take its place as a frequent topic in the dispatches of European ambassadors involving as it did the fundamental balance of power in Northern Europe. To complicate matters, there was also the question of the 'conversion' of Catholic Scotland, and the bible as well as the sword were to be weapons to this end. Further, the position of the Scottish Queen was a factor which would always loom large. Of one thing Somerset was sure in the late summer of 1547: that Mary Queen of Scots should marry Edward and not the Dauphin.

Scotland, then, was an important constituent in the delicate position of England at the beginning of Edward's reign. In the three years of Bollani's residence, it was to demonstrate the terrible weakness of England and her vulnerability to European interests. Events showed that her safety in the end depended on the balance of power between Henry II and Charles V, neither of whom, in the final analysis, could contemplate the supremacy of the other in England. The Venetian ambassador in 1547—1549 was to observe an almost complete collapse in English affairs, and Domenico Bollani found that he had a quite unsuspected role in international diplomacy. Drawn to the French ambassador — perhaps by natural inclination as a Venetian whose state bordered the Empire — he became an important link in the chain of intelligence to France from England on which French policy in Scotland must have been based.[76] It is clear from Selve's dispatches to the French court that much of the intelligence arriving in France from England on the position in Scotland had been through Bollani's hands.[77]

The situation in Scotland had been worsening since the early summer of 1547. In late June, Leo Strozzi had sailed into Scottish waters with troops and twenty-two galleys and recaptured St. Andrews from the English. The effect of this was growing confidence in Scotland; the Queen Mother began to press her claims that Mary Queen of Scots should marry the Dauphin, and behind all this, Somerset had every reason to fear the claims to the English succession of the young Mary Stuart. Agitation and guerrilla tactics in Scotland and at Boulogne seemed to indicate strong action, but Somerset could not allow his forces to be dispersed on two fronts. Further, England was in no position to provoke Henry into open war, as Boulogne remained vulnerable. There was also the fact that Charles V, strengthened after his victory at Mühlberg in April 1547, was unwilling to allow complete French domination in England, though he would not offer concrete assistance to the English. For Charles, the treaty made with Henry VIII in 1543 still held, but, importantly, it covered neither Scotland nor Boulogne.

So harassment continued while open war was avoided. On August 6, Domenico Bollani had arrived at Hampton Court to be received by the Privy Council, the Young Edward and the Protector Somerset before his departure for what was to be the battle of Pinkie on September 4.[78] At this point, Somerset decided that a decisive initiative was necessary from England while France, restrained by fear of the Emperor, was still hesitant about full-scale intervention. In September, therefore, the Protector invaded Scotland with 18,000 men, supported on his Eastern flank by 60 ships which followed him up the East coast. Although a superior army, the Scots were tempted down from their strong position and were totally routed by the English under Somerset at Pinkie Cleuch on 10th September.

The English victory in the battle of Pinkie was quickly reported in Europe. Odet de Selve reported to Henry with a full description in dispatches of 17th and 22nd September[79] based on information which he had had from Paget. Their meeting and conversations were characterised by some wrangling over the actual number of dead — which de Selve frankly refused to believe — but the victory was decisive nonetheless. Domenico Bollani wrote in similar terms to his government on 15th and 17th September, as these dispatches were acknowledged by Venice on 15th October.[80] True to her non-alignment in far-off Northern European affairs, Venice instructed Bollani to 'congratulate the king on his success, and, as the Protector will have returned to the Court, to repeat the same to him.'[81] Bollani must have done this towards the end of October.

From the dispatches of the French Ambassador at the English Court, it is clear that a two-way exchange of information was in operation early in Bollani's term of office. The first evidence of this occurs in October 1547, when Bollani supplied information to de Selve about a possible Imperial agent whose arrival in London was rumoured.[82] De Selve might have been able to return the courtesy after 20th October, as Bollani asked him for information about the rumoured Imperial treaty involving Brescia and Crema.[83] Apparently, Bollani 'n'avoit advis d'ailleurs que par les marchantz quy avoint eu ceste nouvelle de Flandres' and 'est fort en poyne d'en sçavoir la verité.'[84] We do not know whether such an exchange took place on this occasion, but such intrigue between resident foreign ambassadors was the rule rather than the exception in the sixteenth century, and Bollani had obviously established a *rapport* with de Selve for mutual benefit.[85]

But it is extremely likely that Bollani was to have far more to impart to de Selve in the coming months as the war in Scotland moved into its next phase. During the winter of 1547—1548, Somerset found himself unable to occupy the territory gained at Pinkie, and had to fall back on a network of strengthened garrisons to retain strongly fortified outposts. When France entered the war on a full scale, de Selve, representing a belligerent participant in the Scottish question, was liable to find his sources blocked.

Meanwhile, the winter news of the war chiefly concerned negotiations over Boulogne, as Somerset, strengthened by his success at Pinkie, attempted to buy French sympathy with Boulogne. His offer to restore the town to France carried little weight with Henry II, who regarded its restitution as the return of booty illegally plundered by Henry VIII. Agreement was never reached, and winter gave way to spring. Fine weather brought the return to hostilities, as well as an attempt by the Protector to convince the Scots that good Anglo/Scottish relations were in their best interests. The Spring also brought the intervention of France, and it can be no accident that de Selve — fully supplied with information from first-hand sources from October to February, while Somerset still hoped to avoid French intervention — found himself relying more and more on the Venetian ambassador during the period from February to July. For in February and March extensive troop movements had been reported all over Northern France, and Boulogne had never been more seriously threatened. Somerset had even found it necessary to dispatch a special ambassador to the Emperor to establish what assistance might be forthcoming from that quarter.

For Domenico Bollani, reports continued about the renewed hostilities. He passed information about the siege of Broughty-Craig to Ode de Selve on February 15[86] and his dispatches to the Doge and Senate also reported this event, as well as the taking of Dundee by the Scots with French assistance.[87] But there were lighter moments. In early February, 1548, the three resident catholic ambassadors were treated to a spectacular kind of military tattoo at Greenwich, welcomed and fêted by the young Edward VI 'memes qui nou parla en latin.'[88]

From February to May, Bollani undoubtedly reported the progress of the war in full,[89] and was still in a position to inform de Selve. He described the activities of

Lord Grey and the arrival of Petro Strozzi to Odet de Selve,[90] and gave a full report of the siege of Haddington to Venice.[91] We know the substance of this report, as it was referred to the Turkish government through the Venetian 'Bailo': 'We have heard that Pietro Strozzi, the commander of the French fleet, after his arrival in Scotland, went with the French and Scottish troops and battered a fortress held by the English called Had{d}ington, near which place a skirmish took place with the English cavalry, which is understood to have been routed, with the loss of some thousand horse, and of some of the best commanders in the English force; so Had{d}ington is expected soon to fall into the hands of the Scots and the French, and therefore the English were endeavouring to reinforce their troops, and had sent their fleet {which was said to number 40 large ships} into those parts.[92] There is no doubt that the news was reliable, as the Protector had promised Bollani in late April that he would keep him constantly up to date with the dispatches from Lord Grey in Scotland.[93]

So Bollani's position at the English Court was indeed one of privilege. With England suspended precariously between rival Hapsburg and Valois interests, the ambassador of Venice, as a disinterested party, remained on excellent terms with the governors of England and in a position to retail information to whoever he pleased. He had personal audiences with the Protector on June 16 and 31, 1548, and received news of the siege of Haddington from May to July directly from him.[94] During this period, when English forces were again thrown into battle with some 3,000 German mercenaries, de Selve's intelligence is almost completely dependent on Domenico Bollani. Every detail of the skirmishes and siege around Haddington were communicated by word of mouth or by letter to Bollani. He even received some news direct from Scotland from an Italian mercenary captain serving with Lord Grey,[95] and this correspondence must have continued, as Venice mentioned another letter from Scotland dated August 24.[96]

The Haddington campaign had been less decisive than Pinkie the previous year, and both sides could count little gain. Europe was now more deeply embroiled, with help from Charles V and the declaration of war by France. Henry II had been encouraged by internal risings in England, and the state of order, the economy and the general feeling of instability had discouraged the Emperor from further support. All these events were to lead to the downfall of Somerset and an ignominious peace with France — but by this time, events were being reported by Daniele Barbaro who had replaced Domenico Bollani in London.

Bollani had thus witnessed growing instability in England during his period of office in the first three years of Edward's reign. He had watched heresy (from a Catholic standpoint) slowly being erected into a national church, probably with growing distress. Aware of the requests to Venice from Rome to report on the situation in England, he had undoubtedly described the state of English religion very fully, knowing, too, that his reports would reach Rome and perhaps influence papal policy. Only at two moments — at the outset, when a change of ruler might have brought revolution, and in 1549, when the risings had brought the country to its knees — could he have provided any grounds for hoping for a 'reduction' to Catholicism. He had watched the country crippled by internal dissent and a prey to rival Hapsburg and Valois interests. He had seen England struggling in France and in Scotland, and had been able to report fully on the war unhindered by the disadvantages of partiality.

But he must have gained much in political stature from the experience. For a Venetian statesman he was young and comparatively untried, as the government had only previously employed him in one administrative and one minor fiscal post. If England was a pawn in a game being played in Paris, Germany and Rome, Domenico Bollani was in a position to observe the machinations and intrigues of European diplomacy from a position that was central — and both involved and detached. He had shown a clear talent for diplomacy in his relations with his hosts and with other European ambassadors, and had pleased his home government by 'constant diligence regardless of all cost and toil'.[97] He had also brought face to face with Protestantism, and must have brought a clear memory of the 'divine judgement' visited on England for her heresy to his work later in the codification and implementation of the Catholic Reformation. It is certainly true that the embassy to England, with all its sacrifice and disadvantages, was the foundation of his political career as an examination of his elections to the Venetian Senate in the years that followed will show.

NOTES TO CHAPTER II

1 Cotton MSS., Titus, B. ii, 47, ff. 79–81. See W.K. Jordan, *Edward VI: The Young King. the Protectorship of the Duke of Somerset,* (to which this summary is indebted) (London, 1968), pp. 230–241. For the state of England at this turning point in English constitutional and religious history, see A.F. Pollard, *The Political History of England,* VI, (1547–1603) London, 1910 pp. 1–79; Mackie, *The Earlier Tudors,* (Oxford, 1952), pp. 478–603 and bibliography; A.G. Dickens, *The English Reformation,* (London, 1964), *passim.*; R.B. Wernham, *Before the Armada, the Growth of English Foreign Policy 1485–1588,* (London, 1966) pp. 164–178; G. Elton, *England under the Tudors,* (London, 1955) pp. 202–214. See also Fig. 7.
2 W.K. Jordan, *op. cit.,* pp. 230–231.
3 Alvise Mocenigo the the Doge and Senate, February 10, 1547. *Venetianische Depeschen von Kaiserhof,* Ed. G. Turba, (Vienna, 1892), II, pp. 171–176.
4 *Ibid.*
5 Deputy Keeper of the Public Records, *Twenty-seventh Report,* (1866), App., p. 129.
6 For a detailed summary of the Papal plan, and the events arising from the election of legates, see August von Druffel, (Ed.) *Beiträge zur Reichsgeschichte 1546–1551 (Briefe und Akten zur Geschichte des sechzehnten Jahrhunderts),* I, (Munich, 1873) pp. 52–55, n. 1, and sources cited.
7 *Ibid.* pp. 50–52.
8 *Venetianische Depeschen,* II, p. 172.
9 August von Druffel, *op. cit.,* pp. 52–53. Druffel notes that Capodiferro would have been extremely unwelcome at the French court because of Francis' negotiations with the Schmalkaldner League at this time.
10 Quoted by von Druffel, *op. cit.,* p. 53.
11 See Ribier, *Lettres et Mémoires d'estat des Roys, Princes, Ambassadeurs et autres Ministres, sous les Regnes de François I, Henri II and François II,* (Blois, 1666), I, p. 640, and Wilhelm Maurenbrecher, *Karl V und die deutschen Protestanten 1545–1555,* (Dusseldorf/ Leipzig, 1865), p. 101.
12 *Venetianische Depeschen, cit.,* Alvise Mocenigo to the Doge, 11th February, 1547. (p. 174)
13 August von Druffel, *op. cit.,* p. 50.
14 *Ibid.* p. 51. The Pope hoped also to take advantage of the dynastic motives of Charles V as Princess Mary (la cugina) had claims to the English throne which Charles might be induced to support. For the position of Mary under Somerset, see, for instance, W.K. Jordan, *op. cit.,* pp. 206–209.
15 Rawdon Brown, *Calendar of State Papers (Venetian),* V (1534–1554) (Hereafter *CSPV,* V), (London, 1873), p. 198.
16 It should be said that this embassy was the traditional preserve of young patricians who had reached the stage of *Savio agli Ordini* (for which see below, pp. 49–50) in their progress through government offices. This created opposition among the younger members of the government when Venice yielded to Papal pressure against the appointment of an ambassador in 1578 (to Elizabeth), and there had been murmurings in December, 1546, which the Imperial ambassador in Venice reported to his government. (For this see the letter of 17th December, 1546 quoted by Stella in 'Utopie e Velleità dei Filoprotestant Italiani (1545–1547)' in *Bibliothèque d'Humanisme et Renaissance,* XXVII (1965) pp. 133–182 at p. 157. For the election of an ambassador to Elizabeth, see *Nunziatura di Venezia, cit.,* Nunzio to Rome, July 19, November 15, December 20, 1578, Stella, *Chiesa e Stato . . ., cit.,* pp. 21–22, nn. 17, 18). Ironically, Bollani himself was passing information to the Nunzio in 1578, and assured him on 15th November that the Senate would not displease the Pope by appointing an ambassador to Elizabeth.
17 See Stella, 'Utopie e Velleità . . . cit., p. 157–159, *Idem, Dall'Anabattismo al Socinianesimo nel Cinquecento Veneto* (Padua, 1967) pp. 50–55, for full discussion of the circumstances of the election and its possible relationship with political intrigue, Venetian ambi-

valence towards protestant movements and dreams of 'la libertà d'Italia' among conspirators.
18 *Degli Istorici delle cose Veneziane*, (Venice, 1718) tom. IV, pp. 194–195.
19 *CSPV*, V, pp. 198, 185.
20, *Calendar of State Papers (Spanish)* IX, (1547–1549) p. 508, 19th July, 1547. For discussion of this point see also B. Cecchetti, *La Repubblica di Venezia e la Corte di Roma nei rapporti della Religione*, (Venice, 1874) I, pp. 323–324.
21 For the office and functions of the Venetian Ambassadors, the best summary is in Garrett Mattingly, *Renaissance Diplomacy*, (London, 1955) pp. 64–82, followed, for the early seventeenth century by C.H. Carter, 'The Ambassadors of Early Modern Europe, Patterns of Diplomatic Representation in the Early Seventeenth Century' in Carter (Ed.) *From the Renaissance to the Counter-Reformation: Essays in Honour of Garrett Mattingly*, (London, 1966) pp. 269–296. For background and methods see, respectively, D.E. Queller, *The Office of Ambassador in the Middle Ages*, (Princeton, NJ., 1967) *passim*, and (a popular treatment) J.W. Thompson & S.K. Padover *Secret Diplomacy: Espionage and Cryptography 1500–1800*, (New York, 1937, repr, 1963) pp. 17–40.
22 See Bollani's formal commission minuted in *CSPV*, V, p. 219, and discussion below p. 31.
23 Some indication of the state of England's foreign affairs at this point may be seen in the delay in informing the Venetian Senate officially of Henry's death. Venice must have known this by mid-February, as her replies to the Pope (above) clearly show, but was not officially informed until March 2nd — some five weeks after the event — when Harvel made a speech in the Senate officially confirming the news. W.K. Jordan, (*op. cit.*, p. 234) calls this 'an outrageous administrative neglect' adding that the government 'blamed the slowness of the posts, or delay in Antwerp,' but Venice can hardly have been convinced of this, as dispatches were taking little more than a week at this time. (See Thompson and Padover, *op. cit.*, p. 21)
24 This correspondence is in *CSPV*, V, pp. 203–207.
25 W.B. Turnbull, *CSP., Foreign*, (1547–1553), pp. 5–7. Harvel seems confident of England's strength in the face of the situation and feels that the 'fury and vain blasts of the adversaries will not long endure.' (p. 7)
26 von Druffel, *op. cit.*, p. 53.
27 *Venetianische Depeschen, cit.*, pp. 203–204, Alvise Mocenigo to the Doge, 21st March, 1547.
28 *CSP (Spanish)*, IX, (1547–1549) p. 54. On Charles' attitude and relations with the Pope, see also W.K. Jordan, *op. cit.*, pp. 237–239, R.B. Wernham, *op. cit.*, pp. 165–166, K. Brandi, *The Emperor Charles V . . .*, trans. C.V. Wedgewood (London, 1939) pp. 574–578.
29 'J'ai consideré la raisonable volonté, que N{otre} S{aint} P{ère} a de reduire le Royaume d'Angleterre en l'obéissance de L'Eglise: ce que je desire de ma part aussi bien que lui; mais quant à envoyer le Cardinal Pole en mon royaume, ce seroit mettre en grand difficulté la reddition de Boulogne, laquelle le Roy qui est à present, et son Conseil declarent et assurent me vouloir rendre en bref: se monstrant de très bonne volonté et affection envers moi, ce que la venuë dudit Cardinal en mon royaume pouvoit grandement alterer, pour estre cette Nation subçonneuse . . .' (The King to the French Ambassador in Rome, 13th March, 1547, in G. Ribier, *Lettres et Mémoires, cit.*, I, p. 623.
30 On formal commissions to ambassadors, and the functions, see Mattingly, *op. cit.*, pp. 108–118; for a summary of Ermolao Barbaro's treatise on ambassadors, *ibid.* See also Queller, *op. cit.*, pp. 203–219, and Charles Yriarte, *La Vie d'un Patricien de Venise* (Paris, 1874) pp. 98–135. Bollani's election is in *CSPV*, V, *loc. cit.*, where minutes are recorded also of arrangements for his salary, expenses, horses, trunks and couriers (April 27, and similar arrangements for his secretary Alvise Novello (April 30). His commission from the Senate is in *Ibid.*, p. 219. Besides the Pope's business, he may also have carried with him a commission to facilitate a marriage of the son of the Duke of Ferrara: 'to commune upon the said marriage, being in hope to bring the same to effect,' the ambassador having 'full powers' in this. (Discussed in a dispatch from Harvel to Paget on March 20, *CSP, (Foreign)*, 1547–1553, p. 17).
31 *Op. Cit.*, pp. 194–195
32 *Ibid.* Bollani's success may be seen in the matter of wool export licences. The licence to export wool to Venice had been successively revoked by Henry VII and Henry VIII, but was

42

conceded to Bollani and again to his successor, Daniele Barbaro. For this, see *Calendar of Patent Rolls*, (Edward VI) II, p. 366, II, p. 247, for its relation with the English economy, Mackie, *op. cit.*, p. 476, and for fuller treatment of the point, my 'Domenico Bollani in Inghilterra...' *cit.* pp. 217–218.

33 In a dispatch from the Imperial Ambassador in Venice, Don Juan de Mendoza to Charles V of 19th July, there is reference to Bollani: 'he has been delaying because of illness. It seems they are inclined to reconsider his appointment, and I hear that this was the cause of his hurried departure, and not any other conjecture it was possible to make at the time'. (*Calendar of State Papers* {*Spanish*}, IX, (1547–1549) p. 505).

34 Pietro Aretino, *Lettere*, (Ed. *cit.*) IV, p. 424.

35 Queller, *The Office of Ambassador...*, pp. 160–174, J.C. Davis, *The Decline of the Venetian Nobility...*, pp. 32–33.

36 On the difficulty of obtaining men qualified to fill ambassadorships and governorships, and the economic reasons for this, see J.C. Davis, *op. cit.*, pp. 75–105, esp. pp. 82–83 for this period.

37 *Ibid.*, p. 83 and notes; and D.E. Queller, *Early Venetian Legislation on Ambassadors*, (Geneva, 1966) *passim.*

38 *CSP, (Spanish)*, IX, p. 505.

39 Pollard, *op. cit.*, pp. 132–4; R.B. Wernham, *op. cit.*, p. 166; W.K. Jordan, *op. cit.*, pp. 235–236. See also the dispatches of the Imperial ambassador in England, Van Delft, in *CSP (Spanish) vol. cit., passim.*

40 *CSPV*, V, pp. 218–219. This was by no means an uncommon motion given the traditional reluctance of ambassadors-elect to depart. See V. Lazzarini, 'Obbligo di assumere pubblici uffici nelle Antiche leggi Veneziane' in *Archivio Veneto*, XIX, (1936), and the laws on refusals to serve in *A.S.V., Compilazioni leggi, busta* 198. J.C. Davis quotes a dispensation to Zaccaria Contarini in 1500, who was excused duty as ambassador to Hungary for family reasons. (*op. cit.*, pp. 32–33).

41 Council of X to Alvise Mocenigo, April 20th, 1547, in *CSPV*, V, p. 211.

42 For the MS account of Bollani's journey from Venice to/London by his Maestro di casa, Jeronimo Paulini, see Cairns, 'An unknown Venetian description...' *cit.*

43 For Pole's part in the plans for England, and his letter to Somerset of September, 1547, see, for example R. Biron & J. Barennes, *Un Prince Anglais, Cardinal-Légat au XVIe siècle: Reginald Pole*, (Paris, {1922}) pp. 198–204. For his correspondence, see *Epistolae...* (Ed. Card. Querini) Brescia, 5 vols., 1744–1751. A portrait at Fig. 8.

44 The plan is outlined in a discussion between Pole's representative at the Court of Charles, and the Venetian Ambassador there, reported to Venice on 2nd July. Pole had suggested sending a legate to win over the English by peaceful discussion ('con dolci et charitative ammonitioni'). *Venetianische Depeschen, cit.*, p. 299.

45 'dal Christianissimo Re era stata menata questa pratica in longo senza alcuna conclusione, et da Cesare non si havea mai havuto votiva risposta'. *Ibid.*

46 '... che si vedesse di pigliare quello di Vostra Serenità per far introdure in Inghilterra il soprascritto dottore, et per far qualche buon officio in questa materia.' Ibid. p. 300.

47 The Council of X to the Venetian Ambassador in Rome, 27th June, 1547, in *CSPV*, V, p. 220. Throughout Bollani's embassy, Cardinal Pole never ceased to dream of an English return to Catholicism. He made a third attempt, in the summer of 1549, sending two English gentlemen to Somerset with his letter 'to exhort the Government of England to return to the Catholic religion.' By 1549, however, it was a forlorn hope 'and they had audience with the Protector, but were dismissed rather harshly.' (See *CSPV*, V, p. 235 and notes; p. 238; *CSP (Domestic)* 1547–1580, p. 17.

48 This was done until July, 1549, as appears from a dispatch from Matteo Dandolo, Venetian Ambassador in Rome of 14th September. Having acknowledged receipt of news from Bollani, he notes that the Pope would in future depend on his own envoys for news of England and on Cardinal Pole, rather than on Bollani's reports. (*CSPV*, V, p. 239)

49 Chiefly from the replies to Bollani from the Council of X in *CSPV*, V, but also from the dispatches of the French Ambassador at the court of Edward VI, Odet de Selve, in Lefèvres-Pontalis, (Ed.), *Correspondence Politique de Odet de Selve*, (Paris, 1888). For speculation

about initiatives directed through the Venetian Nuncio, Pietro Lippomanno, see J.E. Law and J.M. Manion, 'The Nunciature to Scotland in 1548 of Pietro Lippomanno...' in *Atti e Memorie della Accademia di Agricoltura Scienze e Lettere di Verona* XXII (1970–71) pp. 435–438.

50 See my 'An unknown Venetian description of Edward VI' in *B.I.H.R.* XLII (1969) pp. 110–115.

51 *Ibid.*

52 See above, pp. 26–27.

53 The Doge and College acknowledged receipt of this on October 15th. (*CSPV*, V, p. 222)

54 For the transmission of information from Paget or Somerset to Bollani — and from him to de Selve (for dispatch to Henry II) see Lefèvres Pontalis, *Correspondence Politique . . . cit.*, almost *passim.* From 15th February, 1548, when Selve reports a series of dinners held by each of the Catholic Ambassadors in turn for the others, Bollani becomes the principal channel for transmission of news of the war in Scotland to France for obvious reasons, see below pp. 36–39. See Selve's dispatches from this date in *Ibid.* pp. 286, 290, 337, 342, 369, 376, 385 etc.

55 This was still true in 1551, when Bollani's successor, Barbaro, reported in his *relazione*: 'The Signory is supposed by the English to be friendly to them; they delight at being reminded of this friendship through the Doge's Ambassadors, and hold it in very great account, so that his ministers are well received as was the case with himself.' (*CSPV*, V, p. 362)

56 , Nor would she have been inclined to do so. For the tension between Rome and Venice arising over disputed territories in the Romagna, and Venetian control of the church within the *Terraferma*, see e.g. P.J. Laven, 'The *Causa Grimani* and its Political Overtones', *The Journal of Religious History*, IV, 3, pp. 184–205.

57 For these tentative first steps in the English Reformation, see accounts in Mackie, *The Earlier Tudors*, (Oxford, 1952) pp. 478–603 and bibliography; A.F. Pollard, *The Political History of England*, VI (1547–1603) London, 1910, pp. 1–79, A.G. Dickens, *The English Reformation* (London, 1964) *passim* (particularly pp. 273–314), and a very fully documented account in W.K. Jordan, *op. cit.*, pp. 125–229.

58 It seems also not unlikely that this practical experience of the early days of English Protestantism had a lasting effect on Bollani, contributing to his religious formation and the strong convictions which he brought to bear on the later sessions of the Council of Trent and afterwards in the Diocese of Brescia. (See Chaps. VII–VIII)

59 Besides its transmission to the Pope, Bollani's news of England was also communicated to the Turkish government by Venice through their ambassador, the *Bailo.* For the importance of, and commercial reasons for this office, and the two-way traffic in diplomatic dispatches, see a colourful account in Thompson & Padover, *op. cit.*, pp. 13–29.

60 In *CSPV*, V, pp. 338–362. Barbaro's career parallels that of Bollani in many respects. Besides occupying the London embassy, they were both vocal at the session of the Council of Trent, when Barbaro had become Patriarch of Aquileia, and Bollani, Bishop of Brescia. For Barbaro, see the unpublished doctoral thesis 'Daniele Barbaro' by P.J. Laven (deposited with the Warburg Institute, London) and bibliography. His portrait at Fig. 10.

61 *CSVP*, V, p. 346.

62 *Ibid.* pp. 348–349.

63 The *relazione* comprises a full description of the state of religion, the Law and the military in 1551. It is published in E. Alberi, *Relazioni degli Ambasciatori Veneti*, (Firenze, 1840) repr. Ed.L. Firpo, (Torino, 1965) pp. 227–271. English trans. Rawdon Brown in *CSPV*, V, pp. 338–362. There are various MS variants (for which see Firpo, *op. cit.*, pp. xv–xvi). R. Brown in *CSPV*, V, p. 282 states that the MS in the *Biblioteca Marciana (Cod. It.*, VII, 908), 'supposed to be a copy of Bollani's report' is in fact a copy of the above *relazione.* Internal evidence supports this, but the mistaken attribution was probably occasioned by the reference on p. 178 to 'cose che ho scritte a V. Serenità a 6 8bre *1548*', which other versions do not have. (Italics mine).

64 The complex amalgram of local anarchy, frustrated grievances, and religious dissatisfaction that provided the causes of the unprisings in that year are well suggested in a

document quoted by W.K. Jordan, *op. cit.*, pp. 450—451. For a detailed account of the state of unrest in England in 1549, see *Ibid* pp. 439—493.

65 The Doge and College to the Venetian Ambassador at the Court of Paul III, July 21st, 1549, reporting Bollani's dispatch of 3rd July in *CSPV*, V, p. 238.

66 W.K. Jordan noted that 'religious conservatism was by no means the exclusive cause, it seeming more probable that the underlying grievances were social and economic and that the movement was 'captured', to use Pollard's apt phrase, by the priestly supporters who were its spokesmen.' (pp. 457—458). For discussion see *Ibid.* pp. 457—458, A.G. Dickens, *op. cit.*, pp. 305—307.

67 '... and having in like manner endeavoured to persuade the Princess Mary, she remained very firm in her determination not to renounce the old religion.'

68 Dandolo to Venice, 31st August, 1549, in *CSPV*, V, p. 239.

69 *Ibid*

70 Cardinal Pole to Cardinal Farnese, July 29th, 1549, (*CSPV*, V, p. 238) in which Pole recommends Dr Hilliard, recently returned from England, to have audience with the Pope.

71 '... and according to what they shall bring back or transmit hither, so will his Holiness decide further, but he is very desirous of secrecy.' (Dandolo to Venice, September 7th, in *CSPV*, V, p. 239)

72 *Idem*, p. 267, September 14th. Pole's efforts to bring back his country to the fold were unceasing down to the accession of Mary, but without fruit. Surprisingly, this activity of his during Edward's reign has hardly been dealt with in detail by Pole's biographers. W. Schenk, in *Reginald Pole*, (London, 1950) omits mention of it altogether, while there are references in M. Haile, *The Life of Reginald Pole*, (London, 1911) pp. 336—366, and a short account in Biron & Barennes, *op. cit.*, pp. 198—208.

73 Mary Queen of Scots, as great grand-daughter of Henry VII had a tangible place in the English succession, and supported by France, might eventually bring all England under French influence.

74 As the Pope had hoped. See above pp. 28—29.

75 *Op. cit.*, p. 168. For a highly detailed account of the Scottish question, see W.K. Jordan, *op. cit.*, pp. 263—304, and for European involvement, particularly R.B. Wernham, *op. cit.*, pp. 168—178.

76 See p. 38 and n. 85. Bollani's relationship with the French ambassador, Odet de Selve dates at least from 1st October, 1547, when he passed information to Selve about an envoy from the Emperor (*Correspondence Politique de Odet de Selve, cit.*, p. 214) and remained constant. It is most clearly stated in February, 1548, when Bollani is described as 'l'ambassadeur de Venise avec lequel j'ay quelque amitié et privaulté ...' (p. 285).

77 Selve acknowledges Bollani as his source constantly in his dispatches. See p. 46, n. 93. It is clear that audience with the Protector or with Paget was often impossible for Selve, but much easier for Bollani.

78 For a description of the welcome accorded Bollani and his suite at Hampton Court on August 6, see the description by Jeronimo Paulini, his *Maestro di Casa* in Ms. Misc. Correr, LV/2266, Museo Correr, Venice, and my 'Domenico Bollani in Inghilterra' in *Commentari dell'Ateneo di Brescia*, 1966 (1967) pp. 207—220, and 'An unknown Venetian description of Edward VI' in *Bulletin of the Institute of Historical Research, cit.*

79 *Ibid.*, pp. 203—206.

80 *CSPV*, V, p.,222. The coincidence of dates and the fact that de Selve frequently obtained the same information as Bollani from the same source, argues that these reports were very similar. Paget and Somerset would have been as concerned to press home the English superiority at Pinkie to a watchful Europe as they would have done to France in her menacing posture.

81 *Ibid*

82 , *Correspondence Politique, cit.*, 'Toutefois l'ambassadeur vient de dire a mondict homme que j'avoys envoyé vers luy qu'il estoit venu ung homme de l'Empereur quand a ledict sécretaire ...' (p. 214). (This turned out to be merely the secretary of the English ambassador to the Emperor, as de Selve explained on 4th October. {p. 216})

83 *Corr. Polit., cit.*, p. 226, Odet de Selve to the Constable.

84 *Ibid.* Brescia particularly was constantly one of the danger points on the Venetian frontier with the Imperial dominions, and was repeatedly subject to Imperial intrigues. Venice was unlikely quickly to forget the welcome accorded to Imperial troops in Brescia at the time of Cambrai. The subject does not appear again in the dispatches.

85 Doubtless the *rapport* continued after Bollani's return to Venice, as de Selve later represented France as ambassador in Venice in the early 1550s. (For this and other biographical details, see *Corr. Polit. cit.*, (intro.) pp. xi–xxvii)

86 *Corr. Polit. cit.*, p. 258.

87 Venice acknowledged this dispatch in theirs to the Venetian 'bailo' in Constantinople on 22 March. (*CSPV*, V, p. 225.)

88 *Corr. Polit. cit.*, pp. 284–285. The French ambassador was much impressed by this show of military skills, as doubtless he was meant to be. In his description of the event, he makes much of the apparent partiality towards him by the king – a partiality which seems not to have been bestowed on the ambassadors of Venice and the Empire. For displays of this kind see S. Anglo, *Spectacle, pageantry and early Tudor policy*, (Oxford, 1969) pp. 229–230 and *passim.*

89 In *CSPV*, V, pp. 225–226, and see also *Corr. Polit. cit.*, pp. 00.

90 *Ibid.*, p. 338.

91 On August 20 (*CSPV*, V, p. 228)

92 Venice to Constantinople, *Ibid.*

93 'Le protecteur luy {Bollani} promict de luy faire part des nouvelles qui luy {Somerset} viendront dudict Grey m'assurant qu'il les me {de Selve} feroyt sçavoyr . . .' (*Corr. Polit.*, p. 342, de Selve to Henry II, May 3, 1548.)

94 *Corr. Polit., cit.*, pp. 349, 352, 363, 372, 381, 395–397, 399, 401, 403–413.

95 *Ibid.*, pp. 403–413, dated 18 July.

96 Bollani's letter was acknowledged by Venice on 28 September (*CSPV*, V, p.,229).

97 *CSPV*, V, p. 282. His Ruighthood (Fig. 6) is also evidence of this.

46

CHAPTER III

'SENATOR DI GRANDISSIMA PRUDENZA'
(1549-1558)

The success with which Domenico Bollani carried out his duties in England was soon to lead to the highest offices in the Venetian government. His dispatches and *relazione*,[1] respectively the studies and the portrait of England and her troubles, had been warmly received by the government at home.[2] Clearly, his talents were recognised in that post and took him rapidly to the most responsible positions in the Venetian Senate (or *Pregadi*) and the *Collegio*, so that the functions of those bodies and their offices need to be briefly summarised.[3]

Broadly speaking, all members of the Patriciate became members of the *Maggior Consiglio* by right at the age of 25. In this huge assembly, were debated many matters of state unless they were delegated to higher bodies, which the Great Council would elect. The most important of these were the *Pregadi*, or Senate, the *Collegio*, and the Council of X.[4] Each stage in this ascending order of importance represented promotion to more responsible office. But it is the *Pregadi* which provides the theatre of Bollani's endeavours during the period 1549—1558, so we shall need to examine this body more closely.

We have seen that one of the concerns of the young nobleman, when contemplating candidature, was the right of access to the Senate.[5] For there were two principal avenues to election to this body — which alone would give access to even higher posts in the *Collegio*, such as the three orders of *Savi*, and finally to the Council of X. Patricians with legal qualifications and leanings would probably enter the Senate by means of the Courts of the *Quarantie*, and this was the avenue finally chosen by Domenico's father, Francesco, as we saw in the first chapter. This progress began with election to the *Quarantia Civil Nuova*, a body, as its name suggests, of forty members dealing with cases from the *Terraferma*. From this, the patrician passed automatically, after the statutory eight months' service, to the *Quarantia Civil Vecchia*. Here he would be concerned with civil causes. Finally he passed to the highest judicial body, the *Quarantia Criminale*, to judge criminal cases, and at this final step, gained access to the Senate. If he were further elected to one of the three posts as Chief of the *Quarantia Criminale*, this would provide access to even higher office, as it gained entry to the *Collegio*.[6] Thus, a single election to the most junior of the courts of the *Quarantie* gave occupation for 32 months and would lead, finally, to a place in the Senate.[7]

The other avenue of access to the Senate was by means of administrative and fiscal posts, many of which carried membership of the *Pregadi de jure*. These minor posts provided a graduated training programme for the Senate, were known as the *Sottopregadi*, and were divided by seniority into three groups which became the *cursus honorum*, or traditional path of advancement by promotion towards full membership of the Senate. It became the custom (rather than the law) for progression in the government to be from the first to the second, and from the second to the third group of offices, and only those who had undergone this kind of 'indenture' and had served in all three groups were considered experienced enough for election directly to the Senate.[8] We have seen evidence that Domenico Bollani had filled offices in the second and third groups at least[9] before this embassy to England, so that it is fair to assume that he was politically qualified for direct election to the *Pregadi* when he returned to Venice in the late summer of 1549.[10]

In fact, by this time, he had already occupied a place in the Senate down to 29 September, 1549, as Ambassadors-elect were traditionally allowed access up to the date of their departure, and after their return until the Michaelmas following.[11] So he was now ready for candidature in his own right, so to speak. Elections to the *Pregadi Ordinari*[12] were held in the Great Council in batches of six per day for ten days beginning in August. In practice, this meant that nobleman might have several chances of election, as we shall see in the case of Domenico Bollani.

It is clear that he considered himself eligible for Senate election on his return, as he was proposed twice during the first election in September, 1549.[13] Although not successful in these elections, it seems likely that Domenico was a member of the Senate three months later, when both he and his father, Francesco, were proposed *3 Savi di Terraferma*, as this post was usually drawn from its membership[14] As neither was successful he probably had to wait until the next elections which took place in the summer of 1550. A year after his return, however, he seemed on far surer ground. First proposed *6 de Pregadi* on 28 August by Lunardo Mocenigo, he was also suggested for the same office three more times (on 7, 21, 28 September) being elected to the Senate on his fourth attempt.[15] Two days later, on 30 September, 1550, he was ballotted in *Pregadi* for the *Saviato di Terraferma*, being elected with 177 votes for and 56 against.[16]

So this point in time, at the end of September, 1550 constituted an important moment in Domenico's career. He was to be re-elected *Savio di Terraferma* three times and *Savio del Consiglio* three times down to 1558 — offices which carried the responsibilities and prestige of cabinet ministers — so it will be necessary to look at the function and position of these posts within the Senate in more detail.[17]

First of all it must be said that the Senate comprised a membership of about 300 by Bollani's time, some elected for the term of a year in the Great Council, and a large proportion of *ex officio* members. The *Pregadi* was directly responsible for the conduct of external and internal affairs of State. Their decisions could declare war and conclude peace; they appointed the most important representatives of the Republic — envoys and ambassadors at foreign courts — and debated the relations of the State with foreign powers. Besides foreign policy, they were also ultimately responsible for domestic affairs, supervising the day-to-day running of the government administration through heads of goverment agencies with *ex officio* membership.[18]

A body of such size and wide responsibilities could not function without an executive. Consequently the Senate appointed a committee of councillors, comprising the three orders of *Savi: agli Ordini, di Terraferma* and *del Consiglio*. This committee, embodying the effective power of the State, planned the agenda of the Senate, dealt with representatives of foreign powers, and was responsible for calling meetings of the Senate. It also met together with the Doge, the six ducal councillors and the three *Capi* of the *Quarantia Criminale* to form the *Pien Collegio*. As Domenico Bollani made his entry into this select committee of officers with ministerial responsibilities in September, 1550, it is to these *Savi* that we must now turn.

The *Savi del Consiglio*, or *Savi Grandi* were six in number by Domenico Bollani's time. Half were elected in the *Pregadi* for six months every three months, so that the incoming *Savi* could benefit from the experience of those already in office. In keeping with the almost obsessively anti-oligarchic principles of the Republic, the *Savi del Consiglio* were not eligible for re-election during the six months following the end of their term of office. For this reason, we shall see that Bollani occupied the posts of *Savio del Consiglio* and *Savio di Terraferma* in continuous alternate periods of six months from 1550 until 1558, with the single exception of his governorship of the Friuli.[19]

The *Savi del Consiglio* were generally officers who had already had a distinguished political career. Maranini noted that 'era usanza sceglierli fra quei patrizi che avevano percorso lunga e gloriosa carriera.'[20] and they had also to have attained the age of forty years before being elected.[21] So important was their function, that they could be elected from other offices and were free to relinquish those offices on election.[22] Further — and this could well have been significant in the case of Domenico Bollani's family[23] — the rule that prescribed freedom from debt as an essential qualification for candidature for the *Savi* was waived in the case of this office. Finally, it was felt that membership of this select body of ministers was incompatible with membership of the Council of X, so that patricians could not simultaneously occupy both offices.

The conditions for election to the post of *Savio di Terraferma* were very similar. A slightly more recently established post, this branch of the *Savi* was consituted to deal with the rising problems of the relations of the central governing body with the subject dominions on the mainland.[24] There were 5 *Savi di Terraferma*, 6 *Savi del Consiglio* and 5 *Savi agli Ordini*. Domenico Bollani was first elected *Savio di Terraferma* in October, 1550, a year after his return from England, and it was with this first excursion into responsibility of ministerial importance that he made his debut in the Venetian government as one of its effective leaders. In his three periods in this office, he would have been particularly concerned with the maintenance of good order in the defence system of Venice and the conduct in detail of affairs with the mainland dominions. For the co-ordination of the efforts of the many *Rettori* and representatives throughout the Republic's dominions fell to the lot of the *Savio di Terraferma*, while dealings with Venetian ambassadors at foreign courts — in short, foreign policy — would be the responsibility of the members of the Council of X.

The Savi di Terraferma were, then, further elected to posts within their committee which denoted their functions. In descending order of importance, these were *Savio Cassier* (a kind of Chancellor of the Exchequer), *Savio alla Scrittura* (Chief of Military Staff), *Savio alle Ordinanze* (Chief of Home Defence), *Savio ai da Mò* (dealt with matters of urgency), *Savio ai Ceremoniali* (received foreign princes), and *Savio alle Relazioni* (who collected and reported on *relazioni*). The first two of these posts were the most important, being ballotted individually. The third went automatically to the third in the poll, and the last two could be held by a *Savio* already elected to a position. Thus the vast area of competence of the body can be seen. In this very brief summary it becomes clear that election to the post of *Savio di Terraferma* constituted membership of the effective 'cabinet' of the Republic, that this post carried great power within the structure of the Venetian constitution, and that Domenico Bollani, in his total of twenty-four months in the office between 1550 and 1558, would have occupied most of the positions with executive power in the Republic.

An account of his detailed participation during those years would be more difficult and is outside our scope, but a generalised picture of the affairs of the Republic during these years will provide an indication of the matters in which he must have had a more or less active hand.[25] In the *Senato Terra* archive, which will be the main source for what follows, names of the members of the Collegio were usually included in the margins of the record, but their participation in the discussions in *Pregadi* and in *Collegio* could only be accurately recounted from evidence from contemporary *cronache* and sometimes foreign dispatches. Evidence of the internal workings of the *Pregadi* from these sources being comparatively scarce, we shall content ourselves with *examples* of measures showing the widely diversified functions of the orders of *Savi* during the 1550s.

When looking at examples of the business of the Senate in the 1550s, it is worth remembering that its agenda was prepared by the *Savi*. Therefore, although ratification of their decisions within the parent body was necessary, these officers of state exercised immense power and influence and their honoured positions and the prestige of their long record of distinguished service to the state would have recommended their actions to the main body of the Senate. Of course, some decisions of major importance would require a reading also in the *Maggio Consiglio* (constitutional reforms, for instance), but the function of the *Savi* as initiators of legislation is an indication of their importance. On the home front, the *Pregadi* were concerned with matters involving constitutional reform and the complicated business of relations with territories on the *Terraferma*,[26] elections of ambassadors and *rettori*,[27] appeals from subjects in Venice or in her dominions,[28] and ecclesiastical affairs and elections which fell outside the scope of the *Inquisitori di Stato*.[29] For the mainland, the organisation of the business of reports, dispatches, and elections of Venetian representatives was dealt with *in pregadi*,[30] including ratification of the decisions of subject parliaments and councils,[31] minority groups (Jews etc.)[32] and relations between subject provinces.[33] The Senate also discussed trade matters, the movement of goods within Venetian territory, and the whole apparatus of financial and fiscal legislation.[34] The military control exercised by the *Savio alla Scrittura* and the *Savio alle Ordinanze* gave rise to proposals in the Senate concerned with elections to military commands, troop movements within the Republic's domains, the arsenal, and the fortification of key positions along Venice's frontiers.[35]

But there were two areas where legislation shows the particular preoccupation of Venice in the 1550s when Domenico Bollani occupied central positions of power in the government. The first, the changing economic position of the Republic towards her subject dominions, was one of his problems throughout

50

almost the whole of his adult life. The second, constitutional reform, gives an indication of self-examination, rethinking and the many changes that were to overtake the Republic during his lifetime. If the seeds of revolt, the atmosphere of change and a foretaste of the internal upheaval in the Venetian Senate in the 1580s are already indicated in the legislation for constitutional reform in the 1550s,[36] then the *Sussidio* from the *Terraferma*, its history and political implications, is also a pointer towards the changing international position of the Republic.[37]

First, then, the question of the *Sussidio* from the *Terraferma* to the Venetian Republic seems to have figured prominently in the business of the Senate during the years of Domenico Bollani's career as a Senator. Both at home, when he witnessed the imposition and re-imposition of this levy on the cities of the *Terraferma*,[38] in Friuli when, as *Luogotenente della Patria* (1555–1556), he would have had to oversee its collection, and again in Brescia, when passing from the position of *Podestà* to the bishopric of that city, he witnessed again the pleas of the subject provinces to be allowed more time to pay.[39] By this time, however, he had acquired considerable experience in financial matters, having chosen the path of fiscal posts to senatorial preferment, and having occupied the important *Luogotenenza della Patria del Friuli* with its complex financial and constitutional structure.[40]

The *Sussidio* was first imposed to aid the war economy in 1529, and was subsequently re-imposed at intervals.[41] It comprised a total revenue of 100,000 ducats, divided between the various communities according to their wealth and size.[42] It was then subdivided by the territories to be contributed to each according to his kind: 'da essenti e da non essenti, priviliegiati e non privilegiati, etiam separati, esclusi gli ecclesiastici.'[43] Fabio Besta states that this tax enjoyed the peculiar benefit of a relief from ten per cent in exchange for prompt payment — a measure whose wisdom the prevarication of the 1550s makes abudantly clear. But the problems of payments arose often at local rather than at provincial level. The Republic was little concerned with the distribution of payments among the population of a province once the total share of the whole levy had been apportioned to it. Locally, the weight was distributed according to the conventional tax return or *estimo*, (subdivided again into fixed quotas for city, clerics and province) so that any problems of assessment and subsequent litigation were liable to be reflected also in the efficiency of the collection of the *Sussidio*.

A good example of the difficulties encountered in the collection of the *Sussidio* — and the abuses to which it was subject — is given by Bernardo Zorzi in his relation of Brescia in 1554.[44] Zorzi notes that the *Sussidio* had been imposed many times 'secondo la urgentia et necessita dei tempi,' and that deferred payments were often permitted (as we have seen) 'per habilitar maggiormente essi nostri sudditi, si come è notorio.' But he also noted the ten per cent bounty for prompt payment, and described how private individuals arrogating to themselves the duty of payment, would pay 90% and claim 100% from the community. Not content with this, some persons 'si temerarii et mal edificati di coscientia' would claim a further 10% from the community, with an overall clear profit of 20%.[45]

So with the new political posture of the Republic since Agnadello, the increasing investment in land in the *Terraferma*, the general shift of commerce to agricultural interests from maritime trade, and the dependance of the Republic more and more on the mainland for its food supplies, the relationship of the central government with its subject provinces was changing.[46] No longer could this be the dominance of an aloof and autocratic conqueror, rather the representatives found themselves intimately involved with the financial, agricultural and constitutional problems of a varied group of local committees. It is no accident that Domenico Bollani was to deal, in the mid 1550s with local feuds, minority groups, foodstuffs for the capital, fiscal and legal reforms, and problems of poverty and local charity in the Friuli. It was as *Savio di Terraferma* that he gained his first insight into this new relationship. The *Sussidio*, evolving from a levy in time of need to a regularised financial dependance, provides one index of this change.[47]

There are at least two views of the effects of the problems of this change in direction (of which the *Sussidio* had provided one example) on the people of the mainland. The statement that 'La radice di ogni male era nello stesso sistema politica e amministrativo, nell'assoggettamento della grande massa della popolazione a una ristretta e chiusa classe dirigente'[48] seems to oversimplify the position. Romanin adds a cautionary note that the contadino 'non va giudicata secondo le nostre idee', that the techniques of fiscal evasion and resentment of Venetian domination — while always present — never amounted to a determined and revolutionary antagonism.[49]

The Constitutional lesgislation in the 1550s, in which Domenico Bollani must have participated, foreshadows a sense of insecurity in the government which was to characterise internal policies for the rest of his life and beyond. His later career, as well as that network of family interests which are always helpful — if not conclusive — in determining the political affiliations of a Venetian nobleman, show him to be clearly on the side of conservatism. Preoccupied with the state of the church before his election as bishop, the election itself, and his long career in the church at Brescia, point decisively to a *casa vecchia*.[50] The discussions of internal procedure and a growing division of opinions in church and state relations must clearly have occupied his mind while directing affairs at home as *Savio di Terraferma, Savio Grande*, or when presiding in Friuli. The measures themselves were of slight importance. They do reflect, however, a feeling of insecurity which bore fruit in the many treatises and records of current problems which follow this period,[51] particularly the statement of intellectual opposition evidenced by Paolo Paruta in his *Della Perfettione della Vita Politica*,[52] and betray an atmosphere of self-examination, change and insecurity.[53] Domenico Bollani would have been concerned primarily with home affairs during his repeated elections as *Savio di Terraferma*, as well as in periods spent as Venetian representative in Friuli and Brescia, so we shall confine ourselves to these aspects.[54]

In January, 1551, a measure was proposed to prevent pluralism in the holding of office in the *Collegio*. It was argued that the holding of more than one office would prejudice the efficiency of the Senator in his principal function.[55] Thus he would be debarred from holding other offices, as membership of the *Collegio* was to be considered an automatic disqualification from other offices. This motion passed through the Senate almost without objection, and went through the *Maggior Consiglio* with an overwhelming majority.

But perhaps a more direct indication of the preoccupations of the rulers of Venice was the Senate motion of April 1552. Elections to the more important posts on the Venetian mainland were to take place in the *Collegio* rather than in the Great Council. The previous year, as the motion mentions, it had been decided to elect the rectors of Padua, Brescia and Verona in the *Collegio* by special vote and the move in 1552 was to extend this to all the more important rectorships.[56] The reason given was the 'sicurtà et benefito del stato nostro', and the measure was designed to be a temporary one ('per questa fiata'). But the process was to continue. In 1554, in fact, it was again proposed that all the important posts on the Terraferma were to be elected in the smaller body. But we have seen in the repeated imposition of the *Sussidio* on the *Terraferma*, and its crystallization into standard legislation, how recurring patterns of legislation soon acquire the permanence of precedent. The law, if passed 'per questa fiata' for the third time might be difficult to remove in future. Accordingly, the Great Council firmly rejected it on its third appearance on 19th March, 1554.[57]

It may be that there is a significant trend here. The *Collegio* had managed to secure almost[58] complete control over elections to the most important mainland posts in 1551 and 1552, but had failed to secure this power on the third occasion. It would be instructive indeed to have an account of this debate. with the views expressed on both sides. Interesting, too, (for students of the 1582 reforms particularly) would be the political backgrounds of its opponents – of those who managed to sway the huge council and cause it to reject the measure. In the absence of this, however, and whatever the truth, this rejection perhaps administered a warning to the members of the *Collegio*. In the present context, it indicates that the relative functions of these two bodies, their constitutional powers and respective places in the Venetian government machine must have been at least under discussion in 1554.

Another pointer towards constitutional insecurity in the 1550s is the whole question of *broglio* or canvassing in elections and malpractices with votes. This was an old problem that was to continue well beyond the 1582 reform, but it is probably significant in our present context that legislation against it appeared in 1555, and was strengthened against increasing malpractices in 1588 and 1677.[59] The practice of canvassing for political office had apparently reached disquieting proportions by 1555, as bartering and soliciting votes was conducted openly in the Piazza San Marco and at the Rialto.[60] This slightly comical picture that the preamble to the law conjures up hides a sinister fact. For this particular aspect of the Venetian governmental tradition – the acquisition of support for candidature by means of a network of family, commercial or purchased relationships – was to come under heavy fire from that section of the patriciate that felt itself excluded from power by its poverty.[61] The law of 1588 refers directly back to this legislation of 1555, as does the one passed over a century later in 1677, so that it is clear that, in this field at least, there is a direct link between the troubles in the 1580s and Venetian insecurity at home in the 1550s.

Domenico Bollani's part in this remains obscure. It can clearly be shown, however, that his family was one of the *vecchie* group, and that his commercial connections were probably such as to aid his promotion in government circles.[62] It is even tempting to remember the laudatory letter about him published by Aretino in his *Primo Libro delle Lettere*, in 1537, and to note that he first entered government service in 1537–8.[63] Possibly his path to high office had begun in this way. But for this, there is no concrete evidence. He must have joined in the discussions of *broglio*, however, during his occupation of important government posts.

Finally, we have noted that he spent a period as *Riformatore dello Studio di Padova* between June and November, 1552.[64] On his qualification for this post there is little concrete information, unless the evidence for a literary relationship with Pietro Aretino is adduced, and this is hardly conclusive.[65] It seems very likely, on the other hand, that this post conveniently filled a period of *contumacia* between his periods of office as *Savio di Terraferma* and *Savio del Consiglio*, and provided convenient continued access to the Senate.

The *Riformatori* were originally elected to control and direct studies at the Studio or University of Padua. This function, formerly exercised by Bishops, and then by the Venetian rectors in Padua, was taken over by the *Riformatori* in 1516. Not only were they responsible for the general organisation of the *Studio*, but also supervised teaching methods, choice of texts and election of professors. In fact the evidence from the *Senato Terra* archive denotes Domenico Bollani's function in this last respect.[66]

But the office carried much wider responsibilities, and its function was gradually extended in the sixteenth century to cover almost the whole field of culture and learning. All public and private schools (except seminaries under ecclesiastical control and the military college at Verona) came under their jurisdiction, and they were responsible, in addition, for censorship of books, the issue of printing licences, libraries, galleries, museums and the preservation of manuscripts and works of art.[67] Particularly important was their function in the fostering of the flourishing Venetian printing presses, as standards in typography and the value of texts would depend on their judgement in the final analysis.

Possibly this post filled a gap between two more important posts — or perhaps it provided Bollani with a real chance to return to academic life in some respects — discontinued in the responsibilities of political office since his youth. At any event, he was soon to return to political prominence in his re-election as *Savio Grande* in the autumn of 1552.

The years 1549–1558, then, had seen Domenico Bollani's growing experience of the ways of the Venetian government. At home, he had occupied the main posts of administrative power and influence, and, aided by the reputation gained by his diplomatic experience of England, had moved from the uncertain status of apprenticeship in minor offices to the dignity and reputation associated with the *Savi*. He had become intimately acquainted with the complex procedures of Venice's fiscal and diplomatic relationships with her subject dominions, and had witnessed a period of her growing financial dependance on them. He had also seen a sense of insecurity within the governing class, and probably participated in discussions of the exclusive nature of the top posts, and felt the growing opposition to electoral malpractices — an opposition aimed primarily at his own sector of the Venetian nobility.

54

It was this experience of the machinery of government — particularly for what concerned the *Terraferma* — that formed the traditional basis for elections to important posts on the mainland, and an experience that was to count for much in his elections to the *Luogotenenza della Patria del Friuli* in 1555 and to the post of *Podestà* of Brescia in 1558. It is to this former post, and the years 1555—1556, that we must now turn.

NOTES TO CHAPTER III

1 Tragically lost. On its fate and relationship with the later *relazione* of Daniele Barbaro, see pp. 34–35 above, and my *Domenico Bollani in Inghilterra*, cit., p. 219.

2 The *relazione* must have been read in the Senate between September and December 8, 1549, when a Senate motion paid testimony to its quality in the traditional motion to allow Bollani to keep the gold chain, presented to him on his departure by Edward VI, had been passed. (*CSPV*, V, p. 282).

3 The best study of the Venetian constitution is Giuseppe Maranini, *La Costituzione di Venezia dopo la Serrata del Maggior Consiglio*, (Venice/Perugia/Florence, 1931) to which this summary is widely indebted. For the Senate, the fullest account (and a fully documented one) is in Enrico Besta, *Il Senato Veneziano*, (Venice, 1899). Also useful are simplified summaries in Horatio F. Brown, *Studies in the History of Venice*, (London, 1907) I, pp. 293–334, and in Charles Yriarte, *La Vie d'un Patricien*. cit., pp. 83–89, particularly for the functions of the various committees of *Savi*.

4 For the detailed functions and interaction of these main bodies, see Maranini, *op. cit.*, pp. 325–383.

5 Above, Chapter I.

6 The *Collegio* comprised 26 'cabinet ministers': The Doge, six Ducal Councillors, and the three orders of *Savi*.

7 See Maranini, *op. cit.*, pp. 145–148; H.F. Brown, *op. cit.*, I, pp. 299–303.

8 Maranini, pp. 170–179. In the *first* group were included the Camerlenghi di Comun, the provv. sopra uffici, the provv. sopra conti, the ufficiali alle Cazude, the ufficiali alla camera degli imprestidi, the *patroni* of the Arsenal, the Cattaveri; in the *second*, the esecutori alle acque, the provv. sopra banchi, the provv. sopra pompe, the provv. alla Sanità; in the *third*, the provv. di comun, the provv. sopra camere, the provv. sopra Cottimi (Damascus, London and Alexandria) and the ufficiali alle rason nuove, vecchie, and ai dieci uffici.

9 *'Acque'* (second group) and *Provv. al Cottimo di Damasco* (third group).

10 Statutary prerequisites for membership of the *Pregadi* were nobility and age (at least 32). Exclusions included those with five members of the same family already sitting, state debtors, criminals etc.

11 See Maranini, *op. cit.*, pp. 171–176.

12 As opposed to the *Zonta*, the additional body of sixty members of the *Pregadi*, comprising Magistrates who entered *de jure* – mostly those concerned with commerce, navigation etc.

13 20 and 22 September (*Raccolta de Consegi*, MS. cit., XI, pp. 244, 245). Votes for Bollani were respectively: +437, –735; +401, –790. This election would be held in the *Maggior Consiglio*.

14 'Li eleggeva in pregadi traendoli generalmente dal proprio seno, sebbene nessuna legge lo prescrivesse . . .' (Maranini, *op. cit.*, p. 331). So it is possible that the proposal was to elect Bollani from outside the Senate, which may account for its failure. For *Savio di Terraferma* see below pp. 49.

15 It is interesting to observe his progress on successive days of what was essentially one election. In the four ballots above, an idea of his progress may be obtained by subtracting the negative votes from the positive. From this, he had respectively counts of –205, –5, +119, +325.

16 See the *Raccolta de Consegi, cit.*, for the above elections and votes cast: XI, pp. 315, 317, 320, 321, 323.

17 On the three orders of *Savi, agli Ordini, di Terraferma* and *del Consiglio*, (the most senior) see in general, Maranini, *op. cit.*, pp. 331–337, Besta, *op. cit.*, pp. 64–70, Yriarte, *op. cit.*, pp. 83–89, H.F. Brown, *op. cit.*, pp. 299–303. See Fig. 9.

18 Maranini, *op. cit.*, pp. 226–271, Besta, *op. cit.*, pp. 171–275, W.J. Bouwsma, *Venice and the Defense of Republican Liberty*, cit., pp. 60–63.

19 It may be useful to summarise Domenico's elections to office during this period as follows:

Oct. 1550 – March 1551: *Savio di Terraferma*
Oct. 1551 – March 1552: *Savio di Terraferma*
June 1552 – Nov. 1552: *Riformatore dello Studio di Padova*
Oct. 1552 – March 1553: *Savio del Consiglio*
Oct. 1553 – March 1554: *Savio del Consiglio*
Oct. 1554 – March 1555: *Savio di Terraferma*
1555–1556: *Luogotenente della Patria del Friuli*
1557–1558: *Savio di Terraferma*
(See A.S.V., *Deliberazioni del Senato, Terra, Registri* 38 (1551–1552), 39 (1553–1554), 40 (1555–1556), 41 (1557–1558), 42 (1559–1560). For *Riformatore dello Studio di Padova*, see below, p. 54, and for *Luogotenente . . .*, Chap. IV *passim.*
20   *Op. cit.*, p. 331.
21   Domenico was first elected *Savio del Consiglio* in October, 1552, eight months after his 38th birthday. The 40 years rule was lowered to 38 in the case of ambassadors and *Capitani da Mar*. (Maranini, *loc. cit.*,)
22   Except in the case of *Procuratori di S. Marco, Avogadori, Auditori,* and *Provveditori alle Biade* – in which posts, continuity of tenure was essential.
23   The comparative poverty of the family is suggested in Chapter I (q. v.) although the evidence suggests that a rise in the family fortunes had taken place by 1552. If this had not happened, and perhaps in spite of it, the English embassy might well have again reduced the family to its former modest financial position by this time. In the present context, however, this was not to hinder Domenico.
24   See Maranini, *op. cit.*, pp. 333–340, Besta, *op. cit.*, pp. 65–70, Yriarte, *op. cit.*, pp. 86–89. Whereas the *Savi del Consiglio* exercised a more general controlling influence on the work of the other two orders of *Savi*, the *Savi di Terraferma* had a more specifically defined influence. The first, in the words of Maranini, 'costituiscono quasi una commissione esecutiva e preconsultiva del Pregadi, con una sfera di competenza che si estende quanto la vasta e crescente sfera di competenza di quell'autorevole assemblea'; the latter were divided into sub-groups with titles denoting specific areas of competence. The *Savi agli Ordini*, the most junior body, constituted the traditional training-ground for promising younger members of the patriciate, as the post provided an access to the senate, the *Savi agli Ordini* being elected from outside it. They could propose motions in the Senate, and their arena of competence covered matters connected with the navy, naval armaments and the arsenal. (*Ibid.* pp. 341–343).
25   Evidence of elction to the body of *Savi* in its three orders is provided by the registers of the *Segretario alle Voci* in the A.S.V., as well as by the *Raccolta de ˙ ˙nsegi, cit.* Evidence of Bollani's participation in discussions of specific issue is provided by the records of Senate proceedings in the *Deliberazione del Senato,* 1) *Secreta,* 2) *Terra* and 3) *Mare* in the *Filze*, containing reports *in extenso* and the *Registri,* containing shorter accounts, in the A.S.V.
26   For examples of constitutional reform and the extortion of the Sussidio by Venice from her subject territories, see below resp. pp. 51–52 and pp. 52–53.
27   See for example *Senato, Terra* (A.S.V.) Ro. 38 (1551–1552) pp. 1–3, where a Michiel was elected to accompany the King and Queen of Bohemia through Venetian territories to Germany, Michiel Surian is allowed to enter the Council of X before taking up his embassy with the King of Rumania, so that he might be fully informed of affairs of state, and a successor to Domenico Morosini was elected in the important embassy to the Emperor Charles V. At this point (September, 1551) it was again felt necessary to underline legislation against refusals to serve in embassies to crowned heads of state: 'E quello che sarà eletto non possa refudar sotto le pene contenute nella ultima parte del mazor conseglio contra li refutadi le Ambassarie a teste coronate . . .' We have seen (Chapter II, *passim*) the machinery for election of ambassadors and their function, as well as the difficulty in obtaining qualified men to fill hazardous and expensive embassies. Domenico Bollani, recently returned from Venice's furthest embassy, was now observing the phenomenon from the other side, so to speak, from his legislator's seat in the *Pregadi.*
28   See for example the case of Antonio Priuli, permitted to pay off his debts in instalments, 17 October, 1551 in A.S.V. *Senato Terra,* (Ro. *cit.*) p. 17. We have already noted Domenico's

undoubted experience in this matter: in the case of the plight of his own father, in July 1536 (above, p. 9), now, as legislator, as *Savio di Terraferma*, and yet again as governor of Friuli, in 1556.

29   For example, a gift was voted to the retiring Papal Nuncio on 26 September 1551 (Ro. *cit.*) p. 11. Much more important was the question of elections to ecclesiastical sees within Venetian territories (for example, the Bishopric of Famagosta in October 1551) as the problem was crucial in the delicate relations between Venice and the Papacy down to Bollani's death and beyond. The history of this problem will be dealt with in the discussion of the election of Bollani himself to the Bishopric of Brescia (Chapter VI). For the *Inquisitori di Stato*, see Cecchetti, *La Republica di Venezia e la Corte di Roma . . . cit.*, I, *passim*, Romanin, *Storia Documentata . . . cit.*, tom. 6, Chap. III, p. 67 *et seq.*, and particularly, Maranini, *op. cit.*, pp. 350—353. See also Cozzi, *Niccolò Contarini, cit.*, pp. 21—22, bibliography and notes, on ecclesiastical elections and their political repercussions.

30   For reform of procedure for these elections, see below p. 81. Typical of the business conducted by the Senate under this heading was an event of October, 1551, which, apart from his passage through the city on his way to England in 1547, was probably Domenico Bollani's first contact with the affairs of Brescia. Letters were sent to the rectors of Brescia and Verona in that month about the passage through Venetian territories of Imperial troops under the Conte Zuanbattista Lodron. It was hoped that damage to property and persons 'come e intervenuto li giorni passati a quei de Valcamonica con nostro gran dispiacer . . .' (Ro. *cit.*, pp. 14—15) might be avoided by discreet politics on the part of local rectors.

31   For example, the ratification *in pregadi* of measures decided in the Council of Portogruaro on 10 December, 1551. On the question of subject Councils, see A. Ventura, *Nobiltà & Popolo nella Società Veneta del '400 e '500*, (Bari, 1964) *passim*.

32   The problem of the Jews in Venice and her territories is one in which Bollani was to find himself involved again and again. Perhaps his first contact with it was in 1551 (17 October, 1551, Ro. *cit.*, p. 22), but see below, Chapter IV, pp. 67—70.

33   For example, *loc. cit.*, p. 11, where the rectors of Brescia are advised to settle the quarrel with Gussago over the corn levy.

34   During Bollani's early periods in office as *Savio.* the economic measure which seems, from the reports, to have loomed largest, was the imposition of the *Sussidio* (for which see below, pp. 51—52). Much minor business of a financial nature would have been formulated in the *Pregadi* by the *Savio Cassier*.

35   The *Senato Terra* registers of the A.S.V. are full of elections during this period to military commands, as the delicate structure of the Republic's defence — depending, as it did, on mercenary soldiers and salaried non-Venetian officers — needed constant attention. Examples of the kind of legislation Bollani would have participated in are the reduction in the number of troops stationed on Venice's Bergamasque frontier (from 300 to 50) in September 1551, (*loc. cit.*, p. 2), the voting of 2,000 ducats for the upkeep of the Venetian fortress at Peschiera (*ibid*, p. 28) and the list of elections of army officers given in Ro. 38, (1551—1552) pp. 120—121, for 27 June, 1552. The question of Venice's defence, and the border conflicts associated with her gradually weakening position in Europe in the second half of the 16th Century, will be taken up again in the discussion of the river Oglio (Chapter V) where Bollani was to be more directly and obviously involved.

36   Gaetano Cozzi has clearly shown that the causes of the victory of the *giovani* over the *vecchi* in 1582—3 go back to the 1550s and before. For the contribution of constitutional reform and legislation to the delineation of the factions, see his *Niccolò Contarini, cit.*, pp. 7—12. For description of the *giovani*, their character and standpoints, see *ibid*, pp. 1—53, and for their theoretician, Paolo Paruta, see W.J. Bouwsma, *Venice & the Defence of Republican Liberty, cit.*, pp. 232—292.

37   For the shift from the sea to the land, and general economic implications of this shift, see S.J. Woolf, *Venice & the Terraferma, cit.*, and for the history of the *Sussidio* in particular, A. Ventura, 'La Politica Annonaria di Venezia in Terraferma e la lotta intorno al commercio dei grani' in *Nobiltà & Popolo*, cit., pp. 375—440.

38   It may be useful to summarise the measures which formed part of Domenico's direct

experience. On 6 February, 1552, when he was *Savio di Terraferma*, requests to the Senate from subject cities to defer payment of the *Sussidio* were received in Venice (A.S.V. *Senato, Terra*, Ro. 38 (1551–1552) p. 67). On July 8 and 21, 1553, the *Sussidio* for the Terraforma to a total of 100,000 ducats was officially re-affirmed (*Ibid*, Ro. 39 {1553–1554} pp. 28, 141–142). And further requests for delayed payments were received in the same period (*Ibid*, pp. 33, 35, 65 {Verona}, 71 {Padua}). The Sussidio was again re-affirmed (perhaps in response to this widespread prevarication) in July, 1554 (Ro. *cit.*, pp. 141–142).

39 Ro. 42 (1559–1560) pp. 32–35. The problem was still clearly unsolved as requests for deferment were granted to Verona, Rovigo, Brescia, Padua and Friuli at this time.

40 See Chapter IV, *passim*.

41 For what follows, see, for example, F. Besta, *Bilanci Generali della Repubblica di Venezia*, I (Venice, 1912) p. clxxx, and doc. *cit.* at p. 218, and Marino Sanudo, *Diarii, cit.*, L, cols. 25–28, for the origins of the *Sussidio* in 1529. (I am indebted to Prof. Pullan for information here). For its mechanics, and a somewhat slanted view, see A. Ventura, 'sperequazioni ed evasioni fiscali' in *Nobiltà e Popolo nella Societa Veneta nel 400 e 500*, (Bari, 1964) pp. 405–416. For a contemporary account (1554) see the *relazione* by Bernardo Zorzi from Brescia in A.S.V. *Collegio, Senato, Secreta, Relazioni, busta* 32, (tom. 2) pp. 57–59. The first imposition is in A.S.V. *Senato, Terra* Ro. 25, p. 110. It was reimposed on, for example, 12 June, 1540, (Ro. 31, p. 30), 16 April, 1544 (Ro. 33, p. 81), and in 1553, 1554 and 1559, as we have seen in our period. (F. Besta, *loc. cit.*, M. Sanudo, *loc. cit.*).

42 On this division of overall financial responsibility between the provinces, see A. Ventura, *op. cit.*, p. 407, n. 59. In 1542, the *Sussidio* of 100,000 ducats was divided as follows: Padovano, 10,300; Trevisano, 10,300; Friuli, 5,500; Veronese, 14,700; Colognese, 1,000; Bergamasco, 8,000; Bassanese, 600; Cividale, 1,700; Feltrino, 1,300; Rovigo and Polesine, 2,200; Cremasco, 2,600; Bresciano, 25,000; Vincentino, 16,800. By this purely utilitarian standard, then, Brescia contributed ¼ of the whole *Sussidio*.

43 F. Besta, *Bilanci Generali, loc. cit.*

44 A.S.V. *Relazione, cit.*, pp. 57–58.

45 '... et conducati 90 ne pagano 100, tolendo in loro quel guadagno del X per cento, et non contenti di questi come doveriano {essere}, si fanno et pagar di giònta le pene di essi comuni de altri X per cento come se fussero la istessa camera phiscal arrogando et assumendo in se dette pene, quale aspettano alle camera della Ill.ma Sig.ria ita che con ducati 90 ne consequiscano usura di ducati XX cosa che non viene ne veniva mai tolerate dei hebrei quali fenerano pubblicamente con permission della S.ia nostra. Et non essendo da tolerare che nel stato nostro li poveri communi et homeni siano cusi expilati et deglutiti si potria pòner parte...' (*Relazione, loc. cit.*). Zorzi went on to propose a motion to the effect that this practice be stopped by law. It is worth remembering that the scene of this practice was Brescia, and that 20% of the *Sussidio* would have amounted to 5,000 ducats. For further difficulties in collection, the relatively minor part played by the Venetian rectors, and local obstacles to the completion of the *estimo* (on which contributions to the *Sussidio* would be based) see A. Ventura, *op. cit.*, p. 406 and n. 58. *et seq.* For the place of the *Sussidio* in the overall tax yield of the Republic, see S. Romain *Storia cit.*, VI, p. 445.

46 Examples of this were the transport of grain to the capital, the problem of meat supplies, reclamation of land in the *Terraferma* (for which see the summary of recent work by S.J. Woolf, *cit.*, in B. Pullan, *Crisis and Change, cit.*, pp. 180–181 and sources cited.). The preoccupation of Senate legislation in the Registers cited (1550–1559) with woodcutting licences from the Arsenal, corn imports and local problems of supply in general only serve to support the point.

47 'Venetian authorities... increased the pressure of taxation. It seems that this last factor was more important than legislative and administrative intervention in preparing the way for, or protecting, private economic penetration of the mainland.' (S.J. Woolf, *loc. cit.*, p. 192)

48 A. Ventura, *op. cit.*, p. 416.

49 *Storia, cit.* VI, pp. 499–501. For the next stage in the history of the *Sussidio*, see the reaction against the Padua *estimo* in 1561 and abuses in Ventura, *op. cit.*, pp. 414–415, and reactions to the *Sussidio* of 1548 in Stella, 'La Crisi Economica Veneziana...' in *Archivio Veneto*, LVIII–LIX (1956), pp. 17–69, and for the history of the problem up to the crisis,

ibid. 'La regolazione delle pubbliche entrate e la crisi politica veneziana del 1582' in *Miscellanea in onore di Roberto Cessi*, (Rome, 1958) II, pp. 157–171.

50   The almost complete lack of private archival sources necessarily brings the question of family relationships into the range of speculation. However, Domenico Bollani was related to the Capello, Memmo and Longo families: his mother was Benedetta Capello, his sister-in-law Marietta, sister of the brothers Francesco and Marcantonio Longo, and it is very probable that his aunt Lugrecia married a member of the Memmo family. (See Barbaro *Alberi, cit.,* p. 40, and for the Memmo, the will *cit.* of Giacomo Bollani. For the political affiliations of these families, see A. Stella, *Chiesa e Stato, cit.* especially p. 7, n. 13 and p. 152. At p. 152, the favourable disposition of Francesco Longo towards the church is commented on particularly in the question of his disputed inheritance from Domenico Bollani. Bollani's affection for his brother-in-law is nowhere clearer than in his will, where he emphatically underlines the close friendship between the families, instituting the brothers Longo as his executors (see Domenico Bollani's will in App. I, p. 243) Important on this point, too, is the evidence and sources cited by A. Stella, 'La Regolazione delle pubbliche entrate . . .' in *Miscellanea in onore di Roberto Cessi,* (Rome 1958), II. p. 169. But the overwhelming evidence for Domenico Bollani's political affiliation must lie in the circumstances of his election as bishop (for which see Chapter VI *passim.*) For the opposition between the 'giovani' and 'vecchie' families, see the fundamental work by Gaetano Cozzi, *Niccolò Contarini, cit.,* pp. 1–52, and for the support given in general by these factions for, respectively, France and Spain, pp. 12–18. For the respective positions vis-à-vis the church, Stella, *Chiesa e Stato, cit.,* pp. 1–16. For a typical reaction against the Papal policy towards Venice of a 'giovane', see Seneca, *Leonardo Donà, cit.,* pp. 165–168 and for details of the constitutional crisis of 1582 in which these movements resulted, Romanin, *Storia, vol. cit.,* pp. 364–370.

51   See the contemporary writings of e.g. Francesco da Molino, D. Giannotti, Z.A. Venier and Alvise Michiel quoted by Cozzi, *op. cit.,* pp. 5–7, and contemporary sources and histories quoted by him. For content summaries of most of the treatise literature of the period, see W.J. Bouwsma, *Venice and the Defence of Republican Liberty, cit., passim,* and for Paruta's dialoque, *idem.* pp. 199–231. The fact that Professor Bouwsma's conclusion have depended solely (as far as can be seen) on secondary sources and contemporary comment have seemed to demonstrate the disadvantages of such an approach. We are here concerned, however not with any conclusions in the 1582 movement that may be drawn from such commentaries, but with their value as a measure of constitutional insecurity within the Venetian government.

52   The opposition in the dialoque was between the active and contemplative life, represented by churchmen and politically oriented speakers, with Francesco da Molino, as the representative of the 'giovani', or new faction, forming a third party, and supposedly representing the views of Paruta himself. On this, see above, introduction, *passim,* and below, pp. 232–234.

53   For the international picture in the 1550s, Venice's position from Agnadello to Lepanto, see e.g. F. Chabod, 'Venezia nella politica Italiana ed Europea nel Cinquecento' in *Idem, Scritti sul Rinascimento,* (Turin, 1967) pp. 665–683, Roberto Cessi, 'Venezia e Carlo V' in *Idem, Storia della Repubblica di Venezia,* II, (Milan/Messina, 1968) pp. 86–117, Romanin, *op. cit.,* VI, pp. 226–243.

54   There were two incidents – of a minor nature – in which he did play a part in international affairs. After his return from Udine, Domenico was again *Savio di Terraferma* in 1557 (See above p. 57, n. 19). He was elected with Marcantonio da Mula to call on the French and Spanish Ambassadors resident in Venice to dissuade them from appearing in the Procession in April of that year. The relative places of these ambassadors had been in dispute, and the government had resolved to compromise by allowing neither to be present. (For the full story, see A. Morosini, *Degl'Istorici delle cose Veneziane,* (Venezia, 1719) Tom. II, pp. 133–134; mentioned also in Cicogna, *Delle Inscrizioni Veneziane, cit.,* IV, pp. 451 *et. seq.*). The rivalry of the ambassadors – almost on the eve of Cateau-Cambrésis – had caused some embarassment in Venice, and Bollani had been elected to deliver this message, probably because of a neutral and impartial reputation. Another exception was the motion in the Senate of March 27, 1557, when Bollani was clearly the *Savio* on duty. The proposal, from Hieronimo Zane (*Savio del Consiglio*) and Domenico Bollani (*Savio di Terraferma*) was to subsidize the Secretary of the Venetian Ambassador in England (Antonio Mazza, Secretary to

60

Giovanni Michiel) 'having remained in Flanders by reason of illness, and he from poverty not having the wherewithal to maintain himself.' He was awarded 150 ducats. (*CSPV., cit.*, VI, ii (1557–1558), no. 845, and original in A.S.V. *Senato Mar,* Ro. 33, p. 117)

55 'Che alcuni di essi hanno altri carichi, alli quali volendo attender, convengono mancar necessariamente dal carico suo principal, essendo impossibile che non possi attender bene a più d'un carico solo...' (A.S.V. *Senato Terra,* Ro. 38   1551–1552   p. 63, January 19, 1552)

56 *Luogotenente della Patria del Friuli, Podestà* and Captain of Crema.

57 The 1552 proposal is in Ro. 38 (1551–1552) p. 89. This move met some opposition in the Council, as it was read on March 29, 1552, and reread on 1 April. The third motion of 18 March, 1554 (Ro. 39 {1553–1554} p. 7) went through the Senate on that day (for: 116, against: 70, abst.: 4) but was rejected on its reading in the Great Council on 18 March (for: 592, against: 788, abst.: 24).

58 Not quite complete as the candidates were still proposed 'per quattro mani di elettori' in the Great Council.

59 It should be remembered that Domenico Bollani was by now in Udine as *Luogotenente...*, but he would certainly have been an observer (if not a participant) of the practices described. The law is in *Maggior Consiglio, Raccolta di Leggi Statuarie,* tom. XXX (1550–1560) pp. 107–110: 'Circa Pratiche et Preghiere nelle Concorrenze'. The law of 1588 took the question much further and invited secret denunciations of malpractices in the exchange or sale of votes. (*Consiglio de X, Parti Commun, busta CLXXV,* for 13 October 1588.) See also, for the law of 1677, Museo Correr, MSS *Fondo Dandolo, Prov. Div.,* p. 977, Ins. 27 for September 1, 1677, for the history of *Broglio,* Maranini, *La Constituzione, cit.,* p. 440, A. Pilot, 'Un Capitolo inedito contro il Broglio' and 'Ancora del Broglio' in *Ateneo Veneto,* 1903–1904. See also the commentary of the contemporary, Francesco da Molin in his *Compendio* ... (Biblioteca Marciana, MS It. VII, 553 (8812) pp. 142–143. For the most recent discussion of the question, see also G. Cozzi, 'Authority and Law in Renaissance Venice' in *Renaissance Venice,* Ed. J.R. Hale (London, 1973) pp. 293–345.

60 'Sono tanto moltiplicate le pratiche che si fanno pubblicamente et senza alcun rispetto nella corte del Palazzo, et Piazza di San Marco et di Rialto con numero di parenti, et amici per quelli che pretendeno (*sic*) alcuna dignità intertenendo li Nobili nostri, che passano per le strade ch'è indignità della nobiltà, et con mormorazione così di questa città...' (*Raccolta di Leggi, loc. cit.*)

61 '... era in grande stima chi sapea meglio adulare, e chi avea piu parenti e aderenti...' etc. (Francesco da Molino, MS *loc. cit.*)

62 For Bollani's family, see Barbaro, *loc. cit.* A strong probability of his family having been aided by family and commercial relationships is provided by the following example. A. Stella quotes a list of families with commercial links: ('La Regolazione...' *cit.* p. 169) Contarini, Priuli, Badoer, Querini, Sanudo, Bembo, Da Molin, Michiel, Bollani, Bragadin, Capello, Longo, Morosini Valier, Zane and Zen. First we have seen from his brother's will (above p. 19, n. 25) that he was joined to the Contarini in a trading as well as parental link. Further a glance at the family genealogies shows that for Domenico Bollani, his sister married a Contarini, his maternal grandmother was a Badoer, his niece married a Da Molin, both his paternal grandfather and his great nephew married a Bragadin, his brother married a Longo, his mother was a Capello, etc. (See family trees above, p. 16, *et seq.*)

63 See above pp. 11–12 (Aretino), p. 13. (*Provveditore sopra le Acque*)

64 Above p. 57, n. 19.

65 Above pp. 11–12.

66 His name appears in the registers in the elections of professors reported in the Senate proceedings (Ro. 38 {1551–1552} pp. 95, 96, 113, 136).

67 For the *Riformatori,* see S. Romanin, *Storia cit.,* VI, pp. 455–466, particularly for the printing trade. For the history of this office of three magistrates, see Da Mosto, *loc. cit.,* Maranini, *loc. cit.* The archival source in the A.S.V. (*Riformatori dello Studio di Padova*) does not contain significant records which throw light on this period. Only one *Filza* (No. 284) contains details of the period, and these are only a miscellaneous collection of printing licences extending over a wide span of years.

CHAPTER IV

LUOGOTENENTE DELLA PATRIA DEL FRIULI
(1555–1556)

The election to the post of *Luogotenente* was almost certainly a recognition of merit. By the summer of 1555, Domenico Bollani had served as *Savio di Terraferma* twice and as *Savio del Consiglio* twice. It was sometimes true that a troublesome senator might be elected to a mainland post, and thus removed to a post far enough away from the central administration to cause a minimum of embarrassment. There is not a trace of evidence for this in Bollani's case, however, and the *Luogotenenza* was an office of vital importance to the republic in the second half of the century.

Domenico Bollani emerges as a lieutenant who probably concerned himself far more with internal and social problems. Archival sources in Venice and Udine yield many instances of his concern and legislation for the problems of the people. It is not unreasonable to suppose that he had begun to display those decidedly philanthropic tendencies which ultimately fitted him for candidature for the bishopric of Brescia. A brief summary of the condition. in Friuli, their background, and the role of the Venetian *Luogotenente* will provide the context in which he was active from May, 1555 to August, 1556.[1]

The region which came under Domenico Bollani's direct control was torn with strife at all levels. Struggles over conflicting interests throughout the whole century took place between communes, especially Udine and Cividale, between rival feudatories, and between the different factions of the local nobility. Citizens and peasants suffered universally from the violent periodic clashes between nobles and petty rulers, jealous to preserve their ancient jurisdictional rights. If the continuing problem of the Patriarchate of Aquileia, which passed into Austrian hands after Agnadello is added to this, then Francesco Michiel was right to conclude that almost total confusion remained.[2] Udine, Cividale and Aquileia had retained independent civil and criminal jurisdiction, for instance, and appeals based on different systems would reach the Venetian Lieutenant. Through all this ran the unending stream of border incidents between the inhabitants of Friuli and the subjects of the Archduke of Austria, and the problem of supply routes through Friuli for German grain destined for Venice. When Bollani arrived in 1555, too, mature citizens could still remember the Turkish invasion of 1499, in which his grandfather and namesake had played a part.[3]

Under Venetian government many aspects of the ancient constitution of Friuli had continued unchanged, and Venice had been forced to recognise pre-existing feudal rights.[4] The *Castellani*, or noble feudatories, so-named from the castle fortresses which they inhabited, were the virtual rulers of the province, and proved a thorn in the side of Venice throughout the sixteenth century. Vaunting medieval privileges, they were given to crimes and violence of every description, committed against the people and against each other, arrogating to themselves the right to dispense a rudimentary form of justice.[5] The *cittadini*, on the other hand, or 'people', comprised members of the professions and resident citizens with full rights as such, and these played a significant if minor part in the running of the affairs of the province through the parliament, which elected a smaller council to deal with problems of daily administration.[6] In Udine itself, the communal government was in the hands of a *Consiglio* of 150 members after 1513 (when the *arengo*, or general assembly, had been abolished) which would elect 7 members to an inner council.[7]

The establishment of this structure of provincial and communal government at the beginning of the century had been preceded by popular unprisings of great ferocity, and it is not the complete picture. Spurred on by poverty and the abuses of the *Castellani*, and encouraged by similar peasant movements in Germany, the agricultural labourers hoped to gain a measure of freedom from the serfdom to which they were subject.[8] The reforms that resulted were remarkable in one respect. The Venetian government was concerned to promote conditions which would facilitate the supply of agricultural products to the capital, to remove conditions of social unrest, and therefore allowed an effective opposition to develop in the form of peasant representation at both the provincial and local level — bodies in opposition to the civic government potentially, and to the noble feudatories.

For these reasons a party of *contadini* evolved in the first quarter of the century. Both the Friulan parliament and local *consiglio* at Udine comprised nobles and citizens, but not peasants and the poorer classes. Independent of the parliament, an 'order of peasants elected by the mayors of the villages of Friuli'[9] was allowed, and, just as in the Udine communal government, a right of assembly was granted to the poorer classes in the city in 1550.[10] In Bollani's time, therefore, these representatives — genuinely democratic voices speaking for sectors of the populace without hereditary privileges or property — were able to acquire some influence, especially in the important field of tax distribution, and (in the case of the province) formed a significant opposition party to the larger *parlamento*, whose wings were, by now, well clipped by the Venetian central government.[11]

This was the political structure which Domenico Bollani was to inherit in 1555. By 1536, in fact, the pattern was set in a mould that was to last until the fall of Venice. The Province was firmly controlled by the central government under the Venetian *Luogotenente* who exercised supreme power.[12] The jurisdiction of the *Parlamento* was circumscribed at every turn, and in spite of this moderate concession to representative government — with its built-in opposition factor — Venice retained firm control through her lieutenant.[13] A good picture was given of the respective positions of the *Parlamento* and the *Luogotenente* in 1567 by Girolamo Porcia:[14] 'Non si può fare questo parlamento in altro luogo, se non in quello si trova il Clarissimo Luogotenente, rappresentante il Serenissimo Dominio, il quale siede in mezzo alli Deputadi, poi tutti gli altri per ordini ... I Deputadi propongono le materie, le quali vengono disputate, ed è in arbitrio di ogn'uno il contradire, e dire quello che gli piace ... e le materie, che immediatamente concernono l'interesse del Dominio, come dimandar Sussidi, o dinari per fabricar Castello, o simili, il Luogotenente propone, e se gli risponde in voce, accioche niuno ardisca negare: ma si dimanda dilagazione, o altra scusa per diferire.'

The Lieutenant had therefore specific controls to exercise in conjunction with the officials provided for him by Venice and with officials elected locally (Deputies, lawyers, and *sindici*, or representatives of the peasants). He would have to attend Council meetings, judge cases of conflicting legal jurisdiction, and apply to the letter the instructions received from Venice. Much vigilance would be needed in case the weaknesses of local officials needed supervision and correction,[15] but he could not exceed his prescribed powers. Few Venetian lieutenants, in the short space of sixteen months in office, were able to bring lasting benefits and reforms to the region.[16]

The few references in general works to Domenico Bollani's period as *Luogotenente* in Friuli give no idea of the wealth of problems with which he had to deal in the years 1555–1556.[17] A glance at the records of the Venetian representatives in Udine shows his example to have been conspicuous and the tribute of the people just.[18] During his period of office, he was concerned with legal and fiscal reforms, complex negotiations over the movement of foodstuffs to Venice, relief from plague, the questions of the Jews and reforms and improvements of charitable institutions. It may be convenient to examine his participation in economic, social and diplomatic spheres and to take them in this order.

We have seen in some measure the extent to which Venice had become economically dependent on the mainland subject territories as a result of the decline in maritime trade, the economic 'penetration' of the mainland, and the economic crisis.[19] Bollani's tenure of the post at Udine was to be far from the 'vita calma e facile' that has been suggested, principally because of the temporary but recurring problems of famine and plague. The problems of Friulian agriculture at this time have been summarised as being due in the main to a conservative and static local political and social structure, the restrictive policies of the Venetian government, frequent wars and aggressive movements by neighbours, recurring epidemics of plague, restricted mobility of the people for political reasons, lack of a middle class and investment problems.[20] For Domenico Bollani, these problems were clearly in evidence by the harvest of 1555, and aggravated by a second bad harvest and the onset of the plague by the autumn of 1556.[21] Possibly the problem with which he was most personally involved in this period as Venetian representative was the soul-searching question of the export of grain from Udine to Venice. His letters from Udine bear eloquent testimony to the struggles necessary to equate the demands of Venetian restrictive legislation and acute local shortages occasioned by famine and plague.

The policy of Venice governing the passage of grain supplies from Udine to Venice, and the attempt to encourage imports from Germany in times of shortage was general throughout the *Terraferma*. From the mid-fifteenth century, a special license was needed for the transport of grain between different parts of the mainland to anywhere other than Venice — such as to ensure a virtual import monopoly for the central government.[22] The laws were designed to prevent the hoarding of grain — with consequent price fluctuations — and to ensure a constant supply for Venice.

But the problem was bound to become acute when plague and famine had created hunger and misery in the province, and when the exigencies of the home

64

market would not be met because of the restrictions imposed by Venice. Not for the last time, Domenico Bollani was attracted by dual loyalties: on the one hand, the conditions which surrounded him cried out for some alleviation of Venetian policy in the granting of licences to patricians to take food supplies from Udine, and on the other, the *Luogotenente* had a precise brief from his government, and instructions to adhere to it to the letter. For famine and plague were by no means confined to the *Patria del Friuli*. Bollani himself summarised the problem in April, 1556, having appreciated its difficulties during the 1555 harvest, and now, being faced with the second bad harvest and the plague. He wrote to his government to say that the city had been outlawed by German exporters as a direct result of the plague, 'ma ancho {posto in bando} dagli proprii nostri . . . il che ha posto questo fidelissimo popolo in grandissimo timore che gli sia per mancare il vivere.'[23] He went on to recount that the *Castellani* were seeking refuge outside the city, taking supplies with them, and thus nourishing the old enmity between the nobility and the people: 'cominciorno a dire molte parole fastidiose, minacciando che se gli nobili haveano modo di salvarsi alla loro possessioni, et gli poveri si convengono restare in la citta appestata nelle soe misere case, non sarebbono mai per soppor- tare che gli cavassero de qui gli formenti . . .' Thus the old rancour (whose terrible results at the beginning of the century must have been fresh in the minds of all parties) again threatened, and Bollani's weariness after a year of adjudication of their problems ('le discordie degli Popolari contra gli nobili, nelle quale ben sanno Vre. Ecc.tie quanto mi è convenuto sudare per quetarle') is easily comprehensible.

But the letter has further interest in the lengths to which Bollani was drawn in the attempt to reconcile both Venetian and local demands in times of extreme hardship. It had been noted for other areas of the *Terraferma* how Venetian representatives were often forced to plead with their government for release from the letter of the law — even resorting to disobedience in extreme cases of local hardship.[24] Bollani had clearly resorted to a fiction at this time — refusing to allow a census of grain supplies in the city through his fear that these could be in- sufficient for local needs, and that the news would aggravate an already tense situation.[25]

This situation had occurred many times before April, 1556, when this letter was written, but perhaps not with the same urgency and intensity.[26] Bollani reflects with some bitterness that he has had to struggle 'con le discordie civili, con la fame, e con la peste', but that he has always tried to prevent discord among the people. He hopes that in the present 'travagliosissimo stato' he will not have to order grain out of the city as so many times in the past.[27]

Bollani cannot be accused of not having attempted to carry out the orders of his government in this matter. Early in his term of office, he had dutifully reinforced Venetian policy in local proclamations. In an edict of 7 July, 1555, he had for- bidden the export of corn, with severe penalties for transgression: on 13 of the same month, had blocked a loophole in the law by preventing payment of rents in kind to any other person than the legal landlord.[28] It is clear that the situation was much worse a year later, as his proclamation of July, 1556 attempted to remove delays in the movement of grain caused by the plague.[29]

So Bollani's position by the Spring of 1556 was difficult indeed. He had summarised the dual tenets of Venetian policy himself: 'L'una che non sia posto impedimento a quelli che hanno da condur formenti di questa Patria in quella inclytta città {Venice}', and 'l'altra che di Alemagna ne fusse condotta quella maggior quantita che le Ecc.tie Vre. desiderano,'[30] in his letter of December 4, 1555, and as resident Venetian representative, his first duty lay in the execution of his instructions from Venice. Yet he was bound to sympathise, too, with the population of the province, on whom the economic effects of plague and hunger must have been painfully obvious to him.

The conflict between patriotic duty and local expediency is nowhere better illustrated than in Domenico Bollani's desperate letter of August 6, 1555. He confesses that 'non ho per tutto il tempo della mia vita mai sentito maggior discontento' on receiving letters from Venice which amounted to an accusation of disobedience.[31] The incident was a minor one: a merchant had accused him in Venice of delaying grain supplies against the dictates of his commission — probably through motives of personal gain. But the incident illustrates another facet of the position of the *Luogotenente*. Not only would he receive complaints from both the *Popolari* and *Nobili*, but grievances might be aired also in Venice through the agency of the *oratori* elected to represent the interests of Udine in Venice.[32] It must certainly have been a situation that would require a maximum of tact and diplomacy, and it is probable that the question of restrictions on the movement of grain in times of famine and plague provided his most testing diplomatic experience to date.[33]

If Domenico Bollani had sympathised with the citizens of his province over their supplies of corn, he was quick to seize opportunities to encourage institutions which might bring lasting benefits to the poor. His intervention in favour of the *Fondaco del grano* and of the *Monte di Pietà* was probably backed by two factors. First of all, he had had experience of fiscal measures in his early posts in the Venetian government,[34] and secondly, there are indication that the family had a tradition of interest in such matters. It is certainly true that his grandfather had played a part in the foundation of the original *Monte de Pietà* in Udine in 1499, and that this fact was important enough for inclusion in the preamble to the new law promulgated by Bollani in the *Consiglio* in 1555.[35] Here, then, was a field in which Bollani's contribution was not soon to be forgotten — measures which Battistella called 'movimenti {ispirati} piuttosto che da chiaro e largo concetto di previdenza sociale, da un sentimento di pietà e da un obbligo di religione.'[36]

The *Fondaco*, or communal granary, was one of the oldest charitable institutions in the province. Its aims principally were to distribute food to the poor of the city, particularly in periods of high prices, and to provide a stable and secure supply of grain for the poor at fixed rates irrespective of price fluctuations. It was possible for the institution to provide direct charity in times of real emergency, but generally it exercised a stabilizing influence on food prices by fixing prices in accordance with availability of supplies and its own capital.[37]

The service to the poor that this institution could provide was, therefore, strictly controlled by two factors; the availability of grain, and, importantly, the state of its capital funds.[38] Domenico Bollani initiated a gradual increase in the capital of the *Fondaco* by rising it from 2,000 ducats to 4,000 ducats (over ten years), from which it was again raised to 5,000 in 1574, until it stood at 7,000 by the time Fiducio wrote his treatise at the end of the century.[39]

With this important measure, Bollani helped to provide a stable fund for relief from poverty — almost an insurance, so to speak, against future effects of plague and famine — whose effects he had witnessed at close quarters for the past year, and a providential measure which might help to relieve the pressure created by Venice's grain policy. It is clear that this measure — along with the others proposed at that momentous sitting[40] — was due in the main to the personal intervention of Domenico Bollani, as the records of the *Consiglio* for June 9, 1556, constitute a personal note of gratitude which even the traditional laudatory tone of these records cannot explain.[41]

In fact he had paved the way for this move early in his term of office. On August 20, 1555, he had encouraged private lending to the *Fondaco*, 'onde S. Mag.a desiderando al tutto, che questo predetto cavedale non resti per alcuna via, che imaginar si possa diminuito de la detta suma de li duc. 2M.,'[42] and had provided a graded system of repayment of loans thus given to the institution from public funds.[43] He had then gone on, at the same sitting of the Council, to ensure the perpetual observation of these two provisions, by introducing a complex law obliging the Deputies to review the accounts of the *Fondaco* every June, and requiring that these decisions be regularly read to new Deputies. In this way, he hoped to make abuses more difficult, and to secure for the poor a communal granary whose capital would not be subject to the incursions of expediency.[44]

Perhaps Bollani had been spurred on by the measures his government had forced him to take against the interests of the local population in Friuli, or perhaps it was simply his first-hand contact with the effects of plague and famine. In any event, his intervention in favour of the *Monte di Pietà* in Udine is entirely consistent with the pattern of his activity now gradually emerging.[45] To realise the full significance of his measures to introduce the principle of interest-bearing loans to the structure of a Christian charitable institution in 1556, it will be necessary briefly to sketch in the background, particularly as, in the context of Bollani's formation, this, and the related question of the Jews, were to provide a strong link of continuity between his legislation as a layman and his activity as bishop.[46] It was, after all, a field in which lay and ecclesiastical jurisdiction might coincide in their principal aim to bring relief to the poor, but could also lead to a clash of interests, as in the case of Cardinal Pisani's claim to the revenues of a Paduan hospital in 1544.[47]

There are two significant developments in the evolution of the *Monte di Pietà* (a communal charitable institution providing loans at little or no interest to the poor) in the sixteenth century in the Venetian dominions. In both, Domenico Bollani played a direct and significant part. Firstly the evolution of this charitable institution from a sacred foundation from which economic considerations were entirely absent — to a utilitarian, economically reasoned, interest-bearing deposit bank, took place in Udine as a result of his initiatives. Secondly, this new foundation replaced the Jewish lending tradition throughout the *Terraferma* with the expulsion or persecution of Jewish communities — and for this in Udine, he shares the responsibility.

For it was no accident that the expulsion of the Jews from Udine and the introduction of a 4% rate of interest on loans to the local *Monte di Pietà* were proposed at the same sitting of the Udine Council on June 9, 1556 — the same sitting, in fact, at which the doubling of the capital holding of the *Fondaco del Grano* from 2,000 to 4,000 ducats had been proposed. It was an historic moment for the history of social legislation in Friuli. At one sweep, Domenico Bollani with the Deputies firmly behind him, proposed the drive the Jews from the city of Udine, putting two charitable institutions in a secure position to take over their functions.

But the plague, together with a generous ration of mediaeval superstition,[48] had certainly been a major cause of this outburst of reforming zeal and pious expurgation of non-Christian elements. It is difficult to read the lurid contemporary accounts of the witch-hunt in Udine in the Spring of 1556 without feelings of revulsion at the action taken by the city authorities. In pious satisfaction of recent papal decrees, gratification of a general relief at the passing of the scourge, and less than scientific attribution of the cause of the infection to Jewish families, it was proposed to drive them from the province once and for all. But it is difficult, too, to countenance the situation which the *Luogotenente* and his Deputies had to face. Two contemporary accounts provide telling evidence of the misery occasioned by it, and the need to find a scapegoat to satisfy the fears and anger of an ignorant people.[49]

Whatever the truth, contemporary chronicles and the seventeenth century history of the event agree that the plague had begun with the import of bedding materials from Capodistria via Venice, and had propogated itself through a network of Jewish families.[50] Jews were then strictly forbidden to conduct any kind of business in the city, their property was burnt or sequestered, and a variety of bestialities and acts of violence were committed against them.[51] At this point, orators were sent to Venice to request permission to expel the Jews permanently from the city.[52]

It is difficult to assess the role of Domenico Bollani in the affair, but he was probably able to exercise a pacifying influence, with his brother Giacomo Bollani, once the fury of the city had abated.[53] At any event, the evidence points to an extremely difficult situation administratively. The people, motivated largely by vengeance and ignorance could hardly be allowed free rein in a city slowly recovering from the plague. On the other hand, the Jews had been hounded from the Papal States as a result of specific tenets of Papal policy. It is clear that the demands of local expediency and religious conscience here coincided to produce a force of great strength, and the phenomenon of an infuriated populace after a period of extreme hardship is not confined to Bollani's age. The expulsion of the Jews satisfied contemporary doctrinal and emotional feelings — not to say economic considerations — and found perhaps its most cruel expression in Udine because of the accident of the Plague.[54] Its coincidence in time with a relaxation of the mediaeval censure of the sin of usury brings us back to the *Monte di Pietà*, and the historic sitting of the Udine Council of June 9, 1556.

The possibility of interest being paid on loans to a *Monte di Pietà* had long been complicated by the doctrine of usury.[55] Opposition to the restrictions on interest

68

from an institution designed solely to dispense Christian charity had begun in the fifteenth century, and was crystallised in Papal approval shortly before our period.[56] It had transpired that lending at interest to a *Monte* was not sinful provided that the charitable intention could be preserved in a *lower* rate of interest than that paid by other investment. Thus the lender, whose money might be more profitably employed elsewhere, would be involved in a genuinely charitable act in lending to an institution designed to benefit the poor.

There is every sign that Domenico Bollani had made sure of his ground before proposing this radical modification for the institution at Udine. As Venice's permission had been asked for the expulsion of the Jews, and the fury of that expulsion modified by the Bollani brothers, so Domenico must have been well aware of the developments elsewhere — and particularly of the Papal concession to the *Monte di Pietà* at Vicenza in 1555. Thus he was associated with the proposal to request the bishop of Ceneda to intercede with the Pope to obtain approval for the Udine innovation, 'siccome in tutte le altre citta ove sono state espulsi li hebrei prudentemente.'[57] He was concerned, then, to bring to Friuli social benefits that were already in evidence elsewhere, and the clear intention of replacing the Jewish system of lending at interest with a communal one is here explicitly stated. In this way Bollani was able to contribute — spurred on, perhaps, more by the local effects of plague and famine than by principles of economic far-sightedness — to the evolution of the *Monte di Pietà* at Udine. These institutions were gradually assuming a more secular function 'acting as savings banks which provided a safe security for investors who could not or would not employ their money in more enterprising pursuits, and by acting as cheap loan banks serving all classes and social estates.'[58] By a piece of adroit political timing, catching the wind at its most favourable direction and strength, he had succeeded in combining measures acceptable to the local populations, to Venice, and to the Papacy — yet bringing significant benefits to the depressed classes in Friuli.[59]

Although legislation for the improvement of charitable institutions was probably Bollani's major contribution to the *Patria del Friuli*, his position involved much wider responsibilities. The character of his concern was constant, however. Surviving records show that his action — particularly in the field of social welfare — was constantly directed towards the improvement of conditions of life for the poor, the reform of abuses, and the preservation of law and order and the principles of religion.

At the first signs of plague, his concern was for its control, and his legislation prohibited gatherings where the infection might be spread as early as June 18, 1555.[60] It was clear that these provisions had a dual function: 'per ovviar . . . alle risse, homicidii, et scandali che soleno el più volte avenir per cause delle feste et balli . . .' and 'per ovviar con ogni possibil mezo alli pericoli della peste'. This proclamation was reinforced by others in October, 1555, and June, 1556, at which point licences would be required for gatherings. Again, once the plague had been clearly sighted in a village near Udine, Bollani wrote to the Mayor giving him 'amplissima authorità et libertà . . . per ovviar che quelli de ditta villa amorbata, et altri che passano de luoghi sospetti non venghino ne conduchino robbe d'alcuna sorte . . .'[61] By July, the plague had clearly caused some concern in Venice, as

Domenico's proclamation of 29 of that month refers to the visit of the *Provveditori alla Sanità*. Citizens were instructed to give them every facility, and also to allow free passage to those who had obtained a certificate of good health.[62] Entirely characteristic of Bollani's legislation at this time was the licence granted for a party in July, 1556, provided that: 'tutti li denari che si caverano dalli soprastanti di essa festa siano reposti in man del Cameraro della chiesa d'esso loco, et quelli siano spesi in tanto oglio et cera per illumniar essa chiesa.'[63]

But far more serious was the proclamation of 20 July, 1556, when the plague must have been at its height, which has the unsavoury taste of things to come. Whether the measure carried the force of personal conviction, or was a political expedient designed to allay the fears of a superstitious and ignorant people, cannot be shown, but the terminology is strongly reminiscent of episodes from the Milanese plagues of the seventeenth century, immortalised in Manzoni's *Promessi Sposi*:

> '. . . che siano state trovate diverse sorti di robbe che dano sospetto che siano sparse et gietate da persone scelerate et diaboliche per infestar di peste questa Mag.ca città, et volendo sua Magnificentia ovviar con ogni possibil mezo a tal diaboliche operatione . . .'

Anyone finding such material was to report it for burning to the authorities, and penalties for infringement would be severe. But the proclamation continued with even more sinister overtones — clearly indicating the prevailing atmosphere in the city:

> '. . . che persona alcuna cosi Christiana come Giudei non ardisca di alloggiar in case ne altrimente accettar or dar recapito di giorno o di notte ad alcun giudeo forestiero che venisse in questà città . . .'

The identification of Manzoni's *'untori'* with the Jewish community is revealing. Finally:

> '. . . che passato una hora di notte alcuna no debba andare atorno per la terra senza lume . . .'[64]

Domenico thus faced a difficult situation when dealing with a superstitious and ignorant people. It seems likely that legislation was designed to strike a balance between myth and hygenic good sense.

Finally, Bollani was also concerned with the relief of misery caused by the plague. He ordered a grant of money to be made from the *Monte di Pietà* towards the extra expenses of the plague, and throughout July, took extensive measures to relieve the suffering of the poor at Cesereto, imprisoned in their houses and facing starvation through the sequestration of their food supplies.[65]

All these measures were the results of a state of emergency. Domenico Bollani could not have foreseen the arrival of the plague in Friuli. The experience had taught him much, however, and was to serve him again in the terrible plague of

70

1575, the so-called 'Peste di San Carlo'.[66] More predictable had been his concern with the good order, justice and religion in the everyday life of the city. A block of legislation of this kind was entered in the registers on 8 June, 1555. Possibly this may reflect the legislative zeal of the newly-arrived lieutenant; it may even betray the conduct of his predecessor. Certainly it reflects the state of Friuli when he arrived in the early summer of that year, and gives a good idea of the variety of problems with which the *Luogotenente* had to deal. It also mirrors various aspects of the life of a province to which he was to return in Brescia.[67]

The orders which he issued during his first months of office included penalties for blasphemy and a tightening of the laws governing convents, particularly those affecting visiting doctors and lawyers. It was forbidden to climb convent walls, and carnal relations with nuns were severely punished. Laws restricted the carrying of arms, crimes were to be reported, and doctors were to report wounds. Penalties were increased for harbouring bandits, obstructing officials and for extortion or illegal sequestration of goods. There was even a ban on games of dice and cards, 'per obviar alle bestemmi, furti et altri scandali et male operationi che nascer soleno da li giochi.'[68]

The list does not end there, but in a nutshell can be seen the picture of a province. With minimal education and a natural tendency to abuses of all kind, continuous vigilance was necessary for the orderly conduct of everyday affairs. Much minor legislation was repeated at regular intervals — underlining the difficulties in law-enforcement. For Domenico Bollani, philanthropy and experience of abuses in ecclesiastical institutions were the background to the Catholic Reformation. They were the background for the future reformer and bishop. Close contact with such aspects of life in a Venetian province would lend conviction to his opinions at the Council of Trent and to his actions in the diocese of Brescia.

In this way Bollani governed his province, striving to steer a path between local conflicts to bring order and justice to a turbulent people in a time of almost continuous natural disaster. It is worth looking briefly at his representative function, however, for although in the fields of social legislation and reform there were wide opportunities for personal initiative, it should not be forgotten that he was a servant of the Venetian state — part of a machine whose hub was still the Council of Ten in Venice.

Bollani was never to be allowed to forget that he was a Venetian even — as we have seen in the case of grain exports to Venice — when a conflict of interests was involved. This delegatory side of his activity had a purely formal aspect, and such was the case in the visit in 1556 of Bona Sforza, daughter of Giangaleazzo Sforza, Duke of Milan, to the *Patria del Friuli*. Bona Sforza was Queen of Poland, and was to pass through the province on her way to Padua, so the Republic was anxious to honour her visit in various appropriate ways.[69] The matter was debated in the Senate on 6 March, 1556,[70] when Bollani, the representative of the state resident in Udine, was commissioned to meet her at Venzone and accompany her to Padua 'con cavalli 25 fin 30 a spese della Signoria nostra.'[71] He was to greet the Queen with 'quelle parole che giudichera a proposito,' and could spend up to 500 ducats of Venetian money.

The mounting of this elaborate piece of pure theatre clearly cost Domenico Bollani no little effort — but preparations for Royal Visits have hardly changed down the centuries. Roads were to be repaired for the Queen's 'cochi, carretti e cavalli',[72] and elaborate preparations are described in his proclamation of January 30, 1556: provisions were to be provided by the local inhabitants for horses and men, a bridge was put across the river Tagliamento 'non dissimile a quello sopra il quale passò l'Imperatore Carlo Quinto',[73] and instructions were left for accommodation at Spilimbergo, where the Queen would stay. In February and March, preparations were still in progress, but Bollani was clearly dealing with details — with the order of goats, calves, lambs, capons and hens.[74]

The event itself was sumptuous and courtly, reminiscent in some ways of Bollani's reception at Hampton Court in the summer of 1547.[75] At his meeting with the Queen, 'pose piede in terra esso Luogotenente con cento di quei gentil' huomini. Fece allora la Regina fermare la seggietta, e da quella discese. Passò con essa il Luogotenente un grave et affettuoso complimento osservando tutti i comodi possibili. Gradì la Regina con dimostrazioni cortesi l'officio.'[76]

In this way, Bollani had fulfilled a formal and ceremonial function as well as an administrative one. He had also been occupied with other affairs: reforms of tariffs,[77] and perhaps even reforms of legal procedure.[78] He had certainly had to sit in judgement on hundreds of civil and criminal cases in the courts in his short term of office.[79] With the passage of the plague and the end of the summer, his term of office drew to a close, and preparations were made for his return to Venice. The demonstrations of gratitude made to him at that time by the people of Udine — for his social reforms, just mediation and care of the affairs of the *Patria* in times of plague and famine — must have made him feel well satisfied with his efforts on the completion of a difficult and arduous task.[80]

His contribution had been a notable one in a particularly difficult period. Choosing his moment, he had been able to initiate a programme of reforms that would outlive the temporary emergencies that had given rise to them. His care for the problems of the populace had been demonstrated in various fields. Elections to the Venetian Senate were to follow his return from Udine[81] before his talents in administrative and diplomatic affairs were again to be put to good use in the province and diocese of Brescia, and it is here that he will appear in the next Chapter.

The scribe who recorded the minutes of the Council in Udine for the historic sitting of June 9, 1556, must have been quite unaware of the prophetic nature of his description of Domenico Bollani as 'padre universale de la città nostra.'

NOTES TO CHAPTER IV

1 Much has been written on the *Patria del Friuli*. Indispensable as a general guide in this period is A. Battistella, *Udine nel Secolo XVI*, (Udine, 1932) which provides a detailed but not always fully documented history of the province. P. Paschini, *Storia del Friuli*, 2 vols. 2nd. Ed. revised (Udine, 1954) II, is also useful, particularly for religious history, whereas G.F. Palladio degli Olivi, *Historie della Provincia del Friuli*, 2 vols. (Udine, 1660) but repr. (Bologna, 1966) II, is rather a chronicle of events from month to month. On the state of the province, the *Relazioni* of the *Luogotenenti* are indispensable. I used those in A.S.V. *Collegio, Secreta, Relazioni, busta* 32 (1557, 1559, 1561), and *ibid. Relazioni Miste*, (1552, 1553). For Domenico Bollani, there are 15 letters in A.S.V. *Capi/Consiglio dei X, Dispacci dei Rettori*, (Udine), Filza 170 (1531–1559), and much information of value in *Ibid. Luogotenente della Patria del Friuli, Processi*, CLXX, (169) (1555–1556). Far from the indication given by the title, this source contains, besides the many hundreds of law-suits, *proclami* an almost daily record of decisions taken and exchanges of letters. A similarly rich source is in the Biblioteca V. Ioppi, Udine, *Archivio Civico Utini (A.C.U.) Annalium*, Tom. 54 (1554–1559), which contains almost day-to-day records of the Udine Parliament. Much detailed bibliography exists on a diversity of topics, of which there are indications in the following notes. (Figs. 12, 13)
2 'In questa paese è una totale confusione. Tante e diverse gurisdizioni coi loro privilegi sono causa di tutti i moti ed errori che funestano il Friuli, perchè sotto il Luogotenente stanno 16 communità, 16 prelature 54 castelli, avente giurisdizione chi in prima istanza, chi in seconda, chi in terza, onde cio molti dottori ed avvocati si mette difficoltà nelle cose chiare e tutte {sic} apprezzano tanto i propri privilegi, che per ogni minima causa nascono discordie e tra loro si amazzano.' (Relazione, 1553 in Marchese, *Le Relazioni dei Luogotenenti della Patria del Friuli*, { Udine, 1893} pp. 15–16).
3 For Domenico Bollani, grandfather, see, for example, Barbaro, *op. cit.*, p. 40, G. Priuli, *Diarii*, in *Rerum Italicarum Scriptores*, tom. XXIV, P. III, vol. I, pp. 128, 141, 148, 166, 199, P. Paschini, *Storia cit.* II, 352–355, M. Sanuto, *Diarii cit.* III, col, 19. Domenico himself had been well instructed in his grandfather's career, in common with Venetian family traditions, as the measures he took in the interests of the *Monte di Pietà* were a continuation of his grandfather's policy, and are remembered as such. (*In Archivio Civico Utini* { henceforth A.C.U.} *Annalium*, tom. *cit.*, c. 81, and see below p. 66). Opinion was by no means unanimous on the success of Domenico's grandfather, as a contemporary source described him during his government of Cremona as 'homo diabolicus, crudelis, partialis et sine lege.' (G. Sommi Picenardi, *Cremona durante il dominio dei Veneziani* {1499–1509} (Milan, 1866) pp. 60–62 at p. 61).
4 See Marchese, *op. cit.*, p. 16 for examples.
5 *Idem.* pp. 14–19. We have seen a contemporary picture of the Castellani shortly before Bollani's term of office (1553). By the end of the century, the situation had hardly changed: 'I Castellani ampliano il più che possono le loro gurisdizioni e s'arrogano un'autorità assoluta, contrariamente a ciò che venne dichiarato dai Dieci. La loro autorità reca danno ai sudditi e ruina alla Patria.' (Stefano Viario, *Relazione* {1599} in Marchese *op. cit.*, p. 17. See also Battistella, *Storia cit.* p. 11.
6 For the history of parliamentary institutions in Friuli. see A. Marongiu, *Il Parlamento in Italia nel'Medio Evo e nell'età moderna*, (Milan, 1962) pp. 189–194, 263–277, 369–389 etc. (Eng. trans, in *Idem. Medieval Parliaments* { Ed. and trans. S.J. Woolf} { London, 1968} pp. 119–123, 177–192 etc.)
7 Paschini, *op. cit.*, pp. 380–383, Battistella, *Udine . . ., cit.*, pp. 7–13, and for a contemporary account, M.A. Fiducio, *Del modo di governo della communità di Udine . . .*, {1602} (Venice, 1862) *passim*. Fiducio (1518–1615) had been a prominent lawyer in Udine for almost the whole century. For his career, *Idem. loc.cit.*, p. 1, n. 1.
8 See the account of these uprisings in P.S. Leicht, 'Un movimento agraria nel Cinquecento' in *Idem, Scritti vari di Storia del Diritto Italiano* (Milan, 1943) I, pp. 73–91, and pp. 77–87 for the conditions under which the *contadini* had lived. Cf. also V. Marchese, 'Il Friuli al tempo di Cambray' in *Nuovo Archivio Veneto* VI (1903) pp. 518–527, and A. Battistella, 'La Servitù di Masnada in Friuli . . .' in *Ibid*, n.s. VI (1906) tom. XI, pp. 3–62, XIII,

pp. 169–191, 320–321, partic. pp. 183–191, and D. Tassini, 'La Rivolta del Friuli del 1511 . . .' in *N.A.V.*, n.s. XXXIX–XL (1920) pp. 142–151.

9 S.J. Woolf, 'The Problem of representation in the Post Renaissance State' in *Liber Memorialis Antonio Era*, (Cagliari, 1961) pp. 78–79.

10 Paschini, *op. cit.*, II, pp. 382–383: 'fu riconosciuto a ciascuno dei borghi chiuso entro le mura il diritto di tenere vicinanza cioè un'assemblea di tutti i borghigiani sotto la sorveglianza del luogotenente ed alla presenza dei sette deputati per trattare gli interessi ed i bisogni del borgo stesso.'

11 On the peasant body in opposition to the *Parlamento* (i.e. the provincial deliberative assembly), see also Leicht, 'Un movimento . . .' *cit.*, pp. 90–91, and particularly *Idem*. 'La rappresentanza dei Contadini presso il Veneto Luogotenente della Patria del Friuli' in *Studi e Frammenti*, (Udine, 1903) pp. 125 *et seq.* For its functions see Battistella, *Udine . . .*, *cit.*, pp. 22–24. A. Ventura in his *Nobiltà e Popolo, cit.*, pp. 194–214 describes the peasant uprisings in some detail, and includes the undeniable fact that the public representative body, or *Arengo* was suppressed as a result of these movements, and that attempts to reconstitute it in 1518 and 1521 had failed (p. 213). He then concludes that 'Questa attaccamento alla libertà pubblica e privata, che sembra farsi ora più viva e radicata nell'animo ˛egli ottimati . . . era indizio di una piu sicura coscienza aristocratica, per cui l'ideale del vivere libero postulava l'incontrastata supremazia della nobiltà sulle altre classi sociali, non meno che l'uguaglianza tra tutti i membri di essa.' (p. 214). This author makes no mention of the concessions within our period (and his) to peasant participation – particularly of the concession on January 3, 1550, of the *Vicinanza* or peasant assembly (for which see Battistella, *Storia, cit.*, pp. 22–24, Paschini, *loc. cit.*, etc.). The omission of this significant detail gives a decidedly biased view of the situation during the period in which Domenico Bollani held office (1555–1556), and it seems that the question of the relations between Venice and her subject dominions fits uneasily into the modern framework of class-struggle which this author has given it. A. Tagliaferri, in his recently published *Struttura e Politica Sociale in una Communità Veneta del '500 (Udine)* (Milan, 1969) carries much more conviction when he states that, in spite of the exploitation of Friuli by the Republic, 'essa non può rifiutarsi oltre, quando, dopo una serie di moti contadini del primo Cinquecento . . . e allo scopo di frenare la preponderanza e gli abusi giurisdizionali dei feudatari, concede il suo assenso alla creazione di una forza contadina organizzata nell'istituto *contadinanza*.' (p. 21). See also pp. 42–44.

12 After 1513 'il lavoro legislativo si fermò, e le istituzioni entrarono in un periodo di vita facile e calma . . . ed ora { 1536 } per decreto del eccelso Consiglio dei Dieci, le chiavi della citta venivano portate ogni notte in Castello { the residence of the *Luogotenente* } ed i cavalieri del Luogotenente scendevano ogni mattina ad aprire le porte.' (A. Measso, *I Deputati al Reggimento della Magnifica Comunità di Udine*, (Udine, 1884) p. 22. See also Fiducio, *Del modo di governo . . ., cit.*, p. 39.

13 For a summary of the areas of competence of the *Consiglio* and its impotence in the absence of the Luogotenente, see Measso, *op. cit.*, pp. 22–23, Fiducio, *op. cit.*, pp. 1–3, Marongiu, *op. cit.*, pp. 219–235 especially pp. 231–232.

14 *Descrizione della Patria del Friuli con l'utile che cava il Serenissimo Prencipe e con le spese che fa*, (Udine, 1897) p. 21.

15 One *relazione* expressed it that 'se la vigilanza del retore rallenta un po', le fraudi hanno luogo e le cose di quella povera gente sono male trattate, perchè i sindici miserabili procurano ad ogni potere qualsiasi civanzo a loro pro; gli avvocati operano col solo oggetto della professione e i deputati attendono al beneficio della principale rappresentanza, cioè dei castellani . . .' (quoted by Marchese, *Le Relazioni, cit.*, p. 13).

16 'L'azione dei luogotenente pertanto, oltre che a mantenere la sicurezza e la tranquillità e rafforzare l'autorità del governo centrale, nessuna innovazione poteva tentare nell'intima costituzione del paese: s'intravvedevano le necessità, ma mancava l'energia e forse anche la possibilità di trovare e applicare rimedi necessari ed efficaci.' (Marchese, *Brevi giudizi . . ., cit.*, p. 67, and see pp. 46–47).

17 These derive without exception from Palladio degli Olivi, *Historie della Provincie del Friuli*, II, pp. 173–177, which Cicogna, (*Della Inscrizioni Veneziane, cit.*, IV, pp. 451 *et. seq.*) quotes, and is followed almost *verbatim* by Fè D'Ostiani, *Il Vescovo Domenico Bollani, cit.*,

pp. 5–6, Petroboni, thesis *cit.* pp. 35–40, Zanotti, thesis *cit.* pp. 35–40 (early life). None of the above works contains references to archival sources either in Venice or in Udine for what concerns Friuli.

18 See Marchese, *Brevi giudizi . . ., cit., passim.* There was, of course a complete range of involvement of the lieutenant in the affairs of Friuli, from the saintly example of Pietro Canal in 1794, whose social reforms were extensive, to other far less distinguished incumbents, whose services to the province were commemmorated by the citizens *cum sterco humano* on city walls bearing their arms (1501). The arch bearing the Venetian lion and inscription at the foot of the steps leading to the castle, erected to the memory of Domenico Bollani, stands to this day. (Fig. 11)

19 Above, p. 11 and notes.

20 In A. Tagliaferri, *Struttura e Politica Sociale, cit.*, pp. 45–46.

21 For the plague of 1555–6, see below, pp. 69–71.

22 The original restrictive law was of 20 April, 1451, reinforced many times by subsequent legislation. See the *Capitolare di tutte le ispezioni e leggi del Magistrato Eccellentissimo delle biavi*, (Venice, 1772) p. 27. For the history of this legislation, A. Ventura, *Nobiltà e popolo, cit.*, pp. 379–381, esp. p. 381, notes.

23 A.S.V., *Capi/Consiglio dei X, Dispacci dei Rettori* (Udine) *filza* 170 c. 198. April 24, 1556.

24 Leonardo Emo, Podestà of Padua in 1523, had attempted to prevent the movement of grain to Venice, in the face of a secret export licence granted by the government, and had pleaded unsuccessfully in the interests of the local inhabitants. In 1539, the rectors of Verona had disobeyed a Senate decree for similar reasons. For these and similar analogies, see Ventura, *op. cit.*, pp. 382–398.

25 'Io son ogno giorno sollecitato da questi Sp. li Deputati che si facci la descrittione delle biavi in questa città, dubitando loro che non ne sia bastanza, et massime che ne da vicini, ne dal novo raccolto si può sperare in questa città pur un grano di biava mentre che durerà questo sospetto {di peste} ma io non ho loro mai voluto consentire perchè conosco che non si trovarebbe la quantità che *io per contento del popolo faccio creder che vi sia . . .*' (Italics mine).

26 See Bollani's letters on this in A.S.V., *Dispacci dei Rettori, cit., filza* 170, cc 184–199 dated 24, 27, 28 July, 25 August, 4, 30 December 1555.

27 The situation was common also in other parts of the mainland: 'Non è un caso che il contrasto su tale materia tra il governo centrale e i magistrati inviati nelle province fosse uno dei remi ricorrenti dell'amministrazione veneta.' (Ventura, *op. cit.*, p. 382.)

28 A.S.V. *Luogotenente della Patria del Friuli, Processi, Filza* 169, *Proclamationum Liber Primus*, under 7 and 13 July, 1555.

29 *Ibid*, 29 July, 1556, 'Havendo inteso per relation et gravame de molti che alcuni degani, podestà et zuradi delle ville si fanno liciti di non lasciar che li coloni et massari conduchino le biave delli afitti, Livelli, et entrade alli lor parroni {patroni} sotto pretesto di sospetto di peste, assumendosi di se stessi authorità di commandar et far tale indebita prohibitione in grave pregudizio delli parroni con incomodo della città . . .' (there follow the usual penalties for holding up supplies.) (*Processi, cit.*, 4 December, 1555.)

30 *Dispacci, cit.* c. 193. It is clear from the records of his legislation that Bollani was also actively concerned to encourage the import of grain from Germany. He had issued a proclamation on January 1, 1556 whose effect was to remove obstacles in the way of the passage of German grain from the frontier to Venice via Gemona (A.S.V., *Processi, cit.*, for this date) and was almost continuously concerned with the state of the roads between the 'chiusa', or head of the pass at Venzone, and Udine, through which supplies were bound to pass. (See legislation for October 9, November 29, December 6, 1555 for instance in *Ibid.*) From December, the question had the added incentive of preparing the way for the coming visit of Bona Sforza, Queen of Poland.

31 'col vedermi nelle lettere di Vre. Ecc.tie de ultimo del passato stimare manco pronto di quello che con verità io sia alli mandati suoi in materia di lasciar trazer biave di questa patria per quella inclytta città, ne posso fare che questa mia si mala sorte non mi apporti rammarico, conoscendo io che la diligentia che ho usato in eseguir le deliberationi di quel Ecc.mo cons.o

di 3 del mese presente, hor mi ritova forse a qualche importatione de inobedientia.' (*Lettere di Rettori, cit.*, p. 190.)

32 As was the case in the affair cited.

33 'confesso che mi trovo in tale dubbio che non so come governarmi, prememdomi da l'un canto l'esecution che debbo dare alli mandati suoi, e dall'altro dolendomi . . .' etc. (*Ibid.* c. 190). Domenico does not himself mention the problem of contraband and the difficulties of the passage of goods from the northern frontier to Venice, but it was clearly a difficult problem during his term of office as legislation in the senate of May, 31, 1557 shows (A.S.V., *Senato Terra*, Ro. 41, and see C. Shalk, 'Rapporti commerciali fra Venezia e Vienna' in *Archivio Veneto* n.s. XXIII, pp. 52–95, 284–317).

34 For instance *Provveditore al Cottimo di Damasco* in 1543.

35 See above, p. 73, n. 3 'a proposta del Cl.mo M. Domenico Bollani di felice memoria, avolo suo, fu istituito a beneficio pubblico il Sacro Monte di Pietà del 1499.' (A.C.U., *Annalium*, tom. 54 (1554–1559), c. 46).

36 Battistella, *Udine nel Secolo XVI, cit.*, p. 295.

37 For the background of this institution, see N. Mantica, *Degli ordinamenti del Comune di Udine sul pane dal 1300 in poi e dei prezzi del frumento e del pane*, (Udine, 1888) *passim*. For its state in our period, Battistella, 'Udine nel Secolo XVI. Condizioni e provvisioni annonarie' in *Memorie Storiche Forogiulesi*, XVII (1921) pp. 83–102, and Tagliaferri, *op. cit.*, pp. 107–112. For brief mention of Bollani's measures, Battistella, *Udine . . ., cit.*, (1932) pp. 293–295.

38 The relation between capital and actual stocks and types of grain has been studied by Tagliaferri, *op. cit.*, pp. 108–111.

39 1602. *Del modo di governo, cit.*, p. 24, 'L'andera parte che si propone esso Cl.mo S. Logotenente et Mag.ci Deputati che il fontego di questa città nel quale al presente si trovane ducatti 2M. di cavedale sia aumentata de li denari pub.ci di questa Mag.ca città di altri ducatti due milia in anni X prossimi a' duc. 200 al'anno . . .' (A.C.U., *Annalium, cit.*, tom. 54, p. 78). See also Battistella, *op. cit.*, pp. 293–295, Tagliaferri, *op. cit.*, pp. 110–111.

40 For which see immediately below.

41 See the repeated expressions of gratitude in *Annalium*, tom. *cit.* p. 78: (the *Fondaco*) 'solamente per opera e pietà del Cl.mo M. Domenico Bollani cavalier . . .' '. . . si sono con la sua singolar vigilantia et prudentia felicemente rimossi tutti i pericoli de la fame nel presente anno . . . et ridotta questa città in amor, quiete, et unione . . .' The expulsion of the Jews was 'ottenuta per opera, e diligentia del Cl. M. Domenico Bollani . . . {etc.} padre benemeritissimo di questa città . . .' etc. That Bollani himself proposed these measures in the Council is clear from the wording, but the above would seem to indicate a considerable measure of initiative and participation.

42 *Ibid.* c. 47.

43 'cioè la mità su la prima paga de li datii publici, et l'altra mità su la seconda paga de essi datii . . .' (*Ibid.*)

44 The accounts were apparently ready for the current year by 1 September, 1555, for which toil, the labours of the *Censor*, Bernardin Pavona, were rewarded with ten ducats on that day. (*Ibid.* p. 54) Again, on 15 September, Bollani urged the Council to pass a motion that any future change in the *Fondaco's* constitution should be supported by three-quarters of the votes (pp. 56–57), and finally, for maximum security, the capital of the granary should be deposited 'sopra il Sacro Monte di Pietà in una cassa forte.' (p. 80)

45 For the history of this institution, and in particular, for its relationship with the Jewish lending tradition in Italy, see the fundamental work by Brian Pullan, *Rich and Poor in Renaissance Venice. The Social Institutions of a Catholic State to 1620* (Oxford, 1971) *passim*. (I am indebted to Professor Pullan for allowing me to consult his work prior to its publication). For the Udine *Monte*, see the detailed and fully documented study in A. Tagliaferri. *Strutture e Politica Sociale, cit.*, pp. 119–192 and appendices. See also Battistella *Udine . . ., cit.*, pp. 295–299, Marchese, *Le Relazioni . . ., cit.*, p. 34 (of slight value). For discussion of archival sources for the *Monte* at Udine, see Tagliaferri, *op. cit.*, pp. 131–134. There is also discussion in Ventura, *op. cit.*, pp. 416–419, but on this, see Tagliaferri, p. 146 n. 36.

76

46 Pullan, *op. cit.*, pp. 340–1, 541–2.
47 Pullan, *op. cit.*, pp. 327–337, for this story and discussion of lay and ecclesiastical control of charitable institutions. For further conflicts in jurisdiction, see Aldo Stella, *Chiesa e Stato nelle relazioni dei Nunzi Pontifici a Venezia: Ricerche sul Giurisdizionalismo Veneziano dal XVI al SVIII secolo*, (Vatican, 1964) *passim*.
48 'Quanto agli ebrei, non era possibile che anche qui, nella quasi generale ignoranza, non dominasse il comune preconcetto che, appoggiandosi sopra un fondamento di fede religiosa grossolanamente materializzata, s'era via via rafforzata per ragioni economiche e sociali. Un superstizioso e malevolo sospetto che, supponendo in loro forze occulte, faceva attribuire ad essi le le ignote cause di pubblici e privati malanni (Battistella, *Udine . . ., cit.*, p. 281). For the growth of anti-semitic legislation to its present disagreeable climax, see *Ibid.*, pp. 133–134, 280–283.
49 , The two contemporary accounts, by Vincenzo Giusti, *Cancelliere dell' Ufficio della Sanità*, and Pagano de Susanis, *Sovrastante alla guardia delle porte*, (pub. in *Pagine Friulane*, XII pp. 103–133) purport to contain a record of sanitory provisions for the guidance of future generations, but contain also a large measure of anti-semitic prejudice. The extent to which they agree on the attribution of the cause of the plague to the Jewish community smacks of a prearranged, largely 'political' decision.
50 In *Ibidem* and Palladio degli Olivi, *Historie, cit.*, II, pp. 175–176.
51 'In questo medemo tempo forno alquanti ben creati di questa città che dettero ordine de ammazzar tutti li hebrei ancora che fossero sequestrati et sachizarli, qual commina essendo venuto ad orecchio al Chiarissimo Bollani Luogotenente in quel tempo et justificata, parte ne fece apicare et parte banditi de terra in lochi etc.' {sic.} (Chronicle Susanis, *cit.*, p. 106). It should be added that there is not a trace of such an order either in the acts of the Council (*Annalium*) nor in the record of Bollani's Proclamations (A.S.V., *Luogotenente, cit.*) but rather that his measures to control the infection and prevent its spread point in an opposite direction. (See below, pp. 69–70)
52 *Ibid.*, p. 106. Battistella, *Udine . . ., cit.*, p. 282, *Annalium, cit.*, p. 71. Three orators were elected on April 9, 1556.
53 A compromise was, in fact, reached through the agency of Giacomo Bollani in Venice. (For whom, see above pp. 12, 13 etc.) It was agreed that the Jews should have six months in which to settle their affairs before leaving. There had clearly been bitter feeling between Jewish representatives in Venice and the above orators from Udine, which Giacomo had managed to resolve, as the agreement was finally signed by eleven Jews, the orators, and Giacomo himself. (See Battistella, *Udine . . ., cit.*, p. 283, Pullan, *Religion, the Poor . . ., cit.*, pp. 526–7. The full text of the agreement is in A.S.V. *Senato Terra, Filza* 23 (1556) March 17, 1556.
54 Needless to say, the situation did not last. The property sequestered by the authorities in Udine was returned to the Jews by a decree of the Venetian Senate a year later; Jews continued to reside in the city, as the expulsion was again attempted in 1622; and a successor of Pope Paul IV, Sixtus V, conceded wide liberties to Jews in the last quarter of the century. (See Tagliaferri, *op. cit.*, p. 174 and n. 35)
55 See a full discussion of the debate in Pullan *Religion . . ., cit.*, p. 589 etc., and Tagliaferri, *op. cit.*, pp. 121–128.
56 Papal briefs granting the right to pay interest to *Monti* at Modena in 1542 and Vicenza in 1555 were conceded. See Pullan, *loc. cit.*
57 *Annalium*, tom. *cit.*, p. 81, June 9, 1556.
58 Pullan, *op. cit.*, p. 587.
59 In fact, Bollani's role in the period of tumult following the passing of the Plague must have been essentially one of pacification. Far from exciting the people to violence against the Jews, he had tried to divert their energies into expressions of thanksgiving and communal efforts to convert a volatile situation into some lasting benefit for the community. To this atmosphere of goodwill may be attributed the speed and success of the measure of June 9, and its outward manifestations, once tempers had cooled, were the traditional ones of church and procession, prayer and charity: 'Considerando il Cl. mo M. Domenico Bollani cavalier Locotenente meritissimo de la Patria, et li Mag. ci Deputati del città li molti e grand. mi

beneficiy ricevuti nel presente anno da la Providentia del S. Dio, et prencipuamente la felice et presta liberatione dal morbo contagioso de peste, fame, et altri innumerati travagli, et volendo con quelli più efficaci modi che si possano, dimostrare la gratitudine, che si deve avere a S. divina Maestà per un tanto beneficio ricevuto, pero mettono parte, che de cetero ogn'anno per voto publico di questa mag. ca communità conceputo per la salute universale si debba in una delle tre feste de la Pentecoste, celebrare nel domo di questà città une solenne messa con quelle più efficaci orationi che si possano, per render gratie al S. Dio autore di ogni bene ne la quale etiam si debba pregare per la felice salute del cl.mo S. Logotenente, padre universale de la città nostra; et dapoi, finita la messa, si habbia a fare una solenna processione per l'istesso effetto con quella maggior frequenza di persone che si possa a eterna gloria del S. Dio, et conservatione et augmento di questa città.' (*Annalium, cit.*, c. 77r)

60 A.S.V., *Luogotenente della Patria del Friuli, Processi, Filza* 169, 'Proclamatorium Liber Primus', June 18, 1555.

61 *Ibid.*, July 3, 1555.

62 'et similmente ciascuno debba accettar, dar pratica et transito a quelli di Udine che haverano la fede de sanità dal officio de Sp.li provveditori della città di Udene . . .' (*Ibid.* July 29, 1555). Of the visit of officials from Venice there seems no trace in the archive of that name in the A.S.V., just as the records of the letters that Domenico Bollani 'di continuo scrivo alli sig.ri sopra la sanità' (*Lettere di Rettori, cit.*, p. 198) do not seem to have survived.

63 *Processi, Filza cit.*, July 2 1556.

64 *Ibid.*, July 20, 1556. The proclamations also contained injunctions against those who went 'stravestidi o imbianchadi di notte' because it could not be supposed that they could be engaged in anything lawful.

65 See measures in *Ibid.*, 11, 16, 30 July, 1556.

66 See below, pp. 156–159.

67 See below, pp. 80–83.

68 A.S.V., *Luogotenente . . ., cit.*, June 8, 1555.

69 This event has, perhaps, slight interest for us here, being more to the taste of such 'chronicle-histories' as the *Historie* of Palladio degli Olivi (*cit.*). The statements of this author, where not supported by material from archival sources, have not been regarded as conclusive in the present work. Possibly an exception can be made in this case, however, as the account of Bollani's meeting with the Queen of Poland carries all the conviction and ingenuous enthusiasm of an eye-witness account. In all probability it is based on a contemporary source now lost. (*op. cit.*, II, p. 175) Mention is included here as it indicates the thoroughness and conscientious way in which Domenico prepared for an event in which the prestige of the Republic was involved. Bibliography on Bona Sforza is plentiful; suffice it to mention here the bibliography in the *Enciclopedia Treccani*, VII, p. 378, or the name entry in the British Museum Catalogue.

70 A.S.V., *Senato Terra*, Ro. 40 (1555–1556) p. 94, March 6, 1556.

71 *Ibid.*: 'Non si dovendo mancar si usar ogni ufficio per honorar la Ser.ma Regina Bona qual presto si diè ritrovar nel Dominio nostro per venir in la città di Padova nostra secondo è sta sempre solito della Signoria nostra di usar verso ciascun principe acciò che la Maestà Sua possi conoscere l'affettione che le portiamo . . .' Significantly, Palladio degli Olivi speaks of 200 or more horse on the day itself (*op. cit.*, p. 175), but this may have been the enthusiastic exaggeration of an eye-witness account. Bollani was thus granted expenses by the Senate, and also by the Deputies at Udine (A.S.U., *Annalium*, tom. *cit.*, c. 70, 27 March, 1556, and Battistella, *Udine . . ., cit.*, p. 53) so that the number may have been an aggregate. Clearly Venetian hospitality was not to out-do the Friulian welcome.

72 A.S.V., *Processi, cit.*, December 6, 1555, and January 17, 1556.

73 Bollani's instructions for the bridge in *Ibid.* January 30, but the analogy is Palladio's (*loc. cit.*)

74 *Ibid.* 15 February, 13 March, 1556.

75 See Cairns, 'An unknown Venetian description . . .' etc. *cit.*

76 Palladio degli Olivi, vol. *cit.*, p. 175. 'Havesse seco essa Regina quattrocento persone fra huomini e donne, e tra questo otto Damigelle di Polonia di estraordinaria bellezza e due d'Italia di maggior età {!} . Viaggava in seggietta coperta di veluto negro . . .' There follows a

78

full description of the magnificence of the costumes worn with great attention to detail.
77 *Tariffe della Patria del Friuli intorno ai pagamenti degli Ecc. Signori, Curiali, cancellieri, nodari, ed altri*, (Udine, 1612), and *Tariffe etc.* (Udine, 1736). These acts date from 1555, being revised during Bollani's term of office by a committee of three previous *Luogotenenti* elected in the Senate. For this, see A.S.V. *Senato Terra* Ro. 40, cc. 32–41, March 6, 1556, *Ibid. Luogotenente, Processi, cit.*, June 26, 1555.
78 'Seguî anche la riforma di quel Foro per opera del Luogotenente', Palladio degli Olivi, *op. cit.*, II, p. 174, transmitted to Cicogna, *loc. cit.*, and Petroboni, thesis *cit.*
79 Reports of these cases are in A.S.V., *Luogotenente . . ., Processi*, vol. *cit.*
80 Besides tributes made him in June (above, n. 59), a laudatory poem was composed and presented to him at an appropriate ceremony by one Gioseffo Sporeno 'Udinese Poeta' (Palladio degli Olivi, *op. cit.*, II, p. 177), but of this and its author, there seems to be no trace. The 'Arco Bollani', a Palladian arch standing at the foot of the steps to the castle, bears testimony to his measures in times of famine and plague to this day: 'DOMENICO BOLLANO EQ./ PRAETORI/ OB. LIBERATUM FAME/ PESTILENTIA/ CONIURA/TIONE PROVIN-CIAM/ FOROLIULIENSES/ ARCUM HUNC/ EREXERUNT/ M.D.LVI.' (Cicogna, *Delle Inscrizioni Veneziane, cit.*, IV, p. 451), (Fig. 11)
81 See above, p. 57 n. 19.

CHAPTER V

BRESCIA AND THE RIVER OGLIO
(1558–1567)

Before his election as bishop of Brescia in 1559, Domenico Bollani had served his government in fiscal, ambassadorial and administrative posts. His abilities had been demonstrated in a wide field, but particularly in the fields of diplomacy and social legislation. With his election to the post of *Podestà* of Brescia in 1558, opportunities were given him for further demonstrating his abilities in these two fields. He was able to consolidate his experience — briefly in the administration of the province of Brescia, a city of fundamental importance on Venice's frontier with the Duchy of Milan — and importantly, in the complex negotiations over the uses of the river Oglio. His experience of Venice's mainland subjects was to be deepened in a new theatre of activity, and his diplomatic training was to be exercised to the full in a local dispute — but one with international repercussions. The focus of this chapter narrows, therefore, to examine his activity in these two fields, so that the suitability of this training may be seen for the administrative, diplomatic and vocational functions of the new Counter-Reformation Bishop that the Council of Trent was to create.

For Venice, Friuli faced the Empire in the north and the Turk in the east. Udine was also close enough to be of vital importance for her supplies. Brescia faced west — towards Milan and western Europe — and that part of northern Italy much used by northern invaders during the first half of the century, with its centre, the city of Milan, the principal theatre of French and Imperial rivalries.[1] To the south, lay Cremona — once Venetian, where Domenico's grandfather had administered the city as *Podestà* in 1500 — but now tied to the changing fortunes of Milan and a potentially dangerous encircling influence on Venice's western frontier.[2] Not half a day's ride from the city of Brescia, the river Oglio flowed down from Lake Iseo in the north to Cremona in the south, dividing the Cremonese and Bergamask subjects of Milan from the Brescian subjects of the Doge. Brescia, therefore, constituted an outpost of the Venetian empire of considerable strategic importance when Domenico Bollani made his entry into the city in 1558.[3]

The post involved many duties similar to those of the *Luogotenenza* at Udine. With the Republic of Venice weakened after Cambrai, the questions of her subject provinces and her somewhat tenuous hold over them, had assumed crucial importance. If Friuli would be first in the line of attack for advancing Germans or Turks, then Brescia was the first fortress to fall if the Emperor or France were to decide again to fish in the troubled waters of Italy. Venetians of the generation of Domenico's father, Francesco Bollani, had had direct experience of this during the first quarter of the century.[4] Their memories of that war-torn period had taught them that the loyalties of the frontier provinces could not necessarily be counted on in case of attack, and the preoccupation of Venetian rectors with the attitudes of Brescia towards the Republic may be easily understood.[5] It should not be forgotten, too, that the year of Domenico's entry into Brescia was 1558 — one year before the Treaty of Cateau-Cambrésis — when Spain replaced France in the field of Italian politics, to play a dominant role for the rest of the century. For

80

the rest of Bollani's life, Venice was to be flanked on both sides by the potentially hostile forces of Spain (to whom had passed the Dutchy of Milan in 1555) and Turkey. The power of the former was soon brought to his notice in the coming negotiations with Milan and Cremona, and the menace of the latter was to involve him closely at Lepanto.[6]

But Brescia resembled Udine for Bollani in other respects. The first impression of a biographer who examines his legislation in that city is its similarity to his legislation in Friuli. In part, this was certainly explicable in terms of Venetian policy towards the *Terraferma*,[7] for the central government was not quite so negligent of the interests of its subjects as has sometimes been assumed.[8] But in part, also, it reflects the initiatives of the *Podestà*, who, in internal affairs at least, had a fair measure of independent power.

The functions of the *Podestà* were not dissimilar from those of the *Luogo-tenente* in Udine,[9] except that general responsibility was shared with the *Capitano* — a post amply justified by Brescia's strategic importance. Bollani was again to exercise a representative, legislative and judicial function, attempting at all times to reconcile the interests of the local population with those of his government. Like Udine, Brescia had had a record of unhappily chosen incumbents, and like Udine, their passage had been celebrated in traditional ways. In fact, shortly before Bollani's arrival, Brescia had requested that their rectors be chosen with more care — by *scrutinio* rather than by *sorteggio* in the Council.[10] We have seen that the success of such requests was likely to be affected by internal constitutional prerogatives in Venice itself, but its importance here resides in the fact that Domenico Bollani was carefully chosen for his qualifications and experience, not by lot (*sorteggio*) but by selection (*scrutinio*).

He was to have little time during which to initiate programmes of the kind begun at Udine — less than four months, in fact[11] — before he was deputed by Venice to arbitrate in the Oglio dispute, but even in that sort time, the records show a block of legislation designed, as before, to implement Venetian government policies for the *Terraferma* on the one hand, and to improve the internal conditions of a disordered province on the other.[12] Like Udine, Brescia was a prey to social disorders of every kind: rivalry between local aristocratic families led often to violence, vengeance and bloodshed,[13] against which Venetian and local measures were often powerless to act.[14] The struggle against the carrying of arms was as continuous in Brescia — a noted centre of their manufacture — as Bollani had found it in Udine.[15]

As before, the conditions of the province of Brescia must have impressed Bollani unfavourably on his arrival in June 1558. Three years (almost to the day) after his series of initial proclamations in Udine, he took similar stern steps at the beginning of his term of office to stem the tide of abuses and disorder in the everyday life of the city. In the fight against crime, he ordered restrictions on parties and dances, prohibition of the carrying of arms without licence, and sterner legislation against fights. Law suits were to be registered centrally, and doctors should declare wounds inflicted. In the interests of decorum, he followed the policy of his government with a law against ostentation in women's clothing, and, in an attempt to preserve the sanctity of religious life and institutions, he increased penalties for abuses of monasteries and for blasphemy.[16]

On April 27, 1557, Bollani's predecessor in Brescia, Domenico Gradenigo, had presented his relation in the Senate. Although a brief summary has survived in written form, Gradenigo did provide a concise statement of the problems that were to face his successor, Domenico Bollani a year later. The principal problems were first, 'gratificando a tutta la citta, sedar le discordie et ponervi pace' and secondly, 'satisfacendo al populo procurar di far condur entro la citta la solita sua limitatione di biave che sono somme 80m. all'anno'.[17]

Even if the documentation of Bollani's interest in measures to preserve the city's grain supplies is not as complete as for those at Udine,[18] there is no doubt that he had the matter well in hand. The problem was not as acute as at Udine – where the enforced export of foodstuffs to Venice was always liable to conflict with local needs in times of hardship[19] – but as Gradenigo had stated in 1557, the principal aims of the Venetian rector must be to encourage imports of grain from regions where it was more plentiful, and to prevent its export. Reserve stocks were held by the *Sacro Monte delle Biade* in Brescia from 1525, and by other charitable institutions,[20] but the preoccupation of Bollani in 1558 was to ensure adequate supplies within the city itself.

On June 6, his first published edict was against the export of grain, with penalties including loss of carts and animals for those contravening. He continued on June 8 with a measure to ensure that the correct amount was imported, and from this point, set out to reform the procedures for handling grain within the city. Orders for porters were issued on June 8, a renewed ban on exports on 22 June, and a measure to ensure adequate reserve stocks on 23 June.[21]

Thus the pattern that we have seen for Udine was again in action – but without the urgency that enforced exports and famine had occasioned there. With the gathering in of the harvest, Bollani was concerned to take every possible step to ensure adequate supplies for winter. Finally in August he published an edict setting out the position in clear and unequivocal terms – reminiscent, in some respects, of his legislation against private usury in Friuli. This proclamation (of which a fine printed copy survives in the archives), spoke out in strong terms against private speculative hoarding, against 'alcuni li quali contra il debito della carità, et contra la mente della Serenissima Signoria, et non senza grave danno de poveri, compravano biave per incanevar,'[22] and ordered that those who bought grain at attractive prices outside the city to lay in stocks for the winter should present a note of this to the 'cancelleria di sua Magnificentia'. This measure against speculation must have been difficult indeed to enforce, but its motivation is quite clear: Bollani was concerned first and foremost with the benefits to the whole community of judicious buying at harvest time, and was anxious that private speculation should not exclude the poor from these benefits. He had a direct experience of the hardships suffered by a similar community in times of famine, and was not to let slip this opportunity of ensuring adequate reserves in Brescia. Given the fact that the various beneficent lending institutions were well established and functioning at this time,[23] his insistence on this point through legislation reflects his experience.

Bollani had thus made a significant start in the provisions of his first four months in Brescia in an attempt to bring some order to the everyday life of the city, and to regulate the supply situation — much in the same way as he had begun in Udine. His administration of the city of Brescia was to be interrupted, however. By August, the long history of disputes between Brescia and Cremona over the uses of the river Oglio was about to erupt into crisis, with troop movements already causing alarm on both sides of the frontier river. It is to this dispute — an event of major importance in the career of Domenico Bollani — that we must now turn.

The importance of the dispute over the river Oglio and the deviation of part of its waters into the *Naviglio* (canal) *Cremonese* can hardly be overestimated. The solution finally obtained by Domenico Bollani and his co-arbitrator, Giovanni Anguissola in 1561 posited a definitive solution to a problem which had begun possibly as early as 1191, and was to endure through many vicissitudes down to the Treaty of Vaprio in 1755, which substantially confirmed its provisions. Domenico Bollani acted alone, relying on his experience and talents in negotiation and diplomacy, to find a solution to a problem that had already caused countless diplomatic incidents between Venice and the rulers of Milan in 350 years, and was to cause further disputes for a further 200 years. In a very real sense his achievement is removed in time from the vicissitudes of the era in which he lived, to stand alongside his enduring achievements in the diocese of Brescia. If the chronicle of events that follows at times seems excessively detailed, it should not be forgotten that the richness of surviving documentation itself bears witness to the importance of the dispute, and reflects the measure of his achievement.[24] Few of his measures in the diocese of Brescia have stood the test of time for so long, been so often quoted, and formed the basis and *sine qua non* of all future legislation. The importance of Bollani's participation in the first phase of the dispute in his election as bishop of Brescia will emerge from the next chapter.

Before examining the political background to the dispute, it may be wise to provide a brief description of the issues at stake. The *Naviglio Cremonese* was first dug in the fourteenth century and occupies substantially the same function in the life of the respective provinces to this day.[25] The river Oglio flows south from Lake Iseo in the foothills of the Alps, curving south-westwards to encircle the southern half of the province of Brescia, and providing the provincial boundary between Brescia, Bergamo and Cremona. In the sixteenth century it was the international frontier between the Republic of Venice and the Duchy of Milan (except for the brief French occupation of the western Venetian *Terraferma*). The *Naviglio Cremonese* has its mouth in the Oglio in its western bank slightly north of the town of Calcio, and is now overlooked by the main Brescia/Milan railway line which crosses the river at this point.[26] Two canals take water from the river at this point, the northern (major) *Naviglio Cremonese*, and the southern (minor) *Seriola* or *Roggia Antegnata*.

The river course bends naturally towards the province of Brescia, and provides irrigation for a host of minor tributary canals. The Naviglio flows from its mouth in the Oglio east and then south, crossing the province of Cremona to reach the city itself, and providing irrigation for the province via subsidiary canals, and (in

Domenico Bollani's day) driving mills. To divert the flow of water from its main bed into the canal, a spur, or *Predata* was built, jutting out into the stream. To divert water into the *Seriola Antegnate* from the *Naviglio* a smaller spur (or *Sperone*) was constructed, jutting similarly into the *Naviglio* (Figs. 15–17).

It will be seen that the volume of water diverted, and the volume remaining in the river (irrigating, respectively, Cremona and Brescia) were regulated by three main factors: the length of the *Predata*; the depth of the *Naviglio* at its mouth (depth levels are referred to as *Soglie*); and the size and number of the openings breached in the *Predata* to allow some of the water to return to the river. (These openings are called *Finestrelle*). It emerges therefore, that the measurements of these three elements — regarding the volume of water in both courses — were of crucial importance. An increase in the length of the *Predata* would divert more water into the *Naviglio*, leaving the Brescian fields high and dry. The destruction of the *Predata*, or blocking the canal, on the other hand, would divert water from the *Naviglio*, and thus from Cremonese fields and mills. Brescian ingenuity was to find a third expedient, diverting the whole river into a new course in 1558, which had substantially the same effect. This, in substance, was the problem that Domenico Bollani came nearest to solving in the long course of its history: to find an equable distribution of the water in the river that would meet the needs of farmers in both provinces.

The origins of the dispute in the middle ages are somewhat obscure[27] and all subsequent accounts of the history of the *Naviglio* have a decided and unambiguous bias.[28] The Brescian view was that the Cremonese had obtained a charter for the derivation of waters from the river from the Emperor Lodovico 'Il Bavaro' in 1329, but their rights were subsequently annulled by the Pope when he declared Lodovico an usurper of the Empire, and all his treaties null and void.[29] The Cremonese account omits this last detail, but states that the above concession was later confirmed by *Sigismondo* in 1411, and by Charles V in 1546.[30] Brescia on the other hand, fills in the gap in the above chronology with the confirmation of the annulment of Lodovico's acts in 1335, restoring Brescian rights over the river Oglio. But the writer notes that, by this time, the *Naviglio* had been built and that subsequent events forced Brescia to accept the existence of the *Naviglio* as a *fait accompli*, provided that it was not widened, deepened, or its dimensions otherwise altered.[31]

The first incident seems to have occurred in 1350, when Cremona widened the Canal (according to Brescian sources), drawing more water into it from the river, doubtless to meet the needs of a dry summer. The Brescian susceptibilities were at once offended (accounts do not specify whether the *real* issue — whether the river was capable of supporting both claims on its resources — was in any way affected). The Bresciani 'con mano armata distrussero le operazioni' and the resulting legal process was decided by the Archbishop Giovanni Visconti on 28 February, 1351 in favour of Brescia.[32] Cremona protested that this had taken place without their being involved in any way (perhaps not without justification in modern eyes): 'cio è fatto tra altri, a loro non pregiudica'.[33] Thus the dispute dragged on through periodic exchanges of hostilities, each city protesting its ancient rights: Brescia, to complete control over the course of the river, Cremona,

84

to extract water from it. It could hardly reach a definite solution because of the coincidence of variables at any point in time: first it was only in times of drought that the volume of water irrigating both provinces would depend on measurements at the mouth of the canal, and secondly, both Cremona and Brescia had changed hands between 1499 and 1520 (the former suffering occupations by French, Venetians and Spaniards) so that it was virtually impossible to evaluate the jurisdictional rights claimed and supported by ancient treaties. For agreement was never reached over the definition of a *status quo*, or point of departure. Finally, negotiation was so rarely in the hands of those directly involved (France for Milan for Cremona — and Venice for Brescia in our period), so that the economic and agricultural realities were frequently overlooked, being considered of secondary importance to factors of international prestige and diplomacy. When suspicion and distrust already existed between the negotiator and the community he represented, it was difficult indeed to arrive at a solution acceptable to all parties, and the discontent thus caused would build up in preparation for the next dry summer.[34] Finally it should be added that the primitive state of water engineering created walls and spurs ill-fitted to stand up to exceptional climatic conditions, and that the slightest minor repair carried out at the mouth of the *Naviglio* as a result of normal wear and tear would be regarded with infinite suspicion by the other side.

With the comparative calm of northern Italy after 1509, the state of affairs at the mouth of the canal speedily took the form and shape that Domenico Bollani was to find in 1558. The original *Penello* (or *Predata*) had been destroyed by Brescia in 1462, and Cremona took advantage of the sack of that city by the French to rebuild it in 1512. Venice regained Brescia in 1516, however, so that the city was now to gain the support of the Doge for her claims on the river Oglio. Cremona came under the rule of the Sforzas in 1525, (but with the Emperor in control, ultimately)[35] so that the affair of the division of the waters now became the preserve of princes — a bone of contention between the Empire and Spain, now invested with new strength, and the Republic of Venice, anxious to preserve the inviolability of her hard-won frontiers.[36]

The events of the sixteenth century show a gradually growing tension until the events of 1558 led to the deployment of armies on the banks of the river near the disputed *Naviglio*. While Brescia lacked effective support, remaining outside Venetian control, the *Predata* remained in the river, sending much of its water down the canal and out into Cremonese fields. When Venice regained Brescia, however, the city lost no time in restating its claims. The events of 1526 and 1529, when diplomatic exchanges took place between Milan and Venice,[37] were caused by a complex of events which now involved, additionally, Brescian ownership of Mills in the Province of Cremona.[38] So by 1530s and 1540s, there were two related but distinct questions impinging directly on the territorial susceptibilities of the Duchy of Milan and the Republic of Venice: the rights of Venetian subjects within Milanese territory, and the existence of the *Penello*, remade by Cremona while Brescia was under French domination.

It would seem that the first attempt at negotiations between Milan and Venice in an attempt to find a peaceable solution to these problems dates from 1533. As it is principally this form of negotiation — the nomination of a delegate by both sides to meet at the river and reach agreement — that was adopted in successives phases of the dispute, and because Domenico Bollani would have studied documents of this first negotiation in preparation for his mission, it is worth closer attention. The facts themselves are unimportant in the present context,[39] but the form of the negotiation and its failure throw some light on subsequent events.

Venice deputed Giovanni Bassadonna, then Venetian resident in Milan, and Milan elected Egidio Bosio, a member of the Milanese Senate, to meet at the River Oglio where the road from Brescia to Cremona crosses the river at Pontevico. 'Stettero per molti giorni l'uno a Rebecco con advocati cremonesi, e l'altro a Pontevico con advocati bresciani. Fu disputato assai insieme, ma alla fine si partirono re infecta.'[40] Even the start of negotiations was delayed by definition of the *status quo* — and this was to happen many times — as it had been the intention of Venice that things should be 'ridotti in pristino' before discussions could begin, and this had not been carried out.[41]

The correspondence of the *Deputati all'Oglio* from Pontevico to Brescia describes the discussions in full: demands were exchanged, heated arguments took place, the mills were inspected, but no concrete conclusions were reached.[42] Already a pattern was emerging in that balance of political and juridical elements that was to defeat better men than Bassadonna. First the *riduzione al pristino* (always the prerequisite of talks) caused some swallowing of Brescian pride, as, in the burning of the mills, the last card to be played had been theirs. Then followed the exchange of *sentenzie*, or statements of the respective positions, and much play with documents, treaties and contradictory concessions. Finally talks began, but were centred on the difficult question of constitutional ownership of the river: that is to say, an attempt was made to decide which city was *possessorio* and which *petitorio*.

Bassadonna pinpointed the difficulties of the negotiations in his *relazione* over the treaties and concessions produced by both sides: 'E cosi con repliche e tripliche si devene alle allegazioni, con le quali si vene in difficoltà se fossimo giudici legitimi delle sentenze allegate per bressani, non si havendo mandato nè dalla Illustrissima Signoria, nè dall'Illustrissimo Sig. duca di giudicar le cose giudicate, nè meter in controversia atti giudiciari, ovver assumerli a giudicio nostro.'[43] Bassadonna was understandably at a loss when confronted with this mass of mediaeval documentation, complaining that his function was not to judge decisions taken in the past, but to agree on a solution for the present, seeing it as a *political* rather than a legal function, and lamenting the fact that this seemed an affront to his commission and his authority: 'E tolendo rispetto ambi noi delegati, non avendo scritto nel processo la nostra opinione, ne considerato in alcuna parte *il caso principal, videlicet a chi aspettava la giurisdizione de Oglio*, (Italics mine) la causa si devolse sopra quest'articolo: se l'era conveniente che questo Illustrissimo Stato concedesse che 'l mandato nostro si estendesse alle giudicature e sentenze fatte.'[44] Clearly, much time had been wasted in discussion of the competence of the arbitrators to assess the documents produced, and the central issue, in Bassadonna's view — the total jurisdictional rights of the river — had hardly been touched on. At his stage, it seems that no compromise was possible: each side claimed judicial rights to the exclusion of the other, each side claimed to be the offended *possessorio* party, and that the status of the other should be that of the *petitorio*. It is therefore small wonder that the talks broke down at this point.[45]

From this single example, it can be seen how the attempt to adjudicate had produced the seeds that would germinate further disputes. In a return to the *status quo* Brescia was left with a slight advantage, and Cremona quite unsatisfied.[46] Either side would quickly take advantage of circumstances favourable to its own interests, and the state of deadlock is accurately reflected in the contemporary sources: the formulation of instructions, memoranda and reports of the situation was invariably preceded by an account of *le novità che hanno fatto i Bressani*, or *le novità che hanno fatto i Cremonesi*. From this immovable position, there was no effective departure until Domenico Bollani took the matter in hand.

By 1546, the theatre of action widened to include the governments of Milan and Venice themselves in a more direct way. The cause of this was certainly the procalmation of Charles V of February 6 of that year to the effect that the subjects of the Empire were forbidden to pay taxes, dues or pensions to any other prince than the Emperor himself, with particular reference to the mills in the lower sections of the river Oglio.[47] For Venice and Brescia, this constituted a frontal attack. If Brescia was *possessore* of the river and Cremona *petitore*, then dues paid to Brescia for the use of the waters were just (and, incidentally, had not before been challenged). If Brescia was not the legal owner of the river, then mills and other buildings on Imperial territory would come under Milanese, and therefore Imperial jurisdiction, with consequent taxation rights. Thus Venice and Brescia sent representatives to the Imperial court at Ratisbon in an attempt to obtain the annulment of this decree.[48] Predictably, little was accomplished. It was hardly to be expected that the Emperor would retract his proclamation, as Chizzola had hoped.

The influence of previous attempts at negotiation may be seen even in the preliminary exchange of correspondence between Don Alvaro de Luna, *Podestà* of Cremona, and Milan, as well as between Don Alvaro and the Imperial Ambassador in Venice. Already in June, Don Alvaro had tried to start negotiations in Venice by suggesting the appointment of judges, but had met resistance in the Venetian unwillingness to negotiate before the proclamation of Charles V had been revoked restoring thus the *status quo*. This fundamental objection apart, it seems that both sides shared the opinion that this would be the only way towards a just settlement at this point: 'non si potria in questa material dar ispediente megliore che mandare commissari sopra il luogo con auttorità de puoter conoscer et terminar tutte le differentie che vi sono, et retrattione ogni novità che si ritrovasse fatta.'[49] Milan had proposed the election of *commissari*, but Venice refused to consider this without the usual return to the *status quo*, and, bearing in mind that this was now the retraction of an Imperial proclamation, the dispute seemed further than ever from a solution. According to Venice, Brescia had been 'turbata et spogliata di quello *de fatto* (Italics mine)' and should be restored to its former position *vis-à-vis* the river as a fundamental prerequisite to the re-opening of negotiations ('la qual restitutione se guida desiderando noi de metter fine a tutte le discordie che sono fra tutte questi parti').[50]

The Milanese reasoning behind the suggestion was clear in a letter from Don Alvaro de Luna (*Podestà* of Cremona) to the Imperial Ambassador in Venice: 'Pretendendo una parte esser fatta innovatione et l'altra presentando esser fatta giuridicamente.'[51] Cremona admitted seeing the difficulties of principle involved, and invited the election of delegates. But it should not be forgotten that Don Alvaro was arguing from a position of strength. There would be no future in a political discussion between delegates if the central issue — the ownership of the river — had already been settled by Imperial decree. In essence these were the unenviable tasks facing the ambassadors at Ratisbon. The principle of deputing *commissari* had been agreed — it remained to define the basis from which their talks should begin.

The Ventian ambassadors Mocenigo and Contarini reported the proceedings to their government on July 8. Granvelle had kept them waiting until he received full reports of the dispute from Milan and Cremona, but made a gesture towards them by sending them the documents from Milan as soon as he received them. Having obtained audience, the ambassadors represented to Granvelle the importance of a return to the *status quo* — and the retraction of the proclamation — before delegates could meet. It was too easy, they said, for a people to obtain advantage by violence, then calling in elected judges to settle the dispute: 'de facto spoliatus, de facto restitui debeat'.[52] Granvelle replied that his information alleged innovations by the Brescians against the Cremonese, whereupon the ambassadors pointed out that their own statement alleged innovations by the Cremonese. The logical move, then, would be to elect judges to settle the question of what innovations had been committed and by whom, suggested Granvelle, but the Venetians here objected that this had been precisely the tactic of de Luna in his recent letter to Venice, and that Venice was little inclined to consider it. At this point, Chizzola for Brescia suggested that they should return home, and the talks broke down.

This was the position in July, 1546 — stalemate, with one issue left open: the question of the Emperor's proclamation, which the ambassadors had failed to have revoked. It only remained, therefore, for the establishment of complete deadlock and maximum discomfort for those whose lives were regulated by the waters of the river Oglio for Venice to issue the same proclamation forbidding the users of the waters to recognize any other ruler than Venice and Brescia — and this duly followed on August 7, 1546, within days of the ambassadors reaching Venice.[53] In addition, the *Podestà* of Brescia received instructions to proceed against subjects of Cremona who committed acts prejudicial to Venetian sovereignty over her territories.

This was the background to Domenico Bollani's involvement in the affair in 1558: a complete deadlock, with rival claims to ownership of the river, contradictory proclamations in force against the owners of mills in the river (who must have survived in a kind of stateless limbo for twelve years), and countless subsidiary problems awaiting solution of the main issue. The one point of agreement had been the decision to send delegates. It might have been thought that action would soon follow. Twelve years were to elapse, however, before further developments were to put the dispute in very urgent need of settlement, and at this point Domenico Bollani was elected to adjudicate. But before this the already tense relations between the Republic of Venice and the Duchy of Milan were to be worsened by new factors.

The original plan to cut a new canal in the Brescian bank of the river above Urago d'Oglio to rejoin it below the mouth of the *Naviglio* goes back to 1529, when the idea had been mooted as a reprisal for the rebuilding of the *Predata* by the Cremonese. It was re-introduced in 1546, the result of a secret decision in the Venetian Senate, as a counter-measure to the offensive Imperial proclamation of that year. The engineers' report of that time is preserved in the *Registrum Olei* and concludes that the new canal was certainly practicable, but it was not undertaken as it was felt that the Brescian bank would be left too exposed to attack thereby, and also because there were objections to its construction by Count Gaspare Martinengo, owner of the land near Urago in which it was projected.[54]

The event which precipitated a start in the excavation of this new canal was the decision by Cremona to widen and deepen the *Naviglio* at its mouth. It is almost impossible to know the truth of this incident, as the description of a Cremonese writer represents it as normal running repairs due to wear and tear ('perche in vero essa bocca per un gran tempo era quasi derelitta'),[55] but, predictably, it was a red rag to Brescia. The *Deputati* at once informed the Brescian orators in Venice and a Ducal letter dated 22 March authorised a start to work on the new excavation. By April, 400 workmen were at work on the construction.[56]

The reaction of Cremona was immediate, as was to be expected. Once the new canal was open it would divert the river into a course which would by-pass the *Naviglio* and would leave Cremona without water supplies. Not only would irrigation suffer, but also the moat round the castle would be left dry and there would be little water in the city itself.[57] Letters couched in the strongest terms went to Milan and Venice, and a Cremonese emissary was dispatched to Brescia to treat with the Venetian Rectors and the *Deputati all'Oglio*, obtaining little satisfaction.[58] Violence was the inevitable result. An armed party of Cremonese crossed the river at Urago and forced the Brescian engineers to fill in the excavation. In reprisal, a superior force from Brescia virtually destroyed the mouth of the *Naviglio*, filling it with rocks and stones, and re-opened the mouth of the new canal, allowing water to enter it for the first time 'et facendo caminar barche.'[59]

The sequel to this aggressive move is well known and recounted with evident relish by Brescian historians:[60] there was an immediate build-up of troops on either bank of the river, the establishment of two forts facing the mouth of the *Naviglio*, and the creation of a bridgehead on the Bergamask bank where the town of Calcio now stands. A special levy to meet the expenses of this force was ordered by the city council on May 7,[61] and Brescian canals were breached to swell the river to dimensions that would make fording by the Cremonese hazardous.[62] The inevitable skirmishes took place before the gravity of the situation was brought to the attention of the respective governments.

Venice ordered the removal of the temporary bridge that had been thrown across the river, the withdrawal of troops to Venetian territory, and sent Sforza

Pallavicino with an armed force to the scene to ensure that these instructions were carried out. The Brescians also received orders to hold the east bank, not to provoke action and to reduce the number of forces encamped near Urago. For the Republic was extremely reluctant to allow the situation to develop into a border war.

It was at this point, in May, 1558, that the decision to elect adjudicators — a method already tried in the past — and one that had been mooted and agreed in principle in 1546, finally became reality. Domenico Bollani was elected to represent Venice in the Senate shortly after his election as *Podestà* of Brescia, but before he had left to take up his new post,[63] on May 13, 1558. He was about to undertake the most difficult and important commission of his career. After countless incidents of a minor nature on the banks of the river Oglio and at the mouth of the *Naviglio*, the affair had been the weary subject of endless correspondence, proclamation and counter-proclamation, and finally had brought Brescia and Cremona, subject provinces of Venice and Milan, to the brink of war. Domenico's commission, in which he was to 'decider, et terminar per giustitia le difficulta et controversie . . . la terminatione d'i quali debba esser dall'una parte et l'altra inviolabilmente eseguita,' reflects the urgency and gravity of the situation. Count Giovanni Anguissola, Milanese Senator, was elected to represent Milan and Cremona on August 10, 1558.[64] (Fig. 18)

It is now appropriate to examine Bollani's participation in the dispute between 1558 and 1561, to see how his experience in diplomacy and his natural talents were employed. It is also an episode in the history of Venice and Milan which has never been fully told.[65]

Initial movements took the form so often seen before in the history of the dispute: definition of the *status quo*, and arguments over the areas of competence of the delegates. For talks to begin, Brescia was to rebuild the *predata* to its former specification which they had destroyed in the summer offensive, and was not to allow the waters to flow into the new canal. Bollani wrote to Venice on 11 July anticipating the difficulties ahead.[66] Anguissola had sent a messenger to Brescia to arrange the date for the delegates to meet, and had expressed the Milanese commission in rather one-sided terms. This messenger had spoken of the insolence of the Brescians and Anguissola's commission to settle the grievances, whereas, as Bollani reminded him, it would be prejudicial to the outcome to prejudge the issue, and he noted that his commission was also rather restricting. He recommended to Venice that the commission should be similar — so as to allow maximum freedom for the delegates. This was clearly arranged, for the first meeting was arranged for 12 September, but there was still doubt in his mind about the possibility of a successful agreement on September 7.[67]

As it turned out these fears were justified. Bollani rode out to Urago d'Oglio on September 12, where he was the guest of Count Giulio Martinengo in the Castle,[68] to meet Anguissola and to hear the representations of the offended parties. As in the past, talks were still hindered by considerations of principle, claims to dominion *de jure* over the river, and much production of previous adjudications and mediaeval treaties. Bollani attempted to propose an equable solution — a *political* agreement for the present — in a reduction of the *Naviglio* and its *predata* to their former dimensions, and guarantees that Brescia would not divert the water into their new canal. The Cremonese objected to this on grounds of principle, producing proof positive of their rights to exclusive use of the river, for Bollani 'sue vane pretensioni di assoluto dominio nel fiume Oglio'.[69] It is clear that neither side had yet grown out of the by now classic struggle for dominion *de jure* of the river. Perhaps it was for reasons of political expediency that Bollani himself took this stand in his report to Venice of the talks. For he wrote that 'dalle lunghe allegationi[70] fatte per una parte et l'altra,[71] innanzi a noi delegati, ho chiaramente conosciuto che Cremonesi non hanno alcuna, ne anco apparente, raggione ne fiume Oglio, et la citta di Brescia ne ha raggioni chiarissime per titoli, per giudicature, et per possesso continuo.'[72] So the old clichés were abroad at the meeting — a currency of treaties and legalistic reasoning for absolute control of the river.

But there was much at stake in this question of principle. The questions of taxation rights on merchandise travelling by river, and the possibility of a widened *Naviglio* creating a navigable waterway down to Cremona, with consequent threat to Brescian security and trade, were only two of the considerations in the minds of the negotiators. If a final *political* solution was to be possible, then it was perhaps important not to lose the battle for *possessore* rather than *petitore* status. While one side proposed this question, diplomatic decorum required that the other should resist. But the very introduction of this vexed question — as Bassadonna had found in 1533 — precluded discussion of the real issue: the regulation of the waters by measurement. If one looks ahead — at the history of the use of the river down to 1960 — it is interesting to note that this question was never decided.[73]

After 12 days of talks Bollani left Urago for Brescia and Anguissola returned to Milan with no conclusion reached. Bollani was careful to leave the situation open, however, suggesting tactfully that perhaps the terms of reference of the Cremonese agents had been too restrictive, and that this was the only reason that agreement had not been reached. 'Ho anco voluto, nel partire dall'abboccamento mostrare con Cremonesi ogni amorevolezza.'[74] and he was ready at any time to re-open negotiations.

If negotiations had been temporarily broken off, much was going on behind the scenes. Venice had recently appointed a Tiepolo to the embassy at the court of Philip II of Spain (who was, after 1559, also Duke of Milan) and it was natural that he should be fully informed of any matters in dispute between the two governments. Thus, Giacomo Chizzola had been commissioned to write a statement of the Brescian position in the Oglio dispute,[75] which, together with a design of the mouth of the *Naviglio Cremonese* and a copy of Bollani's letter of 25 September reporting on the talks, was to be among the new ambassador's equipment for his journey to Spain. The Brescian orator in Venice, Calini, duly reported that this material had been delivered and acknowledged by Tiepolo.[76] In Brescia, Bollani was dealing with minor incidents,[77] and had returned to the everyday administration of the city which was to occupy the winter. For the moment, the river flowed undisturbed, and it would be spring before the irrigation of the crops in the provinces of Brescia and Cremona brought the matter again to the fore.

The next phase of the talks took place in April, 1559, after the peace of Cateau-Cambrésis, and Domenico Bollani had become bishop of Brescia.[78] He wrote to the Doge on April 3, 1559, reminding him of his commission to settle the Oglio dispute still outstanding, especially as with the dry weather, the crops in the province of Cremona were suffering from lack of water. In order, perhaps, to forestall the spring 'offensive', he arranged to meet Anguissola again at Urago for further talks. Bollani rode out to the river on April 4, and after mass at Urago, met Anguissola for preliminary discussions.

On the second day, long discussions took place at the mouth of the *Naviglio* with the respective engineers, Battista Masino de Pontevico for Brescia, and Zaniboni de Acquanegra de Mantova for Cremona, and this was followed by talks between the two delegates until 1 a.m. The whole party returned again to the river on April 6, when signs of genuine progress began to appear. The engineers took exact measurements of the widthe of the river,[79] the length of the *predata*, and the terms of the agreement were thrashed out and written down on the spot. The talks were protracted until 3 a.m. 'restando in conclusione della maggior parte delle difficoltà'.[80] April 7 saw the finishing touches to the document — made in the presence of both parties — which was then witnessed by Counts Alvise Martinengo, Curtio Martinengo and Gio. Antonio Rodengo, and copies taken by Faita for Brescia and Zanibon for Cremona.

Bollani himself described the negotiations in his report to the *Signoria*, noting that the agreement was based on a written document copies of which were held by both sides, but which would not be drawn up in legal form.[81] The success of his negotiation had produced two tangible advantages. First, an attempt had been made to divide the waters of the river according to systematic criteria so that they might serve the irrigation needs of both provinces, and second, the precise definition of the amount of water the Cremonese were to extract from the river was tantamount to a recognition of ultimate Brescian dominion over it.[82] Bollani reinforced this point in his letter to Venice of 29 April. The Cremonese had wanted a specific declaration that the Brescian diversionary canal would not be used — a limitation, in fact, of Brescian dominion over the river — but the agreement had been concluded without this clause, to Bollani's infinite satisfaction.[83] Meanwhile Rodengo had been sent from Brescia to compare the Brescian copy of the agreement with the Milanese one, to certify this, and also, it seems, to convey gifts to Anguissola.[84]

The agreement had been signed, and peace between the provinces was to be hoped for, but it did not seem that the Bishop of Brescia was to have more time to devote to his diocese. For it remained to put the agreement into practice, as it had been argued that no new work should be carried out in the river without supervision and approval of the other side. The Cremonese had begun work on the cleaning of the mouth of their canal almost as soon as the talks were over, and there were at once protests from Brescia that the terms of the agreement were being exceeded. Anguissola assured Bollani that this had taken place not from a wish to evade the conditions, but from mistaken interpretation of them.[85] Bollani pressed his advantage adding that the Cremonese had also fortified the *predata* against the terms of the agreement and without Brescian supervision. His method of negotiation here was subtle and expert: having won the friendship and esteem of Anguissola, he now proceeded to represent every innovation by Cremona as an affront to an agreement privately concluded — and therefore, a slight on the personal honour of them both. Bollani's letters to Anguissola of 26 and 29 April are an eloquent demonstration of this method.[86] Honour was soon satisfied when Anguissola promised that all future work would be supervised by a Brescian engineer, but the episode has one curious postscript. It seems that Brescia (with Bollani's connivance) was operating in secret in at least one respect, perhaps deepening the river opposite the *Naviglio*, or merely taking measurements of Cremonese constructions in the river, as an exchange of letters between Bollani and Faita can only be understood in this respect. Perhaps the man concerned was only an observer. Whatever the truth, the event casts a somewhat sinister light on the above expressions of good faith.[87]

In the end, the constructions in the river were reduced to the size specified by the agreement, as the correspondence of Bollani and Anguissola for May, 1559 shows,[88] and Bollani was able finally to report to the *Signoria* that the terms of the agreement had been carried out in full.[89] There were, however, longer term projects specified in the agreements, and work was far from complete. The *Predata* was not finished by October, as Anguissola informed Bollani of this on 8 October, citing certain difficulties over its construction.[90] Bollani replied that the engineers should meet at the mouth of the canal during the following week to settle the problem.[91] At this point, the correspondence ceases so that it may safely be assumed that the work was carried out to the satisfaction of both parties.

Thus at the end of the first delegation, much ground had been covered. Not only had agreement been reached — as never before — in an equable division of the resources of the river, but experience had been gained in carrying out its terms, with each side understandably cautious to preserve its own concessions, and almost continuous resort to the elected deputies. This was not the end of the matter, and there were various difficulties still to be resolved in the events which led up to the second and definitive delegation of July, 1561, two years later.

The preservation of documents relating to the dispute makes it clear that, in the successive phases of the controversy, it was the aggravated party whose political activity behind the scenes was the more energetic. Bollani's own collection of letters omits almost entirely the year 1560, and Brescia's *Registrum Olei* also has little material for this period, indicating that, for Brescia at least, satisfaction had been obtained and calm achieved. Before events precipitated the further crisis that was to bring Bollani back to the Castle at Urago from the Council of Trent, the scene switches to Cremona, where there was much diplomatic activity afther the 1559 agreement.

It seems fair to add that Brescia had had the best of the dispute so far: Bollani had convinced Anguissola of the justice of the agreement for Cremona and Brescia, and gained for Brescia the recognition of an implicit dominion over the river. He had written himself that, had he allowed the introduction of a clause limiting Brescian use of the diversionary canal, then Cremonese demands would have been incessant. But the point is a fine one. For by an agreement which contained the specific right to extract water by the Cremonese, he had admitted a not insignificant limitation of this dominion. For the story of Domenico Bollani, the point is worth making in the context of his tenacious *Venezianità* — a concept of the *Ragion di Stato* operating in the minor sphere of Brescia — which drove him to dogged support for Brescian causes, and even to duplicity. A persistent note in his correspondence at this time with the Count Anguissola is a species of aristocratic disdain for the problems of the two provinces. To Anguissola, he was the friend and ally in the cause of internal peace, and to Brescia, he was, both now and later (in his own words) 'bono et schietto bresciano'. For Venice he was always the devoted servant, giving equal weight (in a controversy which concerned Venice and Spain) to local needs in irrigation, and the frontier-conscious susceptibilities of the Republic. In these terms can be seen his diplomatic skill in this first phase: a dignity and adaptability to situation that was to win the admiration of Anguissola and even the Cremonese negotiators. But for the history of the river, the significant landmark had been the division of the waters, symbolised by the official and legal existence of the *Predata* jutting out into the main course of the river.

During the winter of 1599–1560, there was much diplomatic activity at Cremona, and it seems more than coincidence (bearing in mind Bollani's secret pact with a group of individuals from Urago) that she was complaining that the river had been significantly deepened towards the Brescia bank early in 1560, so that 'quasi il corrente dell'acqua e drizato a quella banda'.[92] At that time, Cremona had instructed Paolo Fossa, her agent in Milan, to represent various matters to the Milanese Senate on behalf of the *Deputati al Naviglio*,[93] and the intention to replace two stakes in the river, and to lengthen the *Predata* was clearly stated in February. Cremona wrote that he would be advised of the date fixed to meet the Brescian Engineers to settle these matters, but the deepening of the river was to be represented to Anguissola in the strongest terms.[94] Anguissola agreed to take the matter up with Bollani, and suggested that a house be built near the mouth of the canal so that these innovations should not go unobserved.[95]

Whether Anguissola mentioned the complaint to Bollani is not known, but his letter to him of March 23 refers to the repairs to the two stakes, the laying of the *soglie*, and the arrangements for a Brescian engineer to supervise this work in the spring.[96] Bollani replied in a friendly and confidential tone on April 1, fixing the date for completion of work to fulfil the terms of the 1559 agreement.[97]

Meanwhile Cremona had been active in quite a different direction. Having last gained the initiative at the time of Charles V's proclamation in 1546, it was natural to suppose that the same should be attempted with Philip II, now Duke of Milan. The request for an official licence to extract water from the river for the *Naviglio*, 'confirmate ultimamente per li felice memoria del Ser.mo Imperatore Carlo V padre di V.M.' exists in draft from among the papers of the Deputati, and emphasised with understandable cunning, the territorial considerations involved. The request was couched in the form of a demand for a licence to open a new canal in the region of Soncino, but the clause referring to the Brescians makes its general intention only too clear: an attempt to obtain a further Royal proclamation for use against Brescian pretensions to dominion over the river.[98] It was unlikely, however, that Philip II would make the same strategical error as his father in 1546, and the reply in August came in the form of a request for more information.[99]

During the spring of 1560, Cremonese agents continued to apply pressure to the Milanese Senate and to Anguissola in an attempt to convert Bollani to a point of view acceptable to them.[100] The *Deputati* proposed to take measurements for laying the *soglie* from the gate of the canal, and, anticipating Brescian objections, hoped that Anguissola 'con la sua solita destrezza operarà ch'l detto R.mo sij conforme a tal opinione' and 'con sue lettere operarà d'produrre il sudetto R.mo a favor nostro'.[101] In August, it was reported from Toledo that Anguissola was in agreement with the interpretation put on the agreement by the *Deputati al Naviglio*, and that he was to write to Bollani to convince him of its justice.[102]

According to the pattern, by now familiar, diplomatic activity ceased with the passing of the urgent need for water and the arrival of the autumn rains. Possibly agreement over the interpretation of the agreement for the laying of the *soglie* was reached. This is unlikely, however, as the subject was on the agenda for the first commission in the early summer of 1561. Certainly, there remained at least two problems unsolved at this time: the Cremonese complaint that Brescia had deepened the river bed, and their intention to lengthen the *Predata*, thus drawing more water into their *Naviglio*. The formation of a crisis situation in the spring of 1561 was swift and dangerous — fruit of the experience both sides had gained since the 1530s of reprisal, adjudication, appeals to higher authority and unilateral action.

With the return of fine weather, routine work continued on the canal as the Cremonese agent Nicoli reported on April 3, 1561, under the suspicious eyes of the Brescians.[103] He commented prophetically that 'li Bressani credo vorriano atrovar qualche cosa di dolersi di noi e spesso vengono a guardar la boccha del nostro Naviglio e veddeno che quella poca acqua che e nel Oglio vene nella nostra boccha.'[104] But the Brescian observers who had visited him early in April had clearly been called by Andrea Prandi, that tireless worker in the interests of Brescian security,[105] as he had reported 100 workmen engaged in construction work in the mouth of the *Naviglio* 'et ancho come rompeno lo muro vecchio che è dinanci alle soglie verso Oglio qual cosa mi pare cosa non dovrebbeno far, a danno e pregiudicio grande del Bresciano.'[106] Events moved with great speed on this occasion, as it appeared that the Cremonese had lengthened and strengthened their *Predata* unilaterally ('una predata si longa, larga, soda et ben inlottata, che gioza alcuna de acqua non andasce per il fiume Oglio' wrote the *Deputati all'Oglio* to Bollani in June.)[107] By May 20, Calini had already received instructions to bring the matter before the *Collegio* in Venice, and the Rectors of Brescia had written to their government.[108] The attitude of the *Savi* and the Doge to the dispute at this point is admirably documented by Calini's report on his conversation with them — a letter all the more fascinating as not designed for the eyes of posterity, and even less for the Venetian Rectors of Brescia.[109]

The letter provides an eloquent document on the Venetian attitude to the whole dispute, particularly to this final phase, and, by implication, to relations with Spain, and deserves closer attention. The news of the latest developments in the river had reached Venice through the Rectors of Brescia, Paolo Corner and

Sebastian Venier, and their letters had been read in the Senate, but without a resolution. Calini had been called for interview in the *Collegio*,[110] in case he should wish to add to this report, and put a strong case for armed intervention to the assembled *Savi*. The reluctance of the government to support the use of force is transparent, and Calini was offered a variety of different suggestions by the senators who were by no means unanimous in their view, and argued among themselves.[111] The future Doge, Nicolò da Ponte, suggested sending a secretary to Milan to negotiate for a return to the *status quo*, but Calini objected that this would bring the inevitable delay associated with the gathering of information by the Governor of Milan, the Marquis of Pescara, (and this had been precisely Cremona's difficulty in their representations to the Court of Spain).[112] The *Collegio* remembered only too well the *impasse* of 1546, when conflicting Venetian and Imperial proclamations had been in force, and was anxious to avoid a repetitions of this situation. Brescia should try to see things 'amorevolmente'. Pietro Morosini now suggested informing the Venetian secretary in Milan (Antonio Mazza), but Domenico Moro objected that this course would bring similar timewasting disadvantages.

The result was that no resolution was to be taken. Brescia was deemed prudent enough to handle the affair alone, and no instructions were to go to the Venetian Rectors in Brescia. It was felt that Domenico Bollani, now immersed in the affairs of the Council of Trent, might again advise, and Calini proposed that the Venetian Rectors in Brescia be instructed accordingly. But again any kind of direct intervention was condemned, and it was felt that as 'padre spirituale' of Brescia, he would naturally have the best interests of the city at heart without need of further instruction. The attitude of the Venetian government is clear from the discussion. Venice could not be seen publicly to support Brescian use of force against the Cremonese 'innovation', but must have known that it would be the inevitable result.[113]

The *Savi* had been accurate in their judgement of Domenico Bollani. When Brescia wrote to him on June 4, 1561, the city had already resolved to 'fargli quella debita provisione che si conveniva e si come questa città ha sempre fatto . . .'[114] Bollani replied in terms which clarify this intention and leave no doubts as to his solidarity with Brescian interests: 'havendo loro operato di fatto contra la capitulatione {the lengthening of the *predata*} . . . Habbino le Signorie Vostre volutto per li medesimi termini provveder alla indennità.'[115] For events were moving exactly as before. Reprisal on both sides, in the interests of preservation of the *status quo*, or 'balance of power' in the river, ended in force, and the Brescians destroyed the *Predata* filling the mouth of the *Naviglio* with the débris.[116]

Cremona naturally protested at once to the governor of Milan and to Anguissola, and one of their *deputati* was dispatched to Milan to help Fossa argue the case. There was talk of utilising Spanish troops in the enterprise, as Cremona (remembering 1558) noted bitterly that 'se noi gli andaremo con ducento soldati li adversarij gli venirano con mille perchè sono ricchi.'[117] Venice, meanwhile, had not informed their secretary Mazza in Milan, as Calini had been told they would not, so that his reaction was one of surprise when called for interview by the

Marquis of Pescara, governor of Milan. Mazza wrote to the Doge arguing from his knowledge of the dispute that Brescian action *de facto* must have followed unilateral action on the part of the Cremonese, reporting this conversation on June, 14, and enclosing a copy of Nicoli's report on the damage.[118] He was obviously keenly aware of the established pattern of reprisal, as he wrote again to confirm that there were no troop movements near Milan that could be connected with a possible Cremonese intervention of a military nature.[119] Meanwhile Calini had had a further disturbing interview with the Doge and College in Venice. The government showed evident concern at the turn events were taking, as Pietro Morosini and Andrea Barbarigo, *Savi grandi*, stated that Brescia should have destroyed only that part of the *Predata* which exceeded the terms of the established agreement.[120]

At last Venice was forced out of her pose of anonymity to act, having received information from Mazza in Milan, the official Cremonese complaint and the account from the Rectors of Brescia.[121] She wrote to Mazza suggesting the appointment of the traditional adjudicators to decide what innovations had been perpetrated, so that these might be restored to their former state at the expense of the perpetrators.[122] Thus the dispute had reached its traditional conclusion: Milan elected Don Emmanuel de Luna, Governor of Cremona and Venice elected Sebastiano Venier, Captain of Brescia, to represent the respective factions.[123]

Detailed reports of the negotiations were sent to Brescia, Cremona and Venice — negotiations which, as inconclusive, need only brief summary here.[124] Given the terms of reference, it was unlikely indeed that a conclusive agreement would be reached, and the talks were soon to give way to the return of the original adjudicators: Giovanni Anguissola and Domenico Bollani. Brescia accused Cremona of having strengthened, lengthened, widened and moved their *predata* nearer to the Brescian bank, and also of unilateral alterations to walls and levels in the mouth of the *Naviglio*. They produced as witnesses the owners of lands in the southern part of the province who testified that they had discovered the dimension of the spur altered after noting a diminution in the amount of water reaching their crops. Brescia further alleged that work had been carried out in the river without reference to their officials — in violation of the agreement. Cremona denied any alteration in the dimensions, as well they might with the evidence destroyed, and denounced Brescian intervention. Brescia then objected that 'innovations' could not be charged to the legal owners and possessors of the river, while Cremona noted that their legal right to extract water was in direct contradiction of this. Once again, negotiations descended into the morass of jurisdictional rights, provincial pride and legalistic argument. Cremona naturally demanded that the *Predata* be rebuilt at Brescian expense, hoping that the work would start at once (as little water was reaching their crops), while Venier adhered firmly to the Brescian view that *de facto* intervention had been the logical reply to Cremonese 'innovations'. In short, discussions — needlessly protracted yet again by the production of the whole apparatus of mediaeval charters — continued for three days in this vein. The question of precedence became all important. Venier objected for Brescia that the *soglie* stipulated in the agreement had not been laid, and a tedious dispute ensued over whether Brescia should rebuild the *predata* first (of benefit to Cremona) or whether the *soglie* (limiting the water in the canal, and therefore of benefit to Brescia) could be commenced first. The Cremonese were unlikely to agree to this in high summer, as the canal gate would have to be closed for work to begin, with consequent lack of water in the province of Cremona. There was also the further unsolved problem of the measurements of the *soglie*. Almost no new ground was covered; the arguments were those of 1558 and 1559; and the adjudicators parted without agreement having been reached.

In fact, Sebastian Venier was to shine in quite another field[125] and doubtless lacked Bollani's tact and subtlety.[126] Emmanuel de Luna had resorted to tactics which left him open to charges of deception.[127] Both were content to stand on their dignity, and left the river without reaching a conclusion. The stumbling block for Brescia had been the Cremonese suggestion that a clause limiting Brescian interference with the *Naviglio Cremonese* should be written into the agreement, as Venice noted with displeasure in her dispatch to Mazza in Milan.[128] This was in direct conflict with Brescia's concept of her rights in the river Oglio. So in mid-July the situation had regressed considerably. Far from any admission of the possibility that the waters might serve both provinces in an equable division, the negotiations had foundered on broad questions of legal principle.

It was clear at the end of the talks that serious problems stood in the way of the complete fulfilment of the 1559 agreement and that the situation was dangerous. As things stood, no water was reaching the Cremonese fields, and direct action must have been a matter of hours away. The logical move was to consult the original arbitrators, and within two weeks the complex diplomatic machinery necessary to extricate Bollani and Anguissola from their present occupations had accomplished this end.

Domenico Bollani at the Council of Trent had been kept fully informed of developments near the river,[129] and was now sent copies of the correspondence and reports of the unsuccessful negotiations.[130] Anguissola had written to him with his views on the placing of the *soglie* in the mouth of the canal, as this had been requested by the recent delegates.[131] Meanwhile, the Brescian orator Lanterio Appiano had made an important speech to the *Pien Collegio* in Venice, making much of the reflected prestige attached to Venetian support for Brescian pretensions to ownership of the river, and Venice decided to write to the Marquis of Pescara, Governor of Milan, and Philip II, proposing that the affair be adjudicated by the original delegates.[132] Hoping as always for Bollani's support and encouragement, the *Deputati* had dispatched Vincenzo Stella, one of their number to Trent to relate the latest development. Bollani replied that 'non mancarò mai di porgere quell'aiuto maggiore in questo importantissimo negotio.'[133] By the beginning of August, Venice had obtained permission for Bollani to return to Urago from Pope Pius IV, as well as from the delegates at the Council.[134]

But before Bollani arrived in Brescia there were further complications. With undeniable justice and in the interests of an equable settlement, the Venetian Senate had passed a motion on August 2 ordering Brescia to rebuild the *Predata* provided that Cremona remade the damaged wall at the mouth of the canal. Possibly the senators had not fully appreciated the situation. In any event, this move aroused a storm of protest in Brescia, as it was felt that a return to the *status quo* should have included the fulfilment of the agreement — and this would include the laying of the *soglie*, inconceivable, as we have seen, in the hot summer months. In an attempt to have this decision reversed, the Brescian orators in Venice went to the lengths of calling on Nicolò da Ponte and the Doge at their homes.[135] They argued that the *predata* should not be rebuilt before Bollani's arrival as this action (unbalanced by a Cremonese initiative) would destroy the balance of initiative in the river to Cremonese advantage. They were unable to obtain such a decision, however.

So even the hour of Bollani's arrival assumed crucial importance. The order for the rebuilding of the *predata* had been in force for two days when he reached Volargne, as he wrote from there on August 4.[136] In Cremona, the significance of this battle of wits had not been lost on the *Deputati al Naviglio*, nor on their agent in Milan, Paolo Fossa. His correspondence of 31 July shows the urgency of the situation that had provoked the motion in the Venetian Senate. Antonio Mazza, Venetian Secretary, had informed the Milanese Senate that Bollani would be in Brescia within three days, as the Senate had resolved to rebuild the *predata* before his arrival, and a heated argument had taken place.[137] Apparently the Venetian decision to rebuild the spur had come just in time to prevent Cremonese intervention. Not in time, however, to prevent the use of that well-tried diplomatic weapon, the proclamation. This move was almost poetic in its timing, though news of it did not reach Venice until August 9. On August 1, the senators of Milan and Cremona published a proclamation ordering all Brescian subjects with holdings in the province of Cremona to declare these at the appropriate office in Cremona. The expected retaliatory proclamation came by return of post, when the Signoria informed the rectors of Brescia of the form their proclamation should take.[138] Meanwhile Brescia had remade the *predata*, bowing to the inevitable, according to the terms of the original agreement, as the engineer who had been present on both occasions certified.[139]

Domenico Bollani was not slow to take up the threads of the dispute — even before reaching Brescia — but felt that the Senate motion ordering the rebuilding of the *predata* had left him at a certain disadvantage.[140] For, in that subtle balance of initiatives that had always characterised the dispute, a similar gesture had not been forthcoming from Milan. The Venetian motion was the cause of considerable delay in the start of negotiations, as having obtained this concession, Cremona was determined to start the talks with this advantage, and pressed Anguissola not to leave Milan before the *predata* was finished, using a variety of excuses.[141] To Bollani's query, Venice replied that she was prepared to allow the *predata* to be rebuilt first, provided that the regulation of the walls and *soglie* followed.[142] As we have seen, however, the reconstruction of the spur was an urgent matter of priority for Cremona, and the rumours of Cremonese intervention that had prompted the motion may not have been entirely unfounded. So Bollani was forced to wait impatiently in Brescia for Anguissola to agree to meet him, referring to the Doge, in the meanwhile, reports of the intense political activity in Milan.[143] Finally, the elected delegates met at Urago d'Oglio on August 25, 1561, for the negotiations that were to prove conclusive.

It is not overstating the case to attribute the success of these talks to Domenico

Bollani's diplomatic ability. He had to work hard to overcome the by now traditional objections of provincial pride, excessive punctiliousness and legalistic reasoning, adopting new methods to arrive at a settlement. His accounts of conversations with Anguissola have an almost modern ring. They illustrate a battle between reasonableness and adaptability — and that obstinate adherence to abstract principle that had dogged the progress of the dispute since the fourteenth century. The result was also the triumph of intelligence and experience. No-one more than Bollani knew the infinite variety of suggestions possible, the importance of the river for the agricultural well-being of the respective provinces, and the importance of the various constructions in the river bed. For he had been an almost continuous participant since the spring of 1558.

He first wrote to the Signoria on the evening of the first day's talks — a day which had seen an energetic survey of all the issues, and particularly the order in which the remaining work should be carried out (the *Predata*[144] and the *soglie* in particular). Bollani defined his aims in this letter: to sweep aside the whole paraphernalia of previous acts, reprisals and indemnities, to found a new agreement in a new spirit of co-operation: 'La mira principale di chi tratta li accordi et le paci dovette esser di fondarle sopra amorevolezza et confidenze, et non sopra amaritudine de puntigli, che le facevano poi poco stabili.'[145] In this spirit, Bollani suggested that the work might be carried out at the same time,[146] but Anguissola, clearly acting on instructions from Cremona, proposed a new regulation of the mouth of the canal which would have had the effect of draining most of the water from the river.[147] Bollani then parried this thrust with a series of compromise suggestions to Anguissola, who, limited by instructions received from the Governor of Milan, did not feel able to accept them. At his point, Bollani tried a far subtler gambit, representing to the count that the agreement was a question of honour for them both, and that to leave without an agreement would reflect seriously on them both. He further suggested that copies of his suggestions should be sent to the Governor of Milan to see whether he felt able to accept them.

For this was an essential part of Bollani's method of negotiation. He believed implicitly in the justice of the Brescian cause, and in his proposals, and was prepared to attempt any method — diplomatic or psychological — to reach an agreement. Having won the personal esteem of Anguissola, he was able to convince him of his point of view as an individual, forcing him to blame others for the stringency of his terms of reference. As we shall see, it was the reduction of the affair to a *personal* level that enabled him to reach agreement in the end. Anguissola agreed to dispatch the proposals to the Marquis in Milan, but Bollani remained pessimistic about the outcome.[148] The reply came much as expected: either the 1559 agreement was to be executed according to the Cremonese interpretation of it, or a new agreement must be concluded.[149]

At this point, deadlock seemed inevitable, and there seemed little to be gained in protracting talks. But Bollani now branched out in another direction, playing, as before, on the mutual respect and esteem between the two delegates. He began by stressing again the element of personal honour involved in the dispute, and then suggested that he and Anguissola, assisted only by the respective engineers, might visit the site and reach a personal agreement — between two individual

100

consciences — unhindered by the ministrations of the interested parties. His plan, therefore, was to convince Anguissola personally of the justice of his argument, and having convinced him, enlist his support for the defeat of the Milanese and Cremonese factions. Anguissola lamented that already the Cremonese were complaining that his loyalty to their cause was suspect, 'et essi dicono che la moglie che io ho Bresciana,[150] et l'amicitia vostra meco mi fanno poco galgliardo in sua difesa.'[151] But here Bollani played a master card. He replied that the Cremonese had also accused him of partiality towards the Brescians by virtue of a small canal which irrigated lands belonging to the bishopric, and he suggested that the Cremonese were using these arguments to besmirch the honour of them both. By this means, he had shown that both he and Anguissola were fundamentally in similar positions, and were working towards the same end.[152] Psychologically, the tactic yielded excellent results, for the next meeting of the delegates brought a resolution, and agreement in principle between the two men. On taking the agreed proposal to the Cremonese, Anguissola met the expected opposition, but, importantly, he sympathised with it himself, and departed for Milan in a rage to convince the Governor of the justice of its terms.

It is here that the subtlety of Bollani's tactics becomes apparent. He had reduced the dispute to a personal level, convincing Anguissola, and it would now appear that they were both arguing on the same side — against the restrictions of Anguissola's commission, and the political necessity (for the Marquis) of preserving good relations between Milan and Cremona. Anguissola was to return in two days; Bollani was not to move from Urago; and the battle seemed almost won.[153]

In spite of these hopeful signs, it did not seem as if the struggle was over. Bollani had informed Antonio Mazza in Milan as usual, whose industry in the Venetian cause failed to produce the necessary approval. He had had talks with the Marquis of Pescara, and with Anguissola, but apparently Anguissola was to return to the river with new suggestions. Mazza had also been concerned with the rumours abroad in Milan about Bollani's possible self-interest in the outcome of the talks, spending time with the governor of the city to discuss these and producing Bollani's letters. He was able to report that the Marquis was fully convinced of Bollani's intentions, and agreed that they were malicious rumours.[154] Having received this news, Bollani wrote again to the Signoria, expressing his sorrow that obstacles were being placed in the way of the freedom of the elected judges to dispute according to their individual consciences. He stated that 'non mancharò mai di haver l'occhio a due principali cose, l'una di non lasciar l'accordo disconcluso, et l'altra di sostener quanto più mi sarà possibile la riputatione publica, che tanto relieva in tutte le cose.'[155] In spite of these initial setbacks, he still felt he had a clear brief: to preserve the dignity of the Republic of Venice in the negotiations, and to gain for Brescia as favourable an agreement as possible. Venice, meanwhile, had written in support of the agreement to Milan as he had suggested, and warm words of praise for Bollani had been spoken in the Senate.[156]

From this point Bollani was concerned to press the advantage gained. Having convinced Anguissola that the function of the elected delegates was to decide as their consciences dictated — and not as dictated by the electors — he was now able to represent the Milanese refusal as an affront to the dignity and honour of them

both. His expert manipulation of the Count in this is only too clear. Anguissola
had agitated in Milan for a harder line with the Cremonese agents, and had
obtained a statement of intent from the Marquis to the effect that: 'gli voleva però
disingannare di qualche loro persuasione intorno al moversi le armi per tal conto.
Il che si come egli non mai farebbe senza espresso ordine del suo Re, così Sua
Maestà non mai divenirebbe a si fatta rissultione, per la buona pace che ha con
quel Serenissimo Dominio.'[157] Apparently the Cremonese were no longer to count
on Spanish arms in support of their rights in the river Oglio. So, for Bollani at
least, an agreement had been reached between the elected delegates. Those obstacles which remained were in Milan and Cremona. Finally Anguissola suggested
taking the matter to the King, and leaving the negotiations in suspense, to which
Bollani, true to his Brescian sympathies, pointed out that this 'reduction to the
status quo would involve destruction of the *Predata*, as this had been replaced
by order of the Venetian Senate and had not been followed by the repairs to the
walls and the laying of the *soglie*. This, of course, was not to be contemplated, so
that on September 7, the dispute seemed as far as ever from final settlement.[158]

In the meantime, vigorous efforts were being made by both sides to support the
proposals made by the delegates at the river. Bollani had asked for pressure from
Venice to be brought to bear on the Governor of Milan, and the Marquis had
delegated two secretaries, Hernandez and Spinoza, to represent the Milanese view
to the Doge. A Cremonese gentleman was also deputed to represent his case to the
Venetian government.

Lecturing with a map of the mouth of the canal, the Cremonese gentleman
expounded the view of his city, noting, probably not without justice, that the
Naviglio provided the life-blood of the province of Cremona, whereas the Oglio
was of relatively minor importance for Brescia.[159] He alleged legal rights, proved
by the inevitable charters, to extract 2,000 *once* of water from the river Oglio,
and expressed the damages arising from the recent Brescian destruction of the
Predata as 40,000 ducats. If this was true, the strength of the case is undoubted.
But we have seen that an economic argument was unlikely to make much headway against the Venetian 'reasons of state': the support for Brescian dominion
over the river, and the control of Cremonese expansion of the canal for commercial and security reasons. The *Signoria*, conscious of her weakness, the importance
of her frontiers and the necessity of preserving the loyalty of her subject
provinces, was more impressed by Bollani's view that the *Naviglio*, if made navigable down to Cremona, would constitute a source of commercial competition for
the Republic, and a security risk on her frontier.[160] The gentleman also alluded (at
length) to the difficulties with the *soglie*, and here it does seem as though Anguissola had accepted Bollani's proposals initially without realising their full implications, being forced to retract subsequently.[161] The Doge replied to this speech
with a renewed request to Milan, to be referred to the Marquis, that the delegates
be permitted to judge according to their individual consciences, as it had clearly
transpired throughout the course of the negotiations, that Bollani was the more
expert of the two delegates. It was overwhelmingly in Venetian interests for
negotiations to be conducted in this way.

Negotiations between the two governments behind the scenes at last bore fruit.

Bollani had emphasised to Anguissola (and the point had also been made by Venice in her correspondence with the Marquis of Pescara) that talks could not continue in this way unless the *Predata* was again destroyed. For, having been reconstructed by orders of the Venetian Senate, it remained a point in favour of Brescia, so to speak, in the balance of initiatives in the river. If the remaining parts of the 1559 agreement were not to be carried out, then it would have to be destroyed. The strategic pressure applied by this produced the desired effect. The Marquis of Pescara finally agreed that Anguissola should have freedom to judge without reference to Cremona, but impressed on him very forcefully that he should not neglect the interests of the Cremonese. He complained bitterly to Bollani that this freedom seemed less than complete ('potete vedere, Monsignor Vescovo, come mi trovo, et che libertà è questa tutta legata.')[162] The principle had been established, however, and provided a spur to greater efforts, so that, to the immense relief of all parties, an agreement was finally reached on September 24, 1561.[163]

The remaining events are the logical sequel. For maximum security, Bollani was instructed to remain at Urago until the construction work at the mouth of the canal was finished, and Venice was to urge strongly that Anguissola be given liberty to do the same.[164] High praise for Bollani's efforts in the negotiations were expressed in Venice, Brescia and Milan, with general unanimity on the judgement and dignity with which he had brought the affair to a successful conclusion.[165] Domenico noted with evident satisfaction that the agreement had two main advantages from the Venetian point of view: first it removed once and for all the danger that Cremona might make her canal navigable down to Cremona, and secondly, he felt that it brought an effective end to Cremonese pretensions to dominion in the river Oglio.[166]

Thus Bollani had managed to reconcile those driving forces which had made him a powerful negotiator and were to place him in the forefront among those Venetian noblemen on whom the Republic was to rely in the coming two decades. Conscious of the patrotic duty imposed by the Venetian *Ragion di Stato*, he had also endeared himself to Brescia by his tenacious insistence on their rights in the river. In the three years during which he had been concerned with the dispute, he had become 'bono et schietto Bresciano' without once losing sight of his responsibilities to the Republic. Beyond this, he had brought a broad comprehension and incisive intellect to bear on the problems of negotiation — adopting new methods to convert his opponent to his cause — often against the fixed odds of vested interest. Essentially he emerges as a practical politician in the broadest sense. He had known precisely when to appeal to the highly developed sense of honour and dignity in his aristocratic opponent, when to exhibit a genial tolerance in the face of strong opposition, and when to encourage secret manoeuvres which might secure an advantage for Brescia. This practical sense was perhaps the supreme quality. For it was only by the formulation of a practical and modern agreement for the division of the waters, that the irrelevancies of former adjudications, reprisals, charters and claims to overall dominion could be cleared away. For all his claims at the end of the talks in 1561 that Brescian dominion in the river was now secure, he must have been conscious of the fact that a settlement which *divided* the waters (and with them, ultimate jurisdiction) was the only one with any chance of success.

By the end of the first week in October, the future of the *Predata* — that construction whose existence had been precarious in the extreme since 1329 — was assured, and the floor levels (*soglie*) had been laid in the mouth of the *Naviglio*. The river now flowed down across the *Bresciano* undisturbed, dividing its strength at Calcio, precisely as it does today after 400 years. Never again was this small section of countryside — unspoilt and served only by a rough track even today — to be the scene of such concern, action and counter-action, politics and war.[167]

Domenico Bollani had earned the gratitude of two nations, and had established himself as a forceful diplomat, a loyal servant of Venice, and a competent and tactful negotiator. From this position of power and influence, as bishop on Venice's western frontier, he was never to retreat, and was to be a vital tool in disputes for his government. As a member of the church he would have a particular responsibility in those important years for Venetian/Papal relations, and in the significant period of the growing momentum of the Tridentine Reformation. The use to which Domenico Bollani was able to put his experience of the river Oglio and the *Naviglio Cremonese* in these two fields will be examined in the second half of this study.

1   For Venice and the Hapsburg/Valois rivalry over Milan, see, for instance, H.G. Koenigsberger & G.L. Mosse, *Europe in the Sixteenth Century*, (London, 1968) pp. 64–66,
180–182, 185 etc. Romanin, *Storia di Venezia, cit.*, V, pp. 188–192, 281–318, VI, pp. 17 *et
seq.* for the position of Venice in the politics of northern Italy from Cambrai to Cateau-
Cambrésis.

2   For the fortunes of Cremona up to 1535, see F. Guicciardini, *Istoria d'Italia*, 4 vols.
(Fribourg, 1775), I, p. 374, II, 390, III, 335, 369, 409, IV, 178. For Domenico Bollani
grandfather, Barbaro, *loc. cit.*, and above, p. 73, n. 3.

3   For Brescia in the sixteenth century, fundamental is the recent *Storia di Brescia*
(Fondazione Treccani, various dates) Vol. II, *passim*, with its wealth of references to local
printed and local archival sources. For a balanced view, it should be supplemented by (e.g.)
Romanin, *op. cit.*,, pp. 488–489, and vol. VI, *passim*, but particularly the texts of the *Relazioni* in Carlo Pasero (Ed.) *Relazioni di Rettori Veneti a Brescia durante il secolo XVI*,
(Brescia, 1939), and Agostino Zanelli, *Delle Condizioni interne di Brescia dal 1426 al 1644, e
del moto della borghesia contro la nobiltà nel 1644*, (Brescia, 1898).

4   Brescia had followed the example of Bergamo and capitulated to the advancing French
troops, expelling the Venetian rectors in 1509. (See Romanin, *op. cit.*, V, p. 216, Sanuto,
Diarii, cit., VIII, May 1509, and *Storia di Brescia*, vol. *cit.*)

5   From 1525, almost every Venetian *Relazione* of Brescia shows this preoccupation, and
significantly, the fidelity of the city invariably comes first in the document – as if this were a
point on which Venice constantly needed to be assured after 1509. See Pasero (Ed.) *Relazioni, cit., passim*, A. Zanelli, 'La Devozione di Brescia a Venezia e il principio della sua
decadenza' in *Archivio Storico Lombardo*, fasc. XXXIII, (1912), pp. 30–100, *Storia di
Brescia, cit.*, pp. 381–382.

6   For a concise summary of the Italian political situation after Cateau-Cambrésis (1559), see
Romolo Quazza, *Preponderanze Straniere*, (Milan, 1938) pp. 23–26. For Bollani and Lepanto
see below, pp. 156.

7   Bollani's proclamations clearly show that – as was to be expected – his measures were
often taken in pursuance of Senate and Council of X legislation in Venice, both in Friuli and
in Brescia. For the examples of laws against blasphemy and abuses in monasteries, see
immediately below.

8   'Generalmente mancò un vero e proprio intervento da parte del governo con leggi e
provvidenze communi a tutte le province della sua Terraferma. Ogni luogo, ogni città doveva
provvedere alle proprie necessità . . .' (*Storia di Brescia, cit.*, II, p. 362), A. Ventura, *op. cit.*,
p. 416 etc.

9   'Il Podestà aveva veste civile, politica e giudiziaria . . .' (Pasero, *Relazioni, cit.*, pp. 11–12).

10   See the full discussion of this point in *Storia di Brescia, cit.*, II, p. 380, and sources cited.
The request had been first made in 1556 to Venice which 'l'acontentò per due reggimenti
successivi' (including Bollani's election in 1558) but was later discontinued. This author states
(*Ibid.*, p. 380) that the request made by Brescia in 1562 was 'perchè i mediocri e i piccoli
della capitale temettero di essere altrimenti delusi nelle loro speranze di ottenere gli ambiti
reggimenti provinciali'. It should be noted, however, that this statement quotes the opinion of
the Brescian orator in Venice who had spoken about the question to various patricians,
including the *Savi della settimana*, and had met reluctance to introduce the matter in the
Collegio. See the letter of Lodovico Calini to Brescia in Biblioteca Queriniana, Brescia,
Archivio Civico Storico di Brescia (henceforth A.C.S.B.), *Letter Autografe*, MSS. F.II.1133,
December 21, 1562. In this letter the above explanation is preceded by 'penso che voglia
dir . . .' and could well be a somewhat embittered reaction. It is not impossible that questions
of constitutional prerogative in the various councils were again involved – as in the decision
to elect rectors in the Great Council rather than the Senate (above, pp. 52–53). The orator
may have been more accurate when he noted that election by lot was 'causa contro il broglio'
(*Ibid.*, and see above, pp. 53–54).

11   June to September, 1558. From September, Bollani was at Urago d'Oglio engaged in

negotiations over the Oglio dispute with Anguissola. Proclamations from 14 September bear the name of Pietro Morosini (*Capitano* and *Vice-Podestà*), who had clearly taken over the administration in the city, until Bollani's election as bishop in 1559. At this point, Morosini became *Podestà*.

12 Contemporary sources for Brescia in this period may be found in the A.C.S.B., (Biblioteca Queriniana, Brescia), with some sources for the sixteenth century in the *Archivio di Stato*, Brescia (henceforth A.S.B.). Bollani's proclamations are in A.C.S.B., *Proclami*, (1528–1598), Ro. 1094, cc. 108–122. The acts of the Brescian Council are in *Provvisioni*, (1557–1558). Important for relations with Venice are the series of *Lettere Autografe, Lettere Pubbliche*, which contain the dispatches of the Brescian orators in Venice. Specialised published sources will appear in following notes.

13 See *Storia di Brescia, cit.*, II, pp. 375–378, and sources cited, particularly pp. 375–376 for the murder of Giorgio Martinengo and its repercussions.

14 *Ibid., loc. cit.* In 1557, the Podestà Domenico Gradenigo spoke of these quarrels in his *relazione (Relazioni*, ed. Pasero, *cit.*, pp. 87–88), stating that the city 'al presente si ritrova in molta quete et contentezza' owing to his efforts to pacify the disputes between the Avogadro and Martinengo families. It is certain that this view was more calculated to please Venice, and represent its author in a favourable light than to represent fact, as will appear in Bollani's legislation. For the difficulty in the administration of justice, see *Storia di Brescia, loc. cit.*

15 *Ibid.* p. 376. See also the *Relazione* of Catterino Zen of 1553 in Pasero Ed. *Relazioni, cit.*, pp. 67–69, Zen wrote a long description of Brescian habits in this respect, concluding: 'Diro reverentemente che meglio lassarli portar l'arme che no perchè si fanno manco homicidii nella citta et territorio' (p. 68). Bollani's severe restrictions, on the carrying of arms (following a motion in the Council of X) both in Udine and in Brescia on June 6, 1558, seem the wiser course.

16 In the context of blasphemy and abuses of Monasteries, (as in his measures of 1555 in Udine) Bollani followed the lead of the Venetian government. Motions fixing penalties for these transgressions had been passed on 9 January, 1544 and 29 september, 1543 respectively in the Council of X. In the latter case the measures had been requested by Brescia (already an indication of a local situation that was to face the future bishop). But these provisions concerning monasteries were substantially the same as those Bollani made for Friuli: visitors (even relatives) were to carry licences, it was forbidden to climb monastery walls, and corruption of monastery officials was severely punished. Severe penalties were prescribed for traffic in letters or messages to nuns reflecting on their honour etc. The seriousness of this problem is further attested by the fact that the city council had legislated against the climbing of monastery walls as recently as January 8, 1550, and the prizes for informers were unusually rich (50 and in some cases 100 ducats). For abuses of Monasteries, see also *Storia di Brescia, cit.*, p. 369 and notes, and for the above measures, with preceding legislation, A.C.S.B., *Proclami, cit.*, pp. 110–111, June 11, 1558.

17 *Relazioni, cit.*, p. 87.

18 Whereas Bollani's letters on this point are in the A.S.V. from Udine to Venice in 1555–6, a systematic search has not discovered any from Brescia during Bollani's brief tenure of the post (see above, pp. 64–66 particularly, and Chapter IV *passim*).

19 *Ibid.*

20 For charitable institutions in Brescia in the sixteenth century, see Carlo Pasero, 'Notizie sul Sacro Monte delle Biade di Brescia e sugli Istituti di Beneficenza bresciani durante il secolo XVI' in *Atti e Memorie del Terzo Congresso Storico Lombardo*, (Cremona, 1938) pp. 3–28, *Storia di Brescia, cit.*, II, p. 362.

21 For these measures, see A.C.S.B., *Proclami, cit.*, cc. 108–114 for the month of June, 1558.

22 *Ibid.*, August 6, 1558. (Fig. 14)

23 See Pasero, 'Notizie sul Sacro Monte . . .' *cit.*, p. 19 for the streamlining and coordination of the various Institutions in 1548.

24 Documents on the Oglio dispute have survived in all the cities whose interests were involved. The negotiations involved Brescia and Cremona most closely, so that in the *Archivio Civico Storico* (Biblioteca Queriniana, Brescia) (A.C.S.B.), quite fundamental is the *Registrum*

106

Olei, a massive collection of MSS, from all sources tracking the city's participation and concern for its water rights. Numerous other MS sources exist in the A.C.S.B. which will appear in the notes, along with printed sources. Further documentation is found in the *Archivio di Stato di Cremona* (A.S.C.), particularly in *Eredità Po, Oglio, Adda, Busta* IX, and those sections of the *Archivio del Naviglio Cremonese* which have passed to the state archives, particularly *busta* VI (1560–1561) (but see immediately below), recording the Cremonese participation in the dispute and the concern for its canal. A further rich source is the vast and virtually unexplored *Archivio del Naviglio Civico di Cremona* (Arch. Nav. Crem., now in A.S.C.), besides technical documents, a wealth of MSS and early printed sources from the Middle Ages to the present day, including historical sources of great richness and variety above and beyond the implications of its title. For Brescia, the interests of the Republic of Venice were always involved, so that the *Archivio di Stato di Venezia* (A.S.V.) contains important material under *Provveditori alla Camera dei Confini (Confini)*, particularly *busta* 16 (1546–1639) and *busta* 17 (Relazione Baitelli, 1639), besides dispatches and reports in the deliberations of the various councils. For Cremona, the interests of Milan were involved, so that much documentation exists in the *Archivio di Stato di Milano* (A.S.M.), particularly in *Fondo Acque, busta* 727bis, and *Confini (parte antica), busta* 315 (1500–1599), as well as dispatches etc. in *Estado, busta*, 1212. During the period under discussion, Milan passed from French to Spanish hands, so that an exhaustive history of the Oglio disputes should take account of the possibility of documents in Paris, Spain, and in the various depositories of documents relating to the Emperor Charles V. This, however, is beyond the present scope. Finally, Domenico Bollani himself left a permanent record of his letters and documents from Urago d'Oglio so that future negotiators might avail themselves of them. One copy is in the Biblioteca Marciana, Venice (Ms. It. Cl. II, 6926) and one in the Biblioteca Queriniana, Brescia, (A.C.S.B., K. VII, 1) bearing an autograph *postilla* and elaborate seal, dated 22 November, 1561: 'Registro delle delegationi, lettere, e altre scritture . . .' (I should like to express a long-standing debt of gratitude to Ing. Bruno Loffi, for his tireless assistance and encouragement, as well as for permission to consult documents in his offices.)

25 See, for instance, VI Congresso delle Acque, *Notizie sui principali cavi irrigui e di colo della provincia di Cremona*, (Cremona, 1932) p. 17, Consorzio dell'Oglio, *Il Consorzio dell'Oglio nel primo decennio della sua costituzione*, (Milan, 1938) pp. 248–249, Società Anonima Canali d'Irrigazione derivate dall'Oglio etc., *Il Lago d'Iseo e L'Irrigazione in provincia di Brescia*, (Brescia, 1926), pp. 11–12 and for a recent account of its origins, B. Loffi, 'Le Antiche Misure Cremonesi dell'acqua irrigua' in *Bollettino Storico Cremonese*, XXIV (1969) pp. 5–11 of offprint.

26 And certainly not between Urago and Rudiano, as stated by Fè d'Ostiani, *Il Vescovo Domenico Bollani, cit.*, p. 7.

27 It has been stated, for instance, that it was a contributary cause of the battle between Brescia and the combined forces of Bergamo and Cremona at Rudiano in 1191 (Società Anonima . . . *Il Lago d'Iseo . . . , cit.*, p. 11).

28 For instance, Fè d'Ostiani, *op. cit.*, pp. 7–12, 23–25, (a brief summary of events of 1558–1561 based on Bollani's letters alone), Co. Cav. Federico Mazzuchelli, 'Relazione Storico-Politico-Economico-Topografico del Fiume Oglio' MS in A.C.S.B., Cod. D.I.10, pp. 99–121, for Brescia, and, in Arch. Nav. Crem., *Scritture diverse concernenti a favore del Naviglio per causa della Predata et novità che fanno li Bresciani*, (Collection of printed unnumbered documents and instructions of 1644–1645), for Cremona. The question of prior rights, jurisdictional control by previous treaties was to confuse the issue beyond all belief, so that every dispute would start with a running battle over the validity of medieval treaties which each side held, and there was much delving into archives for these. In this brief summary of the early history, it is impossible to judge the validity of such claims – real or imaginary.

29 *Relazione, cit.*, pp. 100–101: 'dichiarato illegitimamente intruso nella dignità Imperiale, scommunicato, ed aboliti tutti gli atti da lui fatti . . .'

30 Arch. Nav. Crem., 'Scritture diverse . . .' *cit.*: 'qual privilegio fu confermato per Sigismondo l'anno 1411 e ultimamente per Carlo Quinto l'anno 1546.'

31 *Relazione, cit.*, pp. 100–101. Brescia produced further charters to sustain their point of

view. That conceded by the Emperor Corrado in 1037 gave them full rights over the river, but 'essi producono un Capitolo solo' complained the Cremonesi (*Scritture diverse, loc. cit.*). The charter conceded by Henry VI of 1192 was also produced by Brescia as evidence of her rights, but here Cremona could produce an annulment of this (*Ibid.*) The dispute had begun when both Brescia and Cremona had been under one ruler in the second half of the fourteenth century. Without effective backing, Brescia was unable to prevent its construction (*Relazione, cit.*, p. 100).

32 *Ibid.*

33 *Scritture diverse, cit.*

34 Domenico Bollani clearly realised that a solution acceptable to the *four* parties in all respects was flatly impossible – when he proposed solution by two individual consciences in 'single combat' so to speak. See below.

35 For the history of the domination of Cremona, see the summary in Monteverdi, *Storia di Cremona*, (Cremona, 1970) pp. 85–93.

36 This susceptibility on the part of Venice was not wholly unjustified when intelligence of secret attempts to infiltrate the province of Brescia are borne in mind. (See correspondence on such moves quoted in *Storia di Milano*, vol. *cit.*, pp. 253–254 {1547}.) The vulnerability of Venetian frontiers is amply shown in the many frontier disputes in this period. River frontiers were particularly susceptible, (for which see disputes over the Po and Adda in *Storia di Brescia*, II, *cit.*, pp. 382–384, *Storia di Milano*, IV, pp. 253–256). For an important analogy concerning the Venetian frontier in the Val Brembana see G. Cozzi, 'Politica e diritto in alcune controversie confinarie tra o Stato di Milano e la Repubblica di Venezia' in *Archivio Storico Lombardo*, 78–79, (1951–1952) pp. 10 *et seq.*

37 See Ducal letter of 1 May, 1526, 29 April, 1529 in A.C.S.B., *Registrum Olei, cit.*, resp. Vol. G, pp. 291–292, 310–312. See also Mazzuchelli, *Relazione, cit.*, p. 102, and Arch. Nav. Crem, *Scritture diverse . . ., loc. cit.*, for a totally different account of the events. Engineers widening the *Seriola Piumenengo* (a lower canal leading out of the Oglio) for Galeazzo Pallavicino had been attacked by Bresciani, and one killed. Further attempts to widen the canal had been begun by Cremona. The respective sources are not specific about the mills. For Brescia, Mazzuchello states that several were owned by Brescians who paid taxes to Cremona, for Cremona, the author of *Scritture diverse* recounts how Brescians burnt mills. (*Ibid.*)

38 The owners and taxes paid are in Mazzuchelli, *Relazione, cit.*, p. 103, quoting the documents (*Provvisioni, Instrumenti* etc.) in the A.C.S.B.

39 The dispute concerned water mills in the river, burnt by the Brescians as prejudicial to the irrigation in the southern half of the province: 'Dominando il Ducca Francesco Sforza Secondo doppò la pace de Bologna fecero Bresciani notabile novitade in detto Fiume, percioche abbruggiorno Molini de diversi particolari in esso . . .' (See A.S.C., *Scritture diverse, loc. cit., A.S.C.B., Registrum Olei*, correspondence under date 1532–1533).

40 *Registrum Olei, cit.*, H, c. 338 *et seq.* for copies of the respective commissions. It was doubtless felt in Venice that Bassadonna's experience in Milan would facilitate his negotiation with the Milanese representative. See his admirable summary of the events and of the dispute in his *Relazione* from Milan in 1533, in A. Segarizzi, (Ed.) *Relazioni degli Ambasciatori Veneti al Senato*, (Bari, 1912) II, esp. pp. 52–56. This became the classic form of such negotiations: each representative diplomatically placed in his own territory on either side of the river, 'assisted' by the representatives of the offended parties (usually the *Deputati all'Oglio* of Brescia, and the *Deputati al Naviglio* of Cremona).

41 *Registrum Olei, cit.*, c. 339, letter from the Doge to the rectors of Brescia.

42 See *Registrum Olei, loc. cit.*, and *Relazione* of Bassadonna, *cit.*, pp. 52–56.

43 *Relazione, cit.*, p. 53. But compare the remarks of G. Cozzi in 'Politica e Diritto in alcune Controversie confinaries tra la Repubblica di Venezia e lo Stato di Milano (1564–1622)' in *Archivio Storico Lombardo*, 78–79 (1951–1952) pp. 7–44, esp. pp. 17–23. Cozzi explains this fusion of juridical and political elements in the two states as inherent in their constitutional diversities. Whereas in Venice, 'la compenetrazione delle attività politiche, amministrative, giudiziarie, era comune in quei tempi' (as we have seen amply illustrated in Domenico Bollani's career), for Milan, a concept of legality apart from and almost above politics had had a long tradition, particularly within the Milanese Senate and its organs. But the dispute in

which Bassadonna played a part was in 1533 – thirty years before Professor Cozzi's examples – and it is perhaps significant that both he and Domenico Bollani (1558–1561) may be considered to have got the better of their Milanese adversaries.

44 , *Relazione, cit.*, pp. 53–54.

45 , Bassadonna had been an astute negotiator, in spite of these difficulties of principle, having suspended the talks at a point at which Brescia appeared with a slight advantage: 'e sta' ordinato che revocate le lettere sopradditte, come quelle che erano sta' fatte, accioche bressani stessero quieti e che la causa fusse definita, le cose siano reduti da' bressani nel stato che erano avanti che avesseno il pristino da noi delegati, come e conveniente e giusto.' (*Ibid.*)

46 Negotiations continued in the endless exchange of demands and counterdemands between the various authorities (for which see *Registrum Olei, cit.*, for the years 1533 onwards).

47 'Per virtù della presente Crida fa monicione bando, et comandamento a ogni persona de qual si voglia stato, grado et conditione, qual habbia tenga, et posseda molini bine de Molini vadi over vho in detto Fiume in quanto si extende il Cremonese che non ardisca, ne presuma per se medesimo, o per sottomessa persona ne per diritta, ne indiretta via pagar dinari, cera, o altra cosa, ne recognoscer Principe Republica, o communità particolar persone ne soi agenti . . . o dominio per causa di detti Molini Bine, et vadi de detto Fiume eccetto li Agenti della prefata Cesarea Maestà, et Communità di Cremona . . .' (Arch. Nav. Crem., *Scritture diverse, cit.*).

48 For Brescia, Jacomo Chizzola (later to play an important part in the dispute over the Adriatic at the Congresses of Udine and Cormons in 1562–1563, for which see *Storia di Brescia*, vol. *cit.*, p. 384 and sources cited), for Cremona, Lodovico Cauccio and Giulio Stanga, and for Venice, the ambassadors Mocenigo and Contarini. (For this phase in the dispute, see *Storia di Brescia, cit.*, pp. 382–384, *Storia di Milano, cit.*, p. 255, A.S.V., *Provv. ai Confini, busta* 16 letters of Mocenigo and Contarini from Ratisbon of July 8, 1564 and A.C.S.B., Registrum Olei, cit., vol. L, pp. 327–333 { Chizzola's letters to Brescia from Ratisbon and other documents}). See also A.C.S.B., Mazzuchelli, 'Relazione . . .' *cit.*, pp. 103–104.

49 A.S.V., *Provv. ai Confini, busta* 16, unidentified letter of 11 June, 1546 (probably from the Venetian Secretary in Milan to Venice).

50 *Ibid.*

51 This was in fact the nucleus of the problem. For a discussion of the functions of political, juridical and *de facto* elements in bargaining in a later dispute between Milan and Venice, see G. Cozzi, 'Politica e diritto . . .' art. *cit. passim.* (letter from Don Alvaro de Luna reported in above.)

52 'il privar altrui di possesso violentemente, et poi dimandando giudici a volere mentre dura la lite godere quello che non e suo.' (A.S.V., *Provv. ai Confini*, 16, Mocenigo and Contarini to Venice, July 8, 1546)

53 See A.C.S.B., *Relazione* (Mazzuchelli) *cit.*, p. 103, and *Ibid. Registrum Olei*, Vol. L. p. 341 for full text.

54 See copies of letters from the Rectors of Brescia to Venice in A.C.S.B., *Registrum Olei*, L, p. 345, and sketch-map above figs. 15–17. For the vulnerability, *Ibid.*, p. 330, and Mazzuchelli, MS *cit.*, pp. 104–105, and for Martinengo's representation to the Rectors of Brescia, letter of May 22, *Ibid.*, p. 336.

55 'Instruttione sopra la differenza tra Cremonesi e Bresciani per conto delle acque del Fiume Oglio' in Arch. Nav. Crem., *Scritture diverse, cit.* (unnumb. pages)

56 , Mazzuchelli, *Relazione, cit.*, p. 105.

57 , Arch. Nav. Crem. *Scritture diverse*: 'et in oltre si privava la fossa del Castello di Cremona, et della Ditta d'acque . . .'

58 The conversations of this emissary are reported in full in *Ibid.* Apparently the *Podestà* of Brescia (Domenico Gradenigo, for whose unpopularity see Pasero, *Relazioni di Rettori, cit.*, p. 24) had assured him that only 25–30 workmen were engaged in the construction. He passed the site on his return, however, and counted more than 300. Naturally, this incident is not recounted in Mazzuchelli, *op. cit.*

59 Mazzuchelli, *Relazione, cit.,* p. 106. 1500 *Guastadori,* 100 armed men, 1200 infantry 'andarono con sommo coraggio! '

60 For instance, *Storia di Brescia,* II, *cit.,* p. 384 citing contemporary chronicles and printed works such as Fè D'Ostiani, *op. cit.,* pp. 7–12, Odorici, *Storie Bresciane,* (Brescia, 1882) pp. 213–214. etc.

61 A.C.S.B., *Provvisioni, Atti del Consiglio Cittadino,* MSS. C. VIII, 544, p. 160.

62, Mazzuchelli, *Relazione, cit.,* p. 107.

63 , 'che il diletto Nobil nostro Domenego Bollani Cavaliere che va Podesta a Brescia . . .' Copies of his commission are widely dispersed: e.g. A.S.V., *Confini, loc. cit.,* Arch. Nav. Crem., *Scritture diverse, loc. cit.,* A.C.S.B., *Registrum Olei, cit.,* 0, p. 108 etc.

64 *Registrum Olei,* 0, p. 30 for his commission, reproduced in A.S.V., *Confini, loc. cit.,* and elsewhere.

65 The nearest attempt was by Fe D'Ostiani, *op. cit.,* pp. 7–12, 23–25, but this was based on Bollani's letters almost entirely, the 'Registro delle Delegationi . . .'. The two copies of this collection of documents were made by Mario Trusso, Bollani's assistant as *Podestà* and as Bishop, having followed him into ecclesiastical office by special decree of the City Council, (for which see A.C.S.B. *Provvisioni, Atti dei Deputati,* for June 23, 1559, and B. Zamboni, MSS 'Notizie spettanti al vescovo Domenico Bollani' in Biblioteca Queriniana, Brescia, MSS. F. IV. 9). It was natural, therefore, that for this collection a selection of available documents was made, and choice would depend on documents showing Bollani in a favourable light (whether this choice was made by Trusso or Bollani himself). It is also confined to the dates of the meetings themselves, whereas there are many documents, including many letters between Bollani and Anguissola, in *Registrum Olei, (cit.)* especially for 1559. For other printed accounts, see sources cited in *Storia di Brescia,* II, *loc. cit.,* and above, pp. 106–107, n. 24.

66 For the rest of this chapter letters cited are from the 'Registro delle Delegationi . . .' where not specified.

67 Bollani to Venice, September 7, 1558: 'e grandemente da dubitare che della presente delegatione, ne sia per succeder l'istesso, che si e veduto di tante altre fatte per li tempi passati: le quali tutte sono riuscite senza alcuna conclusione,'

68 The fifteenth century castle in which Bollani spent long periods between 1558 and 1561 still stands, overlooking the former Martinengo lands and the river Oglio. For the Castle, see F.D. Pietro, *Urago d'Oglio, Memorie Parocchiali,* (Brescia, 1941) and for Giulio Martinengo, noted for his friendship with Tasso, see P. Guerrini *I Conti di Martinengo,* (Brescia, 1930) pp. 317–318. (Figs. 19, 20)

69 Bollani to Venice, September 7, 1558.

70 The representations of the Brescian and Cremonese lawyers had lasted four days, and the discussions between delegates, eight. (Chizzola report below).

71 It is clear that for Brescia, Giacomo Chizzola had been principal spokesman for Brescia, and represented the river as the legitimate property of Brescia: 'All'Hora per l'ecc. d. Giacomo Chizola di detti Mag.ci Deputati gli fu rispoto prudentemente che quello {che} era sta fatto per Bressani era sta legitimamente, essendo chiaro che per la disposition de la legge commune e lecito al patron ovver legitimo possessore d'un Vaso tuor et otturar tutta l'acqua.' etc. (Gabriel Faita, one of seven *Deputati all'Oglio* present at the talks to Lodovico Calini, Brescian Orator in Venice, September 24, 1558, in *Registrum Olei, cit.,* P, pp. 14–16.) The speeches of both groups of advocates are reported in full by Faita with much partiality and provincial pride.

72 Bollani to Venice, September 25, 1558.

73 For subsequent agreements, see Loffi, *op. cit.,* p. 10, n. 15, and sources cited above, n. 25.

74 Bollani to Venice, September 25, 1558. He had, in the eyes of the Brescian delegation 'essendosi molto con grandissimo prudenza fatticato, et promossi partiti dal canto nostro molto honesti che non si potria dir di piu.' (Faita to Calini, *cit.*) Interestingly, the Brescian *Deputati* wanted to observe Bollani's movements in the matter, as Faita asks Calini in Venice to procure copies of Bollani's letters for the *Registrum Olei.* The presence of these letters indicates his success.

75 Chizzola's account (*Reg. Olei., cit.*) is substantially the same as above.

76 Calini to Brescia, 17, 22 October, 1558 in *Reg. Olei*, P, p. 19.

77 'E stato fatta querela nanti al molto Mag.ca et Clmo. Sig. Podestà di Brescia che alli giorni passati, et al tempo di notte alcuni mascharati debbano essere andati alla casa del Portinaro al Porto di Urago sopra il fiume Oglio con dargli delle bastonate . . .' etc. (Letter January 29, 1559 in *Registrum Olei*, P, p. 21.) It was suspected that they were from Calcio on the Cremonese side of the river.

78 Bollani certainly did not know the outcome of the Treaty of Cateau-Cambrésis (2–3 April, 1559) when he rode to Urago on April 4. For the changing fortunes of Milan from 1555 to 1559, see *Storia di Milano, cit.*, IX, pp. 163–169, and for the European situation, R. Quazza, *Preponderanze Straniere, cit.* pp. 23–26. For Domenico Bollani's bishopric, see below, Chapter VI, *passim.*

79 'fecero spogliar tre huomini quali intratti nel fiume et tirata una corda della Seriola d'Antegate Andagando in su per il filo et colmo della schena del vaso si mesurete doppo la longezza di detta corda tirata fin al luogo dove Cremonesi potessero far detta predata.' (*Registrum Olei, cit.* P, p. 24t.) Discussions of materials from which the *predata* was to be built ensued, and measurements were taken 'della ripa inferiore della bocca di esso Naviglio al loco dove havesse a principiar detta predata.' See map above, Fig. 16.

80 'Cavalcata fatta per il Clmo. Sr. Domenego Bollani delegato per la citta di Brescia per la causa di Ollio al luogo di Urago' (report of Gabriel Faita, undated, but April, 1559, in *Ibid.*, p. 24.)

81 See Appendix II for the full text of the declaration. 'hora si e finalmente stabilito in fede fra di noi, con haver tenuta per nostra memoria nota particolar di tutte le cose che habbiamo terminate.' (Bollani to Venice, April 8, 1559) The private rather than public nature of the document was to cause further trouble, however. The *Deputati* again asked Calini in Venice to obtain a copy of the certified agreement (which Bollani had sent to Venice) as they said that their copy was not 'authentic' (Brescia to Calini, *Reg. Olei*, P. p. 25.) It is clear that the long and turbulent history of the dispute had produced a situation where every conceivable precaution was to be taken. On this occasion, Calini had to obtain permission from the *Savi* to obtain this copy, which he duly sent with copies of Bollani's letters on April 15. (*Ibid.* p. 25.)

82 Bollani is specific and almost exultant on this legal point. He felt that 'In oltre sarà con questa via dell'haver limitate a'Cremonesi la bocca del loro Naviglio, fatto grande e securo acquisto dal canto nostro, intorno al libero Dominio del fiume Oglio:percio che l'essere limitato a'Cremonesi l'acqua che ha da entrare per la bocca del loro Naviglio, esclude senza dubbio ogni sorte de dominio che essi hanno sempre preteso nell'Alveo principale di detto fiume.' (Bollani to Venice, April 8, 1559, copy in *Reg. Olei*, P. pp. 25–26.)

83 'Dal che senza dubbio sarebbe causato, che in ogni minima cosa che havessero voluto operar in Oglio, essi Cremonesi si sarebbono opposti.' (Bollani to Venice, 29 April, 1559) This was precisely what happened to Cremona.

84 , Antonio Rodengo's certificate is in *Reg. Olei,* P, p. 28. Anguissola's reference to a horse seems to indicate that Brescia had paid homage to him in this way: 'El cavallino si e havuto et anchor sia piccolo, a soddisfatto assai per che e bello et hora che la pace { of Cateau-Cambrésis } e gridata di commun consenso et accordo di questi principi . . . de ambi li Re alli confini, et per tutte le stadi, valeranno tanti i cavalli piccoli come li grandi . . .' (Anguissola to Rodengo, 20 April, *Reg. Olei*, p. 28.) This was not an abnormal procedure in this period.

85 Anguissola to Bollani, 22 April, *Reg. Olei*, P, p. 28.

86 In *Registrum Olei*, P, pp. 29–30.

87 Bollani to Faita, 1 May, (*Reg. Olei*, P, 30–31.): 'Hora e venuto qui a me il Camparo d'Urago, il quale mi affirma esser stato per tre notti con alcuni suoi *in Ollio* et haver fatta buona opera di quel modo che ne ragionai, egli fa conto che gli siano da pagare quatordeci opere, Io senza dubbio stimo che sia bene intratener costui perche vadi seguendo cosa tanto proficua al bisogno nostro, et pero pagategli le dette opere et tenetelo animato a continuar, con ordine che lo facci *secretamente,* et venghi ogni dominica a darmene conto perche lo soddisfaremo *simil opera e ottimo da fare in questi giorni che non luce la luna et che l'acqua e grossa.*' (Italics mine) Rodengo's reply is similarly secretive, relating how he had been to the river with this man 'per veder quello che havea operato, e appresso gli ho dato ordine, accio la

cosa riesca meglio sia possibile.' (*Ibid.*, p. 30.) There are further letters from one Andrea Prandi, 'Camparo de Ollio' referring to similar enterprises (e.g. 15 April, in *Ibid.*, pp. 69–70), and it seems highly likely from this and the evidence of the Cremonese reaction in the following weeks (for which see immediately below) that Bollani's men were surreptitiously deepening the river bed towards the Brescian bank, working at night so as to be unobserved from the Cremonese bank.

88 *Ibid.*, pp. 31–33.

89 Bollani to Venice, May 6, 1559. With this letter, Bollani ends his own account of the first delegation ('Registro . . .' *cit.*)

90 Anguissola to Bollani, October 8, 1559, *Reg. Olei*, P, pp. 35–36. There had been disagreement over the width of the *Predata*, Cremona wanting this to be 6 *cavezzi*, and Brescia 4 *cavezzi*. Anguissola suggested 5 as the logical compromise.

91 Bollani to Anguissola, October 11, 1559, (*Ibid.*, pp. 35–36.)

92 'Istruttione al M.co Sr. Paolo Fossa della Conseglia { of Cremona } da trattar per il Naviglio della Mag.ca citta di Cremona' in A.S.C. (Arch. Nav. Crem), *Atti dei Deputati, busta* 6 (1560–1561), n. 5.

93 A similar body to the *Deputati all'Oglio* in Brescia. The instruction was signed by Raphael Brumano, Antonio Pesce, Jacomo Bagarotto, and Christofero Schinchinello.

94 Fossa to Cremona, 21 February, 1560 (*Ibid.* n. 11): 'con abbassar il fondo di esso dietro la sua ripa, il che haveria causato subversione di tutte le provisioni fatte per S. ill.ma et il R.do Bolano poi che quello abbassamento causava che le acque non sarebbeno andate al nostro naviglio . . . facendo lamenta grandissima che non si potesse da questi Bressani sperar che subversione di tutte le cose stabilite . . .' etc.

95 Bollani had probably been a party to this, as we have seen, but the agreement at this stage of its evolution had not contained clauses prohibiting the deepening of the river, and he doubtless felt that it was a justifiable manoeuvre in the light of recently established Brescian dominion over the river. A house stands on this spot today, the home of the canal gatekeeper. (Fig. 17)

96 Anguissola to Bollani, *Reg. Olei, cit.*, P, pp. 69–70.

97 Bollani to Anguissola, A.S.C., *fondo cit.* n. 32. This letter was almost certainly intercepted by Cremona and referred to Anguissola by the Cremonese Deputati. (*Ibid.*)

98 'Et perchè puotria essere che Bresciani sudditi della Ill.ma S.ria di Vinegia facessero qualche novità per le pretensioni loro in ditto fiume V.M. sarà contenta dar l'ordine che le parrà opportuno che cessi tal impedimento over mandare che contra ogni forza, et impedimento de Bresciani siano essi Cremonesi mantenuti et difesi atteso che la extractione dell'acqua si ha da fare qua verso il territorio de V.M. { the reference is to the Soncino canal} ne si passa per altro territorio che di V.M.' (draft request in *Ibid.*, n. 39, Cremona to Philip II; the text reproduced in *Ibid.*, n. 89, Philip II to Vargas, August 7, 1560.)

99 Philip II to the Spanish Ambassador in Milan, Vargus, from Toledo August 7, 1560 (*Ibid.*): 'Al Governador { de Milano} che lo comunq. con los del sen{a}do y los del Magistrado {y} las otras personas che le parescera avise se puede trajer algun prejudicio al publico o privato . . .' It will be remembered that Charles' proclamation, after the fruitless congress at Ratisbon, had produced only a retaliatory proclamation from Venice. (See above, p. 88). In fact, strenuous efforts had been made by the Cremonese agent at the Court of Philip II at Toledo to obtain royal sanction both for the *Naviglio* and for the Soncino canal. On 16 June, he reported that the King 'prese il memoriale allegramente et disse che non mancharia di far tutto quello che potesse' and that the Courtiers 'promettevano di favorirci' (Anselmo Tristo to Cremona from Toledo, June 16, 1560, *Ibid.*, n. 84). A month later, it was clear that the request would not be granted without extensive enquiries, and on protesting at the expense of such enquiries, Tristo was told that 'S.M. non sol far simili concessioni senza haverne informatione'. (Same to same, June 16, *Ibid.*, n. 88) There is no doubt that this request failed, for by the spring of 1561, new factors were at stake, the Brescians had again operated 'di fatto', and the crisis was again to be placed in the hands of adjudicators. (It is interesting to compare the reception of the Cremonese request at the Court of Spain with that of the Brescian orator, Calini, in the *Collegio* in Venice in the following year. See below, pp. 102–103 and Appendix III.)

112

100   Raphael Brumano to Cremona from Pavia, April 28,1560, *Ibid.,* no. 44. This is also clear from the much mutilated and corrected draft of a letter to Anguissola in May, 1560 (undated).
101   *Ibid.* no. 44. The *soglie* were to have been laid by April, 1560, according to the agreement (for which see Appendix II, pp. 245–250) so that this work was already late.
102   Toledo to Cremona, August 12, 1560, and same to same 16 July, *Ibid.* nos. 87, 88.
103   A full account of his meeting with two Brescian riders near the mouth of the *Naviglio* was recorded by Nicoli and dispatched to Cremona from Fontanella on April 3 (A.S.C., *fondo cit.*, n. 132) The observers had argued with him about repairs to a wall on two occasions.
104   *Ibid.*
105   See above, p. 94 and notes.
106   Prandi to Brescia, April 15, 1561, in *Reg. Olei*, P, pp. 69–70.
107   *Deputati all'Oglio* to Bollani, at the Council of Trent, June 4, 1561, *Ibid.* p. 69.
108   Calini in Venice to Brescia, May 21, 1561, *Ibid.*, pp. 71–72. See the full text also in Appendix III, pp. 251–253.
109   Appendix III p. 251–253. Calini expressly requested that the letter be destroyed, and that it should not reach the eyes of the Rectors in Brescia. He would write another (probably far less revealing) letter for their benefit.
110   The conversation took place between the Doge, Gerolamo Priuli, Nicolò da Ponte, Matteo Dandolo (a prominent member of a family of the 'giovani', with anti-clerical and pro-French inclinations. See e.g. Alvise Michiel, *Annali, cit.*, 12.iii.1586, G. Cozzi, *Nicolò Contarini cit.*,) Hieronimo Zane, Pietro Morosini and Domenico Moro. In the context of Paruta's *Della Perfezione,* four members of the group were protagonists: Da Ponte and Dandolo in the *vita activa* group, and Bollani and Valier (bishop of Verona) in the *vita contemplativa* group (both referred to in the letter). It is interesting to find, at this early date, already a microcosm of the society that Paruta was to describe nearly twenty years later in a document of accurately reported fact. It is tempting to ascribe the argument reported by Calini, and the division in the Senate ('senatori che contradissero gagliardamente') to the tensions among the members of the patriciate that were to develop in 1580s (especially, perhaps, at this short distance in time from the definite establishment of Spanish power in Italy at Cateau-Cambrésis), but this interpretation seems to put undue strain on the facts.
111   The argument was between Matteo Dandolo and Hieronimo Zane, for the record, of 'giovani' and 'vecchi' families respectively It might reflect a fundamental difference of political orientation towards Spain, therefore. See Appendix III, p. 251–253.
112   See above, pp. 94–95 and notes.
113   See Calini's conversation with Zane (*Ibid.*). He may well have made an astute observation when referring to the division in the Senate over the previous Brescian action in 1558, supposing that Venetian support for direct action would have been condemned by those senators of the 'vecchie' families whose political orientation inclined towards the Church and Spain. It will be remembered that it had been *secret* Senate approval that had authorised the cutting of the diversionay canal in 1546. This episode was the third example of Venetian policy of this kind. The document further illustrates the faith of the *Collegio* in the political abilities of Domenico Bollani, and here documents his continuing function as Venetian *political* representative after his bishopric.
114   *Deputati all'Oglio* to Bollani at Trent, *Reg. Olei, cit.*, P, p. 69.
115   Bollani to Brescia, June 7, 1561 (*Ibid.*). In this letter, Bollani promised to act as 'bono et schietto bresciano' when informed officially, and thanked the delegates for having given him advance warning informally.
116   The official report to Cremona concluded that 'si e inteso ancora che quest'opera e statta fatta di Ordine della communità di Bressa e con partecipatione de suoi Rettori perche fu visto la mattina per tempo da otto o diece cavalli armati de quelli del Barigello di Bressa e altri huomini d'arme a cavallo da circa vinti ancora.' (Nicoli to Cremona, June 4, 1561 in A.S.C., *fondo cit.*, n. 169).
117   Nicoli from Milan to Cremona, June 20, 1561, *Ibid.*, n. 165.
118   Antonio Mazza to Venice, June 14, 1561, in A.S.V., *Confini, busta cit.*, under this date, and A.C.S.B., *Registrum Olei.*, cit., vol. Q, pp. 1–2.

119 *Idem* to *Idem*, June 17, 1561. But the Rectors reported hearing from Mazza on June 21 that the Cremonese were preparing a possible attack 'non a Calzo dov'e il luoco della difficolta, ma altrove dove darebeno grandissimo dano a Bresciani.' (Rectors to Venice, June 24 *Ibid.*, Q, pp. 4−5). Reports were also reaching Venice from spies in the area of Piacenza that a large force of Imperial cavalry was gathering there (Rectors to Venice, June 26, *Ibid.*, p. 8).

120 Calini to Brescia, June 16, 1561, *Ibid.*, p. 1. They had also wanted to know whether the intervention of 'Barigello of Brescia' (alleged by Nicoli in his report on the damage for Cremona, and adduced as evidence for the participation of the Venetian Rectors) was true, but Calini was not able to answer this. (Doubtless Barigello occupied a post of authority in the city, and therefore was taken to represent the establishment.)

121 For the Cremonese complaint and the account of the Rectors, see *Reg. Olei, cit.*, Q, pp. 2−4.

122 Reported by Mazza in his letter (*cit.*) of June 14.

123 Respectively, Mazza to Venice and Venice to Mazza, 25 and 21 June, in A.S.V., *Confini, cit.* The commissions were to decide on a return to the *status quo* in the terms of the Bollani/Anguissola agreement: 'se Bresciani hanno fatto innovatione contra quello che fu capitulato per il R.do Vescovo di Brescia et il Conte Zuan Anguissola, che abbiano a refar a spese loro, essendo certo che se da Cremonesi sarà stato innovato, Sua Ecc.tia similmente lo farà retrattar.' (Venice to Mazza, 21 June, 1561, *Ibid.*) The impossibility of the task is evident. If the Cremonese had lengthened their *Predata*, the Brescians had now destroyed the evidence for this. Brescia realised this, of course and would now enjoy the full benefit of the river in the important period of drought until a settlement was reached. Anguissola could not be called in, as apparently suffering from a long illness (which Brescia did not believe). Domenico Bollani was in Trent, but was kept informed of developments by the *Deputati all'Oglio* (e.g. 29 June, *Reg. Olei, cit.*, Q, pp. 16−17.) Brescia doubted that any good could come of the negotiations as Don Emmanual was Spanish, and probably had orders to 'farlo cosa che potria apportar et pregiuditio et dano et al S.o D.o { Venice} et a questa città.' (*Deputati* to Venice, June 26, *Ibid.*, p. 9).

124 The report to Cremona was made by Fossa in Milan, partly at Calcio and partly on his return to Milan, consisting of 11 closely packed draft sheets dated 13 and 14 July, 1561 (A.S.C., *fondo cit.*, n. 173) while Venier reported progress in his letters of 11, 13 and 14 July, 1561 to the Signoria, (A.S.V., *Confini, cit.*) and sent copies to Mazza in Milan for his information on 16 July (*Ibid.*). For Brescia, Jacomo Chizzola and Count Camillo Capriolo were again in attendance (see their report to the *Deputati all'Oglio* in *Reg. Olei, cit.*, Q, pp. 20−28) and Bartolomeo Ossio and Carlo Ponzono for Cremona.

125 See P. Molmenti, *Sebastiano Veniero e la Battaglia di Lepanto*, (Florence, 1899) *passim.* He became Doge of Venice in 1577.

126 For example he had placed great emphasis on questions of rank and dignity, and reported datails such as dismounting from horses, invitations to dinner faithfully to his government as diplomatic triumphs or defeats. Bollani had won the respect of all parties by his conciliatory and diplomatic manner.

127 Emmanuel de Luna at one point attempted to convey to the Brescian delegation that he would deceive the Cremonese in order to reach agreement. Venier was not deceived, however.

128 Venice to Mazza, July 16, 1561, in A.S.V., *Confini, cit.*

129 His reply to the *Deputati* shows his displeasure at being away from Brescia at this time: 'non perchè puotesse essere bisogno di me in aiuto vostro ma per quella sattisfattione, che sole sentire ogni uno nel trovarsi presente, se ben senza forse di aiuto, nelle quali mi si stima molta interessato.' (July 11, *Reg. Olei*, Q, p. 30.)

130 *Deputati* to Bollani, July 18, *Ibid.*, pp. 30−31.

131 June 17, *Ibid.*, p. 32.

132 Appiano to Brescia, July 19, *Ibid.*, pp. 35−36. Appiano had been elected with Count Antonio Martinengo and Bernardino Stella to represent the Brescian case to the Doge at the meeting of the city Council on July 16 (*Ibid.*, pp. 33−34, and see their report from Venice at pp. 37−40.)

133 *Ibid.*, p. 37, July 24, Bollani to Brescia from Trent. He had not heard that he was to return to the river by this date.

114

134   Venice advised the rectors of this on August 2 (*Ibid.*, pp. 40–41.) and notified Bollani
of 28 July in a letter which was to become his new commission (pp. 45–46), enclosing the
favourable reply from the delegates at the Council, and the Papal brief in their letter to him of
12 August (p. 46.) The above letters also appear in the *Registro delle delegationi . . ., cit.*, and
were published by Fè D'Ostiani, *op. cit.* pp. 161–166.
135   Antonio Martinengo from Venice to Brescia, August 4, *Ibid.*, p. 42. Da Ponte replied
'che queste vostre raggioni sonno pontigli, et che questo Serenissimo Dominio vol star in pace,
et levar l'occasione alli ministri Catolici di far ne tentar cosa contra la pace et contra al voler
della Maestà del Re.' Clearly the motion was intended as a conciliatory gesture. See also Da
Ponte's remarks to the Brescian orators in their letter of August 4 (*Ibid.*, p. 43.) to the
Deputati. Da Ponte had been *Savio di Settimana*, so had proposed the motion himself,
obtaining 170 positive and only 3 negative votes in the Senate. He insisted that the point was
insignificant in the general context of peace between the two nations.
136   Bollani to Brescia, August 4, 1561, *Ibid.*
137   In fact the statement of Mazza that Bollani would be in Brescia within three days was
taken as a joke in Milan: Fossa wrote to Cremona that 'Il R.mo Bollani era huomo di settanta
anni, che li caldi erano tanto eccessivi, et che era Venetiano, il costume de quali è non tuorre
le cose molto in fretta, oltra che il termine de tre giorni appena era bastante ad arrivare in
Brescia a chi fosse insuto correre a mezza posta, et che questa non era voler dir altro che
burlarsi la terza volta del mondo . . .' (See Fossa's three letters to Cremona all dated July 31,
in A.S.C., *fondo cit.*, nos. 184, 185, 186, for this episode. Bollani was in fact only 48 in
1561.)
138   ,Calini to Brescia, August 9, *Reg. Olei*, Q, p. 44, and Venice to Venier and Corner,
August 14, for the text of the Venetian proclamation (*Ibid.*, p. 45.)
139   *Ibid.*, report of the engineer. The *predata* was finished on the evening of August 6.
140   'Mi e anco maggiormente cresciuto questo dubbio con l'aviso che li Magnifico Deputati
di Brescia mi mandano della deliberation fatta nell'Ecc. Senato alli due del presente, per la
quale veggo esser commeso . . .' (Bollani to Venice from Volargne, August 4.) He asked for
greater clarity in his commission.
141   See Fossa to Cremona, 8, 11, 14, 16 August (A.S.C., *fondo cit.*, nos. 189, 190, 185,
199). Fossa was engaged in complex political negotiations in Milan, as timing was crucial.
Cremona had to ensure that water returned to the *Naviglio* (or irreparable damage to crops
would ensue) by the rebuilding of the *predata*, and was concerned to delay the *soglie* (for
which the water would have had to be cut off).
142   Venice to Bollani, 4 August, 1561.
143   Bollani to Venice from Torbole, 18 August. Anguissola's excuses for the late start were
the temporary absence of the Marquis of Pescara, the unpreparedness of the accommodation
and recent rains which would have made inspection of the site difficult.
144   It appears from the letter that work was still incomplete on the *Predata*, as first, it had
been rebuilt by the Brescians, and second, had been damaged in recent rains. (Bollani to
Venice, August 27.)
145   *Ibid.*
146   'Così continuavamo la trattattione per me proposta de l'essequire ad uno istesso tempo
le due operatione suddette, cioè la regola della bocca et la reduttione della Predata'.
147   Bollani to Venice, August 28, 1561: 'non si potendo essequirla senza che si divenga a
nuova et molto profonda escavatione del loro Naviglio, che levarebbe del tutto l'acqua del
principale alveo di Oglio.'
148   'pur io temo assai, spiacendomi non poco il proceder che veggo in questi Ministri Regii,
et molto più l'insolenza de' Cremonesi . . .' (*Ibid.*) He went on again to regret the Senate
motion about the *Predata*, and to note that the Cremonese had obtained certain secret letters
from Venice to Venier. It seems that both sides had secret services active in intelligence work,
and the interception of dispatches was no uncommon thing. Bollani had sent Vincenzo Stella,
Deputato all'Oglio to inform Antonio Mazza in Milan of the developments, so that he might
use what influence he had with the Marquis of Pescara.
149   Bollani to Venice, August 31.
150   Anguissola had, in fact, married a Martinengo, the sister of Count Alvise. See e.g.

'Relatione per noi Bernardino Gallarato, & Carlo Ponzono de quello è stato trattato . . . con l'Ill. Conte Aloigi Martinengo' in Arch. Nav. Crem., *Scritture Diverse, cit.*, (A.S.C.): 'il Sig. Conte Anguissola suo Cugnato . . .'

151 Bollani to Venice, August 31.

152 He noted that this seemed to have been favourably received by Anguissola, and that the latter had dropped the proposal that Brescia should fill the divertionary canal, constructed in 1558. Had Anguissola insisted on this, Brescia would have been deprived of that ultimate answer to Cremonese aggression: the diversion of the waters.

153 Bollani seemed confident of success: 'Parmi, Serenissimo Principe, che l'accordo si possa tener per assai sicuro, se non vi sarà un colmo di mali voleri, et pur non posso credere ch'l Marchese, col udirsi affermar dal Conte, che questo per sua coscienza sia guiditio suo libero, debba pigliarsi carico di metter impedimento all'accordo et a l'ultima terminatione di si antiche et travagliate differenze.' (Bollani to Venice, September 1.) He also added that he felt it advisable to inform the Spanish Ambassador in Venice of the facts, so that Anguissola's departure might not be construed as a sign of failure.

154 The allegations concerned a promise Bollani was alleged to have made, and his hypothetical interest in the result in favour of his canal. (Antonio Mazza to Bollani, September 3.)

155 Bollani to Venice, September 4, 1561.

156 Venice to Bollani, September 6.

157 Bollani to Venice, September 7.

158 Bollani had been forced to ask Venice to convey his excuses to the Pope for his delayed return to the Council. The government had obtained papal blessing on Bollani's continued absence by September 9. (Venice to Bollani).

159 'non hanno altro che due seriole, una che serve a macinar due ruote de molini, l'altra per adacquare alcuni pochi terreni' ('Isposizione del Gentilhuomo Cremonese alla Ser.me Signoria' enclosed with Venice to Bollani on September 11.) I am informed by Ing. Loffi that this statement would not be an inaccurate description of the present-day situation.

160 See Bollani to Venice, September 14, for a re-statement of the case, quoted many times in his correspondence.

161 'perche credendone dar due oncie più di aqua, ne dava due di manco, essendo questa terza soglia piu alta della seconda quattro oncie et due punti . . .' ('isposizione . . .' *cit.*) It should be noted that the term *'oncia'* is here used *first* as a measure of water, or 'yield' from the canal, and *second*, as a measure of height. For an explanation of contemporary units of measurement, with modern equivalents for the terms *Once, Cavezzi, Bracci* etc., see B. Loffi, 'Le Antiche Misure Cremonesi . . .' *cit., passim*, with sources cited.

162 Bollani to Venice, September 19.

163 For the full text of the agreement concluded, see below, Appendix IV, pp. 254–256. The 1559 agreement (Appendix II) was confirmed in full, except that the measurements of the *soglie* were more clearly defined, and the width and structure of the *Predata* were more precisely described.

164 Venice to Antonio Mazza in Milan, 25 September. Permission was granted at once (Mazza to Bollani, 28 September).

165 Venice to Bollani, 25 September, Mazza to Bollani, 28 September, and see the letter from the city of Brescia to Bollani on 26 September, which followed the relation on the conclusion of the dispute by Ludovico Terzi di Lana in the city Council (A.C.S.B., *Registrum Olei, cit.*, p. 69).

166 Bollani to Venice, 29 September.

167 Domenico continued to advise the *Deputati all'Oglio* long after the conclusion of the agreement, as his letters from Trent clearly show. In the spring of 1562, Count Alvise Martinengo (Anguissola's brother-in-law) took the law into his own hands and partly filled in the Brescian divertionary canal (dug by Brescia in 1558, it will be remembered), as it remained unused on his land at Urago. Much diplomatic concern, including further embassies to Venice, was caused by this, as the Brescian plan had always been that it remain open as the ultimate answer to future Cremonese aggression. The Counts Martinengo, feudatories of the lands around Urago, clearly had their own reasons for opposition. (*Deputati* to Bollani, May 24, June 1, 1562, and Bollani to *Deputati*, June 3 1562, in *Registrum Olei, cit.*, Q, respectively,

pp. 65–66, 67, 67–68). The intention of the *Deputati* to submit all their major decisions to his judgement and experience is clearly documented in the correspondence: 'Perche l'anima et rissolution nostra massime in questa materia di Ollio, la quale ora mai e fatta sua creatura, passi per le man sue ... (*Ibid.*) In the same year, Bollani was asked again to 'favorir sua creatura' in the minor affair of the Soncino canal (*Ibid.*, Q, pp. 65–73, R, pp. 1–10 etc.) and he replied full of goodwill to the city and its problems (*Ibid.*, pp. 8–9, July 19, 1562). There is thus no doubt that he was fully and continuously involved in the affairs of this magistracy while at the Council of Trent.

But even after his return to Brescia, when he was involved fully in the application of the Tridentine decrees in the diocese, he continued to exercise a guiding influence in this political sphere. An exchange of letters between Anguissola and Bollani shows the upkeep of the *Naviglio* progressing normally, with routine repairs to the *sperone* (the spur which divides the *Seriola Antegnate* from the *Naviglio*; see above, map, Fig. 16) after damage by the waters (15–18 April, 1562, *Ibid.*, p. 23). But in 1567, trouble flared up again, when Cremona proposed to build a two-storey house at the mouth of the *Naviglio* where the gate-keeper's house now stands, as this was construed by Brescia as a violation of the 1561 agreement, and a security threat. The continued absolute reliance of the Venetian Senate on Bollani's assistance in this matter is clear from the Ducal letter of March 16, 1567 to the rectors of Brescia: 'operandosi però il tutto per nome del detto R.do Vescovo.' (Doge to the rectors, *Archivio di Stato*, Milan, (A.S.M.) *Confini, busta* 315 {*parte antica*}. A representative was to be sent to Milan bearing Bollani's letter of introduction (Bollani to Anguissola, March 17, 1567, *Ibid.*) to discuss the matter with Anguissola. Lanterio Appiano, the *Deputato* in question reported his conversation in full on April 4 (Relation of Appiano in *Ibid.*), and referred Anguissola's suggestion that a Brescian be present for the construction to see fair play. The affair assumed the traditional pattern. Cremona began work on the house, insisting that it was merely a depository for working materials for the canal and a lodging for the gate-keeper, while Bollani sent an emmissary to Cremona (Bollani to *Deputati al Naviglio*, April 5, 1567, *Ibid.*) and Cremona sent Schinchinello to see Bollani in Brescia (Anguissola to Bollani April 14, *Ibid.*) who, 'lo soddisfece compitamente'. And the affair did not end there, but this relatively trivial episode serves to illustrate two important facts: first the importance of the river Oglio in the life of the respective provinces continued to be such that a minute account of the foundations of the house had to be approved by both sides, and second, that in the diplomatic affairs of Brescia – for what concerned the river at least – Domenico Bollani continued to provide advice as consultant and father-figure throughout his period as bishop of Brescia.

Recognition of the importance of such disputes came in Venice in 1564–1565, when the magistracy of the *Provveditori ai Confini* was set up, and two such officials were elected to keep close watch on the continuing problem of Venice's frontiers (See A.S.V., *Compilazione Leggi, busta* 145, V. Adami, *I magistrati ai Confini nella Repubblica di Venezia* (Grotto-ferrata, 1915), and for further analogies, 'Emmanuelle Filiberto e la Repubblica di Venezia' (1545–1580) in *Miscell. di Storia Veneta*, 2nd. Series, (Venice, 1901) pp. 108–109) An account of this importance, and Brescian devotion to it, was given by the Venetian Captain, returning from his post in Bergamo in 1565: 'Et il fiume Oglio continua poi a dividere il Bresciano dal Cremonese per spatio di miglia 36 in circa, che va poi a mettere cappo nel Po, ma non lasserò de dire alla Serenità Vostra come quivi vicino doi o tre miglia al fosso Bergamasco si ritrova il luogo delle difficoltà d'Oglio, che è tra Bresciani e Cremonese, nella quale difficoltà già cinque anni quella magnifica sua città di Brescia si dipportò così valorosamente et honoratamente, come intese la Serenità Vostra. Et invero questo fiume de Oglio è de tanta importantia al territorio Bresciano, ch'io ho sentito dire a principali gentil-huomini di quella magnifica città che per sustentare le sue raggioni torrebbono sempre da se stessi a fare la guerra, et spendervi uno o doi millioni d'oro' (A.S.V., *Collegio, Secreta, Relazioni, busta* 35).

CHAPTER VI

'A PRAETURA AD EPISCOPATUM'[1]
1559

It is in some ways ironical that Bollani's election to the bishopric of Brescia was tied so closely to the affairs of England and to the workings of the Roman Inquisition, as he had had some three years experience of English Protestants under Edward VI.[2] His appointment to the see of Brescia was, however, far less the result of his hypothetical energetic repression of heresy, and any credit he might have gained while reporting the affairs of England via Venice to the Pope in 1547–1549, than his suitability as a Venetian politician at the summit of his power, combining the advantages of a family in favour with the Papacy and enormous local popularity in Brescia. The election was a transparent compromise in the controversy between Venice and Rome over the election of Venetian incumbents to vacant sees within the Venetian *Terraferma*. It constitutes a milestone in the path towards the Interdict in the troubled relations between Rome and Venice in the second half of the sixteenth century, and foreshadows the principal achievement of Bollani himself in the political arena: the solution of disputes arising from conflicts of lay and ecclesiastical jurisdiction.

The dispute over the bishopric of Brescia was precipitated by the death in 1558 of Cardinal Durante, the then bishop, but really goes back to the election of Durante to the see of Brescia in 1551. On the death of the Venetian Cardinal Andrea Corner in that year, the traditional dominion of Venetian noble families over this key bishopric on the frontier of the Republic was interrupted by the election of the Brescian Durante Durante.[3] This had already been the subject of Venetian protests, and the compromise solution reached between Pope Julius III and the Republic of Venice had been the concession by the Pope of the right of accession to the see of Brescia to the Venetian Alvise Priuli.[4]

Thus it seemed that the Venetian hold over the important bishopric of Brescia was secured. Priuli would succeed Durante automatically on the latter's death, and the see would pass back into one of the strongest Venetian noble families, and one with a strong tradition of ecclesiastical perferments.[5]

But in 1555 the position became infinitely more complex. On May 1, Cardinal Carafa succeeded to the Papacy becoming Pope Paul IV. The affair of the bishopric of Brescia, which occupied him sporadically for three years, was to find in him a tough and dedicated negotiator, devoted to the sense of his own dignity, and personal control of the affairs of the Papacy, as the principal bargainer on the Venetian side, Bernardo Navagero, was soon to find.[6] Moreover, he began at once a systematic reform of curial procedures which was soon to cut back severely the system of accession to bishoprics by *accesso* and *regresso* — a system much favoured by pluralist Cardinals and Papal courtiers — and a system which had allowed Venetian noble families to retain their control over their *Terraferma* bishoprics without overt jurisdictional conflict.[7] In this way, the Pope abolished all the rights of *accesso* and *regresso* granted by his predecessors in previous years,

118

and with them, the right to the bishopric of Brescia granted to Alvise Priuli by Julius III.

Priuli himself was less affected by this turn in his fortunes[8] than was the Republic of Venice, who saw an important frontier bishopric slipping from her grasp and the possiblity of another non-Venetian occupying the see, as had been the case with Cardinal Durante.[9] As soon as Venice realised this danger, she instructed her ambassador accordingly so that every possible pressure might be brought to bear on Paul IV in the interests of the preservation of Venetian control over the diocese of Brescia.[10]

In fact Venice was unable to obtain any satisfaction from the Pope for more than a year, as Paul IV was totally involved in the war with Spain from September, 1556.[11] When at last he could turn again to his favourite preoccupation of internal reforms, Bernardo Navagero and his government appeared to him in a new light. But before this moment came, a new element was introduced into the controversy: suspicion of the religious orthodoxy of Cardinal Pole and his circle — and this circle included the bishop-elect of Brescia, Alvise Priuli.

If the Spanish war impeded negotiations with Venice over the bishopric of Brescia, it did nothing to halt the devastating work of the Inquisition — so much favoured by the Pope and his principal lieutenant, Cardinal Ghislieri.[12] Suspicion of heresy now fell on Cardinal Pole, at this time working for the restoration of Catholicism in England under Queen Mary, who found his legation cancelled on March 30, 1557. Mary interceded at once on his behalf, so that he did not depart for Rome to clear his reputation as ordered, but the accusation remained, and the stain spread to others of his acquaintance.

For the moment, no measures were taken against Alvise Priuli, though Venetian hopes for his occupation of the see of Brescia must have faded perceptibly at this point. The Pope now appointed William Petow to succeed Cardinal Pole in the legation to England (a man quite unsuited to a diplomatic post, as in his dotage), and confirmed the nephew of Cardinal Durante in the coadjutorship of Brescia.[13] Thus, Priuli was now definitely excluded from the Bishopric of Brescia, and Venice could visualise the post going to a non-Venetian, as Cardinal Pisani, a Venetian present in the assembly where this was decided, objected. Pisani lost no time in informing Navagero of the turn events were taking, relating to him his own efforts to remind the Pope of the concession of Brescia to the Republic under Julius III. These efforts had produced an angry response from Paul IV, who added that 'nessuno doveva più osare parlargi di accessi nè per sè, nè per altri, fossero pure sovrani; perchè egli durante il suo pontificato non aveva fatta riforma più bella di quella di abolire questa inventione et operatione diabolica; e col togliere quanto era stato concesso in antecedenza a favore della repubblica voleva chiarir tutti c'havessero accessi di non poter sperare cosa alcuna.'[14]

Thus the official position had become quite clear: the Pope would be immovable on the question of *accessi* in general, and the see of Brescia in particular. Navagero wrote a further letter to the *Signoria*, based on information obtained from Cardinal Pacheco, in which the position of Alvise Priuli became finally hopeless. The abolition of *accessi* had been aimed principally at Priuli and 'nella casa del Cardinal Polo, dove c'erano persone infette d'eresia, non c'era alcuna peggiore del Priuli.'[15]

Venetian reaction to this was predictably strong though cautious. The Republic expressed its great disappointment that the see of Brescia was to be given to a non-Venetian, especially as this was in violation of the contract made with Julius III, 'tanto più che Brescia era una fortezza di grande importanza, ed era necessario ci fosse un vescovo gradito alla Signoria.'[16] Navagero also received instructions to speak to the Pope's nephews, Cardinal Carafa and the Duke of Paliano, if he felt it appropriate. There was a postscript to this containing a favourable report on the person and religious orthodoxy of Alvise Priuli, added by the *Savi di Terraferma*, Benetto Pesaro and Domenico Bollani.[17]

Navagero's interview with the Pope on July 2, 1557, brought little response, and no change in the situation.[18] Two events brought the affair to a head: the news reached Venice that Cardinal Durante was dying, and peace was concluded between the Pope and Spain. The news from Brescia occasioned further urgent motions in the Venetian Senate, urging Navagero to present the case yet again, and the peace created a more favourable atmosphere for the Venetian ambassador than he had seen for some time. For Paul IV remembered that Venice had not aligned herself with Spain.[19] Yet the coming interview was to be a fateful one for Alvise Priuli. Navagero's report is a historic document for the history of the Inquisition, and for the methods used by Paul IV to repress heresy. Although he was now well-disposed towards the Republic of Venice, and ready to concede the bishopric to a Venetian he still adhered stubbornly to the (quite unproved) view that Priuli was a heretic, describing various burnings in the course of the discussion with a kind of fanatical pride.[20] Again on November 5, the Pope repeated to Navagero that 'desiderava di contentare la Signoria; ma non lo fara mai a favore di quella persona {Priuli}.'[21] At this point, nothing more was said, until the death of Cardinal Durante on Christmas Eve, 1557, precipitated the crisis. Finally, on January 27, 1559, the Pope stated that he had elected a Bishop of Brescia, and Domenico Bollani was named Bishop on 15 March.[22]

The reasons for the selection of Domenico Bollani are not yet entirely clear, although the fact of his local popularity must be a contributing factor. A document quoted by R. Maiocchi, which contains a deposition under oath by a student of the University of Pavia, is of the utmost importance, although research has not so far confirmed it. 'Flavio Stella, studente in leggi dell'università di Pavia e cittadino bresciano depone sotto giuramento che essa città {Brescia} con ogni sorte di officio procurò et operò perchè Sua Signoria {Bollani} fosse fatto vescovo di quella città.'[23] One would expect to find confirmation of these efforts,[24] but none has so far come to light. Bearing in mind the success of Bollani in the first phase of the Oglio dispute, and the fact that the document is of a legal nature, the source has every claim to serious consideration.

There is another reason, however, which is quoted by most writers on Bollani to date,[25] which argues that Bollani's choice had depended on the fact that he had already gained a firm reputation as an energetic opponent of heresy in Brescia during his short period as *Podestà*. These rely on one source, originally quoted by Pio Paschini in 1919.[26] There are two main reasons why the reliability of this

120

source may be questioned. First, perhaps, because the reason is too obvious, and savours of rationalisation. We have seen only too clearly the extent to which the whole affair of the bishopric of Brescia was bedevilled by the heresy hunt and the unfortunate Alvise Priuli. In his final attempt to present Priuli's candidature, Navagero had been told that the Pope 'non voleva saperne di eretici', and that, while willing to favour the Republic's interests, he would never do this in the person of Alvise Priuli. Further there is abundant evidence that the preoccupation on the part of Paul IV with heretics was, in modern terms, pathological.[27] It is a short step from here to the conclusion that the only candidate for the bishopric with any chance of success would be the one with a reputation for the suppression of heresy.[28] No evidence has survived to support the view that Bollani was involved in questions of heresy in Brescia during his term of office as *Podestà* – a lack of evidence all the more remarkable in a field of scholarship as well-tilled as the Inquisition under the pontificate of Paul IV.[29] The second reason is more subjective. We shall see that Bollani's involvement, after his assumption of the bishopric, with cases of heresy in Brescia[30] tended towards a moderating influence on the more precipitate initiatives of the Inquisition, and it seems hard to reconcile this with the statement of Caracciolo that suppression of heresy was the principal cause of his election.[31]

It seems that the cause of Bollani's election is to be found in the relationship between the city of Brescia and the Theatine, D. Geremia Isachino, unless Isachino was personally acquainted with the Bollani family. A draft of a letter from Cardinal Sirleto to Carlo Borromeo survives to indicate that Isachino and Sirleto were on intimate terms with Paul IV at the moment when the final decision about the bishopric of Brescia was taken.[32] Writing about Bollani in 1575, shortly after having made his acquaintance in Rome during the Jubilee, Sirleto states:

'. . . haveva innanci cognosciuto per nome et relatione Monsignor Rev.mo di Brescia (come che insieme col padre don Hieremia { Isachino } prete di chierici regulari et io { Sirleto } havevamo proposto a Paulo IV santa memoria per il vescovado di Brescia) . . .'[33]

As Sirleto, on his own admission, had had no direct contacts with Bollani before 1575, the conclusion remains that Isachino was chiefly responsible for proposing Bollani's candidature to the Pope. It seems most likely that either the city and church authorities in Brescia had made direct overtures to Isachino in his position of influence at the Pope's side (as a result of Bollani's local popularity in Brescia), or that this contact had been through Padre Cabrino, Bollani's confessor and advisor,[34] or possibly also through Padre Santabuona, whose sphere of activity was the area around Salò, where Isachino was active before 1547. Perhaps the request for Bollani's election from Brescia was channelled through Cabrino and Santabuona, for contacts between these 'prereformers' and the emergent orders in the province have been convincingly suggested, if not proved. It remains for further research to document these links and provide firm support for this hypothesis.[35]

There are two further factors which have been insufficiently stressed. We have seen that at the moment of his election (March 15, 1559) he was fully involved with the arbitration of the Oglio dispute, and that, although talks had broken down temporarily, he had clearly demonstrated his diplomatic skill to Venice, and his total dedication to their cause to the people of Brescia.[36] This trust was to bear conspicuous fruit in the years before the final agreement was signed, but the affair must have had considerable influence on the Brescian request for his election as Bishop. Brescia must have known only too well that the bishop would have to be Venetian to satisfy the Republic — and here was an ideal candidate in the person of the *Podestà* — and one who had filled the post with distinction in a series of bad or indifferent Venetian Rectors. He had shown his tenacity in the Brescian cause to the *Deputati all'Oglio*, who occupied posts of importance in the local government of the city, and they would have been in the forefront of his supporters.[37] From the Venetian point of view Bollani also had much to recommend him, having been in office consistently as a Senator, and having returned three times to the powerful *Saviato di Terraferma* after his initial election in 1550. What is more, his experience of the particular problems of Brescia, and — an all important factor — of Venice's relations with the Duchy of Milan, would have recommended him warmly. No other member of the *Collegio* would have been able to match this experience.

For it was more than a bishop that was required. An ambassador extraordinary, with diplomatic experience and skill, was needed to supervise the work of Venetian Rectors and maintain a strict devotion to the *Patria* in matters of conflicting legislation.[38] For Brescia was a centre of many of problems. Not only was the western frontier the boundary between Venice and Spanish dominion, but Brescia soon became an area of possible jurisdictional conflict with the election of the Pope's nephew to the Archbishopric of Milan in 1560.[39] The city was also in direct line of attack for the penetration of heresy from the north, in the form of an influx of foreign preachers and the growth of emigration.[40] A sure hand and a tried experience would be needed to deal effectively with these problems.[41]

But perhaps the simplest reason for Bollani's selection was that he came from a *famiglia vecchia*, that is, a Venetian family in favour with the Papacy, whose activities in the Senate would have found favour in the dispatches of the papal Nuncio in Venice.[42] He had not married, as we have seen, and had been elected by the family *fraterna* to pursue a career of service to the State, and so was a suitable candidate from every point of view.[43]

The year 1559 was the turning point in Domenico's career. After nearly ten years in the Senate, and two major posts in the *Terraferma*, it would not be unreasonable to expect election to the Council of X in the near future,[44] and possibly even higher promotion. The choice would have been a difficult one, for it lay between the prestige, but small financial yield, of a political future in the Venetian government, and the rich prize that the bishopric of Brescia constituted. There was also the fact that the uncertainty of a career suspended between one short-term appointment and the next had to be weighed against the security of a life appointment. And yet the family was no longer in quite the financial straits that Domenico had witnessed in his youth (although the heavy strain placed on its resources by the provision of dowries for Domenico's nieces was later to take its

122

toll.[45]). Some indication of the difficulties and Bollani's reluctance to accept the post is shown in the efforts of his father confessor, Francesco Cabrino, to convince him to accept. According to his biographer, Cabrino 'operà dunque con detto Signore, et con vive ragioni et efficaci essortationi lo persuadeva ad accettare il Vescovato,' as Bollani 'si dimostrava renitente a tanto peso.'[46] Cabrino apparently brought all possible pressure to bear on Bollani, exhorting others to do the same.[47]

Conscious of the difficulties which lay ahead but strengthened by the popular support he had gained in Brescia, Bollani decided to accept the bishopric, filling the necessary gaps in his educational background as soon as possible.[48] He was not to abandon affairs left unfinished in Brescia, however, particularly, as we have seen, the arbitration of the Oglio dispute, as the Venetian Senate had stipulated this in accepting his resignation from the post of *Podestà*. The situation was an unusual one in many ways, and Bollani accepted the conditions of his appointment fully realising its important ecclesiastical/political nature. In fact, within weeks of his election he was again at Urago in conversations with Anguissola.[49] On March 14, 1559, Bollani had been elected Bishop of Brescia amid general rejoicing in the city.[50] The city council elected five prominent citizens to congratulate him at a ceremony held on March 22, at which the *Cavaliere* Scipione Lana read an oration in honour of the occasion.[51] In early April, he returned to Urago, and then to Venice, to receive instructions from the Senate,[52] and was installed as Bishop in the presence of the Captain, Pietro Morosini, and his brother, Giacomo Bollani, on 17 April.[53] On May 4, he made his official entry into the bishop's palace 'essendo ivi tutto il clero et tutta la città a farli honore. Passo per la pallada essendo messi li panni secondo il solito, et nel suo Reggimento {as *Podestà*} fu bravo . . . et fece morir un ladro solo,' as the diarist Caravaggi noted in his chronicle.[54] On August 15, 1559, he said his first Mass in the Cathedral.[55]

NOTES TO CHAPTER VI

1 The passage from *Podestà* to bishop of the same city is unusual but not quite without precedent (The case of the succession of Ambrogio to the archbishopric of Milan is quoted in R. Maiocchi, 'Mons. Bollani e la Facultà di Teologia di Pavia', in *Brixia Sacra*, 1914, pp. 46). It has particular importance in the context of Domenico Bollani, bearing in mind his political career before and after the election, as will appear.

2 See above, Chapter II, *passim.* The facts of the election are well known, having been recounted by Fè D'Ostiani, *op. cit.*, pp. 13–16, P. Paschino, *Un Amico del Cardinale Pole: Alvise Priuli* (Rome, 1921) pp. 130–145, and *passim*, Petroboni, *op. cit.*, pp. 40–49, Zanotti, *op. cit.*, pp. 76–80. I depart from the standard accounts only in questions of emphasis and interpretation, as the political nature of the election has not before been placed in the context of Bollani's career as a whole.

3 Durante's family was from Palazzolo sull'Oglio, in the province of Brescia. For him, see P. Guerrini, 'La Famiglia Durante ed i suoi Vescovi,' in *Brixia Sacra*, 1911, pp. 80 *et seq.*, *Storia di Brescia*, (*cit.*) II, Gradenigo, *op. cit.*, p. 243, Petroboni, *op. cit.*, p. 40, etc. Durante is caricatured in Benvenuto Cellini's autobiography, for which see P. Paschini, 'B. C. ed un Prelato della Corte di Paolo III', in *Roma*, 1929, (typescript in Biblioteca Queriniana, Brescia).

4 For a detailed life of Priuli and the circumstances of his failure to take up this post, see Paschini, *An amico del Cardinale Pole, Alvise Priuli* (Rome, 1921), *passim.* It was traditional for Venice to submit four names to the Pope from among the Venetian patriciate, and the Pope would make his choice from these.

5 For the preferments of the powerful Priuli family, see the family tree and bibliographical supplement in Logan, 'Studies in the Religious Life of Venice' (un-pub. Doct. thesis) *cit.*, pp. 254, 527 resp. For instance, Matteo and Michele Priuli held the bishopric of Vicenza for 38 years (1565–79 and 1579–1603 resp.). The importance of the see of Brescia was stated by the Doge to the Papal Nuncio in Venice in 1579; when it was hoped that the tradition of Venetian incumbents would be continued (see letter of the Bishop of Massa, Nuncio in Venice to Rome, August 15, 1579 in *Archivio Segreto Vaticano, Nunziatura di Venezia* (henceforth, *Nunz. Ven.*) 19, p. 218, and Rome to the Nuncio of the same date (*Ibid.*, 20, p. 214). For the whole question of ecclesiastical preferments in Venice, see Logan, *op. cit.*, pp. 161–299.

6 On the character of Pope Paul IV, see Ludwig von Pastor, *Storia dei Papi nel periodo della Riforma e Restaurazione Cattolica*, (Giulio III, Marcello II, e Paolo IV) It. Ed. (1550–1559) VI, (Rome, 1922), p. 340 *et seq.* with sources cited. Bernardo Navagero, Venetian Ambassador in Rome at this time, was the principal negotiator for Venice in the dispute. His dispatches from Rome provide an illuminating commentary on Veneto/Papal relations, and are in A.S.V., *Consiglio dei X, Lettere di Ambasciatori, (Roma), buste* 24–26, copies in *Biblioteca Marciana*, Venice, Cod. It. 9445. Because they involve English affairs, and Papal opposition to Cardinal Pole and his circle, they were also calendared by Rawdon Brown, in C.S.P.V., VI, pt. II (1556–1557), VII, (1557–1558), from where they are here cited unless otherwise specified.

7 On the reforms, see Pastor, *op. cit.*, pp. 437–438, P. Paschini, 'Benv. Cellini,' etc. *cit.*, p. 506, Petroboni, *op. cit.*, p. 42. 'Ora {21 agosto, 1556} venne totalemente abolito e cessato ogni accesso a benefizi, da chiunque fosse pur concesso e qualunque clausola contenesse . . .' (Pastor, p. 437). See also Navagero's letters of Dec. 5, 18, 1555, and Jan. 11, 1556, quoted by Paschini, *Alvise Priuli . . ., cit.*, p. 131. Priuli's *accesso* had given him the right of accession *before* the death of the present incumbent, Durante. The system of *regressi* involved the renunciation of a post by its holder to another person before his death, usually to a relative. It allowed the system of ecclesiastical dynasticism rife in the first half of the century to develop, particularly among the Venetian patriciate, but, importantly, it was also a means for continued Venetian political control of her subject dominions. For ecclesiastical dynasticism in Venice in the sixteenth century and the part played by family, Papacy and the Venetian State, see the important section in Logan, *op. cit.*, pp. 177–221.

8 He had never been enthusiastic about accepting the onerous public duties of the bishopric, having accepted 'piuttosto con obedientia che con allegrezza alcuna,' preferring a retired life

124

of study (see the letter to him from Paolo Sadoleto, Bishop of Carpentras of 16 April, 1551, in *Lettere di XIII Huomini Illustri*..., {Venice, 1576} pp. 212–213) and wrote to his mentor and ally in England, Cardinal Pole: 'io mi trovo tanto più contento essendo fuori del pericolo d'haver a sostenere un dî peso molto più grave che non comporteria la debolezza delle mie forze, per la rivocazione degli accessi, che V.S. averà già inteso il quale ho accettato per un dono gratissimo di Dio...' (A. Querini { Ed.} *Epistolarum Reginaldi Poli*..., {Brescia, 1744}, V, p. 345).

9   This was not immediately apparent, as Venice did not believe that the Priuli accession was affected by the new reform, being the result of a political compromise with Julius III, rather than a move dictated by motives of personal gain. (Paschini, *Priuli, cit.*, p. 132, n. 4)

10   See his reply of Oct. 2, 1556 (*Idem,* p. 133). Navagero was unable to move the Pope from his stated position on reform at this point.

11   see, for instance, Pastor, *op. cit.*, pp. 397–421.

12   Paschini, *Priuli, cit.*, p. 133. A succession of heresy arrests took place in 1557–8, including the Venetian, Vittore Soranzo, Bishop of Bergamo (for whom, see Paschini, 'Un Vescovo disgraziato nel Cinquecento italiano,' in *Tre Ricerche sulla Storia della Chiesa nel Cinquecento*, (Rome, 1945) pp. 91–151), and on 31 May, 1557, Cardinal Morone, friend of Cardinal Pole, and a member of the Viterbo circle of Vittoria Colonna, that was to come so prominently under the lash of the Roman Inquisition. In the case of Morone, the affair was to start a chain of heresy hunts that was to reach Alvise Priuli, a close friend and confidant of the Cardinal of England.

13   Bernardo Navagero to Venice, June 18, 1557, in *C.S.P.V.*, VI, (II) p. 1169, Paschini, *op. cit.*, p. 135. Alessandro Durante was manifestly unsuited to the Bishopric of Brescia, being 25 years of age, and 'illiterato', according to later reports which reached the Pope (*Ibid., loc. cit.*, n. 1).

14   Navagero to Venice, *C.S.P.V.*, vol. *cit.*, n. 937 quoted by Paschini, *op. cit.*, pp. 135–136.

15   *C.S.P.V.*, VI, n. 939, Paschini, *op. cit.*, p. 136.

16   For the importance of Brescia at this point, see above, pp. 80–81, etc.

17   *C.S.P.V.*, VI, n. 944, Paschini, p. 136. There is no reason to suppose that there is any significance in the fact that this motion was proposed by the future incumbent. It shows merely that he was in the forefront of the affair, at the height of his political influence, and a likely candidate for the Pope's short-list for the see of Brescia.

18 , Navagero emphasised again the importance of Brescia, being on the frontier between Venice and Milan (and none was better qualified to know this than Domenico Bollani, as we have seen, for he must have participated in the discussion which produced Navagero's instructions).

19   'Il Navagero, dunque, presentandosi al Papa il 23 ottobre, cominciò col congratularsi con lui per quella pace, ed il Papa rispose col fare le lodi di Venezia, la quale, a differenza del Duca Cosimo di Firenze, non si era voluta legare cogli Spagnoli.' (Paschini, p. 139).

20   Paul IV stated quite openly to Navagero that he had abolished *accessi* on Priuli's account, that he was certain that Priuli was a heretic as he belonged to that 'casa apostata del cardinale d'Inghilterra'. He went on: 'Il Cardinal Pole era il maestro ed il cardinal Morone, che abbiamo in castello { afterwards proved innocent and reinstated } è il discepolo, ma il discepolo è andato più innanzi del maestro. Il Priuli va al pari di questi e di Marc'Antonio Flaminio, il quale so non fosse morto, sarebbe già bruciato; e noi habbiamo fatto abbrugiare nella Minerva in publico Cesare Flaminio suo fratello...' The Pope continued in the same tone, obsessively preoccupied with the heresy hunt, mentioning a distant relative of his who had flown to Geneva to prove that heresy was an insidious evil whose roots extended even into the Vatican. He concluded: 'Magnifico ambasciatore, non fateci parlare su questa materia, perche se nostro padre fosse eretico, portassimo le fascine per abruciarlo.' (Paschini, *op. cit.*, pp. 139–140, *C.S.P.C.*, VI(ii), n. 1067, Navagero to the Doge and Senate.) But compare Cantimori, 'Italy and the Papacy', *New Cambridge Modern History*, (Cambridge, 1958) II, pp. 251–274 at p. 267.

21   Paschini, *op. cit.*, p. 141. Clearly the Pope was firmly convinced of the existence of a heresy ring, and was anxious to include all the members of the Pole/Priuli circle. He was

particularly keen to capture Soranzo (for whom see above, p. 125, n. 12) 'perchè doveva sapere qualcosa dei personaggi sopradetti.'

22 *Ibid.*, pp. 144–145, Fe D'Ostiani, *op. cit.*, pp. 13–16. Fe D'Ostiani was well wide of the mark when he stated (p. 14) that the Pope had elected Bollani, *serbando il Priuli per altra sede*, as Petroboni (*op. cit.*, p. 45) noted.

23 R. Maiocchi, 'Mons. Bollani e la facoltà . . .' *cit.*, p. 46. Testimonies were required to Bollani's character before a degree in Theology could be conferred, and Stella, a citizen of Brescia, apparently added this detail for good measure. Possibly such initiatives on the part of the city were directed at Rome, rather than Venice, as otherwise one would expect to find mention of it in the correspondence of Brescia with her orator in Venice. (For Bollani's

24 Normally, such a campaign would involved the Venetian rectors, but in this case, of course, the *Podestà* was Bollani himself. But see below, pp. 121–122.

25 Fe D'Ostinai, *op. cit.*, p. 14, P. Paschini, 'Un Umanista disgraziato nel Cinquecento: Publio Francesco Spinola' in *Nuova Archivio Veneto*, (1919) pp. 63–186, Petroboni, *op. cit.*, pp. 46–47.

26 Antonio Caracciola, 'Vita et Gesti di Gio. Pietro Carafa cioè di Paolo IV' MS. no. 349 in the *Biblioteca Casanatense*, Rome, p. 405. (A Manuscript life of Paul IV, which I have been unable to see, nor to discover further details as to date and reliability. *Cit.*, in P. Paschini, 'Un Umanista disgraziato nel Cinquecento . . .' *cit.*, p. 120).

27 Besides the sources quoted above, see also F. Church, *I Riformatori Italiani* (trad. Cantimori) (Florence, 1967) I, pp. 373–391 for a non-Catholic view of the Inquisition under Paul IV. On the death of Paul IV, the roman populace 'took the opportunity to sack the buildings of the Inquisition nad burn its records.' (A.G. Dickens, *The Counter Reformation*, {London, 1968} p. 119).

28 The names of the other three Venetian noble candidates presented to the Pope by the Republic would indeed be revealing, but do not appear to have survived.

29 Of course, lack of evidence does not, in itself, provide proof of this. Among MS sources where notice of heresy cases in Brescia during the period 1558–1559 would be most likely to be found would be Bollani's dispatches to the Council of X when *Podestà* and the dispatches of the Papal Nuncio in Venice. The former have not yielded any such cases, and the latter has not survived, the *Nunziatura di Venezia* archive in the *Archivio Segreto Vaticano* being interrupted between July, 1554 and March, 1566. In general it seems that Brescia was a noted centre of heresy up to about 1550 and after the Council of Trent, when Bollani himself was concerned with it as Bishop (for which see below, pp. 201–211). In general, see Cesare Cantù, *Gli Eretici d'Italia* (1865–6) (Turin), E. Comba, *I nostri Protestanti*, (Florence, 1897) II, P. Tacchi-Venturi, *Storia della Compagna di Gesù in Italia . . .*, (Rome, 1931), I, and on relations between Venice and Rome, Pio Paschini, *Venezia e l'Inquisizione Romana da Giulio III a Paolo IV*, (Padua, 1959), pp. 117–146. For Brescia and heresy in particular, see the fundamental study by P. Guerrini in *La Congregazione dei Padri della Pace*, (Brescia, 1933) pp. 71–94 ('Le Condizioni Religiose di Brescia intorno alla metà del '500'), and for details, for example, A. Zanelli, 'Gabriele ed Eraclito Gandini e i processi d'eresia in Brescia nel secolo XVI' in *Archivio Storico Italiano*, Ser. V, Tom. XL (1907), P. Guerrini, 'Due amici bresciani di Erasmo da Rotterdam: E. Emili, V. Maggi' in *Archivio Storico Lombardo* (1923), pp. 172–180, and E.A. Rivoire, 'Eresia e Riforma a Brescia' in *Boll. Soc. Studi Valdesi*, (1959).

30 See below, pp. 201–211.

31 It should also be noted that there was another candidate of which Venice may or may not have been aware. The Brescian Muzio Calini, Archbishop of Zara, apparently made strenuous efforts to gain election in 1559. He was a subject of the Republic of Venice, but not a Venetian. (On this see, Pasero, 'L'estremo supplizio dei Carafa {1561} e altre notizie Romane in una raccolta di lettere di Mons. Muzio Calini' in *Commentari dell'Ateneo di Brescia*, CXXXVII {1938} A, pp. 42–43). Calini's cause was favoured by the Cardinals Pacheco and of Trent, as well as the Spanish ambassador (see the *Lettere* of Muzio Calini, MSS in Biblioteca Queriniana, Brescia, Fe., 16, pp. 255–256. 260–263, 263–264. These MSS have been on loan from the Queriniana to the Vatican Library for some five years, and I have been unable to consult them.).

32 , The letter was discovered by Pio Paschini and published by Guerrini as an appendix to his 'Il IV Centenario della nascita di San Carlo,' in *Memorie Storiche della Diocesi di Brescia*, (Brescia, 1938) pp. 187–234 at pp. 227–229. On Isachino, see *Ibid.*, p. 227, n. 2, P. Paschini 'San Carlo e i Teatini, notizie storiche,' in *Scuola Cattolica*, II (1922), pp. 287–296, *Idem.*, 'Guglielmo Sirleto prima del Cardinalato,' in *Tre ricerche sulla storia della Chiesa del Cinquecento*, (Rome, 1945) pp. 82, 244–245, 266–267, and *Idem, San Gaetano Thiene, Gian Pietro Carafa e le origini dei Chierici Regolari Teatini*, (Rome, 1926) pp. 88–89.

33 The unfinished rough draft is in Arch. Segr. Vat., Cod. Lat. 7093. Sirleto goes on to praise Bollani's efforts in the Diocese of Brescia, particularly his *Costituzioni per il Clero*. Sirleto had long been an ally in Rome for Bollani, and they must have been frequently in correspondence. Bollani has great praise for him in his letter to Roveglio of February 4, 1576 (*Carteggio Bollani-Roveglio, cit.*). There is no evidence of a relationship before the Council of Trent, however, so that it seems unlikely that Sirleto was directly involved in proposing Bollani's candidature to the Pope.

34 The most recent short biographies of Cabrino and Santabuona are in Guerrini, *La Congregazione dei Padri della Pace, cit.*, pp. 95–128. Cabrino's intimate relationship with Bollani – even before his election – is documented below. If Cabrino was instrumental in persuading Bollani to accept the bishopric and if his contacts with Isachino (suggested by Guerrini) can be proved, it seems a logical conclusion that Isachino acted on advice from Brescia itself.

35 It appears that Isachino was in Venice between 1547 and 1556 when he became *preposto* of San Silvestro in Rome (Guerrini, 'Il IV Centenario . . .' *loc. cit.*). It is not impossible, therefore, that he knew Bollani in Venice. On the foundation of a branch of the Oratory of Divine Love at Salò on Lake Garda during the early 1540s, with the suggestion that Isachino was numbered among its members, see Paschini, *San Gaetano Thiene . . ., cit.*, pp. 88–89.

36 See above, Chapter V.

37 Their affection for him was tellingly documented – down to 1567, at least – in the *Registrum Olei*, it will be remembered (Chapter V, *passim*).

38 It is clear that Bollani acted in an advisory capacity to the Venetian Rectors in Brescia throughout his term of office. See for example, the *Relazione* of Antonio Bragadin (1569) in Pasero, *Relazioni, cit.*, p. 113, the acknowledged intervention of Bollani in civil affairs under the *Capitano* Domenico Priuli in 1572 (Pasero, pp. 120–122), and the dependence of the *Podestà* Soranzo on Bollani's advice in the plague years 1576–77, reported in many of Bollani's letters to his vicar-general, Giacomo Roveglio (for which see below, pp. 158 seq). For conflicts in jurisdiction, see below, Chapter IX, *passim.*

39 Carlo Borromeo. Brescia, although part of the dominion of the Republic of Venice, came under the ecclesiastical jurisdiction of the Archbishop of Milan.

40 See P. Guerrini, *La Congregazione .,. ., cit.*, pp. 78–94. On Bollani and heretics in Brescia, see below, pp. 152–153, 201–211 etc.

41 , The necessity for Venice of a Venetian nobleman to occupy the see of Brescia is nowhere better documented than in the situation reported at Bollani's death by the papal nuncio in Venice, Bolognetti, in his *Relazione*, published in Stella, *Chiesa e Stato . . ., cit.*, pp. 218–219. It seems also very probable that the award of the bishopric to Bollani was, in part, a reward for services rendered in state service.

42 See above, p. 60, n. 50.

43 It must be added that there was no tradition of church posts in the Bollani family as far back as it can be traced. This would tend to emphasise even further the political and 'local' nature of the appointment.

44 The genealogist, Barbaro, was certainly mistaken when he stated that Bollani 'fu Ca{p}o del Consiglio dei X' (*loc. cit.*). For purposes of comparison, Sebastiano Venier, who had *failed* to solve the Oglio dispute in 1561, became Doge of Venice in 1577, when Bollani had two further years of activity before him.

45 See above, pp. 10–11.

46 Padre G.B. Saraceno, 'Storia della Congregazione della Pace ora detta dell'Oratorio di S. Filippo Neri in Brescia' MSS preserved in the library of the *Padri della Pace*, Brescia, Book I, Chap. XV, pp. 61–63. With understandable exaggeration, Saraceno attributes

Bollani's election almost solely to Cabrino's exhortations, prayers and penance. The MS contains a skeleton life of Bollani (at pp. 183–188), which must be the earliest, (about 1650) though is not always accurate, (see attribution of Bollani's knighthood to the Venetian Republic, p. 183).

47 *Ibid.*, pp. 62–63.

48 See below, p. 130.

49 April 4–8, 1559 (above, pp. 92–93). The unusual nature of the passage *a praetura ad episcopatum* was commemmorated by the city in a tablet set into the wall of the recently constructed Loggia (See Fè D'Ostiani, *op. cit.*, p. 15).

50 B. Zamboni, *Memorie intorno alle Pubbliche Fabbriche di Brescia*, (Brescia, 1778), p. 74, Fè D'Ostiani, p. 15.

51 *Ibid.*

52 As it may have been about this time (1559) that Bollani sat for a portrait in Venice, traces of which have come down to us, a note on existing portraits may not be out of place. The only known portrait of him is in the Great Hall, in the Bishop's Palace in Brescia, and is certainly later than contemporary. As part of the decoration of the *Municipio* in Brescia, the city had ordered frescoes to be painted by Titian (on these, see Zamboni, *op. cit.*, p. 143 etc., and more recently, C. Pasero, 'Nuove notizie d'archivio intorno alla Loggia di Brescia' in *Commentari dell'Ateneo di Brescia*, {1952} pp. 49–91). The city had complained that these were not entirely by the painter's hand, and a dispute broke out between Titian and the *Deputati* of Brescia. On June 3, 1569, Titian wrote to Bollani to persuade him to mediate in this dispute, giving as his reason for doing so: 'L'amor che la molta sua cortesia mi porta, e *per l'antica mia servitù e divotione verso di lei*' (letter published in full in Zamboni, *op. cit.*, p. 143, Italics mine.). From this is appears that Titian had received commissions from Bollani in the past, and, indeed, the two men could well have been brought together by Pietro Aretino. Further evidence of this relationship exists in the affair of the request by Orazio Vecellio, Titian's son, to carry arms against threats on his life by Leone Leoni. For this, see Cadorin, *Dello Amore ai Veneziani di Tiziano Vecellio*, (Venice, 1833) pp. 50 *et seq.*, 103 *et seq.* etc., and G. Dalla Santa, *Studi di Arte e Storia a cura della Direzione del Museo Civico Correr*, I (Milan/Rome, 1920) pp. 262–263 etc. Orazio's final petition to the Venetian Senate, on 20 March, 1562, (A.S.V., *Consiglio dei Dieci, Parti communi, filza* 84) was rejected, but its timing is perhaps significant: 'et io con molta faticha et spesa restai con il divino agiuto liberato in capo de doi mesi volendo tornarmene a casa per potermene sicuramente venire feci sapere questa mia occorsa desgratia al Reverendiss. Vescovo di Brescia *padrone amorevolissimo del suddetto mio padre, et di me*, et pregai sua S. Rev. che mi provedesse di securtà et fidata scorta d'huomini che mi levasse salvo dalle insidie di questo mio accerrimo nemico, et con tal mezzo mi son condotto nel gremio di questo felicissimo dominio...' (Italics mine. I am grateful to Mr. Charles Hope for drawing my attention to this latter episode.) The earliest known engraved portrait of Bollani was published in 1608 in the volume *Acta Ecclesiae Brixiensis ab illustriss. et reverendiss. D.D. Dominico Bollano eius Episcopo, promulgata anno Domini MDLXXIIII* (Venice, *apud* Varisoum), reproduced in *Storia di Brescia (cit)* II, p. 444. Fe D'Ostiani published what appears to be a mirror image of this portrait in a new engraving in his *Il Vescovo Domenico Bollani...*, *(cit.)* in 1875. In this latter engraving (not otherwise identified), the portrait appears in an elaborate frame, which includes the Bollani arms, the Venetian Lion, and the date: 1560. There seems to be no justification for the inclusion of this date in the engraving unless, either it has some basis in historical fact, or it is based on an original in which the date appears. If the hypothesis to which this evidence points – that Titian painted Bollani's portrait from sittings possibly in 1559-60 – is true, then the moment of his assumption of the bishopric would have been the appropriate time for it, and the later engraving, (1608) and derivatives, are probably based on a portrait by the artist now lost, or not so identified or firmly attributed. For the record, Titian was in Venice in the period under discussion, firmly established as the first rank portraitist in the city, and the obvious choice for a ceremonial portrait commemorating the new dignity. (Copies of the Fè D'Ostiani engraving were also published in Maiocchi, *op. cit.*, {1914} and Cairns 'A Distinguished Correspondent...' *cit.*, {1966}). See Figs. 22, 28.

128

53 *Archivio di Stato di Brescia* (A.S.B.), *Cancelleria Pretoria, Ducali*, (1557–1562) pp. 65–66.
54 A.S.B., *Diario Caravaggi*, May 4, 1559. (This observer was not noted for his charity towards Venetian Rectors, as Pasero { *Relazione . . ., cit.*, p. 27} noted. On this source, see also, Pasero, 'La Cronaca bresciano cinquecentesca di Lodovico Caravaggi' { N.p. 22.iii.1935}).
55 *Ibid.*, August 16, 1559.

PART II

CHAPTER VII

THE COUNCIL OF TRENT:
DOMENICO BOLLANI AS PARTICIPANT AND PRODUCT
1561–1563

The timing of Domenico Bollani's appointment as Bishop of Brescia — two years before the opening of the final sessions of the Council of Trent — was to have a decisive effect on his own formation and on the Diocese. If he had lacked previous ecclesiastical experience and any sense of vocation towards the Church, it was precisely because of this lack of experience that he came, in succeeding years to personify the spirit of the Catholic Reformation. He 'grew up' ecclesiastically, so to speak, at the Council itself, bringing his undoubted and proven gifts of diplomacy and arbitration in a civil sphere to bear on the problems of the reformation of the Church that were placed before him.[1] Although his family connections had been with that section of the Venetian patriciate most prone to favour Papal initiatives, and most involved with ecclesiastical dynasticism,[2] he had not been involved in any direct ways with the trafficking of benefices between relatives, family traditions of Church preferment, or any of the current practices of ecclesiastical politics in Venice.

He was, therefore, in an ideal position to undertake the reformation of a diocese for two reasons. First because he had been involved in problems of pacification, arbitration and organisation for his government over a wide sphere of political activity, and secondly he had none of the vested interests of tradition, family, and built-in opposition to reform that some of his colleagues at the Council, and opponents in the diocese in the years ahead were to demonstrate.[3] Domenico Bollani as Bishop of Brescia was *created* by the Council of Trent, and so it is small wonder that he turned out to be one of its most successful exponents, and, for the next 20 years, a faithful adherent to its principles.

The influence of the Council on Bollani's future activity was, therefore, immense. Besides providing him with a concrete programme of action for his diocese, to which all his efforts, practical skill and broad human understanding were to be dedicated, it was also the theatre of his first endeavours in ecclesiastical government — a congregation of the finest theological and political minds of the age — against which he could measure his skill in discussion, speech and debate. Even here, the outlines of his reforming personality were laid down: a judicial balance of the broad human tolerance that had won him respect in Udine, Brescia and Milan, and the serious dedication to study that was to put his reforms on a secure Catholic doctrinal and liturgical basis.

In fact he had devoted himself to the study of Doctrine, Theology and the works of Aquinas since his election in 1559, taking lessons from the Dominican Theologian Benedetto Erba,[4] and the Carmelite Friar, Giovita Garzoni,[5] and had brought himself up to date on the complex controversial questions in dispute

130

between the Catholic and Protestant Churches that were to receive a full airing at the Council.

The year of Bollani's election coincided with the arrival of a new Pope. In 1559, after a conclave which had lasted four months, Gian Angelo de Medici was elected, taking the name of Pius IV. The peace of Cateau-Cambrésis had also cleared the way for the re-opening of the Council, interrupted since its closure by Julius III in 1552. Laborious negotiations ensued between the Papacy and the various Christian heads of state, until in 1560 a formula was found that would satisfy both the French and Spanish kings,[6] and the Council was officially called in November 1560.[7] In principal aims were the reformation of the Roman Catholic Church, the eradication of heresy and an attempt to heal the rift between Catholicism and Protestantism. Trent was elected as the site for the meetings, as being most suitably situated to satisfy all susceptibilities.[8]

But it is worth pausing at this point to consider the problems that were facing the Council in which Domenico Bollani was to play a minor if significant part. Pius IV was faced with new problems when he called the Council in 1560. No longer were the hopes of the Emperor Charles V for a solution to the problem of a disunited Germany the spur that was urging the Pope towards a Council. Now the King of France was facing possible anarchy and civil war unless a strong hand could be found to steady the ship. The Calvinist threat had crystallised into a political hazard with the General Synod of Calvinist Churches in Paris in 1559, and the King's reaction in the Council of the French Church constituted both unity and polarity. Importantly, this latter move could also be construed as an attempt at the erosion of Papal power, unless the Pope acted in his own right. The spread of Protestantism throughout northern Europe and the political situation this caused in the relations between European Heads of State and the Pope, were not the only factors impinging on the Pope, and giving rise to Councils, but the contribution of Northern European politics as an influence on four Popes should not be forgotten. Furthermore, 1558 had seen the accession of Elizabeth in England. The old European uncertainty about England's religious future which Domenico Bollani had seen in 1547 was about to have a similar outcome.[9]

The heritage of the final sessions at Trent was the problems raised by previous sessions of the council. Above the enduring preoccupations of internal reforms, eradication of heresy, and the definition of dogma against Protestant assaults on it, hovered the perennial problem of the Papacy. The Popes wavered between genuine desires for reform, and the fear that the Council might alter the image of the Papacy in an assertion of supremacy over it. Fundamentally, it was always going to be difficult to reconcile the idea of a Council — a 'democratic' concept — with the doctrine of Papal supremacy as conceived by Renaissance Popes. From inside the Church of Rome, definition of dogma was to build the bulwark against attacks on it from the heretical north. From north of the Alps, abuses in the Church itself might have seemed the supreme priority. Charles V had seen his own future political stability in the Council. When these factors are compounded with political sympathies, which divided the prelates into more or less strictly defined nationalist camps, the immense complexity of the whole enterprise may be seen, and the endless argument over such details as precedence, ritual at the Council and the order of business may be understood.

In 1560, exterior threats were as powerful a stimulus as before. Heresy in France and the Netherlands was gathering strength. But some ground had been covered in the intervening period, particularly by the new Religious Orders. Earlier Councils had made some progress towards a definition of dogma, too, with a consolidated attack on some Protestant tenets in 1545–1547.[10] But little advance was made in the field of the reform of the Church itself, and great resistence was experienced to the principle of Residence.

In the Council called by Julius III, the prelates had re-affirmed the presence of Christ in the Sacraments, and manifested support for oral confession, but the presence of Protestants for the first time proved its undoing. The Catholic bishops present felt unable to accept their demands, and the session dissolved.

So the sessions of 1561–1563 inherited a host of problems both political and spiritual, procedural and formal. It is sometimes difficult in modern times to conceive of the extent to which sympathies in religious matters were dictated by national affinities and considerations, and the way in which opinion on any given problem would polarize into more or less strictly defined nation viewpoints. But it is perhaps sufficient to remember the character of the Venetian *Ragion di Stato*[11] (with which this study is supremely concerned) to understand the national camps into which the corpus of over one hundred bishops at the Council soon divided.[12]

It remains to examine those aspects of the Council in which Bollani was directly involved in particular, and in general, their effect on his reforming activity in Brescia.[13] His participation had been interrupted, as we have seen, by the demands of the Venetian Senate,[14] but he had already arrived in Trent by April, 1561,[15] and even before the official opening of the assembly, by the time he was called away to the Oglio dispute, had already achieved a reputation as a valuable member of the Council.[16] In late October, the Brescian, Muzio Calini, Archbishop of Zara[17] reported to Cardinal Corner in Rome that Bollani had gone to Venice to report on the Oglio dispute, and was expected in Trent within a few days.[18] During his period at the Council, Bollani participated in discussion of the Indes, the invitation to the Council of heretics, and the perennial problem of Residence, as well as serving on committees, involving himself with the reform of monasteries and engaging in various activities of a political nature.[19]

The Index of Prohibited Books was an early topic at the Council. Ever since the pontificate of Paul IV, increasing embarrassment had been felt by the Papacy over the severity of the restrictions enforced by him, and a gradual mitigation of this severity had taken place under Pius IV.[20] At the Council, the Index was one of the few topics not complicated by the question of whether the assembly was to be considered a continuation of the last or not, but the continued condemnation of Protestant texts would have the function of excluding Protestants from the Council.[21] The further complication that the discussion of the Index might be construed as the correction of the work of a Pope was avoided by a Papal brief ordering the delegates to reform the Index.[22] By January, 1562, the subject was already on the official agenda, and the Council had decided to undertake this task, but much discussion ensued and five separate congregations (from January 30 to

132

February 12) were required to air preliminaries. Finally a Commission representing all the churches represented at the Council was suggested by Domenico Bollani,[23] and nominated on February 17, with Bollani as a member.[24] The group adopted as its principal aim the examination of works already on the Index and those suspect, basing its judgements on the acquaintance of members with the works themselves, rather than on second-hand opinions, as had happened previously. This long study necessitated copies of such works, and a series of initiatives was necessary to obtain these from Antwerp, Germany and Venice.[25]

The work of this group brought tangible results as much revision of the Index of Paul IV was found to be necessary. Formerly, the list had contained merely the descriptions of those books felt unsuitable or damaging to Catholic morality. Now the so-called *Ten Rules* were prefaced, so that works published in future could be classified according to the canons established by the Council, and three categories of prohibition were distinguished. Books by heretics caused the whole of the literary production of such authors to be condemned; individually described books were prohibited; and some books were prohibited until expurgated.[26] Bollani and his colleagues were concerned above all to moderate the harshness of the previous Index. Many works were transferred from the second group to the third,[27] permitting access to them after they had been brought into line with the requirements of the Church. Further, the wording of the description of the first group was modified so that the inclusion of a work in it was no longer tantamount to an outright accusation of heresy. Its author was to be described as 'heretical or suspected of heresy'.[28]

This work must have occupied Bollani for long periods during the winter of 1562, and was one for which his humanistic leanings had well qualified him. It was also a task of which he had had direct experience in the service of the Venetian Government.[29] After the Council, the results of the commission were further studied by a committee of 4 members in Rome before their final publication by the Pope on March 24, 1564.[30]

Like the Index of Prohibited Books, the question of the invitation of heretics to the Council was an early topic for discussion. Many of the prelates at Trent could remember the effect of Protestant presence at the Council in 1552. The calling of this Council had indeed been partly a political compromise between Julius III and Charles V, and was to have been the fulfilment of the latter's dreams of Christian Unity springing from a free discussion of their differences between Protestants and Catholics. But the Germans had come reluctantly,[31] and it could hardly be said that a spirit of co-operation characterised the sessions. The Protestant Princes had stipulated that they would only attend a 'free' (non-Papal) Council, while Charles V had used their apparent commitment to press the renewal of the Council on the Pope.[32] They had argued at Trent that previous decisions taken in their absence would have to be reviewed. The Papal legates, on the other hand, refused to allow Protestants to take part in the business of the Council. War had then brought a menacing Protestant army dangerously close to Trent, and the Council had quickly dissolved.

But by 1560, as we have seen, the Pope had new reasons for calling the Council. Direct threats to Catholicism from possible political unions of Protestant (in both

France and the Netherlands) urged a more cautious approach, and invited a more conciliatory attitude. On February 26, 1562, therefore, the Council published an edict inviting Protestants to Trent to participate in the discussions, 'pervaso da spirito di nobile sentimento pacifico'.[33]

Predictably, this spirit was by no means universally shared by the prelates at Trent in 1562, and was traditionally bound up with the question of German religious disunity. The decision had been to draw up a form of *Salvocondotto* for Protestants, as in the past, and the details of his document were to arouse heated discussion in the days ahead. Calini described these discussions in his letter of 26 February, noting that the matter would arouse Spanish opposition from those legates concerned to safeguard the interests of the Spanish and Roman Inquisitions.[34]

Having decided that a *Salvocondotto* was to be granted, its precise form caused further heart-searching and discussion,[35] and it is here that Domenico Bollani entered the debate. First the document previously issued to Protestants at the request of Charles V was read as a basis for discussion. The question was then put as to whether this concession could be extended to other nations.[36] Daniele Barbaro expressed doubts at this point, wishing to have a copy of the *Salvo-condotto* before him before giving his vote.[37] This was agreed, and caused a suspension of the talks while copies were obtained.

To understand Bollani's contribution to the debate, it is necessary to consider the function of the Imperial representatives.[38] The Imperial conclave at the Council was vitally interested in the problem of the *Salvocondotto*, still hoping, that if Protestants could be induced to attend the Council, the rift in the Church might be healed. This lay behind the Emperor's efforts to promote concessions over the use of the Chalice by the laity and clerical marriage, as he hoped that many Protestants might be so induced to return to the Catholic fold.[39]

The Archbishop of Prague and the Bishop of Cinquechiese had only just arrived at Trent on February 2, 1562, and were still awaiting their lay colleague, Von Thun.[40] The question of their status at this point — whether, not having presented their letters of authority from Ferdinand, they should enjoy participatory rights as ambassadors or bishops — was a delicate question on which Calini commented in his letter to Cardinal Corner on February 2.[41] Their letters of authority were read and accepted, but their position at the Council continued to be the subject of some heated discussion.[42]

Returning to the debate on the form of the *Salvocondotto*, less than three weeks after the above events) the Archbishop of Prague stated that he would have preferred that the number of heretics permitted to attend the Council be specified in the document.[43] Bollani now said that he had taken careful note of the words of the speaker, more particularly as he was the representative of the Emperor Ferdinand, and requested some clarification of the point.[44] The Archbishop replied with some heat that he had spoken as bishop, and not as *Oratore*, and that his only motive in proposing this limitation of numbers had been the reflection that the concession to the Bohemians at the Council of Basle had contained such a clause. Calini's description of the episode makes it clear, moreover, that the Archbishop of Prague had spoken from the position assigned to him in the

134

assembly as Archbishop rather than that assigned to Imperial representatives.[45] As a Venetian, Bollani had been perfectly entitled to suspicion of Imperial motives, when the dispute over the position of the Imperial representatives in the preceding weeks — and the history of the Emperor's overtures towards Protestants — are borne in mind. It was, however, unfounded in this case.[46]

In this way, Bollani gained experience in ecclesiastical politics, and could bring his political and diplomatic skill to bear on the problems he now faced. Conscious of the national and political divisions in the Council, he had nevertheless been wise enough not to pursue the debate with the Archbishop of Prague, when he saw that a decision was imminent.[47] But even before the Council had become fully operative after the arrival of the Imperial representatives in the winter of 1562, he had had a chance to employ his own experience in arbitration in the service of the Church. Remembering, perhaps, Bollani's absence from the Council in the service of the Venetian Republic, the legates elected him to a committee to adjudicate in the unending dispute over precedence which clearly demonstrated throughout the troubled course of the final sessions of the Council the degree to which the prelates present were a prey to wordly ambition and squalid considerations of self importance.[48]

But Domenico was to make his mark at the Council in matters of far greater importance, notably the question of Residence — a problem that had bedevilled the Council since its inception. He became closely involved in the discussions on whether the obligatory residence of bishops was *de iure divino*, and the conviction that the place of the priest was near his flock was to become an important principle for him in his work in the diocese of Brescia.[49]

The question of Residence — of bishops in particular — was to divide the Council of Trent most sharply, accentuating political and national antagonism, and was to be the rock on which the Council almost foundered. Since 1547, the question had been under active discussion, and Cardinal Seripando was able to write in 1562 that if these final sessions were to see a solution of the problem, then the superiority of such recent efforts over all other Councils would be clearly demonstrated.[50]

Since the pontificate of Paul IV, whose reforms of *accessi* and *regressi* we have seen,[51] attempts had been made to induce bishops to abandon the easy and politically satisfying life of the Roman Court and to reside in their sees, devoting themselves above all to the cure of souls. But the severity of Paul IV had only served to drive prelates to seek another Rome in Naples and Venice, and they had flocked back to Rome on his death.

Pius IV had shown similar determination in the matter, ordering bishops to return to their sees in a congregation of February, 1560, and, when the Council was late in starting, repeating this order in September.[52] The great crisis which threatened to disrupt the Council had a complex of causes. First the elimination of non-residence would hit hard at Italian ecclesiastical habits, especially at pluralism, and Italians outnumbered all others at Trent. The Spanish bishops particularly, and the French reforming party desired a greater degree of authority for bishops, which met stern opposition from the Curial party. Finally, the proposal that residence of bishops was *de iure divino*, made by Pedro Guerero,

Archbishop of Grenada, in the congregation of April 7, 1562, split the Council into two irreconcilable parties.[53]

The Spanish bishops were solidly behind their spokesman, but the opposition, led by Cardinal Simonetta, had realised the dangers inherent in the dispute: the supremacy of Papal decisions would become questionable: new attacks by Protestants would be facilitated; and the dangerous thesis that the Pope be subject to the Council would be brought out into the open. There followed further discussions and voting on April 20, with a maximum of confusion — a significant number of prelates basing their answer on the question of the Pope's hypothetical opinion on the matter. Domenico Bollani, at this point, had voted for *de iure divino*.[54] As a result of this confusion, two dispatches went to Rome: one asking the Pope to decide the question himself, and a minority view deploring the fact that he had been asked for this.

The same day, a special commission was elected to draft a decree on the reforms so far dealt with, and Bollani was among the six bishops elected whose clear and unequivocal statement on Residence and sustained loyalty to the Papacy had recommended them.[55] The question of Residence had been too much for the Council, and was again deferred, but it is worth noting that even the decision to defer, hotly contested by the Spaniards, was arrived at by a subtle compromise, and would soon be on the floor again.[56]

By this time Bollani had clearly achieved a position of usefulness at the Council. Although not openly espousing the Curialist cause, his reputation had been such as to warrant his election to a six man commission to draft a decree on which all members would be asked to vote.[57] The accounts of the situation at this point by both Sarpi and Calini give Bollani an even more important role in the events taking place behind the scenes — and one which reflects his growing reputation for diplomacy in arbitration. His task was to convince other members of the Council of the wisdom of a policy which would not conflict openly with Papal interests: '{Mantoa e Simonetta} trattarono strettamente come dar compita soddisfazione al Papa e alla corte in materia della Residenza, e quai prelati sarebbono atti a manneggiarsi a persuader gli altri. Quelli che già erano scoperti per ristretti negli interessi pontifici o della corte, se ben atti del rimanente, stimarono non buoni per mancamento di credito. Messero due di stima per bontà, e molto destri nel negoziare, li vescovi di Modena e Brescia.'[58] Later, Sarpi described the success of this type of negotiation, in which Bollani was involved again, this time with the bishop of Nola and the Archbishop of Otranto, and it appears from his efforts in private discussions that he was prepared to adopt a policy of moderation — giving priority to the continued stability of the Council, as a general indicator of the health of the Church — over the dispute on Residence which was threatening it.[59]

The accuracy of Sarpi's statements is less important in the context of Bollani's participation at this crucial stage in the Council's progress. When it came to the point, the opposition of the Curialist party and Spanish reforming zeal were in the end irreconcileable, given the slight likelihood that the Papacy would consent to alter its function and image radically. Subtleties of theological definition were not the factors that would open a breach in the main body of the Church, causing the dissolution of the Council, and admitting disunity and disagreement to

136

Protestant observers, who would be quick to take advantage of the ensuing confusion. A united front was desperately needed if the Council of Trent was not to do more harm than good.

In this light, Bollani's efforts to persuade the bishops shows how necessary to its progress was an expert political hand. In the confusion of political, national and religious motivations at Trent — and nowhere more so than over the question of Residence — the experience of arbitration and negotiation of men like Bollani could be used to relieve the tension, and perhaps help to save the Council from ruin. In spite of his slight training in Theology and the Scriptures, political moderates were indispensable in such a crisis, and perhaps it was only due to the efforts of men like Morone (whose experience from both sides of the fence, as it were, was unequalled[60]), of Simonetta, the expert in Canon Law, (aided by negotiators experienced in the art of compromise,) that the final sessions of the Council of Trent were not wrecked by the problem of Residence.[61]

, Even without a dogmatic definition of the obligation of Residence, the Council had brought the problem to the attention of the whole Church. No-one could deny that the principal function of a bishop — as defined by the Council[62] — was the cure of souls, and that this could best be done in residence. By 1564, the Pope had again reminded the bishops of their duties in this respect, and finally, had insisted that his instructions to them be carried out.[63]

There is further evidence of Bollani's participation in the discussions and voting of the Council, but perhaps none where his experience of civil life had been used to such good effect.[64] Having declared unequivocally in favour of the obligation of Residence *de iure divino*, he had yet been prepared to work energetically in support of the referral of the whole question, when he saw the dangers into which it was leading the Council. There is perhaps insufficient evidence to reach detailed conclusions about his personal behaviour in the sessions, but the indications we have seen point to skill in negotiation and tactful compromise.[65] The experience of government and the solution of disputes — in short, a talent for the handling of men — he had effectively translated from civil order to the order of the Church, in perhaps the greatest opportunity for influencing the progress of his civilisation that his generation was to produce.

Bollani emerged from the Council of Trent its product in every sense. Convinced of the justice of the principles it decided, he was to spend his life in realising its projects. With almost no experience in the government of the Church before the Council, he began his reforms without the hindrance of preconceptions — the embodiment of its precepts. It is now appropriate to examine, in a brief survey, those aspects of the Council's achievement that had influenced him most deeply and those which he adopted personally in the diocese of Brescia.[66]

The Council of Trent influenced Bollani in two distinct ways. The definition of dogma and establishment of the principles of Catholicism from the authoritative basis of the vast assembly, as a bulwark against Protestantism, gave him security, conviction and a sense of mission. The renewal of ecclesiastical discipline in the delineation of a new image for the bishop, gave him a framework in which to act. In the first case, he had participated in the discussions and joined his colleagues in the signing of the final decrees in 1563; in the second he had been in close contact with those prelates who were to translate discussion and decree into reality through their example. It was, therefore, not only the intellectual edifice of the Council's achievement that contributed to his formation as a reformer, but also the example of those whose work before and after the Council contributed much to the making of a new Church.

The formal achievement of the Council consisted of the advances made in the final sessions in the summer and autumn of 1563. The threads of earlier discussions were drawn together after Cardinal Morone had succeeded in finding a compromise between the varied demands of the Spanish, French and Imperial parties, embodying the results in the final decrees.[67] In part the possibility of a resolution of such disputes had been caused by a new spirit and a new priority. The conviction that the principal function of the Church was the cure of souls seems a truism today, but the sense of mission created by this, a concept which had been lost sight of, carried all before it in 1563, and created the possibility of a successful conclusion to the Council.[68]

This pastoral duty for the bishop, as the Church's chief officer, thus defined by the Council, was not new in 1563,[69] but was crystallised by it and formalised to some degree by those decrees which specifically defined the function of the bishop. This new function — an ideal of charity, austerity and personal dedication, the 'imitation' of Christ in a far more real sense — had an indelible effect on Domenico Bollani. Together with the example of his reforming colleagues at Trent, particularly Borromeo, it created his reforming personality. Bollani's Brescian period demonstrates, in a varying balance, his dependence on these two influences.[70]

The debate on Residence, formalised in the decree in which it was strongly recommended, goes back to Gasparo Contarini's treatise *De officio episcopi* at least, where it was seen as a fundamental prerequisite of the cure of souls.[71] Taking Pietro Barozzi as his model,[72] Contarini described the attributes of the ideal pastor/bishop.[73] The decision of the Council of Trent — in the long debate we have seen — was the culmination of much discussion on the subject in earlier Councils.[74] Further, the obligation of Residence was a foundation principle for Borromeo.[75] For Domenico Bollani, there is no doubt that this principle played a very large part in his administration of his diocese in Brescia, as well as his own rule of life. His preoccupation with his absence from Brescia on Papal commissions,[76] as well as his orders to the clergy to return to their posts after the plague of 1577, provide a continuous testimony to his conviction on this point.[77]

One of the great achievements of the Council of Trent had been the duty to found seminaries imposed on bishops, and here, the Council was probably influenced by the examples of Giberti and Cardinal Pole.[78] Domenico Bollani participated actively in the discussions on clerical education,[79] and we shall see that his foundation of the Brescian seminary in 1568 was a victory over stern opposition, and a cornerstone of his reform policy. His letters on the subject to Ormanetto and Borromeo show the extent to which he was personally dedicated to this project.[80] As Dr. Logan has noted, Domenico Bollani, Agostino Valier, Matteo Priuli and Giorgio Corner were the first to found seminaries in their dioceses in Venetian dominions.[81]

138

On the question of the *Visita Pastorale*, Bollani was probably inspired chiefly by the example of Borromeo, whose visitations of his diocese of Milan and of other regions in the sphere of his archbishopric as Apostolic Visitor, provided a pattern to be followed by all the important reformers during the period following the Council. Borromeo himself had probably been influenced by the visitation conducted by Giberti in his diocese of Verona.[82] Again we shall see the extent to which Bollani adopted the principle of regular inspection of churches, priests and the conduct of religion in his *Visita Pastorale* of the Diocese of Brescia, and in his *Acts*, left valuable testimony to the state of the diocese before the impact of the Catholic Reformation had been felt.[83]

But in a sense, these are only examples of Tridentine decrees that were to play a major part in Bollani's reforms — measures which will emerge in the discussion of the reforms themselves. They formed part of the concept of the cure of souls. The young priest was to grow up in a specific atmosphere, according to principles laid down by the Church; he was to reside in his parish, the better to exercise his pastoral function; and he would be regularly inspected to ascertain whether he was fulfilling his duties satisfactorily. It was towards the establishment of this (simplified) system that the Council of Trent had been working, and this was to be Bollani's principal legacy to the Diocese of Brescia.[84]

But it is with the exponent of the Catholic Reformation in Brescia that we are here concerned, and it was with its agents, the bishops, that the Council concerned itself supremely.[85] A concept of an ideal Bishop had been evolving ever since the days of Gasparo Contarini and his *De officio Episcopi*, which had been transmitted to Borromeo through Giberti and Ormanetto.[86] What is certain is that Giberti's reforms were studied in the earlier sessions of the Council.[87] By 1563, the year of Bollani's 'graduation', so to speak, from the Council of Trent, the idea was firmly rooted of a bishop who would follow a rule of sanctity of life and customs, a frugal existence with devotion to study and meditation, a life of preaching and visits to the afflicted, and a wise custody of his rich benefice, with the distribution of its fruits to the poor and needy parts of the diocese.[88] Barozzi had been the example for Contarini: Giberti must have been the ideal for many of the prelates at Trent. Further, the arrival of Bartolomeo de Martyribus, Archbishop of Braga, with his treatise on bishops, furnished the Council with an up-dated and current ideal.[89] If the Council did not legislate precisely for these qualities in its bishops, it was perhaps because such qualities are not produced by laws. Flexibility of interpretation would allow reformers as different as Carlo Borromeo and Domenico Bollani broad scope for their individual talents. The ideal of the Council — a distillation of much pervious thought — found its theoretician in Bartolomeo de Martyribus. It found its chief exponent in Carlo Borromeo, assisted, in the Republic of Venice, by Agostino Valier, Domenico Bollani, Nicolo Ormanetto and Matteo Priuli. These were men of widely diversified gifts, however, and contributed to the edifice of the Catholic Reformation in different ways. Borromeo was the star by which they were led, the ascetic, saintly and self-denying figure, whereas Bollani was the human and tolerant disciple whose gifts in diplomacy and organisation were, broadly, 'managerial'. Much work has yet to be done on these figures individually, and their relations with Borromeo (especially, for instance, his *Acta Ecclesiae Mediolanensis*) before these differing functions in the fabric of the reform movement can be effectively described and understood.[90]

In our present context — the role of civil experience in the Catholic Reformation — Domenico Bollani had also taken much from his colleagues at the Council of Trent.[91] A glance at a sample of the important reformers whose relations with him are documentable will serve as a measure of this influence, though its precise nature would be harder to document. The mainstream of influence, as regards the ideal bishop, has been seen as Contarini — Giberti — Ormanetto —Borromeo — Valier.[92] At Trent, Bollani was clearly on friendly terms with Ormanetto, as his letter to him of May 5, 1569, describing his plans for the seminary shows.[93] On Ormanetto's death in 1577, Bollani wrote warmly of him to Roveglio.[94] There is every indication that he was also in close touch with Agostino Valier, after his assumption of the bishopric of Verona in 1566.[95] Valier had himself composed a treatise on the bishop, the *Episcopus,*[96] perhaps taking Borromeo as his example. A comparison between Valier's foundations of charitable institutions in Verona with those of Bollani in Brescia, and the study of the derivation of both from initiatives from Borromeo would be revealing. Further, Valier was a Venetian patrician, at short range from Brescia, so that the friendship and the possibility of reciprocal influence is not hard to believe in. We shall see that Bollani's role as a Venetian bishop in the 1570s — as principal advisor in delicate questions of church/state jurisdiction — was probably taken over by Valier, who undertook the extremely delicate task of the Apostolic visitation of Venice in 1581, two years after Bollani's death.[97]

We have seen that Bartolomeo de Martyribus had assumed the function of principal theoretician of the image of the bishop at the Council of Trent, and that his proposals received widespread attention through his personal participation as well as through his treatise. Bollani must have known him in the winter of 1562, when they were both members of the commission elected to revise the Index.[98] A similar case is that of Egidio Foscarari, Bishop of Modena, who had shared Bollani's experience of the commission on the Index, and had also been elected with him to attempt to solve the problem of Residence by persuasion.[99] Foscarari had shared Morone's experience of the Inquisition in Rome, and was the co-author of the definitive Catechism with Muzio Calini and Leonardo Marini, Bishop of Laodicea.[100] Morone himself — perhaps nearer to him in spirit in that combination of theological expertise and political sagacity — was numbered among Bollani's prized colleagues at Trent, as his letter to Roveglio undeniably documents.[101]

The list could be lenthened almost indefinitely. Bollani's relations with Muzio Calini and Cardinal Corner we have seen; his correspondence also shows contacts with Cardinals Colonna, Seripando and Sirleto, and all could have exercised an influence on him. Finally, his contacts with his Venetian colleagues like Daniele Barbaro, of which Paruta's dialogue *Della Perfezione della Vita Politica* is probably an accurate reflection, must have been frequent and hardly need to be further stressed. These contacts undoubtedly exercised an important formative influence on him, particularly those who represented already at Trent, or who were shortly to represent, various aspects of the Catholic reform movement.

Thus it can be seen that Bollani emerged from the Council of Trent with a programme of action, models to follow and allies to call upon in his work in the diocese of Brescia. The prelates at the Council had provided him with a guide not only in what he was to do, but above all, in what he was to be. We shall see in the ensuing chapters his constant reference to these guidelines, both in the Tridentine decrees and in the influence of personalities on his personal image. In a broad sense, the Council of Trent had been the university for the Reformation Bishop. For Bollani, its timing had been crucial, as he had grown to maturity in church government at its sessions.

But this reformation personality or spiritual maturity was not built in a vacuum. Bollani had come to the fore at the Council in those matters in which his conscience had driven him most strongly, and in those where his experience had been useful. He had been culturally prepared to discuss the Index, politically prepared to undertake a lobbying function over Residence, and prepared in civil government to add the weight of this experience to demands for the reform of monasteries. He was not to forget his preparation in the years ahead in his reforms in the diocese of Brescia, reforms which are discussed in the next chapter.

1 Looking back, at the beginning of the seventeenth century, the Venetian Senate must have had men like Bollani in mind when it said: 'We have seen clearly in the past that those who have held secular appointments and offices and have experience of worldly affairs, have proved to be better prelates than those recruited from libraries and bare monastic cells' (Quoted by B. Pullan in 'The Occupations and Investments . . .' *cit.*, pp. 497–8.

2 He was, for reasons of family relationship, commercial interest, or friendship, connected with the Dolfin, Soranzo and Corner families. (For the ecclesiastical dynasticism of these families, see Logan, *op. cit., passim.*) For example, he was related to the Dolfin; was connected with them commercially (see the will of Giacomo Bollani, *cit.*) was on cordial terms with Cardinal Alvise Corner (to which many letters of Muzio Calini to Cardinal Corner bear witness. See for example, Muzio Calini, *Lettere*, (a cura di Alberto Marani) (Brescia, 1963) pp. 87, 101–2 etc.; and was on friendly terms with at least two members of the Soranzo family. (see Bollani's liaison with the *Podestà* of Brescia, Giovanni Soranzo, described in his letters to Roveglio in *Carteggio Bollani-Roveglio, cit.*, for 1577, and his friendship with the Venetian Ambassador to the Emperor, Giacomo Soranzo on the latter's passage through Trent in 1561, documented in Calini, *op. cit.*, p. 91).

3 The most tangible example of this was the opposition of Cardinal Francesco Gambara, for whom see below, pp. 167–170.

4 Benedetto Erba (1517–1576), from Mantua, became Bishop of Casale Monferrato in 1570 (See R. Maiocchi, *op. cit.*, p. 54). He followed Bollani to Trent, and continued to provide him with instruction during pauses between the sessions; as he later testified as a participant on the committee which awarded Bollani a degree in theology from Pavia: 'ne mai in questa letione gli dissi cosa alcuna per difficile che fusse, che Sua Signoria R.ma non la pigliasse et bene intendesse, et in tutta la longa pratica per il detto tempo che ho avuto di sua Signoria Rev.ma, l'ho conosciuto per persona di buona vita et bonissimi costumi et di grande iuditio, ingegno et prudentia' (Maiocchi, *op. cit.*, p. 50.)

5 Garzoni became Vicar General of the Carmelite Order, and died in the plague in 1577.

6 The controversy concerned whether the Council was to be considered a continuation of the last, or an entirely new venture. (See Pastor, *op. cit.*, VII, pp. 135–137, 155.) See also H. Jedin, *Crisis and Closure of the Council of Trent*, (London, 1967) pp. 1–21, particularly pp. 15–21.

7 *Ibid.* The 'General Council' had been opened by Julius III at Trent, and closed a year later. On the achievements of previous councils and their relationship with the final session, see, for example, G.R. Elton, *Reformation Europe*, (London, 1963) pp. 176–209, and for a summary of the issues facing the Council in 1561–2, J.H. Elliott, *Europe Divided (1559–1598)*, (London, 1968) pp. 145–152.

8 It will be remembered that the transfer of the Council from Trent to Bologna (within the Papal States) had offended the Emperor Charles V in 1547, and put an end to the idea that a General Council of the Church might solve the religious split in Germany. (For example, Elton, *op. cit.*, pp. 252–253).

9 For Bollani's involvement in the question of whether to send a Venetian ambassador to Queen Elizabeth, see below, pp. 219–220.

10 The bishops decided that there was no fundamental difference between the reverence accorded to the Apostolic tradition of the Church and that accorded to Scripture. Protestant translations of the Bible were vehemently rejected in favour of the Vulgate as the only true Work of God. The protestant doctrine of Original Sin was rejected in favour of greater stress on Baptism. Human Free Will was defined as playing a fundamental part in Justification through Faith, and the traditional function of the Sacraments was re-affirmed. (Besides works cited above, see also the summary in Koenigsberger & Mosse, *Europe in the Sixteenth Century*, {London, 1968} pp. 165–166 etc.)

11 For Domenico Bollani and the *Ragion di Stato* see below Chap. X.

12 For a convenient summary of the various national positions in broad outline see Elliott, *op. cit.*, pp. 145–148, Jedin, *Crisis and Closure . . ., cit.*, pp. 22–40. By 1563, the Council had become 'no longer an assembly of prelates and theologians, but a great international

council, in which national delegations voted in accordance with the instructions of their princes.' (Elliott, *op. cit.*, p. 148). See also Pastor, *op. cit.*, VII, pp. 192–236, Leopold von Ranke, *Storia dei Papi* (Florence, 1959) pp. 240–256.

13   Bollani's reforms in the diocese of Brescia will be seen in the next chapter.

14   See above, p. 98.

15   See discussions of the date of his arrival in Petroboni, *op. cit.*, p. 51.

16   'sono pochi prelati che abbiano le degne qualità che troviamo in lui onde la persona sua ci vien ad essere non solo di satisfactione ed utile, ma necessaria et tanto più avvicinandosi il tempo di doversi per noi far delle faccende' (Cardinals Seripando and of Mantua to Borromeo from Trent, July 31, 1561, in *Registro delle Delegationi, cit.*, published in Fè D'Ostiani, *op. cit.*, p. 163). See also correspondence between Bollani and the Venetian Senate (*Ibid.*, pp. 163–164).

17   On Muzio Calini, see Alberto Marani, in *Muzio Calini, Lettere*, (Brescia, 1963) pp. 5–32, Fè D'Ostiani, 'M. Calini, Vescovo di Zara, Memorie del Secolo XVI,' in *Archivio Veneto*, XXI (1881) II, pp. 232–248, Pasero, 'L'estremo supplizio dei Carafa (1561) e altre notizie romane in una raccolta di lettere di Mons. M. Calini,' in *Commentari dell'Ateneo di Brescia*, CXXXVII (1938) A, pp. 29–58. Besides the fact that Calini was Brescian, Bollani's friendship with him is documented widely in his *Lettere (cit., passim.)* through their mutual esteem for Cardinal Corner, Calini's patron in Rome. The identity of their views on *Residence* is documented in Calini's letter to Rome of November 5, 1562, ('et mio può essere paricolarmente buon testimonio Mons. di Brescia, chio {sic} ho discorso lungamente con S. Sria del modo che si potesse tenere per fuggire in quest'articolo tutti li scogli ne' quali siamo dati altre volte.' *op. cit.*, p. 305.)

18   Muzio Calini, *op. cit.*, p. 46.

19   The bibliography on the Council of Trent is vast. Besides the classical histories by Pallavicino and Sarpi and the modern one by Jedin, it is perhaps sufficient to mention the *Concilium Tridentinum* (Friburgi Brisgoviae, 1903), which collects many of the available contemporary documents, and the still useful bibliography in Pastor, *op. cit.*, VII, pp. xxxi–xlvi. Until the publication of Jedin's volume on the period 1561–1563, his *Crisis and Closure . . ., (cit.)* remains the best concise modern summary of the final sessions. Specialised modern studies will appear in the following notes. (For the *Concilium Tridentinum*, I have been guided in the main by the summaries in Petroboni, *op. cit.*, pp. 57–64).

20   See Pastor, *op. cit.*, VII, pp. 280–282.

21   *Ibid.*, p. 282.

22   January 14, 1562 (Pastor, *op. cit.*, p. 282). Muzio Calini wrote: 'Ma prima che si cominiciasse a dire i Voti, i SS. Legati fecero leggere un Breve mandato da S. Santità per il quale appareva che quella materia de' libri era stata rimessa da lei al Concilio, il che fu necessario a fare, et forse era più a proposito che si facesse prima che fosse proposta simil causa, perciochè essendo già stato pubblicato l'Indice Romano con l'auttorità di Paulo IIII fel. mem. se il Concilio havesse preso a giudicarne senza commissione di S.B., sarebbe parso in cosa di maggior importanza per questo esempio, che il Concilio potesse giudicare delle cose già determinate dal Papa.' (*op. cit.*, pp. 107–108, Calini to Corner, February 11, 1562).

23   *Concilium Tridentinum, cit.*, Gabrielis Paleotti, *Acta . . .*, III, p. 260. (Petroboni, *op. cit.*, p. 57).

24   The Commission comprised about 22 members, under the chairmanship of Antonio Brus Von Muglitz, Archbishop of Prague, and met at his house. Copies of documents relating to the Index of Paul IV were supplied for the group. (Pastor, *op.cit.*, pp. 283–4). Besides Bollani, the members of the commission were the ecclesiastical leaders of Venice, Naxos, Ragusa, Sorrento, Braga, Cava, Ariano, Modena, Sinigaglia, Oviedo, Lerida, Cremona, Verona, an abbot, and the Generals of the Francican and Agostinian orders. (*Ibid.*)

25   See examples quoted by Pastor, *op. cit.*, p. 285, in the correspondence of Antonio Brus Von Muglitz. (Bollani was soon to meet him in open debate, see below, p. 134).

26   For instance, Boccaccio's *Decameron*, with its eloquent satire on contemporary abuses of the Church, fell into this last category. On the whole question of the Index, see Pio Paschini, 'Letterati ed Indice nella Riforma Cattolica in Italia' in *Cinquecento Romano e Riforma Cattolica*, (Rome, 1958) pp. 239–273, Jedin, *Crisis and Closure . . .*, cit., pp. 43–45.

27 Notably the works of Erasmus.

28 Pastor, *op. cit.*, p. 287.

29 See his friendship and discussions with Alvise Corner and his term of office as *Riformatore dello Studio di Padova*, an office which included literary censorship (above, p. 54). It is clear that he had a reputation for humanistic interests at this point even in Brescia, as he was invited to become patron of a literary and scientific academy there (the *Academia degli Occulti*) in 1563 (for which see the dedication to him quoted by Fe D'Ostiani, *Domenico Bollani, cit.*, p. 147, nn. 3, 4.)

30 Pastor, *op. cit.*, p. 286. An indication of the new spirit in which the Index was compiled is the fact that Cardinals were now permitted to read forbidden books, and to issue licences for others to do so. Calini was a member of the final review committee.

31 H. Jedin, 'Die Deutschen am Trienter Konzil 1551–2' in *Historische Zeitschrift*, CLXXXVIII (1959), quoted by G.R. Elson, *op. cit.*, p. 257. See also *Ibid.* pp. 258–267 for Imperial policy at the Council.

32 Elton, *op. cit.*, p. 258.

33 Pastor, *op. cit.*, VII, p. 194, and see bibliography on this question in nn. 4, 9.

34 'Vero è che del salvocondotto agli heretici et penitenti che volessero venire al Concilio, non gli fu aggiunto altra determinatione, percioche li Spagnuoli s'haveano fatto prima intendere, che non volevano che si facesse niun pregiudicio all'Inquisitione di Spagna et di Roma, similmente i Sigg. Legati hanno avuto aviso che procedessero con rispetto verso quel S. Tribunale.' (Calini to Corner, February 26, *Lettere, cit.*, p. 120). A clear indication of the delicacy of the situation and the wish of many legates not to offend Protestants is the length of the discussion over the title of the Decree. The Archbishop of Grenada had proposed that the title include 'the Universal Church' (*universalem ecclesiam representans*) (*Ibid.*, pp. 118–121). In this session, it was decided 'non ne parlare altrimenti, ma solo decretare, che si potesse dare salvocondotto per Congregatione Generale . . . perchè in questo modo si potrà dare a chi lo domanderà, et insieme provedere che questo non sia con pregiudicio dell'Inquisitione di Spagna o di Roma . . .' (pp. 120–1).

35 'Per tutti questi giorni dopo la sessione i SS. Legati hanno fatto fra loro et con molti prelati periti nelle legii molte consulte sopra la forma del salvocondotto che si debba dare . . . vedendosi gran difficultà in questa concessione . . .' (Calini to Corner, March 2, *Lettere, cit.*, p. 123).

36 *Concilium Tridentium, cit.*, tom. VIII, Part V, p. 304.

37 'Ma perchè sei o otto (de' quali è stato capo Mons. d'Acquileia) hanno detto che non potevano così all'improviso rispondere senz'havere veduta et considerata diligentemente questa forma, i Sigg. Legati hanno ordinato che Mons. di Tilesio Segretario ne dia a ciascuno la copia . . .' (*Lettere, cit.*, p. 124). It is not unreasonable to suppose that this group could have represented the Venetian interest, and that it included Barbaro and Bollani. (Bollani and Barbaro had met in London in 1549, it will be remembered, when Barbaro replaced Bollani as ambassador. They had, therefore, shared similar experience of the schism under Edward VI and the activities of English Protestants. The identity of their views on heresy seems here further supported.)

38 Ferdinand I, Emperor, was represented at the Council by Antonio Brus Von Muglitz, Bishop of Vienna, and from 1561, Archbishop of Prague, and by his principal advisor at Innsbruck, the Count von Thun, a layman. As King of Hungary, Ferdinand was also represented by Giorgio Draskovich, Bishop of Pècs (Hungary) ('Vescovo di Cinquechiese'). For the problem of Imperial representation and the efforts of the nuncio Dolfin, see Pastor, *op. cit.*, VII, pp. 186–187. Calini described them as 'di natura assai terrible et difficili molto da contentare' (*Lettere, cit.*, February 12, 1562, p. 114).

39 For example, J.H. Elliott, *Europe Divided, cit.*, pp. 146–147.

40 Calini, *op. cit.*, p. 108, Pastor, *op. cit.*, pp. 187, 193–194.

41 A special session would have had to be held for the letters of authority to be read, so that 'le loro Sigg. Ill. mandarono Mons. di Tilesio Segretario ad intender se essi volevano essere ammessi a quest'officio come persone publiche oppure come Prelati per nome privato'. At first they decided that they would only participate as orators of the Emperor, and then on

reflection, that they did not wish to contribute before the arrival of von Thun. (Calini, *Lettere, cit.*, p. 108).

42 'Prima che si entrasse in Congregatione gli Oratori Cesarei si mostrarono assai mal sodisfatti con i SS. Legati del luogo che era stato assegnato loro ... et sopra ciò fecero molte difficultà ...' (*Ibid.*, p. 114).

43 , 'havendo detto l'Arcivescovo di Praga oratore Ces. *al luogo della sua promotione come Prelato* (Italics mine) che gli piaceva la forma del Salvocondotto, ma giudicava a proposito che si esprimesse il numero delle persone alle quali si dovesse concedere ...' (Calini, *Lettere, cit.*, March, 2 1563, p. 124). See also *Concilium Tridentinum, cit.*, Gabriele Paleotti, *Acta Conc. Trid.*, Tom. III, p. 282, quoted in Petroboni, *op. cit.*, pp. 57—59. (There are slight differences between these two accounts of the episode, and it may be that Calini's description is a more summary account, while Paleotti had reported it in full.)

44 Calini, *op. cit.*, p. 124, Petroboni, *op. cit.*, pp. 57—59, where Paleotti's account is quoted *in extenso*. The query is comprehensible given the Imperial policy on heretics since 1547, and the fact that Bollani and Barbaro were Venetians. It must have seemed strange that an initiative which might effectively *limit* the Protestant participation in the Council should come from the Imperial camp.

45 Specific positions in the assemply were assigned to the different ranks in the ecclesiastical and lay hierarchies. Further, we have seen that the Imperial orators had not been satisfied with theirs, a fact which may further explain Bollani's stand.

46 The decision was taken not to specify numbers in the *Salvocondotto.* on March 4, after speeches from the Archbishop of Grenada and the Archbishop of Prague, it was agreed that any dangers inherent in the Protestant presence would be safeguarded by Divine Providence. (Calini, *op. cit.*, pp. 126—127, letter of March 5, 1562).

47 In his final speech on the form of the *Salvocondotto*, the Archbishop of Prague had referred again to Bollani's intervention, but this time there was no response. (Calini, *op. cit.*, pp. 126—127, Petroboni, *op. cit.*, p. 59.)

48 Grande impaccio sara al Concilio questo delle precedenze, poiche simile ambitione entra ancho nei religiosi ...' (Calini, *op. cit.*, p. 74). The dispute was chiefly between the various religious orders, who had taken the matter to Pius IV. The Pope replied that the order of previous Councils was to be observed, but the interpretation of this caused further trouble. 'Questi Ill. Legati per levar questa discordia senza strepito haveano eletto per compositori i Vescovi di Tilesio e di Brescia et di Lerida, li quali non havendo trovato altra forma d'accordo fu ordinato che gli Abbati soli di S. Justina venissero hieri in processione ...' (*Ibid.*) See also Fè D'Ostiani, *op. cit.*, p. 25.

49 Particularly in his *Visita Pastorale* of the Diocese, for which see below, pp. 175—178. For unfounded accusations of his own absence during the Plague of 1577, see below pp. 157—158. Bollani constantly lamented the fact the Papal commissions were to keep him from his diocese in the years ahead.

50 Seripando to Borromeo, May 17, 1562, quoted in Pastor, *op. cit.*, VII, p. 319—320.

51 Above, pp. 118—119.

52 Pastor, *op. cit.*, VII, p. 320.

53 'Chi coll'arcivescovo di Granada votava in questa questione pel diritto divino, pronunziavasi nello stesso tempo per l'opinione che nell' ordinazione episcopale venisse immediatamente conferita da Dio una certa ancora indeterminata podestà di governo, mentre il Papa, conferando un vescovado, non avrebbe che designati i sudditi, ai quali dovesse riferirsi tale podestà di governo.' (*Ibid.*, p. 192).

54 See the MS (Cod. cart. N.A. 1346, p. 187) in the Biblioteca Barberini, Rome, quoted by Fè D'Ostiani, *Domenico Bollani ..., cit.*, p. 170.

55 'elessero sei vescovi che per riputazione di zelo, e per uniformità di parere sopra quell'articolo, erano in confidenza con essi {the Spanish bishops whom they were to oppose} e da cui scambievolmente per la rettitudine della intenzione, e per la riverenza verso la Sede Apostolica, i Legati si promettevano sincero aiuto.' (Pallavicino, *Istoria del Concilio Tridentino*, quoted by Petroboni *op. cit.*, p. 61) Bollani's colleagues were Pavesio of Sorrento, Nocchiante of Chioggia, Foscarari of Modena, Sfondrato of Cremona and Della Rovere of Sinigaglia.

56 Pastor, *op. cit.*, VII, p. 200.

57 It is perhaps significant that Sarpi, looking at the Council through decidedly Venetian eyes, described Bollani as 'non . . . pontificio scoperto, ma guadagnato' (*Istoria del Concilio Tridentino*, 3 vols. (Bari, 1935) II, pp. 456–457. Sarpi's view of the episode mentions only Bollani and Foscarari, however (pp. 439–440). We have seen that Bollani discussed the question of Residence at length with Muzio Calini. For Calini's detailed arguments on Residence, see Alberto Marani in Calini, *Lettere, cit.*, pp. 23–26, and Calini in *Ibid.*, pp. 145, 165–168, 175–178 etc.

58 *Ibid.*, pp. 439–440. Calini's account (perhaps the more accurate one) attributes this function to the six-man commission already noted. The results of these negotiations were not encouraging in this tortuous and difficult question: 'Hora V. S. ha da sapere che queste pratiche si son fatte, et è stato risposto massimamente dalle nationi oltramontane, che si contentavano purchè nel decreto della prossima sessione si statuisse che quest'articolo {Residence} si avesse a definire nella susseguente immediate, la qual cosa i SS. Legati non solamente non hanno voluto fare, ma havendo come deliberato fra loro di farne una promessa con una polizza sottoscritta di mano di tutti . . .' (*Lettere, cit.*, Calini to Corner, May 25, 1562, p. 183). Infinite complications ensued, driving Calini to exclaim: 'io non so aspettar altro che nuovi travagli et confusioni . . .' (*Ibid.*)

59 'Queste pratiche fecero tornar in campo quelle della residenza essendo li medesima li desiderosi che il Concilio si finisse e della residenza non si trattasse. Quest'apertura diede occasione a Mantoa e Seripando di adoperarsi, e mostrar al papa con effetto che s'accomodavano al voler suo, secondo l'istruzione che Lanciano gli aveva portato. Adoperavano per far gli uffici con buon modo l'arcivescovo d'Otranto, li vescovi di Modena, Nola e Brescia . . . Questi superarono molti Italiani, inducendoli non a mutar opinione e contradirsi, ma a non promuover più quella materia: da molti ebbero promessa che, cessando gli spagnoli, essi sariano stati quieti; e li quattro suddetti prelati fecero insieme una nota delli persuasi, si che si travorono aver quadagnato molto.' (Sarpi, *op. cit.*, II, pp. 456–457.)

60 For Morone's imprisonment by the Inquisition, see above, p. 125, n. 12.

61 For the ensuing debates on Residence – protracted until the end of the Council, when the matter was deferred – see Pastor, *op. cit.*, VII, pp. 202–242.

62 The Council's definition of the bishop is discussed below, pp. 139–140.

63 For the gradual implementation of Papal instructions to reside, and the part played by Borromeo, see *Ibid.*, pp. 319–323.

64 Possibly the single exception is Bollani's intervention in the reform of monasteries. For this, see *Concilium Tridentinum*, (Paleotti, *Acta . . ., cit.*, tom. III, p. 411), Zanotti, *op. cit.*, p. 87. Bollani's particular concern for the state of monasteries has been seen in Udine in 1555–6 (above, pp. 71) and in Brescia (p. 82 and n. 16), so that he was in the best possible position to report on the abuses current in the Venetian *Terraferma*. For his application of such reforms in Brescia, see below, Chapter VIII.

65 For another example of compromise, see Bollani's suggestion at the end of the Council of a tactful way of ending the assembly: 'Il vescovo di Brescia propose che si trovasse un modo medio tra il metterli compito fine, e il suspenderlo, perchè il finirlo sarebbe stato il desperare li eretici, e il suspenderlo non satisfare li cattolici.' (November, 1563, in Sarpi, *op. cit.*, III, p. 354). On the ending of the Council, see Jedin, *Crisis and Closure . . ., cit.*, pp. 140–177.

66 There are many views of the chievements of the Council embodying varying degrees of bias. Pastor, *op. cit.*, VII, *loc. cit.*, is particularly useful for the role of the Papacy, but a well-balanced modern summary is in H. Jedin, *Katholische Reformation oder Gegenreformation . . .*, (Luzern, 1946) (Ital. Ed. *Riforma Cattolica o Controriforma* [Brescia, 1957], pp. 71–93).

67 For the decrees themselves, a convenient version in English is in James Waterworth, *Canons and Decrees of the Sacred and Oecumenical Council of Trent*, (London, 1888). For the growth of the ideal of the 'pastoral bishop' up to and after the Council, see H. Jedin, *Das Bischofsideal der katholischen Reformation, passim.* (Fr. Ed. trans. P. Broutin, S.J. {Louvain, 1953}, It. Ed. trans. E. Durini, { Brescia, 1950}, especially pp. 81–91). See also Logan, *op. cit.*, pp. 270–281, 281–283, etc.

68 On this theme, see Jedin, *Riforma Cattolica . . ., cit.*, pp. 71–93.

69 *Idem., Il tipo ideale di Vescovo . . ., cit., passim.* Jedin examines the growth of this ideal

through the theories of treatise literature, the example of Giberti at the earlier sessions of the Council, to the matured concept defined in 1563 and its realisation in the figure of Carlo Borromeo.

70 We shall see examples of this in the succeeding chapters. For the influence of Borromeo on Bollani, see below, pp. 155–156. The relationship between the decrees on the bishop ideal and preceding treatise literature has been studied by O.M.T. Logan. 'Legislation at the Council of Trent was inspired and its execution aided by a substantial body of literature and opinion and also, there is little doubt, by the stimulus of personalities.' (*op. cit.*, pp. 270–271). Dr. Logan wrote, in the context of personalities, of a 'direct line of spiritual descent from Pietro Barozzi (Contarini's model) to Agostino Valier (the disciple of Borromeo in Giberti's diocese of Verona)' (p. 271). It seems highly likely that it is only the relative lack of scholarly attention hitherto devoted to Domenico Bollani that has prevented him from inclusion in this scheme. Of course, Valier's development within the tradition of Giberti, and his *Episcopus*, (Milan, 1575) and other writings, naturally focussed attention on him, although a modern biography is still lacking.

71 Jedin, *Il tipo ideale . . ., cit.*, pp. 83–87, Logan, *op. cit.*, p. 274.

72 Bishop of Padua 1487–1507. See Jedin, *Il tipo ideale . . ., cit.*, pp. 36–37.

73 Gasparo Contarini, *De officio episcopi*, in *Opera*, pp. 401–431, at p. 412, Logan, *op. cit.*, p. 274.

74 H. Jedin, *A history of the Council of Trent*, (London, 1957–61) II, p. 317.

75 See M. Petrocchi, 'L'Idea del Vescovo nel Panigarola' in *Rivista della Storia della Chiesa in Italia*, VIII, (1954) pp. 93–94, and, for Borromeo's influence on the Pope during the period following the Council when the latter was active in enforcing residence, Pastor, *op. cit.*, VII, pp. 320–326.

76 Bollani was in Venice from January 7, to March 17, 1576 dealing with the collection of the *Decime del Clero* (for which see below, pp. 216–219). See his letters to Roveglio between these dates in *Carteggio Bollani-Roveglio, cit.*, and Fè D'Ostiani, *op. cit.*, pp. 72–73.

77 See his letter inviting a priest to return to Brescia, and his instruction for a general invitation to the clergy in his letter to Roveglio of September 27, 1577 (*Carteggio cit.*) The accusation of absence from his flock during the Plague (by the biographer of Borromeo, Giussani) has been effectively disproved by Fè D'Ostiani, *Domenico Bollani . . ., cit.*, pp. 118–123, and receives further support from Bollani's letters to the Pope of September 7, 1577 and to Cardinal Gambara of August 27, 1577, (*Carteggio, cit.*).

78 Logan, *op. cit.*, pp. 278–279.

79 *Concilium Tridentinum, cit.*, (Paleotti, *Acta*, III, p. 670), Petroboni, *op. cit.*, p. 91.

80 See below, pp. 161–170.

81 *Op. cit.*, pp. 288–289.

82 Sources discussed by Logan, *op. cit.*, pp. 277–278.

83 See below, pp. 175–178.

84 Chapter VIII, *passim.*

85 Jedin, *Il Tipo Ideale . . ., cit.*, p. 84.

86 *Ibid., passim.*

87 *Ibid.* 'Il Giberti: l'homo aposticus' pp. 38–61. There is already a considerable bibliography on the 'prereformer' G.M. Giberti. For details, see the most recent study, Adriano Prosperi, *Tra Evangelismo e Controriforma G.M. Giberti (1495–1543)*, (Rome, 1969).

88 Jedin, *Riforma Cattolica . . ., cit.*, pp. 83–86. For charity, see below, pp. 153–160.

89 Bartolomeo de Martyribus, *Stimulus pastorum, ex sententiis patrum concinnatus, in quo agitur de vita et moribus episcoporum aliorque praelatorum*, (Rome, 1564); Jedin, 'La forma classica de tipo ideale di vescovo nello 'stimulus pastorum' in '*Il Tipo Ideale . . ., cit.*, pp. 76–80.

90 On Ormanetto, see particularly Enrico Cattaneo, 'Influenze Veronesi nella legislazione di San Carlo Borromeo' in *Problemi di Vita Religiosa in Italia nel Cinquecento*, (Padua, 1960) pp. 123–166. On Matteo Priuli, Bishop of Vicenza, 1565–1579, see G. Fanton, *La Riforma Tridentina a Vicenza nella seconda meta del Secolo XVI* (Vicenza, 1941) and G. Mantese, 'L'origine dei Vicari Foranei e gli inizi della Riforma Tridentina a Vicenza' in *Rivista di Storia della Chiesa in Italia*, XV (1961) pp. 482–491. Giuseppe Alberigo has emphasised the extent .

to which the almost exclusive devotion of scholarly attention to Borromeo, in the field of the
application of the Tridentine decrees, has produced a historical distortion both of Borromeo
himself, and of reformers of fundamental importance like Bollani and Paleotti ('L'applicazione del Concilio di Trento in Italia . . .' *cit.*, p. 246–247).
91 It is r t suggested that this was a one-way influence. Bollani's influence on Borromeo and
other reformers will be seen below.
92 Jedin, *Il Tipo Ideale . . ., cit., passim.* Logan, *op. cit.*, pp. 271–281.
93 Biblioteca Ambrosiana, Milan, MSS. *Carteggio Borromeo*, Petroboni, *op. cit.*, p. 101.
94 Bollani to Roveglio, July 15, 1577 in *Carteggio Bollani-Roveglio, cit.*
95 Bollani described him as 'mio assai amico' on August 9, 1577 (to Roveglio, *Carteggio . . .,
cit.*) and see *Ibid.* (letters of 22, 24 August). For bibliography on Agostino Valier, Logan, *op.
cit.*, p. 531 *ad vocem.* For his contacts in Rome with Borromeo's circle, Paschini, 'Il primo
soggiorno . . .' *cit.*, pp. 131–132. For his Apostolic Visitation to Venice in 1581, see Silvio
Tramontin, 'La figura del vescovo secondo il Concilio di Trento' in *Studi Veneziani* X (1968),
pp. 423–456, Logan, pp. 285–287.
96 Milan, 1575.
97 See Tramontin, 'La figura del vescovo . . .' *cit.* For Bollani's action in church/state disputes, below, Chapter IX.
98 Above, pp. 132–133.
99 *Ibid.*, and p. 145, n. 55. On Egidio Foscarari, see Paschini, *cit.*, p. 53 *Cinquecento
Romano e Riforma Cattolica.*
100 Paschini, *ibid.*, 'Il Catechismo Romano del Concilio di Trento' pp. 35–91, particularly,
pp. 49–56.
101 , May 9, 1576, in *Carteggio Bollani-Roveglio.*

CHAPTER VIII

THE APPLICATION OF THE TRIDENTINE DECREES:
CATHOLIC REFORMATION IN THE DIOCESE OF BRESCIA*
1563–1579

In considering the effect and importance of the application of the Tridentine decrees in the Diocese of Brescia, and Domenico Bollani's initiatives towards a new church and reformed religious life, two principles should be borne in mind. The growing body of scholarly attention devoted to the period immediately following the Council now permits a more comparative approach than has hitherto been possible.[1] The pattern of a reformed church, a result of a complex of initiatives taking place in different dioceses and at different times is gradually emerging from the varied studies undertaken at local level, and is centred principally on the religious life of a single diocese, or the work of a reforming bishop. In arriving at more general and far-reaching conclusions about the Council itself, and its creation of a renewed religious life in Italy, the identification of the differing aspects of reform promoted in different regions for local reasons may only be arrived at by the principle of comparison, and may lead to a more meaningful overall assessment of the historical importance of the Council of Trent in Italy.

With this in mind, it is proposed to examine Bollani's reforms in the Diocese of Brescia not only in the light of local religious life, where its impact is undoubtedly most important, but also in comparison with the reforms of other bishops, taking place in other dioceses. For it is an undoubted fact that the greatest single cause of this coincidence of reforming initiatives in Italy was the Council — a meeting of the future reformers for discussion, debate and decision. Given this direct causal relationship, too little attention has been paid to coincidence and timing, within the more general framework of the Catholic Reformation in Italy.[2]

The recent study by Giuseppe Alberigo has given the measure of any comparative approach to the question of the application of the Tridentine decrees in Italy. Any attempt at exhaustive coverage of the dioceses which have been the subject of study would drown the reformer who is the subject of this study in his vast context.[3] Moreover the particularly noteworthy quality of Domenico Bollani's life was his civil preparation for ecclesiastical office: his continuing experience *astride* the traditionally delineated careers in church and state. This position, within the more specialised field of the Venetian *Ragion di Stato* — his allegiance to Venice, and finally, the use made of him by the supreme church and state authorities to settle disputes between them — led to specific problems and required special talents, as we shall see.[4] The Papal Bull *In Coena Domini* was to lead to Domenico's offer of resignation from his bishopric, thus clearly and sharply delineating his dual allegiance. So it is with the problems of the *Venetian* reforming bishop that we are here concerned. The most important parallels for us will be those reforming bishops who occupied sees within Venetian territories, reformers, in short, who shared Bollani's problems of *Venezianità*.[5]

There are many testimonies to the state of the diocese of Brescia to which

Domenico Bollani returned after his experience of the Council of Trent.[6] During the first quarter of the century, pluralism and absenteeism among clergy had helped to create a materialistic attitude towards church benefices, contributing to a general religious indifference in the diocese. Priests were often uneducated and ill-equipped to carry out their functions, and preaching in the city was often entrusted to itinerant clergy whose fame would attract the faithful, but whose gifts were sometimes oratorical rather than doctrinal.[7] The spread of heretical ideas in Italy through a whole network of nonconformist groups, including some within the aegis of the diocese of Brescia, had produced the reaction that we have seen characteristic of the pontificate of Paul IV: a pitiless and indiscriminate repression in which the fervour of the episcopal inquisition, playing on the ignorance of an uneducated people, acted often without proof beyond that of denunciation, and became, on occasions, the instrument of local feuds or private gain.[8]

In part, the conditions of religious life in the early part of the century, to which the Catholic Reformation was the sometimes immoderate reaction, was a function of the conditions of the times. Ignorance and superstition, often more widespread in communities far from urban life, produced the more bizarre manifestations of the life of a community, cloaking acts of almost mediaeval barbarity in a semi-official framework of formal piety. To this cause may be attributed the witch hunts and consequent burnings which took place intermittently between 1518 and 1545 in the *Val Camonica*.[9] This combination of local superstition and official indifference had brought the Catholic Church to a low ebb in the diocese. Where the principle of pastoral care was missing, the celebration of mass and of Christian feasts was perfunctory, and in the absence of any spirit of dedication to social and religious causes, reaction in the form of the spread of heretical sects in the province became, partly, the search for an alternative.

These manifestations of disorder and decadence were not without a more measured reaction, however, and it was through the New Orders[10] that conspicuous initiatives were taken towards the reform and renewal of religious life — not only in Brescia — but throughout Italy as the century progressed. Giustiniani and Querini had looked forward to a new spirituality in their foundation of the order of Camaldolese monks. Matteo da Bascio had led a movement within the Capuchin order to return to the purity of values of the earliest Francisans. The Oratory of Divine Love in Rome crystallised the efforts towards reform of men like Gaetano Thiene, Lippomano, Sadoleto, and, perhaps supremely, Carafa. The fact that these reformers were connected by bonds of friendship and underwent reciprocal influence, gave this drive towards a reformed spirituality a compactness and unity. In Venetian dominions, the Barnabites and Somaschi were counterparts, springing up just as much in direct response to local conditions, in Venice, Vicenza, Padua and Verona, and in Bergamo and Brescia respectively. They constituted a genuine attempt to combat conditions or moral and physical degeneracy: moral, in the decline of Catholic observance in all its forms, and physical in the urgent need for relief initiatives in times of plague, war, and social diseases of various kinds.[11]

Perhaps, then, only in the independence of the religious orders could a spirit of

Christian charity and genuine pastoral care be kept alive in sharp contrast with the ignorant superstition, the fanaticism of repression, and the formalism of religious habits elsewhere.[12] In Brescia, particularly among aristocratic circles, a number of groups of 'mystical' inspiration were quietly active in an attempt to raise the level of moral and religious life.[13] It has been noted how these currents in the diocese gathered strength and direction in the 1530s; the foundation of new religious orders, as well as a hospital and an orphanage, were notable landmarks in this progress. Particularly noteworthy in this connection was the foundation of the *Compagnia delle Dimesse di S. Orsola* by Angela Merici in Brescia in 1536. Perhaps never before had an order with such socially forward-looking aims deliberately rejected the restrictions of monasticism to perform works of charity for women.[14] Even the lay authorities in the city of Brescia intervened with provisions designed to better the conditions of the monasteries in the diocese.[15] There were also attempts to improve the lamentable standards of the clergy, with the formulation of new constitutions, and the beginning of a Pastoral Visitation by the bishop Duranti. These latter initiatives looked forward particularly to the work of Domenico Bollani, who was to incorporate, revise and enforce such provisions, transforming somewhat pallid initiatives into forceful and telling realities.

Towards the middle of the century, the hunt for heretics assumed the proportions and character we have seen in the affair of Alvise Priuli and the bishopric of Brescia. The general concern with the spread of Lutheranism (and the possibility, now, of its cohesion into a political threat) emanating outwards from the Papacy, involved most of Italy, and not least the diocese of Brescia. The arrival of Cardinal Durante as bishop of Brescia in 1552 was a landmark in the suppression of heresy in the diocese. For the diffusion of heretical ideas — backed by the growing power of the printing press, and reinforced by the physical presence of such men as Pier Paolo Vergerio — was increasing on a wide front.[16] This impetus was probably determined not only by the activities of immigrants from the north — nor exclusively by the corrupt state of the Church — but also by a thirst for novelty, a curiosity about the new movements whose echoes were penetrating south of the Alps, and a timeless spirit of rebellion against authority. Not all the religious deviants who fell into the hands of the Inquisition were rabid iconoclasts gnawing at the roots of the established Catholic Church.[17] On the contrary, many were genuinely searching for a purity of values, a renewed faith, and a personal religious identity which the Protestant persuasions seemed to provide.[18]

The spread of Lutheranism had intensified in the 1530s and 1540s, gradually penetrating the north of Italy by means of the various chinks in Catholic armour. Pockets of Protestant sympathy existed in Piedmont (with French tolerance of Waldensians, and relative freedom in Milan permitted by the civic authorities). In the university towns of Padua and Pavia, traditional centres of ferment, northern students caused growing concern to the Catholic authorities. Dissentient groups grew up at Cremona and Mantua, and Modena, the seed-bed of Anabaptist and Antitrinitarian tendencies, had acquired the reputation of a town 'completely Lutheran and dangerous' by 1540.[19]

Besides the echoes of Luther and Zwingli in Italy, Calvinism also gained ground during these years, with the court of the Duchess of Ferrara providing its focal point. Calvin's visit to the city in 1537 created shock waves of sympathy and reaction emanating from Ferrara, and converts were made not only among the poor and professional classes, but now among the nobility.

In Venetian dominions, the relatively tolerant attitude of the government was demonstrated in the affair of Baldassare Altieri, secretary to the English ambassador, Harvel. We have seen how commercial interests, suspicion of Papal territorial aggrandisement and political non-alignment had favoured a *rapprochement* with England in 1547 when Domenico Bollani had been sent as ambassador.[20] In the 1540s Altieri sheltered successfully behind Venetian diplomatic immunity while conducting propaganda campaigns and establishing contacts with Italian Lutherans down to Harvel's death in 1548. In Vicenza, heretics had established circles of influence in the city and province,[21] and in Venice itself, a synod of Antitrinitarians was held in 1550.[22] Further, there is no doubt that the university of Padua provided a focus of interest in Protestant ideas which was to be a source of friction between the Papacy and the Republic throughout our period.[23] Finally, the strength and influence of the Venetian printing presses provided some outlet for heterodox ideas.[24]

Between 1535 and 1550, therefore, as Delio Cantimori has shown, Anabaptist and Antitrinitarian movements, as well as the circle centred on Juan Valdès, consolidated their strength through a network of informal contacts throughout Italy. The Republic of Venice and her subject province, Brescia, shared this experience through their independence from Roman and Spanish influence, and geographical susceptibility to northern influences.[25] Devoid of formal organisation, the reformers yet made converts among prominent Catholic thinkers like the Pole/Morone/Colonna circle through conversations and correspondence in a way that was to give rise to the first concerted wave of Catholic reaction in the 1550s.[26] Promoted by the intransigent personality of Paul IV, and through a campaign of papal briefs to bishops denouncing heretics, the period saw a growing disquiet in the Catholic Church whose outward sign had been the institution of the Holy Office on 21 July, 1542. The campaign was now centralised. Episcopal inquisition gave way to Roman control of the hunt for heretics, and, in the context of the Venetian bishoprics, the first step had been taken towards the papal interference in local affairs that the Council of Trent (in spite of new powers for bishops) was not to erode, and the Republic of Venice, with her agent, Bollani in Brescia, was to resent.

During the period before Bollani's arrival in Brescia, and that leading up to the Council of Trent, Brescia had become established as something of a centre for heresy,[27] and the activities of the Inquisition continued unabated during his bishopric,[28] causing much suspicion and conflict between the jurisdiction of the Holy Office and that of the Venetian Republic.[29] Cases of heresy were discovered in the region with disturbing frequency, particularly in those areas geographically susceptible to influence from the north,[30] but also, importantly among sections of the Brescian aristocracy, and in their dominions, particularly among members of the family of Martinengo da Barco.[31] The Martinengo family possessed vast feudatery holdings in the areas south and south-west of Brescia,[32] and their

152

tolerance and support of deviant sects and later, Jews, was to be a considerable hindrance to the Catholic efforts to eradicate heresy in the area.[33]

A reflection of the crisis that had developed by the beginning of Bollani's bishopric may be seen in the papal order to enquire into the cases of ex-friars, who were notably subject to heretical influences. Sixty-three of these presented their credentials in Brescia in about 1560.[34]

There were, therefore, various, sometimes conflicting, influences at work in the diocese when Domenico Bollani arrived from the Council to take up the reins of its administration. The inheritance from the fifteenth century in conditions of life was one of indifference and corruption, which the efforts of well-meaning reformers had only just begun to penetrate. Above all, order and system were lacking. Reforming initiatives needed a strong hand and coordination to become really effective. Idealism needed to be embodied in an organizational framework which really worked. A sense of mission was needed in those entrusted with the cure of souls, and example would be as important a factor in the Reformation of the diocese as constitutional establishments. The Council of Trent had provided the impetus for these reforms. Bishops returning to their dioceses were to be resident; they were to codify organizational directives in new constitutions; and they were to *be* examples of partoral care in the diocese.

Domenico Bollani arrived in Brescia with strong convictions, therefore, about the organization of reform and about what was meant by example. We have seen the influence on him of debates and personalities in these two fields. But his task was to have special difficulties. Heresy seemed to be on the increase. Local opposition to changes in the *status quo* was deep-rooted where these conflicted with jurisdictional and financial interests. Venice, perhaps, had shown greater determination after the Council to back the eradication of heresy with official measures, but still displayed reluctance to concede the powers arrogated to itself by the Inquisition in her dominions, and was suspicious of the new principles of inspection and visitation laid down by the Council. In implementing his reforms, Bollani was constantly conscious of the susceptibilities of his homeland. In the diocese of Brescia, on the frontier of Spanish dominion, and part of the Archbishopric of Milan, his task was to steer a course between the currents of reform urged by the Papacy in the figure of Carlo Borromeo, and Venice's continuing reluctance to concessions in her dominions. The edifice of the Brescian Reformation was to be built on a reconciliation of these interests, and a preparation for such a task in terms of practical awareness, diplomacy and organizational flair will be recognizeable.

Bollani's precoccupation with his image in Brescia and personal initiatives in the context of charity show that the lesson of example had been well learned at Trent. He returned to the diocese in 1563 clearly fired with enthusiasm about the new role bishops were to assume in the application of the Council's decrees. But even before the Council, he had celebrated his new dignity with a gesture that reflects his experience in times of famine in Udine, and his preoccupation with the city's food supplies during his period as *Podestà* of Brescia.[35] During the famine which struck Brescia in 1559—60, he proposed that each noble family in the city should take a number of the poor under its wing, and offered to feed 88 people himself while the crisis lasted.[36] Perhaps in this example of direct action at the beginning of his bishopric may be seen the transition from an administrative to a pastoral function: previously concerned with the prevention of disaster through administrative measures, he now offered a practical example through his own generosity. In this he anticipated the Council's insistence on the charitable function of the bishop and the division of a proportion of the fruits of the bishopric among the poor.[37]

Charitable intervention was not the invention of the Council of Trent, however. As Jedin has noted, Giberti provided the link between the old self-denying ideal and the concept of practical Christianity that was to find its expression in Borromeo's generosity.[38] What was new in Giberti's approach had been his personal intervention in charitable foundations through the medium of institutions already existing. In Bologna, Bollani's contemporary, Cardinal Paleotti, had complained (in the context of his own financial hardship) that it had only been Giberti's wealth that had allowed him to indulge in such widespread personal charity.[39]

For Domenico Bollani, the concept of wealth as God-given with its inherent duty to distribute a proportion of the fruits of his benefice among the poor was certainly inculcated after the Council. As early as 1564 he defined the three principal outlets for episcopal revenues as the maintenance of churches, the relief of the poor and the upkeep of the bishop.[40] His ecclesiastical tax return of that year also specifies the ways in which direct charity was administered at this point at the beginning of his term of office: 'Fa il vescovato ordinaria elemosina del pane a grande numero di poveri, li quali, trovandosi il vescovo alla sua residenza, hanno ogni giorni il primo riccorso alle porte del vescovato.'[41] He went on to specify the part played by the bishop in the supply of foodstuffs, money and medicine for the work of the visitors of the poor ('l'opera dei poveri vergognosi'). It seems that a definite programme of poor relief was well advanced by 1564, and that the experience of famine and starvation in Udine and Brescia was now given form and substance in personal initiative and example.[42]

After 1565, the impetus for personal charity was to come from Borromeo. If Bollani had been encouraged in his own philanthropical tendencies during the later sessions of the Council by the image of Giberti and the formula of the *Stimulus Pastorum*,[43] it is likely that he had also drawn strength from the views expressed at Trent by Bartolomeo de Martyribus, archbishop of Braga, for we have seen that they had shared in the work of the commission appointed to revise the Index.[44] Bartolomeo had urged a more precise definition of the duties of the bishop at the session of November 24, 1563, and this suggestion included the uses to which ecclesiastical revenues were to be put.[45] Jedin has described how the Council displayed some reluctance to legislate precisely on the qualities of the bishop,[46] preferring to allow the implementation of an ideal to evolve from local councils.[47] In 1565, the first Provincial Council was convened in Milan, and it was at this point that the strength of Borromeo's influence began to be felt. Before examining further examples of Bollani's later charitable initiatives, therefore, brief description of this all-important first forum for the dioceses within Borromeo's

154

jurisdiction is required, as it had a significant bearing on Bollani's later reforming personality.[48]

Borromeo had made his ceremonial entry into Milan on September 23, 1565, having made arrangements for the convening of the first Provincial Council through his lieutenant, Ormanetto.[49] Bollani arrived at the Council at the beginning of October, having shared the duty imposed on bishops by Borromeo of study of the Tridentine Decrees. Each bishop would then present a section of the decrees of which he had made a special study to the assembly, debate would follow, so that a plan of action for use in the dioceses would emerge.[50] The discussions in which Bollani now participated aimed to root the Tridentine Decrees firmly in the example and initiative of bishops.

Bishops were to preserve the purity of the faith by censoring books according to the Index; to instruct priests in the cure of souls through example; to obtain the support of the civil authorities in the implementation of the reforms;[51] to combine with these authorities in the eradication of heresy; to promote religious education, and to keep a vigilant eye on the furnishing of churches, so that the sacred images should represent orthodox catholicism to the exclusion of all superstition.[52]

The Milanese Council also made clear pronouncements on those aspects of the Tridentine discussions that Bartolomeo de Martyribus had failed to have clearly defined. Candidates for ecclesiastical benefices were to undergo examination to test their worthiness.[53] Bishops' conduct was rigorously restricted in sumptuary legislation, and rules were laid down describing their clothing, plate and household. Even the simplicity of the bishop's table was defined, although the spartan diet for which Carlo Borromeo was later to become famous was not imposed. Finally, norms were devised for the regulation and streamlining of the orders, the foundation of charitable institutions and hospitals in the respective dioceses, and the first steps were taken in the controversial question of the collection of revenue for the foundation of seminaries.[54]

Bollani now had a detailed brief for the diocese of Brescia in the transmission of Tridentine procepts through the Milanese Council. The extent to which his policies were the fruit of collaboration is indicated in the voluminous correspondence between the two men which survives.[55] Bollani certainly accepted the principal framework of Borromeo's reforming method — that campaign for spiritual renewal through example and reorganisation of the resources of the Church — but his own personal campaign was rooted in a less ascetic and more practical background experience.[56]

The divergence of Bollani from the Borromeo ideal has already been noted in some of its particulars.[57] Paolo Prodi observed that both Paleotti and Bollani shared some reaction to certain aspects of Borromeo's reforming method, feeling that a more practical approach was necessary for the reformation of the diocese, now that the Council of Trent had formulated the relevant theory. Sometimes the initiatives of Borromeo seemed to them too abstract: decrees of the Provincial Councils seemed remote from local realities in their respective dioceses.[58] Action was to be the keynote of their reforms. 'Non si deve ripetere i decreti del Concilio di Trento, ma incarnarli nella realtà delle singole diocesi in base alla situazione concreta che il vescovo deve in primo luogo investigare.'[59] It was precisely for this practical function that Bollani had been trained by his civil career, and his success in the organisation of the Diocese, while not leading to canonisation — nor even the cardinal's hat — was founded on this principle.

Before leaving Bollani's pastoral image and the ideal of personal charity, various further episodes serve to illustrate the principles which motivated him. His personal gifts and legacy, as well as his behaviour during the terrible plague in Brescia in 1576–1577, throw light on the pastoral image which informed all his work in the Diocese of Brescia. He certainly believed in the fruits of his benefice as a source of charity, but he was not to reject the needs of his family in time of hardship, nor those of his country in time of war. Further, the plague in Brescia provided him with an opportunity to demonstrate to the full the principle of pastoral example — just as it did for Borromeo — while never obscuring for him the dictates of practical good sense. This practical viewpoint — so clearly the result of his experience in politics and diplomacy — was to lead historians into erroneous charges of dereliction of duty: from that generation which lived through the canonization of Borromeo, and was perhaps blinded by the light of sanctity, down to our own day.[60] Bollani's decrees for charitable initiatives in the diocese of Brescia are collected in the *Atti della Visita Apostolica* of Borromeo to Brescia after Bollani's death in 1580.[61] But whereas decrees may indicate dutiful acceptance, his own actions spell conviction, and will give the measure of his ideal. In his will, Bollani left 1000 ducats to the poor in Brescia 'a' luoghi pii, et a' poveri più bisognosi di questa città.'[62] Inspired, possibly, by the example of Seripando.[63] It would be difficult indeed to measure the sacrifice of this gesture, but it may suffice to say that the Foscarini debt was still sizeable at Domenico's death,[64] and that in the last reference to his financial position in 1577 he was still clearly preoccupied with the recovery of assets.[65] He made similar gestures at the time of Lepanto, and here it may be asserted with confidence that the charitable impulse was both religious and patriotic: not only was the battle of Lepanto to be a victory for Catholicism, but it was also to provide some security for the Venetian republic, and to avenge the loss of Cyprus. As we shall see again, there were moments in Domenico's career when his reforming drive and patriotic instincts were to become one in what was more than a utopian dream.[66]

When the Turkish threat had crystallised into the probability of war in 1570, Bollani had united solidly with the rectors of Brescia Antonio Bragadin and Daniele Foscarini to urge the city to contribute to the war in a tangible way.[67] The result was the offer of 1000 infantry from the city (which Venice gladly accepted), and Bollani contributed 1129 ducats to the war effort.[68] The victory brought financial hardship throughout Venetian dominions, in the manner of most victories, and the Pope levied a *decima* on the clergy of 100,000 ducats. Bollani was deputed with the bishop of Bergamo to begin the arduous task of collecting this sum from the Venetian clergy, and contributed 2,000 scudi from his own fortune by way of example.[69]

Perhaps nowhere more clearly does Bollani's personal pastoral image emerge than in the terrible plague which struck Brescia and the whole of northern Italy in 1575–1577.[70] In the realm of personal dedication and sacrifice, this was the first

156

severe test, in some ways, for the bishops that the Council had created: a period when the pastor's example was to make a telling impact on successive generations. It was probably this aspect of Borromeo's pastoral activity that captured the popular imagination more than any other, and produced a flood of images and votive shrines in the years that followed.[71] For Bollani, the experience was backed by first-hand acquaintance with plague in Udine in 1556, and illuminated by the example of Borromeo during the Milanese plague.[72] Yet again, however, the episode illustrates the difference of approach of the two reformers.

For Borromeo, the struggle against the effects of plague was the culmination, in a sense, and consummation of his pastoral image. Through his personal dynamism and energy he represented through his presence the total campaign to eliminate suffering.[73] His personal sacrifice, scorn for danger, and physical presence wherever the contagion was worst stood out in sharp contrast against the relative cowardice and inefficiency of the civil and medical authorities.[74]

Bollani's own comments on the Brescian situation show him clearly following Borromeo's model of practical Christianity through example in his visits to the *Lazzaretto*,[75] his aid for the sick and suffering,[76] and his insistence on being present to administer communion and readiness to cooperate with the city authorities.[77] But his correspondence shows the practical administrator as well. He wrote on April 16, 1577, of having accomplished 40 sermons in one day, having distributed money to the sick, but added that he had always proceeded 'con la debita prudenza,'[78] and noted that he had had to set a good example of practical hygiene and good sense by keeping people at a distance.[79] His criticism of the city authorities in Brescia was constant — particularly when he could observe the same kind of unprincipled exodus from the city that he had reported in Udine — but he declared himself ready to assist them in any way he could to prevent the spread of plague.[80] Possibly, too, his experience at Udine had made him view the scene with almost a professional's eye: for he described in detail the process of disinfecting goods in Brescia and Venice, and noted that stern methods would be required to enforce sequestration.[81] Above all, however, his concern was for the cure of souls, a pastoral enthusiasm tempered by caution and practical good sense:

'Ci troviamo in termini sî miseri e stretti che fa di bisogno pensar solo a poter giovare alle anime de' miseri, e nel miglior modo alla nostra preservazione, purche non sia abbandono o fuga, che questo non voglio sentirla a modo alcuno, rimettendomi in tutto con obbligo del carico mio.'[82]

In short, *cura animarum*, and self-preservation in that order, in accordance with the dictates of duty.

The concept of the duty of residence — especially in times of plague — provides an example by which it is possible to compare the pastoral image of Bollani and Borromeo by the same standard. In this comparison Bollani and Borromeo stand clearly in relief against each other.

We have noted that the accusation of desertion of his post during the plague had been levelled at Bollani, possibly by enemies in Rome in the circle of Cardinal Francesco Gambara,[83] and that he was able quickly to prove that the charge was unjust. Hearing of this accusation, Borromeo had sent a letter of remonstrace to Bollani in which the rigidity of his principle of pastoral devotion is transparent:

> 'Rieda all'antico istituto ad ai suoi costumi e non rapire a se stesso quella lode che finora si è acquistata per la sua pietà verso gl'infermi e per verità *non deve raffreddarsi l'animo quando una necessità di più grave sventura il dovrebbe maggiormente infiammare.*'[84] (Italics mine)

The fact that the accusation was unjust is unimportant for the present discussion. Borromeo clearly regarded adversity as a spur to greater self-sacrifice, and invited Bollani to return to his post in the centre of a plague-ridden city. Bollani, on the other hand, found himself in precisely the same position early in 1576, when his own subordinate Giacomo Roveglio, fled to Salò where he might be safer from the risk of possible infection.[85] Far from the stern recall to greater self-sacrifice, Bollani replied to Roveglio's letter of resignation in human and conciliatory terms. Bollani's broad tolerance and understanding may be seen in contrast with Borromeo's quotation of abstract principle:

> 'Io sono contentissimo di tutto cuore che vi ritiriate in Riviera e dove in pace, fino a tanto che vi pare, poter sicuramente tornar in Vescovado, perchè ad ogni modo saremo tutti scusati del tener sospese le udienze. Vedete in grazia di fare il tutto con minor moto che potete e con dar voce che andate per ricreazione per la vendemmia per dieci or quindici giorni, fra li quali piacerà forse alla divina bontà liberarci.'[86]

Above all, understanding of human weakness is the keynote of his reply — with even the suggestion of subterfuge.

One further example will serve to contrast the pastoral approaches of Bollani and Borromeo in the framework of charitable action: the projected visit to plague-ridden Brescia of Borromeo himself. It reveals again the basic difference of personality which characterised the pastoral images of the respective reformers. Borromeo saw it as a clear duty to visit those in need in the diocese of Brescia, while Bollani, with perhaps more political intuition and forsight realised that there would be practical difficulties. On May 18, 1577, Borromeo announced his intention of coming to Brescia: 'Il morbo che costi prende forza mi mette quasi in una impazienza, mi aggiungo stimolo a recarmi in fretta tra i miei Bresciani,'[87] revealing again that inner compulsion which drove him to greater and greater efforts. Bollani, hoever, conscious of the political difficulties which the Provincial Councils had already caused with Venetian jurisdictional susceptibilities,[88] and anticipating the danger into which Borromeo would be going, replied in terms of practical realities:

> 'Deponga senza dubbio V. Ill. Sig. ogni suo fervorato affetto che la muove a scrivermi di suo desiderio di vernirmi con tanta benignità a vedere, che tutto causerebbe disordine con quelli Signori di Milano et maggiori con questi di Brescia senza punto di utile et il pericolo non sarebbe poco per questo si sparso ed acuto contagio . . .'[89]

For Bollani, pastoral devotion should not ignore the dictates of prudence and should take account of political realities. Here was Bollani the diplomat, avoiding through tact and political awareness the possibility of an unnecessary international incident. For Borromeo, such things were subordinate to the driving force of Christian compulsion: politics should play no part in the cure of souls. For he replied in a manner that ably illustrates his linear concept of pastoral duty: that the practical and political must be subordinate to the spiritual in a defined hierarchy of priorities:

'Tuttavia io sono ancora in questa opinione che tale mio viaggio che avea intenzione di intraprendere appartenga all' officio pastorale che esercito. Poichè codesta città che è forse il principale ornamento della mia provincia sembra aver bisogno della presenza dell'arcivescovo. Questo esigeva pur anche l'amor mio verso di V.S. trovandomi io a Lei legato per tanti titoli, ma specialmente pel vincolo del pastorale officio pel quale l'uno e l'altro di noi siamo reciprocamente congiunti. Tali ragioni pertanto m'indussero a non calcolare menomamente la prudenza della carne ed i consigli troppo umani di certuni i quali distruggono od almeno certamente reprimono la pietà in questi miseri tempi. E volesse Iddio che di tali arti non si servisse il Demonio a diminuire l'ardore dalle carità!'[90]

Throughout this letter (partly quoted above) runs a singleness of purpose and a unity of vision whose hierarchy of values admits no compromise.

Thus the ideal of personal charity was a fundamental part of the Tridentine attitude to reform. It was a tangible way in which the first generation of Tridentine bishops could translate the theory of example into daily practice, and it was also importantly an aspect of their work which would live on in the imitation of successive generations of Catholic bishops. In the present context, the ideal has gone some way towards defining the pastoral image of Domenico Bollani — that element which Paolo Prodi has called the *Spirito Pastorale* — the interaction of the tridentine theory with the personality of the reformer and the particular local conditions in which he was active.

Yet it also throws into relief one of the paradoxes of the Counter-Reformation: that the movement towards uniformity in the Catholic Church was put into practice by a diversity of methods and approaches.[91] Borromeo had been motivated by a self-denying ideal in which political expediency had given way to a 'Christian compulsion.' Cardinal Paleotti had personified the tridentine example, too — while yet giving full weight to the particular local conditions of the diocese of Bologna.[92] Both Paleotti and Bollani tempered the principle of Christian charity with practical humanity. Both were critical of the narrowness and rigidity of the Borromean view, and both were criticised by Borromeo for their humanity. And there were further contrasts and diversities. Nearer to Bollani in patriotic motivation and collaboration with the civil authorities stands the Archbishop of Florence[93] — than Alfonso Carafa, Cardinal of Naples, who would have agreed with Borromeo that the State was the secular arm of the Church, and must conform with tridentine precepts.[94] Furthest from him, probably, was Niccolò

Ormanetto, who, bringing the intransigence and severity of the Borromeo ideal into the heartland of Venetian influence when he took up residence as bishop of Padua in 1570, incurred hostility and opposition from Paduan and Venetian authorities.[95]

But what of Bollani's fellow Venetians? When more is known about the *Spirito Pastorale*, or the individual reforming personality of Matteo Priuli, bishop of Vicenza, and Agostino Valier, bishop of Verona, it is likely that there will be some real evidence for the statement that 'the Venetian Republic was a special case.'[96] After all, Agostino Valier was chosen for the 'diplomatic' task of examining the Patriarch of Venice,[97] and was to experience Bollani's conflict of loyalties in Rome in 1593, when he tried to serve both the Pope and the Venetian Republic.[98] But for the moment, his pastoral image in terms of charity remains obscure, and we must be content with uncritical hagiographical statements like: 'La carità era per Agostino il pensiero che sempre lo preoccupava. Non mancava mai, prendendo occasione da tutto d'incitare i fedeli.'[99] For Valier had been far closer to Borromeo than Bollani; he had been present at the *Notti Vaticane* in Rome; and he carried the Veronese reforming tradition in his blood, so to speak.[100] Given his experience of the *Visita Apostolica* and his part in Church and State disputes, more must be learnt about his reforming personality before placing him alongside Bollani in a 'Venetian reforming spirit.' built on the administrative expertise and diplomacy of the centuries-old traditions of the Venetian patriciate, and standing away from and in contrast with, the zeal and uncompromising policies of Paul IV and Carlo Borromeo.[101]

The need for legislation in the field of ecclesiastical education had been recognised even during the early sessions of the Council of Trent, and had been demanded insistently also from north of the Alps.[102] During its first session, the Council had stipulated that teachers of Latin grammar and theology be attached to cathedrals and religious orders. This move was scarcely adequate to satisfy the growing body of opinion in all sections of the church, and the examples of cathedral schools which had been expanded to fulfil the function of seminaries by Talavera, Archbishop of Grenada, and Giberti, Bishop of Verona, carried considerable weight in the final sessions. Finall, the decree *forma erigendi Seminarum clericorum* was passed by the assembly on July 15, 1563 during session XXII. Even Cardinal Pole had based analogous institutions in England during the restoration of Catholicism under Mary on the statutes of Giberti.[103]

The importance of the Council's legislation in this respect has been rightly stressed. At a time when the Catholic Church was aiming at renewal and internal strength, the education, formation and upbringing of priests was of vital importance at the lower end of the tridentine hierarchy. It was not only in the upper echelons of a society like Brescia that the risk of infection from northern ideas was to be found, as we have seen, and the educational and spiritual weakness of parish priests — tellingly to be documented in the tridentine *visite pastorali* — had contributed significantly both to the infiltration of heretical ideas, and to some reaction from orthodox Catholicism.[104]

The Council decree on seminaries insisted on early training for the priesthood.

160

Bishops were to provide centres for the instruction of boys with a basic grounding in essential disciplines, who had shown clear leanings towards the church, and these institutions should preferably be attached to cathedrals. The seminaries would provide education for boys from poorer surroundings, although the Council did not exclude the sons of wealthier families whose vocational inclinations were demonstrable. Rules were established for the uniform and curriculum of the seminarists, and practical training was to be given in the future priests' offices. Importantly, the bishop should take advice on the establishment of the seminary from two senior cathedral Canons, and should often visit the institution himself.[105] But the most controversial aspect of the decree was that part devoted to the financial support of the seminary — and it was here that widespread opposition was encountered in Italian dioceses.[106]

The situation which gave rise to this need was not dissimilar in Brescia to that in other dioceses. Before Trent, many priests had been virtually self-taught, and it had been left to individual initiatives — particularly in the family context — to ensure adequate educational, spiritual and practical preparation for ordination.[107] Just as church benefices at all levels had been a family affair in a significant number of incumbencies, so educational preparation lacked the necessary formal direction. Local ecclesiastical authorities did, on occasions, institute quasi-formal training to provide priests within a specific local context,[108] and cathedral foundations also yielded some instruction, but it was a natural extension of the tridentine principle of suitability for appointment to church benefices (*idoneità*) to rationalise and standardise education for the priesthood. In some dioceses, the tridentine seminary was to grow out of previous attempts to remedy this defect. Just as the seminary founded by Agostino Valier in Verona in 1567 was built on the statutes of Giberti, so Bollani's seminary (1568) grew from the early initiatives of Francesco Cabrino and the *Monte di Dio*.[109] The foundation of seminaries after the Council of Trent was to cause bishops serious problems precisely because they had been allowed the freedom to devise constitutions that would take account of local needs.[110]

To appreciate the difficulties and obstacles encountered by the first generation of tridentine bishops,[111] we must return to the terms of the Council's decree. The Canon approved during the final sessions was more the theoretical elaboration of an educational ideal than a blueprint for the creation of concrete institutions. At no point had the tridentine bishops conceived these foundations in their detailed structures, so that the formula for success had to be found by experiment, and was by no means uniform in the various dioceses.[112] Again, the provisions for the endowment of seminaries were decidedly vague: provision was made for their support firstly from revenues from certain benefices diverted for the purpose on a permanent basis, and secondly, from a mandatory tax contribution levied on a very wide range of ecclesiastics in the diocese.[113] The decree does not distinguish between these two major sources as to amount or priority — and it is perhaps here that the cause of major difficulties is to be found — but spelled out severe sanctions against any person not cooperating with, or obstructing the foundation in any way.[114]

The earliest documents in Brescia,[115] and the frequency of Bollani's recourse to

Borromeo for advice,[116] testify to his great personal concern for the question of the Brescian seminary, as do his personal initiatives at each stage of its development. His first legislative steps date to January, 1567 (when the first meeting of elected representatives to discuss the foundation was held), but by that time the storm had been weathered, and we must retrace our steps.

From his correspondence with Borromeo in 1565–1566, Bollani's enthusiastic planning for the foundation of the Brescian seminary shows the degree of his involvement and hints at his future difficulties. He had fully realised that the imposition of an extra tax on the clergy for the upkeep of the seminary would arouse protests, and had asked Borromeo's advice on this difficult question. He had also described that pre-tridentine Brescian initiative towards the training of priests, the *Monte di Dio*, to Borromeo, and had conceived the idea of a gradual evolution from this existing and laudable institution to a new foundation conceived in the terms laid down by the Council.[117] In the light of subsequent events, the wisdom of this is abundantly clear, and it was perhaps a lesson which Agostino Valier had taken longer to learn in Verona. It is not impossible that Borromeo himself had learned something of the virtues of patience and diplomacy in Bollani's adaptation of the merits of a pre-existing institution to the new foundation.

In February, 1566, Bollani described the first reactions to his plan to levy a full *decima* on the Brescian clergy, and thus obtain financial backing both for the foundation of the seminary and for the rebuilding of the cathedral. These plans had been discussed the previous December,[118] but go back to 1564 at least. The plan caused a storm of protest among the Brescian clergy: 'infatto mi trovo un tanto gridare in ogn'uno per causa delle tante gravezze che hanno ch'io ne resto poco consolato, vedendo che tutto si fatta contribuzione habbia a essere violenta con ciascuno et non punto volontaria, come sempre vorrei vedere riuscire le attioni che partengo al spirito et alla lode di Dio.'[119] The letter contains Bollani's plan for the solution of this difficulty, and merits close examination. He suggested to Borromeo that the *decima* might be rendered more palatable to the clergy is its products were seen to benefit *two* urgent needs in the diocese: the foundation of the seminary and the rebuilding of the cathedral.[120] He requested Borromeo's help to convince the Pope of the wisdom of this course, as Pius IV had already given permission for a tax to aid the rebuilding of the cathedral. There is no evidence in subsequent events to suggest that this proposal was to satisfy the objectors.

The years 1566–1568, before the foundation of the seminary in the latter year, constituted Bollani's most severe test in his control of his diocese. The opposition raised to the proposals for the seminary were not dissimilar to those occasioned by the proposed publication of the acts of the first Milanese provincial council. In both cases, the complaints were local, but they soon fused into a general criticism as soon as the decrees of the Council of Trent had really begun to bite, and produced the involvement of the civil authorities. If the Council of Trent and the Provincial Council had written into their respective legislation the use of the *braccio secolare*, then conservative elements whose interests (in terms of regular duties and taxes on benefices) were affected would be bound to complain to the civil authorities. Further, the situation of Brescia under Milanese ecclesiastical but

162

Venetian civil control, meant that a determined opponent of the Catholic Reformation could, if influential, worry the reformer in the courts of Venice, Milan and Rome.

So the opposition to Bollani's imposition of the *mezza-decima* for the benefit of the seminary flourished in the soil of dissent already caused by the proposed publication of the *Concilio Provinciale*. It cannot, therefore be seen separate from it.[121]

Negotiations over the printing of the acts were under way by September, 1566, when one of Borromeo's secretaries reported delivering copies to Bollani — at the time engaged in his visitation along the *Riviera di Salò*, near Gargnano. At this point Bollani was cautiously optimistic about the willingness of the diocese to accept the implementation of the tridentine decrees, 'trovando i popoli ben disposti.'[122]

Three months later, Bollani made a clean breast of his difficulties to Borromeo, abandoning the fairly mild façade of optimism he had presented to the secretary in September. ('sono andato differendo di dirle i miei affanni, con desiderio di poterle pur dire qualche migliore successo . . .'[123]). His attempts at a conciliatory attitude are clear: he had held meetings of the canons of the cathedral each evening to read them the decrees of the Provincial Council; he had published the decrees widely throughout the diocese; but seemingly to no avail. Besides the comprehensible initial reaction of conservatism to novelty, they objected to the proposal to tax them for the upkeep of the seminary, and were deeply resentful of the tridentine prohibition of cohabitation with their womenfolk.[124]

So by 1566, the currents of opposition to the tridentine decrees were gathering strength. The nature of the action now taken by the Brescian canons was fore-shadowed by the Venetian reaction to the council in September, 1565. An edict of the Council of X had distributed copies of a motion to all Venetian rectors in the *Terraferma* prohibiting them from allowing their subjects 'pubblicare nè giubileo, nè indulgenza alcuna, che fosse a comodo dei sudditi di principe forestiero senza licenza di esso Consiglio.'[125] In this particular incident, the difficulties were soon resolved,[126] but the complexity of Bollani's position emerges clearly. The use by self-interested opponents of the tridentine reforms of Venetian jurisdictional susceptibilities was the continuing pattern of his bishopric. When Venice herself was not directly suspicious of reforming initiatives — in that delicate political posture in which the league of Cambrai had left her — appeals to the Republic by Brescian clerics were bound to cause embarrassment, and were a secure delaying tactic. With this recent demonstration of Venetian susceptibilities fresh in their minds, the canons laid their case before the Venetian rectors of Brescia, requesting the Republic to refer their complaints to the Pope through their ambassador in Rome:

'Hanno fatto secreto ricorso a questi clarissimi Signori Rettori, con esporre loro a bocha et in scritto molti suoi agravii di esso Concilio, per li quali dicendo che volevano haver ricorso a Sua Santità, supplicavano la Serenissima Signoria a dar ordine al suo Ambasciatore in Roma che pigliasse in protettione li loro agenti con favorirgli appresso la Beatitudine Sua; così questi Clarissimi Rettori, senza dire altra parola a me, con assai favore accettorono da essi canonici la sudetta scrittura, et l'hanno mandata a Vinetia, et a me hanno fatto sapere ch'io non proceda ad altro atto di pubblicatione di esso Concilio se prima intorno ciò non intendano il volere della Signoria . . .'[127]

The Rectors had further added that they had discerned in the acts of the council various things prejudicial to the Venetian national interest, and even Bollani's offer to explain these to them failed to move them from their purpose.

This incident set the tone for Bollani's period as Bishop of Brescia. The jealousy of Venice for the letter of the law in her control of her subject dominions was to provide Bollani's opponents with fuel for their attack. In this case, the Rectors had probably been naive in supposing that the acts were prejudicial to Venetian interests, but this was not always to be the case. Bollani reflected soberly that the application of the tridentine decrees would suffer sadly if the protection and support of the secular arm was not extended to the church in these times,[128] and correctly forecast that, since Venice had supported the decisions of the Council of Trent, so she would not stand in the way of the promulgation of the acts of the Milanese Council,[129] but noted sadly that the episode had produced a campaign against his person in Venice and Rome, as well as in Brescia.[130]

Bollani had not been alone, however, in encountering serious obstacles to his plans for the seminary and the implementation of the acts of the provincial council. In Milan, Borromeo was meeting considerable opposition to the decrees — particularly that forbidding the cohabitation of priests with female relatives.[131] As far as the seminary was concerned, the objections in Milan centred on the control to be exercised by the Jesuits, but this was a Roman problem.[132] The objections to the *decima* in support of the seminary were far more general. In Venice, Giobatta Contarini succeeded in extracting a subsidy from the Senate only after repeated insistence, and the decision to finance the seminaries from the fruits of benefices allocated specifically to them (Bollani's final solution, as we shall see) did not come until 1579.[133] In Rome, objections to the tax were predictably strong after a 14-man commission of cardinals had decided to entrust the running of the institution to the Jesuits.[134] Again, the canons attempted to call the bluff of the censures threatened to see what action would be taken. In Bologna, the picture was very similar. The proverty of many dioceses made the collection of this tax extremely difficult, and the interests of those whose pensions came from the fruits of Bolognese benefices made them natural opponents. As in Bollani's case, the foundation of the seminary was delayed until 1568 for this very reason.[135]

So in this first phase, Bollani's problems were those of most of the rest of Italy. Before the foundations of the tridentine seminaries, objections had been principally on economic grounds, as the interests of every cleric had been affected where it hurt most. The problem of the extension of Jesuit influence, through Jesuit control of seminaries in Rome and Milan is yet another chapter in the tortured history of that order. The protests caused by the publication of the acts of the first Milanese Council, particularly in the case of the cohabitation of priests with their female relatives, has provided the first minor incidence of jurisdictional

164

conflict, since Borromeo's jurisdiction overlapped with that of the Venetian Senate precisely in the dioceses of Bergamo, Brescia and Crema. It should not be forgotten that Borromeo represented for Venice, not only Milan under Spanish dominion, but also Rome. If Venetian discussions of her policy in the attempted publication of the acts of the council had been recorded, it would probably emerge that the rectors of Brescia had procrastinated through lack of official directives — just as in that other case of Venetian/Milanese conflict of interests with which this study has been concerned — the Oglio dispute.[136]

In this atmosphere of strife and suspicion, Domenico Bollani still pressed forward with his plans for the institution of a seminary in Brescia. The first meeting of representatives elected to supervise the construction was held in January, 1567 — three months before the rectors yielded to pressure to permit publication of the acts of the Milanese Council.[137] Before this action had produced relative calm in the relations between the bishop and his clergy, then, Bollani moved strongly forward with the seminary, backed by the legal force of the Provincial Council, and spurred on by Borromeo. On January 10, the canons elected four representatives to supervise building,[138] and on February 15, the official order went out for the exaction of the *mezza-decima*, to be collected every October, until such time as revenues could be found from the allocation of vacant benefices.[139] Finally, Bollani himself sold an area of land belonging to the bishopric in the city for the erection of the seminary.[140]

His concern that the future of the seminary should not be rooted in the quicksands of tax collection is seen in the events of 1569. By this time, the building had begun, and Bollani had personally laid the foundation stone on September 27, 1568,[141] but the allocation of vacant benefices for the upkeep of the institution would perhaps free the whole question from the deleterious effects of dispute and controversy:[142] he assigned thirteen benefices to the upkeep of the seminary as soon as they should become vacant,[143] thus assuring the long-term security of the institution. To complete the foundation, Bollani made a gift of land next to the seminary site to the order of twelve priests, the *Padri della Pace*, and made detailed arrangements for its internal organisation which was to be placed in their hands. His letter of 1569 to Ormanetto in Rome reflects the general practice of entrusting instruction and the administration of seminaries to independent orders:

'Sono andato sempre più pensando le vie più sicure nel poter dare lunga durazione a questo nostro, {seminario} già per gratia del signor Dio molto bene eretto in questa città, ne che ho sempre avuto non pocho dubbio che non appoggiando a migliore governo che di {sacerdoti} mercenarii, o la pocha cura di sifatti ministri, o di peggio qualche loro mala costumatezza a interrompere si santa opera.'[144]

The new foundation of the *Padri della Pace* was to occupy the site adjacent to the seminary, and one of their number, Bollani's friend and confessor, Francesco Cabrino, was responsible for the election of Francesco Landino di Bibbiena as the first rector.[145]

The problem of the upkeep of the Brescian seminary continued to cause Bollani

endless difficulty. The constant references in his letters to 'il nostro povero seminario' indicates both the extent of his identification of it with the reformed
Brescian church, and his regret that it continued to be a battle ground, in a sense,
for the struggle with the opposition to the reform movement in the city. The
import of most accounts of the early life of the institution is perhaps coloured by
some optimism about its growth in the first ten years of its life, while the evidence
of Bollani's letters shows clearly that it had become the focus of serious disputes
by the end of Bollani's life. It is now necessary, therefore, to look more closely at
the opposition that Bollani faced in Brescia as the first phase in the post-tridentine
reformation gathered momentum.

We have seen how opponents of the reform movement were able to harness the
jurisdictional susceptibilities of the Venetian Republic to their cause by appealing
to the Venetian Rectors in the affair of the first provincial council. They were
further able to enlist the support of the powerful Brescian Cardinal, Francesco
Gambara, whose personal differences with Bollani regularly punctuated his
bishopric, and who also constituted a sympathetic authority outside Brescia to
whom complaints about innovations in the city might be addressed.

Gambara represented, in some respects, the classic type of pre-tridentine curial
careerist — in spite of his participation in the later sessions of the Council. Feuda-
tory lord of vast areas of land in the *basso Bresciano*, on the Brescian side of the
river Oglio from Verolanuova to the town of Gambara, his family also controlled a
significant number of ecclesiastical benefices in the diocese.[146] Related to Carlo
Borromeo, and enjoying similar inherited benefits and opportunities, his career
may be seen as diametrically opposed to that of the self-denying cardinal of Milan.
Gambara's court in Rome became the natural haunt of those Brescian clerics
whose financial interests and ancient privileges were being eroded by Bollani's
energetic application of the tridentine decrees. From the details of clerical life
— such as the cohabitation of priests with female relatives — to the inroads on
individual benefices made by 'tridentine taxes', such as that for the seminary,
Brescian clerics could always appeal for support against Bollani to Gambara.
Among the protégés of this cardinal were Panfilo Manerba, Francesco Soldo,
Orfeo Tolina, Giulio Caravaggi and Paolo Franzoni, canons of the cathedral in
Brescia.[147] The problem of Gambara's previous feudal right to confer church
benefices was to cause endless disputes in the city and seriously threatened the
stability of Bollani's control.

There is little doubt that Gambara's opposition to the seminary was one of
economics rather than any objection to the institution itself. Naturally, those with
the largest and most numerous pensions from Brescian ecclesiastical livings would
be contributing most to the institution while it relied for its support on direct
taxation of the clergy, and we know that Gambara owed 50 ducats per year to the
seminary at this time. Later he was to oppose the union of benefices planned by
Bollani in support of the seminary. From 1569, there was a gradual escalation of
incidents of this kind whose cumulative effect united in a solid front Gambara's
followers in the diocese, and produced the main opposing force against which
Bollani's diplomatic experience was to be pitted.

In the early 1570s, Bollani was clearly using the full range of his political experience against this opposition. He was obliged to marshal his friends in Venice and Rome to this end, and demonstrated a tenacity and singleness of purpose in his dedication to the tridentine formula that brought him unpopularity and sorrow.

The re-opening of the question of the financing and future of the seminary in 1572 was certainly prompted by two facts: the election of Gregory XIII Buoncompagno as Pope, and the Venetian war against the Turks. The former event prompted Bollani again to recommend the cause of his seminary to Rome, in the hope that a better response might be received than that from Pius V, and the latter produced the levy, or *decima*, imposed by Gregory to aid the Venetian war effort, which replaced and cancelled that imposed for the seminary.[148] Bollani wrote to Borromeo on May 20 with these two thoughts in mind, and it seems from this important letter that he had previously met opposition from Pope Pius V. Perhaps fortunately for the diocese of Brescia, Bollani had had occasion to become acquainted with Buoncompagni at Trent,[149] and possibly his fortunes turned at this point.

Bollani requested Borromeo to favour the Brescian seminary in his discussion with the Pope, in particular by means of the union of benefices decreed by the Council of Trent.[150] He further noted that the cause of the present disturbance was a dispute over a benefice yielding some 500 scudi of annual revenue, which he had allocated to the support of the seminary. Without this, the institution — now deprived of its revenues from direct taxation — would fall on evil times.[151] In this last dispute, Bollani proposed to avail himself of his friendship with Cardinal Palleotti, archbishop of Bologna, in order to 'far levar esse si stravaganti clausoli derogatorie al Sacro Concilio di Trento.'

The precise nature of Bollani's difficulties at the hands of Pius V remains somewhat obscure. He pressed forward, however, in his campaign to obtain relief from the problem facing the seminary, again requesting Borromeo to intervene with the Pope on its behalf,[152] and further, enlisting the support of the bishop of Vercelli.[153] In the same letter there are indications of the nature of Gambara's opposition, since it will be remembered that the cardinal's chief supporters were canons of the cathedral in Brescia — those same clerics who had caused Bollani such difficulties over the publication of the acts of the first provincial council. In fact Bollani requested stiffer penalties for lapses of duty by these canons. It is clear that some polarization had taken place between Bollani and the tridentine initiatives in Brescia on the one hand, and Gambara, supported by a section of the influential clergy on the other.[154] The struggle between the forces of conservatism, with interests in the conferment of benefices as articles of patronage, and in freedom from taxation for new institutions — and the reform movement striving to root the foundations on a local level in a secure financial and disciplinary framework, was to reach open rupture at Bollani's diocesan synod in 1574.[155] Before looking at this climax to Bollani's struggles, however, it is worth considering in more detail the influence of Gambara in the diocese, as it can probably be regarded as typical of the vested interests which Catholic reformers everywhere had to combat. In this the focus moves forward to further problems.[156] The relationship between Bollani and Gambara is also fundamental in assessing the role of civil, diplomatic and political experience in the implementation of the tridentine decrees.[157]

Some foretaste of the lengths to which Gambara was prepared to go is already provided by the affair of Savallo in the spring of 1576.[158] It seems that a certain Achille, described as 'arciprete di Savallo', was enjoying the protection of Gambara and using this — to put it at its broadest — as protection against the tridentine decrees.[159] By March 10, 1576, Bollani had clearly had recourse to friends in Rome, and the affair was further complicated by his absence in Venice as *collettore* for the Pope in the exaction of the new *decima* for the war with the Turks. Importantly (and whatever the precise details of the dispute), the episode demonstrates that the episcopal authority re-created by the Council of Trent would not always be sufficient when recalcitrant clergy sought the support of powerful members of the Roman Curia.[160] On April 4, Bollani confided in his vicar-general, Roveglio (who was dealing with the affair in his absence) showing the complexity of the negotiations that the case had necessitated, as well as the bitterness that Gambara's obstruction of his jurisdiction had caused him.[161] We learn too, that a friend in Roman circles was promoting his interests,[162] and Bollani was able to report a successful conclusion to Roveglio on May 2 of the same year.[163]

But relations between Bollani and Gambara were to worsen in the following year, engaging the full range of Bollani's political strength both in Venice and Rome in the face of an outright threat from Cardinal Gambara.[164] The dispute was a direct confrontation between the tridentine principle of episcopal control of reform initiatives and the enduring problem of Papal preferment and privileges which could still override it. Of minor importance in itself, it yet gives the measure of the role of diplomatic experience and skill in the implementation of the Council's decrees by the first generation of Catholic bishops entrusted with the task. From our present standpoint, it shows Bollani's experience in this field being used in its fullest range, and, more generally, points to the usefulness of Venetian traditions of political 'indenture' (broad diplomatic and ambassadorial experience) in the Catholic Reformation in this critical period of re-assertion of Papal dominance in religious affairs. The course Bollani steered was not here between the Venetian Republic and Roman direction of the reform movement (as will appear in the affairs of the Inquisition in the next chapter), but between Roman initiatives, and tridentine episcopal control. It is perhaps natural, therefore, that Bollani should ally himself with Cardinal Morone, the symbol of conciliar strength for his generation of bishops,[165] in the same way as he had perhaps been influenced by Cardinal Seripando in the matter of sanctity of life.[166]

The facts of the dispute may be briefly told.[167] We have seen that the Council of Trent had responded early to the widely-expressed need for improvements in the education of the clergy in the creation, in the fifth session, of permanent teaching posts attached to cathedrals in all dioceses.[168] These posts, the *Teologale* and *Penitenziera*, were to be financed by the union or allocation of vacant canonries or benefices, just as the later seminaries were to be supported by this means. The first vacant canonry had occurred in Brescia in 1568, and Bollani had attempted to bring into force the Council's decree with the election of Girolamo Monti to the lectureship in theology on the death of the Canon Vincenzo Bona.[169] Unfor-

168

tunately, the *Capitolo* of the cathedral opposed this move, claiming rights of election to the vacant post itself, so that again Bollani was experiencing the objections to tridentine directives of pre-existing traditions. Probably to relieve Bollani of the embarassment of compromise, Monti renounced the post, and Bollani was left with the unsatisfactory expedient of temporary measures,[170] while the tridentine directive remained unfulfilled.

It seems certain that, in response to these objections, Bollani now made sure that he would be supported by strong backing in any future allocations of benefices to these two posts. He secured Papal briefs giving him permission to allocate the next vacant canonry — one in support of his own future action in the diocese of Brescia, and one in support of Borromeo for the whole province. It was this security, almost certainly, that prompted him to move so strongly when the next vacancy, the death in the plague of 1577 of the canons Orfeo Tolino and Pietro Bocca, brought the whole matter again to the fore.[171] Now, however, his opponent was Cardinal Gambara, a powerful force in the Roman Curia, but by this year, Bollani must have felt in a strong position. Strengthened by the Papal brief directed to him personally, and availing himself of that conceded to Borromeo for the province, he now proposed to apply the two vacant canonries occasioned by the above deaths to the *Teologale* and the *Penitenzieria,* electing his vicar-general, Giacomo Roveglio, and Roveglio's deputy, Domenico Ettore, respectively to these two posts.[172] Further, he proposed to direct to the use of the seminary a benefice held by Paolo Franzone, Prior of San Giacomo del Mella, who had also perished in the plague.

Gambara reacted strongly against what he saw as an intrusion on his patronage. He claimed absolute rights of conferment of the canonry vacated by his relative, Tolino, and similar rights in the conferment of the Priorate. It seems that Domenico Ettore, elected to the post of *Penitenziere* by Bollani, was the only creation at this time that was to go unchallenged, although the candidate himself was none too willing to accept in this case.[173] Gambara wrote twice to Bollani in the strongest terms, and backed his objections with further letters to the Venetian Ambassador in Rome, Paolo Tiepolo, and to the *Podestà* of Brescia, Giovanni Soranzo,[174] warning Bollani with cynical realism 'che {aveva} più bisogno di amici che di benefici.'[175]

However true this statement turned out to be in subsequent events, the fact remained that Bollani now needed not only the force of the tridentine decree to carry out what the Council had ordered, but also political strategy and agents at the Papal court.[176] He proposed to further his case against the pretensions of Cardinal Gambara by means of these agents, and also with the support of the Papal Datary, Mons. Speciano, Mons. Frumento, the Venetian Ambassador in Rome, and even Cardinal Morone. Further, he enlisted the aid of his brother-in-law, Francesco Longo, who was to transcribe letters to eliminate any prejudice that might surround letters from the plague-ridden city of Brescia.[177]

The care with which Bollani prepared his campain illustrates the degree of his commitment. The first round, as it were, had perhaps produced little effect, as a report of one of Bollani's agents in Rome has survived to show that, in matters relating to preferments, the Cardinal's rank and proximity to the Pope would benefit his cause. Gregory XIII had perhaps acquiesced in Gambara's demands, in spite of the promptings of the Datary that the post had already been conferred, because of his presence in Rome.[178] Bollani now went to great lengths to ensure that his case would receive a fair hearing, by duplicating his initiatives: one request for support with the Pope was to go to Tiepolo, and the other to Morone.[179] Either of these might bear fruit, but Bollani's preference for Morone is interesting. 'Per l'humore tanto contrario tra ambi loro Cardinali { Morone e Gambara },' was Bollani's explanation, 'onde son certo, che non gl'haverà in questo alcun rispetto, come per l'ordinario hanno i cardinali, l'uno all'altro.'[180] For, apart from an astute observation of the probably solidarity of cardinals in defence of their privileges, there emerges from within the college of cardinals, just that opposition that Bollani was here facing: the struggle between conciliar reforming initiatives, and the vested interest of patronage.

In spite of the legal backing for his case (both tridentine and Papal), Bollani did not underestimate the strength of his opposition. He anticipated the loss of face in Rome that would accompany any concession to him, and prepared to sacrifice one benefice in the interests of the canonry for Roveglio.[181] The final outcome is not clear, and it has been noted that the failure to institute the permanent teaching posts that had been recommended in 1546 was general,[182] but the affair has demonstrated the use of political agility in the service of the application of the tridentine decrees.

Bollani had been prepared to use all the resources at his control in political contacts in Rome which dated from his days at the Council of Trent — as well as the diplomatic machinery of the Republic of Venice — to push through the decree in Brescia, and, perhaps more importantly, to make a stand for the new tridentine episcopal administration against the feudal privileges of the Roman college of cardinals. It seems certain that his civil career in politics, diplomacy and administration had taught him these things.

The outcome of Bollani's initiatives in 1568 to institute permanent teaching foundations of enduring educational value was probably interrupted by his death in 1579. Their parallel, the seminary, undoubtedly continued to suffer setbacks to the progress he had hoped for when he laid the foundation stone in 1568. In spite of Bollani's energetic promotion of the institution, it seemed to be in a poor state in 1575 when compared with Borromeo's flourishing foundations in Milan,[183] and when Borromeo visited Brescia on September 27, 1580 (twelve years, almost to the day, since its foundation) the seminary was found wanting in various respects.[184] Within our present context, however, Bollani's efforts on behalf of tridentine educational institutions have brought out some of the elements of opposition to the Catholic Reformation, and shown the use of practical political skill in combating it.[185] Perhaps the most propitious moment for Brescian seminaries was to come in the second half of the eighteenth century.[186]

If the battle against opposition — when supported by conservative elements in the Roman Curia — had engaged fully Bollani's political talents, these talents were not less useful in the sphere of local diocesan organisation. The events of the Diocesan Synod of 1574 again demonstrate the extent to which political expertise

170

was to be necessary to the reform movement, and constituted an undoubted success for the bishop of Brescia. The events also document the strength of local opposition,[187] and point to another important aspect of Catholic reform: the codification of rules for the reformed life of the clergy.[188]

The Diocesan Synod of 1574 was an attempt to unify all the reforms so far promulgated in Brescia and to obtain the sanction of the diocese for their codification in one document. It was also a forum which would allow broad scope for dissent: on a local level, the last confrontation, as it were, between the pre-tridentine principles of privilege and exemption, and the consolidation of reformation initiatives in episcopal authority. It was only as a result of these turbulent discussions in November of 1574 that the most far-reaching tridentine precepts were to become law in Brescia. Bollani may not have been able to count as an unqualified success his individual struggle with Gambara — for the latter was backed by the power of the College of Cardinals. On a local level, however, the battle with the *Savi del Clero* for dominance in the diocese was of fundamental importance for the reformation of the clergy.

It is worth pausing at this point to consider briefly the powers and function of the cathedral canons, whom, as we have seen, were prominent among leaders of opposition to Bollani's reforms and his authority in the diocese; also to consider the situation in two other dioceses on which information is available.[189] The canons enjoyed a traditional exemption from episcopal authority before the Council of Trent, being responsible ultimately only to the Papacy. They were therefore a natural centre in the diocese for opposition to the tridentine decrees,[190] just as the independence of the monastic orders was to cause problems for some reformers. Before the arrival in Brescia of Domenico Bollani, the feudal nature of the power of these canons retained many ecclesiastical benefices within a restricted circle of the local nobility.[191] In a sense, therefore, the problems facing the first generation of bishops after Trent were ones of conflicting jurisdiction, and the diplomat-bishop continued to be the one who was best qualified to solve them constructively. We shall see later how Bollani's gifts were those of Gasparo Contarini and Gian Matteo Giberti[192] — here we are concerned with Bollani's post-conciliar position.

After the Council, disputes in the diocese of Brescia were analogous with those of a similar kind in Milan and Bologna,[193] but Bollani's methods of solving them were individual. Cardinal Paleotti indicated the traditional functions of canons in his treatise on episcopal government, showing them to be the consultative body of the bishop's councillors, partaking in decision-making, and sharing the responsibilities of the bishop. This meant in tridentine terms also a share in 'episcopal perfection',[194] but was firmly consecrated by precedent and canon law.[195] The Council of Trent had confirmed these traditions, defining more closely those matters in which the bishop was bound to consult his canons, but importantly, had re-affirmed the power of the bishop over the canons.[196] As in the case of the tridentine seminaries, however, disputes arose from a lack of precision in the definition of these powers, and the recourse to higher authority by canons was a general result of the application of its decrees.[197] Paleotti's problems in this respect arose from the legalistic jurisdictional susceptibilities of his canons, but it is interesting to find that he too was to appeal to Cardinal Morone for support in the matter,[198] and was to obtain a papal brief similar to that conceded to Bollani for the reform of the canons.[199] It seems that Paleotti managed successfully to avoid open rupture, except, perhaps, in the case of Giovan Francesco Cannobio in 1569.[200]

In Milan, rupture was not avoided, but almost invited. It was a sector of reform activity 'in cui si fecero energeticamente sentire le misure repressive dell'arcivescovo.'[201] Bollani's approach to this much needed reform of patronage and privilege was conciliatory but firm – winning a decisive victory for the tridentine principle of *idoneità* in office, both in qualification and function, but not alienating the canons in the moment of victory, as we shall see. Paleotti had been forced to insist on his rights of episcopal jurisdiction in the dispute with the canon Cannobio – in an affair in which the secular authority played a part[202] – but Borromeo stamped hard on abuses in the colleges of canons, forcing them to renew their penance on the anniversary of their chief transgression for ten years.

The most celebrated case was the affair of the canons of S. Maria della Scala, which documents the intransigence and tenacity of Borromeo's method. This college had obtained direct dependence on the Holy See and exemption from episcopal jurisdiction from Clement VII. The disputes came to a head in Borromeo's proposed 'visit' to the college on August 24, 1569. The canons barred his way by force of arms, resisting an attempt by the archbishop to enter the church with unsheathed swords. As elsewhere, the affair was debated by both civil and ecclesiastical courts (Madrid and Rome) and the canons were forced to bow to tridentine principles, being forced to walk in penitent procession to beg for the release from the censures imposed from Borromeo himself.[203] It may be that such drastic surgery in the way of open confrontation produced a more effective deterrent, and more far-reaching reforms among the many colleges of canons in Milan. However that may be, the affair does little credit to Borromeo's diplomacy, and was a solution which worked only because of Borromeo's immense power and influence. Importantly, it occurred in 1569. When Bollani presented his case to Gregory XIII in the 1570s, he could have been fairly certain of papal support for bringing the canons into line with the decrees of the Council of Trent on the basis of such a precedent.

The diocesan Synod was conceived by the Council of Trent as having two principal functions: to advance the reformation of the diocese through the propagation of information about reforming initiatives, and to provide a real point of contact between the bishop and his clergy.[204] The latter principle had always been present; the former was the new function. Before the Council, Synods had existed chiefly for the propagation of information, while they were now seen as an authentic instrument of reform. Professor Prodi has written that the decline in the regularity and influence of Synods in the period before the Council had been seen by the fathers as a symptom of the general decline of the medieval church.[205] For Bollani, the Synod of 1574 was important in its timing: his *costituzioni* were to be discussed in an open forum, and he hoped for the approval and support of the more influential members of the Brescian clergy. The ideas had passed from their theoretical genesis at Trent; they had been built on from the direct experience of Bollani's *Visita Pastorale*; and they had been ratified in the Provincial Councils from 1564 to 1573, being finally published in the Constitution. The time was ripe, therefore, in the months preceding the jubilee year when bishops would give an account of their work to the Pope, to gather into one document the reforms so far promulgated and present them formally to the diocese. The opening of the assembly was therefore fixed for November 4, 1574.[206]

In the first two sessions, drafts of the new constitutions were discussed by the full assembly, and almost at once, objections began to be heard from the Deacon Davide Odasio and the Canon Antonio Aleni on what are now familiar grounds: 'Protestarono che le publicate Costituzioni ritornavano troppo gravose nella esecuzione, erano contrarie ai Canoni e lesive di molti diritti.'[207] On November 27, Bollani replied to these protests in cautious terms, protesting that his wish had been to keep strictly to the spirit of the tridentine decrees and the provincial councils — both sanctioned by papal approval. He also noted that the document had been discussed at length by representatives of the canons before the assembly.[208] At this point a leader of the opposition to Bollani's constitutions emerged in the person of the Canon Panfilo Rovato, who adopted a position of intransigence. Snubbed by Bollani for presenting a petition purporting to represent the *Savi del Clero* without a specific mandate from them, Rovato was then excluded from the list of eighteen candidates for election of the six *esaminatori del clero* proposed by Bollani.[209]

The fourth and fifth sessions of the Synod on November 6 were stormy and turbulent meetings. The dissident faction, seeing its own exclusion from the candidates for the important *Savi del Clero* elections, interrupted the meeting with noise and much moving from place to place when Rovato was accused of ballot-rigging.[210] In this situation, it is not hard to imagine the position of Domenico Bollani. With experience of Venetian political councils, the turbulence of the city councils of Udine and Brescia, and a personal acquaintance of the principal Brescian noble families dating from his period as *Podestà* of the city in 1558, he would have been as well-equipped as anyone present to deal with such problems. Fè D'Ostiani commented that such turmoil was 'estraneo ed insolito' in a gathering of clerics — but Bollani's experience of men undoubtedly helped him to steer the right course, and even the phenomenon of ballot-rigging must have reminded him of discussions in Venice in the 1550s.[211]

At the sixth and final session on December 7, Bollani used the disorders of the preceding session to gain advantage, and his methods recall to some extent those he had used with Anguissola on the banks of the Oglio: he stated that he wished to leave complete freedom of choice in the election of the *Savi*, but came down hard on fraudulent election practices, issuing a severe decree designed to outlaw them.[212] The election then went smoothly, the elected were sworn in — and the leading opponents of Bollani's reforms found themselves elected.[213] This gave rise to further protests, but the first phase was complete. Bollani had acted with scrupulous fairness and legality — factors that were to count in the days ahead.

Protests and objections continued into mid-January. The chief grounds for dissent were still the jurisdictional ones: that the new constitutions ran counter to privileges and exemptions already in force. Bollani stuck to his guns, repeating in replies to the *Savi* the legality of his position, that this constitutions had been arrived at by all due processes of consultation, and that they embodied principles already ratified by the Council of Trent and Provincial Councils, and sanctioned by the Pope. Against this argument there was no appeal. Two separate issues were referred to the Pope: the affair of the custody of the Episcopal Archives, and the constitutions themselves, and the *Savi* elected Cardinal Gambara as their protector in the dispute on December 22.[214] This time, however, the issue was a purely local one: the struggle was between the bishop and the canons. Bollani's constituions were entirely in keeping with the prescriptions of the Council of Trent, and a hearing of the arguments for and against them produced the papal decision in favour of Bollani's work. On june 14, 1575, Gregory XIII approved the constitutions, censured Rovato, Mangiavino and Franzoni, (precisely as had happened in Milan) and appointed Bollani as one of the judges to decide on measures appropriate to the conduct of these canons. In fact Bollani contented himself with defining more carefully the functions of the *Savi del Clero*, in order that they should not in future obstruct the progress of reform, and reduced them to their ancient pre-tridentine position. It was not until Carlo Borromeo visited the diocese as Apostolic Delegate in 1580—81, after Bollani's death, that the colleges were finally regulated in conformity with the practice in other dioceses.[215]

In this example of Bollani's diplomacy in the reform of the internal diocesan structure may be seen the function of civil experience.[216] The Council of Trent could not have created organisational frameworks for the decrees in the varying local situations of different dioceses. To construct these, it had placed new powers in the hands of bishops. Their task was to ensure their efficient implementation in a variety of political, geographical and constitutional situations. Bollani had been able to use these powers in Brescia, calling upon reserves of experience in legal and diplomatic spheres to push through the codified reforms. He had also been able to use his experience in government, negotiation and the functions of deliberative bodies to impose a new structure on the complexities of a feudally-based pretridentine administration. His success was not always complete. But Bollani proved, just as his forbears, Contarini and Giberti had done, that an administration, a formula, or a working practically-based structure for reforms would have been difficult indeed in the hands of one not experienced in the arts of politics, negotiation and diplomatic protocol. The Catholic Church before Trent was a complex amalgam of privilege and patronage administratively. An accomplished administrator was needed to mould a coherent pattern of reform and graft it on to a diocesan structure that still savoured in many ways in the 1570s of the Rome of Leo X and Paul III. Only with these gifts would a bishop succeed in creating unison, uniformity of purpose and a genuine impetus in the progress of Catholic reform.

Bollani had codified his reforms of the clergy and diocese in progressive stages culminating in the definitive administrative structure established in 1575. He was thus able to give a satisfactory account of the progress of Brescian reform in his audience with the Pope in that year. But we have examined only his legislative

174

battles, and their foundation in the conflict of pre-tridentine establishment and precedent and the norms of the Council. Bollani's concern had been far from solely legalistic and political during these years. He had been concerned also to see with his own eyes, in one of the largest dioceses in North Italy, where reforms of the clergy were most needed through the *Visita Pastorale*. The documentation of this activity has survived virtually complete,[217] and research is showing the extent and depth of his action in this sphere, so it will be sufficient here to summarise Bollani's achievement.[218]

Any complete analysis of the *Visita Pastorale* (indispensable for a religious history of a diocese) cannot come within the scope of a biographical study which is concerned, rather, with the visitor, his method and his success.[219] The acts of the visitations provide a measurable index (of varying reliability) of the state of a diocese, and when a fairly comprehensive coverage and accuracy of recording may be assumed, may give rise to significant conclusions about the progress of reform when two or more visits are compared over a number of years.[220] Such visitations are important in the context of the tridentine bishop for one reason above all others: after the Council of Trent, he began to perform them himself. We have returned often to the principle of episcopal authority as the chief instrument of reform created by the Council. The bishop had been noticeably absent from this sector of his pastoral duty in the middle ages, and where visitations had been performed, they had often been delegated, expensive, formal and (in tridentine terms) perfunctory. After the Council, therefore, the *Visita Pastorale* constituted the possibility of real contact between the bishop and the clergy and people in the diocese at large — in fulfillment of the tridentine 'pastoral' ideal — as well as a means of control and the direction of reform initiatives by the bishop himself.[221] For the success of the visitation, much would depend on the visiting bishop. Justice and fairness in tridentine terms in his method might bring real advances in the reform of religious life in the diocese, while exaggerated severity and a strictly legalistic approach might prove ineffective.[222] In examining Bollani's visitations, it is possible to compare his approach with that of a variety of reformers, illustrating this range, and reaching some conclusion about visitors themselves,[223] though more must be known about Venetian bishops in our present context.[224]

The practice of episcopal visitation after the Council of Trent owes much to the system established by Giberti in Verona. From a document surviving among the papers of Cardinal Morone, we know the formula used by Giberti,[225] and can gauge the conscientious care with which the reformer approached his task, but perhaps more important than the details, are the principles which Giberti left to the Council of Trent and the first generation of tridentine bishops. Giberti reduced the apparatus of the visit and participated personally in it, travelling widely in his diocese and establishing a personal relationship with the clergy and people. The effects of this were immediate — and find their echos in the experiences of Giberti's successors — as a contemporary account shows: previously, 'li vescovi ricchi non solevano fare la visita, ma farla mezzo d'altri, parerà maraviglia ad alcuna che hora {1530} il vescovo faccia l'officio suo.'[226] The shock value of personal visitation by the bishop after the council must have brought benefits in many dioceses, and is probably accurately reflected in a contemporary account of Paleotti's visitation in Bologna: '{1566} ma anche li putti per dove passava si gettavano a terra domandando la benedittione et erano quasi tutti tali che mai havevano visto vescovo, poichè erano uno secolo che vescovo nissuno havea visitato personalmente questa diocesi . . .'[227] And Borromeo's use of the cult of pastoral personality is too well-known to need further elaboration here.

This was the kind of impression Bollani was to make in his visitation of the diocese of Brescia, begun in 1565 and continued in 1567.[228] The diocese had indeed scarcely seen its bishops in almost a hundred years, so that the novelty of a personal visitation would have made its impact.[229] Further, the state of the diocese cried out for an energetic programme of reform of clergy, customs and people.[230]

Bollani's method in his visitation of the diocese was not dissimilar to that adopted by Giberti before him and Borromeo after him.[231] He had been preceded by visitations by twenty parish priests, whose results would serve as a guide for his personal visit.[232] He finally began his own visitation on September 2, 1565, starting with the western Bresciano, and was accompanied by Girolamo Cavalli and Gianpaolo della Corte. All the evidence points to the examination of the diocese having been one of the most scrupulous of all those of which evidence has survived. It has even been suggested that Bollani's was the first visitation since the council.[233] Like Giberti and Borromeo, he was concerned by reducing to an absolute minimum his accompanying suite not to create hardship for the parish priests whose duty it was to provide hospitality for the visitors. Throughout the diocese, Bollani inspected churches, preached sermons, personally interviewed parish priests. He took particular note of the cultural and educational levels of the clergy (in keeping with the tridentine principle of *idoneità*), examining the books read by the clergy, and prescribing others where necessary. He also heard complaints from the people, sat in judgment over cases of abuses of all kinds, and administered sanctions where necessary in an attempt to bring the local situations into line with the decrees of the Council of Trent. Just as the reform of ecclesiastical institutions in the city required tactful handling, so the correction of abuses in the diocese would need a firm hand and legislative experience.

Doubtless Bollani's experience of men in various capacities helped him most in the examination and correction of the Brescian clergy. Among these, he was to find pluralism, poverty and ignorance on a grand scale, as was certainly true in the majority of Italian dioceses at the time,[234] although it is perhaps dangerous to interpret the state of the diocese solely from the published Acts of Bollani.[235]

A few examples will show Bollani's scrupulous attention to detail in the implementation of the tridentine decrees. He commented frequently on the educational level of the clergy, requiring priests deficient in preparation to remedy this deficiency and present themselves for examination in due course.[236] Bollani further distributed catechisms, and often recommended specific texts for study, doubtless remembering his own recent theological formation — a factor which perhaps brought him closer to the problem than many of his reforming contemporaries.[237] A number of priests totally failed to satisfy the visitor, being culturally inadequate or even illiterate,[238] and were therefore suspended.

Nor would Bollani have been a newcomer to scandal and a lifestyle inappropriate to the tridentine priesthood. The courtroom atmosphere conveyed by a reading of these cases recalls his legal functions when *Luogotenente della Patria del Friuli*, and it may well be that understanding and justice might do more for Bollani in this sphere than, perhaps, rigidity and condemnation might accomplish elsewhere.[239] At Chiari, Bollani was informed that the priest played cards in public (reminiscent of the 'giochi et balli' that we have seen so often condemned in Bollani's civil legislation), and was constantly confronted with the spectacle of priests cohabiting with women. At Acqualunga he ordered that the priest 'licenzi la perpetua {of Manzonian overtones} nè più la riceva in casa.'[240] This recalls the tridentine prohibition of cohabitation with female relatives, which had, from the first Provincial Council, caused so much protest in Brescia and Milan. There were, of course, examples of conduct unbefitting a priest of all descriptions.[241]

There is perhaps one aspect of Bollani's visitation — and as aspect of his reforming personality — which was a result of his background and training in a special way: the solution of disputes. This is not to deny the value of Bollani's thorough examination of the Brescian church in all its aspects — church, liturgy, clergy and people[242] — but to select one aspect particularly relevant to the present contest. It is no exaggeration to say that an ability in the solution of disputes had been the foundation of Bollani's career, and continued to be his chief strength throughout his period in Brescia.[243]

On his arrival in a town, it was frequently true that Bollani would be confronted with a local situation demanding tactful handling and judgement. The opportunity to redress wrongs — or revenge grievances — was not to be missed when a fair hearing from the visiting bishop was perhaps possible for the first time. Bollani would often have to judge disputes, assess accusations, and administer sanctions, as he had done so many times before.[244] At Palazzolo, he successfully managed to settle a dispute between the archpriest Giuseppe Durante and the canons.[245]

It may be that the image of the pacifier was the keynote of Bollani's pastoral image. We have seen that his skill in such matters certainly contributed to his election to the bishopric, but a more famous example survives in Bollani's correspondence with Roveglio. It was during the celebrations of the jubilee in 1575 that he took the opportunity offered by the procession to resolve the long-standing dispute between the warring Maggi and Palazzi families, bringing the heads of these families together before the altar in the cathedral, in a touching scene which he described with evident pride to Giacomo Roveglio.[246] Examples of this kind of activity multiply in the acts of Bollani's *visita*, and evidence the new authority and prestige of the tridentine bishop. Further, the similarity of Bollani's activity in this respect with that of Agostino Valier in Verona — that scholarly bishop whose formative years had also included the diplomatic experience of that consummate diplomat Cardinal Bernardo Navagero — tempts one to see this expertise as a result of Venetian 'political identure'.[247]

There were further initiatives in the diocese which undoubtedly gained from Domenico Bollani's experience of government in the civil state, and at the Council of Trent, notably, perhaps, in the reform of monasteries and convents,[248] and the promotion of charitable and Christian associations.[249] In both these fields his work as bishop was a natural extension of his administrative experience. But we are not concerned here merely to enumerate examples. It is already clear that catholic reformation and spiritual revival in a diocese made very specific demands; it is worth summarising the reasons for this to assess Bollani's value and function in the reformation of the diocese of Brescia.

One thing has emerged overwhelmingly: just as the early Catholic Reformers needed power, influence and very 'diplomatic' skills, so the Council of Trent did not replace this need. The Council did not supply the reformer with a package of reforms and a vacuum in which to insert them. For the triumph of the Council of Trent was perhaps its organisational and dogmatic achievement in consensus: its failure, perhaps an inability to check the reviving absolutism of the Papacy. Perhaps inevitably in times when reform was conceived in a rigidly defined hierarchy of authority — to be applied by Borromeo, arch-exponent of this system — the Papacy was to grow in stature and individual strength. The result was conflicts on a wide front, and successes in the implementation of the decrees would reflect credit on the individual reformer. But tridentine administrations were also to conflict with civil administrations, as in Milan, with the power of Spain, and in north-eastern Italy, with the power of Venice. In short, therefore, among the first generation of reforming bishops after the Council, very 'secular' virtues were required for the successful conclusion of disputes in compromise and negotiation.

Of course the pattern varied from diocese to diocese. Borromeo had the power of the Papacy behind him, enjoyed immense personal prestige, and was sometimes thus able to blunder through disputes through sheer force of dogmatic conviction, though he too had had his share of papal politics. His lieutenant, Ormanetto, having ventured into Venetian temporal jurisdiction in Padua, was not to enjoy such far-reaching success. When the principle of the occupation of a Venetian see by a non-Venetian is considered, the case of Giberti comes strongly to mind. But Giberti's duality of experience, both political and spiritual (1493–1543), were employed in the first phase of the reformation. It was a phase that ended in the years 1541–1543. In this short period, with the deaths of Gasparo Contarini and Gianmatteo Giberti, the flight of Ochino, and the assumption of control of the Inquisition by the Papacy, the Catholic reformation became aggressively self-sufficient, and its products, men like Ormanetto, could back their reforms with conciliar law, and ride roughshod over tradition and precedent.

With Cardinal Paleotti in Bologna, we reach the second generation of reformers: for him, like Agostino Valier and Domenico Bollani, the success of the new structure would depend on the skill of the architect — rather than the tridentine blueprint. For Valier and Paleotti, the background had been both diplomatic and devotional. And they came, perhaps, to represent, in the eyes of contemporaries, the fusion of the diplomacy of organisational reform with the piety of religious revival. This meeting of those two complementary sides to the Catholic Reformation — organising skill and spiritual revival — happened most obviously in the person of Carlo Borromeo. Domenico Bollani's case, one feels, was rather different.

What, then, had been Bollani's part in the reformation of the diocese of Brescia

178

in its first phase after the Council? His background and experience of the state throw into relief his strengths — but also what he was not. We have seen that the chief needs in the diocese during these critical years were structure and authority, and Bollani's civil experience qualified him to lead and manage this initiative. He could fight battles, negotiate, construct and reform, to build a lasting edifice for the Brescian church. His example was one of rectitude and human understanding — never of saintly self-denial. He remained in the city throughout the plague as devotion to duty rather than from the driving force of urgent conviction. Throughout his bishopric, his work remained architectural rather than devotional. No evidence has survived of his distinction as a preacher, and his published works are manuals for use and blueprints for action. His personal correspondence (a useful proportion of which has survived) betrays a preoccupation with the whole man in his civil, religious and social states, and quotations from scripture are rare.

In Milan, Borromeo personified also reformed spirituality. Brescia had found her true exponents of this aspect of the reformation in Angela Merici, Franceso Cabrino and Angelo Paradisi. Bollani's gifts, which we have called diplomatic and managerial, were, none the less, a vital component of the reformed diocese. Without them the movement might have foundered through lack of structure and authority.

But it could equally well have failed through a failure to reconcile the growing body of jurisdictional differences between Venice and Rome in these years. As far as the tridentine reformation was concerned, one of the frontiers between Venice and Rome was Brescia. Had the diocese become the focus of jurisdictional disputes, much damage might have been done to the fabric of the reform movement. Domenico Bollani was a Venetian of course, and this aspect of his activity — in disputes between church and state — will be examined in the next chapter.

1 For this, the now classic review article by Giuseppe Alberigo is the indispensable guide: 'Studi e problemi relativi all'applicazione del Concilio di Trento in Italia (1945–1958)' in *Rivista Storica Italiana* LXX, (1958) pp. 239–268, which lists much work done in thesis form on individual dioceses and reformers.
2 , 'L'applicazione del Concilio di Trento' *cit.*
3 The problems inherent in a project of this kind have been amply illustratedby G. Alberigo in 'Note in margine a uno studio sulla partecipazione dei Vescovi italiani al primo periodo del Concilio di Trento,' in *Problemi di Vita Religiosa in Italia nel '500, cit.*, pp. 68–69.
4 This is discussed below, chapter IX.
5 Principally Agostino Valier, bishop of Verona (1566–1606), Matteo Priuli, bishop of Vicenza (1565–1579), and Nicolò Ormanetto who became bishop of Padua (1570–1577) after periods in Rome and Milan as Borromeo's lieutenant. Ormanetto was Veronese, but offers some interesting points of comparison. The see of Bergamo was occupied successively after the Council by Federigo Corner (1561–1577) and Gerolamo Ragazzoni (1577–? 1592). Of course, outside the Venetian context, important parallels are to be drawn with such leaders of Catholic Reformation as Cardinal Gabriele Paleotti in Bologna and Cardinal Carlo Borromeo in Milan, particularly because Bollani was on terms of friendship and collaboration with them, and the existence of authorative studies invites some comparison with Alfonso Carafa, Cardinal of Naples, and the Blessed Cardinal Paolo Burali of Piacenza. Bibliography on these figures will appear in following notes.
6 For the state of the diocese of Brescia during the first half of the sixteenth century, see *Storia di Brescia, cit.*, II, pp. 443–6, P. Guerrini, 'Le condizioni religiose di Brescia intorno alla metà del cinquecento' in *La Congregazione dei Padri della Pace* (Brescia, 1933) pp. 71–94, P. Tacchi-Venturi, 'La vita religiosa in Italia' in *Storia della Compagnia di Gesù . . .*, (Rome, 1931). For initiatives towards reform before the Council of Trent, A. Cistellini, *Figure della Riforma Pretridentina* (Brescia, 1955) *passim* is fundamental, and certainly replaces Irma Ricci, 'La Preriforma Cattolica a Brescia' (thesis in the Università Cattolica del Sacro Cuore, Milan, 1938–1939). Particularly useful is the most recent survey, 'Alcuni aspetti della Vita Religiosa a Brescia durante il Secolo XVI' by C. Zanotti (thesis *cit.*,) pp. 23–69, with bibliographical directions to local sources, to which this brief account is widely indebted.
7 Tacchi-Venturi, *op. cit.*, p. 291, Zanotti, pp. 32–34. Particularly noteworthy was the case of G.B. Pallavicino, who preached in Brescia in 1527 to an enthusiastic congregation, and was invited again the following year. He was finally arrested and tried for heresy.
8 In 1518, seventy witches were tortured and burnt in the *Val Camonica*, with the connivance of the bishop, Paolo Zane, often on a single accusation. The element of gain derived from the confiscation of goods of those burnt.
9 See Odorici, *Storie Bresciane* (Brescia, 1860) IX, pp. 130 *et seq.*. In 1545, witches were burnt as responsible for local calamities (recalling the superstitions encountered by Domenico Bollani in the plague years 1555–1556 in Udine). The phenomenon grew to the point where the Venetian government intervened, ordering trials in Venice for those accused, in an attempt to avoid excessive injustice. (Zanotti, *op. cit.*, p. 28)
10 H.O. Evennett, 'The New Orders', in *N.C.M.H.*, II, pp. 275–300, and *Idem, The Spriti of the Counter Reformation* (ed. with 'postscript' by John Bossy) (Cambridge, 1968) *passim*, but particularly pp. 67–88. Of course, the omission of the Jesuits (founded by Loyola in 1540) here does not imply that this order was unimportant. On the contrary, it was soon to surpass others in importance for the future of Catholicism. (Evennett, *N.C.M.H., cit.*, pp. 291–300, and *Idem., The Spirit . . ., cit.*, pp. 43–66, etc.) But we are here concerned with *Italian* foundations in general, and the local conditions in Venetian dominions which gave rise to them in particular.
11 Evennett has shown how the foundations of the Camaldolese, Capuchin, Theatine, Barnabite and Somaschi orders illustrate a complex of reforming initiatives at work well before the Council of Trent. He has stressed the influence on these of the older orders, underlined the network of contacts between the reformers themselves, and pointed to the

180

conditions of the times as causal factors in this Catholic spiritual revival. See also P. Paschini, *S. Gaetano Thiene, Gian Pietro Carafa, e le origini dei Chierici Regolari Teatini,* (Rome, 1926) particularly pp. 41–109 for movements in the Venetian dominions.

12 See Cistellini, *op. cit.*, pp. 64–67 and *passim,* for examples of women reformers in Brescia like Laura Cereto, Laura Mignani, the Beata Stefana Quinzani, and Veronica Gambara, that prominent Brescian contributor to the circle of Renaissance poetesses. See also Zanotti, *op. cit.*, pp. 36–42.

13 They urged reforms of spiritual life and customs through correspondence with notable people and promoted charitable institutions. See *Storia di Brescia*, II, *cit.*, p. 355 *et seq.*, for the renewal of statutes common to various orders in the city documenting the work of renewal of spiritual and practical Christianity.

14 Zanotti, *op. cit.*, pp. 42–50. On Merici, see Guerrini, *S. Angela e la Compagnia di S. Orsola* (Brescia, 1936), Sister Monica, *Angela Merici and her teaching idea,* (London, 1927), Evennett, *N.C.M.H., vol. cit.*, pp. 289–290. The *Congregazione dei Somaschi* was founded in Brescia by S. Gerolamo Emiliani, the *Instituto delle Penitenti o Convertite* by Laura Gambara, and the *Congregazione dei Padri dell' Oratorio* by A. Paradisi etc.

15 See the provisions for monasteries by the city council in *Storia di Brescia, cit.*, II, pp. 445–447. A magistracy for the preservation of the interests of monasteries had been instituted in 1517, but Domenico Bollani, it will be remembered, had himself encountered abuses on a massive scale both in Udine and in Brescia.

16 For Vergerio in Brescia, see Tacchi-Venturi, *op. cit.*, pp. 140–1, Paschini, *Pierpaolo Vergerio, il giovane e la sua Apostasia*, (Rome, 1925), Zanotti, *op. cit.*, p. 51.

17 This impression is obtained from readings of heresy trials in the works cited (above p. 126, n. 29) on heresy in Italy, particularly those reported in Comba, *I nostri Protestanti, cit., passim.*

18 '. . . la reazione cattolica romana e tridentina ebbe forse il torto di non distinguerli dai veri e propri eretici; di non tolerarne, per poi ricondurla alla ortodossia della dottrina cattolica, la confusa aspirazione alla purità delle fede, ad una vita individuale e sociale più morale, ad un'istintiva ricerca della verità.' (Zanotti, *op. cit.*, p. 52) The above 'distinction' represents a Catholic viewpoint. It should not be forgotten, however, that the final sessions of the Council of Trent had debated at great length the question of the *Salvocondotto* for Protestant participation, and that the initiative to limit numbers participating was finally rejected. (Above, pp. 133–135) For bibliography on heresy in Brescia, see above, p. 126, and see particularly Delio Cantimori, *Gli Eretici Italiani del Cinquecento* (various eds.) *passim.*

19 A good summary of the incidence of heresy in northern Italian towns and the Catholic reaction during the first half of the century is in Cantimori, 'Italy and the Papacy' (*N.C.M.H., cit.*) pp. 251–274.

20 Chapter II.

21 See Stella, *Dall'Anabattismo . . ., cit.*, particularly pp. 55–61.

22 *Ibid.*, pp. 63–83.

23 See bibliography above, p. 22, n. 47. The difficulties in this respect were concisely summarised by the Papal Nuncio Bolognetti in his *relazione* of the Republic of Venice of 1581 (published by Stella in *Chiesa e Stato nelle relazioni dei Nunzio Pontifici a Venezia . . ., cit.*, pp. 105–318, at pp. 281–286.). For the evidence of heretical activities in Padua during the first half of the century, see *Idem, Dall'Anabattismo . . ., cit.*, ('Tradizione Razionalistica Padovana e Antitrinitariamo') pp. 39–50, and *Idem, Anabattismo e Antitrintarismo . . ., cit., passim.*

24 It should be noted, however, that the Roman edict against heretical books of 1534 only specifically mentioned Rome, Ferrara and Bologna as centres of publication of heretical works (Cantimori, *op. cit.*, p. 264). In this context, however, see the forthcoming study by Professor Grendler of Toronto on the Venetian printing presses and the Inquisition.

25 Cantimori, *op. cit.*, pp. 264–265, The growth of Anabaptism in Venice and Antitrinitarianism in Italy, have been exhaustively studied by Aldo Stella in the two works cited. See also P. Pachini, *Venezia e l'Inquisizione Romana da Giulio III a Pio IV* (Padua, 1969) pp. 1–30 'Episodi di lotta contro l'eresia nell'Italia del primo Cinquecento' for the events before the formation of the Holy Office.

26 We have seen the reaction of Paul IV to the circle of Cardinal Pole and its effects on the bishopric of Brescia above, pp. 120. See also accounts of the influence of Carnesecchi, Ochino, Vergerio and others in Cantimori, *op. cit.*, pp. 264–269.

27 *Storia di Brescia, cit.*, II, pp 443–446, Guerrini, *La Congregazione . . ., cit.*, pp. 89–93, Zanotti, *op. cit.*, pp. 51, 57–66.

28 See below, pp. 202–212.

29 Particularly in the dispute over the collocation of papers relating to the Inquisition in Brescia in 1568–1569, between the Inquisitor, backed by the Cardinal of Pisa, president of the Roman Inquisition, and Bollani, backed by the rectors and the Venetian Republic. This episode is fundamental for the role of Bollani, here torn between conflicting authorities, and is developed below, pp. 202–212.

30 The valleys north of Brescia were for long the trouble centres for the Inquisition, as we have seen for the *Val Camonica*. At Collio, in the *Val Trompia*, Chiari, Capodiponte, Maderno, and particularly at Gardone, in the *Val Trompia*. (see Guerrini, *op. cit.*, pp. 89–93).

31 See Guerrini, *I Conti di Martinengo, cit.*, pp. 239–243, for the most famous example, Count Ulisse di Martinengo.

32 See map reproduced in Guerrini, *I Conti . . ., cit.*, at p. 1.

33 For Bollani and the persecution of the Jews in the Bresciano see A.V.B. *busta* 'Ebrei'. For heresy in Brescia 1560–1580 (with new documents), below, Chapter IX.

34 The incident is quoted by Guerrini, *La Congregazione*, p. 89, but documentary sources are reserved for a further publication which has not appeared. The incident is referred to 1559 by Cistellini, (*Storia di Brescia, loc. cit.*) and Zanotti, (*op. cit.*, p. 63) in error, it must be assumed.

35 See above, pp. 64–71 and pp. 82–83 respectively.

36 Zamboni, *Memorie delle Pubbliche Fabbriche di brescia, cit.*, p. 9, n. 16, Fè D'Ostiani, *Domenico Bollani, cit.*, pp. 21–22, which quotes a contemporary account of this famine. It should be noted, however, that the number of people fed by Bollani was put at 58 by Luca Antonio Giunti in his printer's dedication of Zaffi's translation of the *Epistole di S. Gerolamo*, (Venice, 1562) to Domenico that year. It may be that the influence of Francesco Cabrino can be detected here, as Bollani had been in close touch with his confessor before and after his election as bishop (p. 123). Guerrini has shown how personal charity was a fundamental part of the pastoral activity of Cabrino, in common with that of the Brescian mystics (*La Congregazione . . ., cit.*, pp. 102 *et seq.*). After 1564, it is likely that his star was eclipsed by the example of Borromeo.

37 '{Bishops shall visit} the eleemosynary {sic} institutions, called *monts de piété*, or of charity, and all pious places by whatsoever name designated . . . and shall take cognisance of and see to the performance of – in accordance with the ordinances of the Sacred Canons – all things that have been instituted for God's worship, for the salvation of souls, or for the support of the poor.' (Session XXII, *On Reformation*, from J. Waterworth, *Canons and Decrees of the Sacred Oecumenical Council of Trent*, {London, 1848} p. 167). For the conception of wealth in the church as a gift from God, of which the bishop is custodian, see the discussion by Gino Barbieri, *'L'etica economica nella legislazione ecclesiatica del Cinquecento* (Padua, 1960) pp. 73–82, especially pp. 78–79. For a practical example of this function as a requirement of duty, see the examination of the Patriarch during the Apostolic Visitation of Venice in 1581 in S. Tramontin, 'La figura del Vescovo secondo il Concilio di Trento . . .' *cit.*, in *Studi Veneziani*, X (1968) pp. 440–441, and bibliography of general works there.

38 *Il Tipo Ideale del Vescovo . . ., cit.*, pp. 45–46. For examples of Borromeo's well-known initiatives towards the poor, see, e.g. P. Giussani, *Vita di San Carlo Borromeo*, (Venice, 1613) pp. 425–427. The bishop, wrote Borromeo, 'maneggia le cose del mondo come fattor di Dio, et non come padrone assoluta; et usale per necessità, et bisogno, non per piacere; et procura cosi passare per queste cose temporali, che non perdi le eterne.' (quoted by Barbieri, *art, cit.*, p. 79).

39 'La Santa Vita di Gio. Matteo Giberti santo vescovo di Verona di immortale e felice memoria con le grandi elemosine redusse la Chiesa sua a questo stato che sa et vidde con l'occhio V. S. Ill.ma; con le elemosine otteneva ciò che voleva, senza quella harebbe fatto

niente . . .' (March 8, 1566, quoted by P. Prodi, *Il Cardinale Gabriele Paleotti* {1522—1597},
II, { Rome, 1967} p. 277.)

40 '. . . sapendosi da ogni uno chiaramente, che per li Sacri Canoni le rendite delle chiese
sono obbligate a tre principali carichi, cioè alli servizi e reperazione di quelle, alla sostentatione de'poveri di N.S.Giesù Christo, et al conveniente sostentamento di chi ha il peso e
governo di esse.' (A.S.V., *Soprintendente alle Decime del Clero, Condizioni*, Ro. 235 (Brescia)
No. 3. For discussion of this source and the full text of Bollani's personal *Decima del Clero*
return, see below. Appendix V, p. 257. For Bollani's activity as *collettore*, below
pp. 216—219. The fact that Bollani refers to 'Sacri Canoni' as his authority (omitting confirmation by the Council of Trent) indicates that he probably completed his tax return before
the publication of the Tridentine Decrees (in the same year, 1564) as he had also written to
Cardinal Paleotti in Bologna shortly before 22 April, asking advice on whether these decrees
could be implemented before publication (*cit.*, in Prodi, *Gabriele Paleotti, cit.*, I,
pp. 199—200 and n. 18). Prodi noted (*loc. cit.*,) that Bollani's request may have been the first
request for confirmation from Rome of the Council's decrees by a bishop.

41 *Ibid.* Doubtless this practice had begun during the famine in Brescia in 1559—60, and had
continued after the crisis was over. It is difficult to say whether this had been regular practice
before Bollani's arrival, although it seems necessarily tied to the duty of *residence* ('trovando
il vescovo alla sua residenza'), and Bollani himself noted elsewhere in the same document (in
the context of rebuilding the bishop's palace) that his predecessors had never been fully
resident in the Tridentine sense: 'non gli si essendo in tanta lunghezza di anni, che li vescovi
sono stati assenti . . .' (*Ibid.*)

42 These initiatives were later formalised in Bollani's *Constituzioni per il Clero* (discussed by
the diocesan synod of 1574). Priests were specially urged to promote charity, particularly
among those who might be reluctant to come forward ('quelli che arrosendo di mendicare
sono nell'indigenza'), and the function of personal charitable initiative was again stressed: 'Ma
{ i sacerdoti} diano prima l'esempio col donare large et hilariter . . .' (Domenico Bollani,
*Costituiones Rev.mi D. D. Dominici Bollani Brixiae Episcopi in Diocesana Sinodo promul-
gatae anno Domini 1574 die 4 mensis novembris*, { Brescia, 1575}: 'De Cura piorum operum'
quoted by Petroboni, 'Domenico Bollani . . .' thesis *cit.*, pp. 141—142.) Bollani's constitutions
(the printed edition) must now be considered unobtainable. Five years of enquiries about a
copy circulating among Brescian scholars have produced the unhappy thought that the last
surviving copy may have perished in the Florentine floods of 1966.

43 Bartolomeo de Martyribus, *Stimulus Pastorum . . ., cit.*, (for which, see Jedin, *Il tipo
ideale . . ., cit.*, pp. 76—80.)

44 See above, pp. 132—133. Pastor, *op. cit.*, VII, pp. 283—284.

45 Jedin, *op. cit.*, p. 85, quoting *Concilium Tridentinum . . ., cit.*, IX, p. 1047.

46 *Ibid.*

47 C. Orsenigo, *Vita di San Carlo Borromeo*, (Milan, 1929³) 2 vols., I, p. 110.

48 Provincial Councils had been prescribed by the Council of Trent in its 22nd session. Four
were held in Bollani's lifetime: in 1565, 1569, 1576 and 1579, and the proceedings have been
published many times in the *Acta Ecclesiae Mediolanensis*. A good modern survey of this is in
R. Mols 'Saint Charles borromée, pionier de la Pastorale Moderne' in *Nouvelle Revue
Théologique*, 79 (1957) pp. 600—622, 715—747.

49 Ormanetto was given precise instructions for lodgings and reception of bishops (Giusanni,
op. cit., p. 24.)

50 Fè D'Ostiani, *op. cit.*, p. 37, Petroboni, *op. cit.*, pp. 113—114. Borromeo had clearly
stated his intentions for the Council in a letter to Pius IV on October 18: 'Sono deciso di
incominciare dai prelati la riforma prescritta a Trento; sarebbe questa la strada migliore per
ottenere l'obbedienza nelle nostre diocesi. Noi dobbiamo marciare per i primi: i nostri soggetti
ci seguiranno più facilmente.' (quoted, without source, by Orsenigo, *op. cit.*, I, p. 111). In this
statement, the function of personal example in Borromeo's thinking on reform and the
hierarchiecal nature of his plan are transparent. Of the 15 dioceses in the jurisdiction of the
archbishop of Milan, 10 were personally represented by their bishops, which included Nicolò
Sfondrato, bishop of Cremona (and later Pope Gregory XIV). Also at the Council representing
the See of Bergamo was Bollani's fellow Venetian, Federico Corner, who was to become his

friend and ally in the collection of the *Decime del Clero* in 1570s. (For the Corner family and their control of the See of Bergamo, see Logan, *op. cit., ad vocem.*

51   Difficulties of various kinds were experienced in this, especially, perhaps, in the Veneto. Borromeo himself had already obtained general approval and cooperation from the Milanese authorities in 1565, though, as the congratulatory letter from Pius IV of October 27 testifies (reproduced in Giussani, *op. cit.*, pp. 26–27). Such difficulties will be the subject of the next chapter.

52   This element has been much studied. See Prodi's discussion of Paleotti's *Discorso intorno alle imagini sacre e profane*, (Bologna, 1582) (but repr. in P. Barocchi, *Trattati d'Arte del Cinquecento*, II, {Bari, 1961} pp. 117–510) in his *Gabriele Paleotti…, cit.*, II, pp. 527–562, and bibliography, nn. 1–2. See, for example, Judith Hook, 'Italy and the Counter-Reformation,' in *History Today* (Nov., 1970) pp. 782–790 for a summary. A summary of the proceedings of the first council from the *Acta ecclesiae Mediolanensis* is in Petroboni, *op. cit.*, pp. 114–115.

53   This had been objected to at Trent by the Germans who pointed to the difficulties of enforcement inherent in the German system of ecclesiastical posts reserved for certain ranks in the hierachy of the nobility.

54   This is discussed below, pp. 160–170.

55   At least 78 letters from Bollani to Borromeo between August 22, 1564 and March 10, 1579 survive in the *Biblioteca Ambrosiana*, Milan, (*Carteggio lettere Bollani–Borromeo*) catalogued by Petroboni, *op. cit.*, pp. 23–26, and see p. 20.

56   Bollani had had 21 years of diplomatic and administrative experience when he decided to accept the bishopric of Brescia. Borromeo was 26 years of age when he made his entry into the archdiocese of Milan, having been in Holy Orders since the age of 7. An accurate reflection of the difference of approach of the two men is provided by those letters by Bollani to his vicar general, Giacomo Roveglio, where he criticised the severity of Borromeo's meticulous and self-denying ideal: '… a me non piacciono questi zeli indiscreti, et che non accompagnano le immaginazioni con la pratica; questo Sig.re è pieno di santa volontà, ma questo procedere con tanto rigore causa senza dubbio minor frutto nel suo governo…' (*Carteggio Bollani–Reveglio, cit.*, letter from the Provincial Council in Milan of 12 May, 1576). '… a Dio piacendo domani si farà l'ultima sessione di questo … tissimo Concilio con li tanti decreti pieni di rigore et sottiliezza di questo Signore pieno di grande bontà ed ardente zelo, ma bisogna nel governo dei popoli ricordarsi che sono huomini et non angeli…' (*Ibid.* 24 May, 1576). In general, however, Bollani's praise for Borromeo is continuous and sincere. Six days after the above letter, Bollani wrote again to Roveglio from Milan: 'Siamo in questa provincia, dove per l'osservanza di decreti, et esempio di questo Santo Arcivescovo ci bisogna andar col compasso assai ristretto, se non uguale al suo, che è cosa inimitable in tutte le cose.' (*Idem.*, 30 May, 1576)

57   Paolo Prodi, 'San Carlo Borromeo e il Cardinale Gabriele Paleotti: due vescovi della riforma cattolica,' in *Critica Storica*, III (1964), pp. 135–151 at pp. 142–143. See also Giuseppe Alberigo, 'Carlo Borromeo come modello di vescovo nella chiesa post-tridentina', in *Rivista Storica Italiana*, 79 (1967), pp. 1031–1052 at p. 1036.

58   Paleotti had declared these doubts as early as 1565: 'non dubito che li decreti che si faranno non debbano essere prudentissimi et santissimi, ma per dirli liberamente *quod sentio*, io stimo sin hora molto di più quel che V. S. Ill.ma con le sue attioni e regolata disciplina havrà dimostrato, perocchè questi sono fatti, de' quali solo abbiamo bisogno, et gli altri sono ragionamenti…' (Paleotti to Borromeo, Prodi, *op. cit.*, p. 142). Bollani complained later in just the same way that (speaking of the fourth Milan Council) 'non so che frutto se ne caverà con tanto aggregato di decreti…' (Bollani to Roveglio, *Carteggio cit.*, May 12, 1576). It was doubtless this similarity of view: a practical concept of action founded on the solid basis of Bollani's knowledge of men that drew him towards Paleotti, and we shall have reason to enlarge on this comparison. Their reciprocal friendship and esteem (dating certainly from the Council) is documented in the Bolognese Archives (e.g. Prodi, *Gabriele Paleotti, cit.*, I, pp. 199–202, II, 21, 149 etc.) and in Bollani's letters to Roveglio, *Carteggio cit.*, Feb. 14, 1576, Dec. 18, 1577. Prodi has further observed that Paleotti's treatise on bishops, the

184

Archiepiscopale Boloniense, (Pub. Rome, 1594) was a manual of work, rather than a theoretical treatise. (*op. cit.*, I, p. 10).

59 Prodi, 'Borromeo e Paleotti . . .' *cit.*, p. 142.

60 P. Giussani, *Vita di San Carlo Borromeo, cit.*, pp. 196–197, where Bollani was accused by Borromeo's biographer of having deserted Brescia during the plague. This error had been corrected by the middle of the 18th Century (see discussion in Petroboni, *op. cit.*, pp. 6–10), but survives still (*Dizionario Biografico degli Italiani*, Vol. 11 (1970) *ad vocem* Domenico Bollani). The story had apparently originated in Rome, and was refuted by Bollani in a letter to the Pope on Sept. 7, 1577 (*Carteggio Bollani–Roveglio, cit.*, and see Fè D'Ostiani, *op. cit.*, pp. 118–123).

61 These are collected in the Archepiscopal Archives in Milan. See particularly, vol. VII: 'Ordini del Vescovo Bollani e del Visistatore San Carlo per le elemosine . . .'. Thus they are catalogued by Guerrini, 'Il IV Centenario della nascita di San Carlo . . .' *cit.*, p. 200.

62 Appendix I, p. 241.

63 There seems little doubt that Bollani was influenced by the example of Seripando when he made his will, and that we have here a concrete example which documents the influence of Seripando on the younger generation of bishops at the Council of Trent. Bollani acknowledged a copy of Seripando's will from Roveglio on April 4, 1576 (*Carteggio cit.*). The correspondence of format and detail between this will (published by Jedin, *Girolamo Seripando, Sein Leben und Denken*, {Wurzburg, 1937} II, pp. 647–652) and Bollani's (reproduced here in full for the first time as Appendix I) is striking, unless the circumstances of Seripando's death are remembered. Dying at Trent while the Council was in session, Seripando must have made a deep impression on the younger bishops as an example of holiness and spirituality, representing to them the authority of the Pope (as Papal Legate), and all that was best in Catholic theology. Comparison of the wills is revealing. First their format is precisely similar, dealing with the penitence of the testator, the sanity of his mind at the time of writing, the care of the body after death and the disposition of material possession, in precisely this order. Further, the similarity of terminology bears poignant testimony to the influence exercised on the assembled bishops of the life-style and devotion of the first of the tridentine reformers to die, (unless both wills were influenced by a common source, which does not explain Bollani's request for Seripando's will). One example must suffice here. Seripando wrote: 'Et perchè varii sono gli accidenti et impedimenti di mente et di lingua, con li quali si suole alle volte venir' alla morte . . .' while Bollani wrote: 'Ma perchè può occorrer per diversi accidenti, che sogliono nell'estremo di essa, impedire la mente et la lingua . . .'

In the present context of charity, the pronouncement of the Council of Trent had been quite clear. 'Also, it wholly forbids them {bishops} to strive to enrich their own kindred or domestics out of the revenues of the Church: seeing that even the Canons of the Apostles forbid them to give to their kindred the property of the Church which belongs to God; but if their kindred be poor, let them distribute to them as poor, but not misapply or waste it for their sakes . . .' (*Canons and Decrees . . ., Ed. cit.*, p. 254: *On Reformation*, Session XXV). Seripando's will was consistent with this up to a point, but it is perhaps significant that both he and Bollani regarded their direct descendents as sufficiently deserving through poverty to receive the majority of the assets. Seripando had written: 'Avanzando però danari per qualsivoglia quantità, dispono che siano dispensati agli luoghi pii della città o terra nella quale morrò, come sono hospitali, monasteri di donne et huomini religiosi secondo il parer degli esecutori . . .' Bollani too, had left similar instructions, specifying that alms were to be distributed in Brescia (and not Venice). It is interesting to reflect that this practice, widely adopted by succeeding generations of bishops, may have started with Seripando, and not with Borromeo, as has been implied. Borromeo, too, left that part of his fortune free from *fideicommessi* to deserving causes, and was followed in this by Cardinal Cusano and Gaspare Visconti, his successor. (For this see Giussani, *op. cit.*, pp. 157, 427). In his *Episcopale Bononiensis . . .*, Cardinal Paleotti had been specific on the point, condemning the practice of leaving goods to relatives, even when papal permission (Bollani's case) had been obtained (Prodi, *Gabriele Paleotti . . ., cit.*, II, pp. 25–26). It would be instructive indeed to know how other *Venetian* bishops had acted – subject, as we have seen, to particular demands in terms of family tradition, solidarity and clannishness. For some, like Ormanetto, the problem did not arise, as he apparently had very little to leave (G. Mantese, 'A proposito del testamento di Niccolò Ormanetto,' in *Rivista di Storia della Chiesa in Italia*, XIV (1960), pp. 121–122), but even he, as a non-Venetian, left what little there was to his sisters. Bollani had not been bound by a *fideicommissum* (Appendix 1), and had sought to provide adequately for his descendents as well as making a conspicuous gesture towards the poor. O.M.T. Logan in his 'Grace and Justification: some Italian Views of the sixteenth and early seventeenth centuries,' in *The Journal of Ecclesiastical History*, XX, (1969) pp. 67–78, sought to trace the possible influence on Venetian wills of 'evangelical' currents in Venice, but did not consider the influence of the tridentine pronouncement on the transmission of wealth, and the treatises on the subject (for example, Paleotti's) to which it gave rise. Among clerics, at least, it must have made a significant impact, although the strength of Venetian family traditions probably militated against it there. For discussion of Venetian wills, see also Logan, 'Studies in the Religious Life of Venice...' thesis *cit.*, pp. 476–481. For Seripando, also Jedin { trans. Eckhoff } *Papal Legate at the Council of Trent: Girolamo Seripando*, (London, 1947) *passim*; for Seripando's death, *Ibid.*, pp. 689–692, 695–697, (only the German ed. contains the important appendices of documents) and *Idem., Crisis & Closure...*, *cit.*, pp. 99–100.

64   Referred to in his letter of June 8, 1577, quoted above, p. 19, n. 16.

65   'Voglio credere che egli a quest'hora haverà ricevuta la scrittura di Vinetia per poter fare in Verona la ricuperation intiera di nostri crediti contra il fillauolo { fittavolo } di Corezo che così anco per il vero ricerca anco li molti bisogni della si gravata commissione nostra...' (Bollani to Roveglio, October 1, 1577).

66   For discussion of this point, see immediately below. At this point in Bollani's career, his dual allegiance was documented by the returning *podestà* of Brescia, Antonio Bragadin, in his *relazione:* '... quel dignissimo prelato non solamente si adopera eccellentemente nel governo di quelle anime a lui commesse, ma anche in tutte le cose dove si tratta l'interesse di V. Serenità, et di questa città { Venice } dimostra tanta affettione che non pretermette cosa a fare che li possi apportare giovamento et benefitio...' (Carlo Pasero, *Relazioni di Rettori Veneti a Brescia, cit.*, p. 113, *Idem., La Partecipazione Bresciana alla Guerra di Cipro e alla Battaglia di Lepanto (1570–1573),* { Brescia, 1954 } p. 62, n. 7). Bollani's identification with the cause of Venice is illustrated in his correspondence with Borromeo after Lepanto, as he described the rejoicing in Brescia in his letter of Nov. 8, 1571 (*Carteggio Bollani–Borromeo cit.,*). See also the letters of November 21, 1572, and November 1, 1571, where the victory seemed almost 'una grande vittoria del regno celeste.' (Pasero, *La Partecipazione..., cit.,* p. 48)

67   *Ibid.*, pp. 7–8.

68   *Ibid.*

69   Fè D'Ostiani, *op. cit.*, pp. 70–71. The *decima* is discussed below, pp. 216–219. The conflicts between these two loyalties, and the problems caused are considered in Chapter IX.

70   On the economic implications of plagues in the sixteenth century in the Venetian republic, see Brian Pullan, 'Wage-Earners and the Venetian Economy, 1550–1630,' in *Idem.* (Ed.) *Crisis & Change..., cit.*, pp. 146–174 at pp. 149–155.

71   See, for instance, the collection reproduced by A. Francesco La Cava, *La Peste di San Carlo...*, (Milan, 1945) and Pietro Gorla, 'Immagini di Sal Carlo,' in *Echi di San Carlo Borromeo* (Milan, 1937–1938) *passim.*

72   The plague struck Trent and Verona in 1575, moving to Mantua, Padua and Venice, and thence to Cremona and Milan. It was said to have arrived in Brescie from Iseo, where it had been trasmitted by a Cremonese merchant in 1576. (See Fè D'Ostiani, *op. cit.*, pp. 103–140, where a range of contemporary documents is quoted.). Both the main sources of Bollani's letters (*Biblioteca Queriniana*, Brescia MSS. B.V. 31, *Carteggio Bollani-Roveglio*, and *Biblioteca Ambrosiana*, Milan, *Carteggio Bollani–Borromeo*) cover the years 1576–1577 when the plague was in Brescia. Many of his letters testify to the measures taken in the city, the dimensions of the problem, and the part played by the bishop.

73   La Cava, *op. cit.*, pp. 200–201.

74   *Ibid.*

75   Bollani–Roveglio, April 9, 30, May 24, 1577, Bollani–Borromeo, August 28, 1577, Fè D'Ostiani, *op. cit.*, pp. 109–110.

76 Bollani—Roveglio, April 30, 1577, April 15, 1577 etc. The influence of Borromeo was also suggested by Logan, *op. cit.*, p. 285, and see Cicogna, *op. cit.*, IV, p. 453.
77 See below.
78 Bollani—Roveglio, April 16, 1577.
79 *Ibid.* May 27, 1577.
80 See, for example, his letters to Roveglio of 15, 19, 17 July, and particularly that of 30 July, 1577, by which time he was clearly helping the *Podestà* Soranzo in measures to alleviate suffering. See also Bollani—Borromeo, August 28, 1577, and Fè D'Ostiani, *op. cit.*, p. 114.
81 Bollani—Roveglio, respectively on August 19 and July 15, 1577. It had been found necessary to erect a gallows at the end of a street where the plague had taken hold.
82 Bollani to Roveglio, July 8, 1577 quoted by Fè D'Ostiani, *op. cit.*, p. 113.
83 *Ibid.*, pp. 118—123.
84 *Ibid.* p. 119.
85 *Ibid.*, pp. 106—107: 'ho voluto per ogni debito mio pigliar licenza da V. S. R.ma pregandola a contentarsi che per mera necessità mia possa partire per Bedizzole ovvero per altri parti di Riviera con animo di attender solo alla mia salute . . .'
86 *Ibid.* p. 107.
87 *Ibid.* p 111: Borromeo to Bollani, May 18, 1577.
88 There was to be interminable discussion of Borromeo's Apostolic Visitation to Brescia between Venice and Milan.
89 *Ibid.* p. 111: Bollani to Borromeo, June 13, 1577.
90 *Ibid.*, pp. 112—113, July 9, 1577. Borromeo himself seems to have been much concerned about the principle of exposure to the plague. According to his biographer Giussani (*op. cit.*, pp. 156—157) he called a committee of advisors to deliberate and advise him on the problem. Their conclusion was that he was not obliged to expose himself to infection as a necessary duty of his archiepiscopal pastoral function (much as Bollani would have concluded) 'che questi erano termini di perfettione, non d'obbligo necessario.' Borromeo had replied that the office of the bishop is the office of perfection ('lo stato del vescovo è stato di perfettione') but he did not go to Brescia, as we have seen. The question of Borromeo's intention to visit Brescia and Bollani's reply was discussed by P. Felice Murachelli, (*Il Vescovo Domenico Bollani . . .*, {Brescia, 1959} *cit.*, p. 25) but the real point, (Venetian political and juridictional susceptibilities) seems to have been missed. See also below, pp. 214—216 for discussion of this point.
91 See the recent discussion of this point by Eric Cochrane, 'New Light on post-Tridentine Italy: A note on recent Counter-Reformation scholarship,' in *The Catholic Historical Review*, LVI (1970), pp. 291—319 at pp. 308—313.
92 *Idem.* pp. 310—311, Prodi, *Gabriele Paleotti . . ., cit., passim.*
93 See bibliography cited by Cochrane, *op. cit.*, p. 311, n. 64.
94 Romeo De maio, *Alfonso Carafa, Cardinale di Napoli* (Vatican City, 1961) pp. 167—178.
95 Paolo Preti, 'Un aspetto della Riforma Cattolica nel Veneto: L'Episcopato Padovano di Niccolò Ormanetto,' in *Studi Veneziani*, XI (1969) pp. 325—363.
96 Cochrane, *op. cit.*, p. 312.
97 Silvio Tramontin, 'La figura del Vescovo secondo il Concilio di Trento ed i suoi riflessi Veneziani nell' interrogatorio del Patriarca Trevisan,' in *Studi Veneziani*, X (1968) pp. 423—456.
98 F. Masotto, 'Agostino Valerio, Vescovo di Verona e la sua attuazione dei decreti del Concilio di Trento,' (Unpub. thesis, Università Cattolica del Sacro Cuore, Milan, {1936—1937} p. 94).
99 *Idem.* p. 109. For Valier's initiatives in connection with the *Monte di Pietà*, see Brian Pullan, *Rich and Poor in Renaissance Venice*, (Oxford, 1971) pp. 393—394.
100 See, for instance, Innocenzo Cervelli, 'Storiografia e problemi intorno alla vita religiosa e spirituale a Venezia nella prima metà del '500,' in *Studi Veneziani*, VIII (1966), pp. 447—476 at pp. 474—476, where the author documents the links between the Veronese Church (Giberti—Navagero—Valier) and Borromeo and his circle.
101 Particularly significant will be the contacts and exchanges between Venetian Bishops.

For Bollani, contacts are already documentable with Valier (above p. 140) and Federico Corner (below p. 218 {Bergamo}). It is hoped that G. Mantese will continue his examination of the episcopal archives in Vicenza to add the pastoral image of Matteo Priuli, bishop of Vicenza to existing information. (See his articles in *Rivista di Storia della Chiesa in Italia*, XIV {1960} and XV {1961} *cit.*, from which Priuli's pastoral image has not yet emerged). It should be noted that Alberigo's scheme of division of the dioceses into ecclesiastical provinces has precluded consideration of a current or style of reform which had specifically Venetian characteristics. (See his fundamental 'Studi e problemi relativi all'applicazione . . .' *cit.*, pp. 239–279.) Further evidence for the alignment of Agostino Valier with Bollani in a 'Venetian' rather than 'Borromean' current of reform is provided by Valier's letter *De cauta imitatione episcoporum*. Valier advised Borromeo's nephew, Federico Borromeo against excessively close imitation of his uncle, and criticised the asceticism and rigidity of the saint – particularly where this had led to conflicts with the government of Milan. This, as we have seen, had been precisely Bollani's attitude. (Logan, *op. cit.*, p. 286, P. Broutin, *L'Evêque dans la tradition . . .*, {Louvain, 1953}, pp. 101–102 {Fr. Trans. of Jedin, *Il tipo ideale . . ., cit.*, with significant additions}).

102 For instance, by Colet, Erasmus, Loyola and Calvin. The point was made recently by A.G. Dickens, *The Counter Reformation.* (London, 1968) p. 128.

103 Jedin, *Crisis and Closure of the Council of Trent* (London, 1967) pp. 115–117. For the Council's decree, see, for example Waterworth, *Canons and Decrees . . ., cit.*, pp. 187–192: 'method of establishing seminaries for clerics and educating the same therein.' For Giberti's example, see Prosperi, *Tra Evangelismo e Controriforma: G.M. Giberti, cit.*, pp. 215–234, particularly pp. 233–234, Jedin, *op. cit.*, p. 117. The latest account of the growing concern with priestly education in the sessions of the Council is in L.E. Halkin, 'La formation du clergé après le Concile de Trente,' (typescript of his contribution to the *Colloque d'Histoire Ecclesiastique de Cambridge:* 22–24 September, 1968, pp. 1–2. The Canon *Cum adolescentium aetas* is reproduced { in French} at pp. 2–7. I am grateful to my friend and colleague Mr. A.C. Duke for making this source available to me.) See also Petroboni, *op. cit.*, pp. 91–94.

104 The *Visita* is discussed below pp. 174–178.

105 Petroboni, *op. cit.*, pp. 91–94 (Italian), Waterworth, *op. cit.*, pp. 187–192 (English), Halkin, *op. cit.*, pp. 2–4 (French).

106 Writing on the tridentine seminaries has been fairly prolific, although comparative studies of the whole position are few, the recent *Seminaria Ecclesiae Catholicae* being the sole exception (Vatican City, 1963), since M.Barbara, 'L'origine dei Seminari a norma del Concilio di Trento,' *Civiltà Cattolica*, XCI, iii (1940), pp. 215–221 is now out of date. Professor Halkin (*loc. cit.*,) urged the collection of information for such a treatment by means of a questionnaire. For the first post-tridentine seminaries in Rieti and Rome, see Pio Paschini, 'Le Origini del Seminario Romano,' in *Cinquecento Romano e Riforma Cattolica*, (Rome, 1958) pp. 3–32; for the all-important Milanese seminaries, A. Bernareggi, 'La fondazione del Seminario di Milano,' in *Humiltas. Misc. Storica dei Seminari*, (Milan, 1929), C. Marcora, 'San Carlo e il Seminario' in *Mem. Stor. della Diocesi di Milano*, V (1964), pp. 642–647, E. Cattaneo, 'Nel IV Centenario del Seminario di Milano,' in *La Scuola Cattolica*, 92 (1964), pp. 291–302, Fondazione Treccani, *Storia di Milano* (various dates), IX, pp. 507–720, X, 119–199, XI, pp. 283–331, A. Rimoldi, 'Le Instituzioni di San Carlo Borromeo per il clero diocesano milanese,' in *La Scuola Cattolica*, 93 (1968), pp. 427–458. For Venice, see S. Tramontin, 'L'Istituzione dei due seminari veneziani,' in *Studi Veneziani*, VI (1965), pp. 363–378; for Vicenza, some information in Masotto, thesis *cit.* pp. 80–82, 139–152. The situation at Bologna is discussed by P. Prodi, *Gabriele Paleotti . . ., cit.*, II, particularly pp. 138–145; and for Brescia, Paulo Guerrini's essay, published in various places, but finally in *La Congregazione dei Padri della Pace . . ., cit.*, pp. 159–175, is fundamental. See also Petroboni, thesis *cit.*, pp. 91–111 and, with new documents, (but almost without commentary) G.L. Masetti-Zanini, 'Le origini del seminario di Brescia,' in *Brixia Sacra*, (1967) pp. 64–77. For the facts in Brescia, the present account does not differ substantially from the standard ones by Guerrini and Petroboni, except for conclusions drawn from placing it in Italian, Venetian and biographical contexts.

188

107 The substitution of a formalised hierarchical institution for a family based practice in Tridentine legislation is a point to which we shall return (below, p. 236).
108 For Brescia, at Chiari, Rezzato and Salo (Guerrini, *op. cit.*, pp. 159 *et seq.*, Petroboni, *op. cit.*, p. 93, Masetti-Zanini, *op. cit.*, p. 64). In Venice, for instance, the 'Collegium *perpetuum duodecim pauperum clericorum*, {reflecting the tridentine emphasis on poor students} istituito nel 1441 dal primo Patriarca, San Lorenzo Giustiniani{,} e quello creato verso il 1450 dalle benemerite nove Congregazioni del clero *ut ipse clerus possit litterarum studiis indulgere*, ma generalmente la formazione e l'educazione del clero erano riserbate alle scuole parrocchiale potenziate nella nostra Venezia attraverso delle scuole sesteriali erette intormo al 1520 dal Patriarca Antonio Contarini.' (Tramontin, *op. cit.*, p. 363). On the point in general, see Halkin, *op. cit.*, p. 1, Jedin, *Crisis & Closure . . ., cit.*, pp. 115–117.
109 On the growth of Valier's seminary and its relationship with Giberti's *Scuole Acolitali*, see Masotti, thesis *cit.*, pp. 139–152. In this case, the very strength of existing tradition caused opposition to the new foundation, leading, apparently, to an attempt on Valier's life (pp. 80–82). It had been feared that the new foundation would replace the old – a fear perhaps not without justification when the reaction of Valier to the coexistence of the two institutions is seen: 'Questo seminario aperto è superfluo è deve essere tutto uno seminario; il voler vesti differenti è metter schisma.' When this statement is compared to Valier's later comments on the Venetian seminaries during his Apostolic Visitation in 1581, the strength of the tridentine drive towards uniformity of practice among some bishops may be seen: 'Si spera gran frutto dai duoi seminari . . . l'altro seminario ch'è di più di sessanta chierici vive d'elemosine che è cosa meravigliosa, et perchè il frutto di questa visita maggiore et la speranza della riforma della discipline ecclesiastica consiste nello stabilmento di questi duoi seminari, s'è pensato . . . che fosse bene unirgli et stabilirgli col governo di qualche religione di preti . . . potendosi molto temere che non seguendo questa unione né l'uno né l'altro porti molto beneficio a questa città . . .' (Arch. Segr. Vat., *Nunz. Ven.*t. XXII, f. 163. quoted by Tramontin, *op. cit.*, pp. 369–37).
We have seen that Francesco Cabrino had probably been close to Bollani even before his assumption of the bishopric in 1559. Cabrino had founded his own institution for the training and education of the priesthood, the *Monte di Dio*, in a house on the *Ronchi*, a hillside location some way from the city centre. It seems that 'la prima attuazione di questa idea seguì l'anno 1548 a Cisano {San Felice di Scovolo} molto prima che il Concilio di Trento rendesse obbligatorio in ogni Diocesi la istituzione provvidenziale, vivaio perenne del clero diocesano,' (Guerrini, *op. cit.*, pp. 160–162, Petroboni, *op. cit.*, pp. 94–96, quoted from Guerrini by Masetti-Zanini, *op. cit.*, p. 64). Cabrino was a member of the *Padri della Pace*, and this brotherhood was to play a significant part in the early growth of the Brescian seminary.
110 Bollani shared the problem of the financial endowment of his seminary with virtually all the bishops of the cities mentioned above. Hubert Jedin has further made the point that the implementation of the Council's decrees on seminaries was even slower in Germany, France and Spain for this reason (*Crisis & Change . . ., cit.*, p. 119). It should be added that the reformers at Trent had never conceived of the seminary as the only method of ensuring that priests should be adequately prepared for their office: 'Il decreto lascia ai vescovi la massima libertà nella attuazione pratica di questa nuove instituzione, L'istituzione dei seminari fatta dai padri tridentini non intendeva affatto sopprimere i modi tradizionali di formazione del clero, allora in use, e tanto meno abolire od anche ostacolare la formazione culturale del clero fatta nelle facoltà teologiche esistenti nelle università.' (Antonio Rimoldi, 'Le istituzioni di San Carlo Borromeo per il clero diocesano milanese,' in *La Scuola Cattolica*, 93 (1965), pp. 427–453, at p. 428). Halkin added the observation that the Canons fixing the conditions for ordination to the priesthood contain no reference to the seminary (*op. cit.*, p. 7).
111 These obstacles were ably summarised by F. Molinari, 'Il Beato Paolo Burali, Cardinale Teatino e le origini del seminario a Piacenza,' in *Regnum Dei*, pp. 24–39 (*cit.*, Rimoldi, art. *cit.*, p. 429, n. 5): 'Ostacoli di vario genere vi si opponevano: dalla mancata o ritardata promulgazione dei decreti tridentini (è il caso della Francia) alla penuria dei fondi sufficienti (è il problema di molti diocesi esigue) alla difficoltà di reperire il personale dirigente e il corpo insegnante (è un po' la crisi generale del clero post-tridentino, cui si vuol ovviare mediante una

più adeguata educazione nei seminari). Ma erano appunto anche gli ostacoli, specie l'ultimo, che sottolineavano l'urgenza dell'iniziativa.'

112 *Ibid.*: 'non si impose universalmente un 'tipo ideale' di seminario, ma fiorirono per un certo tempo varie specie di convitto. Qui nacque un collegio universitario per ecclesiastici, altrove un convitto maggiore per preparazione di ordinandi oppure un libero pensionato a pagamento per chierici . . .'

113   For this range, see, for instance, Waterworth, *Canons & Decrees . . ., cit.*, pp. 187–192, or Halkin, *op. cit.*, p. 4. It was envisaged that almost every ecclesiastical foundation (except other seminaries) and every benefice should make its contribution.

114   Such persons 'pourront être contraints par l'évêque du bien, par des censures écclésiastiques et autres moyens de droit, et même, si cela paraît utile, en recourant au bras seculier.' (*Ibid.*, p. 5)

115   The *Annali Cronologici ed economici* of the seminary in A.S.B., and the *Fondo di Religione* in A.V.B., reviewed by Masetti-Zanini, *loc. cit.*

116   The fact that the subject appears so often in Bollani's letters to Borromeo also underlines the role played by Borromeo in the whole enterprise. Touched on many times, the seminary is discussed chiefly in letters of Jan. 13, 1566, Sept. 2, 1568, May 5, June 29, 1569, May 20, Sept. 5, Nov. 21, 1572. Also in those of Feb. 27, 1566 and Dec. 23, 1572 (*Carteggio Bollani-Borromeo, cit.*). For his later difficulties, particularly in connection with the opposition of Cardinal Francesco Gambara, Bollani confided his troubles to Giacomo Roveglio (*Carteggio Bollani-Roveglio, cit.*). These letters will be the most important source for what follows. Enrico Cattaneo has shown how Borromeo had been involved in the tridentine decree at every stage, having been ordained a priest himself on June 17, 1563, two days after the decree on seminaries had been agreed at Trent. His involveme it may be seen in the provision made for poor priests (Borromeo was certainly one of the richest prelates of his generation, having been loaded with benefices by his uncle { See list in Pastor, *op. cit.*, II, p. 85, n. 4}). On this, see Cattaneo, 'Nel IV centenario della fondazione del seminario di Milano,' in *La Scuola Cattolica*, 92 (1964), pp. 291–302, particularly 'Il pensiero di San Carlo sul seminario,' pp. 292–296 at p. 295.

117 , This is clear from Borromeo's reply of December 27, 1565, quoted in full by Petroboni, p. 97, and in part by Fè D'Ostiani, *op. cit.*, p. 50, and A. Sala, *Documenti circa la vita e le gesta di San Carlo Borromeo*, 3 vols. II (Milan, 1857), p. 272: 'Et poichè V.S. ha quel monte, dove al presente s'allevano figlioli tanto ben creati et timorati di Dio, oltre il profitto delle lettere, potrebbe al presente fondare il seminario serrato, con istituire un certo numero di putti; et col tempo poi, quando andrà trovando qualche buona pianta nei seminari foranei, i quali dice voler instituire, metterla dentro che anch'io voglio fare il medesino.'

118 *Ibid.*

119   Bollani to Borromeo, February 27, 1566 (*Carteggio, cit.*,). It is significant that these two items, the seminary and the cathedral, were given pride of place among the expenses sustained by the bishop in Bollani's own *decima* tax return (below, Appendix V, pp. 257–267 'Vi è la spesa del seminario ordinato per decreto del Sacro Concilio di Trento, il quale è anche posto in esenzione nella nostra Metropoli di Milano con gravezza di 5 per 100 . . . anche noi in Brescia per non mancare della debita nostra ubbidienza, et procurare un tanto beneficio della chiesa di Dio di allevare buoni sacerdoti, et ben disciplinati nella via christiana.' (For the Cathedral, see below.) The Papal brief authorising the tax on ecclesiastical benefices in Milan is dated July 6, 1566, and reproduced in A. Sala, *op. cit.*, I, p. 182.

120 *Ibid.* Bollani had invited Andrea Palladio to Brescia in 1567, but this project – which might have yielded a Palladian cathedral on the site of the present one – was doomed to be a victim of just such opposition as that described here (Fè D'Ostiani, *op. cit.*, pp. 30, 34, Zamboni, *Memorie delle pubbliche fabbriche . . ., cit.*, p. 74, Petroboni, *loc. cit.*).

121   The latest treatment of the Brescian opposition to the *Concilio Provinciale* is Carlo Marcora's 'I primi anni dell'episcopato di San Carlo,' in *Memorie Storiche della Diocesi di Milano*, X, (1963) pp. 517–617 at pp. 520–526. See also Petroboni, *op. cit.*, pp. 110–124, where, however, I do not agree with the author's standpoint.

190

122 Marcora, 'I primi anni . . .,' *cit.*, p. 521, Bernardo Cathaneo to Borromeo, September 27, 1566.
123 Bollani to Borromeo, December 23, 1566, quoted in full in *Ibid.* pp. 522–525.
124 *Ibid.*
125 September 24, 1565, quoted by G. Soranzo, 'Rapporti di San Carlo Porromeo con la Repubblica Veneta,' in *Echi di San Carlo*, fasc. XII (1938) p. 451. A copy of this rather rare periodical, which ran from 1937 to 1938, not catalogued in the *Union list of Periodicals*, is, however, to be found in the Bodleian Library.
126 In this decree, the most obvious 'suddito di principe forestiero' was Carlo Borromeo. It had been aimed at an indulgence published by him on the occasion of the Milanese council.
127 Bollani to Borromeo, *cit.*, (Marcora, 'I primi anni . . .' *cit.*, p. 523).
128 The necessity for this was underlined by Borromeo in his letter to the Pope on November 3, 1565 (*cit.*, in Marcora, 'Nicolò Ormanetto . . .' *cit.*, p. 342): 'habbiamo pubblicato molti casi pertinenti a layci prohibendo molti costumi, et de superstitioni de pompe et spese superflue, nel che non havrei messo mano se non havesse veduto infinito desiderio universale oltre la disposizione del Principe et magistrati essendomi io governato di maniera che non ho pur fatto uno ordine pertinente a'laici, che prima non sia stato concertato, et approbato dal Governatore et Senato, et promessomi di mandar fuori dal canto loro editti suoi, in conformita dei miei per dar maggior caldo alla essequtione.'
129 Borromeo had sent a copy of the acts to the Venetian Senate, and had written to the Pope on Bollani's behalf. Venice finally approved them, urging her rectors to facilitate their publication in Brescia. (See the letter of the Doge to Borromeo of Oct. 3, 1566, published by A. Sala, *op. cit.*, I, p. 187, Soranzo, *op. cit.*, pp. 489–490, Petroboni, *op. cit.*, p. 117). The success of this manoeuvre is documented in a letter from Ormanetto to Borromeo of January 11, 1567, where he relates how he had presented Bollani's difficulties to the Pope 'per l'executione del Concilio . . . quale si è mostrato prontissimo a porger ogni aiuto et favore et così di sua mano ne pigliò il memoriale col suo stilletto, dovendo andar quella mattina l'Ambasciatore de Vinetia a S. Stà. per farne caldo officio et si farà in questo anche il resto.' (Marcora, 'I primi anni . . .' *cit.*, p. 525. See also correspondence in Sala, *op. cit.*, II, {1566–1568} pp. 270–277).
130 'Sono andati dell'un canto diffamandomi per Vinetia, dove piu piace qualche destrezza nelli governi, ch'io sia il piu rigido huomo del mondo, et in Roma, dove piacciono le intrepide esecutioni, mi mordono per troppo rimesso.' (*Ibid.*). This characterization of Roman and Venetian attitudes is discussed below, p. 236.
131 Marcora, 'I primi anni . . .' *cit.*, p. 526 *et seq.*
132 For this, see E. Cattaneo, 'Nel IV centario della fondazione . . .' *cit.* p. 297, A. Bernareggi, 'la fondazione . . .' *cit.*, in *Humiltas . . .*, *cit.*, p. 253. For the opposition to Jesuit control of the Roman seminary, Paschini, 'Le origini del seminario romano,' *cit.*, *passim.*
133 'Mancavano i danari, mancava la casa, mancava soprattutto ogni appoggio: nè il clero, eccetto il patriarca, nè la Repubblica sembravano ben disposti . . . Giobatta Contarini espone ripetutamente le sue idee in Senato, ottiene dei sussidi . . .' (S. Tramontin, 'Gli inizi del seminario . . .' *cit.*, p. 365). In Venice the clergy were equally resentful of the incursions made by the *decima* into their benefices, (*Ibid.*, p. 364).
134 Paschini, 'Le origini . . .' *cit.*, pp. 11–19.
135 , P. Prodi, *Il Cardinale Gabriele Paleotti . . .*, *cit.*, II, pp. 141–143. According to Masotti, (thesis *cit.*, pp. 137–140) Valier's seminary was financed at first partly from revenues formerly allocated to the *scuole acolitali*, and later from the union of benefices. This work makes no mention of a *decima* in support of the seminary. For later objections to the tax on Brescia, see below pp. 165–166.
136 On the delay by the rectors of Brescia, see A. Sala, *loc. cit.*, Fè D'Ostiani, *op. cit.*, pp. 46–47, Petroboni, *op. cit.*, pp. 121–126. It is certainly significant that although Venice had declared her willingness to promote the publication of the acts (on October 3, 1566) the rectors of Brescia and Bergamo had delayed permission. Apparently, on the insistence of Borromeo, Venice had renewed orders to facilitate publication. Yet one month after this, Borromeo wrote to the Nunzio in Venice that the rectors of Brescia and Bergamo 'si sono

mostrati molto freddi et quelli di Brescia in particolare hanno risposto che havevano ordini di ritardare l'essecutione fin tanto che si faccia più matura considerazione sopra alcune cose, le quali portano pregiudizio alla Serenissima Signoria.' (quoted Petroboni, p. 122). The Pope had to intervene with the Venetian ambassador before the rectors of Brescia and Bergamo yielded. If the situation that confronted the Brescian orator Calini in Venice, when he had pleaded unsuccessfully for Venetian arms for support of Brescian rights in the Oglio, is remembered, it may be seen that this policy was precisely true to the form established after Cateau-Cambrèsis: not wishing to speak openly on the matter and declare her hand, Venice had replied positively to Borromeo – but had probably not countermanded orders already in the possession of the rectors of Brescia and Bergamo, leaving the order to delay publication in force – as a delaying tactic.

137   On March 11, 1567, the Canons renewed their complaints by presenting a document to Mons. Girolamo Cavalli, at that time Bollani's Vicar-general. Cavalli replied to this at a general meeting stating that it was no part of a vicar-general's function to decide in favour or otherwise of acts decreed by the Provincial Council and approved by the Pope, 'confortandoli poi ad ubbidire agli ecclesiastici mandati, li assicurò che in quelle cose che al vescovo o suo vicario appartengono avrebbe usato temperamento di giustizia e clemenza, con speranza non sarebbe sorta giusta causa di lamento.' (doc. from 'Raccolta de' Sinodi' in A.V.B., quoted by Fè D'Ostiani, *op. cit.*, and not further identified). This 'temperamento' could equally well have described Bollani's method: a formula of justice tempered with humanity, and doubtless Cavalli was acting on instructions.

138   See documents in A. V.B., *Annali Cronologici... (Seminario),* quoted by Masetti-Zanini, 'Le origni del seminario di Brescia ...' *cit.,* pp. 66–67.

139   *Ibid.* pp. 67, 73–77. This may indeed have been the formulation by which a compromise with the canons had been reached (the classic 'temporary' nature of all taxes). In the document dated May 13, 1567, no mention is made of the provisional nature of the tax, while in that printed, embellished with the bishop's arms, and dated May 31, Bollani states that 'habbiamo co'l conseglio delli medesimi reverendi deputati (fin'a tanto che si farà provisione per altra via alle suddette necessarie spese) imposto mezza decima ...'. Logically it would seem that the compromise (if such it was) was reached between these dates. Bollani also added that 'ne havendo potuto per hora far provisione per le necessarie spese di esso per via di unione di benefice semplici, come sarebbe stato il nostro desiderio.' It will be remembered that these two methods of raising revenue had been indicated by the Council of Trent, but that no further instruction had been given as to amount or priority.

140   'vendette ai deputati al seminario un fondo in contrada San Pietro e Marcellino,' on which the seminary was eventually built. The road is now known as Via Callegari, and the building has become a military hospital. For its subsequent fortunes down to the present day (with photographic documentation) see Anon., 'Ha quattro secoli il seminario di Brescia,' in *Il Seminario ...,* XXI (may/June, 1969) Brescia, pp. 4–8.

141   The building was entrusted to the architect Lodovico Beretta in July, 1567. (Masetti-Zanini, *op. cit.,* p. 71, Fè D'Ostiani, *op. cit.,* p. 51, and sources cited there, Petroboni, *op. cit.,* p. 103)

142   We have seen that the difficulty of collection had been the main obstacle to the seminary's progress in Bologna. Bollani's difficulties transpire from his edict of November 20, 1567, in which he threatened recalcitrant subscribers with 'escomunicatione come della invocatione del brazzo secolare ...' if payment had not been made within 15 days. (A.V.B., Seminario, doc. 5, in Masetti-Zanini, *op. cit.,* p. 77).

143   These benefices were assigned on July 30, 1569, according to a document in the *Annali...,* (Masetti-Zanini, *op. cit.,* p. 71) and were distributed widely through the diocese (Quinzano, Pompiano, San Giacomo del Mella, Orzinuovi etc.). The first of these whose revenues could actually be applied, however, fell vacant on the death of the incumbent, Barnabò Maggi, on August 23, 1570. The importance of this is clear: the benefice consisted of six *piò bresciani* p.a., plus the revenue from a house. A substantial proportion of the revenues necessary for the unkeep of the seminary, therefore, would continue to be drawn from the yield from the *Mezza-decima,* and it was to be precisely this need that was to give rise to Bollani's war with Cardinal Francesco Gambara. Only the dates of the further vacancies in the

remaining twelve benefices, and the accounts of the seminary in its infancy would yield the economic background to this great dispute − one which was central to Bollani's career, and significantly impeded the progress of his reforms in Brescia − but these documents do not appear to have survived.

144 Bollani to Ormanetto, May 5, 1569, quoted in full in Petroboni, *op. cit.*, pp. 101−102. Bollani seems to have received conspicuous aid for his reforming initiatives in the diocese from the Brescian orders − always a possible source of jurisdictional conflict, as not subject to episcopal control. A separate educational initiative seems to have come from the *Padri di Sant' Antonio* in 1564, when a school for pirests was founded. (It will be remembered that the Council of Trent had not sought to *replace* other forms of education for priests with seminaries). On the arrival of the Jesuits in Brescia in 1568, they were first welcomed by this order, which finally adopted the statutes of the Society of Jesus in a union approved by Borromeo in 1569. (See Fè D'Ostiani, *op. cit.*, pp. 53−54, for the detailed history, and Petroboni, *op. cit.*, pp. 104−105 for Borromeo's letter to Bollani of February 8, 1568). It is interesting to find that the sources have not yielded any trace of conflict between these orders and the tridentine impetus in Brescia, when the opposition to Jesuit control of seminaries in Rome, Milan and Naples is remembered. In fairness it should be added that the Jesuits arrived in Brescia at a point coincident with the launching of the seminary, and also that Bollani had diplomatically entrusted control of the seminary to an order with which he had been closely associated even before his assumption of the bishopric. (Bollani remembered the 'Collegio delli Reverendi Padri Giesuiti' in his will, leaving them a legacy of 50 ducats). The Jesuits were also in control of a number of French seminaries (Halkin, *op. cit.*, p. 13). For the Brescian *Padri della Pace,* see the exhaustive monograph by P. Guerrini, *La Congregazione dei Padri della Pace*, (Brescia, 1933), chap. VIII and *passim.*

145 Guerrini, *op. cit.*, pp. 167−168 etc.

146 Francesco Gambara was born in 1533, of the union of the powerful Gambara and Pallavicino families. He became provost of Verolanuova at the age of 15, and entered the papal court as *Cameriere segreto* to Julius III, enjoying the protection of his uncle Uberto Gambara, a Cardinal. He became a Cardinal under Paul IV in 1561, and, as bishop of Viterbo, built the luxurious Villa della Bagnaia at huge expense and was castigated by Borromeo for this. He died in 1587. On his career, see the summary and sources in Petroboni, *op. cit.*, p. 106.

147 Petroboni, *op. cit.*, p. 106, n. 2.

148 Bollani to Borromeo, May 20, 1572: 'ora che gli {il seminario} è levata la mezza-decima del clero, per la tansa che pagha alla Signoria {di Venezia} in sanctione della guerra contra il Turco . . .' This dramatic change in the fortunes of the seminary marked a significant landmark in its history, and seems to have been missed by Guerrini, Petroboni, Masetti-Zanini etc. Indeed it may have been in direct response to this measure that the principle of fee-paying students was introduced into the Brescian seminary. Some three years later, the rector of the Seminary was to complain in a 'secret' correspondence with Borromeo, that the benefits of the institution − particularly its educational benefits − were being eroded by the poverty and consequent inability to maintain themselves at the seminary of the young priests: 'Ma perchè quelli che vogliono entrare in esso sono astretti a pagar donzena (eccetto trei, ai quali si fanno le spese gratis, però, vestendosi del suo come gli altri), da qui viene che ogni anno la maggior parte di detti figliuoli si partono per non haver il modo di continuare a pagare essa donzena; sicchè la buona disciplina incominciata resta imperfetta, con grande pericolo delle anime loro.' It will be remembered that there was nothing in the tridentine decree to ensure *free* education in seminaries, although its emphasis was clearly to be directed towards the benefit of poor children. He went on to remark that 'si vede chiaramente et l'esperienza ce l'insegna che chi vuole mantenere il Seminario di buon spirito et cavarne quel frutto che il Santo Concilio desidera, bisogna che la sua propria entrata (già) applicata o contribuita la mantenga, altrimenti è impossibile che possa durare.' (P. Stefano Giroldi, rector of the seminary, to Borromeo, October 1575, quoted by Guerrini, *La Compagnia dei Padri della Pace, cit.*, pp. 170−171.

149 See a late copy of Bollani's letter to Gregory XIII, congratulating him on his accession to the pontificate in Museo Correr (Venice), MSS, P.D. 397. p. 21, of June 12 {1572} .

150 'et massime nell'unione che se gli farà de beneficii semplici, rivocatemi sempre dal
precessor {Pius V} con clausole stravagantissime derogatorie nominatamente a essi decreti
{del Concilio di Trento}...'
151 He mentioned the 'lite sopra un beneficio {...} di cinquecento scudi di entrata senza il
quale è impossibile a fatto che questo nostro povero seminario si possa mantenere...'
152 'Mi consoli d'ottenere da sua santità la gratia della giustissima causa di questo nostro
povero seminario, che non resti oppresso et destrutto dalla pervicacia di quel primiero suo
avversario {Cardinal Gambara}, ancho con la sostentatione di tanti poveri chierici, potiamo
fare di quelli operarii nella vigna di Dio, che tanta ne è bisognoso...' (Bollani to Borromeo,
September 3, 1572).
153 'L'affettuosa lettera ch'è piacuta alla pietà di V. Ill.ma Sig.ia scrivere a Mons. Ill.mo di
Vercelli m'ha data grandissima consolatione in confidare ogni bene nella giusta causa del mio
povero seminario, tanto vessato da violenza di favore di quel suo pertinace avversario...'
(Bollani to Borromeo, quoted Petroboni, pp. 109–110).
154 'Supplico parimento la sua grande pietà a procurare di Roma una particolare confer-
matione di quel santo decreto nostro primo concilio provinciale intorno all'assiduo et debito
servitio dei canonici et altri ministri della cattedrale nel culto divino, ch'a certi tempi vedo
quasi in tutto abbandonato nella mia chiesa...' Bollani proposed to add 'doi parole di
maggior dichiaratione sulle pene che si danno alli disubbidienti...' (*Ibid.*)
155 This is discussed below, pp. 170 seq.
156 See below, p. 170 for the fortunes of the seminary in 1575–1580.
157 The main source for the affair of the priest of Savallo (as well as that for the later more
serious confrontation) is the letters from Bollani to Roveglio (MSS., B.V. 31. Biblioteca
Queriniana, Brescia *cit.*), for 1576–1577. They have the advantage of great confidentiality,
and the range and treatment of subjects is such as would never have been communicated to
Borromeo.
158 Savallo is a small parish in the Val Sabbia, just north of the city of Brescia. The
Gambara lands were, as we have seen, in the southern part of the Bresciano, but his influence
clearly extended much further, and the connection with Achille was almost certainly one of
family relationship. (For the extent and character of the Gambara land holding of some 8828
piò in the early 17th century, see, for example, C. Pasero, 'Giovanni da Lezze e il suo
catastico,' in *Il Catastico Bresciano*... 1609–1610 , {Brescia, 1969}, p. 59 n. 171, and
C. Magni, *Il Tramonto del Feudo Lombardo*, {Milan, 1937}, p. 239 etc. for comparison with
holdings of other noble families in the Bresciano.
159 It is not clear precisely in what way, although, in the light of subsequent events, it seems
likely that Bollani planned to allocate the benefice to the seminary, depriving this priest of
the living conferred by Gambara. There seems no evidence of the pre-conditions for this,
however, to be expected in Bollani's *visita pastorale* of this area.
160 On the emergence of a reinforced political power in the Roman Curia after Trent, see
P. Prodi, *Lo Sviluppo dell'Assolutismo nello Stato Pontificio* (Bologna, 1968).
161 'Il Trappa mi dice che mi manderà col presente corriero una fede del modo che ricercate
per conto di Savalo, onde voglio sperare che quel negocio passerà bene et noi resteremo
coperti col prudente modo che vedo che caminate, et vi so dire che con quelli satrapi non vi
bisogna meno, per l'affetto grande che ha Gambara a questo suo Mo.{ }? di casa...'
(Bollani to Roveglio, April 4, 1576, *Carteggio cit.*,).
162 'piacemi grandemente il confidente tratenimento dell'amico nostro col Datario, et
particolarmente per l'occasione del negocio di Savallo con quelli satrapi di Gambara...'
(Ibid.) (See also the letter of 16 March, in *Ibid.*).
163 'Che si paghino a esso S. Achille scudi 70 di pensione all'anno sopra la detta chiesa...
et così si farà finito questo intrico, et levato anche a noi simile impazzo...' (Bollani to
Roveglio, May 2, 1576).
164 What follows is based on Bollani's letters to Roveglio of September 1, 3, and 12, and
that of Cardinal Gambara to Bollani of August 10, 1577 (all in *Carteggio Bollani–Roveglio,*
cit.), as well as that from Bollani to Pope Gregory XIII of September 10 (also published in Fè
D'Ostiani, *op. cit.*, pp. 133–136) in *Ibid.* The relevant sections of these documents, of

fundamental importance as indications of Bollani's methods in diplomacy, are collected below as Appendix VI.

165 See, for instance, Hubert Jedin, *Crisis and Closure of the Council of Trent, cit.*, pp. 101–159.

166 Above, p. 185, n. 63.

167 Fè D'Ostiani, *op. cit.*, pp. 132–133, was content only to examine Bollani's letter to the Pope, while the documents in Appendix VI, below, throw light on the range of Bollani's political activities while bishop.

168 *Super lectione et praedicatione:* June 17, 1546, for which, see Waterworth, *Canons and Decrees . . ., cit.*, pp. 24–27, Rimoldi, *art. cit.*, p. 427, and above, p. 160.

169 Bona's death had occasioned a vacancy which was to be filled by the Caonon Della Corte. Bollani proposed to allocate the vacancy caused by this shift to the support of the lectureship. (Fè D'Ostiani, *op. cit.*, p. 55, quoting 'Atti della Curia Vescovile {di Brescia}', (not further identified) which I have not seen.

170 Bollani was convinced that the benefits of some teaching of the scriptures in the city should not be lost in the affair, and elected Giacomo Zurlera di Cavalgese, *Cappellano* of the cathedral, to teach theology, and Francesco Landino as *Vice-Penitenziere. (Ibid.*, p. 55).

171 These briefs were constantly quoted by him in the correspondence about the dispute (Appendix VI). The link between the 1568 and 1577 initiatives – with the suggestion that Bollani had obtained these Papal briefs in response to local oppostion earlier – is strongly suggested by the facts, but has not been noticed before. The Papal concessions were almost certainly the work of Borromeo, as we have seen that Bollani had repeatedly requested his help.

172 Fè D'Ostiani, *op. cit.*, p. 133.

173 For this reluctance to accept the duties of the post, see Bollani to Roveglio, *Carteggio cit.*, September 22, 1577.

174 Gambara to Bollani, August 10, 1577, doc. 1 (Appendix VI), Bollani to Roveglio, September 1, doc. 2. Bollani's letters to Roveglio contain much criticism of Soranzo, from the amusing account of his huge suite of retainers which descended on the city on his arrival, to his behaviour during the plague and certain inconveniences arising from the presence in the city of a Venetian doctor whose links with the Soranzo family meant that he could not be contradicte.

Paolo Tiepolo had been requested to promote Gambara's case in August, but since Bollani himself felt able to entrust his cause to the Venetian Ambassador, it does not seem as if he could have enjoyed much success: 'se è vero ch'l Papa non habbia voluto udire il Cardinal Gambara intorno al nostro canonicato, non senza grande contento, perchè esso cardinale ha scritto al Cl.mo {Paolo} Thiepolo dolendosi die me et dicendo ch'l faccia ufficio meco per esser solito che si porti sempre rispetto alli benefici vacanti de famigliari de Cardinali; et così esso Cl.mo {Thiepolo} ha fatto ufficio col Cl.mo nostro {Francesco} Longo, che mi scrive di ciò.' (Bollani to Roveglio, August 22, 1577, *Carteggio cit.*,)

175 Appendix VI, doc. 2: Bollani to Roveglio, September 1, 1577.

176 A certain 'Marini' and 'Gio. di Camerini' are alluded to in the correspondence, as well as a 'Zerbino'.

177 Appendix VI, doc. 6: Bollani to Roveglio, September 12, 1577.

178 *Ibid.*, doc. 5: Gio. di Camerini to Bollani, August 3, 1577.

179 *Ibid.*, doc. 6: Bollani to Roveglio, September 12, 1577.

180 *Ibid.*

181 'Ho scritto al Marini un partito a proponer a quel di loro Sig.ri {Morone or Tiepolo} che farà l'ufficio col Papa, che è di dar con mia quiete a Gambara la mansionaria, et che S. Santità gli {Gambara} commandi non più parlare del cononicato . . .' *(Ibid.)* He was therefore anxious to leave his supporters room to manoeuvre realistically.

182 '. . . a Bologna come universalmente in Italia, le indicazioni positive date dal concilio a questo riguardo rimasero quasi senza applicazione . . .' (P. Prodi, *Il Cardinale Gabriele Paleotti . . ., cit.*, II, pp. 225–228 at p. 226.)

183 See the report to Borromeo of P. Stefano Giroldi, rector of the seminary, of October, 1575, quoted by Guerrini, *La Congregazione . . ., cit.*, pp. 170–171. Besides the problem of

paying pupils (already mentioned), the questions of the exemption from local taxes and the quality of the teaching staff were also raised.

184 *Archivio Arcivescovile di Milano* (A.A.M.), *Visita Brescia*, II, p. 85, quoted in *Ibid.* pp. 171–172, n. 12. Borromeo's report contains a detailed description of the state of the seminary. The building, the income of the institution and the standard of teaching were all considered inadequate. Guerrini has compared Bollani with Borromeo in this context, writing that he 'tirava avanti con stento fra mille difficoltà; non aveva potenze di aderenze, diffettava di mezzi pecuniari, era oppresso da avversari potenti, vicini e lontanti, *non aveva spirito combattivo*{!}' (Italics mine). This brief examination of Bollani's letters to Roveglio should correct the impression given by this last statement.

185 A further example of local opposition will be seen in the Diocesan Synod of 1574 (below, pp. 171–174).

186 Giovanni Molino, Bishop of Brescia (1755–1773) founded three seminaries in the diocese. (See P. Paschini, 'Vescovi Veneti nel giudizio di un Nunzio a Venezia,' in *Rivista di Storia della Chiesa in Italia*, IX, (1955), pp. 413–416 at p. 413.

187 This opposition was also supported by Cardinal Gambara, as we shall see. The events of the Synod (for Brescia alone) were fully recounted by Fè D'Ostiani, *op. cit.*, pp. 75–88, drawing on the *Atti Sinodo Bollani* in A.V.B., to which this account is widely indebted. See also Petroboni, *op. cit.*, pp. 135–149, for an account of the content of Bollani's *Costituzioni per il Clero.*

188 The 'Constitutions for the Clergy' had been Bollani's first step in the direction of a codification of these rules for Brescia, having been first published in 1564: *Constitutiones R. Rmi D. D. Bollani*, Brix. Ep., (Brixiae, ad instantiam I. B. Bozolae, 1564). They were republished in 1574, with the acts of the diocesan Synod we are about to discuss, and again in 1575 (apud V. Sabbium). Bollani's *Rituale Sacramentorum ex Rom. Eccl. ritu Rmi. D.D. Bollani Ep., Brixiae, jussu editum ad usum suae ecclesiae*, (Brixiae, 1570) was adopted beyond the bounds of the diocesan boundaries, notably by Cesare Speciano, bishop of Cremona (for instance), whose name appears often in Bollani's correspondence. On the publications, see *Storia di Brescia, cit.*, II, pp. 459–460, Fe D'Ostiani, *op. cit.*, pp. 57–59, and Petroboni, *op. cit.*, pp. 125, 127–129.

189 The similarities and contrasts between Bollani's case and those of Cardinals Borromeo and Paleotti in Milan and Bologna make interesting comparisons with these reformers possible.

190 The influence of Giberti on the fathers at the Council has already been noted. It is highly significant, therefore, that the tridentine emphasis on episcopal authority followed just such a contest for power in Giberti's diocese in the 1530s as Bollani was now facing in 1570s. A. Prosperi noted that 'queste battaglie { between bishop and canons on residence} non si svolsero in Verona, ma in Roma e a Venezia,' which we have seen to have been true in Bollani's fight with Gambara. Further, Giberti 'dovette mobilitare tutta la sua abilità diplomatica e mantenere in piedi tutta la rete dei suoi precedenti rapporti per assicurarsi la possibilità di realizzare il suo programma in Verona.' (*Tra Evangelismo e Controriforma, cit.*, p. 151). This was precisely Bollani's case *after* the Council, which, it becomes clear, had sharpened rather than diminished the need for diplomatic ability. The similarity of of Bollani's problems in this sphere to those of Giberti before the Council, their respective appeals to higher ecclesiastical and civil authority (Rome and Venice in *both* cases), and the victories finally obtained, show yet again that the way to reform had been clearly indicated by Giberti in Verona, and that the Council's insistence on episcopal authority as the main strength of the reform movement, was the valid (if not totally effective) response to problems that had been clearly seen and to battles that had been clearly won.

191 *Storia di Brescia, cit.*, II, p. 443; see also P. Guerrini, 'Per la storia dell'organizzazione ecclesiastica di Brescia nel Medio Evo,' in *Brixia Sacra*, (1925–26), and *Idem*, 'Sviluppo cronologico dell'organizzazione parrocchiale diocesana dal secolo XV in avanti,' in *Memorie Storiche della Diocesi di Brescia*, 25 (1958).

192 Below, p. 234–235.

193 For Borromeo's position in Milan, see M. Bendiscioli in *Storia di Milano, cit.*, X, pp. 187–189: 'Abusi e riforma sulle collegiate di canonici'; for Bologna, P. Prodi, *Gabriele*

Paleotti. . ., cit., II, pp. 23–24, 48–56, 357–360, and Idem, 'Lineamenti dell'organizzazione diocesana durante l'episcopato del Card. G. Paleotti (1566–1597)' in *Problemi di Vita religiosa in Italia nel Cinquecento* (Padua, 1960) pp. 323–394, now trans. and ed. E. Cochrane, in *The Late Italian Renaissance 1525–1630*, (London, 1970) pp. 226–243. (but without the text of the 'Governo Arcipiscopale . . .' fundamental to the present discussion.)
194 Prodi, *Gabriele Paleotti . . ., cit.*, pp. 48–49, *Idem,* 'Lineamenti . . .' *cit.*, p. 343.
195 *Gabriele Paleotti . . ., cit.*, p. 49.
196 *Ibid.* The Council's provisions are in Session VI, chap. iii; XXIII, chap. xviii; XXIV, chaps. xii, xv.
197 Professor Prodi quotes an article by F. Ceredda, 'El litigio de los cabildos y su reprecussion en las relaciones con Roma 1551–1556' in *Razó y Fe*, 130 (1944) pp. 215–234 in support of this.
198 P. Prodi, *op. cit.*, p. 356.
199 *Ibid.*, p. 52.
200 *Ibid.*, pp. 357–360. Cannobio had refused to obey the reform edicts of Paleotti, enjoying the support of powerful interests in Rome through family connections with the Bolognese Pope Filippo Buoncompagni. Cannobio headed the opposition to reform of the canons in just the same way as Panfilo Rovato was to do in Brescia (for whom see immediately below). The Bolognese story runs parallel to the Brescian situation: Paleotti, like Bollani, received Papal support for his 'constitutions' in his audience with the Pope in the Jubilee year (1575), as well as support for the founding of the *Teologale* and *Penitenzieria*. Given their friendship, it may well be that Bollani's actions in these important years continued to be influenced by Paleotti through correspondence, as we have seen for the 1560s. They would certainly have discussed these difficulties in Rome in 1575.
201 *Storia di Milano, cit.*, X, p. 187.
202 P. Prodi, *Gabriele Paleotti . . ., cit.*, II, pp. 357–360.
203 *Storia di Milano*, X, p. 189.
204 Session XXIV, chap. ii.
205 P. Prodi, *Gabriele Paleotti . . ., cit.*, pp. 152–163.
206 The edict giving notice of this was published by Fè D'Ostiani, *op. cit.*, pp. 177–179. The convocation of the Synod found more than 600 Brescian clerics gathered in the old cathedral for the election of officers, an oration from the bishop, and an eleaborate procession. (*Ibid.*, pp. 76–77).
207 *Ibid.*, p. 77.
208 A.V.B., *Sinodo Bollani, Atti Annessi*, quoted in *Ibid.*, p. 78.
209 This was a tridentine prescription (Session XXIV, chap. 18, q.v.). Bollani was in close touch with Borromeo at this stage, requesting his help with the drafting of his constitutions on October 26: 'ho sempre tanto desiderato che restino raffinate dal prudente giudicio suo.' On December 15, he poured out all his bitterness at the actions of the Canon Panfilo Rovato, and on December 22, requested Borromeo's help with the presentation of his case to the Pope. (Bollani–Borromeo, *carteggio cit.*, Oct. 26, Dec. 15, Dec. 22, of which the last letter has hardly withstood the test of time, being only legible in very small part.)
210 'Tumultuousa e non senza frodi del partito oppositore fu la proposta dei savi di città, fra i quali però non poté ottenere de' suoi che il canonico Senna, mentre gli altri, cioè il proposto della Corte, Antonio Averoldi, Tranquillo Doldo, G. Battista Averoldi, e Pietro Durante più o meno aderivano ai principi riformatori del Bollani. Senonchè, avendo voluto, durante la proposta dei Savi della Diocesi, il Promotore Fiscale, Ammonire pubblicamente il Rovato delle arti illegali che andava operando, ne naque tal rumore ed un muoversi dai posti ed un protestare ed un insolentire si estraneo ed insolito a queste radunanze, che il Vescovo, raccotil sollicitamente i nomi dei proposti e presa occasione dell'ora tarda, dichiarò sciolta la sessione.' (Fè D'Ostiani, *op. cit.*, pp. 80–81).
211 See the discussion of *broglio* above, pp. 53–54. This consciousness may perhaps be seen in Bollani's opening remarks at the Synod, when he warned against electoral malpractices. (*Ibid.*, p. 77).
212 'De mandato di Monsignor Rmo. si comanda sotto pena di scomunicazione a ciascuno della presente congregazione che non ardisca dar più del suo voto nel balottare, ma che dia

ciascuno il proprio, di mano propria, ne ardisca partirsi dal suo loco mentre si balotta, nè far pratiche direttamente od indirettamente, strepiti nè cenni sotto l'istessa pena di scomunicazione ad arbitrio di S.S. Rma. et questo restando anche fermo il Decreto già fatto in materia di balottare pubblicato il giorno primo del presente Sinodo.' ('Memorie del Not. Glisenti', {*Sinodo Bollani: Atti annessi*}, A.V.B., quoted in *Ibid.*, p. 81).

213 Panfilo Ravota, Mangiavini and Franzoni were recognised as opponents of Bollani's reforms. They were elected with Camillo Gambara of Gambara, clearly a relative or protégé of the Cardinal.

214 See *Ibid.*, pp. 86–88 for the facts in detail.

215 *Ibid.*, pp. 87–88. Borromeo's formula for the Brescian canons is in A.A.M., *Visita Brescia, cit.*, and see Guerrini, 'La Visita Apostolica...' *loc. cit.*

216 No attempt is made here to discuss exhaustively Bollani's minor reforms in the diocese – a process more appropriate to a history of the Catholic Reformation in the diocese. Rather the attempt has been to choose aspects of this reform important for the movement as a whole, and those which demonstrate the function of civil experience. To *measure* the impact of Bollani's *costituzioni*, comparison needs to be made with those of the bishop Durante in 1550s, and the result related to the *Atti della Visita...*, of Bollani, and Borromeo's visitation in 1580. It is worth stressing again that the progress of the Brescian Reformation in the first critical years after the Council, for what concerns churches, liturgy and clergy, will also emerge in important respects from comparison of the *Decime del Clero* returns for this period of years (preserved in the *Archivio di Stato*, Venice, *loc. cit.*).

217 See the notes on the conservation of the MSS acts of Bollani's *visite* (in A.V.B.) in Guerrini, *Atti della Visita Pastorale del Vescovo Domenico Bollani alla diocesi di Brescia*, 3 vols. (Brescia, 1915–40) I, pp. 4 *et seq.*, and Petroboni, *op. cit.*, pp. 71–75. The former work has published the majority (though not all) of the documents themselves, which have contributed significantly to knowledge of Bollani's place in the Catholic Reformation (see, for example, the review by H. Jedin, in *Il Concilio di Trento*, II (1943) pp. 411–413, and Alberigo, 'Applicazione del Concilio...' *cit.*, esp. p. 264). Bollani's *visite* are an area of active research at the present time, with work concentrating particularly on the Val Camonica and the area of the diocese not covered by Guerrini's publication. Two recent theses for the *Università Cattolica del Sacro Cuore*, Milan, reflect this interest: T.A. Moreschi, 'Vita e Istituzioni ecclesiastiche nella valle Camonica del Sec. XVI: Visita Pastorale del Vescovo Domenico Bollani dell'anno 1567' (1968–1969), and E. Cattane, 'La Pieve di Cemmo in Valle Camonica nel periodo della Riforma Tridentina,' (1969–1970), which attempted a 'pilot' comparison of Bollani's visit to this village with Borromeo's later visit. Its conclusion yields little that is useful, however. More promising, perhaps is the thesis by Sig. V. Gazich, which deals also with heresy centres in the Bresciano, and may be the first Italian thesis on Brescia to take proper cognisance of the importance of Venetian sources: Vincenzo Gazich, 'La Visita pastorale del Vescovo Domenico Bollani alla Valle Trompia nell'Anno 1567' (Univ. Catt. Sacro Cuore, Milan, 1969–70). I am grateful to Sig. Gazich for mutually stimulating discussions and the loan of his unpublished thesis. Still useful in this context, are the articles by Guerrini in *Brixia Sacra* (1910–1911) and 'Il IV Centenario...,' *cit.*, in *Mem. Stor. Dioc. Brescia* (1938) etc.

218 The best summary of Bollani's findings remains that by Petroboni *op. cit.*, pp. 71–90, to which the present remarks are indebted. See also Fè D'Ostiani, *op. cit.*, pp. 34–35, 38–40.

219 As A. Prosperi noted: *Tra Evangelismo e Controriforma...*, *cit.*, p. 203.

220 It should be added that the state of the documentation itself has probably prevented widespread use of this method in the past, especially before 1563, as the keeping of accurate parish and diocesan records was itself a preoccupation of the council.

221 Prosperi, *op.cit.*, p. 203, and see immediately below for the popular reaction to this.

222 Below, p. 178.

223 On this, the visitations of Giberti are fundamental, of course, influencing Pole, Morone and Borromeo (Prosperi *op. cit.*, pp. 204–205) in *Ibid.*, pp. 202–209. The influence of Giberti on Ormanetto is also documentable, so that the latter's visitations in Padua are important (Marcora, 'Ormanetto...' *cit.*, in *Mem. Stor. Dioc. Milano*, VIII {1961} p. 446, and for Padua, Preti, 'L'Episcopato Padovano di N.O....' *cit.*, in *Studi Veneziani*, XI {1969}, pp. 341–350). Giberti's influence was also acknowledged by his successor in Verona,

Agostino Valier, for whom see Masotto, thesis *cit.*, pp. 103–135 (a full treatment which deserves to be better known). For a broader picture, Alberto Monticone's description of the tridentine visitations in Rome up to Sixtus V throws up particular problems: 'L'Applicazione a Roma del Concilio di Trento. Le Visite 1564–1565' in *Rivista di Storia della Chiesa in Italia*, VIII (1954) pp. 23–48, for Bologna, see Prodi, *Gabriele Paleotti...*, *cit.*, II, pp. 162–178. Bollani's vicar-general and confidant, Giacomo Roveglio, himself became bishop of Feltre after Bollani's death, so that comparison of his methods in the Feltrino with Bollani's might prove illuminating. (Information in A. Pellin, 'Giacomo Rovellio { *sic* } {1584–1610} e la sua prima visita pastorale nel Feltrino,' in *Archivio Storico di Belluno*, XXIV {1953}).

224 Particularly, perhaps, in the cases of Vicenza and Treviso, within Venetian temporal jurisdiction but outside the Patriarchates of Venice and Aquileia (but see the articles *cit.*, by Mantese in *R.S.C.I.* 14, {1960} 15 {1962}, for Vicenza).

225 On the influence of Giberti, see Prosperi, *op. cit.*, pp. 204–205, and the text of the *formulario* in *Archivio Segreto Vaticano, Arm.*, 62 (Conc. Trento), vol 94, pp. 98–121, reproduced in *Ibid.*, pp. 205–206 n. 64.

226 *Ibid.*, p. 203.

227 Francesco Palmio (who accompanied Palcotti in the diocese of Bologna) wrote these words (*cit.*, Prodi, *op. cit.*, II, pp. 31–32).

228 Fè D'Ostiani, *loc. cit.*

229 Brescia had had a succession of absentee bishops inadequate to the task of reform of abuses: Paolo Zane (1481–1532), F. Corner (1532–1542), A. Corner (1542–1551), and D. Durante (1551–1558). See summaries in Petroboni, *op. cit.*, pp. 71–72.

230 Above, pp. 150–153, Guerrini, *La Congregazione...*, *cit.*, pp. 71–94, *Idem.*, *Atti della Visita...*, *cit.*, I, *passim*, Petroboni, *loc. cit.*, Storia di Brescia, II, pp. 443–450, etc.

231 For Giberti, see Prosperi, *loc. cit.*, for Borromeo, for example, Giussani, *Vita di San Carlo...*, *ed. cit.*, pp. 54–65, esp. p. 55.

232 The relation of Giacomo Pandolfo, describing his progress through *Franciacorte* and the *Valcamonica* in 1562 (A.V.B.) seems to be the only surviving evidence of this.

233 Fè D'Ostiani, *op. cit.*, p. 34, Petroboni, *op. cit.*, p. 75. However it is clear that Cardinal Savelli had visited 93 Roman churches in 1564 (Monticone, *op. cit.*, pp. 227–228): 'in una vera e propria visita pastorale secondo i decreti tridentini.' And there are doubtless other examples. There is no general survey work on tridentine *Visite Pastorali*, so that questions of precedence, timing, and therefore possible influence are difficult to establish.

234 See, for instance, Tacchi-Venturi, *op. cit.*, I, *passim*. In Brescia about 120 parish priests were non-resident.

235 Petroboni, *op. cit.*, p. 88. Firstly, the visitation was to correct and reform, so that the acts may give an unduly pessimistic picture of the diocese. Secondly, the MSS themselves should be consulted, since Guerrini, on his own admission, felt free to edit and select his material.

236 The priest at Roncadelle had two months to prepare for this (*Atti...*, *cit.*, I, p. 8), while the one at Rovato was to present himself in three months (*Ibid.*, pp. 26–27).

237 A Catechism by B. Pietro Canisio recurs in the Acts, along with a life of Jesus by Ludolfo Sasso (1340). Perhaps these had played a part in Domenico's own formation in 1558–1563. Specific reference to books in the acts shows the degree of Bollani's concern with educational matters – but they have yet to be used in the context of orthodoxy and the influx of heretical ideas.

238 For example at Cologne and Corzano, as well as in the Valcamonica (cases cited by Petroboni, *op. cit.*, p. 84.)

239 Comparisons with Borromeo and Ormanetto spring to mind. In Padua it is clear that Ormanetto's severe reaction to the problem of non-resident priests worried the Republic of Venice. Such was the number of suspensions for non-residence, that the Council of X suggested to Ormanetto that 'era molto meglio avere alla cura delle chiese preti di mediocre eruditione che non ne haver alcuno.' (A.S.V., *Capi del Cons. dei X, Secreta*, Ro. 9, p. 30: June 13, 1573, quoted by Preti, *op. cit.*, p. 347.)

240 Petroboni, *op. cit.*, p. 85, *Atti...*, *cit.*, I, p. 114.

241 At Manerbio, 'Messer pre Giulio Luciago e diffamato di havere tenuto et che tenga una putta che si chiama Checca ovver la boffa et del gioco et dela biastema lui è diffamatissimo . . .' (*Ibid.*, resp. pp. 86, 96).
242 Examples in Petroboni, *op. cit.*, pp. 76–90.
243 This will be seen in the next chapter.
244 Above, Chapters IV–V.
245 *Atti . . ., cit.*, I, p. 45, Petroboni, *op. cit.*, p. 76.
246 Bollani–Roveglio, *carteggio cit.*, April, 25, 1576, Fè D'Ostiani, *op. cit.*, p. 98.
247 For Valier's treatment of disputes during his visitation, see Masotto, thesis *cit.*, pp. 114–116, 121–124 etc. For his formation, *Ibid.*, chap. I, *passim* (based on printed sources).
248 This was one of Bollani's enduring preoccupations, as we have seen both in Udine, and Brescia. He had recognised the need for widespread reforms, and promoted repressive legislation. It had also been a subject which had occupied him at Trent. On the reform of Brescian Monasteries, see the fully documented section in *Storia di Brescia*, II, pp. 444–446, and the reforms printed in *Atti della Visita . . ., cit.*, pp. vii–xxv. Besides the local sources and bibliography in *Storia di Brescia*, see also Guerrini, 'Monasteri, conventi, ospitali e benefici semplici della dicesi di Brescia,' in *Brixia Sacra*, (1911) 323–240. Bollani's involvement is further documented in his letters to Borromeo (for example, Jan, 16, 1572, Oct. 21, 1577, Jan. 11, 1578, Feb. 22, 1578, in *Carteggio cit.*). For the decisions at Trent, see Waterworth, *Canons & Decrees . . ., cit.*, pp. 237–252 etc., and for the position in other dioceses, (Vicenza): G. Mantese, 'Nota d'archivio . . .,' *cit.*, (Verona–Valier): Masotti, *op. cit.*, pp. 154–171, (Padua): Preti, 'Ormanetto . . .' *cit.*, pp. 350–353, where Ormanetto fell foul of Venetian monastic traditions, predictably. For the situation in Milan, see the excellent introduction to the whole question in *Storia di Milano*, X, pp. 178–180, and the decrees in *Acta Eccl. Mediol.* there referred to. See also, Paschini, 'I monasteri feminili in Italia nel '500' in *Problemi di Vita religiosa . . ., cit.*, pp. 31–60, and R. Creytens, 'La Riforma dei Monasteri femminili dopo i decreti tridentini,' in *Il Concilio di Trento e la Riforma Tridentina, cit.*, I, pp. 45–83, for a much more modern approach.
249 In general, see the *Storia di Brescia*, II, pp. 461–465, for a good summary of local research in this field, one in which Bollani was particularly active in the 1570s. The *Congrega del Duomo* assumed new functions of a charitable kind under his episcopate; he supported the foundation of the *Pio Luogo del Soccorso* in 1570, which did valuable work for *fanciulle traviate*, and in fact composed its 'constitutions' (pub. in *Acta. Eccles. Brixiensis, cit.*, pp. 281–287). Finally, the *Scuola della Dottrina Cristiana*, founded by bishop Durante in 1554, gathered strength under Bollani, chiefly owing to the efforts of Cabrino and Paradisi. On this, see A. Cistellini, *Il Padre Angelo Paradisi e i Primi Gesuiti in Brescia* (Brescia, 1955) which also documents Bollani's interest in the question of the Jesuits in Brescia from Jesuit sources, and Guerrini, *Catechismi e Scuole della Dottrina Cristiana in Brescia* (Brescia, 1940).

CHAPTER IX

VENICE AND ROME : DOMENICO BOLLANI
IN DISPUTES BETWEEN CHURCH AND STATE
1563–1579

The Council of Trent, partly a reaction against the dangers of a political cohesion of 'heresy' north of the Alps, did not kill Italian dissent, although the Catholic Reformation was to emphasize uniformity and frustrate sectarianism. After the Council, the Venetian Republic became, in a sense, a sounding-board for secular reaction to religious reform. The Republic had been conscious of the weakness of her hold on those outlying parts of her dominions most susceptible to protestant influence since Agnadello, and the *Ragion di Stato* — almost a religion of patriotic allegiance — dictated a particular kind of political function, even to Venetian ecclesiastics appointed to posts on her frontiers. On one hand the political cohesion of religious uniformity (piety apart) made Venice a devout ally of the Catholic Reformation, since sedition and heresy, using the same channels, were easily identified in Venetian minds:[1] but on the other, the interests of the state required suspicion of initiatives by Spain in Italy since 1559, and by the Pope as the ruler of a foreign state. Thus areas of conflict between the Catholic Reformation and the Venetian Reason of State in the first twenty years of the application of the Council's decrees were likely to be two: the impetus for reform began in Rome, and was directed through Spanish Milan in the person of Carlo Borromeo; and conformity was to be enforced from Rome by the activities of the Holy Office from 1542. Brescia, as we have seen, was potential theatre for such conflicts for two reasons. First, as a buffer city on the Venetian frontier, she would be the first region to fall under Milanese domination if religious reformation brought Spanish influence. Secondly, she was susceptible to heretical influences from her open northern valleys, and had become, already before the Council, something of a centre for heresy.

In this situation had lain at least one important reason for the appointment of Domenico Bollani, a tried government servant, to the bishopric of Brescia, and it was to be an important side of his activity in the diocese. We have seen him acting 'diplomatically' in his efforts to implement the decrees of the Council in Brescia, but it should not be forgotten that Venice also required him to *be* a diplomat: to further the secular aims of the republic in disputes with Rome. Not only does this evidence further demonstrate the breadth of Bollani's ability, but it also weaves the pattern in minor incident and susceptibility of Venice's growing distrust of Rome. It is perhaps an early chapter in the story that ends with the Interdict.

The measure of Venetian susceptibility in this respect, and a reflection of the situation which confronted Bollani throughout his bishopric almost continuously, is given by an incident in Brescia in November, 1565, on the passage of Borromeo through Brescia, which has not yet been fully told according to available sources.[2] Bollani was called on to resolve a problem of great delicacy — in perhaps his first experience of such disputes as a prince of the church. As the incident foreshadows

Bollani's diplomatic function in Brescia as a Venetian agent, it deserves full consideration.

Soon after the close of the Council of Trent, the Pope had entrusted to Borromeo a diplomatic mission of some importance: he was to journey to Trent to conduct the Archduchesses Barbara and Giovanna, daughters of the Emperor Maximilian, to Florence where they were to marry the Duke Alfonso D'Este of Ferrara and Francesco dei Medici respectively.[3] The conditions of his commission make it clear that his mission was far from solely diplomatic, however. He was also to investigate and examine those parts of his archdiocese through which he passed, and carried full powers to correct any divergencies from recently-established tridentine law. The first stop on his journey was Brescia, and the events which occurred there make it clear that he had taken this authoritative function seriously.[4]

Borromeo arrived in Brescia on November 16, 1565, being met by Bollani and Girolamo Morosini, the Venetian Captain, some two miles outside the city, and by Corner and Sfondrato, bishops of Bergamo and Cremona at the gates. The first Provincial Council had just concluded, and the protagonists had returned to their dioceses to put the decrees into practice. Borromeo was perhaps at the height of his intellectual power, though relatively inexperienced, as yet, in the jurisdictional susceptibilities of Spain and Venice. His influence, supported by his uncle, Pope Pius IV (who was to die shortly after this event), could never have been greater, and his confidence was indomitable.

At a dinner the same evening, to which the Venetian rectors of Brescia had been invited, a disputation occurred which recalls the *Notti Vaticane* in Rome, and evokes, too the spirit of free discussion conveyed by Paruta's imaginary discussion *Della Perfettione della Vita Politica*. But the main speakers were all Venetian except Borromeo in this case. The discussion ranged over philosophical and literary subjects,[5] and dealt with the interpretation of certain passages in the scriptures, notably, the place of Faith and Works in the Christian life: 'Et disse il podestà {Francesco Tagliapietra} che chi haveva vera fede conveniva necessariamente bene operare et che la vera Chiesa cattolica era la congregatione dei buoni cristiani, dicendo anco altre parole che non ho' così tutte a memoria in risposta di quello che ragionavano detti Prelati.'[6]

After the event, almost everyone was agreed that this had been rather a proposition for the sake of argument than a statement of personal belief, but it touched a nerve in the delicate constitution of the Catholic establishment in the person of Borromeo. The next morning at six o'clock, Bollani and Corner had already been in touch with Borromeo, and had succeeded only with difficulty in preventing him from making a formal denunciation of heresy against the *Podestà:* having expelled all servants from the chamber, there occurred a conversation which Morosini reported in these terms:

'{Bollani} cominciò a dire che il cardinale non haveva mai dormito quella notte, et che era tutto affannato et voleva ispedire un corriere a Roma a Sua Santità et un altro al Legato di Venetia, nè pero diceva la ragione. Pure io {Gerolamo Morosini} 'non poteva contenermi che non le dicessi: che cosa è questa? che vogliono riferire queste parole? Concludete Monsignore? All'hora disse il Rev.mo di Bergamo: horsu signor Podestà, voglio io parlar liberamente: siamo tutti Gentihuomini Venetiani et Figliuoli di quella religiosa Repubblica. Il Cardinale { Borromeo } ha havuto a male quelle parole che voi diceste a tavola et vuole darne conto a Roma et a Venetia et per questa causa è levato alle X hora et voleva all'hora ispedire doi corrieri et partirsi. Habbiamo operato assai { per } tenerlo, sino che vi parliamo et per rimediare andò ad un altro inconveniente dicendo che il Cardinale voleva ordinare che andando il Podestà le fusse detto che era occupato et che non fusse admesso, che questo sarebbe di gran murmuratione nella città. Et continuando con parole efficaci disse: bisogna risolversi di soddisfar al Cardinale, altrimente veggo gran fuoco contro voi { Tagliapietra } perchè ha fatto notare tutti gli casi che havete detto con testimonii solo per mandarli a Roma. Sarà bene che andiamo al Cardinale et dirle che sete cattolico et obbediente alle chiesa et così venirete a dirle, ma advertite che non basta stare sopra i generali di chiesa cattolica, che è forza che dicciate d'assentire et essere ubidiente alla chiesa Romana con molte altre parole. Il che udendo, io rimasi stupido. Et il Podestà rispose al Rev.mo Vescovo: Questa è una strana cosa et massimamente a me che ho dell'entrate sopra quello di Ravenna. Quelle cose che ho detto sono tutte colle auttorità della Scrittura Sacra, et dell'Evangelio et ho sempre parlato gratia disputandi essendo anco invitato et provocato con altre parole. Il Vescovo di Bergamo continovava dicendo che havevano fatto ogni officio, per acquetare questo moto, et che laudava se acquetasse: Il Podestà disse: farò quello che mi consigliarete et le fu replicato quasi il medemo detto di sopra, dicendo che andarebbero al Cardinale et come fusse l'hora, lo mandarebbero a chiamare. Et così partorno restando il Podestà et io soli, et poco dopo egli fu chiamato.'[7]

The episode shows the sensitivity of the Catholic Reformation to any suspicion of contravention of the dogmas recently confirmed by the Council of Trent. It illustrates the vast ground covered by the movement in a comparatively short time. A discussion of Justification by Works might have entered freely into conversations of 1530s — one of those many free discussions of broad issues which characterised the literary Renaissance in Italy — or might not have sounded strange from the lips of Gasparo Contarini at the time of Regensburg. But the phrases cited tell their own tale. Justification by Faith *and* Works, the 'double justification', had been accepted by Contarini in his *Epistola de Justificatione*,[8] yet was denounced by Caraffa in 1541, and condemned by the Council of Trent. The Council had also outlawed Luther's priesthood of all believers in a quite unequivocal way. At a distance of just two years from the close of the Council, it is not hard to see how Tagliapietra's statements must have impinged on the feverish reforming sensibility of the young Borromeo. The significance of the episode for us here is that not only was such free discussion now outlawed by the new agressiveness of the impetus for reform from Rome and Milan, but that this aggression was susceptible of a political interpretation in Venetian eyes.

The circumstances of the fateful interview were graphically described by Morosini: the Venetian rectors grew impatient at being kept waiting; Bollani ran back and forth from them to Borromeo, concerned to choose the most propitious moment. Finally Tagliapietra agreed to a prepared statement read to him which covered the controversial points in his statements the previous evening, 'Io no dico all'incontro, anzi laudo et bene,'[9] and Borromeo departed from Brescia to resume his journey to Trent and Rome.

Understandably, the episode left an unsavoury taste in many mouths then, as it does now, for we have seen that there had already been tension between Borromeo and Venice in the delay in publication of the decrees of the first Provincial Council. In her prohibition of the publication of an indulgence, Venice had also implied that Borromeo was 'suditto di Principe forestiero,' which was not calculated to facilitate his work as Apostolic Visitor of the dioceses of Brescia and Bergamo. But to ascribe a 'political' motivation to Borromeo in an attack on the Venetian representative in Brescia as a reprisal or show of strength, seems to do less than justice to the dedication and singleness of purpose of the Cardinal of Milan.[10] Through the many jurisdictional disputes of the period, there is no evidence that Borromeo ever specifically protested to the Venetian Republic.[11] On the other hand, the traditional view of Tagliapietra as naturally loquacious and impetuous is now supported by Bollani's description of him as 'alquanto più loquace di che bisognarebbe, che questa et non altra tendo essere la sua infermità.' Apparently Tagliapietra had been understandably chastened by the experience which 'l'haveva morcata da vero, et {insegnatolo?} il tacere.'[12]

In the present context, the episode is a backcloth for Bollani's future preoccupations in Brescia, and foreshadows his function as arbiter in such disputes. Firstly, the event produced significant echoes in Rome and Venice, and became a talking-point in Brescia itself. In his report of his Brescian experience, Tagliapietra suggested that he may have been victimised by enemies in the city,[13] and Bollani reported the reaction of Brescia in his letter to Borromeo.[14] As this previously unknown source also documents the strength of reaction in Venice, it will deserve close attention.

It appears that Borromeo had perhaps considered proceeding with the imputation of heresy, unless, as Cistellini has suggested, the request for the statement of Tagliapietra was a threat to encourage Brescian participation in the reform movement. He had written to Bollani within days of his departure from Brescia, from Rome, asking him for the papers containing Tagliapietra's answers to the questions put to him. Bollani's reply was to enclose these ('che restarono sopra la tavola del mio studio'), but impressed secrecy on Borromeo. He justified this by describing the furore the affair had caused in Brescia: 'perocchè essendosi qua divulgata per ogni cantine di Brescia et non senza qualche solita morsicatura contra di me che io habbia addetto el pottestà che si presenta la persona del prencipe a fare, come questi bresciani la vogliono chiamare, una abiuratione.'[15]

Venice, on the other hand, had dispatched a patrician of importance, Alvise Mocenigo,[16] to Brescia, who had demanded to know from Bollani whether the interests of the Venetian State had been threatened in the person of its representatives, and particularly what records of the event had been taken by Borromeo.[17] Clearly, the incident could well have developed into an international quarrel of the type we shall see again, had Bollani not managed to pacify the disputants. To

Mocenigo's questions, Bollani replied in terms which do not betray the facts, but paint Borromeo's role in the episode as possibly more lenient than it was: 'col voler ancho credere che nel dirle non vi fusse stata mala voluntà di fare ad esso {Tagliapietra} lui quel charitativo ufficio che fece . . .' The three Venetian civil authorities in Brescia now forgathered with Bollani to discuss what action was to be taken. It is again significant that the decision to report the episode to the Council of X — that stronghold of Venetian patriotic sensibilities — was taken in case the news should reach them by other means.

In his letter, Bollani attempted to block any further action on the part of Borromeo or the Roman Inquisition by subtly hinting that Borromeo would never embark on a policy of alienation of the Venetian Republic, counselling silence, and diverting the argument into the more acceptable channel of the officially constituted Inquisition in Brescia. Thus Bollani drew an implied parallel between legality and autocracy: the constituted court of the Brescian Inquisition was the body to stamp out heresy by legal means; the after-dinner chatter of a garrulous magistrate was no matter for the Church. The experience of a life-time emerges from this use of tact and subtlety. Bollani even managed to suggest that the rectors themselves would be instrumental in promoting the activities of the Holy Office.[18]

Bollani's role as pacifier is here sharply delineated. His letter to Borromeo betrays a keen sense of duty in a delicate situation. He explained fully the action taken to his superior, and complied with the request for vital evidence. But between the lines, the mature tactician advised the younger and less experienced diplomat how best all parties might be satisfied: the necessity of not exaggerating a trivial incident, and of not alienating Venetian opinion, (for which he personally would have to answer) — potentially essential to the progress of Tridentine reform in Brescia. Mocenigo for Venice, Borromeo for the Inquisition, and Tagliapietra for himself — all three must have been well-satisfied with his conduct of the affair.

'così pero ancho che come questi miei bresciani havevano un pezzo di ciò raggionato nel modo che loro pare, s'acqueteranno, et fra tanto lo passerò il tutto consolatamente, essendo io ben averso alle detrattioni et croci, come ben sa Vra. Ill.ma Sig.ria . . .'[19]

The affair of the dinner in Brescia in 1565 is symptomatic of the tensions existing between the Inquisition based on, and directed by, Rome, and Venetian reluctance to concede papal jurisdiction over her subjects. There is no evidence to suggest that Venice was herself lukewarm in facilitating the eradication of heresy — on the contrary, she was well aware of the political advantages accruing from uniformity of religious practice — but there are areas of common ground in jurisdiction where she was sometimes sensitive of her own prerogatives, to the point, on occasions, of being overtly obstructionist. One such area was the carrying out of the death penalty on convicted heretics. This sentence would be carried out by the 'braccio secolare', and was fertile soil for minor disputes. Another, perhaps, was the influence exerted by Venetian Rectors in heresy trials. In the period 1565–1568 there were a number of incidents of this kind, insignificant in themselves, but amounting to a significant trend cumulatively.[20] Domenico Bollani, of course, was liable to be centrally placed in such matters, having a foot in both camps.

By 1566, Venice had managed to secure the participation of her representatives in the work of the Inquisition,[21] and it may be that their influence sometimes impeded its work. In the case of the two relapsed heretics, Stefano Planerio and Artoldo Francese, the persistent obstruction of the policy of the Inquisition by a succession of rectors of Brescia was a thorn in the side of the Papacy for fully ten years. As Bollani was, in a sense, the cause of the dispute, it is worth consideration.

Stefano Planerio had been tried for heresy about 1556, and condemned to be burned in 1558–9, when Domenico Bollani was *Podestà* of Brescia. According to current procedure, the man was handed over to Bollani for sentence, but, for reasons we may only conjecture — humanitarian, legal or, perhaps, political motives — Bollani wrote to Facchinetti, the Nuncio in Venice, requesting permission to be excused this disagreeable task.[22] The Nuncio's reply at that time (reported much later) suggests that his motives may not have been free from that jurisdictional susceptibility which coloured many contemporary events. Bollani may not have been the only Venetian rector whose obduracy contained an element of resentment at the civil authority having to carry out the dirty work of the Inquisition. Bollani and his successors no doubt felt that their image (not always immaculate) of justice and mercy, as representatives of the Venetian Republic, was not served by the public burning of a man over seventy, however deviant his religious views. The Nuncio had replied:

'Io gli risposi che nelle attioni nostre si dovevano considerare la voluntà et la pottestà, che se bene essi volevano usar gratia et clemenza verso costui non però era in facolta loro di farlo, perchè i giudici et prencipi temporali senz'haver risguardo alcuno erano obbligati a far morir gli heretici che erano rimessi da gli ecclesiastici al braccio loro secolare . . .'[23]

In the light of later dispatches of the Nuncio in Venice, it appears that Bollani's action had set a powerful precedent for future rectors. Between 1558 and 1566, a total of eight Venetian rectors had been demonstrably reluctant to carry out the execution,[24] taking upon themselves that responsibility, to avoid, perhaps, the accompanying unwelcome image, until Francesco Tagliapietra (whose own orthodoxy, by a stroke of irony, had been recently challenged) was faced with the problem. By this time, pressure was building up from Rome through the channel of the Nuncio in Venice to expedite the sentence.[25] Tagliapietra wrote fully, and at tedious length on the problem to the Chiefs of the X on July 26, 1566,[26] but before this, a variety of initiatives had been taken by the Inquisition. On June 6, the Venetian Inquisition inquired of its opposite number in Brescia why the sentences had not been carried out.[27] Bollani replied on behalf of himself and the Brescian inquisitor in terms which show a fine appreciation of the legal problem. He explained that both judicial bodies — the inquisition and the secular arm — had carried out their functions correctly, but implied that the function of the former was to sentence, and that of the latter was to carry out sentence, reserving the right to commute or alter that sentence:

> 'et io Vescovo habbiamo desiderato d'intender dalli Clmi. Rettori, che qua si sono trovati per Tempora ciò che si fa intorno ad altre essecutioni contra essi rei, ci hanno risposto moversi a pietà nel differir loro l'ultimo supplicio della morte, trovando come le loro Sig.rie Cl.me dicono, che per la informatione che pigliano di continuo, et che da essi stessi rei gli è fatto dire, essi mostrano qualche pentimento delli suoi errori, et che gli dimandano qualche miseri-cordia, anzi in particolare il Francese gia supplica di poter esser rialdito { ? } per esser sententiato in contumacia con proferirse di voler giustificare che quando fu ritenuto veneva per {   } fatta supplicatione; *Il Rev.do Padre Inquisitore, et io habbiamo sempre risposto alle loro Cl.me Sig.rie ch'l santo Officio per quel che pertiene a esso, ha fatto quanto può, et che'l restante tocca al brazzo secolare* . . .'[28] (Italics mine)

The point is a fine one. For Bollani omitted to mention here that the attitude of the rectors derived in origin from his own actions in 1558—9, and we shall see that he undoubtedly encouraged them to defer the executions. A week later, the rectors themselve were also asking the Council of X for a clear brief in the matter.[29]

Tagliapietra's letter of July 26 illustrates the difficulties of the case and demon-strates Bollani's involvement. He quotes the decision to delay execution of the *Podestà* of Brescia, Lorenzo da Mula in 1562—63, apparently much moved by the plight of the penitent octogenarian. For the other heretic, Francese, 'pareva pur che non fussero così bene giustificate le imputationi et colpe sue, et oltra di questo, essendogli stata ritrovata adesso una scrittura quando fu retenuto, per la quale supplicava la S.tà { Santa } Inquisitione che dovesse udire delle ragioni sue, Mons. Rev.mo nro { Bollani } stava con l'animo molto sospeso, et li pareva dover' havere la coscienza sua aggravata quando costui dovesse morire . . .'[30] Tagliapietra further complained that 'ne pare cosa dura esser rimproverati, che non l'habbia esseguito quello che non sentiva ne Mons. Rev.mo { Bollani } ne 'l Padre In-quisitore.'

This represents a significant departure from the legal position as described by the Nuncio: Bollani's original doubts as rector had been followed by a succession of rectors and were now expressed in his new function as a participant in the Brescian Inquisition. In this case, he had carried the Inquisitor with him. There followed requests for full documentation of the facts from the Nuncio in Venice, and as these were forwarded directly to Cardinal Francesco Gambara in Rome as a member of the central inquisition, it is hardly surprising that renewed requests were to come from that quarter to carry out the execution of Planerio.[31] By now, however, the susceptibilities of the Republic were fully engaged. The Nuncio's reports show his insistence that Venice should reach a resoltuion on the matter, and document the Republic's conspicuous failure to do so.[32]

The dispute was settled by the usual series of compromises. The precendent set by Bollani's example as rector in 1558—9 had had a durable influence on the senators, as, of the 26 members of the *Collegio*, several had been rectors of Brescia, 'i quali stimano che vi vada dell' honor loro per non haver fatto morir costui . . .'[33] Finally the formula reached was that only a spontaneous request for confession and communion should save the man's life. He should be put to death in the absence of this. In any case he was to remain in prison.[34] The Nuncio appended a report on ways of dealing with Venice when she might show reluctance to act with zeal and effectiveness in the eradication of heresy:

> 'che questi signori nelle materie d'heresie faranno sempre quello che N{ostro} S{ignore}si risolverà di volere, ma bisogna parlare in modo all'ambasciatore {di Venezia in Roma} che non possa sperare che S. B.ne s'habbia da mutare; la quale se si mostrasse anco di sentir dispiacere, per l'affettione che porta a questi signori, che diano occasione tal'hora col modo di proceder loro a gli altri popoli di credere che non siano quei religiosi et catholici che poi sono in effetti, saria come io credo sempre a proposito perchè veramente, per esser molti al governo, hanno bisogno di sprone, ma con quel zelo carità et prudenza che S. B.ne sa usare.'[35]

In the end Planerio was to eke out his last days in prison, having complied with the demands of the Inquisition in the form of penitence. In the light of past events, however, it may not be out of place to suspect some hint of Venetian subterfuge even in this final chapter: 'dico che N.S. à restato sodisfatto del successo di quel relapso di Brescia, poichè si è voluto confessare et communicare come ella scrive con molta contritione, *benchè si ricercava in simil atto la presentia del padre inquisitore ancora.*' (Italics mine).[36]

It may be that a year later Rome had become conscious of Bollani's readiness to compromise. The rectors of Brescia had been asked to speak to him in 1567 on a matter concerning the Inquisition, and Bollani had replied that he would write directly to Cardinal Alessandrino in Rome. By May, 1568, this was certainly true. Bollani had received specific orders from Borromeo to retain and imprison Don Lucio Martinengo, brother of Count Camillo Martinengo da Barco. In the attempt to reconcile both demands on his conscience, he complied precisely with the instruction, but referred the information to his compatriot, Gasparo Renier, the *Podestà.*[37] Such a compromise always involved some sacrifice however. The Pope himself had transmitted his orders to Bollani, that Borromeo was to be obeyed 'con uno Breve da Sua Santità nel quale ad esso Rev.mo Episcopo che ad instantia della Santa Inquisitione et per estirpar le heresie *debbi operar con vero effetto et segreto* quanto esso Ill.mo Borromeo gli dirà . . .' which contains an element of reproof. But Renier also noted that Bollani 'l'haveva mandato a chiamare et eseguito il tutto *del che haveva voluto dar notitia a me.*' Not for the last time would Bollani's solution involve a lapse of confidentiality.

These events had tried Bollani's loyalties and shown the conflict possible between his duty to Venice and that to the authority of the Pope and the Inquisition. They were only a hint of things to come, however, as the years 1568–1569 saw the differences between Venice and Rome notably sharpened. Bollani faced severe tests at the time of the *Bolla in Coena Domini.* For Brescia,

the above tensions perhaps had two results within the sphere of the Inquisition:
Rome attempted to tighten her control over its affairs in the city, and Bollani fell
out with the Inquisitor.

The difficulties in Brescia were shared in varying degree in other parts of the
Venetian Terraferma. Since this moment at the end of the 1560s is significant for
Bollani in a polarization of jurisdictional interests in the diocese, it is appropriate
to set his experience for those years against the background of other parts of the
Terraferma. For virtually all bishops, imbued with a personal sense of the *Ragion
di Stato*, were in the habit of referring information received from the Pope and
the Inquisitor to the local rectors for transmission to, and approval of, the Council
of X. They consistently delayed carrying out orders from Rome so that this
permission could first be obtained.[38] When it was not forthcoming, they found
themselves sometimes in the most desperate plight. We shall have occasion to
compare Bollani's actions under such stress with those of similar circumstances of
Agostino Valier, bishop of Verona, and Matteo Priuli bishop of Vicenza, both of
whom were faced with this problem in 1568–9.[39]

It is quite clear that the initiatives of the Inquisition in Venetian dominions in
1568–9 show mounting anxiety — probably because of the inefficacy of local bodies in stamping out heresy — and possibly also as a result of Venetian obstruc-
tionism. At this point, the Inquisition seemed to be making efforts to free itself
from Venetian participation and surveillance of its working, as these privileges were
based on pre-tridentine decisions. Individual bishops were asked for reports of the
success of their local branches of the Holy Office,[40] and some were also asked to hand
over to the Inquisitor himself the papers of the body.[41] Further, a papal decree of
1569 described elaborate legal protection for the Inquisitors themselves.[42] All this
was to come to a head, so to speak, in the revival of the *Bolla in Coena Domini*,
but possibly some causes of the need for legislation and definition in the eyes of
the Papacy were attitudes prevalent in those Venetian bishops that we shall now
examine and compare.[43]

It seems that the request from Rome to hand over to the Inquisitor all papers
relating to the Holy Office had come first to Domenico Bollani in Brescia. His
reply to the message of displeasure passed on from the rectors shows the difficulties into which he was thrown by this situation, and documents his attempt to
serve two masters. He emerges as a very conscientious Venetian agent:

'Non havendo io mai stimata alcuna cosa piu, doppo la gratia del Sig. Dio et la
salute della mia anima ch'l viver et morire buon cittadino della mia carissima et
amatissima patria, da me per si lungo tempo, et in tante occasioni, cosi in
questo come in altro habito, servito sempre fidelissimo et sincerissimamente;
confesso che mi è stato pur troppo grave il sentire cio quasi metter in dubio
con lettere di quel Ill.mo Consiglio lettemi da questi Cl.mi rettori, per le quali,
in risposta del buon et sincero ufficio per me con loro fatto, come rappresentante la Ser.ta Vra. circa l'ordine venutomi sotto censure ecclesiastiche da Sua
Santita ch'io dovessi subitamente metter in mani di questo inquisitor le scritture della Santa Inquisitione, mi dicono l'Ill.me Sig.e Vre. che oltre la suddetta

communicatione dovevo ancho metter tempo a ubbidire si efficace comandamento . . .'[44]

Bollani requested the protection of the Republic in this, describing the duplicity of the Inquisitor who had become his enemy after Bollani had refused to grant the benefice of the church at Calvisano to the Inquisitor's brother, who, 'ne fu per ogni rispetto conosciuto indegno.' The following week, the rectors reported further moves and complications. The Inquisitor had complained to 'Il suo Rev.do Priore' (sent to enquire about the progress of the Inquisition in Brescia)[45] that the position vis-a-vis the documents was unsatisfactory, administratively inconvenient and possibly dangerous. Bollani's view was that the attitude of the Inquisitor was a facade, concealing the wish for complete control over the workings of the Inquisition.

By March, 1569, the affair had reached a stalemate position. Bollani had received further instructions from Rome to hand over the documents to the Inquisitor, and was again faced with conflicting orders. The Council of X, jealous of ancient privileges (expressed through Venetian bishops in the Episcopal Inquisition before 1542), and anxious to retain control of judicial measures taken against her subjects for heresy, ordered him not to allow them to be removed. On the other hand, the Cardinal of Pisa, president of the Roman Inquisition, had specifically ordered him to hand them over, 'onde che ha mostrato Sua Signoria Rev.ma esser in assai travaglio per la intimazione che da noi rettori gli fu fatta contrario a nome di quell'Ill.mo Consiglio.'[46] Bollani's view remained that the whole affair had been caused by the personal ambition of the Inquisitor 'per farsi tenere come capo principale nel maneggio di questa santo Tribunale, et che'l vescovo gli fosse come assessore.'[47] He had by now managed to convince the rectors of the truth of this, as they wrote warmly of his fidelity to the Venetian State in the episode.[48]

It may well be that the cause of the dispute was to be found in local ambition, according to Bollani's assessment. If so,[49] it struck a chord in Venetian jurisdictional susceptibilities, and had repercussions throughout the Terraferma. Venetian rectors at once received instructions that, if a similar request was received from Rome, they were to delay action, and the rectors acknowledged these instructions.[50] Perhaps reflected in the Brescian dispute — rooted fundamentally in personal antipathies — is the extreme delicacy of relations between Venice and Rome. Perhaps the Brescian Inquisitor, in his attempt to save himself the journey from the monastery where he lived to the bishop's palace, and to add prestige to his function in the city, had succeeded in stirring up a hornet's nest.

There were many types of conflict possible during the crucial years 1568–1569, that will form part of the history of jurisdictional conflict in Venice and Rome.[51] Bollani's personal plight in the above situation may be usefully compared, for our present purposes, with that of his compatriots in Verona and Vicenza,[52] in incidents which bring out their attitudes. Within two months of Bollani's confession that he was caught between the opposing forces of Papal and Venetian instructions, Agostino Valier found himself in a similar position. It is hardly possible here to enquire into the background of the affair,[53] but it is clear that Valier had been

210

criticised for his actions both by Venice and Rome. He complained that Venice had criticised him 'perchè io habbi fatto intendere alli Padri di S. Zorzi de questa città che mi aspettassero per il giorno seguente {havendo a} ragionar con essi nel loro capitolo.' Valier stated that his express intention had always been to serve equally well God, the Pope and the Republic of Venice:

> 'voglio rengratiar il nostro Sig. Dio che non attendendo io ad oltro che al servitio di S{ua} D{ivina} Maestà et alla satisfattione di quell'Ill.mo D{ominio} . . .'[54]

and lamented bitterly the fact that his actions had been criticised by both sides ('negligentia et di fredezza nel eseguir li ordini di quella Santa Sede'). His double loyalty was protested as Bollani's had always been, and it is interesting to find that he specifically recognises the difficulties of his compatriots in Venetian bishoprics:

> 'VV. SS. Ill.me si degnino tenermi per quel figliolo et servitor ch'io son di quella Ill.ma Repubblica: degnandosi appresso haver compassione non solo a me ma a tutti gli altri vescovi di questo Dominio, dandoci qualche lume quel che habbiamo a rispondere in simili casi.'

Possibly Matteo Priuli in Vicenza was made of less durable material than Bollani and Valier.[55] His reply to the Chiefs of the X was written two days before Valier's, its subject is similar, leading to the hypothesis that they were written in response to a general admonition from Rome. However this may be, Priuli's letter is a desperate plea, and illustrates the very tangible difficulties of a Venetian bishop in this moment of minor crisis. He feared far-reaching consequences as a result of the dispute, 'ond'io, trovandomi confuso, et temendo qualche repentina disgratia, alla quale io non sia bastevole provedere, con vergogna e danno forse anche di Casa mia e di miei fratelli.'[56] Like Bollani and Valier, Priuli protested his loyalty to the Serenissima; he noted that his liaison with the rectors had always been close; but thought that his position was different to that of other Venetian Bishops (remembering, perhaps, the recent attempt on the life of Agostino Valier):

> 'Supplico però humilmente la serenità Vostra degnarsi di considerar il mio stato facendolo differente da quello di tutti gl'altri vescovi del Dominio e protegermi, se possibile, che io non sia del tutto escluso dalla gratia di S. S{ereni}ta. Il che spero fara, se pensara solamente questo, cioe: quanto S. B.ne voglia esser obedita da suoi ministri et esser io nell'istesso grado, che sonno questi Cl.mo Rettori con V. Ser.ta da i quali la vole esser obbedita. Ond'io, che pur sopra modo desidero servir alla S{ereni}ta Vostra et Dio col pericolo della propria vita mi vedo molto confuso . . .'

In spite of Priuli's confusion, the dilemma of all three was succinctly put: perhaps without Bollani's skill and experience in negotiation and compromise, the future looked bleak for a Venetian bishop caught between rival demands of religious duty and patriotic conscience. Significantly, Priuli offered to resign his see if required to by the Republic as Bollani was later to do.[57]

From the evidence discussed it is possible to perceive the difficulties and problems facing the Church in Venetian dominions in the first decade after the closure of the Council. The new powers for bishops in the realisation of reform initiatives were still hedged about by the specific demands of Venetian patriotic duty, and those just as specific from the Pope through his Nuncio in Venice. Heresy provided fertile soil for disputes between these jurisdictions. Venice had won participation for her rectors in the work of the tribunals before the Council, and was understandably reluctant to relinquish this. So the rectors and bishops were constantly asked to report fully on local cases — both to Venice and Rome — as each side spied warily on the activities of the other, and the organisation of the inquisition at local level was a matter often at issue. Other delicate problems were the *brazzo secolare* in heresy cases, the immunity of inquisitors and clerics, and countless minor problems. From the evidence of surviving documentation, there seems to have been an increasing pressure of such disputes in the period 1568–9, with requests for information, reports, admonitions and conflicting orders culminating in the winter of 1569.[58] It can be no accident, therefore, that the order from the Venetian government forbidding publication in her dominions of the *Bolla in Coena Domini* was dated April 22, 1569.[59]

The Bull had already had a somewhat chequered history by 1569 and the objections to its new form raised storms of protest not only in Venice.[60] But Venetian objections to the new clauses were based on very specific principles. The affair constituted a confrontation and a climax to the events we have just described — events which may have played no small part in causing this stiffening in the Papal attitude.[61]

On April 20, 1568, the Bull with its new additions — directed principally against areas of disputed jurisdiction between the lay and ecclesiastical authorities — began to be distributed to bishops in their dioceses, who were to make its contents known. Excommunication was now the price to pay for any appeal to a Council against Papal authority. Greater protection for ecclesiastics was to be provided by prohibition of lay adjudication of crimes by ecclesiastics, regardless of any Papal privileges or concessions claimed in the past.[62] Perhaps most importantly for Venice, the Bull attacked (at least in the eyes of the Republic's ambassador in Rome) the state's right to tax her own subjects — lay and ecclesiastical alike.[63]

Venice protested energetically through Paolo Tiepolo, her ambassador in Rome, and Cardinal Grimani. Even the new ambassador, Michele Surian, failed to make any impression. And precisely the same objections were being received in Rome from Spain.[64] When Rome demanded to know in what specific ways Venice felt the *Ragion di Stato* was being compromised, Venice instructed her ambassador to keep the discussion to general terms,[65] and the repeated insistence of the Papal Nuncio in *Collegio* failed for long to obtain any clarification of this.[66] By March, 1570, the Nuncio in Venice was receiving instructions to urge Venice to unite with Spain and the Pope against the Turkish threat.[67] Right up to the eve of the Cyprus war in 1570, the polemic continued with unabated heat,[68] and it was only

212

when necessity brought a temporary union of Venice, Spain and the Papacy, that a short respite was enjoyed.[69]

After the dissolution of the League, the dispute over the publication of the Bull *In Coena Domini* continued as if nothing had interrupted it. Compromises were reached, however, which allowed relative stability in relations between Rome and Venice, for this, as we have seen, was the constant practice of the Republic (with her agent, Bollani, in Brescia), and of the Pope (with his agent, the Nuncio, in Venice). Looking back over the dispute in his 'relation' of Venice in later years, the Nuncio Bolognetti showed a masterly understanding of Venice's posture, an appreciation of Venice's difficulties over the controversial clause concerning the taxation of ecclesiastics, and an accurate expression of the readiness to find compromise solutions by both sides.[70]

Among the attempts to find a compromise solution, Bolognetti described that by which the Bull should simply not be published in places where it aroused passionate opposition.[71] Alternatively, it might be published in Latin and not generally distributed in a diocese, fulfilling the outward form of Roman directives, but causing a minimum of embarassment to the temporal authority.[72] But before such a compromise had been reached — as happened in 1575 when a motion of the Council of X lessened the possibility of a bishop being subject to conflicting orders — it is clear that the affair had assumed the proportions of a minor crisis. Two episodes document this, showing again that brand of 'compromise diplomacy' that Bollani and his colleagues in Venetian bishoprics were using.

An episode in Verona demonstrates the identity of the policies of Bollani and Valier in disputes between Church and State. Bolognetti complained that Valier had leaked information about his instructions for the Bull to the Venetian rectors of Verona: 'Vero è che ultimamente[73] i rettori di Verona, quando scrissi la di questo {certainly to Agostino Valier}, procurorno di haver copia della mia lettera, la mandorno subito per corriero a S. Ser.ta la qual poi insieme con quei Signori di Collegio si dolsero meco ch'io havessi dato tal ordine senza farne nota ad essi signori, et senza scrivere prima a Roma la dispositione della Signoria intorno a questo.'[74] Bollani too had done the same in 1578, when fresh orders to publish the Bull had arrived from Borromeo.[75]

The affair has special significance for Domenico Bollani, for it refers his 'political primacy' among Venetian bishops to the year 1575. In 1580, in the course of a heated discussion in *Collegio* of the issues raised by the accusations levelled against the Archbishop Michiel, the Doge Niccolò da Ponte quoted the case of Domenico Bollani, the Bull *In Coena Domini*, and Pope Gregory XIII, as an example of connivance, conciliation and accommodation, which the Holy See and the Republic of Venice would do well to emulate. Leonardo Donà had observed:

'Se ben i sacri canoni in alcuna cose disponeno ad un modo, non di manco pro bono pacis dal Papa, che ha la omnipotentia sono alle volte dispensate, et conniventibus oculis vengono tollerate alcune cose ad instantia delli principi per causa della quiete et tranquillita universale, per non sempre si osserva il rigor de canoni, ma quando si ha il troncon et la midolla della religione et buona volontà d'un principe come si ha di questa Repubblica, si può condonar qualche cosa pro bono pacis, come ho detto.'

To this the Doge Niccolò da Ponte added the example of Domenico Bollani:

'Sua S.ta ha anco fatto con un nostro vescovo, tanto più lo può fare con la Rep.ca, perchè essendo andato a Roma il vescovo di Brescia { Bollani in 1575} di buona memoria, parlando con Sua Santità in proposito della bolla in Coena Domini le disse, che desiderava renontiar il vescovato, perchè non poteva obedir la S.tà Sua senza incorrer in contumacia con la sua patria, il Papa a punto oculis conniventibus li diede libertà per le assolutione . . .'[76]

Since Bollani's audience with Gregory XIII in 1575, it seems fairly clear that he had become one of the chief spokesmen in the debate on the Bull.[77] Perhaps his gesture had represented the difficulty of the Venetian situation to the Pope; at least it must have left no doubt of the troubled consciences of Venetian bishops. As Matteo Priuli had done in Vicenza, Bollani was prepared to resign his bishopric over this issue, and his action had produced a workable compromise. Moreover, as we have seen, the case was a precedent in the way of concession at this point in Veneto-Papal relations, to be used five years later by the Doge as fuel for his argument with the Nuncio. Further, the episode is entirely characteristic of Domenico Bollani's methods — and of his philosophy. Had he been alive and in *Collegio* in 1580 at the time of the above conversation, he would have endorsed the view of his compatriots in every way. His own life demonstrates the efficacy of negotiation and compromise. His views on the possibility of agreement, on the finding of common ground in dispute — so firmly established in his experience on the banks of the Oglio — brought him to a position of pre-eminence in the eyes of the Venetian government in these last four years of his life.[78] As a member of a *casa vecchia*, such views were not incompatible with those of Niccolò da Ponte, Leonardo Donà, and later, Niccolò Contarini, his contemporaries from *giovani* families, and demonstrate that, in times when the security and health of the Republic were at stake, all pulled together to find a compromise solution to serious problems.[79]

Some indication of the esteem in which Bollani was held by the Venetian government is also provided by this stage in the debate over the Bull *In Coena Domini*. Like Valier, Bollani had also received new orders about its publication in July, 1578. Like him, too, he relayed the information at once to the rectors of Brescia, Giovanni Soranzo and Alvise Grimani, who duly reported to the Council of X on July 23.[80] Apparently the matter was complicated in Brescia by local events connected with the restrictions on absolution promulgated in the Bull.[81] The reply of the Council contained fulsome praise of Bollani's actions — indicating, perhaps, the primacy that he now enjoyed among Venetian bishops — and the motion received 25 votes for, none against, with one *non sincero* in its reading in the Council of X and *Zonta*.[82] The body found no need to do more than endorse the action already taken by Bollani.[83]

On April 22, 1575, Gregory XIII deputed Carlo Borromeo to visit the dioceses

214

of Bergamo and Brescia in the Republic's dominions, together with other dioceses in his sphere, as Apostolic Visitor.[84] There is no evidence to show that Venice ever objected to the visit in principle — as indeed it was never to be an issue of principle when the Republic herself was to be visited — but the proposal naturally excited much interest and speculation.[85] The Visit of Borromeo to Bergamo had been attended by predictable Venetian interest, and the rectors, Gabriele Corner and Antonio Memmo were warned to keep a close watch on their distinguished Visitor, noting particularly anything that could be construed as prejudicial to Venetian interests in the province, any difficulties in connection with the application of the Bull *In Coena Domini*, and also in the complex question of the control over Bergamasque hospitals claimed by the Cardinal.[86] They were, however, to receive him with due reverence and honour. In Brescia, the projected visitation caused much speculation, and was not, in fact, carried out until after Bollani's death, in 1580. Echoes of this speculation may be found in many of the documents which have survived in this period.[87] For we have seen that Borromeo's last visit to Brescia in 1565 had not been in entirely happy circumstances,[88] and that important political reasons had induced Bollani to prevent him from visiting the city during the plague.[89]

News of the projected visit first reached Brescia in June, 1575, when Bollani informed the rectors, who had also received it from the Jesuits.[90] At this time, Bollani was preparing to leave for Rome and his audience *ad limina* with the Pope. Venice certainly did not want Borromeo to visit Brescia when Bollani was not there to protect her interests, so Bollani managed to persuade Borromeo to defer his visit until his return. Bollani described his success in this to the Council of X with his customary diplomacy, evading the question of the protection of Venetian interests, but stressing the necessity of providing Borromeo with an appropriately honourable escort.[91] Having convinced the Council that Borromeo would not leave before his return, he left for Rome on September 1, 1575, for his all-important interview with Pope Gregory.[92]

On Bollani's return, he was armed with new powers, having obtained the dispensation discussed above. This, however, was shrouded in a veil of secrecy and could hardly be used against Borromeo's actions in the diocese, should the Cardinal wish to legislate in Brescia on matters covered by the Bull *In Coena Domini*. The fears of the Republic were ably summarised by the rectors of Brescia in June, 1579 (by which time the projected visit was again on the cards). They noted that difficulties over the Bull had not occurred in Brescia precisely because of the dispensation granted to Bollani in 1575, but now that Borromeo was coming to inspect the diocese, trouble might be caused in those key areas covered by clauses in the Bull which Venice had found unacceptable:

'ma perchè il cardinale in alcune cose contenute nella bolla in coena domini intorno la immunità de preti dalli datti et altro non ritrovera che le cose passino qui secondo il desiderio suo, ne tampoco che le costituioni delli suoi sinodi provinciali, nelle quali s'intende pur esserne alcune che intaccano l'ordinaria iurisdittione temporale, habbino quella esecutione che egli potrebbe ricercare ch'havessero in queste parti.'[93]

They also had occasion to note a characteristic of Borromeo's which we have contrasted with Bollani's diplomatic formation: his intransigence and inability to negotiate:

> 'Et a questi si aggiunge che per esser il cardinale nelle sue opinioni così costante, che con gran difficoltà suol dar luogo al parere de gli altri, il negociar seco per quanto { intendiamo } riesce sempre opera assai difficile.'[94]

So Bollani could not make use of his papal dispensation, as this had been granted to him 'sotto profondo silentio.' The rectors forsaw possible difficulties during the visit to the Scuole, monasteries and hospitals which claimed independent status.

The Council of X in Venice must have discussed the matter in detail on June 10, 1579, and praised Bollani's action in informing them with such speed. They were resigned to the visit in principle, but fearful in case 'il cardinale con quella sua severità potesse causar qualche moto d'importantia.' They hoped that above all the visit might proceed quietly, but resolved to request its deferral through the Venetian Ambassador in Rome.[95] By the beginning of August, both the discussions in the Council and the reports of the Nuncio show mounting concern for Bollani's health, as his last illness had by that time taken a firm hold.[96] Even when Borromeo had travelled to Brescia to assist Bollani on his deathbed in the second week in August, the Council was still concerned in case he might begin the Visitation of the diocese.[97]

These preoccupations were to continue in the following months — almost to the eve of Borromeo's Apostolic Visitation in Brescia in 1580.[98] But Bollani had died on August 12, and so the controversy was deprived of his diplomatic talents.

The episode and its aftermath show the absolute trust in Domenico Bollani of the Republic in matters of dispute between Church and State. He had been the one to pioneer a compromise in the disputed application of the Bull *In Coena Domini*, possibly finding a satisfactory remedy to satisfy the consciences of other Venetian bishops[99] — at least in the mind of the Doge Niccolò da Ponte. It was a cruel stroke of ill fortune that his death removed the possibility of his bringing the affair to its logical conclusion: a successful outcome for Borromeo's visit to Brescia.[100]

We have suggested that Bollani's reputation and prestige as a mediator and pacifier in disputes between Venice and Rome was at no time higher than during the last four years of his life. During these years (1575–1579) he was deeply involved in one further major area of controversy: the collection of the Decima del Clero conceded by the Pope in the 1570s. This episode will show him at the height of his powers, and will go some way towards defining his political stance, his standpoint in the Catholic Reformation, and the principles on which his life had been based. The all-important key to this latter question is provided by his relationship with the Papal Nuncio in Venice, Alberto Bolognetti.

Documents relating to the collection of the *Decime del Clero* are widely scattered among Venetian sources.[101] The background to the dispute in which Bollani was involved during the period 1575–1579[102] goes back to the Cyprus war in 1570, when a 100,000 ducat *sussidio* was granted to Venice by the Pope as a contribution towards the expenses of war against the Turks.[103] This was to be raised by a tax on Venetian clerics imposed for one year in 1570,[104] and renewed for a further five years in 1571.[105] The chief problems were the difficulties in the collection of such a tax, and the classic problem of exemptions, as Domenico Bollani himself had noted in his *decima* return of 1564 from Brescia.[106] It seems that by mid-March, 1570, the plan in Rome was that Giovanni Dolfin, bishop of Torcello,[107] and Daniel Barbaro, Patriarch-elect of Aquileia, were to be deputed to collect the tax, which was to be levied on the real value of benefices. There were to be no exemptions, except that the mendicant orders were to pay half.[108]

As a result of the inevitable strain placed on the Venentian economy after the battle of Lepanto, the Republic was naturally anxious to recoup losses, particularly as only 80,000 of the original 100,000 ducats conceded had been collected. There was long discussion in the College in Venice in 1574 of the question of *decima* or *sussidio*; and the advantages of each system to the Republic. It was claimed that the *sussidio* involved a more equable distribution of the load, as not subject to the classic exemptions – particularly Cardinals. It is difficult indeed to assess the justice of such claims, particularly in the light of what follows, but the Nuncio, Giovanni Battista Castagna was clearly concerned to reach an acceptable compromise with the Republic in details. Not least among his preoccupations was the thought that Venice might take it upon herself to tax ecclesiastics, in contravention of the Bull *In Coena Domini*. Moreover, Venice was in urgent need of financial assistance, and continually pressed her claims to expenses on the Pope for the costly upkeep of forces in Candia.[109]

The continuing threat from the Turks was a strong argument when the Doge, Alvise Mocenigo, took the Nuncio to task in *Collegio* on collection methods employed in the past. Castagna reported this conversation to the Pope on December 18, noting that the Republic preferred the *sussidio* 'perchè la summa è più certa, manco esenti, et manco difficultà,' and added that Venice was particularly anxious to get back some three years of arrears.[110] But most importantly, perhaps, the Nuncio enclosed a sheet by which he intended to show sample yields for one *decima* from monasteries, convents and bishoprics throughout the Venetian *Terraferma.*[111]

It appears that the first major difficulty arose out of the decision by the Pope to exempt both Cardinals and the religious orders. Venice complained that in the past only one of these categories had been exempt.[112] Not without justice, it seems, the Doge complained in the College to the Nuncio that 'facendosi queste esenzioni, tutto il peso del sussidio viene a restar sopra i poveri,' and reiterated the claims of Venetian forces in Candia, increased since Lepanto from 300 to 6,000 men. The Nuncio, for his part, took the opportunity to request a note of the value of benefices of Venetian Cardinals.[113] By early February, the *Collegio* was still pressing for a contribution from Cardinals, having employed the Venetian Ambassador in Rome to this end. When this failed, the Doge complained to the Nuncio in a long argument on February 4, and resolved not to accept the concession in this form.[114]

Meanwhile the Papal brief was published nominating Domenico Bollani and Federico Corner, bishop of Bergamo as collectors, on September 23, 1575, and

Bollani's arrival was expected in Venice by mid-October.[115] The first report of the three collectors (the Nuncio, too, was named) was dispatched to Rome on November 26. They resolved to point out to the Pope some of the difficulties in the task ahead, particularly that, with the expenses of collection and exemptions deducted, they would need to impose a *sussidio* of 3½ *decime* on the clergy to realise the required sum. This evaluation was based on the value of the 1564 *decime*, and they predicted that it would arouse a storm of protest. The only alternative seemed a completely new tax, 'argumentando il valore già tassato {1564} et attribuito alli frutti.' They also observed that it would be difficult to collect in any case at the end of 1575, with benefices for that year already committed.[116]

At the same time, Domenico Bollani was negotiating independently with the *Serenissima* from a commanding political position in Venice. It may be that the subject was his recent interview with Gregory XIII over the Bull *In Coena Domini*, and the problems of conscience of Venetian bishops in the Republic's dominions. However that may be, he was clearly at the centre of any discussion of relations between Venice and Rome by the autumn of 1575.[117]

Throughout the winter of 1576, minor problems of taxation were discussed, and the collection continued,[118] until, during the week preceding March 24, the Nuncio reported that Bollani and Corner had returned to Brescia and Bergamo.[119] Before Bollani left Venice, however, there are indications that again point to his special relationship as a negotiating channel between the Pope and Venice.[120] But almost as soon as the collectors had departed, serious difficulties arose in the collection of the *Sussidio*, particularly, perhaps, in the diocese of Verona. A long letter to the bishop, Agostino Valier, setting out the complaints of the Veronese clergy, was approved in a congregation of clergy on April 4, 1576. They complained of exemptions, local difficulties, injustice by comparison with the relatively fertile Padovano and Bresciano, and the growing threat of plague. Agostino Valier himself summarised the problems in an eloquent letter to the Council of X.[121]

Valier hoped that the collectors might use their authority to sweep away all pre-existing structures to institute an entirely new tax, and declared himself ready to concede to them that authority which had been conceded to him (for collection from the clergy of Verona) by the Pope. In doing so, he perhaps took up a 'Venetian' stance in regard to the Bull *In Coena Domini* which even Bollani had not overtly expressed:

> 'potranno in questo caso le SS. VV. Ill.mi {Council of X} risponder che SS. SS.rie RR.me {the collectors} usino della loro auttorità et faccino una nova tassa, che per me restero contento di cederli tutta quella pottestà, che mi fosse stata data in ciò dalla sede apostolica . . .'[122]

By the time Valier wrote this letter, the plague was making its presence felt in northern Italy, complicating and aggravating the already complex task of collecting the tax. Again, Bollani was the object of special attention and favour by the Papacy, as the Nuncio reported, in the summer of 1577, that the Venetian government was pressing for urgent collection of the tax, but that he had special orders from Rome not to 'molest' the plague-torn diocese of Brescia. It will be remembered that the Republic, too, had advaced a loan to the city at this terrible time.[123] In his letter to the Council of X, Valier expressed the hope that one of the collectors might be deputed to give special and sympathetic consideration to the case of the Veronese clergy. On the evidence so far adduced, it is now predictable that this was to be Domenico Bollani.[124]

Bollani replied personally to Valier's letter of April 4 on 17 of that month, justifying the procedure adopted by the collectors in a situation where natural, jurisdictional and economic factors had combined to render the tax almost impossible to collect.[125] Ironically, some six months later, he was to address a personal plea to the Pope, requesting personal relief from the tax[126]— a request which was clearly sympathetically received, given his 'special' position in the eyes of the Papacy at this time: 'V. S. Ill.ma resti sicura che al sudetto Mons. {di Brescia} non solo non si farà aggravio, ma la sua persona sara tenuta in quel rispetto ch'ella commanda.'[127]

It falls outside the present scope to follow successive events in the exaction of the *sussidio* from the clergy in the Venetian *Terraferma*. For Domenico Bollani, the episode documents a growing power and significance. From 1577 until his death, he became the central authority on matters pertaining to Church and State jurisdiction in Venice, and the remaining events of his life serve to reinforce his prestige.

From 1577, Alberto Bolognetti was the Papal Nuncio resident in Venice. Bollani had had to convince him of the justice of his claim to special consideration for tax relief, and of the real value of his benefice, as Bolognetti justly observed that relief 'aprirebbe la strada di pretendere esentioni de simili benefici.' But this was no doubt settled by the summer of 1578, when Bollani was again anxious to return to Venice to take up the cause of the *sussidio* — and that central bargaining position we have seen for 1577.[128] Bollani was in Venice from September, 1578[129] until shortly before his death in August the following year, and developed an enduring relationship of mutual esteem and trust with the Nuncio Bolognetti during that time. He was in a position now to advise both the Republic and the Nuncio on the best way to solve differences, and was politically active in ways consistent with the breadth of his experience.

The first example of this was the suggestion that Venice might send an accredited ambassador to the court of Elizabeth I of England — contested by the Nuncio on behalf of the Pope for obvious reasons. In July 1578, Bolognetti had already expressed concern, reflecting that the Grand Duke of Tuscany would probably follow the Venetian example. He feared too that, if an ambassador was not sent, Elizabeth might treat with someone 'che fosse heretico scoperto.' Meanwhile, Bollani was at work introducing the new Nuncio to the complexities of the *sussidio del clero*.[130] In November, Bollani had sent Bolognetti information about the ambassador which was the beginning of a secret correspondence between them, in which information was systematically 'leaked' from the *Collegio* to the Pope's representative by Domenico Bollani:

'Uno di quelli co' quali ho ragionato intormo a questa prattica di mandar
Amb.re in Inghilterra e stato Mons. Rev.mo di Brescia, che fu gia Amb.re
residente presso a quella corona in tempo del Re Odoardo,[131] il quale hoggi
ancora m'ha mandato a confermare il medesimo per una sua poliza, nella quale
usa queste precise parole: Potra V. S. dar quasi total sicurezza a S. Bne che non
si fara intorno a cio altra deliberatione. So che alle volte si resta ingannato in
simil cose dal creder troppo; nondimeno credo che Mons. si guardaria molto
bene di scrivere una cosa tale, massime contentandosi d'esserne fatto auttore,
se ben mi prega a mandar subito al fuoco la poliza sua.'[132]

Bolognetti's judgement was certainly accurate: Bollani would not have laid himself open to charges of disloyalty to the Republic had he not been sure of his
ground. His influence and central bargaining position emerge clearly from the
event — the more so since he had been approached by the Grand Duke of Tuscany
to favour the sending of a Venetian ambassador to Elizabeth.[133]

This point, in November 1578, perhaps marks the high point in Bollani's usefulness and influence in the cause of the unity of Roman and Venetian initiatives.
With a lifetime of experience of bargaining and compromise behind him, he was
prepared to use all methods in his power — and the present ones recall certain
devices employed in the cause of Brescian pretensions on the banks of the Oglio —
to bring together these two great preoccupations of his life: the greatness of the
Republic of Venice and the advancement of the reformed Catholic Church.
Having accomplished much in the diocese of Brescia with his own Venetian brand
of reforming statecraft, he had come home to Venice at the end of his life in an
attempt to aid the reconciliation of these two ideals on a broader canvas. A
conversation he held with Alberto Bolognetti towards the end of November,
1578, expresses perfectly the sincerity of his belief in such a union, the position in
his mind of these two mainsprings of all his activity, and the unity — rather than
duality — of his philosophy:

'Mons. il Vescovo di Brescia . . . et hieri ancora mi replico il medesimo che
havendo sempre l'occhio al servitio di S {ua} S {erenità} et al beneficio di questa
Sante Sede, et conoscendo che questo consisteva principalmente nell'unione
del Sommo Pontefice con questa Serenissima Repubblica et nel credersi ancora
che tal unione veramente vi fosse, sentiva molto dispiacere che il mondo
potesse far congiettura del contrario dal vedere che ne l'Ambasciatore costi
{Rome} andasse in Capella, ne qui {Venice} il Nuntio andasse col Prencipe ai
luoghi pubblici, et che pero nell'occasione di questa sua venuta a Vinetia,
haveva fatto offitti sopra cio con molti gentilhuomini, persuadendosi di farne
cosa grata a Nostro Signore {Gregory XIII} perche intendeva che Sua Santita
ne trattava costi con l'Ambasciatore {di Vinezia}. La conchiusione del
ragionamento fu, che io ne scrivessi a V. S. Ill.ma per intender se a Sua Santita
occorreva dargli sopra ciò avvertimento alcuno particulare per facilitare
l'effetto di questa sua buona intentione. Ho voluto riferire a V. S. Ill.ma quasi
le parole istesse dettemi da Monsignore perche possa meglio far giuditio et
ordinarmi quanto havro da rispondere. S. S. Rev.ma mi ha pregato che io voglia

scrivere appartatamente a V. S. Ill.ma a stracciar subito questa carta, accio non capiti alle mani d'alcuno altro.'[134]

By August 1579, news had arrived in Venice from Brescia that Bollani was seriously ill. The Republic was naturally concerned at losing one of its most trusted servants, but worried also in case the bishopric might go to someone less trustworthy than Bollani. The rectors of Brescia, Leonardo Donà and Francesco Duodo, were instructed to convey the sympathy of the Council of X to Bollani, and to ask him to name a successor.[135] The Nuncio in Venice had also received the news, and noted that Francesco Longo, Bollani's brother-in-law, had departed hurriedly for Brescia. He probably took with him Antonio Bollani, Domenico's second nephew, as he had been Antonio's guardian since the death of Giacomo Bollani in 1568. The Nuncio further noted that among the candidates for the bishopric, 'oltre i Cardinali di Venezia et Mons. vescovo di Torcelli, intendo che concorreranno anco il Procurator Barbaro, il Cav. Michiel, il S. Francesco Longo et il { Leonardo } Donato, Podestà di Brescia . . .'[136] In this list may be seen the story of the Brescian bishopric: Longo was Bollani's close relative, member of the Council of X, and by association, had been in close touch with Veneto-Roman relations; Donà was the future Doge, and a member of a *giovane* family. The political necessity of a trusted diplomat (whatever his precise orientation within the Venetian caste system), reflects again the function Bollani had fulfilled for so long at the outpost of the Venetian empire.

A few days later, Bollani's illness had become 'una dispositione di qualche importantia,' when the Council of X wrote to the Venetian ambassador in Rome about the bishopric of Brescia. He was instructed to represent the importance of Brescia to the Pope in the usual way, that the successor should be Venetian, 'diligente et bono' as Bollani had been.[137] On June 10, Borromeo was already at Bollani's bedside, and the Nuncio reported from the Longo household in Venice that his stomach would no longer take food. In this state Bollani lingered for fully two days, before dying at 11 a.m. on Wednesday, August 12, 1579, assisted by Borromeo and the members of his immediate family.

'Scrissi di poi anco in conformita per le lettere di sabato come {   } Mons. { Bollani } andava declinando a poco a poco non potendo lo stomaco contener cibo d'alcuna sorte, in tal termine si è trattenuto il povero prelato sino a mercoledi mattina a XI hore, in qual tempo passò a' miglior vita lasciando nome di prelato molto essemplare et intelligente, massime nelle cose di stato.'[138]

On that note — and with an epitaph whose accuracy the preceding pages have attempted to demonstrate — it is appropriate to end this account.

1 Certainly not without a certain justification. For example, we have seen the case of Baldassare Altieri, who used diplomatic immunity for religious ends in Venice (*NCMH*, II, pp. 262–263). Milanese designs on Bergamo and Brescia had been real enough in 1547, when the governor had clear designs in this direction (*Storia di Milano*, IV, pp. 253–254).

2 Contemporary documents on this key episode for the future of the Inquisition in Brescia are three. Girolamo Morosini, Captain of Brescia, reported the incident in a long report to the Council of X on December 1, 1565 in response to a specific request from them (ASV, *Capi, Consiglio dei X, busta* 22, doc. 153). The *Relazione* of 1567 of the *Podestà*, Francesco Tagliapietra, centrally implicated, contains a full report of the episode (pub. in Pasero, *Relazioni...*, *cit.*, pp. 110–111). The incident was first discussed by G. Soranzo in *Echi di San Carlo, cit.*, pp. 451–454, and again by A. Cistellini, 'La prima visita di San Carlo a Brescia,' in *Mem. Stor. Dioc. Brescia*, XV, (1948) pp. 9–18. Cistellini unaccountably described the episode as 'finora ignorato,' yet acknowledges Soranzo's account of some ten years earlier. Neither of these authors was aware of Domenico Bollani's letter to Borromeo of November 22, 1565 (*Carteggio cit.*), which internal evidence and date relate to the event beyond any shadow of doubt. This letter throws new light on the episode.

3 See the commission of Pius IV to Borromeo of Oct. 5, 1565 in Sala, *Documenti circa la vita... di San Carlo..., cit.*, p. 165, and the letter of introduction of Borromeo to Cosimo dei Medici, *Ibid.*, p. 166.

4 Cistellini, *op. cit.*, pp. 10–11.

5 For instance, there was some argument over whether Cicero had denied the immortality of the soul.

6 Report of Morosini *cit.*, Cistellini, *op. cit.*, p. 12, where, however, the passage is incorrectly quoted, without the word 'cattolica' (a not unimportant detail), and in Soranzo, *op. cit.*, p. 452, where the reading 'tutte' for 'tratte' is to be preferred.

7 Gerolamo Morosini, letter *cit.*, partly pub. in Cistellini, *op. cit.*, pp. 13–14, where some 29 errors of transcription should be corrected.

8 Quoted by A.G. Dickens, *The Counter-Reformation, cit.*, p. 105.

9 Morosini, letter *cit.* For the statement, see below, p. 317.

10 The theory was suggested by Cistellini, *op cit.*, p. 17.

11 Giovanni Soranzo, op. *cit.*, (fasc. XIII, April, 1938) p. 489.

12 Bollani to Borromeo, 22 November, 1565, *cit.*, (*Carteggio* Bollani-Borromeo, MSS f, 106, f. 206, *Biblioteca Ambrosiana*, Milan).

13 Pasero, *Relazioni..., cit.*, p. 111.

14 Immediately below.

15 Bollani – Borromeo, *cit.*

16 Described as 'P{rocura}tor' in the document. He had been the Venetian Ambassador in Rome in 1558, who had had wide experience of heresy cases in Venetian dominions, and was Doge of Venice 1570–1577. (Paschini, *Venezia a l'Inquisizione Romana*, cit., pp. 123, 126–138).

17 'et ciò che si era fatto di certa scrittura che gli fu letta, se fu rogata e come...' The anxiety was clearly directed at the possibility of the document being used as evidence by the Inquisition. Bollani had sent it secretly to Borromeo; he had assured Mocenigo that 'quanto alla scrittura io non sapevo che si fusse volsuto far altro che adunare insieme tutti li capi nelli quali havuto esso pottestà dato s▪andolo, et di essi haverne più secura sattisfattione...' Morosini had replied to the specific request of the Council of X that he had no knowledge of the document, that he thought Borromeo had taken it with him, but managed to learn its gist from the inquisitor for inclusion in his report. Bollani believed that no further action was to be taken (as he had informed Mocenigo) but he had not, of course, divulged the fact of having dispatched the paper to Borromeo. His use of subterfuge here in a conflict of loyalties is characteristic of him.

18 'Ho ancho detto che per il mio credere non sarebbe ne da Roma ne da altro loco fatto intorno questo alcuno moto per el benigno ufficio profferto da Lei, *la quale conosco amore-*

volissima a' ogni interesse di ciascun privato non che de questa religiosa repubblica; et che non vi era il più sicuro modo di tener ferma Vra. Ill.ma Sig.ia in si benigna premessa, et finalmente a sopire il tutto, che astenersi loro totalmente de parlare di simili materie de fede, con lasciar carico a' quelli che, come ella loro disse, sono chiamati a si fatta vocatione, et essi fra tanto ad ogni assiduo spirito attender a' congregarsi al tribunale della Santa inquisizione et perseguitare le iniqui et perfidi, se vi ne sono; *così ambi loro* {Francesco Tagliapietra and Gerolamo Morosini } *rettori affermavano di voler prontamente fare con haversi havuto ancho dato ordine di fare la congrega al meno una volta alla settimana . . .'* (Bollani to Borromeo, *cit.*, Italics mine).

19   *Ibid.* There is every reason to suppose that Francesco Taglipietra emerged unscathed. In his relation, he mentioned the good account given in Rome of his character (probably to the Pope via the Venetian ambassador), indicating that Borromeo had taken the matter up with Pius V. Subsequent documents containing no reference to him indicate that Bollani's estimate had been accurate, and his efforts successful.

20   For the background to heresy in Brescia in the sixteenth century, see bibliography above, p. 126, and particularly the fully documented account by Cistellini, 'Penetrazione e diffusione dell'eresia,' in *Storia di Brescia*, II, pp. 447–450. For what follows, some incidents are described in Soranzo, 'Rapporti di San Carlo . . .' in *Echi di San Carlo, cit.*, based on A.S.V. *Lettere di Rettori* (Brescia), *busta* 22. Important documents concerning the Inquisition were extracted from this source, however, to be replaced recently in A.S.V. *Santo Ufficio busta* 161 (1560–1569), which have not, I believe, been previously available to modern writers. (I am indebted to Professor Gaetano Cozzi for this information). Important in this context, too, are the reports of the Papal Nuncio in Venice in *Arch. Segr. Vat.*, Rome, (microfilms used in the *Fondazione Cini*, Venice), referred to as *Nunz. Ven.* For the period 1566–1569, the dispatches are published in Aldo Stella, (Ed.) *Nunziatura di Venezia*, VIII (Rome, 1963), which will be given the full title.

21   See Bollani's letter quoted above, and A.S.V., *Lettere di Rettori* (Brescia), *busta* 22, Rectors of Brescia to the Chiefs of the X, July 20, 1566. It appears that they attended the deliberations of the Brescian Inquisition two or three times a week. See also Soranzo, *op. cit.*, p. 454.

22   This information appears in a much later dispatch, when the affair had reached international proportions: Facchinetti to Bonelli, November 2, 1566 (*Nunziatura di Venezia*, VIII, p. 126).

23   *Ibid.*

24   This again appears from the later dispatch of the Nuncio, for which see below.

25   Facchinetti to Bonelli, July 6, 1566, in *Ibid.*, p. 71, where the Nuncio first reported progress to Rome.

26   A.S.V., *Lettere ai Rettori, busta cit.*, Rectors {but Tagliapietra } to the Chiefs of the X, July 26, 1566.

27   Deputies of the Inquisition of Venice to the same of Brescia, June 6, 1566 in *Ibid.* They had also sent the same request to the rectors Tagliapietra and Gussoni (*Ibid.*, dated July 9, 1566).

28   Bollani to the deputies of the Venetian Inquisition, July 12, 1566 (*Ibid.*).

29   Rectors of Brescia to the Chiefs of the X, July 20, 1566 (*Ibid.*).

30   Tagliapietra and Morosini to the Chiefs of the X, July 26, 1566 (*Ibid.*).

31   Facchinetti to Bonelli, August 31, 1566, *Nunziatura . . ., cit.*, p. 99. See also same to same, September 7, (*Ibid.*, p. 103). By the following week, the Nuncio hoped that the execution could be carried out secretly (September 14, *Ibid.*, p. 105), but discussions in *Collegio* had produced two contrary votes. By November 2, the Nuncio felt it desirable to relate the story of Bollani's involvement in full (*Ibid.*, p. 126, *cit.*) as the Republic had by now dug her heels in.

32   See those of November 16, 23, September 14, 1566 in *Nunziatura di Venezia, cit.*

33   Facchinetti to Bonelli, November 16, 1566, (*Ibid.*, p. 132).

34   Reported in Facchinetti to Bonelli, November 23, 1566, and same to same, November 30, in *Nunziatura . . ., cit.*, pp. 137, 139.

35   *Ibid.*, November 30, p. 139.

36   On December 13, 1566, the affair was still in the balance (A.S.V., *Santo Ufficio, busta* 161 rectors of Brescia to Chiefs of the X) but the conclusion was reported to Rome by the Nuncio in Venice on December 21, (*Nunziatura . . ., cit.*, p. 149, Bonelli in Rome to Facchinetti in Venice)

37   Gasparo Renier (*Podestà*) and Sebastiano Miani (Captain) to Venice, November 12, 1567, and Renier to Venice, May 10, 1568 (*Santo Ufficio, busta cit.*).

38   For example, the rectors of Padua had received orders from the Nuncio in Venice to capture one Gasparo Parma, a man eighty years of age, and a public figure in the city. They found it prudent to 'metter con buon modo tempo di mezo,' obtaining the consent of the Council of X before proceeding (A.S.V., *Santo Ufficio, loc. cit.*, Rectors of Padua to Venice, March 26, 1568). A similar case in Udine recalls the affair of Stefano Planerio in Brescia. After specific instructions from the Council, the heretic Ambrosio Tedesco was put to death in great secrecy, his body being smuggled out of the city for burial. Further, the *Luogotenente*, Francesco Venier, in the face of an imputation of heresy against the man's wife, secretly advised her to depart from Venetian dominions with all speed (*Luogotenente . . .*, to Venice, November 5, 1568, *Ibid.*). Similarly, Agostino Valier was at great pains to point out that he had only acted unilaterally in the capture of the heretic Pompeo Bagno after the most elaborate attempts to trace the Venetian rectors (Bishop of Verona to Venice, Nov. 26, 1568, *Ibid.*). In the most heart-rending attempt at self justification, Matteo Priuli spoke with pride of such delays, (see below, Appendix VII, doc. 3).

39   See immediately below.

40   Agostino Valier reported such a request from Cardinal Alessandrino, in particular 'se io havevo difficultà nelle cosa dell'Inquisitione . . .' (Valier to Council of X, November 26, 1568, *Ibid.*), and Priuli was reporting to Rome once a week through the Nuncio on his own admission (below, Appendix VII doc. 3).

41   At Brescia, Verona and Udine. See respectively, Domenico Bollani to Council of X, January 19, 1568, Rectors of Verona to same, January 17, 1569, and *Luogotenente . . .* to same, January 18, 1569 all in *Ibid.* (see below).

42   The text of this long document entitled 'Constitutione del Santiss. S. N. Papa Pio Quinto contra quelli che offendono il stato, cose et persone dell'off.o dell'Inquisitione dell'heresia,' dated April 1, 1569, is in A.S.V., *Santo Ufficio, loc. cit.* There is no reference to Venetian policies, of course, but only to the growth of heresy itself: 'crescendo adunque ogni giorno piu la forza di questi tali empii, li quali, con tutte le mali arti, tentano di ruinare il pte. off.o.'

43   It is not suggested that these were the only causes. Professor Stella wrote that conflicts due to jurisdictional disputes sharpened progressively after Trent, since the Republic had no intention of relinquishing privileges gained from Paul III and Clement VII, while the Papacy considered that these had been swept clean by the Council (*Chiesa a Stato nelle Relazioni dei Nunzi Pontifici a Venezia*, {Vatican city, 1964} pp. 5–7). This author was concerned primarily with attitudes within the patriciate and their possible polarity, and was not aware in 1964, as far as can be judged, of the collection of documents at present under discussion (A.S.V. *Santo Ufficio, buste* 161–162). On the polarization of views in the patriciate, and Bollani's political stance, see below, pp. 232–233.

44   Domenico Bollani to Council of X, January 19, 1569 (*Ibid.*, reproduced in full as doc. 1, Appendix VII). This interview with the rectors of Brescia, Gasparo Renier and Giacomo Emo, was described in detail by them in their dispatch to Venice on Jan. 17, (*Ibid.*) which, compared with Bollani's account gives an accurate record. However, Bollani had protested his loyalty to Venice to the rectors, adding that 'che voleva confidentemente dire {not respected, clearly} che questi frutti al presente con la baldezza grande che hanno del {?} Papa, fanno di poco buoni offitij et che in questa materia del consegnar esse scritture, gl'havevano fatto scriver in forma si efficace et sotto censure si strette {. . .} fosse stato ribelle di S.ta Chiesa, et che pero non puote far di meno senza metter tempo di meggio, de consegnargliele perchè altrimente detto Inquisitore diceva esser sforzato de scriver a Roma con il primo spazzo . . .'. The rectors had then interviewed the Inquisitor according to their instructions, and found him pliant and obedient to the wishes of the Republic, pleading his own illness and administrative inconvenience as reasons for the projected transfer of the documents. The Inquisitor agreed at this point to restore the documents to the bishop's palace, 'onde il tutto si tornara al suo loco

senza strepiti' (Rectors of Brescia to Venice, January 17, 1569. The relationship of this letter to Bollani's { above } refers Bollani's to Jan. 1569 {1568 *more veneto*}, or a slip of the pen that often accompanies January correspondence).

45   He advised the Inquisitor to keep the documents well guarded 'apresso lui, et che di ciò haveva anco esso Priore a darne aviso alla Santità Sua,' (reported in Rectors of Brescia to Venice, January 25, 1569, postscript by Captain Giacomo Emo, Jan, 26).

46   Same to same, March 15, 1569, *Ibid.*

47   *Ibid.*

48   'con la sicurezza che vedemo poter avere di esser dalla sincerità di questo Rev.mo vescovo in ogni caso avvisati { noi } di quel tutto che sia per venire a sua notitia, come di continuo costuma di fare con noi in tutto quello in che può conoscersi esser alcun interesse della dignità et ... della patria sua, da lui per tanti anni diligente et fedelmente servito ...' It is clear that the affair was still in the balance some six months later, when the rectors of Brescia reported a conversation with Bollani, in which they advised him not to publish the *Bolla in Coena Domini.* He had readily consented to this with characteristic adaptability 'non intendendo di mai partire dal volere et sodisfattione della patria sua.' He then returned to the subject of the *'scritture'* of the Inquisition, and reported that the Cardinal of Pisa had written again urging compliance with his previous order to pass them to the Inquisitor. The Rectors enclosed a copy of this to Venice (Rectors of Brescia to Chiefs of the X, September 24, 1569, encl.: Cardinal of Pisa to Domenico Bollani, September 3, 1569, in A.S.V., *Santo Ufficio, loc. cit.*).

49   If this move had not been prompted in some way by the Brescian situation (i.e. if it had been a general instruction to all Venetian Bishops from Rome), then Bollani's explanation of it in purely local terms hardly makes sense.

50   Udine (January 18, 1569), Verona (Jan. 17), Bergamo (Jan. 20), Vicenza (Jan. 17), Treviso (Jan. 16), Padua (ditto), all dispatches in A.S.V., *Santo Ufficio, loc. cit.*

51   For example, the dispute leading to the Interdict at Desenzano; disputed inheritances of heretics; the discovery of a cache of heretical books in the Veronese, condemned because printed in Geneva; and a dispute over the imprisonment of an ecclesiastic at Cividale (docs in *Ibid.*). This is not to suggest that there were not conspicuous examples of cooperation. The rectors wrote to Venice from Vicenza on January 6, 1569, reporting the successful conclusion of five heresy cases with their cooperation; and the rectors of the same city had written with pride of their part in the public abjuration of one Alessandro della Pace (Rectors of Vicenza to Venice, July 21, 1568, *Ibid.*).

52   This corpus of three letters to the Council of X from Domenico Bollani, Agostino Valier and Matteo Priuli, written between January and March, 1569, document the position of the Venetian bishop at this moment shortly before the crisis over the *Bolla in Coena Domini* was to erupt. They are therefore reproduced in full for the purposes of comparison below as Appendix VII.

53   There are at least three subjects of some controversy which emerge from the reports of the Nuncio in Venice during 1568–69: the affair of the interdict at Desenzano; cases of vacant benefices which Valier (like Bollani) planned to divert to the use of the seminary; and the aftermath (prosecution and trial) of the attempt on Valier's life, Details are likely to emerge from local research, and A.S.V. *Lettere ai Rettori, (Verona)* etc. See *Nunziatura . . ., cit., passim.*

54   Agostino Valier, bishop of Verona to Venice, March 20, 1569, A.S.V., *Santo Ufficio, loc. cit.*, (reproduced in full below Appendix VII, doc. 2).

55   It will be remembered that both Bollani and Valier had had considerable political experience – Bollani as a lay magistrate, and Valier in the suite of his uncle, Cardinal Navagero.

56   The Priuli family were a well-known Venetian ecclesiastical dynasty. (See Logan, *Studies in the Religious life . . .*, thesis, *cit.*, p. 527, and particularly the Priuli family tree, p. 254, where, on the above evidence, the tree needs some correction. Matteo (1528–1595) resigned his bishopric to his nephew Michele (1547–1607) in 1579.

57   'offerendomi sino a privarmi della Chiesa per suo servitio.' Matteo Priuli, bishop of Vicenza to Chiefs of the X, March 18, 1569, in A.S.V., *Santo Ufficio, loc. cit.*, reproduced below as doc. 3 Appendix VII. For Bollani's resignation, see below p. 214.

58 A good example of this was reflected in the attitude of the Nuncio on September 21, 1566 (Facchinetti to Bonelli, *Nunziatura . . ., cit.*, VIII, p. 111): 'conoscendo io che i vescovi hanno havuto tempo assai da essequire quanto sono obligati per lo Concilio di Trento, io sono d'opinione di scrivere a ciascuno d'essi domandandogli conto di tutti i capi del Concilio annotati nella inchiusa scrittura, parendomi che questo uffitio, oltre al servir quasi per visita, habbia a svegliare i negligenti et accender di piu quei ch'hanno fatto il debito loro . . .' Facchinetti also seemed to be reflecting the mood of stringency in his suggestion that 'l'usar una severa monitione contro qualch'uno di questi vescovi (in this case Valier) sarà un freno di contener gl'altri nei termini loro . . .' (Same to same July 21, 1568, *Ibid.*, p. 414), and see his comments on Venetian bishops quoted above, p. 208.

59 A.S.V., *Senato, Deliberazioni Roma Ordenarie*, II, p. 67, Soranzo, *op. cit.*, pp. 534—535; the Bull was first read on April 15, 1568 (Pastor, *History of the Popes*, XVIII (London, 1929) trans. Kerr, p. 35).

60 'l'opposizione assume anzi dovunque caratteri e manifestazioni pressocche uniformi, si da lasciar apparire che i governi degli stati si siano scambiati note.' (Soranzo, *op. cit.*, p. 587).

61 This is suggested, but not proved by Stella, *Chiesa e Stato . . .*, pp. 5—6. For the general nature of protest, see Soranzo, *op. cit.*, pp. 534—535. For a good modern bibliography on the Bull, see S. Tramontin, 'La figura del Vescovo . . .' *Studi Veneziani*, X (1968) p. 439, n. 73, and particularly, F. Claeys Bouaert, 'Bulle in Coena Domini,' in *Dict. de Droit Canonique*, II (Paris, 1937), *ad vocem.* The following article was too general to be of use here: M. Bendiscioli, 'La Bolla in Coena Domini e la sua pubblicazione a Milano nel 1568,' in *Archivio Storico Lombardo*, LIV (1927) pp. 381—399.

62 Pastor, *History of the Popes*, ed. *cit.*, XVIII, pp. 35—38, an extremely one-sided view, and for the text of the clauses added, *Ibid.*, App. 2, 3.

63 Romanin, *Storia di Venezia, cit.*, VI, pp. 255—258, and see the Nuncio's relation in Stella, *Chiesa e Stato . . ., cit.*, pp. 113—114.

64 Pastor, *op. cit.*, XVIII, pp. 36—70.

65 Soranzo, *op. cit.*, pp. 588 *et seq.*, quoting A.S.V., *Senato, Deliberazioni Roma, Ordin.*, dispatches of May 7 1569 to Jan. 20, 1570.

66 Arch. Segr. Vat., *Nunziatura di Venezia* (microfilmed in the Fondazione Cini, Venice), dispatches of the Nuncio of August 13, September 3, 7, 13, 24, 1569 etc.

67 Cardinal Alessandrino to the Nuncio, March 9, 1570, *Nunz. Ven.* On the difficulties of the alliance before Lepanto, see Pastor, *op. cit.*, XVIII, pp. 363—365, Soranzo, *op. cit.*, p. 589.

68 A. Stella, *Nunziatura . . ., cit.*, (preface) p. xii.

69 On the reasons for the speedy dissolution of the League, see M. Brunetti, 'La crisi della Sacra Lega, 1573,' in *Misc. in onore di Roberto Cessi*, (Rome, 1958), II, pp. 145—155.

70 I take issue quite fundamentally with the assessment of Bolognetti by Professor Stella in his *Chiesa e Stato . . .*, (*cit.*, almost *passim*, particularly p. 64). Far from a naive appreciation of the polarity of views in Church and State disputes in a patriciate torn by strife into *pro* and *contra* views of the Church, Bolognetti, like Bollani, was conscientiously striving for a union of aims, a closing of the gap, and a harnessing of Venetian opinion to the twin ideals of the greatness of the Venetian State and the success of the Catholic Reformation. We shall see this more clearly in the relationship between Bollani and Bolognetti, but in the present context, perhaps the Nuncio's description of the dispute over the Bull lays more serious claim to consideration than Professor Stella allows. (See the important review article by G. Benzoni, *Studi Veneziani*, VIII (1966) pp. 560—578, and G. Cozzi, *Niccolò Contarini . . ., cit.*, p. 38).

71 Bolognetti in Stella, *op. cit.*, p. 113.

72 *Ibid.*: 'dove conoscono che questa pubblicatione possa avere qualche difficultà, la facciano senza strepito con intimare la bolla ai confessori . . .' This is clearly a reference to the Venetian decision in 1575, to have the Bull published in Latin, 'et a tempo che niuno l'udirà ne advertirà; et fatto questo, li vescovi non possono essere imputati di mancar al loro debito . . .' (A.S.V. *Consiglio dei X, Roma*, 1, p. 59, in Tramontin, *op. cit.*, p. 439, n. 73.).

73 The episode is undated but refers to Bolognetti's own Nunciature (1578—1581), and may probably be dated 1578.

74 Bolognetti in Stella, *Chiesa e Stato . . ., cit.*, p. 113.

75 A.S.V., *Consiglio dei X, Libro primo da Roma*, Council of X to rectors of Brescia, July, 1578.
76 A.S.V., *Esposizioni Roma* (1580–1582), quoted by Stella, *op. cit.*, pp. 26–27, n. 31.
77 This further supported by the fact that Bollani had had secret audience with the Doge at this time (mentioned by the rectors in their dispatch to the Council of X, July 23, 1578, A.S.V., *Santo Ufficio, busta* 162).
78 1575–1579
79 See also below, p. 232 for discussion of the polarity of views on Church and State among the Venetian patriciate.
80 A.S.V. *Santo Ufficio, busta* 162, Rectors of Brescia to the Council of X, July 23, 1578.
81 'havendo l'arciprete delli Orzinuovi fatto certo moto in questo proposito, gli scrisse che'l si astenesse da qualunque moto in questa materia, et pur egli stando pertinace in non voler assolvere quelli che in quella terra scuodeno la masena et tasse di soldati, lo fece venir qui, et dopo molti officij, trovandolo saldissimo et fermo nella sudetta opinione di non dar essa assolutione, Sua S.ria Rev.ma { Bollani } mandò a posta nel detto luoco alcuni padri confessori, che sopplirono ad ogni bisogno.' (*Ibid.*)
82 A.S.V., *Consiglio dei X, Libro primo da Roma*, p. 142, motion in the Council to the rectors of Brescia, July, 1578.
83 The rectors were to thank Bollani 'con parole amorevoli et grate della continuata ottima volontà che dimostra verso le cose nostre, le diciate, che quanto questa materia possa apportare travaglio et dispiacere, tanto all'incontro ci deve dar soddisfattione et contento, la confidenza che potemo haver che S. S.ria R.da colla sua destrezza et prudentia, sapera divertir le cose che potriano esser cagione di scandalo, si come altre volte ha fatto, quando sono venute occasioni de simili moti, ben ricordevole di quanto altre volte ne referi haverle detto sua S{antit}a a medesima di propria bocca in questi propositi, { doubtless a reference to Bollani's report on what had been said to him by the Pope in 1575 } et ben certa, intentione della S{antit}a Sua non poter esser mai che si metta disturbo nelli governi temporali delli Principi liberi, et pero la pregarete a'voler operar colla solita destrezza et valor suo che le cose passimo con quella quiete . . .' (*Ibid.*) For an incident in Bergamo reflecting local difficulties analogous with Bollani's (and involving Bollani's brother-in-law, Francesco Longo, *Podestà*), see documents quoted by Soranzo, *op. cit.*, p. 636, n. 1.
84 A. Sala, *Documenti . . ., cit.*, I, pp. 303–306, A. Roncalli, *Atti della Visita . . . Bergamo, cit.*, p. 25, A.S.V., *Dispacci Residenti Milano*, IV (May 28, 1575), Ottaviano Maggi to the Senate, Soranzo, *op. cit.*, p. 591 etc.
85 Soranzo, *op. cit.*, p. 592.
86 A.S.V., *Libro primo da Roma, cit.*, Council of X to the rectors of Bergamo, June 22, 1575, in Roncalli, *Atti . . .*, pp. 32–33.
87 Borromeo to Bollani, August 1, 1575, Borromeo to Gambara, August 22, 1575, Borromeo to the Nuncio in Venice etc., in Sala *op. cit.*, pp. 621–622, 626–645, where Borromeo's plans are set out. See also A.S.V., *Consiglio dei X, Libro secondo da Roma*, (1579–1582) almost *passim*, and docs. in A.S.V., *Santo Ufficio, loc. cit.*, quoted below.
88 The episode of Francesco Tagliapietra, above, pp. 201–205.
89 Above, pp. 158–159.
90 A.S.V., *Santo Ufficio, busta* 162, Rectors of Brescia to the Council of X, June 10, 1575.
91 *Ibid.* Domenico Bollani to the Council of X, August 31, 1575 (signature only autograph).
92 'ella [the Doge] stia sicura che piu presto che mancare di darle questa sodisfattione di trovarme alla sudetta visita, sarei per pigliar ogni incomodo, come anco l'haver tralasciato . . .' (*Ibid.*).
93 *Ibid.* Rectors of Brescia to the Council of X, June 3, 1579.
94 *Ibid.*
95 A.S.V., *Consiglio dei X, Libro secondo da Roma*, the Council to the ambassador in Rome, and to the rectors of Brescia (both unanimous decisions gaining all 27 votes), June 10, 1579.
96 See below, p. 221.
97 *Ibid.*, Council of X to Rectors of Brescia, August 10, 1579: 'Et perchè, come voi sapete, l'Ill,mo Cardinal Borromeo è molto geloso, in certe cose che perturbano il governo temporale,

se ben volemo sperar, che essendo S. S.ria Ill.ma venuta de lî per sola visita del vescovo, et per raccomandarli l'anima, et non per metter mano in alcuna cosa di quel vescovato, non farà alcuna novità, pur quando lo volesse far, o come arcivescovo, o come visitatore . . .'

98 *Ibid.*, same to same throughout February, 1580. In March, the Council discussed controversial areas such as the Great Hospital in Brescia, its independence and freedom from scrutiny, and instructed the rectors that 'andiate temporando il rigor del cardinale siche si faccia quel minor moto, che sia possibile.' They also considered the possibility of a visit to the prison, under lay control. (same to same, March 5, 1580, *Ibid.*).

99 At the present stage of research, this is impossible to prove, but, given its use by the Doge as a precedent, seems likely.

100 For the opposition aroused by Borromeo's Visitation of the diocese of Brescia, see Soranzo, *op. cit.*, pp. 636–637. For the Visit itself, see the research of Paolo Guerrini: 'La Visita Apostolica di San Carlo Borromeo alla Diocesi di Brescia,' in *Brixia Sacra*, (1910) 'San Carlo e la diocesi di Brescia,' in *San Carlo nel terzo Centenario della Canonizzazione*, (Milan, 1910), and 'Il IV Centenario . . .' *cit.*, in *Mem. Stor. Dioc. Brescia*, 1938.

101 A.S.V., *Esposizioni Principi*, Ro. 3, dispatches from 1574; *Ibid.*, *Santo Ufficio*, *busta* 162, 1575–1577; but particularly Arch. Segr. Vat., *Nunziatura di Venezia*, correspondence between the Nuncios and Rome 1570–1579, which contains also autograph letters of Domenico Bollani and Agostino Valier.

102 Bollani was also in Venice for this purpose in 1572 (for which, see Fè D'Ostiani, *op. cit.*, pp. 70–71) but we are here concerned with the later stages in the affair.

103 *Ibid.*, also pp. 94–95, Morosini, *Storie . . .*, *cit.*, (1719) p. 570, Giustiniani, *Degli Istorici . . .*, *cit.*, p. 620, Cicogna, *loc. cit.*, etc.

104 A useful summary of previous concessions to Venice of *decime del clero* is the MS book in A.S.V., *Sopra le Decime del Clero*, Ro. 1. See also *Nunz. Ven.*, Nuncio to Rome, March 9, 1570.

105 *Ibid.*, same to same, June 7, 1571.

106 See below, Appendix V, p. 263.

107 Dolfin was to become bishop of Brescia on Bollani's death in 1579.

108 Cardinal Alessandrino in Rome to the Nuncio in Venice, March 15, 1570 (*Nunz. Ven.*, *cit.*).

109 *Ibid.*, the Nuncio to Rome, December 11, 1574.

110 A.S.V., *Esposizioni Principi,* Ro. 3, Report of the conversation of December 17, 1574. For the state of the Venetian economy after Lepanto, see A. Stella, 'La regolazione delle Pubbliche Entrate . . .' *cit.*, pp. 161–162.

111 *Nunz. Ven.*, Nuncio to Rome, December 18, 1574 and enclosures: The Nuncio gave comparative figures for the total yield from the *Terraferma* in 1536 and 1564. In the former year, one *decima* had been worth 32,000 ducats, in the latter, 47,000, although the loss of Cyprus and other factors reduced this to 40,000. In neither year had it been possible to make the full collection. He added that the Venetian *scudo* was worth slightly more than the Roman unit, and that the total yield from non-mendicant orders was 7780, and that from mendicant orders, 2006 (halved, so 1003). He had not been able to assess revenues from Cardinals, but appended the value of one *decima* in bishoprics, monasteries and convents throughout the *Terraferma* for example, Padua: 4485, Vicenza: 2812, Verona: 2152, Brescia: 2100, Bergamo: 1134, Treviso: 941 etc.). For Bollani's 1564 *decima del clero* return, see below, Appendix V.

112 *Ibid.*, Nuncio to Rome, January 29, 1575, A.S.V., *Esposizioni Principi* 3, January 14, 1575.

113 *Ibid.* The question of their exemption was further discussed on January 28 (*Ibid.*). Provided that their contribution was part of the total agreed figure, the Nuncio was prepared to agree, and wrote to Rome with this suggestion. In his reply, however, the Cardinal of Como was little inclined to favour it, and this news occasioned further heated discussion in *Collegio*.

114 *Nunz. Ven.*, the Nuncio's dispatches to Rome of February 4, 5, 1575, A.S.V., *Esposizioni . . .*, *cit.*

115 A printed copy of the brief (with subsequent additions) is in A.S.V., *Santo Ufficio*, *busta* 162. News of Bollani's arrival was reported in Collegio on October 14, (A.S.V.,

Esposizioni . . ., cit.), and see *Nunz. Ven.*, Nuncio to Rome, October 15, 1575.

116 Castagna, archbishop of Rossano, Bollani and Corner to Rome, November 26, 1575 (autograph signatures) in *Nunz. Ven.*: 'Onde noi la vedemo cosa quasi impossibile et piena di stridi et di ramarico (se ben io Nuntio per virtu di una lettera di V. S. Ill.ma ho gia mandato fuori il monitorio, et ordine che si paghi una Xma sola a buon conto secondo il tenore di detta lettera) restamo nondimeno sospesi di questi due primi intoppi.'

117 'Del negocio che'l Rev.mo Mons. di Brescia dice haver havuto ordine di trattare per parte di N.S. {Pope Gregory XIII} et che gia ne ha parlato in collegio secreto, io lassaro dar conto dal sudetto S. il quale è diligentissimo et piena di eloquentia et come non havera lassato cosa degna da dire, cosi non pretermettera di darne pienissimo ragguaglio.' (*Nunz. Ven.*, Nuncio to Rome, November 26, 1575).

118 Particularly the 5% traditionally exacted by the Holy See. and the question of whether the collectors themselves should be exempted, or paid a salary of 1,000 ducats a year (*Ibid.*, dispatches of January 14, February 16, March 24, 1576).

119 *Ibid.*, March 24, 1576.

120 'et circa Mons. di Brescia non mi sono scordato di quanto V.S. Ill.ma mi scrisse nella sua . . .' (*Ibid.*)

121 Verona was probably not exceptional. Its case is symptomatic of the difficulties in general, however, and a collection of documents (A.S.V., *Santo Ufficio, busta* 162) has survived concerning its difficulties in 1576–1577. See the three 'scritture del clero di Verona' dated April 4, 1576, June 6, 1576, and July 6, 1576, in *Ibid.*, enclosed with Agostino Valier to the Council of X, July 10, 1576.

122 *Ibid.*

123 *Nunz. Ven.*, Nuncio to Rome, September 7, 1577, and for complications arising from the soaring price of grain as a result of the plague, see also *Ibid.* same to same, September 28, 1577. Bollani was prevented by sequestration following the plague from returning at once to Venice, and negotiated from Brescia. See also the further 'scrittura' from the Veronese clergy forwarded with the Nuncio's dispatch of August 6, 1577.

124 *Ibid.*, September 28, 1577.

125 Domenico Bollani to Agostino Valier, April 17, 1577 (forwarded with the above) copy. The letter is a personal and intimate attempt to reconcile Valier to the decision of the collectors. Bollani had heard the claims of the Veronese clergy from a Veronese agent sent to him for this purpose before coming to his decision.

126 Domenico Bollani to the Cardinal of Como, October 1, 1577 (enclosed with the Nuncio's dispatch of that date, *Ibid.*

127 *Nunz. Ven.*, Nuncio to Rome, December 21, 1577. Bollani's claim was based on the suggestion that the real value of benefices had declined since 1564 (see that claim for that date, Appendix V, below) as was later reported by the Nuncio, now Alberto Bolognetti, on April 19, 1578, *Ibid.*

128 Bolognetti to Rome, April, 1578 (*Ibid.*): 'Pero io ho voluto dare conto a V.S. Ill.ma accio ci sara volonta di N. S. di *esimerlo con particolar privilegio per il merito et valore di quel signore* io possa esseguirlo con quella prontezza et humilta che debbo.' (Italics mine).

129 His arrival reported in *Ibid.* September 27, 1578.

130 *Ibid.*, July 26, November 15, 1578.

131 See above, Chapter II.

132 *Ibid.*, Nuncio to Rome, November 15, 1578.

133 MS note appended to the above in Bolognetti's own hand. Bollani had replied in a similar vein to the Grand Duke. Great stress was laid on secrecy: Bolognetti's note (with Bollani's implication) was to be destroyed on arrival. Further, the Nuncio calculated that in response to praise from Rome, Bollani would supply further secret information: 'credo certo che quando Mons. {Bollani} intenda per un verso ch'ella me ne tocchi nella risposta di questa, che la Santita di N. S. habbia havuto cari questi particolari, si movera tanto piu a communicarmi quello che intenda per avvenire.'

134 Reported by the Nuncio on November 29, 1578 (*Ibid.*). From this point, information from Bollani about the doings of the government was consistently reported by Bolognetti in manuscript notes appended to his reports. Bollani was suitably complimented on his informa-

tion from Rome (Nov., 1578); he passed news from Constantinople to the Nuncio (Dec., 1578); he was mentioned again: 'Mons. del vedersi nominato nelle lettere di Lei sente una consolatione troppo grande.' (Dec., 13, 1578). He was again instrumental in informing the Pope of the Turkish situation (Jan., 10, 1579) and passed on further news (Feb., 1. 1579). On March 4, 1579, the Nuncio reported that Bollani would be departing for Brescia the following week, having given an account of the *sussidio* in *Collegio*.
135   A.S.V., *Consiglio dei X, Secondo Libro da Roma*, Council of X to the rectors of Brescia, August 8, 1579. From his deathbed, Bollani had replied: 'che era cosa da considerarsi, et che vi pensaria,' but died without naming a successor (*Ibid.*, Council to the ambassador in Rome, August 14, 1579).
136   *Nunz. Ven.*, Nuncio to Rome, early August, 1579.
137   A.S.V., *Cons. dei X, Secondo libro da Roma*, Council of X to the ambassador in Rome, August 9–10, 1579, *Nunz. Ven.*, Nuncio to Rome, (undated) of about the same date.
138   *Ibid.* Nuncio to Rome, August 15, 1579.

CHAPTER X

CONCLUSION
CIVIL EXPERIENCE: ITS FUNCTION IN THE VENETIAN CHURCH
AFTER THE COUNCIL OF TRENT

Returning to Paolo Paruta, his *Della Perfettione della Vita Politica,* and the literary figure of Domenico Bollani, we are now in a position to attempt a definition of his stance in the post-tridentine Venetian Reformation, his place in the Venetian Patriciate, and to point some conclusions about the function of civil experience in the reformation of the Church in Venetian dominions in the sixteenth century. The compactness of Bollani's ideal, the unity of his inspiration and the constancy of his devotion to the twin ideals of Venetian greatness and Catholic Reformation are beyond doubt. When Bollani expressed his ideal of a Christian society and the shortfall of the Republic in his own day to the Nuncio in 1578, he may have voiced the views of many patricians of his generation. For many of his contemporaries who did not live to see the upheaval of the Venetian government in the early 1580s, which must have caused some polarisation of the patriciate, any division of his generation into *vecchi* and *giovani,* into *pro* and *contra* views of the Catholic Church, proposers and opposers of state freedom from Papal interference, would have seemed a false distinction. History is ever ready to see the division and polarity of the many in the surviving documentation of the few. Rather many patricians who had shared Bollani's problems and his experience of government were devout Catholics and devoted government servants. The experience of probing deep into lives of such patricians whose public views were so divergent in times of national stress as Leonardo Donà and Agostino Valier,[1] to find that strain of devotion to the Catholic Church and the good of the State in combination so characteristic of the Republic in the sixteenth century, must surely sound a note of caution in the enunciation of broad generalisations. Perhaps Bollani's urgent need to engage in political activity in Venice — an idealistic attempt to draw into one unified drive both Venice and Rome — was a personal utopia. Perhaps his relationship with the Nuncio Bolognetti was an example of cynical exploitation of a gullible Venetian for political ends. But these interpretations are at odds with the facts of the story which this study is concerned to tell.

What, then, was Bollani's political stance within the Venetian patriciate? What was his importance for the Catholic Reformation and what light is thrown by his life on the Venetian contribution to it?

Domenico Bollani's life spanned important stages in the evolution of the Venetian Republic. His death in 1579 occurred almost on the eve of those momentous events of 1582–3, when an attack was made on the oligarchical structure of the Council of X by the refusal to elect its *Zonta.* The mantle of his influence fell, perhaps, on the shoulders of Francesco Longo, his brother-in-law, who had shared his trust in a lifelong friendship and esteem,[2] and Marco Bollani, another distant relative.[3] Both were members of the Council of X in 1582. They, like Bollani's colleague in the Veronese church, Agostino Valier, were to live on through the troubled days ahead. Bollani's life had been lived on a plane of practical realities — the search for the truth in a definition of areas of common ground and overlap — which he perhaps learned on the banks of the Oglio. Importantly, those realities were the facts of the first three-quarters of the century.[4]

Bollani's political heritage was the situation of the Republic after Agnadello. His consciousness of the weakness of the Republic — doubtless instilled early from his grandfather's first-hand experience of the Turks in Friuli — had been reinforced when in *Collegio*, on the Venetian frontiers with Austria and Spain in Friuli and Brescia, and in bargaining with Spain over water rights. But his life also spanned important events in the history of the Venetian Church. Eighteen years older than Valier, he had reached maturity in that atmosphere of religious reform at Venice which the career of Gasparo Contarini represents, since he was already 29 when Cardinal Contarini died in 1542. His entry into the Church at the age of 46 coincided almost exactly with that great moment of Catholic rethinking and consolidation: the Council of Trent.

He was born into a Venetian noble family of modest standing; a family without the useful backing either of the highest offices in the government or the church, or the undoubted political advantages of great wealth. Perhaps through individual drive he had broken into the close circuit of major appointments in 1547, by accepting the possibly unpopular embassy to England on the accession of Edward VI. From this position he never looked back, and we have seen how that driving force of patriotic duty, reinforced by a breadth of vision — a readiness to adopt all methods in the pursuit of an aim — and above all, armed with the optimistic conviction that compromise was the key to most disputes between men, informed also his management of the Catholic Reformation in Brescia.

Of his early intellectual and philosophical formation, little is known, and Paolo Paruta does not supply the deficiency. Paruta's dialogue is timely for the present discussion for two reasons: first, its publication coincided almost exactly with Bollani's death, and therefore the configuration of patrician attitudes drawn by its author was intended to reflect the Venetian situation in the years 1563–1579; secondly, the work does not allocate a position of importance to Domenico Bollani. It may perhaps stretch credibility too far to argue an exact resemblance between facts and fiction when relating the *Della Perfettione della Vita Politica* to the situation of the patriciate at the moment of Bollani's death, but recent research has posited a fairly close reflection of Venetian society in its pages.[5] For Domenico Bollani, this means that it was precisely because he did not fit those factions placed in a kind of oppostion by Paruta, that he plays an insignificant part in the work. He was never a *papalista scoperta*, to use a Sarpian phrase, nor was he a statesman whose energies were directed only at the good of the State: he was never a della Torre, nor a Surian. Rather his life demonstrates a union of the principles of active and contemplative life — in a sense, a denial of Paruta's central premise.

To grasp the significance of this, it is necessary again to sketch in Paruta's scheme as it has been interpreted in recent work.[6] The initiators of the debate had been Michele Surian, 'prototipo della grande classe dirigente veneziana,' the states-man and diplomatist *par excellence,*[7] and Michele della Torre, bishop of Ceneda since 1546, and firmest of supporters of the Pope against Venetian pretensions in his bishopric.[8] The debate was centred on the relative merits of the active and contemplative life, a philosophical opposition which had had a good run by Paruta's day.[9] But in Venetian terms, and at this moment in the Republic's history, the opposition reflects the Church and the State. There is no intention here to suggest that Paruta's work was at any stage a discussion of jurisdictional disputes. But his choice of members of the patriciate, and their opposition in the ensuing conversations, does follow a historical alignment which broadly follows the pattern of attitudes to Church and State, and it is within this framework that the significance of Domenico Bollani may be understood.

On the side of the Church, with della Torre, stand also Filippo Mocenigo, archbishop of Cyprus, and Giovanni Grimani, Patriarch of Aquileia. Both these prelates are identifiable with Rome in disputes between Church and State. Behind Surian, as it were, in positions not of unity but of broad similarity, stand Matteo Dandolo and Nicolò da Ponte, Venetian legates to the Council of Trent, and representing that watchful eye of the Venetian government over the affairs of the Church in her dominions.

With the introduction of Daniele Barbaro into the debate, we are perceptibly closer to Bollani's position. Reflecting Bollani's dual experience in Church and State, Barbaro mediated between Grimani and Surian in the work, just as Bollani had mediated in life between Venice and Rome in the affair of the *Bolla in Coena Domini*, the Visitation of Borromeo and the *Decime del Clero*. But Barbaro may have been chosen because of his personal reputation; his qualification as a scholar and philosopher would have recommended him to Paruta's abstract theme.[10] The introduction of Agostino Valier, on the other hand, as the representative of the post-tridentine reformed Venetian Church, was no accident. The other three Venetian prelates, Michele della Torre, Filippo Mocenigo and Giovanni Grimani were all disqualified from the position of eminence.[11] Agostino Valier represented, what is more, that all-important link between Giberti and Contarini on one hand, and the post-tridentine reformation in Venice on the other.[12]

Domenico Bollani could have occupied just such a position, except, perhaps, that he had not acquired the reputation of a writer of philosophical and religious works that many Venetian reformers enjoyed. His experience of civil government matched those of Barbaro and Valier, and his activity as Bishop was similar in many ways to that of Valier. We have further already noticed coincidences of timing that threw Bollani and Barbaro together in London in 1549, and at Trent in 1562–3, and documented Bollani's relationship of respect and friendship with Valier. Both Bollani and Valier had infused the diplomatic skill and adaptability of Venetian patriotism into reform programmes in their diocese, giving those programmes a particular shape and style. They had espoused totally neither the Papal nor the State cause, but had steered a path between the rival claims of patriotic conscience and religious duty to implement the decrees of the Council of Trent and create the second stage of Venetian reform. Moreover, Bollani had engaged in political activity in Venice in an idealistic attempt to draw together the gradually diverging forces of Church and State, and part of this function had been adjudication of the claims for relief from the *decime* of the Veronese clergy.

So *Vita activa* and *Vita contemplativa* had become one in the bishoprics of the Republic after the Countil of Trent. The whole edifice of the Canons and Decrees points in this direction. The contemplative life in retirement, study, scholarship and devotional example found its continuation in the New Orders, but was fused in Borromeo, Paleotti and Valier with the political skill necessary to manage the new initiatives. In Venetian dominions. to narrow the focus, the *Ragion di Stato*, with the whole tradition of family solidarity, political indenture, public duty and participatory government, had quite specific gifts to offer in such a situation. For this generation, the diversion of political traditions into the channel of the Catholic Reformation altered its course not insignificantly, broadened its scope, and enriched its fabric. One has only to recall and compare the treatment of Cathedral Canons — that bastion of pre-tridentine papal privilege — by Borromeo and Bollani, to see the value of 'Venetian' diplomacy in some areas of reform. This, of course, had been the dominant contribution of Domenico Bollani.

Paolo Paruta had attempted to reflect in his work a society far more complex than this simple formula suggests. The introduction of Giovanni da Molino prephesies the upheavals in the government of the 1580s; the broader contrast between Renaissance Society and Counter-Reformation, as one might compare, for example, in a broad sweep, the *Orlando Furioso* and the *Gerusalemme Liberata*, finds a true reflection in Paruta's configuration of characters. For Catholic reform, however the opposition of active and contemplative life had been resolved in the new ideal of the bishop: attempting to be both an example of pastoral devotion and a diplomat, both a spiritually and politically cohesive force within the reformed Church. The fact that Paruta's final word is given to Gasparo Contarini is a tacit recognition of this. For Contarini's presence is always sensed in the debate; his influence on the generation depicted is implicit. In its last pages, he returns in person, as it were, to instruct the new generation in the direction it must take.

Gasparo Contarini's career is too well-known to need retelling. He represented for the generation of Domenico Bollani the Venetian contribution of Catholic reform in its first phase. The fundamental unity between his concepts of Church and State action have also been recently studied.[13] For Contarini, the duty to the state and obligation to serve in government posts, and that attempt to initiate reform from the top, so to speak, which the *Consilium* constitutes, were complementary facets of a classic personality. In him, the attributes of active and contemplative traditions in Italian religion and politics were nowhere better combined.[14] By 1559, Domenico Bollani must have had a clear idea of the possibility of a concrete contribution to the life of the Church of a statesman of Contarini's calibre. His decision to accept the bishopric was in accordance, therefore, with the highest traditions of attainment in the Venetian patriciate. It is not impossible that the influence was actual rather than theoretical, too, in that network of family and commercial interests which always played an important formative part in the career of a sixteenth century Venetian nobleman.[15] Giberti, too, although not Venetian, would have been an obvious model, embodying the diplomacy of an accomplished statesman and the sanctity of life typical of the

234

Catholic Reformation, later to be personified by Carlo Borromeo. His effect on the bishops gathered at Trent in the 1560s is already well documented.[16]

It would be too much to offer Domenico Bollani as a direct heir to the ideal constituted by the figure of Giberti — Valier is far closer to this concept in the tradition of spiritual and meditative works which came from his pen, and with the tangible results of Giberti's ministry all around him in Verona. Nor can Bollani be said to represent the post-tridentine flowering of the Contarini tradition in any complete sense, as his intellectual and spiritual achievement would hardly bear the comparison. But Bollani's attempt to bring the experience of civil government to bear on the problems inherent in reforming the Catholic Church seem the direct outcome of the Venetian political tradition, just as the statesmanship of Contarini and Giberti were important aspects in their success. 'Someone might object, { Contarini had written in his treatise on the bishop } that so far we seem to describe a citizen rather than a bishop. Our answer is that a bishop should not lack in the moral and social virtues, although they do not belong to him alone but also to others. They are the foundations; without them those which are peculiar to a bishop and properly his would necessarily collapase.'[17] Professor Gilbert noted further that 'Contarini saw a close connection between political organisation and the Church. The political society may stand lower than the Christian community in the universal hierarchy; nevertheless the right political organisation is the necessary basis on which to prepare for the development of the life of the Church. This interconnection is strikingly documented in a sentence of the *officio episcopi* dealing with heresy: 'it removes not only the foundations of faith but it also undermines the foundation of any government.''[18] After the Council, in Venice — as in Milan, and Bologna and elsewhere, the theory of the Council needed diplomatic skill for its successful application. Perhaps in the first phase of this application — in the first generation of post-tridentine bishops — where papal privilege, patronage and state suspicion on the part of Venice were all problems with a new urgency, such skill was needed in special measure.

This was the particular contribution of Domenico Bollani in Venice and Brescia in the years 1559–1579. A natural piety, genuine sympathy for the misery of man in his social and spiritual states, combined with diplomatic skill gleaned from experience in many fields, ennabled him to press forward in the construction of a new Church and a new society in Brescia — and in Venice, the hoped for (and perhaps Utopian) new *entente* in Veneto-Papal relations.

The comparison of Bollani with some of his contemporaries in Italian bishoprics yields one final suggestion, and until the modern studies of such Venetian bishops as Agostino Valier and Matteo Priuli, much to be hoped for, are forthcoming, it remains necessarily somewhat speculative. Venetian Bishops reacted with impressive constancy in the face of disputes with Rome over the affairs of the Inquisition.[19] They document the strength of the call to patriotic duty exercised by the *Ragion di Stato*, and not simply the Republic's care in supervising the selection of candidates. Paruta's choice of prelates in his work show that it was not always the case that Venetian prelates would react unswervingly to the call from home when rival demands were made on their consciences by Venice and Rome. But the bishops made a distinct contribution to the 'Venetian' reformation in its second phase. They were the natural heirs of Contarini and Giberti in political consciousness. And this consciousness had always been bred by the Venetian constitution with its piety, its duty of public service, and its broadly oligarchical rather than autocratic structure.

Borromeo's concept of a reformed church was hierarchical. The power of the Pope was clearly the apex of his pyramidal design. We have seen in a number of comparisons between Bollani and Borromeo the differences between 'political' and 'autocratic' methods. A contemporary observed accurately that the Catholic reformation in both Milan and Bologna had seemed like the creation of a little Rome in those dioceses:

> 'whereby it cometh to passe that they have made eche his owne Citie as it were an other Rome {Paleotti in Bologna, Borromeo in Milan} so that for al practises of Devotion and of charitie before mentioned, Milan and Bononie are the verie true daughters of Rome their mother.'[20]

It is not hard to see how this *kind* of transformation would have gone against the grain in Venice. In spite of the creation of individual episcopal powers by the Council of Trent, the Venetian constitution (of which she was never more conscious than in the sixteenth century) encouraged different habits of thought, different administrative structures, and an almost pathological fear of the corrupting influence of individual autocratic power.

Domenico Bollani himself noted a difference of style between Venetian and Roman political attitudes early in his Brescian period.[21] In the background — as perhaps in all his dealings with Borromeo — may be discerned his 'republican conscience'. He may have shared with a majority of his colleagues in Venetian dominions a less than total dedication to the practices of the Inquisition. Thus it may well be that Bollani contributed to a style of reform — based on the particular traditions of Venice's political past and present — and in direct line of descent from Gasparo Contarini. It may be worth elaborating this theory to suggest how different aspects of the Catholic reformation — complementary in their total effect — yet had an individual colour conferred by regional and historical traditions. Such an attempt is not to deny the unity in a broad sense of the movement: indeed, Bollani himself had been a cohesive force as his letters to Borromeo show beyond doubt. But the unity and diversity of Roman and Venetian styles of reform may throw light on contrasting elements within this total unity, and is perhaps one step towards the assessment of 'contribution'.[22]

How may these contrasting currents be identified and described?

In his fundamental discussion of the early Venetian reformers, Hubert Jedin argued from a traditional position of commitment. He described the efforts and achievements of such figures as Paolo Giustiniani and Pietro Querini, authors of the *Libellus ad Leonem X* of 1513, and Gasparo Contarini, author of the *Consilium de emendenda ecclesia* of 1537, as a great river of reform: individual contributions constitute 'molti ruscelli e rigagnoli che in futuro dovranno appunto raccogliersi nel grande fiume della riforma Cattolica.'[23] In the first quarter of the sixteenth century, in an atmosphere of religiosity, a spirit of free discussion, and a

236

unity of aim in the face of the threat, still hypothetical, from Lutheranism, perhaps Venetian and Roman currents were flowing in the same stream. And perhaps symbolic of this unity of aim were the years of friendship and interchange in Venice and her dominions of Gian Pietro Caraffa, Gianmatteo Giberti and Gasparo Contarini. In this cooperation met, after all, the fervour of repressive reform, a model bishop, and a politico-religious personality.[24]

The divergence of Roman and Venetian currents may perhaps be symbolised in a description and comparison of Caraffa and Contarini: 'la sua natura vulcanica appare radicalmente diversa da quella dolce, irenica del veneziano.'[25] In December, 1536, Caraffa had been created a cardinal by Paul III, and was called to Rome in 1537. Perhaps this division of these two early reformers presages much of the development of Catholic reform of the later century: perhaps Roman and Venetian styles diverged at this point. Contarini's theological position — so close at times to those north of the Alps — his attempt to bring union to the whole Christian Church in a reconciliation, a conference, are all activities founded in part in a political conscience: all this was 'Venetian', and looks forward to this descendents, Bollani, Valier, Priuli, in the post-tridentine movement. Caraffa's methods in reform were not to await his assumption of the Supreme Pontificate in 1557, but were the antecedents of the Papacy's developing vigour and strength after the Council of Trent.

Contrasting characteristics became more pronounced in the years 1541–1543, when the divergence of these currents produced a *terminus ad quem* in Catholic Reform, as has been observed.[26] The deaths of Contarini and Giberti, the flight of Ochino and the assumption of control of the Inquisition by Rome, underline the aggressive self-sufficiency of the Roman reform drive. From this moment, perhaps, the figure of Borromeo, that exponent of the Roman style, becomes almost inevitable, and the Venetian 'political' and Roman 'Papal and autocratic' currents were not to flow back into the same channel. In that small sector of reform that this study has examined, many initiatives from Rome have seemed to carry the hallmark of hierarchy, repression and discipline. And in this may doubtless be seen the resurgence of Papal supremacy after the Council of Trent. Venetian initiatives have often appeared diplomatic, conciliatory and flexible. And behind this undoubtedly lie the Republic's particular structure, political consciousness and traditions. The life of Domenico Bollani, with that little that it has shown us of his Venetian contemporaries, points in the direction of a very distinct contribution to the reform of the Catholic Church by Venice.

Domenico Bollani is, however, only an example of the transfusion of the traditions of the Republic into the arm of Catholic Reform. When more is known of other Venetian bishops, their training and methods, we shall be in a position to assess more satisfactorily and more fully the force, characteristics and contribution of Venice to the Catholic Reformation.

1   Valier dedicated his *De utilitate e studio rerum Venetiarum capienda* and his *Qua ratione versandum sit in Aristotole, ad Leonardum Donatum* to Leonardo Donà. Contarini dedicated his *De Perfectione rerum to* Donà. (Cozzi, *Nicolò Contarini . . ., cit., passim*, particularly p. 34, nn. 1–2. The whole of Professor Cozzi's first chapter demonstrates this principle. See particularly the discussion of the religious views of Leonardo Donà and Nicolò da Ponte, and the fact that Federico Badoer, a member of a *famiglia vecchia* supported the *giovani*. While Bollani was alive, at least, state suspicion of papal initiatives and religious devotion were complementary sides to the Venetian character for Bollani and many of his contemporaries.)

2   This appears particularly in Bollani's correspondence with his vicar-general, Roveglio. For Longo in the Council of X, see, for example, Stella, 'La regolazione delle pubbliche entrate . . .' *cit.*, p. 168. He had been *Podestà* of Bergamo in Bollani's day, and became *Podestà* of Brescia in 1584.

3   *Ibid.*, and see Barbaro, *loc. cit.*

4   It may be, indeed, that Bollani's death was timely for his reputation. It is hard to visualise his possible success in uniting the dissident forces abroad in Venice by 1580, and his idealistic view of the possibilities of cooperation may already have been somewhat outdated by November 1578, when he stated his position most clearly to Bolognetti. Certainly his presence would have smoothed the path of the Apostolic Visitation of Brescia, had he lived to see it, but events such as the trial of the Archbishop Michiel might have disillusioned him and left his well-meaning political initiatives far behind. For Church/State disputes in 1580–1606, see Cozzi, *Nicolò Contarini . . ., cit.*, Chap. I, Stella *Chiesa e Stato . . ., cit., passim.*

5   G. Cozzi, 'La Società Veneziana del Rinascimento in un'opera di Paolo Paruta: 'Della Perfettione della Vita Politica," in *Atti della Deputazione di Storia Patria per le Venezie*, (1961), pp. 13–47. See also Innocenzo Cervelli, 'Machiavelli e Paruta,' in *Machiavelli e Venezia, Machiavelli a Venezia*, (Atti del Convegno per il V Centenario della nascita di Nicolò Macchiavelli) (Florence, 1970) pp. 1–84, and *Idem*, 'Giudizi Seicenteschi dell' Opera di Paolo Paruta,' in *Annali dell'Istituto Italiano per gli Studi Storici*, (Naples, 1967) pp. 237–308. See also 'The active and contemplative life' in Oliver Logan, *Culture and Society in Venice 1470–1790* (London, 1972) pp. 49–67.

6   Cozzi, 'La Società . . .,' *cit., passim.*

7   *Ibid.*, pp. 22–23.

8   *Ibid.*, pp. 21–22. See the episode recounted by Logan, thesis *cit.*, pp. 199–200.

9   Cervelli, 'Macchiavelli e Paruta . . .' pp. 35–38, 71–72.

10   See the unpub. thesis, 'Daniel Barbaro . . .,' *cit.*, by Peter Laven, in which Barbaro's learning has been extensively studied. For a summary of works, Paschini, 'Gli scritti religiosi di D.B. . . .' *cit.*, is still useful.

11   Della Torre was not Venetian; Grimani was not on good relations with the Republic; Mocenigo was not in the front line of patricians (Cozzi, 'La Società . . .,' *cit.*, p. 34).

12   Valier had accompanied his uncle, Bernardo Navagero, on his legation to Paul IV; he had been in close touch with Borromeo in Rome at the time of the *Notti Vaticane*; and this friendship was continued through Borromeo's cousin, Federico Borromeo. (Cervelli, 'Storiografia e problemi intorno alla vita religiosa e spirituale a Venezia nella prima meta del '500,' in *Studi Veneziani*, VII (1966) pp. 447–476, at pp. 474–476.) Valier's belief in the nobility of State service is amply demonstrated in his advice to his nephews. His treatise on Venice, *Dell'Utilità che si può ritrarre dalle cose operate dai Veneziani*, (trans, N.A. Giustiniani) (Padua, 1787) proposes to his nephews a formula of moderation, religious devotion and civic consciousness. It recalls Valier's advice to Frederico Borromeo not to follow too closely on the heels of the Saint, and that of Domenico Bollani to his nephew Antonio, 'stimo cosa buona tener Antonio applicato nelle due vie ch'ho di sopra dette, si di chiesa come di viver politico . . .' (Bollani to Roveglio, Oct., 1, 1577, *Carteggio cit.*).

13   I refer particularly to Felix Gilbert, 'Religion and politics in the thought of Gasparo Contarini,' in *Action and Conviction in Early Modern Europe. Essays in memory of E.H. Harbison*, (Princeton, 1969) pp. 90–116, with sources cited, particularly n. 3. Gilbert

has stressed the complementary nature of religion and politics in Contarini and related them to his Venetian background.

14   See also in this connection, H. Mackeson, 'The Diplomatic Role of Gasparo Contarini at the Colloquy of Ratisbon of 1541' in *Church History*, 27 (1958) pp. 312–337.

15   This cannot be proved at the present stage of research, and a glance at the family trees of the vast Contarini clan at this time (Barbaro, *op. cit., ad vocem*) gives the measure of the problem. Bollani's sister, Caterina, married a Contarini, and echoes of commercial contacts survive in the will of Giacomo Bollani. (See above, family tree, p. 27, and the will *cit.*)

16   Prosperi, *op. cit., passim*, E. Cattaneo, 'Influence veronesi nella legislazione di San Carlo Borromeo,' *cit.*

17   Gasparo Contarini, *De Officio Episcopi, cit.*, and trans, in Gilbert, *op. cit.*, p. 109.

18   *Ibid.*, pp. 109–110. Professor Gilbert was at pains to prove that Gasparo Contarini's activities may not be reduced to the formula of active and contemplative life (pp. 106–107, but *passim*). Contarini was, as Bollani was later to become, a result of the Venetian political tradition – in which, as we are here suggesting, the distinction is perhaps no longer meaningful.

19   See below, Appendix VII, for this comparison.

20   Gregory Martin, *Roma Sancta* (1581) Ed. G.B. Parks, (Rome, 1969) p. 248.

21   'sono andati dall'un canto diffamandomi per Vinetia, dove piu piace qualche destrezza nelli governi . . . et in Roma, dove piacciono le intrepide esecutioni . . .' (Domenico Bollani to Carlo Borromeo, December 23, 1566, pub. in Marcora, 'I primi anni dell'Episcopato di San Carlo,' *cit.*, p. 524.

22   'Panoramic' views of the Catholic Reformation have not so far developed the theme of the regional and historical character of contributions to the movement. E. Cochrane, in 'New Light on post-Tridentine Italy . . .' *cit.*, came nearest to a definition of a Venetian school (based alone on Valier and Cervelli's reading of Paruta) at p. 312. In a broader context, however, he suggests that 'Italians may not have lost their political creativity after the death of Macchiavelli. They may simply have transferred it from civil to ecclesiastical institutions, as Alphonse Daudet proposed as long ago as 1935 {'D'un humanisme chrétien en Italie à la fin du XVIe siècle,' *Revue Historique*, 175 (1935) pp. 296–307}. After all the post-tridentine bishops were the direct descendents of exactly the same great families who had governed Italy for over three hundred years.' (p. 313). The present purpose is to suggest that this was true in special measure in Venice, and for special reasons. Alberigo, it will be remembered, in his 'Studi e problemi relativi all'applicazione . . .' *cit.*, divided reform into constituent parts, and not into reformers by region politically. Of course, fundamental for the assessment of the Venetian 'contribution' is Jedin, 'Gasparo Contarini e il Contributo Veneziano alla Riforma Cattolica', in *La Civiltà Veneziana del Rinascimento*, (Florence/Venice, 1963) pp. 105–123, but Jedin is not here concerned with political aspects, and is limited to the first phase (the death of Contarini). See also Paolo Prodi, 'The Structure and organisation of the Church in Renaissance Venice' in *Renaissance Venice*, Ed. J.R. Hale, (London, 1973) pp. 409–430.

23   H. Jedin, 'Gasparo Contarini e il contributo Veneziano . . .' *cit.*, p. 122.

24   For the community of reformers in Venice, see Paschini, *S. Gaetano Thiene, Gian Pietro Carafa . . ., cit., Passim.*

25   *Ibid.*, (quoted from Pastor, *op. cit.*, V,07.) p. 145.

26   Cervelli, 'Storiografia e problemi . . .' *cit.*, p. 476.

A' nome della Santissima Trinità Padre, et Figliuolo, et Spirito Santo, unico Dio, Signor nostro.

Io Domenico Bollani, per la grazia di Dio, et della Santa Sede Apostolico vescovo di Brescia, considerando esser occorsi, dopo l'altre mie ordinationi testamentarie, presentate nella cancelleria inferiore del Serenissimo nostro Prencipe di Vinetia, diversi accidenti[2] nella nostra casa patrimoniale; et in particolare la morte del Magnifico et mio amatissimo fratello M. Giacomo Bollani,[3] con haver lasciati dopo se molti figliuoli, si mascholi come femine;[4] et fatte per suo Testamento diverse ordinationi, rimesse in molta parte al solo mio arbitrio;[5] però ho giudicato esser di bisogno si per questo rispetto, si per quello della gratiosa facoltà concessami dal Santissimo Pontefice nostro Gregorio XIIJ^{mo}, di poter anco testar di qualunche beni a me spettanti per conto del vescovato, non più differir a dar, col mezzo del presente mio Testamento, quella regola et ordine a tutte le predette occorrenze, che aiutato dal lume divino stimarò esser di maggior gloria di Dio, più sicurezza della mia conscienza, et più conveniente al stato della sudetta casa nostra. Et prima ch'Io divenga all'ordinatione dei beni mondani et caduchi, comincio dalle cose pertinenti alla mia anima, pregando con humil core l'Altissimo che sì come sì è compiacuto per sua infinita misericordia crearla, et di poi col mezzo del Sacramento Battismale riporla nel gremio della santa Chiesa cattolica, nella quale sta ogni nostra salute, et farmi dono ch'Io habbia sempre fermamente creduti et tenuti per indubitati il documenti et precetti di quella, onde non mai mi sia di essi occorsi minimo scrupolo nella mia conscienza, così accusando le mie gravissime et innumerabili colpe et neglienze nell'haver, mentre l'ho per il più tenuta nelle mani et governo mio, poco ben operato conforme a quelli, anci con frequente scordanza della legge d'Iddio commessa diverse offese verso la Divina Sua Maestà, per le quali mi conosco et confesso reo dell'eterno suplicio, si degni, quando le piaccia chiarmarmi da questa misera vita, valle di lagrime, concedermi, come ne e tutto il pieno desiderio mio, ch'Io la riponghi nelle braccia clementissime dell' unico Figliuolo Suo, Salvator nostro, con quel vivo spirito di Fede, Speranza, et Carità, ch'egli ricerca dalli suoi eletti, et con tutti quei Sacramenti che la Santa Chiese costuma dare a quelli ch'incorporati in essa, partono da questa vita.

Ma perchè può occorrer per diversi accidenti, che sogliono nell'estremo di essa, impedire la mente et la lingua, ch'Io non potessi all'ora dichiarire questa mia stabile mente et dispositione, voglio et intendo al presente per all'hora, et per sempre haverla, col Divino aiuto, fermamente dichiarita, et confessata, pregando humilmente la sua immensa pietà che si compiaccia d'accettarla per così stabilita nel cor mio, non da propria virtù, ma dal singolar dono della Sua gratia, rinonciando et protestando a tutto quello che da me in quel punto, per qual si voglia accidente, potesse esser pensato, detto, o fatto, contra questa mia ferma intentione et stabilita dispositione.

Del corpo, che anco e conveniente haverne qualche cura per la viva speranza della nostra Resurettione, ordino che mentre a tanto haverò con gl'altri morti, a comparire innanzi al tribunale di Giesù Christo Redentor nostro, stia riposto nella nostra chiesa cathedrale in Santa Maria Rotonda, dove all'incontro sta posta al capo dell'altar maggiore l'imagine di essa Beatissima Vergine, nostra pia avvocata, che e il sito gia dissegnato per la mia sepoltura, la quale occorendo che alla mia morte non sia del tutto finita, prego li miei commissari a sollecitare che quanto prima si la dia fine, per non lasciarla imperfetta, con disconcio anco di quella parte della chiesa.

Può facilmente avvenire per la sudetta et altre spese et dispense che qui sotto ordinarò che non si habbiano a trovare alla mia morte tanti denari contanti che possano sodisfare a tutti essi bisogni, come per il piu in vita mi è occorso, per causa di pagamenti di Decime, Pensioni, Fabriche del vescovato, et altre spese ordinarie et estraordinarie, però siano essi commissari solleciti nella ricuperazione di quanto fino all'hora mi si doverà dalli fittavoli et livellari di vescovato, comprese le rate non mature, ma però de frutti gia per loro levati dalla terra, come di questo ne è fatta particolar dechiaratione nella sudetta gratia concessami dalla Santita Sua; et con ciò sodisfacendosi prima a qual si voglia debito de dinari ch'io havessi, et suplendosi parimente alla spesa della detta sepoltura, voglio che del restante siano dispensati in limosina ducati Mille di moneta Bresciana a'luoghi pii, et a' poveri più bisognosi in questa citta,[6] come a'loro commissari meglio parerà, limosinando però in particolare de ducati cinquanta l'esemplare Collegio delli Reverendi Padri Giesuiti di Santo Antonio, li quali strettamente prego a tener raccomandata a esso begninissimo Salvator nostro nelli loro santi sacrificij la mia anima di quel modo che costumano fare per li suoi Reverendi Fratelli defonti, col darne di ciò avviso a gl'altri suoi collegij. Ordino che siano distribuiti altri ducati Mille tra quelli della mia famiglia di vescovato che al tempo della mia morte si trovaranno per un'anno al meno prima haver servito, et tutta via servite in casa con habitatione continua dando essi commissari a chi piu et a chi meno secondo il merito della fedele et antica servitù di ciascuno, conosciuta dal solo arbitrio loro, onde se alcun di essi beneficiati facesse intorno ciò qual si voglia contradittione, non possa quel tale haverne alcuna parte, dovendo ciascun di loro ben quetarsi alla sincerità di essi commissari, et all'intiera pratica che hanno di tutte le cose mie. Et se occorrerà che oltre le spese, et legati sudetti vi mancino dinari o crediti di qual si voglia debitori, ordino che ne investiscano tanto parte in fondo sicuro, dentro o fuori della città di Brescia, che si possa a loro giudicio haver communemente l'entrata convenie(n)te per la celebrattione di una Messa, da esser cottidianamente detta nella chiesa del Domo all'altare di Santo Martino per un'idoneo sacerdote, da esser di tempo in tempo detto per quello di nostri heredi che sara di maggior età, il quale nell'elettione di esso habbia ogni piena libertà, con poter a'suo arbitrio rimoverne uno et surrogarne un'altro, come a lui meglio parerà, purchè ne tenga uno sempre, per acrescimento del Culto Divino in detta chiesa, et per qualunche suffragio che potesse bisognare alla mia anima, et a quelli di defonti della casa nostra, habbia esso sacerdote obligo di tener continuamente il detto altare ben ornato et proveduto di ogni suo conveniente ornamento, et de vesti sacri di quattro colori, soliti usarsi dalla Santa Chiesa, con fare giornalmente mutatione conforme al rito ecclesiastico; et oltre il celebrare cottidianamante a'esso altare, debba tutti li giorni delle Domeniche, et altre feste conmandate, aiutar in coro la celebratione delle Messe et vesperi cantate, sodisfacendo a tutto cio egli stesso personalmente, et non per sustituti; et sia sempre ubbidiente al suo Reverendissono vescovo, et porti il debito honore alli molti Reverendi et miei fratelli canonici, li quali insieme con gl'altri Reverendi Mansionari et capellani prego a tener caritativa memoria di me nelle loro divote orationi; pregogli anco al tempo della mia morte darne di essa quanto prima aviso al Reverendissima Nostro Arcivescovo di Milano,[7] et alli Reverendissimi vescovi comprovinicali, acciò secondo il pio ordine delle Constitutioni provinciali possano, con divota celebrazione d'uffici, aiutare la mia anima ad eterna pace, come l'istesso confido che farà il nostro Reverendo at amatissimo clero Diocesano di quel modo che per le nostre sinodali constitutioni è ordinato. Et li Reverendi Curati parimente eccitaranno gli loro popoli a porger divoti prieghi per me, et per la buona elettione di un'exemplare et vigilante successore.

Le Robbe di qualunche uso che al detto tempo si trovaranno in vescovato, et in l'altre case di fuori pertinenti a me,[8] per essermi in maggior parte state provedute dalla casa patrimoniale, voglio che restino libere a'uso et commodo di essa casa, comprendendo anco in esse le robbe della mia particolare capella; ma l'altre tutte, gia per me dissegnate a uso della Chiesa cathedrale, cioè il razzi che forniscono nelle solenità il coro, li palij per gl'altari, pianete, et piviali con gl'altri suoi fornimenti per le publice celebrationi, restino libere alla Sagristia, et siano descritte nell'Inventario di essa,[9] come proprie sue; ne si possano prestar fuori sotto qual si voglia pretesto.

Se per gli libri et conti tenuti per il cassiero di vescovato si trovasse alcun deposito de dinari per conto de liveli francati, che fino all'hora non si fusse potuto trovar fondo sicuro et utile da investirgli, ordino che di subito siano, col consiglio del Reverendo Capitolo di canonici, depositati in mano de persona sicura, et col loro giudicio investiti, quanto prima si potrà trovar esso fondo utile et sicuro, si come de simili dinari si è sempre per me fatto; et di tutto ne appare particolar nota et conto in detti libri.[10]

Mi ha fatto lungo et fedele servitio il Magnifico ser M. Trusso,[11] gia Cancelliere di Vescovato, nell'haver tenuta con molta prudenza, amorevole cura delle cose temporali di esso, da che, per Divina dispositione, fui chiamato a'questo grave peso episcopale, mentre mi trovavo per commandamento della cara Patria mia governare, come Podestà, questa Magnifica et amatissima città, in tempo de suoi assai travagliosi affari;[12] però ordino ch'il debito de ducati trecentosettantatrè che egli mi resta per conto de dinari da me commodatigli nelli suoi bisogni, gli sia in tutto rimesso et condonato; ben lo prego a' continuare con l'istessa amorevolezza in aiuto delli miei commissari per quello che loro occorrera di bisogno in Brescia, si per la ricuperatione delli crediti di sopra nominati, si per l'essecutione delle cose per me ordinate nel presente Testamento da farsi in detta citta; come parimente prego il Magnifico M. Hippolito Cocciano, procurator generale di essa Magnifica città, a'prestarsi pronto nel medesimo aiuto con quel vivo affetto ch'ha sempre tenuto nella protettione delle cose mie.

Instituisco et ordino universali heredi di qualunche miei beni, si patrimoniali, come di qual si voglia altra raggione, che spettar mi possano, li miei diletti nipoti Antonio et Vincenzo Bollani,[13] figliuoli legitimi del sudetto Magnifico

M. Giacomo mio fratello; li quali prima d'ogni altra cosa prego, essorto, et commando, che in tutte le loro attioni habbiano per principale mira l'acquisto de gli eterni et celesti beni, col mezo del Santo timore d'iddio, della pronta ubbidienza alla santa chiesa catholica, della caritativa unione tra loro e il prossimo, et della debita riverenza et ossequio a' suoi maggiori, et prencipalmente alla loro Magnifica et cara Madre, et alli suoi amorevolissimi cij et padri li clarissimi M. Francesco et Marcantonio Longo fratelli;[14] li quali da che furono per il testamento di detto mio fratelli instituiti insieme con essa loro madre, et me, commissari suoi, si sono di continuo con granda carita et assidue fatiche adoprati nel governo della sua commissaria, con l' incorporatione anco in essa di tutti li beni patrimoniali et legatari a'me pertinenti: li quali si come ho sempre lasciati in uso et comodo della casa, cosi instituendo io per miei commissari li medesimi sopranominati, voglio et dispongo che tutti le restino liberi sotto il governo et maneggio loro, o'di quelli di essi che si trovaranno sopravivere fino che il minore di detti miei nipoti sara pervenuto all'etta di anni venti; et cosi prego essi commissari a continoare esso governo et maneggio coll'istesse caritative fatiche che hanno sempre fatto; onde espressamente commando alli detti miei heredi, che ne per loro, ne per interposta persona, nè sotto qual si voglia pretesto, ardiscano de dimandar in alcun tempo a'essi suoi clarissimi cij alcun conto o'raggione del sudetto maneggio, ma stiano in tutto e per tutto alla semplice parola et conti suoi con ogni riverenza et ossequio, sicurandomi Io della loro sincerità et lealtà, come se tutto fusse passato o havesse a'passare per le proprie mani mie.

Vuole ogni raggione che le facoltà si conservino, quanto più convenientemente si può, nelle case patrimoniali, però ordino che morendo l'uno di essi fratelli senza figliuoli nasciuti di legitimo matrimonio si mascoli come femine, la parte sua vadi al fratello che sopraviverà o'vero suoi legitimi descendenti con libertà però di poter disponer, dopo finita l'età anni venti, per suo testamento, et non altrimente de ducati diecimille, come a lui meglio parerà;[15] ma se alcun di essi fratelli morirà, con lasciar dopo'se una sola figliuola legitima, l'altro che sopraviverà, o'vero suoi legitimi descendenti mascoli, habbi libero potere di succeder in tutta la parte del fratello morto, con obligo di sborsar a'essa figliuola, tra termini di anni tre, ducati ventimille ogni anno al meno la (. . .); et passati li detti tre anni, non essendo fatta essa intiera sborsatione, sia et s'intenda tutta essa parte dei beni restar libera alla predetta figliuola, overo suoi legitimi descendenti, et se ambi essi fratelli heredi morissero senza legitimi descendenti, succedano le loro sorelle maritate, o che fossero da maritare, overo suoi legitimi descendenti per stirpem et non per capita;[16] risservata però a' ciascun di loro fratelli la predetta libertà di poter disponer delli ducati diecimille come è predetto; Dichiaro inoltre, che occorrendo à essi fratelli di devenir ad alienatione di alcuna parte di detti beni, lo possano ambi di commune consenso fare, et non altrimente; et con obligo appresso, che tutto l'intiero tratto sia di subito investito in altro fondo di più utile et commodo della casa, a' giudicio delli sopranominati commissari che si trovaranno all'hora sopravivere, o'non sopravivendo alcuno di essi, suppliscano per tale bisogno dui communi parenti o amici; altramente l'alienatione sia et s'intenda esser et di nessun valore; nè possano li compratori in detto caso valersi della libertà per me concessa.[17]

Et perchè ho stimato esser bene non stender alcuna delle predette condicioni in altri descendenti dalli sopranominati nostri heredi per rispetto della continova variatione delle cose mondani, onde dificilmente si può così da lontano giudicare ciò che possa esser di maggior bene et commodo delle case et famiglie, però con tutto el core essorto et prego tutti essi descendenti ad haver in ogni tempo prudente occhio et caritativa avvertenza, tra di loro, che si habbiano a conservare le facoltà nella casa, per non lasciar diminuire, in quanto più possano, li commodi et riputazione di essa.[18]

Voglio et espressamente ordino che a tutte le sudette conditioni per me poste in essa heredità, sia et s'intenda ubligata tanto la parte delli miei beni, quanto quella delli beni di sudetto mio fratello, per l'ampia libertà da lui datami per il suo testamento di poter alterar, minuir, et corregger qualunche sua ordinatione si come per il successo di tempo meglio mi paresse.[19]

Appresso ciò, per vigore della detta libertà, ordino che tutti essi beni siano et s'intendano ugualmente ubligati alli seguenti crescimenti de legati, cioè.

Al legato lasciato alla Magnifica Madonna Marrietta Bollani per il sudetto mio fratello, fu suo consorte, voglio sia cresciuto tanto, ch'in tutto ella habbia ducati sessanta all'anno in vita sua.

Al diletto mio nipote, figliuolo di detto mio fratello, frate Domenico professo nella Religione di Santo Domenico,[20] ordine siano cresciuti ducati trenta, si che computati li trenta che esso suo padre gli lascia per il suo testamento, ne habbia in tutto ogni anno sessanta, accio possa meglio provedersi in ciascun suo bisogno, con l'ubbidienza però sempre di suoi superiori, per non contravenir in modo alcuno al voto et obligo della professione sua; il qual obligo fa ch'io non lo nomino per commissario, come lo nominò esso suo padre innanzi essa professione.[21]

Alli legati gia lasciati per li nostri consaguinei a ciascuna delle figliuole di detto mio fratello che monacharanno, ordino che così alle tre gia monachate nel monasterio di Sant'Anna di Padova,[22] come a ciascuna delle altre tre che medesimamente monachasse,[23] sia fatto tanto cresimento, che ogn'una di esse habbia in tutto ducati trenta all'anno, mentre vivaranno.

Ordino che al legato di cinquemille che esso mio fratello lascia per conto di dote a quelle di sue figliuole che si maritaranno, siano aggiunti a ciascuna che si vorrà maritare, quando al tempo della mia morte non sia stata maritata, et stia in proposito di maritarsi più che di monachare, ducati mille delli beni della casa, si che habbia quel tanto che per le leggi della Patria nostra si è ultimamente statuito potersi dare in dote, che è fino a ducati seimille,[24] li quali anco dificilmente si potrebbono crescer, havendosi riguardo alli stretti termini in che si trova la casa per li molti debiti et spese che di continovo sostiene, onde per tale necessità si è convenuto tanto differir il loro maritare,[25] essendovi sempre stata parimente compagnata l'impotenza mia di aiutare caritativamente si pia opera, come ho di sopra dichiarito; nel resto di ciò che pertiene a questo negocio del maritarsi di dette figliuole, confermo ogni altra cosa ordinata per il testamento di detto loro padre, et in partiolare nel cavar esse doti dalle entrate annuali di tutto il corpo della facoltà, et non altrimente.

Non possendo io, come vorrei, mostrarmi ben grato alla grande amorevolezza sempre mostratami dalli sudetti Clarissimi M. Francesco et M. Marcantonio Longo,[26] voglio almeno per segno di mia grata volontà, che dopo la mia morte sia loro di subito consegnato in libero dono il bacile et broncino d'argento, solito da me usati nella celebratione cottidiana della santa messa.

1578, Il Giorno 12 agosto in Brescia.
Io Domenico Bollani Vescovo sopradetto ho scritto il presente mio testamento di propria mano, et così lo sottoscrivo, per haverlo poi a metter sotto il mio sigillo; ordinando che subito dopo la mia morte sia legitimamente levato in pubblica forma con li modi soliti servirsi nella nostra ben istituita città di Vinetia, et mandato ad essecutione, come in esso è disposto; al che se alcun delli heredi da me instituiti ardisse di contravenire in qual si voglia modo in parte o in tutto, sia et s'intenda privato di qualunche nostri beni; nelli quali in tal caso ordino che succeda quello di essi fratelli, overo suoi legitimi descendenti, che non sarà contravenuto; et se ambi contravenessero, succedano le loro sorelle maritate, o che fussero da maritare, overo suoi legitimi descendenti per stirpem et non per capita. Laus Deo.
1578. Il giorno 6 novembre in Vinetia.
Essendo occorso a me Domenico suddetto venir in questa città al presente, per il negocio delle Decime del clero di questo Serenissimo Dominio, impostomi da Sua Santità; et havendo portato meco il presente mio testamento già scritto in Brescia, ho chiamato a me il Magnifico N. Cesare Ziliolo Canceliero nella cancelleria inferiore del Serenissimo Prencipe, et gli ho presentato sigillato in tre luoghi col mio sigillo, accio così tenga custodito in detta cancelleria, da esser poi, quando piacerà alla Divina Maestà chiamarmi a se, levato in publica et autentica forma; et così in tutte le parti sue esseguito; et ho dal medesimo M. Cesare ripigliate l'altre mie due testamentarie ordinationi già presentate in detta cancelleria, rivocandole et annullandole in tutto, si che resti solamente valido il presente mio testamento et ultima volontà nella Santa gratia di Nostro Signor Dio.

NOTES TO APPENDIX I

1 In A.S.V., *Cancelleria Inferiore, Atti* C. Ziliol, *busta* 1257, f. 264. In this transcription, I have retained the punctuation and spelling of the MS, but expanded abbreviations.

2 Among these was certainly the loss of 10,000 ducats in the disastrous voyage to Alexandria during the war against the Turks in 1567. See p. 0.

3 (1518–1571). See family tree p. 00, and his will in A.S.V., *Atti* Ziliol, *busta* 1258, f. 451.

4 Three sons and seven daughters (will cit.).

5 See p. 10.

6 This is referred to in Barbaro, *op. cit.*

7 Carlo Borromeo.

8 See below, Appendix V.

9 It is likely that a complete inventory of these effects is to be found among documents relating to Borromeo's Apostolic Visitation of Brescia the year after Bollani's death in 1580 (*Visita Brescia*, A.A.M. *loc. cit.*). Compare the published inventories of the Visitation of Bergamo in 1575 in Angelo Giuseppe Roncalli (Ed.) *Gli Atti della Visita Apostolica di S. Carlo a Bergamo*, (Florence, 1936 I (i), pp. 227–235.

10 At least some of these have survived in A.V.B. (where re-cataloguing is in progress). For economic considerations of Bollani's bishopric, comparison with his *decima* (tax-return of 1564, below, App. V), would be interesting.

11 See above Chapter V.

12 Clearly a reference to the dispute of the city with Cremona over the *Naviglio Cremonese* (above, Chap. V).

13 See family tree, p. 16.

14 Francesco (1529–1584) and Marcantonio (1538–   ). Sons of Antonio Longo (–1567) were Domenico's brothers-in-law. See Barbaro, *op. cit., IV*, p. 301. After Giacomo's death, much of Domenico's business in Venice was transacted by Francesco Longo. (See *Carteggio* Bollani – Roveglio, *cit.*, passim.)

15 This is the *fideicommissum*, instituted by Domenico to ensure that the family patrimony remained intact in its inheritance by successive generations. The freedom to dispose of 10,000 ducats conceeded by Domenico to his heirs – with the implication that this would not seriously erode the fortune – is already an indication of the size of the fortune. See pp. 9–10, and 15, for discussion of the family patrimony in 1624.

16 This is in fact what happened on the death of Vincenzo Bollani in 1609, as his brother Antonio's son, Giacomo, had been executed the same year without heirs. Thus, Vincenzo was obliged to leave the patrimony to his sister Cecilia, from whom it passed into the Loredan and Molin families in 1624. See family tree p. 16, Cairns, 'Ancora sulla casa dell'Aretino sul Canal Grande' in *Studi Veneziani*, 14 (1972) pp. 211–217.

17 This was common practice in sixteenth century Venice. We have seen that the fortune was invested chiefly in land on the *Terraferma*, and in many house properties in Venice. Domenico thus forbids his heirs to sell this property – unless it be to invest it more profitably alsewhere – and only this with the consent of two senior relatives or friends. On the change in Venetian fortunes from trading to land see J.C. Davis, *op. cit.*, pp. 42–43, and on the application of the *fideicommissum, ibid.*, pp. 68–72.

18 A prudent move. It will be noted that Domenico imposes restrictions specifically only on the next generation of his heirs. It was often the case that the *fideicommissum* was imposed on all subsequent heirs in the interests of conservation intact of the family fortune. See the wills of Domenico Contarini, Nicolò Tron and Giustiniano Contarini quoted by Davis, *op. cit.*, pp. 69–70. In his *continova variatione delle cose mondani*, Domenico must have had in mind the drop in the family fortunes in 1567 and 1572 as a result of war. (See above, p.10 and n.25).

19 See Giacomo's will in A.S.V., Atti Ziliol, Busta 1258, fol. 451.

20 This Domenico had become a Dominican Friar in Brescia between 1568 and 1570, living there under his uncle's wing. (See will of Giacomo Bollani, *cit.* p. 4). He became Bishop of Crete. (Barbaro, *op cit.*, p. 41).

21 Giacomo had left his property to his *three* sons in 1568, but left Domenico out in his *postilla*, in 1570, as he had entered the church as Dominican Friar in Brescia.

246

22 Giacinta, Catarezza (sic) and Lugrecia. (see wills of Cecillia and Jacopo Bollani). The records of the Convento di Sant'Anna are now dispersed. The Monastery was important up to the fall of the Republic, at which point it had become a depositry for books and MSS collected from all over the Venetian Terraferma. At this point, the material was dispersed. See *Relazione Storico-Descrittivo sulla Regia Biblioteca Universitaria*, (Padova, 1872), p. 28. According to Cecilia's will (1624) the family also owned a house in Padua.

23 Elena (married Gerolamo Loredan) and Laura (married Bernardo Molin) and Cecilia. These were the three remaining of Giacomo's four daughters in 1579, as Betta (who married Michiel Foscarini) had died in 1577, (See will of Betta Bollani in A.S.V. Atti Ziliol, Busta 1257, fol. 303). See also above, pp. 18–19, n. 16.

24 For legislation to regulate dowries, see references and discussion in B. Pullan, *Service to the Venetian State* ... cit. p. 137. The law Domenico here refers to is in A.S.V. *Senato Terra, Filza* 67, July 28, 1575.

25 For the 'stretti termini' of the family fortune at this point see above p. 0–0 etc. On the custom of late marriages for economic reasons, see J.C. Davis, *op. cit.* pp. 61–67. It is probable that some, at least of the three daughters not already married in 1579, and had waited for this reason. Laura and Clara obviously took advantage of this provision (by which the wealth personally accrued by Domenico from his Bishopric of Brescia was added to the family patrimony).

26 Domenico's brothers-in-law and executors. See above n. 14.

Note: I am grateful to the late Prof. Carlo Pasero for his patient assistance in the transcription of the MS.

TERMS OF THE AGREEMENT REACHED BETWEEN DOMENICO BOLLANI AND GIOVANNI ANGUISSOLA AT THE END OF THE FIRST PHASE OF THE OGLIO DISPUTE.[1]

April, 1559

Che la Bocca del Naviglio Cremonese si curi fino alla soglia, così di dentro, come di fuori alla equalità delle soglie, cioè la ingerazione fatta nella distruzione, per distanza di cavezzi cento dentro di essa Bocca, si abbiano a fabbricare altre quattro soglie in questo modo, cioè cominciando dalla detta bocca, distante per cavezzi venticinque, sia posta una delle dette quattro soglie, con caduta di oncie una, e per distanza di altri cavezzi ventincinque, si metta un' altra soglia, con caduta di oncie una e mezza, e per distanza di altri venticinque cavezzi sia posta un'altra soglia con caduta di oncie una e mezza, e per distanza di altri cavezzi ventricinque sia posta un'altra soglia con decaduta di oncie due, e ciascheduna di esse soglie sia construtta di pietra battuta, con braccia tre di pavimento fatto di quadrello per ogni parte, a tal che siano in tutto esse saleggiate braccia sei per ciascuna, senza le soglie.

Item che da ogni banda di esse soglie accolte dell'una, et l'altra Riva del Naviglio, si debbano fabbricar li suoi muri di tanta longhezza come sono large le soglie, con la sua salizata, li quali muri si fabbrichino in modo che l'Alveo non ecceda, nè restringa la sua larghezza, che si trova di presente; e se li muri, che si trovano fabbricati dentro della Bocca, averanno bisogno di rifacimento, si rifacciño sopre li fondamenti vecchi. Item che tutte dette Fabbriche siano state in termine di un anno prossimo futuro, cioè per tutto Aprile 1560, e così abbiano da esser mantenute perpetuamente dalli Sigg. Cremonesi.

Item che la Palificata, ovvero sperone,, che serve al suddetto Naviglio, che confina con la Seriola di Antegnate, e si estende nel fiume Ollio, sia riddotta nel termine, che era prima, cioè riempita, e fortificata nell'altezza, longhezza, e larghezza, talmente che non ecceda li Pali, che vi sono al presente, e trovandosi, che vi sia alcun Palo coroso, e più basso degli altri non corosi, siano tutti ridotti all'altezza de' Pali non corosi.

Item si debba fabbricare per i Sigg. Cremonesi un muro di lunghezza di Braccia trenta nella riva che è di sopra della Bocca del Naviglio, dove erano speroni affissi alla Pezza di Terra che soleva esser del Magnifico Sig. Antonio Secco, il qual muro si congionga col muro che è attaccato alla Bocca di esso Naviglio, seguitando l'ordine della Palificata, che di presente si ritrova, la qual fabbrica s'abbia da fare in termine d'anni due prossimi futuri.

Item che il muro che è nel mezzo della Bocca di esso Naviglio, si possa ridurre in quel stato, ed essere, nel quale era per innanzi.

Item che s'abbia da fare una Predata in beneficio del Naviglio, che abbia da principiare di sotto di essa Bocca del Naviglio per braccia n° cinquanta uno, ed estendersi nel fiume all'insù per cavezzi venticinque, situandola sopra il colmo. e filo della schena, che di presente si vede in detto fiume, come ne sono informati detti Ingegneri, costruendo essa predata de sassi solamente, e che per la metà, cioè per cavezzi dodeci, e mezzo continuati in quella parte di essa predata, che a loro Sigg. Cremonesi parerà. Si possano metter cavaletti per sostentzione di essa predata, & al presente a giudicio de' Periti, e questo si faccia per modo di provisione; e si vedrà per la esperienza, che questa Predata fatta al sudetto modo non sia di satisfazione all'una, ovvero all'altra parte, l'Illustr. Sigg. Delegati abbiano a far nuova provisione secondo, per il loro prudente Arbitrio, giudicaranno esser necessario.

NOTES TO APPENDIX II

1 Copies of the agreement are widely dispersed among the archival sources in Chapter V, for example in the 'Registro delle Delegationi . . .' *cit.* (copies in Biblioteca Marciana, Venice, and Biblioteca Queriniana, Brescia), *A.C.S.B., Registrum, Olei*, Vol. P, pp. 26–28, and a printed copy in *Arch. Nav. Crem. Scritture diverse, cit. Trattato fra Sua Maestà l'Imperatrice Regina e la Serenissima Repubblica di Venezia sulla Materia dei Confini* (Treaty of Vaprio, 1755) (Brescia, 1755) pp. 27 et seq.

APPENDIX III

LETTER FROM LODOVICO CALINI, BRESCIAN ORATOR IN VENICE, TO BRESCIA.[1]

May 21, 1561

Hebbi hieri le lettere delle M.V. de 12 con la instruttione circa la Usurpatione fatta per Cremonesi dell'Acqua de Ollio alla Bocca del loro Naviglio, et ne parlai con molti di Sri. del Collegio, dalli quali havendo inteso che le lettere di Clmi. Rettori in questa materia erano statte lette in Pregadi sebbene passato senza haver fatto deliberatione alcuna ne in Pregadi ne in Collegio, raccordai a molti de loro mentre si reducevano la importantia di questa causa, supplicandoli a dar quell' ordine che gli paresse conveniente circa il che non havendosi potuto trattar hieri cosa alcuna ho continuato questa mattina a far l'istesso offitio. Et sono statto chiamato in Collegio, dove S. Ser.ta mi ha detto che hanno viste le lettere di Cl.mi Rettori con le scritture in queste annesse, et inteso il rimedio raccordato per le M.V. oltra al quale s'io haveva altro da raccordare dovessi dirlo, al che resposi ch'io non ho altro se non che essendo questa causa di quella importantia che S. Ser. ta può considerare e da stimare assai, et ha bisogno di presta provisione, perche il differire et lasciar invecchiar questa attione saria di troppo pregiuditio nostro, et per consequente di S. Ser.ta. Rispose il Cl.mo Sr. Nicolo da Ponte che gli pareva bene mandar un secretario a Milano a posta qual insieme col secretario ordinario che è a Milano ricercasse retrattatione di questa novità[2] al quale io replicai, ch'io credeva che questo non fusse bene, perche non si riportaria altro se non che quel Sr. Governatore voria informarsi, nel che si metteria tempo di meggio, et che volendosi informare, o saria statto bisogno che havesse udite anche le nostre raggioni il che saria stato un consentir a un certo modo nel suo giuditio overo non facendo intendere le raggioni nostre, et che si tentasse puoi qualche altro rimedio, pareria che fusse mancato da noi di vederla amorevolmente, et forse nasceria quello che venne nel 1546 quando si fece querimonia con la Maestà dell'Imperatore[3] per novità chiare fatte a pregiuditio nostro per Cremonesi[4] ricercandosi che fussero ritrattate, et non si puote mai operar altro non che haveria datto giudici, ma non volse far ritrattar la novità prima, si come si ricercava et era honesto per il che doppoi quando è occorso qualche difficoltà, si ha atteso ad operare che Cremonesi vengano da S. Ser.ta per non andar noi a contestar lite a Milano ne altrove. Fu poi raccordato per il Cl.mo Sr. Pietro Morosini, fratello del Cl.mo Sr. Carlo che si puotria far che qualch'uno per nome delle M.V. andasse a informare il secretario che è a Milano, qual dovesse poi, come per non lasciar far torto alla citta far qualche offitio al che rispose il Cl.mo Domenego Moro che li inconvenienti allegati per me sopra la prima proposta succederiano anche in questa, et che non gli piace ne questo arricordo, ne anche quello che danno le M.V. nella instruttione, perche vorria in tutte le attioni proceder modestamente, come saria far che il Conte Gio. Anguissola intendesse questa Usurpatione, et tentar se per meggio suo si potesse far retrattar et eseguir solamente la capitulatione fatta per lui col nostro R.mo Vescovo. Sottogionse il

Cl.mo Sr. Hier.o Zane che le M.V. che sonno sul fatto, et sonno prudenti saperanno provedere senza far rissolutione in Collegio. Mi dimanda il Morosini perche causa si ha tolerato che Cremonesi habbano fatto questa novità, et perche non obstargli mentre la facevano, al qual risposi che la predata si è fatta in virtu della capitolatione, et che il lungarla piu di quello [che] si deve, et tenerla lontana dalla Ripa de Cremonesi piu di quello che dovevano, non si puo saper cosi in un tratto, tanto piu che per quel loco passano poche persone, et dieci Homeni in quattro hore puonno allongare la predata trei o quattro braza et che sulla sua Ripa facilmente ponno far quelle novità che vogliono, che non si puo cosi sapere facilmente. Il Cl.mo Sr. Matteo Dandolo mi commise ch'io dovessi dar loco, et per quello che io puosso comprendere, fece offitio perchè non si debba far attione alcuna in questa materia, et esagero molte cose; sapra la gente che le M.V. mandereno gia trei anni a quella impresa, et i Belloardi con artiglierie sopra, et che non è a proposito che il Ser.mo D.o pigli protettione di queste cose, al qual contradisse gagliardamente il Cl.mo Zane et parlorno l'uno et l'altro piu volte. Ultimamente fui richiamato, et S. Ser.ta mi disse che la rissolutione è di non riscrivere cosa alcuna alli Cl.mi Rettori in questo negotio perche essendo le M.V. prudenti saperanno provedere, et che si puotria vedere se il R.mo Vescovo[5] puotesse operar che il Co. Giovanni[6] facesse retratar tutto quello che e fatto contro la capitulatione. Al che risposi che S. Ser.ta scrivesse di questo alli Cl.mi Rettori, S.S.R.ma faria piu volentieri questo offitio, al che mi rispose il Cl.mo Dandolo che non accade altro, perche essendone padre Spirituale, non mancava di ogni offitio possibile. Mi rispose anche il Cl.mo Zane che le M.V. sonno prudenti, et che saperanno proveder. Uscendo il Cl.mo Zane di Collegio ho ragionato con seco dicendogli che l'altra [volta] che le M.V. per non lasciarsi far torto diffesero l'honor et riputatione della città senza saputa di S.Ser.ta, et che si trattò di darlo vi furono senatori che contradissero gagliardamente, et che per questo forse le M.V. non si sonno risolte a far operatione alcuna da se qual mi ha risposto che se ne sonno qualch'uno di questa opinione, ve ne sonno per uno dieci di miglior opinione, et perche loro non ponno trattar questa materia se non tra le muri della sala secretamente senza mostrar di saper altro. Le M.V. ponno provedere loro come da se senza mostrar di saper altro. Ho voluto scrivere alle M.V. particolarmente ogni cosa, essendo la materia della importantia che è, ma la prego a far stracciar la lettera per che elle ponno considerare, et pero gli mando un'altra lettera da puoter mostrar alli Cl.mi Rettori, acciò che non habbino d'aspettar altra risposta in questo negotio da S. Ser.ta. Il D.o Monsig.r Valerio venne hieri da me e mi mostrò una lettera d'un suo agente qual gli scrive in substantia che quelli arbori . . .

[cut by the Cremonese on land between the old and new basins of the river Oglio at Pontevico] . . .

Di Venetia il 21 Maggio 1561.

Lud.co Calino

NOTES TO APPENDIX III

1 Copy in *A.C.S.B., Registrum Olei*, Vol. P, pp. 71–72.

2 The Cremonese had lengthened and strengthened their *Predata*, so that very little water was reaching the southern reaches of the river.

3 Calini refers to the proclamation of Charles V, and the resulting congress of representatives at Ratisbon in the same year.

4 The reference is to the re-construction of the *Predata*, last destroyed by the Brescians in 1462.

5 Domenico Bollani, at this time at the Council of Trent.

6 Anguissola.

TERMS OF THE AGREEMENT REACHED BETWEEN DOMENICO BOLLANI AND GIOVANNI ANGUISSOLA AT THE END OF THE SECOND PHASE OF THE OGLIO DISPUTE.[1]

September 24, 1561

Per la esecuzione della Capitolazione fatta del 1559 dichiariamo, quanto al primo Capitolo del metter delle quattro soglie nel Naviglio Cremonese, che si debba cominciar a misurare li primi venticinque Cavezzi dalla prima soglia vecchia delle tre, che si trovano nelle bocca di esso Naviglio verso il Fiume Oglio,[2] ed in capo delli detti venticinque cavezzi, si metta la prima di esse quattre soglie nuove con caduta di oncie una dalla superficie di essa prima soglia vecchia, che è nella bocca alla superficie di essa prima delle quattro che si hanno a mettere nel Naviglio, e perchè la terza soglia vecchia, che si trova in essa bocca verso il Naviglio, è più alta della detta prima soglia, che si trova verso Ollio un'oncia manco mezzo punto, si dichiara, che essa terza soglia si debba abbassare la detta oncia uno manco mezzo punto, perchè in questo modo le superficie di esse due soglie si troveranno uguali, quando essa prima soglia non sia più bassa di detta oncia una manco mezzo punto. E così si vada esequendo a mettere la seconda soglia di esse quattro soglie nel Naviglio lontana altri cavezzi venticinque della predetta prima di esse quattro, con caduta di oncia una e mezza dalla superficie di essa prima soglia nuova posta nel Naviglio alla superficie di essa seconda, e con questo ordine si metta la terza, e la quarta soglia, cioè alla terza un'oncia e mezza, e alla quarta due oncie da superficie a superficie, e nel resto si esequisca esso Capitolo come sta.

Item il secondo Capitolo si esequisca al presente in tutto e per tutto.

Item il terzo Capitolo sia esequito al presente, e sia osservato come sta.

Item per la esecuzione del quarto Capitolo, dichiariamo che al presente si rimettano due pali, che s'attrovano mancare alla cima di essa palificata,[3] ovvero nel luogo dove erano, e nel resto sia eseguito esso Capitolo come sta.

Item il quito Capitolo sia eseguito al presente come sta.

Item il sesto Capitolo sia osservato come sta.

Item il settimo Capitolo, nel quale si parla della Predata,[4] sia provveduto in questo modo, che dove si dice, che essa predata non si possa fortificare con cavaletti, se non per spazio di cavezzi dodeci e mezzo; Ora dichiariamo, che essa possa essere fortificata con Cavaletti da un capo all'altro,[5] accio si possa più sicuramente mantenere in piedi dall' impeto dell'acqua, o altro accidente, lasciando però in essa predata le sue fenestrelle, siccome furon fatte nel 1559 dopo essa Capitolazione.

Item si dichiara, che la larghezza di essa predata sia di braccia cinque, construtta tutta di sassi solamente, e situata nel luogo, e sito, e con le misure dichiarate in esso Capitolo.[6]

Item si debbano mettere due Pali in piedi in quelli luoghi precisi dove essa predata deve cominciare e finire, acciò si levi ogni dubbio fra esse parti, quando *ut supra*, occorresse rifarla; restando però la libertà ad essi Giudici di poter provvedere in ogni tempo a gravame di alcuna di esse parti, sicchè ella s'intenda esser fatta *per modum provisionis*, come è dichiarato in esso Capitolo, il quale in tutte le sue parti resti valido e fermo.[7]

NOTES TO APPENDIX IV

1 MS copies of the agreement are widely dispersed among the archival sources cited. For a printed copy, see *Trattato cit.* (of Vaprio, 1755) pp. 25–26.
2 The point from which the *soglie* were to be measured was the first of the two chief causes of disagreement which led to the second phase of the dispute.
3 These had provided guide-lines to the form of the *Predata* established in 1559, and their removal had been part of the Brescian complaint in 1561.
4 The size, position and materials of construction of the *Predata* were the second chief cause of complaint by Brescia in 1561, and led to its destruction by them in April, 1561.
5 By 1561, the Predata appeared 'inlottata', or bound together with a kind of cement. the 1559 agreement had forbidden 'cavaletti', but the delegates had clearly realised in 1561 that a more durable construction would produce less possibility of dispute. (See App. II).
6 Brescia had also complained that the *Predata* had been moved nearer to their bank, so as to extract more water. For the measurements of its position, and angle of incidence, see contemporary maps (*A.S.V.*, and *A.S.M.*) above, Figs. 15, 16.
7 Unlike the agreement of 1559, the document was drawn up in legal form and witnessed (see *Trattato, cit.*, pp. 26–27) and a certificate added on November 13 1561 to certify the presence of Bollani and Anguissola throughout the course of the above constructions. (*Ibid.* where may be found also the methods used to fix the angle and position of the *Predata*).

THE DECIMA DEL CLERO OF DOMENICO BOLLANI[1]

1564

Avendosi al presente a mandare a' V. S. Reverendissime, et ... per questo Reverendo Succollettore il Rogito delle Condizioni di queste Vescovato, le quali gli furono li giorni passati dalli miei agenti qua presentate di mio ordine con ogni sollecitudine, acciò similmente li altri di questo clero con l'esempio mio si movessero a prestarsi prontamente ubbidenti alli mandati di Vostre Signorie, perciò ora con questa occasione a maggior chiarezza della verità, oltre le cose, e carichi dichiariti per esse scritture si aggiungono le cose infrascritte.

Che la Chiesia di Rocha Francha, la quale fu altre volte tassada separatamente dal Vescovato, ora che per Brevi Apostolici, dopo l'ultima tassa in tempo delli miei precessori ella si trova unita al Vescovato così hanno essi miei agenti dati in nota unitamente per esse condizioni li Beni et intrade di essa chiesia insieme con il restante delli altri Beni, et intrade, che il Vescovato si trova avere in detta terra di Roccafranca, però saranno contente le Signorie Illustrissime che siccome la loro tassa sarà perciò fatta unita sopra tutti li Beni descritti in esse condizioni così dar ordine che li libri, e scritture siano acconcie, sinchè il nome, e tassa di essa chiesia resti unito al nome et partita del Vescovato, acciò per errore la tassa et il debito non venisse a restare doppiato in due nomi.

Lo stesso ordine saranno medesimamente contente di dare con la Chiesia di Tusculano di Riviera di Salò,[2] li beni et intrade della quale si trovano similmente uniti al Vescovato, et dati in nota per li miei agenti ivi al Succollettore di Salò, acciò da questa regolazione ne segua il predetto buon ordine, che siccome tutti li beni di ambe esse chiesie si trovano, come è suddetto, uniti al Vescovato, così con la medesima tassa unita et solo ad un solo nome si abbia a vedere una sola partita, et fare un solo pagamento quanto veramente a quello che partiene alli carichi di tutte esse intrade mi rimetto a quel conto, che con ogni sincera verità viene esposto nelle suddette condizioni e scritture nelle quali le Signorie Vostre per la loro prudenza saranno anche avvertite, che il callo delli quindici per 100 solito darsi alli grani di altri territorii non può essere a gran giunta bastante a questo del Bresciano, il quale perchè è gravoso produce più per forza delle acque, che per alcuna sua buona qualità onde con l'esperienza si vede, che le robbe che quà si raccolgono calano molto più delle suddette 15 per 100 per esser dal morbido delle acque tutti li grani non solamente di minor peso, ma anche molto male accompagnati, et similmente tutte le altre robbe sono di assai minor bontà, che non quelle che vengono in buona terra.

Occorre anche oltre il callo della predetta tassa, che sia considerato dalle Signorie Vostre per cosa molto importante la grande differenza ch'è delli minori pesi e misure che si costumano nel Bresciano da quello, che sono in Venezia, e nel Padovano, et altri territorij: perochè siccome li campi, che nel Bresciano si chiamano Piò sono minori delli Campi Padovani e Trivisani per forse una quarta parte così tutte le biavi, li fieni, olei, lini, et altre robbe rispondono nel Bresciano a questa libra piccola una terza parte manco che non fanno in Venezia, et Padovano, essendo che in Brescia quasi tutte le suddette robbe passano per via di peso; et è cosa notoria, che cento libre piccole di queste bresciane non rispondono in Venezia più di libre sessanta sei e due terzi, che è giustamente la terza parte manco, siccome anco li vini, che vano a misura rispondono nel modo suddetto che tre carra bresciani non fanno più di due carra Padovani: però innanzi che si dia a esse intrade per il sporco et spesa il sopradetto callo, et che si valutino dovrà essere fatta la ridduzione alla vera quantità delle misure e pesi predetti di Brescia che sono per tanta parte minori da quelli di Padova, Treviso, e Friuli, con li quali è regolata essa limitazione.

Condizione di tutti li beni, possessioni, et intrade del Vescovato di Brescia, la quale io Mario Trusso cittadino di questa città d'ordine di Monsignor Reverendissimo Vescovo, et come suo Procurator per debita obbedienza del Breve, et Monitorio Generale degli Illustrissimi, e Reverendissimi Signori Deputati a fare la nuova tassa del Clero, presento al Reverendo nostro Succolettore[3] quà con ogni sincera verità per quella cognizione, e notizia che io posso avere delli suddetti beni et intrade, avendone, come ne ho il continuo maneggio di esse, e l'obbligo di tenere particolar conto per la imposizione datami per Sua Signoria Reverendissima, dal principio che Ella fu chiamata a questo Vescovado fino al presente, et così per mio giuramento . . . la presente scrittura, sottoscritta di mia propria mano contener tutta quella verità che io posso sapere per il continuo mio maneggio siccome quà sotto sarà per me notato particolarmente e distintamente, e prima.

Nel territorio di Bagnolo[4] Piò di terra 750 circa, la qual misura di Piò è un terzo manco della misura del campo padovano, parte delli quali sono arativi et videgadi, parte sono prativi, et parte arativi solamente e la maggior parte di essi sono giacivi e palludivi, le quali terre sono lavorate per l'infrascritti lavoradori cioè.

Vicenzo Celigata, Battista Marmesion, Giacomo Mazzuccho, Nicolò Viviano, Giovanni Feretto et li eredi del q. Vicenzo Castellino.

Delli quali terreni nelli ultimi tre anni se ne è cavato la intrada infrascritta a rason di somma di Brescia che risponde alla misura venetiana alcuna parte manco di due stara veneziani per ciascheduna somma.

1561 Il primo Anno		1562[5] Lo anno secondo	1563 Lo anno terzo	1564
198	Formento. . . somme	226	138	190
22	Segalla „	28	32	20½
10	Formentada „	14	16	8
98	Miglio e Panica	122	108½	116½
32	Sorgo	27	31	16
18	Biava da cavalli	17	16	24
4	Legumi	5	6	4½
80	Fieno . . . Carra	70	73	79
60	Lino . . . Pesi	72	60	78

1561		1562	1563	1564
	Vino di piano alla misura bressana			
13	carra.	19	15	10½
14	Fassine . . . Migliara	15	13	16

Item ha una casetta in Bagnolo con un ortecello qual è affittada a Caradino Tintore libre dodeci all'anno.

Nella terra e territorio di Rocca Franca[6] una possessione di Piò 590 in una parte delli quali sono arativi solamente, parte arativi e vidgadi, parte prativi, et parte giacivi et palludivi, la qual possessione in gran parte non si può adacquare, e di essi vi sono circa campi 130 vicini al fiume Oglio,[7] che solevano esser Bosco, e delli quali se ne cava poschissimo. Sono essi terreni lavorati dall'infrascritti lavoradori: Paulo Minotto, Masino Gedoli, Antonio Frassine, Domenico di Poli, Antonio Bassano e Battista Lazzarino.
Delli quali terreni si è cavato li ultimi tre anni la intrada infrascritta, cioè
[1561] Il primo anno [1562] Lo anno secondo [1563] Lo anno terzo [1564]

1561 Il primo Anno		1562 Lo anno secondo		1563 Lo anno terzo	1564
146	Formenta	somme	134	150	140
64	Segalla	somme	94	82	62
9	Formentada	somme	12	16	15
165	Miglio	somme	163	142	170
8	Sorgo	somme	15	21	10
82	Fieno	Carra	86	90	90
207	Lino	Pesi	216	196	200
1	Vino di piano	Carra	2	0.8	1½

Item in detta terra alcuna casette vecchissime fatte di terra che rovinano delle quali quando si possono trovare fittaioli che le vogliano si trazerebbe in più partite all'anno L. 60.
Item si affitta de pascoli della parte palludiva et del luogo del boschetto L. 85. Item si affitta un pezzo di terra delli . . . L. 26. Nella terra e territorio di Manerbio[8] Piò 180 circa, parte arativi et videgadi, e parte senza vite, quali sono lavorati dalli infrascritti lavoratori cioè Lorenzo Remondino, e Giacomo Panzera. Delli quali si è cavato li ultimi tre anni la intrada infrascritta cioè

	(1561)			1562	1563	1564
	60	Formento	somme	78	93	57
	31	Segalla	somme	26	31	28
	90	Miglio	somme	90	93	90
	43	Fieno	carra	40	45	50
	155	Lino	pesi	190	200	150
	6	Vino di piano	carra	12	11	5
(legne)	2	Fassine	Migliara	2½	2½	2½

Nella terra e territorio di Milzano,[9] Piò 190 circa, parte arativi et videgadi, et parte senza vite et arbori ma arativi solamente quali sono lavorati dalli infrascritti lavoratori. Bernardino Tassone e Andrea di Guidini delli quali ultimi tre anni si è cavata la intrada infrascritta.

	(1561)			1562	1563	1564
	59	Formento	somme	82	63	55
	27	Segalla		23	27	54
	80	Miglio		86	92	90
	40	Fieno carra		45	40	50
	165	Lino pasi		175	190	160
		Vino di piano				
	3	carra		4	6	2
(legne)	2	Fassine migliara		2	2	2

Nella Contrada detta del Brolo del Vescovato,[10] Piò 65 in circa, arativi solamente senza vite e senza albori quale è lavorato da Vicenzo Erizzardo della quale se n'è cavato li ultimi tre anni la intrada infrascritta.

(1561)			1562	1563	1564
35	Formento	somme	50	57	30
18	Segalla	somme	25	25	15
38	Miglio	somme	25	20	47
28	Fieno carra		22	18	26

Nella terra di Santo Eustacchio[11] e Santo Bartolomeo, Piò 120 circa, parte arativi solamente et parte prativi, li quali sono lavorati da Maffio delle Mesane e Pivino di Poli. Delle quali li ultimi tre anni si è cavata la infrascritta intrada.

(1561)		1562	1563	1564
49	Formento somme	59	62	46
16	Segalla	28	33	24
20	Miglio e Panizo	13	13	14
5	Sorgo	3	2	3
2	Legumi	2	2	1½
29	Fieno carra	26	26	27
8	Vino di piano carra	15	13	7
1½	Fassine migliara	2	1½	1½

Nella terra e territorio di Gavardo,[12] Piò 190 circa, parte arativi e videgadi, parte arativi solamente, et prativi, ma tutti giacivi et sassosi, li quali sono lavorati da Antonio dalla Costa e Gio. Pietro di Bianchi, delle quali si è cavato la intrada infrascritta li ultimi tre anni.

(1561)		1562	1563	1564
10	Formento somme	14	16	8
6	Segalla	6	8	4
4	Miglio e Panizo	3	7	3
2½	Legumi	2½	3½	2½
28	Fieno carra	30	28	32
12	Vino carra	18	20	10

Item vi sono alcuni pezzi di boschi delli quali non se ne cava utile alcuno. Ha nella Contrada di San Pietro Marcellino[13] da circa Piò 3 di prato del quale si è cavato li ultimi tre anni la intrada infrascritta.

(1561)	1562	1563	1564
8 Fieno carra	7	8	9

Ha una porzione del pedaggio di Pontevico[14] per la quale si è cavato li ultimi tre anni la intrada infrascritta.

(1561)	1562	1563	1564
not given	L. 103:15:8	114:2:−	18:13:4[15]
	(Per li due anni fatta la fattura)		

Sono nella soprascritta terra di Gavardo diverse persone al numero di 300 obbligate a pagare ogni anno le robbe e danari infrascritte, onde per tanta divisione et si minuta scodendosi da persone miserabili ne vanno assai in sinistro.

Formento	somme	41½
Miglio		20½
Sorgo		32
Fieno	carra	1
Vino		1

Item sono obbligati le persone sopradette a pagar in dinari L. 63 Sono in Valcamonica livelli e fitti in più posti similmente minute, e da persone miserabili al numero 121, e perciò da farne poco fondamento per le somme infrascritte.

Formento somme 3½, Segalla 4½, Miglio 4½, Mistura 9, Vino carra 2½. Item in dinari L. 518:13:4.

Sono in Brescia e suo territorio diverse persone al numero di 260 obbligate a pagar ogni anno da L. 1000. ma per tanta divisione et tanta minuta vera com'è predetto grande parte in sinistro.

Io Mario Trusso per mio giuramento esser vero quanto si contine nella presente scrittura, la quale ho sottoscritta di propria mano ad ultimo ottobre 1564.

Avendo io Mario Trusso come Procurator e Negotiatore delle cose di Monsignor Reverendissimo Vescovo di Brescia prodotto le polizze delle Intrade dell'anno 1562, 1563, 1564 per li tre ultimi anni secondo la forma del primo editto: ora per ubbidienza dell'ultimo editto, per il quale espressamente si comette, che si diano le entrate del 1561, se bene dalla intrada dell'anno 1561 a quella dell'anno 1564 vi è poca differenza per il maneggio che ne ho Io avuto non dimanco per la sudetta ubbidienza produco la infrascritta polizza dell'intrada cavata dalli terreni del Vescovato l'anno predetto 1561, rimettendomi poi alla intrada delli livelli et affitti continui a quanto è stato dato nelle precedente polizze, e perciò . . . [there follow the figures which I have incorporated above].

Ego Marius Trussius Manu Propriae

Cariche e gravezze che sostiene il Vescovato di Brescia le quali Io Domenico Bollani per volere del N[ostro] S[ignor] Dio trovandomi al presente dettore di essa chiesia debbo per scarico della mia coscientia dichirarire affine che intendendosi li carichi con la intrada di esso Vescovado, la quale ora si presenta in scrittura per li miei agenti, e che ne hanno il continuo maneggio, e ne tengono conto ciascheduno di Voi Reverendissimi et Illustrissimi Signori Tassatori, potiate con satisfazione, e sicurezza della Vostra coscientia aggravare la condizione mia in quella porzione di X^{ma} che giustamente giudicarete col rispetto delli miei carichi potersi per me sostenere, essendo Io sicurissimo che Vostre Signorie Illustrissime e Reverendissime voranno avere sicura considerazione a non mi restringere il modo di poter operare quello che conviene a tanto mio obbligo nel debito servizio di Dio e necessario governo di seicento mille anime, che mi sono commesse sapendosi da ogni uno chiaramente, che per li Sacri Canoni le rendite delle chiesie sono obbligate a tre principali carichi, cioè alli servizi e reparazione di quelle, alla sostentazione de' poveri di N.S. Giesù Christo, et al conveniente sostentamento di chi ha il peso e governo di esse.

Io dunque chiamandomi aggravato con questo obbligho l'anno 1558, come piaque a Sua Divina Maestà, a un tanto peso e vedendo l'abitazione, e casa Episcopale in manifestissimo pericolo e rovina, fui forzato nel mio intrare nel

Vescovato di mettermi a fabricare essa casa con spesa molto grave, per il che oltre quello che la casa mia patrimoniale convenne esborsare per la spedizione delle Bolla e per pormi all'ordine de' vestimenti e mobili convenienti per questo mio nuovo stato,[16] e per molti altri necessarij bisogni, fui sforzato intanare di grossa summa di danari le proprie sostanze di M. Giacomo, mio fratello, aggravato sin quà di dieci filgioli, cioè sette femine e tre maschi,[17] et non solamente da quel tempo in quà non ho avuto modo di sgravare li sudetti miei di si fatto debito, ma mi è stato anco farlo di accrescerlo, non potendo far di manco di refabricare quasi dalli fondamenti, le case e coperti delle possessioni per la manifesta sua rovina non si gli essendo in tanta lunghezza di anni, che li Vescovi sono stati assenti, fatto alcun miglioramente di riparatione,[18] et inoltre convengo similmente dar principio alla fabrica di questo Duomo ridotto a rovinossissimo termine, siccome anche la Magnifica Città si è contentata intuitu Pietatiu et elemosine et in onore del Signor Dio contribuire alla detta fabrica,[19] conosciendo questi Magnifici cittadini, che per fare tale spesa non basterebbero molti Vescovati non che questo solo, il quale anche si trova assai gravato di spese e carichi; onde io non debbo, ne anco per qual si voglia mia impotenza ricercare a modo alcuno di fare si necessaria spesa in le riedificazione di essa chiesia, siccome non ho similmente mancato di farne un'altra molto importante nel provedergli di un gran numero di Paramenti di quali se ne trovava in estremo bisogno, et posso dire spogliata.

Per li quali detti carichi, et per molti altri che quà sotta notarò, è cosa certamente impossibile che io possa continuare nella onerosa tassa, che si trovava per il passato posta a questo Vescovato, la quale senza dubbio non sarebbe stata posta si grave, se quello, che allora lo possedeva, trovandosi Cardinale ricchissimo,[20] et antico Prelato, fosse stato nello stretto termine, et gravi pesi che io mi trovo, e che egli anco fosse stato in obbligo di pagare le decime siccome io le pago,[21] stringendomi più di che porta il mio debole potere con speranza però che il Signor Dio un giorno averebbe permesso, che io ne fossi in buona parte sgravato, siccome ora me ne assicuro, vedendomi Deputati si Religiosi Signori et osservatori della Giustitia e Servizio di Dio.

Trovomi gravato di una pensione di ducati 763 d'oro di camera ogni anno al Reverendissimo Cornaro, Vescovo di Treviso, et di un'altra di scudi 300 d'oro ad un suo nipote, nominato M. Marco.[22]

Item di scudi 20 all'anno ad uno M. Marco Bozzaoli, la qual summa di pensioni mi importa di pagamento in contadi quà in Brescia per causa della grande differenza del corso delli ori, et monete da quà ad altri luoghi . . . 1444:— Ho appresso a questo per la compartita delle biave gravezza di far condurre ogni anno nella città la quarta parte circa delle intrade per conto di monicione al luogo detto il granarolo,[23] dove per l'ordinamento le biave si vendono un terzo manco di quello vagliono da per tutto, la qual gravezza non vi era al tempo della tassa ultima, e questo come ogniun sà non importa manco di ducato uno per somà. Fa il Vescovato ordinaria elemosina del pane a grande numero di poveri, li quali, trovandosi il Vescovo alla sua residenza, hanno ogni giorno il primo riccorso alle porte del Vescovato.

Abbiamo per Grazia del Signor Dio quà in Brescia l'opera dei poveri vergognosi con la deputazione di alquanti buoni servi di Dio in ciaschuna parrocchia a visitare

personalmente tutti li poveri infermi alli quali col persuadere prima la confessione
per assicurarsi che siano ben timorati di Dio, et degni di essere sovvenuti, vengono
subitamente somministrati danari, medici, medicine, et il viver anche per le loro
famiglie, mancandogli per le infermità delli capi chi loro proveda delli suoi bisogni,
et essi deputati hanno continuo riccorso al Vescovo per esser sovvenuti de dinari
accio sia proveduto alle cose necessarie per sostentazione di si importante opera.[24]

Queste cose che si fanno palesamente ho voluto solo così in brevità toccare,
non mi si convenendo nel resto divenire a molti particolari di quantità di danari,
frumento, et altre robbe, che necessariamente mi convengono uscire di casa,
potendo ciascheduna per sua prudenza considerare, che non possono essere di
molte e di assai importanza. Contribuisce il Vescovato ogni anno a tasse di soldati
imbottadi, et altre simili gravezze, che non importano manco di L. 100 all'anno,
et tutte esse gravezze si pagano con il danno delle monete, et ori, che ho suddetto,
siccome con lo stesso danno vengono pagate le decime in questa camera di
Brescia, onde per ogni cento scudi che si devono pagar in essa è bisogno esborsare
116, non pigliando la camera li scudi italiani se non per L. 6:16 a valuta di Venezia,
et li Mocenighi per soldi 24, et non di manco li scudi si contano in ogni scosseda
fuori di camera per la città in ragion di L. 8:—, et li Mocenighi di soldi 28, et cosi
alla rata ogni altra sorte di moneta, et ori, ch'è quà in Brescia un dannonotabil-
issimo. Portano seco le possessioni del Vescovato molte gravezze e spese per esser
divise in più bande del territorio, onde mi fa bisogno tener molti ministri et fattori
con grossi salarij dentro en fuori della città. Il bisogno anco di tenere le possessioni
adacquate alli tempi debiti aggiunge grave spesa per li affitti che si pagano di molta
importanza alli patroni delle acque senza le quali le terre non renderebbero in
Bresciana se non pochissimo, come si sa.[25]

Patisce il Vescovato assai nello scoder le soe intrade, dovendosi scoder con più
rispetto, che non fanno li laici per il che succede molte volte, che si resta col
credito in mano senza poterne fare alcuna ricuperazione.[26] Ha carico il Vescovato
di tenere quattro Capellani cioè, due a Roccafranca, e due a Tusculano per servizio
di quelle chiesie, alle quali si dà di salario fra tutti loro ogni anno D. 120.[27]

Mi bisognano molti ministri per diversi officij del governo spirituale, essendosi la
Diocesi per tanto paese, come fa, et medesimamente mi fa bisogno di buon numer
di persone per l'ordinario servizio della casa et famiglia mia, in che mi va buona
summa di dinaro, non avendo io voluto mai tener a servizio mio persone con
speranza di beneficij di chiesia, se non siano atti a minstrare degnamente, et con li
gradi ecclesiastici al Culto di Dio, et al governo delle Anime,[28] onde che vi vanno
in salariati non manco di scudi 500 all'anno.

Il mio Vicario,[29] che sta ressidente in Brescia ha per sua mercede scudi 200.

Il Predicatore per la quadragesima scudi 70.

Il Predicatore che faccio predicare le Feste per tutto l'anno scudi 50.

Il Lettore[30] che faccio leggere continuamente in Vescovato una lezione di Theo-
logia et casi di coscientia scudi 30.

Vi è la spesa del Seminario ordinato per Decreto del Sacro Concilio di Trento, il
quale di già è anche posto in esenzione nella nostra metropoli di Milano con
gravezza di 5 per 100 sopra tutte le intrade delle chiesie diocesane con la qual
regola bisogna che ... anche noi in Brescia per non mancare della debita nostra

ubbidienza, et procurare un tanto beneficio alla chiesia di Dio di allevare buoni sacerdoti, e ben disciplinati nella via christiana.[31] Convengo appresso per esser la Diocesi ampia come ho sudetto aver molti Vicari Foranei che mi agiutano a tener visitate di continuo le parocchie di fuori, le quali sono in gran numero, e molto distanti dalla città, acciò con le loro frequenti informationi et ajuti, io possi di continuo sapere quello che si opera in ciascheduna parte della Diocesi, et provedere nel modo, che ricerca il servizio di Dio, et la salute di tanti migliara di uomini, e perciò fa bisogno, che la casa mia sia in continuo albergo di non poco numero di persone, oltre le ordinarie della famiglia, di modo che con tanti carichi, gravezze e spese, che ho di sopra dette, oltre li accidenti di tempeste, et altri danni, che ben spesso si travagliano in questo paese di Brescia, mi trovo molte volte intricato a poter supplire a molti occorenti bisogni, s'io debbo continuare così nelle spese di fabriche tanto necessarie, come nel mantenimento di opere si pie, e nel ordinario sostentamento di buon numero di ministri, e di miei famigliari, siccome di tutto ciò supplico il Signo Iddio, che me ne faccia vero testimonio nelle coscientie di Vostre Reverendissime, et Illustrissime Signorie e pur son tutte cose che mi devono stare per l'onore del Signor Dio in continuo pensiero e forzarmi a non abbandonarle, siccome per Grazia di Sua Divina Maestà non son finora mancato, et . . . sicuro, che le Signorie Vostre Reverendissime non vorranno gravare le loro coscientie nel restringermi il modo più che possano comportare in me le intrade del Vescovato con li carichi, gravezze et spese che ho sudette et in loro buona grazia mi raccomando.

Extra presentata fuit.

Decimato per Decima con li limiti cioè Rocca Franca e Tusculano in L. 2061:-

1 A.S.V., *Sopra le Decime del Clero*, R⁰. 235, No. 3. This is the entry in the register for Domenico Bollani by Mario Trusso. The original documents submitted to Venice, with the addition of various legal attestations, are in *A.S.V., Ibid., Filza* 18, no. 3.

2 in *A.S.V., Ibid., Filza* 18, no. 3.

3 Giampaulo Corte, whose sworn testimony to the differing values of money in Brescia and elsewhere appears attached to Bollani's *Decima* in A.S.V., *Sopra le Decime del Clero, Filza*, 18, no. 3 dated February 19, 1565.

4 Bagnolo [Mella] is 13 kilometres due south of Brescia on the main road to Pontevico and Cremona.

5 Dates are inferred from what follows. In the MS, the three years' products are given vertically in a list. I have transcribed them horizontally, omitting to repeat names, for reasons of space and for purposes of comparison. The 1561 figures are brought back from later in the documents.

6 Roccafranca is west of Brescia, between Rudiano and Orzinuovi close to the river Oglio.

7 It will be remembered that the Cremonese had accused Bollani of partiality in their dispute with the Brescians, as his own canal (known today as the *Vescovada*) waters these lands.

8 Manerbio is between Bagnolo and Pontevico, due south of Brescia on the Brescia-Cremona road.

9 Milzano, in the southern region of the *Bresciano*, due south of the city, is near the Brescia-Cremona provincial boundary.

10 A holding in what is now the centre of the city, situated where the New Cathedral, Via Mazzini and the bishop's palace now stand. (See Luigi Francesco Fè D'Ostiani, *Storia, Tradizione e Arte nelle vie di Brescia*, (Brescia, 1927) pp. 271–275).

11 Areas on the north-western fringes of the city, now built-up as suburbs. Bollani owned a villa at Sant'Eustacchio, to which he retired during the plague of 1577, it will be remembered.

12 Gavardo is situated to the east of Brescia on the road to Salò.

13 This holding, on the eastern fringe of the city, was much larger before 1533, when the bulk of the land was bought from the bishop by the Martinengo dei Conti Palatini family to found a monastery of the Agostinian order. Suppressed by Borromeo in 1580, as too open to public view, the monastery became a church of the Capuchin order in 1587. The full history is in Fè D'Ostiani, *op. cit.*, pp. 162–165.

14 It is very probable that this was a share in the toll on the bridge across the river Oglio at Pontevico on the Brescia/Cremona provincial boundary (rather than a road toll at the *place* Pontevico).

15 There is a cross against this figure in the MS, and the discrepancy in the figures seems to indicate a changed system of accounting in 1564. There is no figure given for 1561. There is a document in *A.S.C.B., Registrum Olei*, Reg. R, p. 63 which may be significant in this connection. Bollani bought an island in the river Oglio in 1562 (the sale was engineered by Mario Trusso, for 475 ducats) which may have entailed toll rights on traffic crossing the bridge linking the provinces of Brescia and Cremona. As this item is mentioned in the *Decima del Clero*, it was doubtless a result of re-investment of episcopal revenues resulting from the sale of immobile goods.

16 It will be remembered that the family was less able to contribute in 1558 (when these expenses were incurred) than in 1564 (after the addition of the Memmo fortune on the death of Lucrezia Memmo in 1562).

17 He does not mention, of course, that he was able to contribute significantly to the dowries of his nieces, as Giacomo Bollani acknowledged in his will in 1568. He was technically correct in describing the family patrimony as belonging to Giacomo (rather than jointly owned in a *fraterna*) as their father died in 1564 (according to Barbaro) so that the fortune would have been left to Giacomo in that year, as Domenico was in holy orders. (See tree above p. 16).

18 For Bollani and residence, see above, pp. 135–136.

19 See Zamboni, *Memorie cit.*

20 Cardinal Durante, for whom see, for example, P. Guerrini, 'La famiglia Durante e i suoi

266

vescovi' in *Brixia Sacra*, 1911, pp. 80 ff. Durante had become bishop of Brescia on the death of Cardinal Andrea Corner in 1551. Exemptions, normally conceded to Cardinals, had been extended to certain named prelates in 1556 and 1558 by Paul IV. (See, for example, references in A.S.V., *Sopra le Decime del Clero, busta* 48: 'Collettori, Decreti di Senato in copia (1531–1690)'). Much of this document seems to be a bid for inclusion in this category. For further discussion, and Bollani's role later as *collettore*, see above, pp. 216–219.

21 Bollani was not exempt, as Durante had been, as not a Cardinal.

22 Giorgio Corner, bishop of Treviso, 1538–1577. For bibliography on him, see Logan, *op. cit.*, p. 516, and family tree p. 252 (where, on the above evidence, the tree needs some correction).

23 See above, pp. 81–83, for Bollani's concern with these measures while *Podestà* of the city.

24 For discussion of this, see above, pp. 153–156.

25 See above, Chap. V.

26 The contrast must have been a telling one for Bollani, who had progressed from the traditional income from the investment of capital of the Venetian aristocracy – to the 'image' of the bishop/landlord so carefully circumscribed by the Council of Trent. Perhaps, too, he was remembering Pietro Aretino, who, we have suggested may have occasioned a lawsuit. (Cairns, 'Ancora sulla casa dell'Aretino . . .' *cit.*)

27 Bearing in mind Bollani's insistence that the income from these two churches outside Brescia was declared in separate *condizioni* (above, p. 257), as well as above, his inclusion of these salaries is comprehensible.

28 Doubtless this comment reflects the influence of Borromeo in his reduction of personal staff and the bishop's 'court' to its barest minimum.

29 Leandro Lana de' Terzi in 1564–1565. See biography in Fè D'Ostiani, *Domenico Bollani, cit.*, pp. 195–197.

30 Benedetto Erba (1517–1576).

31 On the seminary, see above, pp. 160 seq.

APPENDIX VI

DOCUMENTS CONCERNING THE DISPUTE BETWEEN
DOMENICO BOLLANI AND CARDINAL FRANCESCO GAMBARA[1]

August – September 1577

1. Cardinal Gambara to Domenico Bollani, August 10, 1577

Molto Reverendo e Illustrissimo Monsignore,

In questa calamità della mia patria[2] m'è stata di molta consolatione l'intender con quanta carità V.S. provveda alla salute di quel popolo, di che oltre al merito ch'ella acquista rispetto a Dio, io me la sento particolarmente obbligato, et se ben io non ho mai havuto avviso della ricevuta d'una lettera che io le scrissi al principio di questo mese[3], non mancai, come V.S. havrà veduto di procurare che N.S.[4] concedesse un giubileo alla città et alla Diocesi di Brescia con quelle conditioni et circumstantie che V.S. havesse dichiarito, per gl'impedimenti causati dalla peste. Ho poi inteso con mio gran dispiacere la morte di M. Orfeo Tolino mio cameriere, et sono stato avvisato (e ben difficilmente m'inclino a crederlo), che V.S. pensava di conferire il canonicato vacante nel Domo per la morte di questo mio servitore, il quale, come ella debba sapere, tocca a dar a me, et questo non ha alcun dubbio, essendo la raggion tanto chiara et tanto ordinaria, che il muovermi difficultà in questo, parebbe un mettermi in lite le cose mie, et un voler travagliarmi espressamente a torto, il che non solo non aspetto dall'amicitia nostra, dalla quale provarei piuttosto aiuto per quelli che mi servono, havend'ella una diocesi così ricca di collattioni, ma non l'aspettarei anche da un mio nimico, potendo ogn'uno esser certo che alla fine doppo simili molestie la giustitia haverebbe il suo luogo. Però quando pur V.S. per qualunque causa si fusse mosso a far questo, la prego quanto posso a desistere, et a non mi metter in questa lite, che nel vero non mi pare di meritarlo, massime da lei, che sa quanto amorevolmente altre volte mi si è offerto a volermi aiutar del suo a beneficia [dei] miei servitori, onde sentirei tanto maggiormente questo torto sino all'anima, et me ne terrei per sempre offeso perchè simili torti non si fanno se non con gran dispreggio di colui a cui si fanno. Col quale fine a V.S. di retto cuore mi offero et raccomando.

Cardinal Gambara

2. Domenico Bollani to Giacomo Roveglio, September 1, 1577

. . . Stimai al proposito scriver al Cardinale Gambara per risposta dell'ufficio fatto dal Cl.mo Thiepolo,[5] et mandai la lettera al Clarissimo [Francesco] Longo[6] da mostrargli, con ordine che egli mandi poi a noi l'istessa copia che gli ho mandata, che penso vi piacera;[7] ma non è bastato a quel Cardinale quella lettera scritta al Thiepolo,[8] che gli vi ha scritto un'altra a questa Pottesta[9] per far l'istesso ufficio meco et in essa dopo una lunga diceria, diviene a dire infine che mi ricordi che ho più bisogno di amici che de benefici; che è pur troppo . . . proceder di un cardinale

con un par mio; di più ha scritto anco a me la lettera che vederete alla quale col
corriero della presente settimana faccio conforme risposta all'altra che vi mandarà,
come ho predetto al Cl.mo Longo . . .
[he also plans to send a further letter in the same vein to Mons. Speciano,[10] and
requests Roveglio to ask Mons. Frumento[11] to advise him on the best way of
proceeding with the Pope].

3.   Domenico Bollani to Cardinal Gambara, September, 1577

Dopo inviata a Vinetia la lettera per me scritta a V.S. Ill.ma in materia del
Canonicato del Rev.do Tolini, ho havuto dal Mons. Soldo la lettera di lei nel
medesimo proposito,[12] come anco nell'istesso giorno me n'haveva parlato questo
Ill.ma Podestà, et perchè non vorrei tardar a rispondere di subito a ciascuna sua
lettera, esser stimato men riverente di quel che le sono, et voglio sempre essergli
come conviene al debito mio, et alli molti obblighi che le tengo per la benigna
amorevolezza che sempre si è compiacuta mostrarmi, vi le dico con ogni sincerità
non haver creduto poterle dar in ciò risentimento per la necessità in che mi sono
trovato di unir essa prebenda alla lettura teologale con li due brevi di N. Sig. l'uno
all Ill.mo Sig. Cardinal Borromeo generale per tutta questa provincia, l'uno a me
per questa nostra particolar Chiesa di Brescia, di così fare con la prima vacante
prebenda Canonicale non ostante qualunque affetto nella corte di Roma, come
V. Sig.ia Ill.ma haverà più particolarmente inteso dalla suddetta mia con la quale
l'ho anco suplicato humilmente di volentieri de veder il fatto bene in questa
Chiesa, et massime in questo tempo, ch'ella se ne trova in tanto bisogno per allevar
idonei ministri nel servitio di Dio per supplimento delli tanti morti in questo si
rabbioso travaglio della peste. Di gratia consideri V. Ill.ma Sig.ia con la molta
prudenza et Christiana pietà sua, che quando ciò si tralasciasse di fare con detta
prima vacanza come dicere i Brevi et parimenti lo comanda il Concilio di Trento[13]
si tendrebbe a pregiudicar di non poter [ciò fare] con altra vacanza, perchè
ciascuno, che ne fosse per altra via provveduto nell'avvenire addurrebbe per favor
[ire] le sue raggioni esser passato il caso di detti Brevi con l'essecutione tralasciata
nel modo ch'essi commandano, et con la chiesa [. . .] restar privata di tanto bene,
et io incaricato nella coscienza et nell'honore. Torno dunque a suplicarla di
riconoscer con la molta benignità sua il sincero mio proceder, et insieme per il
cordiale affetto a questa chiesa, et . . . sua a haver per grato il tanto servitio, che si
le fa col mezzo di detta lettura in honor del Sig. Dio; et io ne considerarò
maggiormente debitore a lei in qualsivoglia cosa che sia per comandarmi; supplico
medesimanente V. Ill.ma Sig.ia a interpretar bene la tardanza mia nel darvi
risposta alla sua capitatami assai ben tarda, . . .
[the rest of the letter comprises a 'relation' on the state of the plague in Brescia.]

4.   Domenico Bollani to Pope Gregory XIII, September 10, 1577

. . . Intendo oltre ciò con mio assai dolore che l'Ill.mo Cardinale Gambara tenta di farmi rivocare parte della benigna gratia già fattami dalla S[antità] Vostra per il mezzo del Rev.mo Datario di due Mansionarie della Cathedrale, col levarmene una, che sarebbe con infinito dolore di detti miei poveri Cappellani, che in essa hanno di continuo in tanti pericoli portato pondus diei et aestus, et con non poco mio incarico, col essersi la gratia già fattami divulgata in Roma, et qui. Ho anco per tutta questa provincia all'Ill.mo Card. Borromeo, et l'altro particolare a me per questa mia chiesa, tanto bisognosa di allevare buoni ministri in supplemento delli tanti morti, unita alla Lettura Theologale una prebenda Canonicale vacata per la morte d'un Canonico, che egli[14] pretende per la sua famigliarita conferire. Non mi vale a fargli dire ch'essi Brevi derogano a qualunque affetto si sia, che mi minaccia di litigio et mali uffici contra di me. In questo dunque tanto travagli d'ogni sorta, prostrato a' piedi della Beatitudine Vostra suplico la paterna protettione con la Santissima Sua Benedittione; et il Sig.re di continuo prego la conservi lunghi anni in accrescimento della Santa Chiesa.[15]

Domenico Vescovo di Brescia

5.   Gio. di Camerini[16] [?] in Rome to Domenico Bollani, August 31, 1577.

Mons. Datario bacia le mani di V.S. Ill.ma et desideroso di servirla, et compiacerla quanto altra persona sua amicissima et se non fosse che li Cardinali possono troppo li farebbe veder con effetto quanto li porta affettione, ma che è alla corte forzato da N. Sig.re quale spesso si lascia espugnar con prieghi, et intercessioni come ha fatto in conferire il Canonicato che V.S. Rev.ma haveva conferito a Mons. Vicario[17] sotto pretesto che non sia compresa sotto l'Indulto che S.S. concesse a V.S. Rev.ma di poterlo conferire essendo il morto famigliare dell'Ill.ma di Gambara; Non ostante che Mons. Datario habbia fatto sapere a S. Beatitudine, che detto Canonicato era conferito, et che la collattione haveva havuto effetto. Sono stato anche avvertito che detto Canonicato ha 60 Ducati di pensione vecchia, pero V.S. potrà pigliare quella provvisione che parerà secondo il suo sano et vero giudicio . . .

6.   Domenico Bollani to Giacomo Roveglio, September 12, 1577

L'aviso che mi scrivete d'haver havuto dal Marini intorno il riporto fattogli da M. Zerbino, mi ha fatto pigliar necessaria occasione di dar conto al Papa delle cose di qua, et far conoscere la malignità d'altri, che principalmente credo che sia stato astuto tiro del Card. Gambara per ottener qualla Mansionaria, col dire che tutto era abbandonato, et che 'l suo verrebbe hora alla ressidenza etc. Hor mostrando intorno ciò il torto fattomi per la gratia già concessami, ho anco introdotto a parlare del vostro canonicato. Et per [. . .] con più di qualche [. . .] ho tirata una lettera a modo mio che dice il tutto ristrettamente et senza punto d'affetta-tione, et ricordandomi che esso Marini scrisse il [. . .] fattogli dal Datario nel presentargli mie lettere scritte di qua per rispetto del contagio l'ho mandata al Cl.ma M. Francesco [Longo] che la trascriva di sua mano, insieme con due altri che scrivo al Card. Morone et all'Ambasciatore,[18] con ordine che'l Marini torvandosi il Morone in Roma, et non impedito da qualche indispositione, faccia prima riccorso a lui con presentargli la mia lettera con la propria insieme del Cl.mo M. Francesco [Longo] che gl'attesta d'haver trascritta in Vinetia ambe le mie del Papa, e di esso Cardinale [Gambara] per le quali viene per ricercato a creder in tutte le cose all'informatione, che gli darà esso agente, col leggergli insieme la copia, che gl'ho mandata della lettera del Papa, et così ad apresentarla a S. Santità; et quando esso Cardinale si trovi absente, o impedito, faccia riccorso all'Ambasciatore per ricercarlo dell'istesso; il qual ufficio di scrivere duplicato all'Ambasciatore oltre il Cardinale [Morone] ho voluto fare a cautela, che senza fallo sia fatto per l'uno o per l'altro, ma più mi piacerebbe Morone per l'humore tanto contrario tra ambi loro Cardinali [Morone e Gambara], onde son certo, che non gl'haverà in questo alcun rispetto, come per l'ordinario hanno i cardinali, l'uno all'altro. Mandai il tutto hieri a Vinetia col cavallaro et hora con la presente mando a voi la copia, che penso vi consolarà assai.[19] Hor di più per sicurar in voi il Canonicato, ho scritto al Marini un partito a proponer a quel di loro Sig.ri che farà l'ufficio col Papa, che è di dar con mia quiete a Gambara la Mansionaria, et che S. Santità gli comandi non più parlare di esso Canonicato. Parmi haver posto il negocio a buon segno, et ne spero buona riuscita in qualche guisa, et che'l Papa debba insieme restar ben soddisfatto delle mie attioni et fatiche, et parimenti che restarà levato il credito a Gambara, et ad ogni altro che volesse far mali uffici contra di me. Facciane mo la divina bontà a suo volere. Haverà già significato essa Manionaria al nostro da bene et fedelissimo Santicoli, ma non si puo altro.[20] Vi ho pur fatto quel bene da lui tanto desiderato del chiericato dato a suo nipote in Valcamonica per la morte del Prevosto di S. Giorgio, che . . . ma senza dubbio è degno, et meritevole d'ogni bene. Diedi a copiar al Morone li dui Brevi in materia della Theologale et Penitentiaria, con ordine a esso Pr[evosto?] Battista, che ve li mandasse, come son certo che haverà fatto, et così rileggendo qui, insieme col nostro amatissimo M. Domenico[21] il particolare concesso a me, lo giudiciamo bastante assai al nostro bisogno abbraciando anco nel non obstantibus le regole di Cancellaria che fa l'attione alli Cardinali, di che ne ho anco avvertito il Marini, perche tutto il fondamento del Gambara è quella sua espressa riserva, se bene egli dissimula essa derogatione per la lettera, che'l mi scrive, la quale vi mando, et poi mi rimanderete, rissolvendomi io de differir la risposta fin a tanto che sappia alcuna cosa dell'ufficio di Mons. Speciano, et di questo che hora sarà fatto da Morone o dall'Ambasciatore col Papa; et se pur egli non restarà quieto, dirò con sua burla, che voi conterete di farne remissione al Cardinale Borromeo con mia anco sodisfatione per rispetto del suo Breve. Ho detto al Marini, che'l confessi e consegli il tutto in Mons. Frumento, onde sarà bene, che intorno si fatta cose, mostrando voi esserne avvisato da me gliene scriviate. Per certo è stata gran cosa la promessa del Papa della Mansionaria a Gambara contra la parola data a Mons. Datario, onde mi pento non haver tenuto altro mezzo in far simili richieste, evadendo io che S. Santità non abbia in ciò stimato il Datario, et egli habbia fatta poca replica . . .

1 These letters are collected in Mss. B.V. 31., Biblioteca Queriniana, Brescia, and were originally collected by Giacomo Roveglio, Bollani's Vicar-General during this period. For the transcription, reference has also been made to the eighteenth century copies made by Baldassare Zamboni in MS. H. III. 7, (Biblioteca Queriniana).
2 Gambara alludes to the plague in Brescia.
3 Bollani refers to the reason for this below.
4 *Nostro Signore*: Pope Gregory XIII.
5 Gambara had clearly attempted to favour his cause with Tiepolo, Venetian ambassador in Rome.
6 Bollani's brother-in-law.
7 Probably the letter which follows as document 3.
8 Of this, there is no trace, of course.
9 Giovanni Soranzo.
10 Cesare Speciano was Borromeo's agent in Rome, and afterwards Bishop of Novara and Cremona.
11 'Un prelato della commissione pontificia' according to Prodi, ('San Carlo Borromeo e le trattative . . .', *R.S.C.I.* 11 (1957) p.234.
12 Doc. 1 above.
13 The establishment of a lecturer in Theology had been decreed in the earlier sessions of the Council – even before the decree establishing seminaries (see above, p. 168).
14 Cardinal Gambara.
15 This letter is published in full in Fè' d'Ostiani, *op. cit.*, pp. 133–136.
16 Doubtless this was the friend alluded to elsewhere in Bollani's letters to Roveglio as 'il nostro amico del Datario'. Although this letter is dated as above, it is placed here, as probably included in a letter of Bollani to Roveglio during the first week of September.
17 Roveglio. Bollani's intention in this is confirmed in doc. 6: ('del vostro canonicato').
18 Paolo Tiepolo, Venetian ambassador in Rome.
19 This compromise was designed to ensure for Roveglio the post of Canon, as appears.
20 Presumably Santicoli's post was to be sacrificed to the *Canonicato* which Bollani hoped to win for Roveglio.
21 Domenico Ettore. (See Bollani to Roveglio, September 22, 1577 in *ibid.*, and Fè d'Ostiani, *op. cit.*, pp. 132–133)

THE REACTIONS OF THREE VENETIAN BISHOPS WHEN
FACED WITH CONFLICTING ORDERS FROM VENICE AND ROME:
DOMENICO BOLLANI IN BRESCIA, AGOSTINO VALIER IN VERONA
AND MATTEO PRIULI IN VICENZA

January — March, 1569

1. *Domenico Bollani to the Chiefs of the X, January 19, 1569.*[1]
Non havendo Io mai stimata alcuna cosa piu, doppo la gratia del Sig. Dio et la
salute della mia anima, ch'l viver et morire buon cittadino della mia carissima at
amatissima patria, da me per si lungo tempo, et in tante occasioni, così in questo
come in altro habito, servito sempre fidelissimo et sincerissimamente, confesso che
mi è stato pur troppo grave il sentire cio quasi metter in dubio con le lettere di
Questo Ill.mo Consiglio lettemi da Questi clarissimi rettori, per le quali in risposta
del buon et sincero ufficio per me con loro fatto, come rappresentanti la Ser.tà
Vra., circa l'ordine venutomi sotto censure ecclesiastiche da Sua Santità ch'io
dovessi subitamente metter in mani di questo inquisitore le scritture della Santa
inquisitione, mi dicono l'Ill.me Sig.e Vre. che oltra la sudetta communicatione
doveva ancho metter tempo a' ubbidire si efficace comandamento; onde suplico la
Ser.ta Vra. che con quel paterno affetto che suole protegger sempre li suoi buoni
cittadini, consideri l'instante necessità ch'in ciò mi era posta, et massime con questo
inquisitore ch'in apparenza si fa tutto servitore di quel ser.mo Dominio, ma poi
con gl'effetti non procura altro ch'ingratiarsi altrove con far il diligente et severo
in queste cose dell'inquisitione, onde m'instava a dirgli la mia rissolutione intorno
l'ordine sudetto con dire che era ubbligato risponder a' Roma per il spazzo
d'al'hora; da che si puo comprendere il manifesto travaglio in che ero per incorrere
senza ancho punto di necessità del servitio della ser.tà Vra., la quale in si fatti casi
dei ministri pocho discreti suole, riguardando con benigno occhio alla salvezza dei
suoi buoni cittadini, provedere, come hora ha sapientissimamente fatto, con la
suprema auttorità di quel eccellentissimo consiglio a' reprimere ogni loro insolenza, et insieme senza ancho strepito dei principi rimediare a' si fatti disordini, come
al sicuro ne viene ad esser proveduto co'l trovarsi le scritture al suo luoco in questa
cancellaria; di che tutto ne sia ringratiata la divina bonta; la quale ben prego con
humilissimo cuore che finalmente da lume a' esso inquisitore di voler hormai
cessare da molti suoi mali ufficij, mostrando in apparenza de parole el miele, et ne
gli effetti il veneno, che mai non ha rimesso contra di me, da che come ben ne puo
dare ampia testimonianza il cl.mo S. Giacomo Soranzo K. per il tempo che stette
ambasciatore a Roma, esso inquisitore si voltò a' perseguitarmi con molti mali
modi per la ripulsa che per debito della mia coscienza io diedi a' un suo fratello
laico che si proponeva a'ottenere la chiesa di Calvisano, et ne fu per ogni rispetto
conosciuto indegno; pensino mo' l'ecc.me Sig.e vostre quale possa essere il mio
tormento nel convenir esercitare questo tanto peso dell'inquisitione con si fatta
compagnia, et pur per gratia del Sig. Dio supporto il tutto in buona pazienza,
perche non si manchi punto in negocio si importante, anci ch'io procuro, come sa

il Sig. Dio, di guadagnarlo a piu mio potere, et massime in questo che pur vorrei
per servitio pubblico ottener da lui, che nel scrivere a Roma intorno li negocij
dell'inquisitione comunicasse con gli cl.mi rettori et meco quanto gl'occorre,
essendo noi tutti ad un medesimo fine per la gloria di Dio et netezza de questa
citta et diocesi; Mi raccomando con ogni mia humiltà insieme con tutta la casa mia
in buona gratia dell'Ill.me Sig.e Vre., alle quali prego sempre dalla divina bonta
acrescimento di ogni felicità:
Da Brescia alli 19 Genaro, 1568.[2]

Il Vescovo di Brescia

2. *Agostino Valier to the Chiefs of the X, March 20, 1569.*[3]

Questi cl.mi rettori mi han detto heri che VV. SS. Ecc. sone restate mal satisfatte
di me peroche io habbi fatto intendere alli padri di san Zorzi de questa città che
mi aspettassero per il giorno seguente [havendo a] ragionar con essi nel loro
capitolo. In rispetto di che voglio rengratiar il nostro S.r Dio che non attendendo
io ad altro che al servitio di S. D. Maestà et alla satisfattione di quel Ill.mo Do.
non succeda [. . .] ripreso [. . .] di negligentia et de fredezza nel eseguir li ordini
di quella S.ta Sede come potrei mostrar per alcune lettere, et non di meno VV. SS.
Ill.me parimente non restano satisfatte il che [. . .] dalla mano di Dio confidando
che la sua bonta non debbi mancarmi di agiuto. Voglio ben dire a VV. SS. Ill.me
che s'io havessi havuto animo esequir ascosamente il breve havuto da Roma sarei
di subito andato a San Zorzi. Ma la verita è et non voglio vergognarmi dicendo il
vero di confessar la tardita del mio ingegno, non mi e mai venuto in mente che
VV. SS. Ill.me fossero per ricever questa attione in mala parte et ho creduto
essendo la bolla stampata gia tanti mesi che la fusse uscita con saputa del Sig.
Ambasciatore [of Venice in Rome]. Deus qui [. . .] scit quod non meritior. Et per
ciò prego quanto piu humilmente posso VV. SS. Ill.me che si degnino tenirmi per
quel figliolo et servitor ch'io son di quella Ill.ma Rep. degnandosi appresso haver
compassione non solo a me ma a tutti li altri vescovi di questo Ill.mo Do. dandoci
qualche lume quel che habbiamo a rispondere in simili casi. Io sapendo non
poterle servir in altro, non macharò al meno di pregar N.S. Dio come son tenuto
per quella Ill.ma Rep[ubblica]: et per le SS. VV. Ecc.me alle quali humilmente in
gratia mi raccomando.
Di Verona li XX Marzo, nel 1569.

Il Vescovo di Verona

3. *Matteo Priuli to the Chiefs of the X, March 18, 1569.*

Io non son cosi balordo ne cosi imprudente che non sappia quanto importano a
noi i commandamenti dei Principi nostri, così temporali come spirituali, et che
non conosca anche dover esser tal volta un picciol cenno loro inteso da noi per
severo commandamento, ma quanto piu mi sforzo conoscendo questo di non
trasgredire, et i cenni et i commandamentidei miei superiori, a me riesce tanto

peggio per cio che ne servo a Sua B.ne [i.e. the Pope] ne alla ser.ta vra., ne se voglio dir [. . .] alla mia propria coscientia. Mando alla Ser.ta Vostra la risposta che mi fece far S. S.ta dal S. Card. Alessandrino quando io sospesi l'esecutione d'un altra bolla di S. S.ta nella translatione de i governi delle Monache da i Frati Conventuali di S. Francesco a [. . .] altri Ordinarij, et da quella lettera potra molto ben comprendere Vra. Ser.ta che mala sodisfatione ne hebbe da me S. B.ne che non pur mi punse cosi mortalmente in quello di che si sentiva mal servita da me, ma etiamdio in cosa che ne anche per haverla io mai imaginata ne sognata potevo meritar tal nota da S. S.ta, ne che la dovesse mover a minacciarmi che questa Chiesa havea bisogno urgente di persona che desse rimedio al suo male, et pur so, che ne anche la Ser.ta Vostra restò sodisfatta di me in quell'atto. Ond'io trovandomi confuso, et temendo anche qualche repentina disgratia, alla quale io non sia bastevole provedere con vergogna e danno forse anche di Casa mia e di miei fratelli, li quali insieme con me, son certi si [. . .] per sertitio di V. Ser.ta, non havendo altro fine nelle mie attioni che l'honor d'Iddio, et il servitio di S. B.ne, et della Ser.ta Vostra: non satisfacendo ad alcuna di queste cose la supplico humilmente ad havermi compasione come quella che p[u]ò molto ben considerar il stato mio. E dirò a V. Ser.ta chiedendole prima humilmente perdono, d'ogni mia transgrettione, e qualmente per l'esecutione di questo breve di S. Sta, copia del quale ne ho dato al Clar.mo Capitano et per lettere che in conformita mi scrive il Card. Alessandro non ho fatt'altro che pigliar i voti de i Padri, se vogliono far la professione, o no, è vero ch'io gl'ho gagliardamente esortati, et impauriti, si per che a Roma si son resoluto di farla tutti, come anche per che so che gli metta conto obedire. [. . .]ch'io habbia mai pensato che a V. Ser.ta dispiacesse questo, ch'io mandai subito havuto l'aviso, e trovata la durezza in quelli Padri di San Rocho, a pregar il Clar.mo Capitano di questa citta, che esortasse ancor esso i Padri all'obbedienza, di che ne puo esser essa Mag.za Clar.ma ben testimonio, il quale come prudente rispose non lo poter fare. E non pensando io che in ciò V. Ser.ta potesse restar offesa da me, andai poi all'altre Chiese di S. Agostino e di S. Fermo. Ma hora comandandomi V. Ser.ta ch'io suspenda l'altre esecutioni, obedirò molto prontamente in doi altri che mi restano di quei di S. Hieronimo di Pisa, ma supplico però humilmente la Ser.ta Vostra degnarsi di considerar il mio stato. Facendolo differente da quello di tutti gl'altri Vescovi del Dominio, e proteggermi se possibile che io non sia del tutto escluso dalla gratia di Sua Ser.ta. Il che spero farà se pensarà solamente questo, ciò e, quanto S. B.ne voglia essere obedita da suoi ministri, et esser io con S. B.ne nell'istesso grado che sono questi Clar.mi Rettori con V. Ser.ta da i quale la vole esser obedita. Ond'io che pur sopra modo desidero servir alla Ser.ta V. et Dio col pericolo della propria vita, mi vedo molto confuso accusandomi massime V. Ser.ta di haver con questa cosa trans-gredito comandamenti che mi furon fatti per nome suo ai dì passati dal Clar.mo Cap.o per occasione delle cose dell'Inquisitione che qui si trattano, nelle quali a me par d'haver osservato quanto mi fu imposto. Ma hora vedendo che ogni di possono nascer nove occasioni contra di me, così dal canto di V. Ser.ta, come di S. B.ne, et per ogni luogo non mancaranno persone diligenti a cercar dette occasioni contra di me, Supplico la Ser.ta V. si degni cavarmi da questo pericolo et liberarmi da queste molestie nel modo che a Lei parerà: Offerendomi sino a

privarmi della Chiesa per suo servitio, se ben son securissimo che mai ne piu fedele, ne piu sviscerato servitor di me sia per servire alla Ser.ta V. ne in questo ne in altro. Et perche potrei anche esser accusato da V. Ser.ta di haver scritto ogni settimana a Roma per conto della Inquisitione mandando le lettere a Mons. Legato [Facchinetti in Venice], le fo sapere che per nome di S. S.ta me lo commanda espressamente Il Sig. Card. di Pisa, che e supremo Inquisitore come dell'inclusa lettera la potrà vedere, le quali lettere supplico V. Ser.ta farle restituire tutte a m. Hieronimo, mio fratello, dandomi licenza ch'io possi continuar a dar conto delle istesse cose a S. B.ne, come ho fatto sin'hora per mezzo di Mons. Nontio et per maggior dechiaratione della fidelissima servitù mia verso V. Ser.ta le faccio anche sapere, che tutto quello che mi è stato di tempo in tempo scritto da Roma per nome di S. B.ne l'ho communicato sempre alli Clar.mi Rettori dandole a leggere le medesme lettere del Card. di Pisa che anche di questo me ne puo esser S. Mag.ze Clar.me bon testimonio si che non havendo che altro dir con questa a V. Ser.ta se non chiederle di novo humilmente perdono d'ogni mio fallo, et del prolisso et forse molesto mio scrivere faro fine, pregando N.S. Dio per ogni felicità et augumente [sic] del suo felicissimo Dominio, et baciandole con ogni debita riverenza le mani.
Di Vicenza, alli XVIII di Marzo MDLXVIIII.

Il Vescovo di Vicenza

1 A.S.V., *Santo Ufficio*, *busta* 161 (autograph). These letters are discussed above, pp. 209.
2 But 1569 (See above, p. 224, n. 44).
3 The MS has suffered somewhat from the corrosive effects of the ink used.

APPENDIX VIII

BIBLIOGRAPHY OF ARCHIVAL AND PRINTED SOURCES QUOTED
IN THE TEXT

A   *The letters of Domenico Bollani*

These are by far the most important primary sources. The two main collections are 1. Bollani's correspondence with Borromeo in *Biblioteca Ambrosiana*, Milan, under various catalogue headings. This source contains at least 78 letters between August 22, 1564 and March 10, 1579, and 2. Bollani's correspondence with his Vicar-General, Giacomo Roveglio, in A.C.S.B. (*Biblioteca Queriniana*) MSS, B.V. 31–32, which contains also letters by Roveglio, Francesco Longo and others. There are also letters by Bollani in various other places; e.g. A.S.V., *Capi, Consiglio dei X, dispacci dei Rettori* (Udine), *busta* 170, *Ibid., dispacci dei Rettori* (Brescia), *busta* 22, and *Ibid., Santo Ufficio, buste* 161–162. There are also letters by him in A.C.S.B., *Registrum Olei.* (See also Brescia I, 8, below)

B.   *Archival Sources most commonly quoted in the text.*

(Material provided in the notes to the text is not repeated here, but reference is made to such notes where appropriate.)

Brescia   I *A.C.S.B. (Archivio Civico Storico Bresciano)*

This source contains many documents for the history of Brescia in the sixteenth century. It is housed in the *Biblioteca Queriniana*, Brescia, under the direction of the archivist, Dott. O. Valletti, and was used particularly for Chapter V (See bibliographical note 12).

1   *Provvisioni* (1557–1558), the acts of the Brescian parliament.

2   *Proclami* (1528–1598) Ro. 1094, for Bollani's edicts, proclamations.

3   *Lettere Autografe* and

4   *Lettere Pubbliche* constitute an important collection of documents containing the correspondence between Brescia and her orators from time to time, and permanently, in Venice.

5   *Registrum Olei.* A massive collection of documents reflecting the work (deliberations and correspondence) of the Brescian magistracy set up to deal with the dispute over the River Oglio, the Deputati all'Oglio (see bibliographical note 24, Chapter V).

6   'Relazione Storico-Politico-Economico–Topografico del Fiume Oglio' by Co. Cav. Federico Mazzucchelli, MS. D. 1 10 (see bibliographical note 28).

7   'Notizie spettanti al Vescovo Domenico Bollani' by Baldassare Zamboni, MS. F. IV. 9.

8   'Registro delle Delegationi, lettere e altre scritture . . .' MS. K. VII. 1.
(Copy also in *Biblioteca Marciana*, Venice, MS. It. Cl. II. 6926)
collects Bollani's own choice of his letters and other documents for
the Oglio dispute. (See bibliographical notes 28, 65 above, Chapter V)

II *A.V.B. (Archivio Vescovile, Brescia)*

This archive has recently come under the expert direction of Padre
Masetti—Zanini, and is now open to all students at a new independent
location. It is undergoing re-cataloguing.

1   *Sinodo Bollani* (1574)
2   *Busta 'Ebrei'* (letters to Bollani about Jews)
3   *Fascicolo 'Varie'* (1579)
4   *Libro della Carità*, account book of alms dispensed during Bollani's
bishopric.

III *A.S.B. (Archivio di Stato, Brescia)*

There are few sources for the sixteenth century here, although it is
expected that it will become the home of the A.C.S.B. at some time.
Sources used were:

1   *Cancelleria Pretoria, Ducali* I (1557—1567)
2   *Cancelleria Prefettizia Inferiore, Ducali*, IV (1558—1563)

Cremona   I *Arch. Nav. Crem. (Archivio del Naviglio di Cremona)*

Formerly in the offices of the *Consorzio Irriguo Cremonese* and now
in A.S.C. (see bibliographical note 24, Chapter V).

1   'Scritture diverse concernenti a favore del Naviglio per causa della
Predata et novita chè fanni li Bresciani', collection of unnumbered
printed documents, 1644—1645 (see above, bibliographical note 28,
Chapter V).

II *A.S.C. (Archivio di Stato, Cremona)*

1   *Archivio del Naviglio Civico di Cremona*, the archive which reflects
the working of the Cremonese magistracy of the *Deputati al Naviglio*,
instituted in connection with the Oglio dispute.
2   *Eredità Po-Oglio-Adda, busta* IX.

Milan   I *Biblioteca Ambrosiana*

1   Carteggio Bollani-Borromeo (see above, A)

II *A.A.M. (Archivio Arcivescovile, Milan)*

Contains the documentary sources for Borromeo's *Visita Apostolica*, to Brescia in 1580 (used in secondary sources).

III   *A.S.M. (Archivio di Stato, Milan)*

1   *Fondo Acque, busta* 727bis. (see bibliographical note 24, Chapter V)
2   *Confini, (Parte Antica), busta* 315 (1500–1599)
3   *Estado, busta* 1212

Rome   I   *Archivio Segreto Vaticano*

1   *Segreteria di Stato, Nunziatura di Venezia* (Nunz. Ven.)
Microfilmed copies in the Fondazione Cini used for the correspondence of the Nuncios 1569–1579, not yet calendared and published.

Udine   I   *A.C.U. (Archivio Civico Utini)*

As in Brescia, this collection is still housed in the *Biblioteca V. Ioppi*, Udine. The source used for Chapter IV was *Annalium*, tom. 54 (1554–1559), the acts of the Udine parliament (see bibliographical note 1, Chapter IV).

Venice   I   *A.S.V. (Archivio di Stato, Venice)*

The documents in the A.S.V. were of fundamental importance to this study. Only the most important are listed below. Explanatory notes appear in the text.

Chap. I   Barbaro, *Arbori dei Patrizi Veneti*
Cancellaria Inferiore, testamenti.
Archivio Notarile, testamenti.
Dieci Savi Sopra le Decime. Condizioni. (1514–1566)
Avogaria del Comun, Ro. 106/1, *Matrimoni . . .* (1400–1560)
Libro Contratti, Ro. 143/4 (marriage contracts)

Chap. III   *Senato Terra, registri* and *filze* used for the years 1549–1558, for examples of the work of the *Savi* (see above, bibliographical note 25, Chapter III)

Chap. IV   *Collegio Secreta, Relazioni, busta* 32 (1557, 1558, 1561)
Collegio Secreta, Relazioni Miste (1552, 1553)
(for *Relazioni* of *Luogotenenti,* see above note 1, Chapter IV)
Capi, Consiglio dei X, Dispacci di Rettori (Udine), *filza* 170 (1531–1559)
Luogotenente della Patria del Friuli, Processi, filza 169 (1555–1556)

Chap. V   *Provveditori alla camera dei Confini, busta* 16 (1546–1639) *busta* 17 (*Relazione Baitelli,* 1639).

Chap. IX   *Capi, Consiglio dei X, Lettere di Rettori* (Brescia), *buste,* 22, 23.
Santo Ufficio, buste 161, 162

Capi, Consiglio dei X, Esposizioni Principi, Ro. 3 (1574–77)
Idem, Primo Libro da Roma (1573–1578)
Idem, Secondo Libro da Roma (1579–1582)
Collegio, Esposizioni Roma, (1580–1582)
Sopra le Decime del Clero, Ro. 235 (Brescia, 1564)

C.   *Bibliography of Printed Sources*

(Only those sources cited in the text are included.)

1 Adami, V., *I Magistrati ai Confini nella Repubblica di Venezia*, (Grottaferrata, 1915).

2 Alberi, E., (Ed.) *Relazioni degli Ambasciatori Veneti*, (Florence, 1840 {Ed. Firpo, Turin, 1965}).

3 Alberigo, G., 'Studi e problemi relativi all'applicazione del Concilio di Trento in Italia (1945–1958)', in *Rivista Storica Italiana*, 70 (1958).

4 *Idem*, 'note in margine a uno studio sulla partecipazione dei vescovi italiani al primo periodo del Concilio di Trento', in *Problemi di Vita Religiosa in Italia nel '500*, (Padua, 1959).

5 *Idem*, 'Carlo Borromeo come modello di vescovo nella chiesa post-tridentina', in *Rivista di Storia della Chiesa in Italia*, 79 (1967).

6 Anglo, S., *Spectacle, pageantry and early Tudor Policy*, (Oxford, 1969).

7 Anon., 'Ha quattro secoli il seminario di Brescia', in *Il Seminario*, (Brescia, May/June, 1969).

8 Aretino, P., *Ragionamenti*, (Cosmopoli, 1660).

9 *Idem., Lettere*, 6 vols., (Paris, 1609).

10 Barbera, M., 'L'origine dei seminari a norma del Concilio di Trento', in *Civiltà Cattolica* 91 (1940).

11 Barbieri, G., 'L'etica economica nella legislazione ecclesiastica del cinquecento', in *Problemi di Vita Religiosa in Italia nel Cinquecento*, (Padua, 1960).

12 Barocchi, P., *Trattati d'Arte del Cinquecento*, II (Bari, 1961).

13 Battistella, A., 'Udine nel Secolo XVI. Condizioni e provvisioni annonarie', in *Memorie Storiche Forogiulesi*, 17 (1921).

14 *Idem., Udine nel Secolo XVI*, (Udine, 1932).

15 *Idem.*, 'La Servitu di masnada in Friuli . . .' in *Nuovo Archivio Veneto*, n.s. 6 (1906).

16 Bendiscioli, M., 'La Bolla in Coena Domini e la sua pubblicazione a Milano nel 1568', in *Archivio Storico Lombardo*, 54 (1927).

17 Bernareggi, A., 'La fondazione del seminario di Milano', in *Humiltas. Miscellanea Storica dei Seminari*, (Milan, 1929).

18 Besta, E., *Il Senato Veneziano*, (Venice, 1899).

19 Besta, F. *Bilanci generali della Repubblica di Venezia*, I (Venice, 1912).

20   Biron, R., and J. Barennes, *Un Prince Anglais, Cardinal-Lègat au XVI siècle: Reginald Pole*, (Paris n.d. {1922})

21   Boerio, *Dizionario del Dialetto Veneziano*, (Venice, 1829).

22   Bollani, Domenico, *Costitutiones R. Rmi. D. D. Bollani Brix. Ep.* (Brixiae, ad instantiam I.B. Bozolae, 1564).

23   *Idem. Rituale Sacramentorum ex Rom. Eccl. ritu Rmi. D. D. Bollani Ep. Brixiae, jussu editum ad usum suae ecclesiae* (Brixiae, 1570).

24   *Idem., Costitutiones Rev.mi D. D. Dominici Bollani Brixiae Episcopi in Diocesana Sinodo promulgatae anno Domini 1574 die 4 mensis novembris*, ({Brescia, 1575})

25   *Idem., Acta Ecclesiae Brixiensis ab illustriss. et reverendiss. D. D. Dominico Bollano eius Episcopo, promulgata anno Domini MDLXXIIII*, (Venice apud Varisoum, 1608).

26   Botero, G., *Relatione della Repubblica Venetiana* (Venice, 1608).

27   *Idem., Discorso intorno allo Stato Della Chiesa*, (Venice, 1608).

28   Bouwsma, W.J., *Venice and the Defense of Republican Liberty: Renaissance Values in the age of the Counter-Reformation*, (California, 1968).

29   Brandi, K., *The Emperor Charles V . . .* (trans. C.V. Wedgewood) (London, 1939).

30   Brown, Rawdon., (Ed.) *Calendar of State Papers . . . (Venetian)*, V (1534–1554) (London, 1873).

31   Brown, Horatio, *Studies in the History of Venice*, 2 vols., (London, 1907).

32   Brugi, B., 'La Nazione Tedesca dei Giuristi dello Studio di Padova nel secolo XVII', in *Monografie Storiche Sullo Studio di Padova* (Venice, 1922).

33   *Idem.*, 'Gli Scolari dello Studio di Padova nel Cinquecento', in *Per la Storia della Giurisprudenza e delle Università Italiane*, (Turin, 1921).

34   *Idem.*, 'L'Università dei Giuristi in Padova nel Cinquecento: Saggio di Storia della Giruisprudenza e delle Università Italiane' in *Archivio Veneto-Tridentino*, 1 (1922).

35   Brunetti, M., 'La Crisi della Sacra Lega, 1573', in *Miscellanea in Onore di Roberto Cessi*, 3 vols. (Rome, 1958).

36   Cadorin, *Dello amore ai Veneziani di Tiziano Vecellio* (Venice, 1833).

37   Cairns, C.S., 'An unknown Venetian description of Edward VI', in *Bulletin of the Institute of Historical Research*, 42 (1969).

38   *Idem.*, 'Domenico Bollani in Inghilterra', in *Commentari dell'Ateneo di Brescia*, 1966 {1967}.

39   *Idem.*, 'Domenico Bollani, a distinguished correspondent of Pietro Aretino: some identifications', in *Renaissance News*, 19 (3) (1966).

40   *Idem.*, 'Ancora sulla casa dell'Aretino sul Canal Grande' in *Studi Veneziani*, 14 (1972).

41   Cantimori, D., *Gli Eretici Italiani del Cinquecento*, (Florence, 1939).

42   *Idem.*, 'Italy and the Papcy', in *New Cambridge Modern History*, II (Cambridge, 1958).

43   Cantu, C., *Gli Eretici d'Italia*, (Turin, 1865—6).
44   Carter, C.H., 'The Ambassadors of Early Modern Europe, patterns of diplomatic representation in the early seventeenth century', in *Idem., From the Renaissance to the Counter-Reformation: Essays in Honour of Garrett Mattingly*, (London, 1966).
45   Cattane, E., 'La Pieve di Cemmo in Valle Camonica nel periodo della Reforma Tridentina', unpub. thesis, *Università Cattolica del Sacro Cuore*, Milan 1969—70.
46   Cattaneo, E., 'Nel IV Centenario del seminario di Milano', in *La Scuola Cattolica*, 92 (164).
47   *Idem.*, 'Influenze Veronesi nella legislazione di San Carlo Borromeo', in *Problemi di Vita Religiosa in Italia nel Cinquecento*, (Padua, 1960).
48   Cava, F., la, *La Peste di San Carlo vista da un medico*, (Milan, 1945).
49   Cecchetti, B., *La Repubblica di Venezia e la Corte di Roma nei rapporti della Religione*, 2 vols. (Venice, 1874).
50   Ceredda, F., 'El litigio de los Cabildos y su repercussion· en las relaciones con Roma 1551—1556', in *Razò y Fe*, 130 (1944).
51   Cessi, R., *Storia della Repubblica di Venezia*, 2 vols., (Milan/Messina, 1968).
52   Cervelli, I., 'Macchiavelli e Paruta', in *Macchiavelli e Venezia, Macchiavelli a Venezia*, (Florence, 1970).
53   *Idem.*, 'Giudizi Secenteschi dell'Opera di Paolo Paruta', in *Annali dell'Istituto Italiano per gli Studi Storici*, (Naples, 1967).
54   *Idem.*, 'Storiografia e problemi intorno alla vita religiosa e spirituale a Venezia nella prima meta del '500', in *Studi Veneziani*, 8 (1966).
55   Chabod, F. *Per la storia religiosa dello stato di Milano durante il dominio di Carlo V*, (Bologna, 1938).
56   Church, F., *I Riformatori Italiani*, (trans. Cantimori), 2 vols. (Florence, 1967).
57   Cicogna, E.A., *Delle Iscrizioni Veneziane*, 6 vols. (Venice, 1824).
58   Cistellini, A., *Figure della Riforma Pretridentina*, (Brescia, 1955).
59   *Idem., Il Padre Angelo Paradisi e i Primi Gesuiti in Brescia*, (Brescia, 1955).
60   *Idem.*, 'La Prima Visita di San Carlo a Brescia', in *Momorie Storiche della Diocesi di Brescia*, 15 (1948).
61   Claeys Bouaert, F., 'Bulle in Coena Domini', in *Dictionnaire de Droit Canonique*, 2 (Paris, 1937).
62   Cochrane, E., 'New light on post-tridentine Italy: a note on recent Counter-Reformation Scholarship', in *The Catholic Historical Review*, 56 (1970).
63   Comba, E., *I Nostri Protestanti*, (Florence, 1897).
64   *Concilium Tridentinum . . .* (Friburgi Brisgoviae, 1903).
65   *VI Congresso delle Acque, Notizie sui principali cavi irrigui e di colo della provincia di Cremona*, (Cremona, 1932).
66   Consorzio dell'Oglio, *Il Consorzio dell'Oglio nel primo decenno della sua costituzione*, (Milan, 1938).

67   Cozzi, G., 'La Societa Veneziana del Rinascimento in un Opera di Paolo Paruta: "Della Perfettione della Vita Politica"', in *Atti della Deputazione di Storia Patria per le Venezie*, (Venice, 1961).

68   *Idem.*, 'Politica e diritto in alcune controversie confinarie tra lo stato di Milano e la Repubblica di Venezia', in *Archivio Storico Lombardo*, 78–79 (1951–52).

69   *Idem.*, *Il Doge Nicolò Contarini: Ricerche sul Patriziato Veneziano agli inizi del Seicento*, (Venice/Rome, 1958).

70   *Idem.* 'Authority and Law in Renaissance Venice' in *Renaissance Venice*, Ed. J.R. Hale (London, 1973).

71   Dalla Santa, G., *Studi di Arte e Storia a cura della direzione del Museo Civico Correr*, I, (Milan/Rome, 1920).

72   Daru, P., *Storia della Repubblica de Venezia*, (Capolago, 1837).

73   Davis, J.C., *The Decline of the Venetian Nobility as a ruling class*, (Baltimore, Johns Hopkins, 1962).

74   Deputy Keeper of the Public Records, *Twenty-seventh Report*, (London 1866).

75   Dickens, A.G., *The English Reformation*, (London, 1964).

76   *Idem.*, *The Counter-Reformation*, (London, 1968).

77   Druffel, A. von, *Beiträge zur Reichsgeschichte 1545–1551 (Briefe und Akten zur Geschichte des sechzehnten Jahrhunderts).* I (Munich, 1873).

78   Elliott, J.H., *Europe Divided 1559–1598*, (London, 1968).

79   Elton, G., *England under the Tudors*, (London, 1955).

80   *Idem.*, *Reformation Europe*, (London, 1963).

81   Evenett, H.O., 'The New Orders', in *New Cambridge Modern History*, II, (Cambridge, 1968).

82   *Idem, The Spirit of the Counter-Reformation* (Ed. John Bossy) (Cambridge, 1968).

83   Elwert, W.T., 'Pietro Bembo e la Vita Letteraria del suo tempo', in *La Civiltà Veneziana del Rinascimento*, (Venice, 1958).

84   Fanton, G., *La Riforma Tridentina a Vicenza nella seconda metà del secolo XVI*, (Vicenza, 1941).

85   Fè D'Ostiani, L.F., *Il Vescovo Domenico Bollani, Memorie Storiche della Diocesi di Brescia*, (Brescia, 1875).

86   *Idem.*, 'M. Calini, Vescovo di Zara, Memorie del Secolo XVI', in *Archivio Veneto*, 21 (1881).

87   *Idem.*, *Storia Tradizione e Arte nelle vie di Brescia*, (Brescia 1927).

88   Fenlon, D. *Heresy and obedience in Tridentine Italy: Cardinal Pole and the Counter Reformation*, (Cambridge, 1972).

89   Fiducio, M.A., *Del modo di governo della communità di Undine . . .* (Venice, 1862)

90   Fondazione Treccani . . ., *Storia di Brescia*, (various dates).

91   *Idem., Storia di Milano*, (various dates).

92   Gaeta, F., 'Alcune considerazioni sul mito di Venezia', in *Bibliothèque d'Humanisme et Renaissance*, 23 (1961).

93   Gazich, V. 'La visita pastorale del vescovo Domenico Bollani alla valle Trompia nell'anno 1567,' unpub. thesis, *Università Cattolica del Sacro Cuore*, Milan, 1969–70.

94   Gilbert, F., 'Religion and Politics in the thought of Gasparo Contarini', in *Action and Conviction in Early Modern Europe. Essays in memory of E.H. Harbison*, (Princeton, N.J., 1969).

95   Gorla, P., 'Immagini di San Carlo', in *Echi di San Carlo*, (continuously through the periodical) (Milan, 1937–38).

96   Gradenigo, D.G., *Pontificum Brixianorum series commentario historico illustrata opera et studio Iohannis Gradonici*, (Brescia, 1755).

97   Guissani, P., *Vita di San Carlo Borromeo*, (Venice, 1613).

98   Guerrini, P., *I Conti di Martinengo,* (Brescia, 1930).

99   *Idem.*, 'La famiglia Durante e i suoi vescovi', in *Brixia Sacra*, 1911.

100   *Idem., La Congregazione dei Padri della Pace* (Brescia, 1933).

101   *Idem.*, 'Due Amici bresciani di Erasmo da Rotterdam: E. Emili, V. Maggi', in *Archivio Storico Lombardo*, (1923).

102   *Idem., S. Angela Merici e la compagnia di S. Orsola*, (Brescia, 1936).

103   *Idem.*, 'Per la storia dell'organizzazione ecclesiastica di Brescia nel Medio Evo', in *Brixia Sacra*, 1925–26.

104   *Idem.*, 'Sviluppo cronologico dell'organizzazione parocchiale diocesana dal secolo XV in avanti', in *Memorie Storiche della Diocesi di Brescia*, 25 (1958).

105   *Idem, Atti della Visita Pastorale del Vescovo Domenico Bollani alla diocesi di Brescia,* 3 vols. (Brescia, 1915–40).

106   *Idem.*, 'Monasteri, conventi, ospitali e benefici semplici della diocesi di Brescia', in *Brixia Sacra* (1911).

107   *Idem., Catechismi e Scuole della Dottrina Cristiana in Brescia*, (Brescia, 1940).

108   *Idem.*, 'La Visita Apostolica di San Carlo Borromeo alla Diocesi di Brescia', in *Brixia Sacra*, 1910.

109   *Idem.*, 'San Carlo e la diocesi di Brescia', in *San Carlo nel Terzo Centenario della Canonizzazione*, (Milan, 1910).

110   Giusti, V., and P. de Susanis, 'Cronache della Peste', in *Pagine Friulane*, 12.

111   Guicciardini, F., *Istoria d'Italia*, 4 vols, (Fribourg, 1775–6).

112   Haile, M., *The life of Reginald Pole*, (London, 1911).

113   Halkin, L.E., 'La formation du clergé après le Concile de Trente', *Colloque d'Histoire Ecclesiastique de Cambridge* (September, 1968) (typescript).

114   Hazlitt, W. Carew, *The Venetian Republic*, (London, 1900).

115   Hook, J., 'Italy and the Counter-Reformation', in *History Today*, (Nov. 1970).

116   Innamorati, G., *Tradizione e Invenzione in Pietro Aretino*, (Messina/Florence, 1957).

117 Jedin, H., *A History of the Council of Trent*, 2 vols, (London, 1957–61).

118 *Idem., Il Tipo Ideale di Vescovo secondo la Riforma Cattolica*, (Brescia, 1950).

119 *Idem., Riforma Cattolica o Controriforma*, (Brescia, 1957).

120 *Idem.*, 'Die Deutschen am Trienter Konzil 1551–2' in *Historische Zeitschrifte*, 188 (1959).

121 *Idem., Crisis and Closure of the Council of Trent*, (London, 1967).

122 *Idem., Girolamo Seripando, sein Leben und Denken*, (Wurzburg, 1937), and *Idem.*, (trans. Eckhoff) *Papal Legate at the Council of Trent: Girolamo Seripando*, (London, 1947).

123 *Idem.*, 'Gasparo Contarini e il contributo veneziano alla Riforma Cattolica', in *La Civiltà Veneziana del Rinascimento* (Florence/Venice, 1963).

124 Jordan, W.K., *Edward VI: The Young King, the Protectorship of the Duke of Somerset*, (London, 1968).

125 Koenigsberger, H.G., and G.L. Mosse, *Europe in the Sixteenth Century*, (London, 1968).

126 Laven, P.J., 'The Causa Grimani and its Political overtones' in *The Journal of Religious History*, 4 (3).

127 *Idem.*, 'Daniele Barbaro . . .' unpub. Ph.D. thesis, *University of London*.

128 Law, J.E. and Manion, J.M. 'The nunciature to Scotland in 1548 of Pietro Lippomano, bishop of Verona,' in *Atti e memorie della Accademia di Agricoltura Scienze e Lettere di Verona*, Ser. VI, XXII (1970–1).

129 Lazzarini, V., 'Obbligo di assumere pubblici uffici nelle antiche leggi Veneziane' in *Archivio Veneto*, 19 (1936).

130 Lefèvres-Pontalis, (Ed.) *Correspondence Politique de Odet de Selve*, (Paris, 1888).

131 Leicht, P.S., 'La Rappresentanza dei Contadini presso il Veneto Luogotenente della Patria del Friuli', in *Studi e Frammenti*, (Udine, 1903).

132 *Idem.*, 'Un movimento agrario nel Cinquecento', in *Idem., Scritti vari di Storia del Diritto Italiano*, I (Milan, 1943).

133 Loffi, B., 'Le Antiche Misure Cremonesi dell'Acqua irrigua' in *Bollettino Storico Cremonese*, 24 (1969).

134 Logan, O.M.T., 'Studies in the Religious Life of Venice in the Sixteenth and early Seventeenth Centuries: the Venetian Clergy and Religious Orders 1520–1630', unpub. Ph.D. thesis, University of Cambridge, (no date).

135 *Idem.*, 'Grace and Justification: some Italian views of the sixteenth and early seventeenth centuries', in *The Journal of Ecclesiastical History*, 20 (1969).

136 *Idem, Culture and Society in Venice 1470–1790*, (London, 1972).

137   Lowry, M. 'The reform of the Council of Ten, 1582–3: an unsettled problem?' in *Studi Veneziani*, 13 (1971).

138   Luzzatto, G., *Storia dell'Età Moderna e Contemporanea*, 2 vols. (Padua, 1955).

139   Luzio, A., *Pietro Aretino nei suoi primi anni a Venezia e la Corte dei Conzaga*, (Turin, 1888).

140   Mackeson, H., 'The Diplomatic Role of Gasparo Contarini at the Colloquy of Ratisbon of 1541', in *Church History*, 27 (1958).

141   Mackie, *The Earlier Tudors*, (Oxford, 1952).

142   Magni, C., *Il Tramonto del Feudo Lombardo*, (Milan, 1937).

143   Maio, R. de, *Alfonso Caraffa, Cardinale di Napoli*, (Vatican City, 1961).

144   Maiocchi, R., 'Mons. Bollani e la Facoltà di Teologia a Pavia' in *Brixia Sacra*, 1914.

145   Marcora, C., 'I primi anni dell'episcopato di San Carlo', in *Memorie Storiche dell Diocesi di Milano*, 10 (1963).

146   *Idem.*, 'San Carlo e il Seminario', in *Memorie Storiche della Diocesi di Milano*, 5 (1964).

147   Martin, G., *Roma Sancta* (Ed. G.B. Parkes) (Rome, 1969).

148   Mantese, G., 'A propositi del testamento di Niccolò Ormanetto', in *Rivista di Storia della Chiesa in Italia*, 14 (1960).

149   *Idem.*, 'L'origine dei vicari Foranei e gli inizi della Riforma Tridentina a Vicenza', in *Rivista di Storia della Chiesa in Italia*, 15 (1961).

150   Mantica, N., *Degli Ordinamenti del Comune di Udine sul pane dal 1300 in poi e dei prezzi dei frumenti e del pane*, (Udine, 1888).

151   Maranini, G., *La Costituzione di Venezia dopo la Serrata del maggior Consiglio*, (Venice/Perugia/Florence, 1931).

152   Marchese, V., *Le Relazioni dei Luogotenenti della Patria del Friuli*, (Udine, 1893).

153   *Idem.*, 'Il Friuli al tempo di Cambray' in *Nuovo Archivio Veneto*, 6 (1903).

154   Marongiu, *Il Parliamento in Italia nel Medio Evo e nell'Eta Moderna*, (Milan, 1962).

155   Martyribus, B. de, *Stimulus Pastorum, ex sententiis patrum Concinnatus, in quo agitur de vita et moribus episcoporum aliorumque praelatorum*, (Rome, 1564).

156   Masotto, F., 'Agostino Valiero, Vescovo di Verona e la Sua Attuazione dei decreti del Concilio di Trento', unpub. thesis, *Università Cattolica del Sacro Cuore*, Milan, 1936–37.

157   Matheson, P., *Cardinal Contarini at Regensburg*, (Oxford, 1972).

158   Mattingly, G., *Renaissance Diplomacy*, (London, 1955).

159   Maurenbrecher, W., *Karl V und die deutschen Protestanten 1545–1555*, (Dusseldorf/Leipzig, 1865).

160   Masetti-Zanini, G.L., 'Le origini del seminario di Brescia', in *Brixia Sacra* (1967).

161   Mazzucchelli, G., *Vita dell'Aretino*, (Brescia, 1763^2).

162   McNair, P., *Peter Martyr in Italy: an anatomy of apostasy*, (Oxford, 1967).

163   Measso, A., *I Deputati al Reggimento della Magnifica Comunità di Udine*, (Udine, 1884).

164   Molmenti, P., *Sebastiano Veniero e la Battaglia di Lepanto*, (Florence, 1899).

165   Monticore, A., 'L'Applicazione a Roma del Concilio di Trento. Le visite 1564–165', in *Rivista di Storia della Chiesa in Italia*, 8 (1954).

166   Mols, R., 'Saint Charles Borromée, pionier de la pastorale moderne', in *Nouvelle Revue Théologique*, 79 (1957).

167   Monica, Sister, *Angela Merici and her teaching idea*, (London, 1927).

168   Monteverdi, M., *Storia di Cremona* (Cremona, 1970).

169   Moreschi, R.A., 'Vita e Istituzioni Ecclesiastiche nella Valle Camonica del Sec. XVI: Visita Pastorale del Vescovo D. Bollani dell'anno 1567' unpub. thesis *Università Cattolica del Sacro Cuore*, Milan, 1968–69.

170   Morosini, *Degli Istorici delle Cose Veneziane*, (Venice, 1719).

171   Muracchelli, F., *Il Vescovo Domenico Bollani: Profili Storici per il IV Centenario della sua elezione episcopale (1559–1959)* (Brescia, 1959).

172   Odorici, *Storie Bresciane* (Brescia, 1882).

173   Orlandini, G., 'Lineamenti di Storia dell'Amministrazione della Repubblica Veneta', in *Ad Alessandro Luzio gli Archivi di Stato Italiani – Micellanea di Studi Storici*, (Florence, undated offprint).

174   *Idem.*, 'Il Veneto Magistrato alle Acque', in *Ateneo Veneto*, (1960).

175   Orsenigo, C., *Vita di San Carlo Borromeo*, 2 vols. (Milan, 1929³).

176   Palladio degli Olivi, G.F., *Historie della Provincia del Friuli*, 2 vols., (Udine, 1660 {1966}).

177   Paschini, P., *Storia del Friuli*, 2 vols., (Udine, 1954²).

178   *Idem.*, *Un Amico del Cardinale Pole: Alvise Priuli*, (Rome, 1921).

179   *Idem.*, 'Benvenuto Cellini ed un prelato della corte di Paolo III', in *Roma* (1929) (Typescript in *Biblioteca Queriniana*, Brescia).

180   *Idem.*, 'Un Vescovo disgraziato nel Cinquecento Italiano', in *Idem.*, *Tre Ricerche sulla storia della Chiesa nel Cinquecento*, (Rome, 1945).

181   *Idem.*, 'Un Umanista disgraziato nel Cinquecento: Publio Francesco Spinola', in *Nuovo Archivio Veneto*, (1919).

182   *Idem.*, *Venezia e l'Inquisizione Romana da Giulio III a Paolo IV*, (Padua, 1959).

183   *Idem.*, 'Il IV Centenario della nascita di San Carlo', in *Memorie Storiche della Diocesi di Brescia*, (Brescia, 1938).

184   *Idem.*, 'San Carlo e i Teatini', in *La Scuola Cattolica*, 2 (1922).

185   *Idem.*, 'Guglielmo Sirleto prima del Cardinalato', in *Tre Ricerche sulla Storia della Chiesa nel Cinquecento* (Rome, 1945).

186   *Idem.*, *San Gaetano Thiene, Gian Pietro Carafa e le origini dei Chierici Regolari Teatini*, (Rome, 1926).

187   *Idem.*, 'Il Catechismo Romano del Concilio di Trento', in *Idem.*, *Cinquecento Romano e Riforma Cattolica*, (Rome, 1958).

188   *Idem.*, *Pierpaolo Vergerio il giovane e la sua Apostasia*, (Rome, 1925).

189   *Idem.*, 'Le origini del seminario Romano', in *Idem., Cinquecento Romano e Riforma Cattolica* (Rome, 1958).

190   *Idem.*, 'Vescovi Veneti nel giudizio di un Nunzio a Venezia', in *Rivista di Storia della Chiesa in Italia*, 9 (1955).

191   *Idem.*, 'I monasteri femminiti in Italia nel '500', in *Problemi di Vita Religiosa in Italia nel Cinquecento*, (Padua, 1960).

192   Pasero, C., (Ed.) *Relazioni di Rettori Veneti a Brescia durante il secolo XVI*, (Brescia, 1939).

193   *Idem.*, 'Notizie sul sacro monte delle Biade di Brescia e sugli Istituti di Beneficenza bresciani durante il secolo XVI', in *Atti e Memorie del Terzo Congresso Storico Lombardo*, (Cremona, 1938).

194   *Idem.*, 'L'estremo supplizio dei Carafa (1561) e altre notizie Romane in una raccolta di lettere di Mons. Muzio Calini', in *Commentari dell' Ateneo di Brescia*, 137 (1938).

195   *Idem.*, 'Nuove notizie d'archivio intorno alla Loggia di Brescia' in *Commentari dell'Ateneo di Brescia*, 1952.

196   *Idem.* 'La Cronaca bresciana del Cinquecento di Lodivico Caravaggi' (N.p. 22.iii. 1935).

197   *Idem., La partecipazione Bresciana alla Guerra di Cipro e alla Battaglia di Lepanto*, (Brescia, 1954).

198   Paruta, P., *Della Perfettione della Vita Politica*, (Venice, 1579).

199   Pastor, L. von, *History of the Popes*, (trans, Kerr) XVIII (London, 1929).

200   *Idem., Storia dei Papi nel periodo della Riforma e Restaurazione Cattolica*, (It. Ed.) {1550–1559} VI, (Rome, 1922).

201   Pellin, A., 'Giacomo Rovellio, (1584–1610) e la sua prima visita pastorale nel Feltrino', in *Archivio Storico di Belluno*, 24 (1953).

202   Petrocchi, M., 'L'idea di Vescovo nel Panigarola', in *Rivista di Storia della Chiesa in Italia*, 8 (1954).

203   Petroboni, C., 'Domenico Bollani e la sua opera nella Controriforma Bresciana', unpub. thesis, *Università Cattolica del Sacro Cuore*, Milan, (1937–8) no. 7889.

204   Pietro, F.D., *Urago d'Oglio, Memorie Parocchiali*, (Brescia, 1941).

205   Pilot, A., 'Un capitolo inedito control il Broglio' in *Ateneo Veneto* (1903–1904).

206   Pole, R., *Epistolae* . . . (Ed. Quirini) 5 vols. (Brescia, 1744–1751).

207   Pollard, A.F., *The Political History of England, VI (1547–1603)* (London, 1910).

208   Porcacchi, T., (Ed.) *Lettere di XIII Huomini Illustri*, (Venice, 1576).

209   Porcin, G., *Descrizione della Patria del Friuli con l'utile che cava il Serenissimo Prencipe e con le spese che fa*, {1567} (Udine, 1897).

210   Preti, P., 'Un aspetto della Riforma Cattolica nel Veneto: L'Episcopato Padovano di Niccolò Ormanetto', in *Studi Veneziani*, 11 (1970).

211   Prodi, P., 'Lineamenti dell'organizzazione diocesana durante l'episcopato del Card. G. Paleotti (1566–1597), in *Problemi di Vita Religiosa in Italia nel Cinquecento* (Padua, 1960).

212   *Idem., Lo Sviluppo dell'Assolutismo nello Stato Pontificio*, (Bologna, 1968).

213   *Idem.*, 'San Carlo Borromeo e il Cardinale Gabriele Paleotti: due vescovi della Riforma Cattolica', in *Critica Storica*, 3 (1964).

214   *Idem., Il Cardinale Gabriele Paleotti (1522–1597)* 2 vols. (Rome, 1959, 1967).

215   Prosperi, A., *Tra Evangelismo e Controriforma G.M. Giberti (1495–1543)*, (Rome, 1969).

216   Pullan, B., 'Wage-Earners and the Venetian Economy, 1550–1630)' in *Idem.*, (Ed.) *Crisis and Change in the Venetian Economy*, (London, 1968).

217   *Idem., Rich and Poor in Renaissance Venice*, (Oxford, 1971).

218   *Idem.*, (Ed.) *Crisis and Change in the Venetian Economy in the Sixteenth and Seventeenth centuries*, (London, 1968).

219   *Idem.*, 'The Occupations and Investments of the Venetian Nobility in the middle and late Sixteenth century', in *Renaissance Venice*, (London, 1973) Ed. J.R. Hale.

220   *Idem.*, 'Service to the Venetian State: Aspects of Myth and Reality in the early Seventeenth Century', in *Studi Secenteschi*, 5 (1964).

221   *Idem.*, 'Poverty, Charity and the Reason of State', in *Bollettino dell' Istituto di Storia della Societa e dello Stato Veneziano* 2 (1960).

222   Quazza, R., *Preponderanze Straniere*, (Milan, 1938).

223   Queller, D.E., *The Office of Ambassador in the Middle Ages*, (Princeton, N.J., 1967).

224   Ranke, L. von, *Storia dei Papi*, (Florence, 1959).

225   Ribier, *Lettres et Mémoires d'estat des Roys, Princes, Ambassadeurs et autres ministres, sous les Regnes de François I, Henry II, e François II*, (Blois, 1666).

226   Ricci, I., 'La Preriforma Cattolica a Brescia', unpub. thesis, *Università Cattolica del Sacro Cuore*, Milan, 1938–39.

227   Rimoldi, A., 'Le Istituzioni di San Carlo Borromeo per il clero diocesano milanese' in *La Scuola Cattolica* 93 (1968).

228   Romanin, S., *Storia Documentata di Venezia*, 10 vols. (Venice, 1925).

229   Roncalli, A., *Gli Atti della Visita Apostolica di San Carlo Borromeo a Bergamo*, 1575, 5 vols. (Florence, 1936–57).

230   Rossetti, L., 'Bibliografia dell'Università di Padova', in *Quaderni per la Storia dell'Università di Padova*, (Padua, 1968).

231   Sanuto, M., *Diarii*, 58 vols. (Venice, 1879–1902).

232   Sala, A., *Documenti circa la Vita e le gesta di San Carlo Borromeo*, 3 vols. (Milan, 1857).

233   Sarpi, P., *Istoria del Concilio Tridentino*, 3 vols. (Bari, 1935).

234   Schenk, W., *Reginald Pole*, (London, 1950).

235   Segarizzi, A., (Ed.) *Relazioni degli Ambasciatori Veneti al Senato*, (Bari, 1912).

236   *Seminaria Ecclesiae Cattolicae*, (Vatican City, 1963).

237   Seneca, F., *Il Doge Leonardo Donà, la sua vita e la sua preparazione politica prima del dogado*, (Padua, 1959).

238   Società Anonima Canali d'Irrigazione derivata dall'Oglio etc., *Il Lago d'Iseo e l'Irrigazione in provincia di Brescia*, (Brescia, 1926).

239   Sommi Picenardi, G., *Cremona durante il dominio dei Veneziani 1499–1509*, (Milan, 1866).

240   Soranzo, G., 'Rapporti di San Carlo Borromeo con la Repubblica Veneta', in *Echi di San Carolo*, (Milan, 1937–38).

241   Stella, A., 'Utopie e Velleità dei Filoprotestanti Italiani (1545–47)' in *Bibliothèque d'Humanisme et Renaissance*, 27 (1965).

242   *Idem., Nunziatura di Venezia*, VIII (March 1566–March 1569) (Rome, 1963).

243   *Idem., Dall'Anabattismo al Socinianesimo nel Cinquecento Veneto*, (Padua, 1967).

244   *Idem.*, 'La regolazione delle pubbliche entrate e la crisi politica Veneziana del 1582', in *Miscellanea in onore di Roberto Cessi*, 3 vols. II (Rome, 1958).

245   *Idem., Chiesa e Stato nelle Relazioni dei Nunzi Pontifici a Venezia: Richerche sul Giurisdizionalismo Veneziano dal XVI al SVIII secolo*, (Vatican City, 1964).

246   *Idem., Anabattismo e Antitrinitarismo in Italia nel secolo XVI*, (Padua, 1969).

247   Tacchi-Venturi, *Storia della Compagnia di Gesù in Italia*. I (Rome, 1931).

248   Tagliaferri, A., *Strutture e Politica Sociale in una Comunità Veneta del '500* (Udine), (Milan, 1969).

249   *Tariffe della Patria del Friuli intorno ai pagamenti degli Ecc. Signori, Curiali, cancellieri, nodari ed altri*, (Udine, 1612).

250   Tassini, D., 'La Rivolta del Friuli del 1511 . . .' in *Nuovo Archivio Veneto*, n.s. 39–49 (1920).

251   Thompson, J.W., and S.K. Padover, *Secret Diplomacy: Espionage and cryptography* 1500–1800, (New York, 1937 {1963}).

252   Tiepolo, M.F., and R.M. della Rocca, 'Cronologia Veneziana del Cinquecento', in *La Civiltà Veneziana del Rinascimento*, (Venice, 1958).

253   Tramontin, S., 'La figura del Vescovo secondo il Concilio di Trento ed i suoi riflessi Veneziani nell'Interrogatorio del Patriarca Trevisan', in *Studi Veneziani*, 10 (1968).

254   *Idem.*, 'L'Istituzione dei due Seminari Veneziani', in *Studi Veneziani*, 6 (1965).

255   Turba, G., (Ed.) *Venetianische Depeschen von Kaiserhof*, (Vienna, 1892).

256   Various authors, *Il Concilio di Trento*, 3 vols. 1943.

257   Valier, A., *Episcopus*, (Milan, 1575).

258   *Idem., Dell'Utilità che si puo ritrarre dalle cose operate dai Veneziani*, (Padua 1787).

259   Ventura, A., *Nobiltà e Popolo nella Società Veneta dell '400 e '500*, (Bari, 1964).

260   Waterworth, J., *Canons and Decrees of the Sacred and Oecumenical Council of Trent*, (London, 1888).

261   Wernham, R.B., *Before the Armada, the growth of English foreign Policy 1485–1588*, (London, 1966).

262   Wilson, A.E. *Andrea Navagero Lusus*, (Nieuwkoop, 1973).

263   Woolf, S.J., 'The problem of representation in the post-Renaissance State', in *Liber Memorialis Antonio Era*, (Cagliari, 1961).

264   *Idem*, (trans. & Ed.) *Medieval Parliaments*, (London, 1968).

265   *Idem.*, *Studi sulla Nobiltà Piemontese nell'Epoco dell'Assolutismo*, (Turin, 1963).

266   *Idem.*, 'Venice and the Terraferma, Problems of the change from Commercial to landed activities', in *Studi Veneziani*, 4 (1962).

267   Yriarte, C., *La Vie d'un Patricien de Venise*, (Paris, 1874).

268   Zamboni, B., *Memorie intorno alle Pubbliche Fabbriche di Brescia*, (Brescia, 1778).

269   Zanelli, A., 'Gabrielle ed Eraclito Gandini e i processi d'eresia in Brescia nel secolo XVI', in *Archivio Storico Italiano*, 40 (1907).

270   *Idem.*, *Delle Condizioni interne di Brescia dal 1426 al 1644, e del moto della borghesia contro la nobiltà nel 1644*, (Brescia, 1898).

271   *Idem.*, 'La Devozione di Brescia a Venezia e il principio della sua decadenza', in *Archivio Storico Lombardo*, 33 (1912).

272   Zanotti, C., 'Aspetti della figura e dell'opera di Domenico Bollani nella Riforma Cattolica Bresciana', unpub. thesis, *Università Cattolica del Sacro Cuore*, Milan (1963–4) no. 35101.

SUPPLEMENTARY BIBLIOGRAPHY

In the time which inevitably separated the completion of a work of this kind and its appearance, a number of works have appeared of interest to its subject. The courtesy of the publisher permits me to append a short list of the most important items of interest to historians of Venice, Venetian dominions and those studies important in a further broadening of the comparative approach to the Counter-Reformation which have been published since the present study was completed in 1971.

1. VENICE AND VENETIAN DOMINIONS

The *relazioni* of Venetian rectors in *terraferma* dominions are now being published, and volumes for Udine, Belluno, Feltre, Treviso and Padua have already appeared: *Relazioni dei rettori in Terraferma*, 4 vols., (Milan, 1973–75). Two more volumes of the dispatches of nuncios in Venice have also appeared: IX (1569–71) Ed. A. Stella (Rome, 1972), and XI (1573–76) Ed. A. Buffardi (Rome, 1972). For Venice itself, Maranini's *La Costituzione di Venezia* has been usefully reprinted (Florence, 1974) and the following studies have appeared: F.C. Lane, *Venice, a Maritime Republic* (Baltimore, 1973), W.H. McNeil, *Venice, the hinge of Europe* (Chicago, 1974), J.C. Davis, *A Venetian family and its fortunes* (Philadelphia, 1975).

BRESCIA: The *Catastico Bresciano* is now complete, with publication of the second and third volumes (Ed. C. Pasero, Brescia, 1973).

VERONA: the important Cardinal Agostino Valier is now better known through his correspondence with Borromeo (L. Tacchella, *San Carlo Borromeo ed il Card. Agostino Valier (carteggio)*, Verona, 1972), and see *Idem, Il Cardinale Agostino Valier e la riforma tridentina nella diocesi di Trieste*, (Udine, 1974).

VICENZA: G. Mantese has continued his *Memorie storiche della chiesa vicentina* with volume IV (1563–1700), Vicenza, 1974.

TREVISO: G. Liberali, *Documenti della riforma cattolica pre- e post-tridentina*, 5 vols., (Treviso, 1971) takes full account of Venetian sources.

2. CATHOLIC REFORM IN ITALIAN DIOCESES

Translations of Hubert Jedin's important *Introduzione alla storia della Chiesa* and *Chiesa della fede, chiesa della storia* into Italian have now appeared (Brescia, 1973, 1972), and a massive two-volume anthology of documents important for Counter-Reformation history has been Ed.M. Marcocchi (*La Riforma Cattolica*, Brescia, 1967, 1970). A useful survey article of recent work is Mario Rosa, 'Per la storia della vita religiosa e della Chiesa in Italia tra il '500 e il '600. Studi recenti e questioni di metodo,' in *Quaderni Storici*, 1970, and R. de Maio has collected essays in *Riforme e miti nella Chiesa del Cinquecento*, (Naples, 1973).

MILAN: the work on heresy begun by Chabod (see above, bibliog. 55) is continued by Domenico Maselli, 'Per la storia religiosa dello stato di Milano durante il dominio di Filippo II: L'eresia e la sua repressione dal 1555 al 1584,' in *Nuova Rivista Storica*, 1970.

FLORENCE: A. d'Addario, *Aspetti della Controriforma a Firenze*, (Rome, 1972).
PAVIA: V. Bernorio, *La Chiesa di Pavia nel secolo XVI e l'azione pastorale del Card. Ippolito de' Rossi*, (Pavia, 1971).
TORTONA: L. Tacchella, *La riforma tridentina nella diocesi di Tortona*, (Genova, 1966).
SIENA: V. Marchetti, *Gruppi ereticali senesi del Cinquecento*, (Florence, 1976).

Frumento, mons., 169, 269, *271–2*
Gambara, Francesco, card., *142*, 157, 166–70, 174, *193, 196*, 207, 268–272
Garzoni, Giovita, carmelite friar, 130, *142*
Gavardo, province of Brescia, 261–2
Gemona, in Friuli, *75*
Geneva, *125, 225*
Ghislieri, card., 119
Giberti, G.M., Bishop of Verona, 6, 138–9, 140, *147*, 160, 161, 171, 175–6, 178, *196, 198–9*, 235, 236
Giorgione, 11
Giroldi, Stefano, (rector of the Brescian seminary), 195
Giustiniani, Paolo, 150, 236
Giovani and *Vecchi*, (See Patriciate, Venetian)
Gradenigo, Domenico (Podestà of Brescia), 82, *106, 109*
Grain, export from Friuli to Venice, 64–65, 66, *75, 76* measures to conserve stocks of, 65, *75*, 82
   import from Germany, 65–6, *75*
Gregory XIII, Pope, 167, 170, 172, 213, 214, 218, 240, 269–70
Grey, Lord, 39, *46*
Grimani, Alvise, (rector of Brescia), 214
Grimani, Giovanni, Patriarch of Aquileia, 233, *238*
Guerero, Pedro, Archbishop of Granada, (at the Council of Trent), 135, *145*
Gussago, (province of Brescia), 286
Haddington, 39
Hampton Court, 33, *45*
Harvel, Edmund, (English ambassador in Venice), 30, 32, *42*, 152
Henry VIII of England, *42*, 26–30, 34, 37
Henry II of France, 28, 32–3, 37
Heresy, 120, *125*, 126, 131–2, 150, 152, 160, *181, 233*
   in Brescia, *120–1, 122, 126, 181*, 201–6, 202–12, *223–4*
   (*See also* heretics, inquisition)
Heretics, 152–3, *180, 224, 225*
   their invitation to the Council of Trent, 133–4, *144*
   (*See also* heresy, inquisition, Planerio, Stefano; Francese, Artoldo; Parma, Gasparo; Tedesco, Ambrosio; Bagno, Pompeo)
Hilliard, Dr, *45*
Holy Office (*See* inquisition)
House owned by Bollani family, home of Pietro Aretino, 20–1, Figs. 3, 3a, 3b
   (*See also* Aretino, Pietro)
In Coena Domini (papal bull), 149, 208–9, 212–14, 215, 217–18, *225–6*
Index (of prohibited books), 132–3, 141, *143–4, 181, 225*
Inquisition, 126, 140, *144, 146*, 152, 178, *182*, 201–12, *222, 224–5*
   (*See also* heresy, heretics)
Interdict, Venetian, 15
Isachino, Geremia, theatine, 121, *127*
Iseo, lake, (province of Brescia), 83
Jesuits, 164, *193, 200*, 241
Jews, *58*, 67–71, *76–7*, 153, *182*
Julius III, Pope, 119, 120, 131, *142*
Justification by Works, 202–5
Lana, Scipione, *cavaliere*, 123
Landino di Bibbiena, Francesco, (rector of the Brescian seminary) 165
Lane, Prof. F.C., 14
Lepanto, battle of, *60*, 81, *105*, 156, *186, 228*
Leo X, Pope, 174
Lodovico 'Il Bavaro' (Louis the Bavarian), 84
Lodron, Zuanbattista, *58*
London, 27
Longo, family, *61*
Longo, Antonio q. Francesco, 16
Longo, Francesco, (brother-in-law of Domenico Bollani), *19, 60*, 221, *227*, 231, 243, *245–6*, 268, 270–1
Longo, Marcantonio, (brother-in-law of Domenico Bollani), 60, 243, *245–6*
Longo, Marietta, (Bollani), 14, 15, 243–4
Loredan, family, 15–6, *246*
Loredan, Gerolamo, *247*
Luna, Don Alvaro de, (*podestà* of Cremona), 87
Luna, Don Emmanuel de, (governor of Cremona), 97–8, *114*
Luogotenente della patria del Friuli, 10, *24*, 51–2, 54, *57, 60–1*, Chap. IV, *passim*, 80, 81, 177
Luther, Martin, 151
Magistrates of the Republic of Venice (*See* Venetian magistracies)
Maggi, Brescian family, 177
Manerba, Panfilo, (Brescian canon), 166
Manerbio, (province of Brescia), *200*
Mantua, 151
Mantua, bishop of, (at the Council of Trent), 146
Manzoni, Alessandro, 70
Marini, Leonardo, bishop of Laodicea (at the Council of Trent), 140
Martinengo, (Brescian noble family), *106, 110*, 152–3

138, 139, 140, *147–8*, 160–3, 178, *180,
187–8, 199, 200*, 210–11, 213–14,
218–19, *224–5*, 231–7, *238*, 252, 274
Vaprio, treaty of, 83
Vargus, (Spanish ambassador in Milan), *112*
Vecchi and *Giovani*, (*See* patriciate,
Venetian)
Venetian magistracies, 210, 213, 216, 221,
222, 231, 273
   Avogador, 24, 57
   Camerlengo a Verona, 13, *23*
   Camerlengo de Comun, 23, 56
   Camera degli imprestidi, 23, 56
   Cinque savi alla mercanzia, 24
   Consolo, 22
   Council of X, 11, 70, 105, 106, 122, 163,
   205, 206, 207, 210, 213, 216, 221, 222,
   231, 273
   *Dieci savi sopra le decime del Rialto,
   22–24*
   Gran consiglio, (Great Council), 8, 11, 14,
   18, 24, 50, 52, 56, 61
   Inquisitori di stato, 50
   Luogotenente della patria del Friuli, (*See
   Luogotenente . . .*)
   Officiali alle rason vecchie, 24, 56
   Pregadi, (Senate), 8, 9, 14, *17*, 40, 47–8,
   50, *56, 57–8*, 105, *113, 115*
   Provveditore sopra le acque, 13, *23, 56*
   Provveditore sopra i banchi, 23–4, *56*
   Provveditore de comun, 14, 24, *56*
   *Provveditore alla camera dei confini, 107,
   117*
   Provveditore sopra i dazi, 23
   *Provveditore al cottimo di Alessandria, 23,
   24*
   Provveditore al cottimo di Damasco,
   13–14, *56, 76*
   Provveditore sopra li uffici, 23
   Quarantia civil nova, 13. *22, 24*
   Quarantia criminale, 17, 47, 48
   Savio del Consiglio, (*Savio grande*), 48–9,
   52, 54, *56–7*, 62
   Savio agli ordini, 48–9, *56*
   Savio di Terraferma, 48–9, 50, 52, 54,
   56–9, 62, 120, 122
   Zonta, (suspension of, 1582), 6
   Other offices, 56
Venier, Francesco, (*Luogotenente . . .* at
Udine), *224*
Venier, Sebastian, (rector of Brescia, later
doge of Venice), 96–98, *114–15, 127*
at Lepanto, *114*
Verallo, (papal nuncio to Charles V), 28
Vergerio, Paolo, 151, *182*
Verona, 15, 53, *58–9*, 150
   (*See also* Valier, Agostino, Giberti, G.M.,
   bishops of Verona)
Venzone, (Friuli), 71
Vicenza, 150, 152
   (See also Priuli, Matteo and Michele,
   bishops of Vicenza)
Visconti, Giovanni, archbishop of Milan, 84
Visita apostolica, Borromeo to Brescia,
   158–9, *187*, 215–16, *228*, 233, *246*
   Valier to Venice, 160, 204
Visita pastorale, 139–40, 151, 173, 175–7,
   139, *198–9*
Waldensians, 151
Witch hunts, 150
Wool export licences, *42–3*
Zambon, (Venetian secretary in England),
   27, 29
Zane, Paolo, bishop of Brescia, *180, 199*
Zane, Hieronimo, (*savio* in Venice), 60, 113,
   252
Zen, family, *61*
Zen, Cattarino, (Venetian recto of Brescia),
   106
Zorzi, Bernardo, 51
Zuccato, Gerolamo, (Venetian secretary in
   England), 29
Zwingli, 151